LET'S GO

BARCELONA
2003

ANNA E. BYRNE EDITOR

RESEARCHER-WRITERS
COLLEEN GARGAN
REI ONISHI
ADAM WEISS

DAMIAN WILLIAMS MAP EDITOR
MICHELLE BOWMAN MANAGING EDITOR
ABHISHEK GUPTA TYPESETTER

MACMILLAN

HELPING LET'S GO
If you want to share your discoveries, suggestions, or corrections, please drop us a line. We read every piece of correspondence, whether a postcard, a 10-page email, or a coconut. Please note that mail received after May 2003 may be too late for the 2004 book, but will be kept for future editions. **Address mail to:**

> **Let's Go: Barcelona**
> **67 Mount Auburn Street**
> **Cambridge, MA 02138**
> **USA**

Visit Let's Go at **http://www.letsgo.com,** or send email to:

> **feedback@letsgo.com**
> **Subject: "Let's Go: Barcelona"**

In addition to the invaluable travel advice our readers share with us, many are kind enough to offer their services as researchers or editors. Unfortunately, our charter enables us to employ only currently enrolled Harvard students.

Published in Great Britain 2003 by Macmillan, an imprint of Pan Macmillan Ltd.
20 New Wharf Road, London N1 9RR,
Basingstoke and Oxford
Associated companies throughout the world
www.panmacmillan.com

Maps by David Lindroth copyright © 2003 by St. Martin's Press.

Published in the United States of America by St. Martin's Press.

ISBN: 1-4050-0085 6
First edition
10 9 8 7 6 5 4 3 2 1

Let's Go: Barcelona is written by Let's Go Publications, 67 Mount Auburn Street, Cambridge, MA 02138, USA.

WHO WE ARE

A NEW LET'S GO FOR 2003

With a sleeker look and innovative new content, we have revamped the entire series to reflect more than ever the needs and interests of the independent traveler. Here are just some of the improvements you will notice when traveling with the new *Let's Go*.

MORE PRICE OPTIONS

Still the best resource for budget travelers, *Let's Go* recognizes that everyone needs the occassional indulgence. Our "Big Splurges" indicate establishments that are actually worth those extra pennies (pulas, pesos, or pounds), and price-level symbols (❶ ❷ ❸ ❹ ❺) allow you to quickly determine whether an accommodation or restaurant will break the bank. We may have diversified, but we'll never lose our budget focus—"Hidden Deals" reveal the best-kept travel secrets.

BEYOND THE TOURIST EXPERIENCE

Our Alternatives to Tourism chapter offers ideas on immersing yourself in a new community through study, work, or volunteering.

AN INSIDER'S PERSPECTIVE

As always, every item is written and researched by our on-site writers. This year we have highlighted more viewpoints to help you gain an even more thorough understanding of the places you are visiting.

IN RECENT NEWS. *Let's Go* correspondents around the globe report back on current regional issues that may affect you as a traveler.

CONTRIBUTING WRITERS. Respected scholars and former *Let's Go* writers discuss topics on society and culture, going into greater depth than the usual guidebook summary.

THE LOCAL STORY. From the Parisian monk toting a cell phone to the Russian *babushka* confronting capitalism, *Let's Go* shares its revealing conversations with local personalities—a unique glimpse of what matters to real people.

FROM THE ROAD. Always helpful and sometimes downright hilarious, our researchers share useful insights on the typical (and atypical) travel experience.

SLIMMER SIZE

Don't be fooled by our new, smaller size. *Let's Go* is still packed with invaluable travel advice, but now it's easier to carry with a more compact design.

FORTY-THREE YEARS OF WISDOM

For over four decades *Let's Go* has provided the most up-to-date information on the hippest cafes, the most pristine beaches, and the best routes from border to border. It all started in 1960 when a few well-traveled students at Harvard University handed out a 20-page mimeographed pamphlet of their tips on budget travel to passengers on student charter flights to Europe. From humble beginnings, *Let's Go* has grown to cover six continents and *Let's Go: Europe* still reigns as the world's best-selling travel guide. This year we've beefed up our coverage of Latin America with *Let's Go: Costa Rica* and *Let's Go: Chile;* on the other side of the globe, we've added *Let's Go: Thailand* and *Let's Go: Hawaii*. Our new guides bring the total number of titles to 61, each infused with the spirit of adventure that travelers around the world have come to count on.

CONTENTS

♜ accommodations 195

♝ daytripping 211

✈ planning your trip 277

▤ alternatives to tourism 303

♘ service directory 313

↰ appendix 318

↗ index 321

✵ maps 331

HOW TO USE THIS BOOK

PRICE RANGES AND RANKINGS. Our researchers list establishments in order of value from best to worst. Our absolute favorites are denoted by the Let's Go thumbs-up (🔲). Since the best value does not always mean the cheapest price, we have incorporated a system of price ranges into the guide. The table below lists how prices fall within each bracket.

SYMBOL:	❶	❷	❸	❹	❺
ACCOMMODATIONS	under €15	€16-25	€26-35	€36-45	€46 and up
FOOD	under €5	€6-10	€11-15	€16-20	€21 and up

WHEN TO USE IT

TWO MONTHS BEFORE. Our book is filled with practical information to help you before you go. **Planning Your Trip** (p. 277) has advice about passports, plane tickets, insurance, and more. The **Accommodations** chapter (p. 195) can help you with booking a room from home.

ONE MONTH BEFORE. Take care of travel insurance and write down a list of emergency numbers and hotlines to take with you. Make a list of packing essentials and shop for anything you're missing. Make any necessary reservations.

TWO WEEKS BEFORE. Start thinking about your ideal trip. **Discover Barcelona** (see p. 1) lists the city's top 20 sights and also includes suggested itineraries, our new **walking tours** (complete with maps), Let's Go Picks (the best and quirkiest that Barcelona has to offer), and the scoop on each of the city's neighborhoods, including what areas to avoid and what you absolutely should not miss.

ON THE ROAD. Once in Barcelona (see p. 23) will be your best friend once you've arrived, with all the practical information you'll need, plus tips on acting like a true Barcelonese. This year, *Let's Go: Barcelona* includes all new features such as **interviews** with locals and the scoop on the **hot topics** in Barcelona news today. When you reach Barcelona, you'll spend your time flipping through the following chapters: **Sights, Museums, Food & Drink, Nightlife, Entertainment,** and **Shopping.** When you feel like striking out, the **Daytripping** chapter will help: it provides a list of options for one-day and weekend trips away from Barcelona into the historic or beachy towns of surrounding Catalunya, or the party-hardy Balearic Islands. The **Service Directory** contains a list of local services like laundromats, tourist offices, and emergency numbers. The **Appendix** has a list of useful Catalan and Spanish words and phrases to help you navigate almost every situation. The **Map** appendix has area maps of all the major neighborhoods in the city with plottings of all accommodation, food, and nightlife listings. Finally, remember to put down this guide once in a while and go exploring on your own; you'll be glad you did.

RESEARCHER-WRITERS

Colleen Gargan   *La Ribera, l'Eixample Dreta, Gràcia, Tibidabo, Horta, Cadaqués, Montserrat, Tossa de Mar, and Mataro.*

A veteran researcher from *Let's Go: USA 2000*, Colleen graduated *magna cum laude* from Harvard University with a degree in Literature and Film and a citation in Spanish. A native of Quincy, Massachusettes, she studies dance, drama, and voice (she seriously considered tap-dancing on Las Ramblas for money). Colleen is currently living in New York City, continuing her work in travel-writing.

Rei Onishi   *Montjuïc, l'Eixample Esquerra, El Raval, Port Vell, Sitges, Tarragon, and Palafrugell.*

Coming straight from *Let's Go: Mexico 2002* where he conquered the Yucatán Peninsula, Rei was excited to research in a city where the tap water is drinkable (even if restaurants refused to serve it). Originally from Naha, Okinawa, Rei has extensive travel experience in Asia, North America, and Central and Western Europe. He enjoys studying social theory, philosophy, and comparative politics.

Adam Weiss   *Las Ramblas, Barri Gòtic, Barceloneta, Pedralbes, Les Corts, Poble Nou, Port Olímpic, Sarría, Girona, Ripoll, Puigcerdà.*

Originally hailing from Merrick, New York, Adam is currently a fellow at the Sorbonne in Paris. He studies the history of Medieval France, particularly those questions concerning issues of gender and sexuality in romance literature. A great linguist who picked up Catalan in a matter of months, Adam graduated *magna cum laude* from Harvard University with a degree in History and Literature.

CONTRIBUTING WRITERS

Sarah Jacoby was a Researcher-Writer for *Let's Go: India & Nepal 2001* and *Let's Go: Spain & Portugal 1999*, as well as an associate editor for *Let's Go: Europe 2000*. While living in Barcelona she worked for an Internet consulting company.

Sarah Kenney was editor of *Let's Go: Barcelona 2002*. A onetime resident of Barcelona, she speaks both Spanish and Catalan. She is currently editing for a spanish-language publishing company in Boston and teaching English for a non-profit organization. She is an avid fan of Floquet de Neu.

ACKNOWLEDGMENTS

LET'S GO

Anna thanks: First of all, a huge thanks to my researchers, Colleen, Rei, and Adam, for being great workers who made my job enjoyable and rewarding. You all are amazing and kept things entertaining. Thanks to Michelle for being a patient and helpful manager—you're the best! Amber, for being my surrogate AE and a cheerful and speedy assistant. To all my City Guide buds in West B: scrobins, for her timely net sends and love for luna; skramer for keeping it cold-to-freezing and for hot love; Ankur for taking over with Eustace when I was too tired; The Eustace for his phone calls; Antoinette for sassiness; the Kwok for her theories; Flany for being the unflappably preppy Club F; and Shannon for witty banter on modern art. To East B: you made us laugh with your tales of disaster; to prod, thanks for not killing me; Damian for his master map-making, Julie and Colin for helping out in the end. And more thanks to Colleen, who swooped in at the last minute and helped me out. You are tireless and have gone above and beyond. Andy, Lucy, Irin, and Josh—thanks for letting me use your islands. Amy and Mare—you taught me everything I know. Also, thanks to you guys who have kept me sane outside of the office: Ryan, thanks for letting me call you in the middle of the night and for always being happy to hear from me; to Cait and Missa, for dinners and scandals, respectively; and to my family, Em, Rach, Matt, Mom and Dad—I love you all so much and wish that I could be with you more.

Damian thanks: I'd like to thank Anna and the rest of Team Barcelona for all their hard work and indefatigable dedication to the book. A special thanks goes to Colin, who worked extremely hard to get the maps polished into a finished product. And finally, I'd like to thank Liz for showing me the true beauty of Barcelona.

Editor
Anna Elizabeth Byrne
Managing Editor
Michelle Bowman
Map Editor
Damian Williams

Publishing Director
Matthew Gibson
Editor-in-Chief
Brian R. Walsh
Production Manager
C. Winslow Clayton
Cartography Manager
Julie Stephens
Design Manager
Amy Cain
Editorial Managers
Christopher Blazejewski,
Abigail Burger, D. Cody Dydek,
Harriett Green, Angela Mi Young Hur,
Marla Kaplan, Celeste Ng
Financial Manager
Noah Askin
Marketing & Publicity Managers
Michelle Bowman, Adam M. Grant
New Media Managers
Jesse Tov, Kevin Yip
Online Manager
Amélie Cherlin
Personnel Managers
Alex Leichtman, Owen Robinson
Production Associates
Caleb Epps, David Muehlke
Network Administrators
Steven Aponte, Eduardo Montoya
Design Associate
Juice Fong
Financial Assistant
Suzanne Siu
Office Coordinators
Alex Ewing, Adam Kline,
Efrat Kussell
Director of Advertising Sales
Erik Patton
Senior Advertising Associates
Patrick Donovan, Barbara Eghan,
Fernanda Winthrop
Advertising Artwork Editor
Leif Holtzman
Cover Photo Research
Laura Wyss
President
Bradley J. Olson
General Manager
Robert B. Rombauer
Assistant General Manager
Anne E. Chisholm

Discover Barcelona

Barcelona loves to indulge in the fantastic. From the urban carnival that is Las Ramblas to buildings with no straight lines; from wild festivals to even wilder nightlife; from bronzed nude beaches to a beloved white gorilla named Floquet, the city pushes the limits of style and good taste in everything it does, with amazing results. As the center of the whimsical and daring *Modernisme* architectural movement, Barcelona holds fairy-tale creations that are like no other buildings in the world; as home to three of the most well-known Surrealist painters, Salvador Dalí, Pablo Picasso, and the lovable Joan Miró, even Barcelona's most famous art is grounded in a reality alternative to the one that the rest of us know.

The time is now for Barcelona. In the quarter-century since Spain has been freed from Franco's oppressive regime, Barcelona has led the autonomous region of Catalunya in a resurgence of a culture so esoteric and unique it is puzzling even to the rest of Spain. The city has prospered and given itself a major makeover that began as preparation for the Olympics in the early 1990s, but was so successful that the image-obsessed Barceloneses have kept it going. The result is a vanguard city squeezed between the mesmerizing blue waters of the Mediterranean and the green Tibidabo hills, flashing with such vibrant colors and intense energy, you will see Barcelona long after you have closed your eyes.

Barcelona is a gateway: the gateway to Catalunya, to Spain, to the Mediterranean, and to the Pyrenees. Pack your swimsuit and your skis, your art history book and your clubbing shoes, and don't worry about the fact that you don't speak Spanish: neither does Barcelona.

BARCELONA BY THE NUMBERS

City population: 1.5 million.

Metropolitan area: 4.2 million.

White geese in residence: 13 (visit the cathedral; see p. 63).

White gorillas in residence: 1 (see p. 74).

Average annual rainfall: 23.2 in. (590mm).

Pork consumed per resident annually: 55.78kg.

Percentage of population that chain smokes: 25%.

Percentage population that is Roman Catholic: 90%.

Number of statues in the Barri Gòtic: 37.

Percentage of those statues that are living: 65%.

Density of mimes on Las Ramblas: 4 every 1m.

Number of words the English language has drawn from Catalan: 1 (it's yacht).

Number of military strongholds turned into parks: 2.

Number of bars with Roman walls running through them: 7.

Number of absinthes required to knock you out: 3.

TOP 20 SIGHTS

If you want to catch as many of the sights as possible, try our walking tours (see p. 20).

20. Poble Espanyol, a recreation of all of Spain's greatest hotspots. Hey, if you can't hit the real thing, go for the tacky imitation (see p. 90).

19. The Aquarium, the largest in Europe, complete with an underwater tunnel that guides visitors through the briny deep (see p. 87).

18. The Sardana, the traditional Catalan dance, performed impromptu in front of the Cathedral on Sunday mornings (see p. 63).

17. Fonts Luminoses, a nighttime show of lights, music, water, and magic (see p. 89).

18. Museu d'Art Modern, showcasing the best and the brightest of Catalunya's painters from the past century (see p. 111).

15. Museu Nacional d'Art de Catalunya (Palau Nacional), a religious experience in and of itself (see p. 120).

14. The Mediterranean, a fool-proof pleaser. Enjoy swimming, fishing, boating, waterskiing, parasailing, jet skiing, diving...(see p. 171).

13. El Barça, Barcelona's world-class soccer team and the stars of some killer matches (see p. 175).

12. Floquet de Neu, the world's only white gorilla. And isn't he dashing! (see p. 74).

11. Els Quatre Gats, the Barri Gòtic hangout of such giants as Pablo Picasso and Ramon Casas, which still serves the best coffee in the city (see p. 130).

10. La Manzana de la Discòrdia, the city block with a Modernist identity crisis, where Modernisme's three most famous sons—Puig i Cadafalch, Domènech i Montaner, and Antoni Gaudí—duke it out to be the tourists' favorite (see p. 79).

9. The Cathedral, the religious center of Barcelona. A cloister, geese, Roman ruins, and mimes out front add to your average Gothic cathedral-going experience (see p. 63).

8. Museu Picasso, one of the best collections of Picasso's works anywhere, from his earliest painting to his late engravings (see p. 109).

7. Fundació Miró, Miró's artistic legacy to his homeland, showcasing his own work and the work of up-and-coming Catalan artists (see p. 118).

6. Palau de la Música Catalana, Domènech i Montaner's amazing architectural tribute to good music (see p. 70).

5. Park Güell, Gaudí's unfinished housing project, now the wackiest park in the world. Hikes lead to spectacular views: buns of steel not included (see p. 91).

4. Passeig de Gràcia, the Fifth Avenue of Barcelona: home to several Modernist landmarks (see p. 79 and p. 81), outdoor dining (see p. 136), and designer-store labels (see p. 189).

3. Casa Milà (La Pedrera), Gaudí's finished masterpiece and the best look inside his work and his head (see p. 78).

2. Las Ramblas, the central and most colorful street in Barcelona's oldest district, complete with mimes, flowers, and baby emus (see p. 58).

1. La Sagrada Família, Gaudí's unfinished masterpiece, and his tomb (see p. 76).

SUGGESTED ITINERARIES

THREE DAYS

DAY 1: MODERNISME 101

Head out to the **La Sagrada Família** (see p. 76) early in the morning to avoid fighting the high-season crowds; grab some *churros y chocolate* at one of the nearby cafes. From there, make your way to the Pl. de Catalunya (M: Catalunya) and take the half-day walking tour through **l'Eixample** (which you have now started in reverse; see p. 6), Barcelona's gridded upper neighborhood that is jam-packed with Modernist sights (including **Casa Milà** (see p. 78) and **La Manzana de la Discòrdia** (see p. 79), where you can pick up the Ruta del Modernisme pass that offers discounts on sights all over the city). After pondering the chimneys of Casa Milà, catch the #24 bus from the Pg. de Gràcia up to your last Modernist stop of the day: **Park Güell** in Gràcia (see p. 91). Wander through the colonnades, park it on the longest and most crooked bench in the world, and snap a photo with the drooling lizard. At the end of the day (and the beginning of a long night), head down to one of l'Eixample's many bars or clubs (see p. 158).

DAY 2: OLD TOWN SUPER-TOURIST

Start out at the Pl. de Catalunya (M: Catalunya), but this time, head down **Las Ramblas** (see p. 58) to see the traditional **Boquería** market, where you can buy pastries or fruit for breakfast (see p. 62). Check out the various offerings of the different sections of Las Ramblas (who on earth buys those baby emus they sell there?), then head into

Inside La Sagrada Família

Balcony at Park Güell

Ducklings for Sale on Las Ramblas

BEST OF BARCELONA

▨ Most aesthetically pleasing bathroom experience: **Els Quatre Gats** (see p. 130).

▨ Best place to see the city from above: **La Sagrada Família** (see p. 76).

▨ Best (and only) white gorilla in the whole wide world: **Floquet de Neu** (see p. 74).

▨ Best place to get an emu or a sunflower: **Las Ramblas** (see p. 58).

▨ Most obscene photo op: the giant phallus in the **Museu de l'Eròtica** (see p. 106).

Best place to take a date: **Mirador de Vila Paula** (see p. 100).

Best place to see the sun set: **Palau Nacional** (see p. 120).

Best place to see eggs: it's a tie! The **dancing eggs** during the Corpus Cristi Festival (see p. 20) are pretty cool, but so are the eggs on top of the **Dalí Museum** (see p. 216).

Best place to make cheesy Teenage Mutant Ninja Turtle Jokes: **Museu de Clavegueram** (see p. 114).

the **Barri Gòtic** via C. Portaferrissa, which will turn into C. dels Boters and drop you at the **Cathedral** (see p. 63). After you've seen the resident geese, mimes, and Roman walls, head to Modernist hangout **Els Quatre Gats** for a quick bite (see p. 130). Get your Ruta de Modernisme pass ready for your next stop just off the Via Laietana, the **Palau de la Música Catalana** in La Ribera (see p. 70). Make your way through La Ribera's twisting alleys to the **Museu Picasso** (see p. 109). Check out the galleries in the labyrinth of streets (see p. 123) and stay in the area for tapas (see p. 132). Finish up the night by heading back into the Barri Gòtic for the clubs and bars around the **Plaça Reial** (see p. 154).

DAY 3: ATHLETIC ART

Eat breakfast before heading up to **Montjuïc,** as culinary pickings are slim on the mountain. Take a quick ride up to the mountain from the waterfront on the **Transbordador Aeri cable car** (see p. 87), then head over to the **Fundació Miró** to explore your inner child (see p. 118). Bring a swimsuit and take a dive in the **Olympic pool** (see p. 174). Wander around the other Olympic edifices and then satiate your desire to visit the rest of Spain in the artificial and nostalgic **Poble Espanyol** (see p. 90). Poble Espanyol is also a reasonable place to grab lunch before you trek onwards to the **Museu Nacional d'Art de Catalunya** (see p. 120). On your way out of the museum, try to catch one of the shows of the **Fonts Luminoses** (see p. 89). If you still have energy and you're ready to party, you can return to Poble Espanyol, which gets much cooler after dark, and party until 6am at **Torres de Ávila** (see p. 165).

FIVE DAYS

If three days just aren't enough, read on....

DAY 4: THE WATERFRONT

Start out your day in the **Parc de la Ciutadella** with a visit to the Barcelona **zoo** and its lovable mascot, **Floquet de Neu** (Snowflake), the world's only albino gorilla (see p. 74). If you can tear yourself away from Floquet (and we understand if you can't), stop by the **Museu d'Art Modern** (see p. 111), which houses a good collection of works by Catalan artists. Get lunch at the cafe in the Modernist **Hivernacle** (see p. 73) before heading out of the park and down to the **Moll d'Espanya** to Barcelona's **aquarium,** the biggest (and some say best) in Europe (see p. 58). If all this family fun is too much for you, swing up **Las Ramblas** to the nearby, ever-raunchy **Museu de l'Eròtica** (see p. 106). The S&M display will clearly whet your appetite; good thing **Les Quinze Nit's** tasty and affordable paella is nearby in the **Plaça Reial** (see p. 128). After dinner, bide your time until 3am and then head to the Port Vell and writhe in the cheesy but irresistible clubs of **Maremàgnum** (see p. 163).

DAY 5: DALÍLAND

Get up early: you've got a train to catch, to nearby **Figueres** (see p. 212). Spend the morning at the surreal **Teatre-Museu Dalí,** the second-most popular museum in Spain, where you can stand on Dalí's tomb (see p. 216), listen to rain inside a Cadillac, or watch a room turn into Mae West. You can make it back to Barcelona before sundown, and after some rest (or getting tattooed and pierced; see p. 193), lose yourself in **Poble Nou's** alternative music and bar scene (see p. 162).

SEVEN DAYS

Still want more? We don't blame you.

DAY 6: EL BARÇA & EL RAVAL

By now you've had plenty of time to get tickets to a **soccer game** (see p. 175), featuring the city's beloved team, **El Barça.** Before you head over to Camp Nou, do some thrift-shopping in El Raval's **Mercat Alternatiu** (see p. 190) and stop by Gaudí's spooky **Palau Güell** (see p. 75). Grab lunch in blue-collar El Raval (see p. 134), then head to the **Museu FCB** (see p. 122), any *fútbol*-lover's personal version of heaven. Follow the crowds into the game at **Camp Nou** (see p. 175), and then follow them to the nightlife on the way out.

DAY 7: DAYTRIPPING

What you'll want to do on your last day depends on the weather. If you're traveling in the summer, a daytrip to beachy **Sitges** (see p. 239) is a great way to enjoy your last day in Catalunya, with its own wild (and very gay-friendly) night-life. If it's too cold for the beach, the nearby mountains and monastery at **Montserrat** (see p. 248) are one of the wonders of Catalunya. If you're looking for some authentic nightlife for your last night in Barcelona, go to where the locals party, the clubs and pubs around C. Marià Cubí in the Zona Alta (see p. 168).

Flamenco Dancer at the Museo de Cera

Fundació Miró

View of Sagrada Família from Roof of Casa Milà

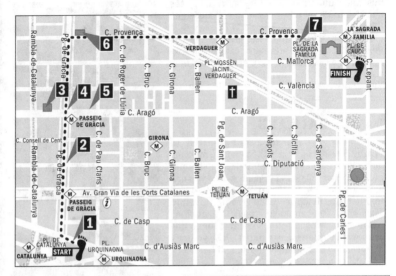

This tour traverses l'Eixample, the newest and most fashionable neighborhood in Barcelona. The walk will pass upscale shopping and the major sights of Modernisme, the intensely visual architectural movement that swept through Barcelona in the late 19th century (see **Life & Times**, p. 50).

Suggested Time: 5hr.

Distance: 3.2km/2mi., or about 21 blocks.

When to go: A weekday afternoon, on a clear day.

Start: M: Catalunya

End: M: Sagrada Família

1 PLAÇA DE CATALUNYA. Start at Pl. de Catalunya, the hub of the city. Stop by **El Corte Inglés** (see p. 190) for a free map.

2 PASSEIG DE GRÀCIA. Exit El Corte Inglés onto Pg. de Gràcia, and let your wallet do the talking as you pass some of Barcelona's hottest designer shopping (see p. 186). A stop in the free **Museu del Perfum** (see p. 115) will compensate for any extravagant purchases that you make along the way.

3 FUNDACIÓ TÀPIES. For those looking for abstract postmodern angst at its finest, you have arrived. Check out the über-hip rooftop sculpture (see p. 114).

4 LA MANZANA DE LA DISCÒRDIA. Continuing on Pg. de Gràcia, just before C. Aragó is the famous La Manzana de la Discòrdia (see p. 79). Enter Casa Amatller (no. 41) to buy a Ruta del Modernisme pass (see p. 57), good for discounts at Modernist sights all over the city, including a free tour of the facades of the three houses that make up La Manzana de la Discòrdia: Casa Amatller, Casa Lleó Morera, and Casa Batlló.

5 THE EATERIES OF CARRER ARAGÓ. Stop for a late lunch at one of the many quality and reasonably priced restaurants on C. Aragó east of Pg. de Gràcia (see p. 136).

6 CASA MILÀ. Return to Pg. de Gràcia and continue north to Gaudí's Casa Milà, a Modernist masterpiece with an unusual rooftop and an even more unforgettable view (see p. 78).

7 LA SAGRADA FAMÍLIA. Exit onto C. Provença and follow it (without crossing the Pg. de Gràcia again; with your back to the Pl. de Catalunya, follow C. Provença to the right) for 11 blocks to La Sagrada Família, the ultimate Gaudí jewel (this one is unfinished—117 years and counting) with infinitely complex views and facades (see p. 76).

LAS RAMBLAS WALKING TOUR

Suggested Time: 5hr.

Distance: 3.2km or 2mi.

When to go: A weekday morning.

Start: M: Liceu

End: M: Drassanes

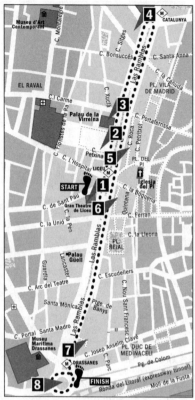

No visit to Barcelona is complete (or even possible) without traversing the famous Las Ramblas first. This promenade is actually a string of five individual Ramblas strung together; each has its own distinct character and plenty of built-in entertainment.

1. GRAN TEATRE DEL LICEU. Start your morning with the 10am guided tour of Barcelona's premier stage, and bask in the history of one of Europe's greatest opera houses (tours M-F; see p. 61)

2. LA BOQUERÍA. Check out the famous all-steel Modernist market and grab a late-morning snack at this wondrous bazaar of fresh and exotic food (see p. 60).

3. PALAU DE LA VIRREINA. Wander in the courtyard of this 18th-century rococo building and see if any exhibitions are going on; if not, visit the building's Cultural Events Office or admire the upscale souvenirs in the giftshop (see p. 60).

4. PLAÇA CATALUNYA. Now you've come to the city's main hub. Every tourist wanders through at least once; can you tell by the crowds? The busy *plaça* makes a great place to people-watch or just relax. It is also where the old city meets the new; turn south to catch the rest of this walking tour, but if you continue farther north you begin the l'Eixample walking tour (see p. 6).

5. MUSEU DE L'ERÒTICA. Swing back around and, if you dare, check out Spain's only erotica museum.

6. CAFÉ DE L'OPERA. Enjoy a cup of coffee at the famous cafe (see p. 127). But don't expect to order to go; Europeans like to enjoy their coffee by sipping it leisurely. If you're having trouble ordering a plain cup o' Joe, see **Can I Get Coffee With That?,** p. 148.

7. MUSEU DE CERA. Enjoy some of Barcelona's still life at this wax museum. There are almost as many statues in here as there are living statues along the street you just walked down; only these people don't move when you drop a euro in their hat. If they do, that's a bad sign (see p. 104).

8. MONUMENT A COLOM. End your tour with the man Spanish cities love to claim as their own. Sevilla purports that he is buried in their city (he's not); Barcelona claims that he was born in Catalunya (he wasn't). Christopher Columbus may have been elusive in birth and death, but at least Barcelona has captured the prophet in a moment of inspiration, pointing valiantly, heroically, epically . . . the wrong way (see p. 62).

LA RIBERA WALKING TOUR

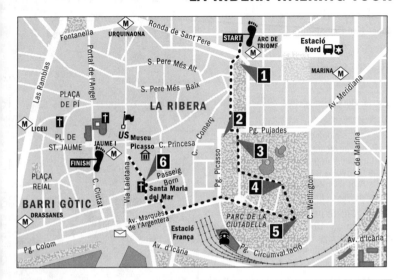

This walking tour is a trip through La Ribera, one of the oldest sections of the city, and the Parc de la Ciutadella. Begin your day early with a light breakfast at a restaurant near your hostel, and stop by your local grocery store for picnic fixings. Take the Metro to Arc de Triomf and get ready to roll.

Time: 5hr.

Distance: 2½km or 1½mi.

When to go: A weekday without rain.

Start: M: Arc de Triomf

End: M: Jaume I

1 ARC DE TRIOMF. This Modernist work was created by Josep Vilaseca to welcome visitors to the 1888 Exposition (see p. 72).

2 MUSEU DE ZOOLOGIA. Follow Pg. Lluís Companys toward Parc de la Ciutadella (about four blocks), one of Barcelona's most beautiful public spaces, great for families with young children and couples on a romantic outing. Domènech i Montaner's Museu de Zoologia (see p. 111) is credited with being one of the first creations that spawned Barcelona's famous architectural movement, Modernisme (see p. 53).

3 CASCADE FOUNTAINS. Directly across from the Museu de Zoologia are the magical Cascade Fountains (see p. 73). Unpack your lunch and relax by the water as children chase pigeons and orange trees sway in the wind. If all the splashing has gotten you in the mood for water sports, rent a **boat** at the nearby pond (see p. 73).

4 MUSEU D'ART MODERN. Gaze at one of the finest collections of Noucentiste (see p. 111) sculpture in the world or study some of Dalí's paintings (the only works of his still left in Barcelona) at the Museu d'Art Modern (see p. 111).

5 PARC ZOOLÒGIC. You may be thinking to yourself, "I can go to a zoo anywhere. Why should I waste my time in Barcelona at this one?" There is one simple answer for you: Floquet de Nou, the world's only white gorilla and Barcelona's favorite celebrity (see p. 74).

6 ESGLÉSIA SANTA MARIA DEL MAR. Come see the widest Medieval nave in the world at Mary of the Sea, a church built in the 14th century to serve the sailors of La Ribera. Another architectural feat of note: if the roof was 2ft. higher it would collapse from structural instability (see p. 71).

NEIGHBORHOODS

CIUTAT VELLA

BARRI GÒTIC AND LAS RAMBLAS

see map p. 338-339

🎯 *Orientation:* *Between Las Ram-blas in the west and Via Laietana in the east. The ocean borders the neighborhood to the south and C. Fontanella borders it to the north.* **Sights:** *see p. 58.* **Museums:** *see p. 104.* **Food & Drink:** *see p. 125.* **Nightlife:** *see p. 151.* **Accommodations:** *see p. 196.* **Public Transportation:** *M: Catalunya, Liceu, Dras-sanes, and Jaume I. Because of the narrow streets, no buses run through the Barri Gòtic, but down the border-ing streets. Buses #14, 38, 59, and 91 traverse Las Ramblas, while buses #17, 19, 40 and 45 drive down Via Laietana.*

Courtyard in the Barri Gotic

As the oldest sections of Barcelona, the Barri Gòtic and Las Ramblas are the tourist centers of the city. Originally settled by the Romans in the 3rd century BC, the Barri Gòtic is built on top of the original Roman city, Barcino, which at times pokes through the surface. Subsequent layers of medieval Catholic rule cover Barcino in a maze of narrow, cobbled streets dense with historic and artistic landmarks. The modern tourist industry has added shops, hostels, and bars to the churches and other monuments left over from the Middle Ages. Amid the museums and tacky tourist shops are some truly unique cul-tural phenomena, such as religious parades of towering plaster dolls and spontaneous perfor-mances of the *sardana*, the traditional Catalan dance (see **May I Have This Dance**, p. 51) Although the Barri Gòtic is one of Barcelona's more tour-isted areas, it has a kind of flavor that captures the essence of Barcelona. Take a stroll down **C. Avinyò** and you'll see some of Barcelona's most treasured architectural landmarks, just meters away from the area's most popular bars and res-taurants. Whether you are drawn in by the new or the old, there is something for everyone in this labyrinthine neighborhood.

Entry of the Liceu Opera House

DON'T MISS...

Sights: Relax in the tranquil cloister of the awe-inspir-ing **La Catedral de la Santa Creu** (see p. 63), along with 13 white geese.

Food & Drink: Els Quatre Gats (see p. 130), an old Picasso hangout, has lots of Bohemian character.

Nightlife and Entertainment: The bars in the **Plaça Reial** (see p. 151) are fun places to pass the night.

Girl with Birdcage on Las Ramblas

Barceloneta Boats

La Boqueria

On the Barceloneta Beach

LA RIBERA

see map p. 341

7 Orientation: *La Ribera is separated from the Barri Gòtic by Via Laietana and is bordered on the east by C. Wellington, past the Parc de la Ciutadella. Often lumped together with its northwestern neighbor, Sant Pere, the* district extends to Ronda de Sant Pere and southeast to Av. Marqués de l'Argentera and the Estació de França. **Sights:** see p. 70. **Museums:** see p. 108. **Food & Drink:** see p. 131. **Nightlife:** see p. 154. **Accommodations:** see p. 201. **Public Transportation:** *The most convenient Metro stops are M: Urquinaona and Jaume I. La Ribera is a fifteen minute walk from Pl. de Catalunya. Buses #17 and 19 drive down Via Laietana.*

As the stomping ground of Barcelona's many fishermen and local merchants, La Ribera has always had a very plebeian feel. However, its confines were witness to two of the most major events to shape Barcelona's history. In the 18th century, Felipe V demolished much of La Ribera, then the city's commercial hub, to make space for the impressive Ciutadella, the seat of Madrid's oppressive control, and now a park. Angry that Barcelona had sought his opponent, the Archduke Carlos, as its leader, Felipe V stuffed the wealthy, and therefore powerful, citizens of Barcelona into its chambers. Luckily, his successors were more lenient on their subjects, most victims were freed, and La Ribera was subsequently rejuvenated. Then, when in 1888 the former site of Ciutadella became home to the Universal Exposition, La Ribera served as the launch point of Barcelona to the world, capturing the new flare of Modernisme and the simplicity of old Spanish architecture and values. In recent years, the neighborhood has evolved into Barcelona's bohemian nucleus, attracting a young, artsy crowd of locals and a few expats and tourists in the know. Art galleries, offbeat shops, chic eateries, and exclusive bars line the major thoroughfares C. Montcada and the Pg. del Born, while you'll find others nearly hidden on smaller side streets. After dark, La Ribera makes for a relaxing evening of delicious tapas, extensive wine and *cava* menus, and fashionable but reasonably unpretentious bars.

DON'T MISS...

Sights: With a great multimedia English tour explaining its every nuance, the **Palau de la Música Catalana** (see p. 70) will leave even the most jaded tourist in awe of the excessive beauty of Moderisme.

Museums: The **Picasso Museum** (see p. 109) has a collection of the early and late works of the father of modern art.

Food & Drink: Enjoy tapas and a glass of *cava* at **Xampanyet** (see p. 132), the most renowned tapas bar in a veritable sea of great tapas bars.

Nightlife: Passieg del Born offers some of the hippest, most diverse bars in Barcelona, and a picturesque backdrop for some serious barhopping (see p. 154).

EL RAVAL

⁊ Orientation: *El Raval is the neighborhood to the west of Las Ramblas. It is bordered on its far sides by Av. Parallel and the Rondas St. Pau, St. Antoni, and Universitat. C. Hospital is the main street that divides the neighbor-*

see map p. 340

hood into two halves: the quainter northern area and the more run-down southern side, the Barri Xino. **Sights:** *see p. 75.* **Museums:** *see p. 111.* **Food & Drink:** *see p. 134.* **Nightlife:** *see p. 155.* **Transportation:** *Metro and bus lines hug the perimeter of El Raval, but do not go into the interior of the neighborhood.* **Metro:** *M: Liceu, Drassanes, Universitat, and Sant Antoni.* **Buses:** *#14, 38, 59, and 91 traverse Las Ramblas.*

The ancient *zona* just next to—but so different from—Las Ramblas and the Barri Gòtic tends to be a favorite of Barcelona's natives rather than its tourists. This ethnically diverse and culturally rich working-class neighborhood has a special charm of its own, with small, quirky shops and eateries, welcoming bars, and hidden historical attractions. Beginning as a small rural area outside of the city walls, El Raval was enveloped by the new city boundaries in the 14th century, and has been squeezing people in ever since. The situation became critical in the late 19th and early 20th centuries, when overcrowding led to an urban nightmare of rampant crime, prostitution, and drug use (see **Big Trouble in Little China,** p. 33). Revitalization efforts, especially since the '92 Olympic games, have worked wonders, however; new museums and cultural centers have paved the way for some of the city's trendiest new restaurants and bars, and today El Raval is emerging as one of Barcelona's most dynamic areas.

DON'T MISS...

Sights: The sumptuous visual feast of Gaudí's psychedelic **Palau Güell.**

Museums: The **Museu d'Arte Contemporani** is a showcase for some of the world's most cutting-edge art.

Food & Drink: Creative international dishes served on **Bar Ra's** intimate outdoor patio; traditional homecooked Catalan cuisine at **Restaurante Can Lluis;** fine dining at its finest at **Colibri.**

Lingerie Ponyride

Bull

Lesbian Tango

11

Girl Running in Park by Sant Pau

Women at a Catholic Festival

Pl. Espanya at Night

Nightlife: Hang out with all your tourist brethren at **La Oveja Negra;** or lose yourself in the Bongo Lounge at **La Paloma.**

PLAÇA DE CATALUNYA

see map p. 344-345

⚑ *Orientation: The most important streets in the city emanate from Pl. de Catalunya. The Aerobus airport shuttle drops off newcomers on the El Corte Inglés side of the plaça. The city's main* **tourist information office** *is directly across the street from the store, underground. On this side of the plaça one can also catch the* **Bus Turístic** *red route (see p. 58), which visits the city's northern areas of interest. Looking out onto the plaça from El Corte Inglés, you'll see the Hard Rock Café side of the plaça on the left. The legendary avenue Las Ramblas begins next to this popular restaurant. Directly across the plaça from El Corte Inglés is the Triangle shopping center, featuring a FNAC store and the crowded* **Café Zurich.** *The line for the Bus Turístic blue route, which hits the southern sights, forms on this side. To the right is the Banco Español de Crédito. Across the street from here is the plaça's underground police station.* **Ronda Universitat** *runs in front of the Banco Español.* **Passeig de Gràcia,** *the city's showcase of modernist architecture and upscale shopping, begins between the Banco Español and El Corte Inglés. The* **Avinguda Portal de l'Angel,** *a wide pedestrian way, and* **Carrer Fontanella,** *which houses a few accommodations, start between El Corte Inglés and the Hard Rock Café block.*

Chances are, visitors to Barcelona will eventually find themselves in Pl. de Catalunya, the gateway between the Ciutat Vella (Old City) and the more carefully laid out l'Eixample. The airport shuttle, a fleet of tourist buses, and almost all city buses pass through here, creating snarling traffic jams several times a day. And as the starting point of Passeig de Gràcia and Las Ramblas, not to mention a bastion of Internet cafes and currency exchanges, it is no wonder throngs of people spill over into the streets. The *plaça* itself contains little greenery but over 26 fountains and statues. Of these, the most visible is the **Monument a Macia** (1991) by Josep Subirachs, the architect now in charge of La Sagrada Família (see p. 76). Subirachs's monument, set on the Ramblas corner of the *plaça*, appears to be two sets of steps piled precariously on top of one another; the bust of Macia, president of the Generalitat in the 1930s, isn't all that aesthetically pleasing either. For over a century, the city has wanted to develop the *plaça* into a space worthy of Barcelona's center, but somehow plans have never taken shape. Today, the *plaça* is known for its commercial shopping centers, busy traffic, and amazingly docile, over-fed (and possibly over-bred?) pigeons.

L'EIXAMPLE

⚑ Orientation: *Bound by C. Ausiàs Marc and Pl. de Catalunya in the south, C. Còrsega in the north, C. Tarragona in the west, and C. del Dos de Maig in the east. L'Eixample is bisected vertically by the Pg. de Gràcia into l'Eixample Esquerra (Left Enlargement) to the west and l'Eixample Dreta (Right Enlargement) to the east. **Sights:** see p. 76. **Museums:** see p. 113. **Food & Drink:** see p. 136. **Nightlife:** see p. 158. **Public Transportation:** Metro lines 3, 4, 5, and the FCG trains run through l'Eixample; about half the city buses pass through this neighborhood, and all Nitbuses originate at Pl. de Catalunya.*

see map p. 344-345

Barcelona's l'Eixample (the Enlargement) is remarkable for the unusual circumstances leading to its development. Right around the time when the oppressive Bourbon walls around the old city were finally demolished in 1854, the Catalan cultural Renaixença was picking up. As the number of wealthy benefactors of industrialization grew, utopian socialist theories circulated like wildfire through philosophical circles, including that of l'Eixample designer **Ildefons Cerdà i Sunyer.** Cerdà's plan for Barcelona's enlargement was to impose an equal social community through uniformity of space and building design; however, once l'Eixample was built, rich industrialists harassed rising young architects to turn the new houses into overt displays of privilege in an early move of gentrification. Land-developers ignored Cerdà's garden designs and maximum height proposals in the interest of greater profits, and the result is what you see today: largely gardenless avenues packed with cars that nevertheless boast hundreds of interesting building facades.

Despite the fact that today's l'Eixample is not an accurate incarnation of Cerdà's original plan, the neighborhood is a fabulous place to wander, particularly for those claustrophobes who feel cramped by the tight spaces of the older neighborhoods. l'Eixample's gridded streets are filled with relatively wealthy residents, designer shops, corporate buildings, and eateries from around the world. Most tourists only see the Pg. de Gràcia and Sagrada Família areas, but if you have the energy to explore the whole neighborhood, you'll get a great lesson in Modernisme, and a better feel for the Barcelona beyond the tourists.

DON'T MISS...

Sights: Modernisme is what made Barcelona famous and L'Eixample is the place to find it in all its glory. No trip would be complete without visits to **La Sagrada Família** (see p. 76), the **Hospital de Sant Pau** (see p. 83), and **Casa Milà** (see p. 78).

Museums: The scintillating scents and sights of delicate perfume holders make the **Museu del Perfum** (see p. 115) a perfect place to indulge in cosmetic aesthetics.

Food & Drink: While Passeig de Gràcia bursts with outdoor cafes and tons of people watching, get in touch with your inner Buddha at **Thai Gardens** (see p. 136), then grab a cafe at **Café Torino** (see p. 137), where Gaudí tried his hand at eatery design.

Nightlife: Run away and join the circus at **La Fira** (see p. 158). L'Eixample Esquerra's thumping LGB nightlife (see p. 158) has earned it the well-deserved nickname, "Gaixample."

POBLE NOU & PORT OLÍMPIC

⚑ Orientation: *Bound by C. de Marina, Av. Diagonal, the Vila Olímpica, and the ocean. **Sights:** see p. 86. **Museums:** see p. 116. **Food & Drink:** see p. 141. **Nightlife:** see p. 162. **Public Transportation:** M: Marina, Bogatell, Llacuna, Ciutadella/Vila Olímpic, and Poble Nou are most central; Glories and Selva de Mar lie at the outskirts of the neighborhood. Bus lines include #6, 7, 36, 41, 71, and 92.*

see map p. 349

While industrial Poble Nou fueled Barcelona's economic growth in the 19th century, it enjoyed little of that era's wealth. Until the last few decades, Poble Nou consisted mainly of factories, warehouses, and low-income housing. Auto shops and commercial supply stores still abound, but the major factories were all removed in time for the **1992 Olympics.** When Barcelona was granted its Olympic bid in 1986, this privilege presented a two-sided problem: comfortably housing 15,000

Barceloneta Church

Barri Gòtic

Barcelona's Center of Government

athletes while beautifying the city's long-ignored coastline. Oriol Bohigas, Josep Martorall, David Mackay, and Albert Puig Domènech designed the solution: the **Vila Olímpica**, a residential area with wide streets, symmetrical apartment buildings, pristine parks, and open-air art pieces. The Vila Olímpica includes a shiny Americanized mall, a municipal sports center, and some restaurants, but most social activity in the area takes place in the L-shaped **Port Olímpic,** home to docked sailboats, more than 20 restaurants, a large casino, and a long strip of brash nightclubs.

In the wake of this development, old industrial buildings are slowly being converted into more apartments and nightclubs. With the exception of the Olympic areas, the atmosphere in Poble Nou is village-like compared to most of Barcelona: nondescript corner bars abound, and the tree-lined Rambla de Poble Nou is more likely to be filled with chatting grandmothers, small children, and gossiping teens than street artists and tourists. Besides its Olympic structures, Poble Nou's claims to fame are its sparkling city beaches and a raging alternative/hard rock music scene.

BARCELONETA

see map p. 350

🚺 *Orientation: Barceloneta lies between Port Vell and Port Olímpic on the waterfront. Pg. Joan de Borbo, running along the port, is the neighborhood's main street, while the Pg. Marítim borders the beach area. **Sights:** see* p. 87. **Museums:** see p. 116. **Food & Drink:** see p. 142. **Public Transportation:** M: Barceloneta. Buses #59 and 14 both run down Las Ramblas to the waterfront area. Also accessible by buses #17, 36, 40, 45, 57, and N8.

Barceloneta, or "Little Barcelona," was born out of necessity. In 1718, La Ribera was butchered to make room for the enormous Ciutadella fortress (see p. 43); the destruction of this historic neighborhood left thousands homeless, and it was only after over 30 years that the city created Barceloneta to house the displaced refugees. This area, a triangle jutting into Port Vell, follows a carefully planned grid pattern, which would later influence the design of l'Eixample. Because of its seaside location, Barceloneta became home to the city's sailors, fishermen, and their families.

It is hard to believe that only twenty years ago Barceloneta was a neglected industrial area. Despite rapid development of the port area for the 1992 Summer Olympics, Barceloneta retains its working-class residential flavor; while not the most touristed area of the city, it is popular with urban beach-bums and seafood lovers.

DON'T MISS...

Restaurants: The **seafood restaurants** along Juan de Borbo are touristy, but they can't be beat for freshness (see p. 142)

The Beaches: Platja San Sebastiá and **Platja Barceloneta** are the neighborhood's biggest draws (see p. 171).

PORT VELL

see map p. 350

▣ Orientation: *At the end of Las Ramblas, by the water. Extends from Av. Parallel in the west to Via Laietana in the east. Facing the water near the Columbus monument (Monument a Colom), the World Trade Center and Trasmedi-*

The Joy of a Chihuahua

terránea ferries are on the right, at the Moll (wharf) de Barcelona. Pg. de Colom and Moll de la Fusta run along the entire port, from the Columbus statue to the post office and Barceloneta. To get to Moll d'Espanya, the pedestrian dock that holds Maremàgnum and other attractions, cross the port at La Rambla del Mar wooden footbridge, the wavy seaside extension of Las Ramblas. **Sights:** *see p. 87.* **Museums & Galleries:** *see p. 118.* **Food & Drink:** *see p. 142.* **Nightlife:** *see p. 163.* **Public Transportation:** *M: Drassanes or Barceloneta. Buses #14, 38, and 59 run from Pl. de Catalunya to the waterfront via Las Ramblas.*

From the thirteenth to the sixteenth century, Barcelona's prime location on the Mediterranean enabled its port to become one of the wealthiest cities in the world. With Columbus's discovery of the New World in 1492, however, the epicenter of world trade moved from the Mediterranean to the Atlantic, and Barcelona's busy port began a long, slow decline. It was only in the frenzy of renovation and development surrounding the '92 Olympic Games that the city's ports, overlooked for centuries and marred by heavy industry and pollution, started to reach for their former glory. Barcelona's drive to refurbish its seafront resulted in the expansion of Port Vell. After moving the congested coastal road underground, the city opened Moll de la Fusta, a wide pedestrian zone that leads down to the beaches of Barceloneta (see **Entertainment,** p. 172), and connects to the bright **Maremàgnum** (p. 191) mall and the **Moll d'Espanya.** The port is picturesque day or night, and clamors with the bustle of seaside eateries, loud discos, overpriced shops, and tourist hordes. Today, the rejuvenated Port Vell—the "Old Port"—is as hedonistic, new, and touristy as Barcelona gets.

Palau Saint Jordi

Funicular

DON'T MISS...

Sights: Meet the sealife you keep eating at **L'Aquàrium de Barcelona** (see p. 87).

Museums: The engrossing **Museu Marítim** (see p. 118) is an interactive experience.

Nightlife: Bar- and club-hop at the 3-storied **Maremàgnum** complex (see p. 163).

MONTJUÏC

see map p. 348

🗾 Orientation: *Montjuïc lies in the southwest corner of the city, bordering the Poble Sec neighborhood.* **Sights:** *see p. 88.* **Museums:** *see p. 118.* **Food & Drink:** *see p. 143.* **Nightlife:** *see p. 165.* **Accommodations:** *see p. 206.* **Public Transportation:** *The Metro has stops on the outskirts of Montjuïc; a few buses run through Montjuïc. M: Espanya is best for reaching the MNAC and Poble Espanyol area, while M: Parallel gives you access to the underground funicular, which is a convenient way to reach the Fundació Miró, Miramar, and the Castell de Montjuïc; it lets you off on Av. Miramar. The funicular runs from inside the M: Parallel station at Av. Parallel and Nou de la Rambla (open daily 9am-10pm). Wheelchair accessible. Bus #50 is useful for reaching Poble Espanyol and the more distant Montjuïc sights like the Olympic area. Catch bus #50 either at the Av. Reina Maria Cristina stop in Pl. d'Espanya (flanked by 2 large brick towers) or as it heads uphill (every 10-20min.).*

Montjuïc (mon-joo-EEK), the hill at the southwest end of the city, is one of the oldest sections of Barcelona; throughout Barcelona's history, whoever controlled Montjuïc's peak controlled the city. The Laietani collected oysters on Montjuïc before they were subdued by the Romans (see **Life & Times,** p. 40), who erected a temple to Jupiter on its slopes. Since then, dozens of despotic rulers have constructed and modified the **Castell de Montjuïc,** built atop the ancient Jewish cemetery (hence the name "Montjuïc," which means "Jew Hill"). In the 20th century, Franco made the Castell de Montjuïc one of his "interrogation" headquarters; somewhere deep in the recesses of the structure, his *beneméritos* ("honorable ones," a.k.a. the militia) are believed to have shot Catalunya's former president, Lluís Companys, in 1941. The fort was not available for recreational use until Franco rededicated it to the city in 1960.

Since re-acquiring the mountain, Barcelona has given Montjuïc a new identity, transforming it from a military stronghold into a vast park by day and playground by night. Montjuïc served as the site of the 1992 Olympics (see **Life & Times,** p. 47), and today the park is one of the city's most visited attractions, with a little bit of something for everyone—world-famous art museums and theater, Olympic history and facilities, walking and biking trails, a healthy/unhealthy dose of nightlife, and an awe-inspiring historical cemetery.

Visitors be forewarned: Montjuïc is a park, not a neighborhood, and as such is not the easiest area to navigate. Street signs are scant, building and renovation projects are ongoing, and the park is immense. In times of need, a simple map marking particular locations and the curves of major roads is most helpful—the Barcelona tourist office map (see **Service Directory,** p. 317) or El Corte Inglés map (see **Shopping,** p. 191) works well, as does the map in the map index at the back of this book.

DON'T MISS...

Sights: The **Castell de Montjuïc** (see p. 88) offers incredible views of the city and the sea; re-live the '92 Summer Olympics with a visit to the **Estadi Olímpic** and the **Anella Olímpica** (see p. 89).

Museums & Galleries: The **Fundació Joan Miró** (see p. 118) will make you a fan of the renowned artist; the **MNAC** (see p. 120) exhibits world-famous Romanesque murals and Gothic murals.

Food & Drink: For a tranquil dining experience, try **La Font de Prades** (see p. 143).

Nightlife: The ethereal bar **Tinta Roja** (see p. 165) hosts regular live music *espectáculos;* or dance the night away at Poble Espanyol's clubs (see p. 165).

ZONA ALTA

Zona Alta ("Uptown") is the section of Barcelona that lies at the top of most maps: past l'Eixample, in and around the Collserola mountains, and away from the low-lying waterfront districts. The Zona Alta is made of several formerly independent towns. Although all of these have now been incorporated into Barcelona's city limits as residential areas, each neighborhood retains its own character and attractions.

GRÀCIA

🄵 *Orientation: Gràcia lies past l'Eixample, above Av. Diagonal and C. de Còrsega, and stretches up to the Park Güell.* **Sights:** *see p. 91.* **Food & Drink:** *see p. 144.* **Nightlife:** *see p. 166.* **Public Transportation:** *M: L700essps, Fontana, Diagonal, and Joanic, or FGC: Gràcia. Buses #24, 25, 28, and N4 serve the area.*

see map p. 346

Originally an independent, largely working-class village, Gràcia was incorporated into Barcelona in 1897, to the protest of its residents. Calls for Gràcian independence continue even today, albeit with less frequency. The area has always had a political streak—a theme that appears in the names of Mercat de Llibertat, Pl. de la Revolució, and others. After incorporation, the area continued to be a center of left-wing activism and resistance, even throughout the oppressive Franco regime. Gràcia still retains plenty of its independent, activist spirit—political graffiti and rallies are common sights.

Gràcia packs a surprising number of Modernist buildings and parks, international cuisine, and chic shops into its relatively small area, making it very walkable. The people here come from diverse backgrounds, fitting nicely into a neighborhood that charms and confuses with its narrow alleys and numerous *plaças*. It is both a solidly middle-class residential area and an up-and-coming young bohemia. And because it is relatively untouched by much tourism, Gràcia retains a local charm that has been sapped from some of Barcelona's more popular sections. If you're in town in August, be sure to check out the *Festa Major* (see p. 20), a weeklong party that draws in Barcelonenses from all corners of the city.

DON'T MISS...

Sights: Spend an afternoon amidst the mosaic wonderland of **Park Güell** (see p. 91).

Shopping: Handmade jewelry dazzles with cheap chic at **Locura Cotidiana** (see p. 186).

Food & Drink: The eclectic international restaurants are sure to charm; be sure to sample vegetarian delicacies served in a fauna-draped courtyard at **La Buena Tierra** (see p. 144).

Nightlife: Drink under the stars with the locals swarming **Pl. del Sol** (see p. 166).

HORTA & VALL D'HEBRON

🄵 *Orientation: Horta and Vall d'Hebron lie past l'Eixample Dreta, in the upper northeastern corner of the city.* **Sights:** *see p. 96.* **Food & Drink:** *see p. 145.* **Public Transportation:** *M: Horta, Vall d'Hebron, Mundet, and Montbau.*

Horta did not lose its status as an independent village until 1904, and its abundance of narrow pedestrian streets and old apartment buildings attest to that small town history. It boasts a few farmhouses and fortresses from the Middle Ages, as well as aristocratic estates dating from the 19th century, when the base of the Collserola mountains were a popular place for wealthy country homes. In contrast, the neighboring **Vall d'Hebron** was built up specifically to serve as one of four main Olympic venues in 1992, serving as the center of the cycling, tennis, and archery competitions. In general, however, the area is a little-touristed home to dozens of apartment buildings, leaving it with a nondescript atmosphere perfect for suburbanites but lacking the adventure and excitement sought for by many travelers.

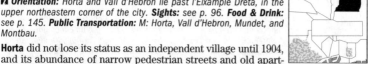

DON'T MISS...

Sights: An afternoon wandering the luscious **Jardins del Laberint D'Horta** (see p. 96).

Food & Drink: Indulge in a cup of *cava* and medieval inspiration in the feudal tower of **Can Cortada** (see p. 145).

PEDRALBES & LES CORTS

🗺 Orientation: *Pedralbes and Les Corts lie above Sants, below the mountains, and west of C. Numància.* **Sights:** *see p. 96.* **Food & Drink:** *see p. 145.* **Public Transportation:** *M: Palau Reial or Collblanc. Buses #22, 63, 64, 75, and 114 run through the neighborhood.*

see map p. 347

Welcome to Pedralbes 90210, home to Barcelona's rich and famous. In the 1950s, the growing University of Barcelona moved most of its academic buildings to the area, but the neighborhood is hardly a "college town," as it remains one of the city's most exclusive residential areas. This part of Zona Alta also has great shopping, particularly along Av. Diagonal.

DON'T MISS...

Sights: Pedralbes was chosen by Queen Elisenda de Montcada in the 14th century as the site of the **Monestir de Pedralbes** (see p. 96), home of the Poor Clares.

Entertainment: Les Corts's most beloved residents are, of course, the *fútbol* superstars on **El Barça** (see **p. 175**), whose stadium **Camp Nou** is here.

SANTS

see map p. 351

🗺 Orientation: *Sants occupies the western end of the city, between Gran Via de Carles III and C. Tarragona, the area's border with l'Eixample. Montjuïc borders on the ocean side and Les Corts toward the mountains.* **Food & Drink:** *see p. 146.* **Accommodations:** *see p. 207.* **Public Transportation:** *M: Sants-Estació and Pl. de Sants. Bus lines include #32, 44, 78, and 109, coming mostly from the outskirts of the city.*

The Sants neighborhood began as a resting post for travelers heading into historic walled Barcelona (the city gates closed shortly after dark). Today, the area still serves as a point of entry for travelers coming through the city's international train station, **Estació Barcelona-Sants,** but its status as a textile manufacturing zone hardly makes Sants a warm welcome for weary travelers. The busy industrial and commercial area features narrow streets, low-level apartment buildings, plazas, and a park where factories once stood. Flooded with locals who do much of their household shopping along C. de Sants, the area attracts few tourists besides those passing through the train station. Sants does have an eclectic display of colorful political graffiti, especially in and around the run-down Parc de l'Espanya Industrial. There are a few good hotels and hostels if you want to stay close to the station.

SARRIÀ

🗺 Orientation: *Sarrià lies at the base of the Collserola mountains and is loosely bordered by Av. Pedralbes and Av. Tibidabo on either side. Divided from l'Eixample and Les Corts by Av. Diagonal; Via Augusta separates it from Gràcia.* **Sights:** *see p. 98.* **Food & Drink:** *see p. 146.* **Public Transportation:** *FGC: Bonanova, Tres Torres, Sarrià, and Reina Elisenda. Bus lines include #66, 30, and 34.*

see map p. 354

Sarrià enjoys both meanings of the name Zona Alta ("Uptown")—economic prosperity and an elevated altitude. The last neighborhood to be incorporated into the city (1921), Sarrià often falls off the edge of Barcelona maps. Its geographical fringe status, however, holds many un-touristed sights and residential splendor. Sarrià is home to some of the city's most coveted apartments, mansions, and chic boutiques, yet the neighborhood's center, Pl. Sarrià, still retains an Old World village feel.

COLLSEROLAS & TIBIDABO

⚐ Orientation: *The Collserola mountain range, 17km long and 6km wide, marks the western limit of Barcelona, and incorporates the neighborhoods of Tibidabo and Vallvidrera. **Sights:** see p. 99. **Food & Drink:** see p. 147. **Public Transportation:** the Tibibus runs from Pl. de Catalunya to Pl. Tibidabo (the very top of the mountain) stopping only once en route (every 30-40min., only when the Parc d'Attracions is open; 285ptas/€1,71). The first bus from Pl. de Catalunya leaves 1hr. before park opening and the last usually leaves Pl. Tibidabo at 10pm, but schedules change frequently; for current details, call 010. Wheelchair accessible. An **FGC train** (U7 line) runs from Pl. de Catalunya to the Tibidabo stop (€1); it stops at the foot of the peak in Pl. JFK, where C. Balmes turns into the Av. Tibidabo. **Bus #58** also runs from Pl. de Catalunya to Pl. JFK. The **neighborhood bus** (every 20 min.; M-F 7:45am-9pm, Sa-Su and holidays 8:10am-9pm; €1) and the 100 year-old **Tram Via Blau** (every 20 min. 10am-8:05pm, every 15-30min.; one-way €1.90, round-trip €2.70) ascend the steep Av. Tibidabo from Pl. JFK. Both the bus and tram take about 5min. to get to tiny Pl. Dr. Andreu, where the **funicular** continues to Pl. Tibidabo (6min. every 30min.; departure schedules change to match the park's hours; one-way €2, round-trip €3; over 60 one-way €1.50, round-trip €2; under 3 free). Not wheelchair accessible. A Metro pass covers the FGC train and funicular on a single ticket; this combination is the cheapest way up the mountain and the only way to reach the church when the amusement park is closed.*

The Collserola mountains hovered between wilderness and civilization for centuries. Remains from the Neolithic and Bronze Ages found in the park suggest it was home to many long before the Romans set up shop in the area. With the fall of the Roman Empire (see **Life & Times**, p. 40), Barcelona became vulnerable to the attack of many German tribes, forcing peasants north to defend their territory. For most of the last 1000 years, the area has been home to agricultural people who built the area's historic chapels and *masías* (traditional Catalan farmhouses). In 1860, with the Industrial Revolution, the people of Barcelona began to notice the area's potential for leisure and summer housing; in the last century, the installation of railtracks, trams, and funiculars has made the mountains easily accessible to urban residents wanting to take advantage of the mountains' offerings.

The **Parc de Collserola** (see **Sights**, p. 100) encompasses essentially the entire chain of mountains; the landscape ranges from almost entirely wild to well-populated. Tibidabo, the highest peak (512m), hosts a century-old amusement park and the popular Sagrat Cor church, while the hilltop town of Vallvidrera and the communications tower **Torre de Collserola** occupy a slightly lower peak nearby (see **Sights**, p. 100).

The man most responsible for the development of Tibidabo and surrounding slopes was Dr. Salvador Andreu, who in 1899 founded the Tibidabo Society and invested heavily in the land, installing transportation and building hotels, the amusement park, and an extravagant casino, now in ruins. Soon after, the Barcelona bourgeoisie rushed to outdo one another in country-home construction, and the hillsides are now dotted with outstanding examples of early 20th-century Modernist and Noucentist (a return to classical forms) architecture (see **Life & Times**, p. 53). Many of these former homes now house offices and schools.

DON'T MISS...

Sights: Gaze down on Barcelona from the heavenly heights of El Sagrat Cor

Food & Drink: Dine in a medieval setting at El Asador de Aranda.

Nightlife: Sip *cava* or cocktails with the glistening lights of Barcelona sprawling before you and your honey at

Museums: Press their buttons and watch 'em go at the Museu d'Automats

WHEN TO GO

The tourist season officially runs from mid-June through late August, when the city is filled to capacity with travelers and the weather is at its most beachy; be aware that July and especially August are also the months when native Barceloneses take advantage of their month off from work and vacate the city. Cheaper tickets and comparably good weather prevail throughout the spring and early fall. Traveling to Barcelona around Christmas can get expensive, as travel companies know that Christian Europeans will pay exorbitant amounts of money to celebrate the holidays with their families.

SEASONAL HIGHLIGHTS

Rest up, because it's time to party Barcelona-style. While Barcelona is quite different from the rest of Spain, the city shares at least one thing in common with the rest of the country—it knows how to have fun. Festivals abound in this happening city; the trick is to know what will be going on during your visit. For information on all festivals, call ☎ 93 301 77 75 (open M-F 10am-2pm and 4-8pm). Below is a summary of the major festivals in and around Barcelona.

SPRING

With the warm breezes and chirping birds, love is in the air every spring in Barcelona. **Día de Sant Jordi,** celebrated on April 23, is a favorite day for the lovebirds out there. A festival in honor of one of Barcelona's favorite saints, the festivities involve men purchasing roses for their girlfriends and women purchasing books for their boyfriends. Check out the flower district on Las Ramblas during this time, as it will be selling both books and flowers just for this special occasion (see p. 59). **Setmana Santa** (Catholic Holy week; the week leading up to Easter) is a huge festival complete with grand processions; Barcelona natives pour into the streets to celebrate. On May 10-11, **Fira de Sant Ponç,** a festival dedicated to the patron saint of beekeepers, is celebrated on C. Hospital near Las Ramblas (see p. 58). To satisfy your inner child, head over to Estació de França for the **International Comics Fair,** held every May.

SUMMER

Festivals dubbed **"Festa Major"** are known for their size and popularity. Poble Nou (see p. 13), Sants (see p. 18), Gràcia (see p. 17), and Sitges (see p. 239) host these huge summer festivals. **Focs de Sant Joan** is held in Girona on June 24 (see p. 218). For those on the life-long quest to find a dancing egg, your journey stops in Barcelona. The **Corpus Cristi** festival occurs in June and includes huge parades, huge carnival figures, and of course, the traditional *ou com balla*—the dancing egg. Theater, dance, music, and movies flood Barcelona's top venues from late June to the end of July during the city-wide **Grec Festival.**

AUTUMN

Bring your Catalan flag and other favorite Catalan-pride paraphernalia to the **Catalan National Day Festival,** held September 11. You'll find people dressed in traditional costumes and homes decorated with the flag and shield pattern. Wine-makers and *butifarra* (sausage)-makers pile into Barcelona from the surrounding areas to present their goods during the **Feria de Cuina i Vins de Catalunya;** for one entire fall week, you can taste food and wine for only a small price. September 24 brings fireworks and devils to town for the **Festa de la Verge de la Mercè,** when *correfocs* (devils) run through the streets, flashing their pitchforks at the nearby residents. To retaliate, people throw buckets of water at the devils. Human towers (see **I've Got the Tower,** p. 244) are also a common occurrence in the streets around this time of year. Come October, Barceloneses trade their pitchforks and buckets for saxophones as the **Festival Internacional de Jazz** comes to town. Be prepared to hear lots of jazz in the streets and clubs, as some of the finest musicians perform for this event. **The Festival del Sant Çito** begins in November, and all in all, becomes one of the best city-wide parties. Make your way to Las Ramblas and let the Barceloneses teach you how to party like you never have before.

WINTER

Christmastime proves to be a major time for festivities, but people do tend to spend more time with their families than on the streets. Rather than a huge celebration occurring on Christmas Eve or Day, Spaniards tend to have a family dinner on *Nochebuena* (Christmas Eve), the most important holiday of the year. While the exact kind of food varies from family to family depending on tradition, some typical foods include: *entremeses de jamón serrano, lomo, chorizo, y queso* (appetizers of serrano ham, red hard sausage, and cheese), *ensalada de escarola y aceitunas y vinagre* (salad with olives and oil and vinegar), *langostinos* and *gambas* (shrimp), *cordero asado* (roasted lamb with garlic), and *pavo* (turkey). There are also many sweets associated with *Nochebuena*, like *turrón* (a chocolate-like treat that can be plain or include goodies like almonds or coconut), *mazapán* (marzipan), and *polvoroneolms* (made from crushed almonds and sugar).

Spaniards hold off on exchanging presents until January 5, the **Epiphany,** the day the Three Kings ride their camels into Spain. The night of January 4th, children put their shoes outside to be filled with gifts and candy by the visiting Kings. That night, people gather to devour *roscón*, an oval-shaped sweet bread with a small toy baked into it. If someone finds the special toy, he or she gets to keep it and is dubbed King or Queen for the year. But if someone finds a bean baked into the *roscón*, the unlucky person must pay for the *roscón*. Speaking of special prizes, the **caganer** ("shitter") become even more popular during this season; just be careful where you step (see p. 214). As residents prepare for the new year, the price of grapes will suddenly skyrocket. Why? For good luck, Spaniards gather all of their friends together on **New Year's Eve,** and when the clock strikes midnight, people begin to pop a grape into their mouth for each chime, twelve in all.

Come February, join natives in celebrating **Festes de Santa Eulàlia,** a holiday dedicated to Barcelona's first patron saint. The Mayor's office organizes events for the city and arranges the special guest appearances by *mulasses* (dragons) in parades. Concerts abound during this time. During **Festa de San Medir,** held in Tibidabo, Barcelona's young and old race to the mountain to be showered with candy by men galloping on horses down the mountain. In February, residents celebrate the end of winter and their last week of indulgence before Lent with **Carnaval.** The more daring head over to Sitges (see p. 239) or Vilanova i la Geltrù (see p. 243) for some especially rowdy partying.

Once in Barcelona

ORIENTATION

Barcelona's layout is quite simple. Imagine yourself perched atop Columbus's head at the **Monument a Colom** (on **Passeig de Colom,** parallel to the shore), viewing the city with the sea at your back. From the harbor, the city slopes upward toward the mountains. Keep this in mind if you need to re-orient yourself. From the Columbus monument, **Las Ramblas** (see p. 58), the main thoroughfare, runs from the harbor up to **Plaça de Catalunya** (M: Catalunya; see p. 59), the city's center. The **Ciutat Vella** (Old City; see p. 58) is the heavily touristed historical neighborhood, which centers around Las Ramblas and includes the Barri Gòtic, La Ribera, and El Raval. The **Barri Gòtic** (see p. 62) is east of Las Ramblas (to the right, with your back to the sea; see p. 62), enclosed on the other side by **Via Laietana.** East of Via Laietana lies the maze-like neighborhood of **La Ribera** (see p. 70), which borders Parc de la Ciutadella and the Estació de França train station. On the west side of Las Ramblas (to the left, with your back to the sea) is **El Raval** (see p. 75).

Beyond Parc de la Ciutadella (farther east, outside the Ciutat Vella) is the **Poble Nou** and the **Vila Olímpic** (see p. 86), with its twin towers (the tallest buildings in Barcelona; see p. 86) and a shiny assortment of malls, discos, and restaurants. Beyond El Raval (to the west) rises **Montjuïc** (see p. 88), crammed with gardens, museums, the 1992 Olympic grounds, the Montjuïc castle, and other tourist attractions.

Directly behind you as you sit atop the Monument a Colom is the **Port Vell** (Old Port; see p. 87) development, where a wavy bridge leads across to the ultra-modern shopping and entertainment complexes **Moll d'Espanya** and **Maremàgnum** (see p. 181).

in recent news

The Melting Pot

Watch out, world! Barcelona, the Spanish Government, and UNESCO are uniting to stamp out racism, ignorance, and poverty! Or so says the mission for the first **Universal Forum of Cultures**, a huge summer-long festival set to bloom for the first time in 2004 right here in sunny Barcelona. The event, which runs from May 9th to Sept. 26th, seeks to promote a "renewal of thought and attitudes" toward cultural diversity, sustainable development, and conditions for peace through a powerhouse of events from six film festivals to over 60 international congresses to over 300 "gastronomic experiences." With this marking the Forum's inaugural event, the sponsors are envisioning a global communal experience akin to the Olympics, with an even more important message. What does this mean for Barcelona? Tons of new parks (140,000 sq. m, to be exact), renewed seashore and beaches, and a sparklingly rejuvenated face to the city which will greet the world. Some are even drawing comparisons to the makeovers preceding the **Universal Exposition of 1888** and the **1992 Olympics**. But while this means fun and games for Barcelona, in the summer, winter, and spring tourists should watch out for unexpected construction as the city beautifies for the Forum.

In front of you, to the North, beyond the Ciutat Vella, is **l'Eixample** (see p. 76), the gridded neighborhood created during the urban expansion of the 1860s, which runs from Pl. de Catalunya toward the mountains. **Gran Via de les Corts Catalanes** defines its lower edge and **Passeig de Gràcia**, l'Eixample's main commercial street, bisects the neighborhood. **Avinguda Diagonal** marks the upper limit of the grid-planned neighborhoods, separating l'Eixample from the **Zona Alta** ("Uptown;" see p. 91), which includes Pedralbes, Sarrià, Gràcia, and Horta, some of the older neighborhoods in the foothills. The peak of Tibidabo, the northwest border of the city and the highest point in Barcelona, offers the most comprehensive view of the city.

GETTING TO & FROM BARCELONA

BY PLANE (EL PRAT DE LLOBREGAT)

All flights land at **El Prat de Llobregat** airport (☎ 93 298 38 38; www.aena.es/ae/bcn/homepage), 12km (8 mi.) southwest of Barcelona. From the airport, there are several options for transport into the city. The **Aerobus** links the airport to Pl. de Espanya and Pl. de Catalunya, the center of town (approx. 40min.; every 15min.; to Pl. de Catalunya M-F 6am-midnight, Sa-Su 6:30am-midnight, to the airport M-F 5:30am-11:15pm, Sa-Su 6am-11:20pm; €3.30).

RENFE (24hr. info ☎ 93 491 31 83; www.renfe.es) trains provide slightly cheaper transportation to and from the airport (43min.; every 30min.; 6:13am-11:15pm from airport, 5:43am-11:24pm from Sants; €2.15). The most useful stops are **Estació Barcelona-Sants** and **Plaça de Catalunya.** Tickets are sold at the red automatic machines. In Sants, buy tickets at the "Aeroport" window (open 5am-11pm). After 11pm, get them from the ticket machines or the Recorridos Cercanías window.

The city **bus** offers the only inexpensive late-night service. Take bus #106 from the airport to Pl. de Espanya (airport to Pl. de Espanya every hr. 6:20am-10:15pm, then 11:35pm, 12:50am, 2:05am, and 3:20am; Pl. de Espanya to airport 7:10am-3:15am with similarly erratic late-night service; €1). The stop in Pl. de Espanya is on the corner of Gran Via de les Corts Catalanes and Av. Reina Maria Cristina. A **taxi** ride between Barcelona and the airport costs €18-27.

Three **national airlines** serve all domestic and major international destinations. **Iberia/Aviaco,** Diputación, 258 (☎902 40 05 00), has the most extensive coverage. Iberia/Aviaco usually offers student discounts (except on already reduced fares). **Air Europa** (☎902 40 15 01; www.air-europa.com) and **Spanair** (☎902 13 14 15) offer fares that are often cheaper.

All major international airlines serve Barcelona, including **British Airways** (☎902 11 13 33, airport office ☎93 298 34 55; open 6am-7pm) and **Delta** (☎901 11 69 46; www.delta-air.com). **Easy Jet** (☎902 29 99 92; www.easyjet.com) also offers flights from Barcelona to Amsterdam, Geneva, Liverpool, and London. For more information on international reservations, visit a travel agency in Barcelona (see **Service Directory,** p. 317).

Walking Over the Miró Mosaic

BY TRAIN

Trains are an easy and affordable way to travel within Catalunya and Spain. Barcelona has two main stations which serve different destinations. When in doubt, go to Estació Barcelona-Sants; while all domestic trains leaving Estació França pass through here, not all trains leaving Barcelona-Sants necessarily pass through Estació França. A taxi between either station and the Pl. de Catalunya will cost approximately €6. For general information about trains and train stations in Barcelona, call RENFE, Spain's main train company (☎902 24 02 02).

Bike Tricks at Miró Park

Estació Barcelona-Sants, in Pl. Països Catalans. M: Sants-Estació. Buses to the station include #30 from Pl. de Espanya, #44 through L'Eixample (stops at La Sagrada Família), and N2. Barcelona-Sants is the main terminal for domestic and international traffic. For late arrivals, the N14 Nitbus shuttles to Pl. de Catalunya (every 30min. 10:30pm-4:30am, €1). Services include: currency exchange (open 8am-10pm), ATMs, pharmacy, tourist office, restaurants, phone center, and touristy shopping. Internet available (€1 for 13 min.) in the back of the station in the video-game room. Large lockers €4.50 per 24hr., small €3; storage open daily 5:30am-11:00pm. Station open M-F 4:30am-midnight, Sa-Su 5am-midnight.

Estació França (☎902 24 02 02), Av. Marqués de l'Argentera. M: Barceloneta. Buses include #17 from Pl. de Catalunya and N6. Open daily 7am-10pm. This recently restored 19th-century station on the edge of the Ciutat Vella serves regional destinations on RENFE, including Girona, Tarragona, and Zaragoza, as well as some international arrivals.

View of Port

BY BUS

Buses are often cheaper and more direct than trains, if you don't mind the lengthy travel times. Most—but not all—buses arrive at the **Barcelona Nord Estació d'Auto-buses,** C. Ali-bei, 80 (☎902 30 32 22). The small Nord station features a sandwich shop, restaurant, candy shop, a butcher, money exchange, and luggage storage. The building also houses an office of the **Guardia Urbana,** the local police. (☎93 265 61 32. M: Arc de Triomf, exit to Nàpols. Info office open daily 7am-9pm.) Buses that go there include #54 along Gran Via (a block from Pl. de Catalunya) and N11. A taxi from Pl. de Catalunya to the station will cost approximately €4. Other buses, particularly **international buses,** arrive at the **Estació d'Autobuses de Sants** station, next to the train station in Pl. Països Catalans (see above). The following companies operate out of Estació Nord:

Eurolines (☎902 40 50 40; www.eurolines.es). Transportation to **London** (25hr., 8:45am and 5:45pm, €92).

Sarfa (☎902 30 20 25; www.sarfa.com). Sarfa buses stop at many beach towns along the Costa Brava, north of Barcelona. Open daily 8am-9pm. To: **Cadaqués** (2½hr., 11:15am and 8:25pm, €15.15); **Palafrugell** (2hr., 13 per day, €11.40); **Tossa del Mar** (1½hr., 10 per day 9am-9pm, €7.50).

Linebús (☎93 265 07 00). Open M-F 8am-8pm, Sa 8:30am-1pm and 5-8pm. To **Paris** (13hr., M-Sa 8pm, €80). Also has daily service to southern France and Morocco. Discounts for travelers under 26 and over 60.

Alsa Enatcar (☎902 42 22 42; www.alsa.es). To: **Alicante** (9hr., 3 per day, €32.46); **Madrid** (8hr., 13 per day, €22.08); **Valencia** (4hr., 16 per day, €20.46); **Zaragoza** (3½-4½hr., 20 per day, €17.74); **Naples** (24hr., 5:15pm, €113).

BY FERRY

Barcelona's prime Mediterranean location makes the city an ideal gateway to the **Balearic Islands,** which are renowned for their beaches, raging clubs, and resorts. The main ferry station is **Estació Marítima,** in Port Vell. (M: Drassanes.) Head down Las Ramblas to the **Monument a Colom.** Columbus points straight toward the Estació Marítima. Cross the street and walk right, along the waterfront, until you see the large Trasmediterránea building on your left. Two companies operate out of Estació Marítima. Both offer discounts for students and seniors. Tickets are available at any travel agency or at Estació Marítima.

Trasmediterránea (☎902 45 46 45; fax 93 295 91 34), in Estació Marítima-Moll Barcelona, Moll de Sant Bertran. In the summer months only to: **Ibiza** (10-11hr., 1 per day M-Sa, €45.43); **Palma** (3½hr., 1 per day, €63); **Mahón** (10½hr., 1 per day starting mid-June, €45.43).

Turbocat (☎902 18 18 88; www.turbocatonline.com), in Estació Marítima-Moll Barcelona, Moll de Sant Bertran. In the summer months only to: **Ciutadella** (3½hr., 1 per day, €65) and **Alcuida** (5hr., 1 per day, €62).

GETTING AROUND BARCELONA

BY METRO AND FGC

Barcelona's public transportation system (info ☎010, claims 93 318 70 74) is quick, cheap, and all-around excellent. The *Guia d'Autobuses Urbans de Barcelona,* free at tourist offices and in Metro stations, maps out the city's bus routes and the five Metro lines; the small book *Guia Facil del Bus per Mour't per Barcelona6* also free, describes the routes in even more detail.

If you plan to use public transportation extensively, consider buying one of the several *abonos* (passes) available, all of which work interchangeably for the Metro, bus, urban lines of the FGC commuter trains, and the Nitbus. The **T-1 pass** (€5.60) is valid for 10 rides and saves you nearly 50% off the cost of single tickets. The **T-Día pass** (€4.20) is good for a full day of unlimited travel, while the **T-Mes** (€36.30) and the **T-Trisemestre** (€100) offer the same for one month and 90 days respectively. The **T-50/30** (€23.40) buys 50 trips in a 30-day period. Finally, for short stays, the **3 Dies** (€10.80) gets you three days of unlimited travel; the **5 Dies** (€16.50) is good for five days. Both save you money if you use the Metro more than three times per day.

Metro (☎93 486 07 52; www.tmb.net). Automatic vending machines and ticket windows sell Metro passes. Stations are indicated by red diamonds with the letter "M" inside of them. Hold on to your ticket until you leave the Metro—an official with a white-and-red pin-striped shirt may ask to see it. Riding without a ticket carries a hefty fine of €40. Most trains run M-Th 5am-midnight, F-Sa 5am-2am, Su and holidays 6am-midnight. €1 per *sencillo* (single ride).

Ferrocarrils de la Generalitat de Catalunya: FGC (☎93 205 15 15; www.fgc.es). Commuter trains with main stations at Pl. de Catalunya and Pl. de Espanya. Service to **Montserrat** (from Pl. de Espanya). Blue symbols resembling two interlocking "V"s mark connections with the Metro. The commuter line charges the same as the Metro (€1) until Tibidabo. After that, rates go up by zone: zone 2 destinations €1.50, zone 3 destinations €2.10. Metro passes are valid on FGC trains. Information office at the Pl. de Catalunya station open M-F 7am-9pm.

BY BUS

Barcelona has a comprehensive bus system, with more than 80 lines connecting different parts of the city. Bus stops have red signs and brown benches under a small roof; bus lines that use the stop will be posted there. Always respect the line at the bus stop. Try to buy a ticket before you get on the bus, as the drivers tend to be cranky about cash and may even refuse to make change. When you get on the bus, you'll see two machines at the front; if you have a Metro pass, insert your ticket into it, printed side facing up, arrow pointing down, and the machine will stamp your ticket. To signal the driver to stop, press the small red buttons on the railing inside the bus. Most major lines are partially wheelchair accessible, meaning that at least some, though not all, of the buses on the line have wheelchair lifts (see Travelers with Disabilities in **Planning Your Trip,** p. 297). Buses keep the same hours and charge the same fees as the Metro (see above). See the *Guia d'Autobuses Urbans* or *Guia Facil del Bus*, free at tourist offices or Metro stations, for more detail. Some of the most useful lines include the following:

#10: Bisects the city from top to bottom, passing by the Parc de la Vall d'Hebron, La Sagrada Família, Teatre Nacional, Parc de la Ciutadella, Museu d'Art Modern, and Parc de las Cascades on the way to its final stop on Pg. Marítim, right in front of Platja Barceloneta. Partially wheelchair accessible.

#14: Begins above l'Eixample Dreta and runs down Las Ramblas, stopping near the Mercat de la Boquería, Palau de la Música Catalana, Catedral, and Gran Teatre de Liceu. Continues from there to the Museu Marítim and Port Vell and then takes Pg. Colom past the Estació de França, Parc de la Ciutadella, Estació de Autobuses Barcelona Nord, and finally Vila Olímpica. Partially wheelchair accessible.

#19: Starts in Port Vell and passes near the Museu Picasso, Palau de la Música Catalana, the Arc de Triomf, and La Sagrada Família. Partially wheelchair accessible.

#24: Runs from Pl. de Catalunya up Pg. de Gràcia to Park Güell, along the way passing by La Manzana de la Discòrdia, Casa Milà, and the Palau Robert. Partially wheelchair accessible.

#50: The most useful part of this line connects Montjuïc to La Sagrada Família, passing by the Palau Nacional, Estadi Olímpic, and Poble Espanyol. Partially wheelchair accessible.

Bus Turístic: Departing from the Pl. de Catalunya, this bus is one of the easiest ways to get to all the tourist attractions in the city.

BY NITBUS

When the regular bus system and Metro close, the Nitbus begins. Sixteen different lines run 10:30pm-4:30am, usually every 20-30 min., depending on the line; a few run until 5:30am. Almost all the buses have stops near the Pl. de Catalunya; a Metro pass is valid on the Nitbus. The buses stop in front of most club complexes and work their way through the Ciutat Vella and the Zona Alta. Maps are available at *estancos* (tobacco shops) and marked by signs in Metro stations. (☎901 51 11 51; single ride €1).

BY TAXI

Taxis are everywhere in Barcelona. On weekend nights, however, you may wait up to 30min. in some locations; long lines form at popular club spots like the Port Olímpic. A *lliure* or *libre* sign in the windshield or a lit green light on the roof means they are vacant; yellow means they are occupied. To summon a cab by phone, try the companies listed in the **Service Directory,** p. 316. Disabled travelers should call ☎93 420 80 88. Taxi prices are set: Monday through Friday the first 6min. or 1.9km cost €1.80; each additional km is €0.66. After 10pm on Saturday, Sunday, and fiesta days, the first 6min. or 1.9km cost €1.95, and each additional km is €0.84.

BY BICYCLE AND MOPED

As you make your way through the streets of the city, be wary of speeding business-men and grandmothers on *motos*. It seems as if everyone in Barcelona owns a moped. To change your status from the hunted to the hunter, visit one of Barcelona's many rental shops. Bicycles are not widely used in the city.

Vanguard Rent a Car, C. Viladomat, 297, between Londres and París (☎93 439 38 80). Min. age 19 to rent (ID required). Mopeds start at €36.95 per day if renting for 3 days or less, €34.56 per day for more than 3 days, and €32.80 per day for more than 7 days. More expensive, 2-person *motos* also available. Insurance, helmet, and IVA included. Open M-F 8am-1:30pm and 4-7:30pm, Sa-Su 9am-1pm.

BY CAR

Public transportation is by far the easiest way to get around the city; cars are more of a hassle than they are useful. Spanish drivers are notoriously aggressive, gas is expensive, and parking in Barcelona is an adventure every day. If you plan to drive in the hazardously tight Ciutat Vella, you had better have nerves of steel and above-average dexterity. To drive a car while in Spain, you must be over 18; an **International Driving Permit** (IDP; see **Planning Your Trip,** p. 295) is highly recommended.

FINDING YOUR PIMPMOBILE

Except for reaching small towns in the Pyrenees with infrequent bus service, travel-ing in Spain and living in Barcelona do not necessitate the use of a car, which will only triple the cost of a trip. For those who desire that get-up-and-go convenience, you can generally make reservations before you leave by calling major international offices in your home country. However, occasionally the price and availability infor-mation they give doesn't jive with what the local offices in Barcelona will claim. Check with both offices and make sure you get the correct price and information. Car rental agencies in Barcelona include:

Avis/Auto Europe, Casanova, 209 (☎93 209 95 33). Will rent to ages 21-25 for an addi-tional fee of about US$5 a day.

Budget, Av. Josep Tarradellas, 35 (☎93 410 25 08). Must be 25. **Branch** in El Prat de Llobregat airport (see p. 35).

Docar, C. Montnegre, 18 (24hr. ☎93 439 81 19). M: Les Corts. Free delivery and pickup. From €13.80 per day plus €9 insurance and €0.15 per km. Open M-F 8:30am-2pm and 3:30-8pm, Sa 9am-2pm.

Hertz, C. Tuset, 10 (☎93 217 80 76; www.hertz.es). M: Diagonal or FCG: Gràcia. Open M-F 9am-2pm and 4pm-7pm, Sa 9am-2pm. **Branch** in El Prat de Llobregat airport (☎93 298 36 37; see p. 35).

Tot Car, C. Berlín, 97 (☎93 430 01 98). Free delivery and pickup. From €27 per day, plus €0.13 per km. Insurance included. Open M-F 8am-2pm and 3-8pm, Sa 9am-1pm.

To rent a car from most of these establishments, you need to be at least 21 years old; very few let 18-year-olds slip by. Some agencies require renters to be 25, and most charge those under 25 an additional insurance fee (around US $5-6 per day). Policies and prices vary from agency to agency. Small local operations occasionally rent to people under 21, but be sure to ask about the insurance coverage and deductible, and always check the fine print. Try to get a policy that includes **roadside assistance.**

Teleferic Cablecar

COSTS AND INSURANCE

Including basic insurance and taxes, rental car prices start at around US$125 per day from national companies. Expect to pay more for larger cars and for 4WD. Cars with **automatic transmission** can cost twice as much as standard manuals (stick shift), and in some places, automatic transmission is hard to find in the first place. It is virtually impossible, no matter where you are, to find an automatic 4WD.

Outdoor Escalator at Park Güell

Many rental packages offer unlimited km, while others offer a set number of km per day with a per-km surcharge after that. Be sure to ask whether the price includes **insurance** against theft and collision. Remember that if you are driving a conventional vehicle on an **unpaved road** in a rental car, you are almost never covered by insurance; ask about this before leaving the rental agency. Beware that cars rented on **American Express** or **Visa/Mastercard Gold** or **Platinum** credit cards in Spain might *not* carry the automatic insurance that they would in some other countries; check with your credit card company. Insurance plans almost always come with a **deductible** (or excess) for conventional vehicles; this means you pay for all damages up to that sum, unless they are the fault of another vehicle. The deductible you will be quoted applies to collisions with other vehicles; colli-

Estació França

sions with non-vehicles, such as trees ("single-vehicle collisions"), will cost you even more. The deductible can often be reduced or waived entirely if you pay an additional charge.

MONEY MATTERS

The quintessential Catalan bank is Caixa Catalunya (www.laCaixa.es), better known simply as **la Caixa**—the Bank. Its distinctive logo, a blue star next to red-and-yellow dots, was designed by none other than Joan Miró, the late Catalan artist. The numbers on its ATM machines often (though not always) include the corresponding letters—a Spanish rarity which is a huge help to password-dependent American users. Special Caixa ATM machine/computers, called **ServiCaixa,** use ATM cards to sell tickets to a wide list of events. Buy tickets here to the opera, FCB matches, movies, and the zoo, just to name a few of the choices. Other, lower-profile banks found in the Barcelona area include **BancSabadell, Caixa Penedès,** and **Banesto.**

HEALTH

MEDICAL CARE

For a complete listing of hospitals in Barcelona, check the **Service Directory,** p. 315.

Should you require a house call for a condition not requiring hospitalization, contact the appropriate number from the list of emergency numbers in the **Service Directory,** p. 314. Any hospital should be able to refer you to a dentist, optometrist, or ophthalmologist. Request documentation (including diagnoses) and receipts to submit to your home insurance company for reimbursement.

EU citizens can get reciprocal health benefits, entitling them to a practitioner registered with the state system, by filling out a E111 or E112 form before departure; this is available at most major post offices. They will generally treat you whether or not you can pay in advance. EU citizens studying in Spain also qualify for long-term care. Other travelers should ensure they have adequate medical insurance before leaving; if your regular insurance policy does not cover travel abroad, you may wish to purchase additional coverage (see **Planning Your Trip,** p. 287). With the exception of Medicare, most health insurance plans cover members' medical emergencies during trips abroad; check with your insurance carrier to be sure.

If you need a **doctor** *(un metge/un médico)*, call the nearest hospital for a list of local practitioners. If you are receiving reciprocal health care, make sure you call a doctor who is linked to the state health care system. Contact your health provider for information regarding charges that may be incurred. Note that the same medicines may have different names in Spain than in your home country; check with your doctor before you leave.

MEDITERRANEAN MANNERS

CHURCH ETIQUETTE. Catalunya's religious buildings are open to the public at various hours; be aware that a visit to these edifices requires a certain dress code and respectful attitude. Shorts and tank tops are considered disrespectful; keep your arms and legs covered if you don't want to be ushered out by a clergy member. Some chapels are reserved for devotional purposes only; please respect these restrictions and only enter if you are worshiping. Camera regulations vary from site to site, but flash is almost never permitted. Noise above a whisper is inappropriate, unless you are participating in a mass.

EUROPEANS WHO DISAPPEAR IN AUGUST. The European summer schedule is quite pleasant for those who work in Europe and quite bizarre for those who come to visit. Many employees have a month off in the summer, which they usually take in August. Barcelona's native residents clear out of the city during this month and head to the nearby beach towns. The city is noticeably deflated at this time of year, although the tourists keep coming; be prepared for some small businesses, such as hostels and restaurants, to close down for a few weeks in the summer.

HOURS. Spaniards observe the siesta, which can be a nap, but also serves to describe an even grander tradition. Excluding larger companies and needed services, all of Spain shuts down for a period of three hours in the afternoon so the family can eat their midday meal—also their largest—together. Businesses generally open around 9 or 10 am, close from 2pm until 5, and open again until after 9.

SMOKING. Spaniards smoke a lot. They also smoke virtually everywhere, even where it is clearly prohibited, such as on Metro platforms. Restaurants, bars, and clubs accommodate a smoking clientele.

TIPPING & BARGAINING. They don't exist. Businesses in Spain expect you to pay no more and no less than the posted price, and may even be offended if you leave more than you owe.

KEEPING IN TOUCH

BY TELEPHONE

How much a given phone call will cost is dependent upon what sort of a call it is; this edition of *Let's Go* has formatted telephone numbers to reflect those price differences. The city code for Barcelona is 93; a number that begins with 93 is a call within the city. Other areas in Catalunya use the code 97. You must dial this city code, even within the city; it is not charged as a long distance call.

Spain is currently ensnared in a phone number format dilemma. Regional phone numbers can be listed either in the 2-3-2-2 format or the 3-3-3 format; that is, a number in Barcelona may appear either as 93 555 55 55 or 935 555 555. *Let's Go* uses the 2-3-2-2 format to visually separate local or regional calls from other sorts of calls, which begin with a three-digit prefix. A number that begins with the three-digit prefix 900 is a toll-free number; other three digit prefixes are toll numbers or mobile phone numbers that will cost copious amounts of money.

CALLING CARDS

Pay phones in Spain always accept coins, but this is not the best way to make a local or international call. Opt for prepaid **calling cards,** issued in denominations of €6 and €12 and sold at *estancos* (tobacco shops, identifiable by brown signs with yellow lettering and tobacco leaf icons) and most post offices. Some *kioscos* (newsstands) and many tourist shops along Las Ramblas also sell calling cards. Choose your phone card based on who you want to call. For **local calls** or calls from **payphones,** the cards that you insert into the payphone are best; for **international calls** or calls made from **private phones,** the telephone cards with a Personal Identification Number (PIN) and a toll-free access number are best. Instead of inserting this card into the phone, call the access number and follow the directions on the card. These cards can be used to make international as well as domestic calls, and may offer discount rates on calls to certain countries.

LOCAL CALLS

The one-and-only Spanish phone company is **Telefónica.** Phone booths are marked by signs that say *Teléfono público,* and most bars have pay phones, though they are coin-operated only and tend to cost more than public pay phones. Local calls cost €0.15 to dial and then €0.05 per min. from 8am to 6pm and €0.02 per min. from 6pm to 8am. Be aware that it is almost five times as expensive to call mobile phones (€0.24 per min. 8am-6pm; €0.12 per min. 6pm-8am; minimum charge €0.66). Phone numbers in Barcelona begin with the area code 93; if a phone number does not begin with 93 or does not have nine digits, it probably connects to a mobile phone (see **By Telephone,** above).

Fax service is available at **Easy Everything,** Las Ramblas, 31 (24hr.; local first page €1.17, additional pages €0.65; international first page €2.70, additional pages €1.77; www.easyeverything.com). Private phone and fax service is also available at **Estació Barcelona-Sants.** For directory assistance or information, dial ☎003.

INTERNATIONAL CALLS

There are two different sets of rates for international calls: *normal* and *reducida*. *Normal* rates apply 8am-8pm, and *reducida* rates apply 8pm-8am. The minimum charge for making an international call is €1.80. The following are the *normal-reducida* rates for calls from Barcelona, using change or a Telefónica phone card. To the US and Canada, €0.54-0.50 per min.; to England or Ireland €0.48-0.44 per min.; to Australia or New Zealand €1.41-1.20 per min.; to South Africa €1.65-1.50 per min. You can also buy competing phone company cards, which vary wildly in per min. charges, but often provide the best deals possible with calls to the US at less than €0.10 per min. To save money, tell the shop owner where you are calling and ask which card gives the best rates to that particular location (he will have detailed rate lists behind the counter). Beware that with some cards, calling mobile phones at home will be significantly more expensive than with others.

It is also possible to bring an international calling card from home, issued by your phone company. Calls are billed collect or to your account. These sometimes have slightly more expensive rates than the cheapest cards that you can find in Barcelona, but the convenience of billing and the security that they provide may make them worth it. You can frequently call collect without even possessing a company's calling card just by calling their access number and following the instructions. **To obtain a calling card** from your national telecommunications service before leaving home, contact the appropriate company listed below. To **call home with a calling card,** contact the operator for your service provider in Spain by dialing the appropriate toll-free access number below:

COMPANY	TO OBTAIN A CARD, DIAL:	TO CALL ABROAD, DIAL:
AT&T (US)	800-288-4685	900 990 011
British Telecom Direct	800 34 51 44	900 964 495
Canada Direct	800-668-6878	900 990 015
MCI (US)	800-444-3333	900 990 014
New Zealand Direct	0800 00 00 00	900 991 836

Call ☎025 for an international Telefónica operator (free). Placing a **collect call** through an international operator is more expensive, but may be necessary in case of an emergency. For **Directory Assistance,** call ☎1003 for numbers within Spain, ☎1008 for numbers within in Europe, and ☎1005 for numbers outside Europe.

MOBILE PHONES

For a longer stay in the city, a mobile phone might be a good investment and a great convenience, but be sure to do comparative shopping between the major companies before purchasing (Telefónica, Movistar, and Airtel offer the best service). For shorter stays, you can rent a Nokia phone from **Rent-A-Phone,** C. Numància, 212. Pay the up-front deposit of €150.25 with a credit card (AmEx/MC/V); the company will charge the same credit card €29.45 per month, in addition to €0.02 per min. for calls in Spain, and €2.10 per min. for international calls (minimum charge of €7.20 per day). The phones work from anywhere in Europe and Rent-A-Phone will retrieve these phones for free from any European country. (☎93 280 21 31. M: Maria Christina. Walk down Diagonal with El Corte Inglés on your right, then go left on C. Numància. Open M-F 9:30am-2pm and 4-7:30pm.) There is another **branch** on the second floor of Maremàgnum. (☎ 93 225 81 06. Open daily 11am-10:30pm.)

TIME DIFFERENCES

Barcelona is one hour ahead of Greenwich Mean Time (GMT), and 2 hours ahead during daylight savings time. Barcelona is 6 hours ahead of New York, 9 hours ahead of Vancouver and San Francisco. Spain observes daylight savings time, and fall and spring switchover times vary between countries. Because of this factor, in Spain's winter, Spain is 1 hour behind Johannesburg, 10 hours behind Sydney, and 12 hours behind Auckland; in Spain's summer, Spain is on the same time as Johannesburg, 8 hours behind Sydney, and 10 hours behind Auckland.

BY MAIL

SENDING MAIL HOME FROM BARCELONA

Airmail (*por avión*) takes five to eight business days to reach the US or Canada; service is faster to the UK and Ireland and slower to Australia and New Zealand. Standard postage is €0.75 to North America. Surface mail (*por barco*), while considerably less expensive than air mail, can take over a month, and packages will take two to three months. Registered or express mail (*registrado* or *certificado*) is the most reliable way to send a letter or parcel home, and takes four to seven business days. Spain's overnight mail is not worth the added expense, since it is not exactly "overnight." For better service, try private companies such as DHL, UPS, or the Spanish company SEUR; look under *mensajerías* in the yellow pages. Their reliability does, however, come at a high cost. Stamps (*sellos*) are sold at post offices and tobacconists (*estancos* or *tabacos*). Mail letters and postcards from the yellow mailboxes scattered throughout the city, or from the post office.

RECEIVING MAIL IN BARCELONA

There are several ways to arrange pickup of letters sent to you by friends and relatives while you are abroad. Mail can be sent via **Poste Restante** (General Delivery) to almost any city or town in Spain with a post office. This is not the

in recent news

Big Trouble in Little China

El Raval has long been considered Barcelona's dirty little secret, the side of the city the image-conscious urban planners don't want visitors to see. In the 19th century, industrialization hit the neighborhood hard. Workers and their families crammed into the low-rent housing, making it one of the most densely populated urban areas in Europe. Pollution, crime, and prostitution followed. The southern half of the neighborhood was given the nickname "El Barri Xino," or Chinatown. No Chinese immigrants ever lived there, but it reminded some of the red-light districts of Chinatowns in other cities, with its brothels and debaucherous atmosphere.

In the early 1990s, with the Olympics coming to Barcelona, city leaders made an effort to revitalize the marginalized neighborhood. Investment poured in, the brothels were closed, and, as social and economic conditions improved, crime dropped. Despite these many advances, El Raval's problems are far from being wiped out. Still, in the last 10 years El Raval has undergone a metamorphosis, and its community—the most ethnically diverse of the city's *zonas*—is coming together with a new energy and vision to leave "El Barri Xino" in the area's long and colorful past.

in recent
news

Workers of the World

Worker strikes in Europe are nothing new; thousands of tourists have stories about being stranded at hotels, airports, and train stations when European workers decide to exercise their right not to work. In Spain, however, and Barcelona in particular, strikes have become a particularly powerful way of capturing the attention of the powers that be. On June 20, 2002, the *Confederación General del Trabajo* (CGT, General Confederation of Labor) organized a strike that paralyzed Barcelona, shutting down all major businesses, halting metro and bus services, and bringing the city to a standstill.

The thousands of workers who mobilized and paraded through the streets addressed the plight of workers in Spain. The CGT accuses the Spanish government of favoring big business at the cost of the worker. The CGT claims that Spanish workers suffer from the lowest purchasing power and the highest unemployment and sexual harrassment rates in the European Union.

For more information (available in Spanish and English), see the CGT website: www.cgt.es.

quickest way to get mail. Address Poste Restante letters:

Ryan Michael WILLIAMS
Poste Restante
Lista de Correos
08070, Barcelona
SPAIN

The mail will go to a special desk in the central post office, unless you specify a post office by street address or postal code. It's best to use the largest post office, since mail may be sent there regardless. Bring your passport (or other photo ID) for pick-up; there may be a small fee. If the clerks insist that there is nothing for you, have them check under your first name as well (i.e. if your name is Amber Musser, have them check under "Amber" and "Musser," and even "Ms."). *Let's Go* lists post offices in the **Service Directory** for Barcelona and the **Practical Information** section for other towns.

BY EMAIL & INTERNET

Internet addicts won't have to worry about withdrawal symptoms, thanks to Barcelona's plethora of Internet cafes. You can surf the Web in almost any electronics store, or try more posh locales where you can surf with a drink and *bocadillo* at your side. Although it will usually be possible to connect to your home server, it may be faster (and thus less expensive) to take advantage of free **web-based email accounts** (e.g. www.hotmail.com and mail.yahoo.com). In general, connections in Spain tend to be more sluggish than those in the US or Canada. Travelers with laptops can call an Internet service provider via a **modem.** Long-distance phone cards specifically intended for such calls can defray normally high phone charges; check with your long-distance phone provider to see if it offers this option.

Internet access costs about €3.60-6 per hour; if you'll be going to the same establishment for email for a while, buying an *abono*, that is, a voucher for a certain number of access hours paid up front, is the most economical option. The website www.tangaworld.com lists nearly 200 cybercafes across Spain by location and name. **Internet cafes** are available all over the city and listed in the **Service Directory**, p. 315. The largest and most popular are also listed below.

▨ **Easy Everything,** Las Ramblas, 31 (www.easyeverything.com). M: Liceu. On **Las Ramblas.** This branch of Europe's Internet chain offers high-speed Internet access in an ideal location. Tourists flock to its 450 computers, equipped with telnet and messaging services like Yahoo, AOL, and ICQ. €1.20 for about 40min. Price fluctuates according to the number of computers in use. A 1-day unlimited pass is available for €5, a 7-day pass is €7, and a 20-day pass is €20. The cafe serves snacks and drinks (€1.20 each). Open 24hr. **Branch:** Ronda Universitat, 35, next to Pl. de Catalunya, with 300 computers at the same prices.

Café Interlight, Av. Pau Claris, 106 (☎93 301 11 80; interlight@bcn.servicom.es). M: Urquinaona. Jarring aqua seat compartments and silver piping give this cafe a futuristic feel. €1 per 15 min., €1.50 per 30 min., €2 per hr. Open M-F 8am-11pm, Sa-Su 4pm-midnight.

Internet Exchange, Las Ramblas, 130 (☎93 317 73 27). From its prime location at the top of Las Ramblas, this few-frills cybercafe has close to 50 computers with a decent connection speed. €0.06 per min. with a €1 minimum: €12 for 5hr., €27.05 for 20hr.; students €15 for 10hr., €30 for 30hr.

TOURIST OFFICES

Tourist office representatives dot the Barri Gòtic from July to September (10am-8pm). Look for officials wearing red vests.

Informació Turística Plaça Catalunya, Pl. de Catalunya, 17S, below Pl. de Catalunya. M: Catalunya. The motherlode of Barcelona information. Provides multilingual advice, maps, pamphlets, transportation passes, hotel information and reservations, currency exchange, telephone cards, email kiosks, and souvenirs for purchase. Updates Barcelona Visitor's Info Line (☎90 730 12 82 in Spain; ☎93 368 97 31 30 abroad). Open daily 9am-9pm.

Informació Turística Plaça Sant Jaume, Pl. Sant Jaume, 1, off C. Ciutat. M: Jaume I. Fewer services and more personal attention than its big mama in Pl. de Catalunya. Open M-Sa 10am-8pm, Su 10am-2pm.

Aeroport El Prat de Llobregat (☎93 478 05 65), in the international terminal at the airport outside the baggage claim area. English-speaking agents offer information on Catalunya and Barcelona, maps, transit passes, and hotel and tour reservations. Open daily 9am-9pm.

Oficina de Turisme de Catalunya, Palau Robert, Pg. de Gràcia, 107 (☎93 238 40 00; fax 93 292 12 70; www.gencat.es/probert). M: Diagonal. The place to come for info all about Catalunya as a whole, including camping, national parks, and driving routes. Also a student office that helps with youth accommodations, sells travel books, and offers computers for searching their website. Open M-Sa 10am-7pm, Su 10am-2pm.

LOCAL MEDIA

TELEVISION

Sadly, for English-language viewing, the small screen is not your best option. Most Spanish television consists of poorly dubbed American programming—*The Simpsons* are all the rage—and some original Spanish fare, including a hefty dose of *telenovelas* (soap operas). Check the *Guía del Ocio* for weekly listings and TV highlights. Daily newspapers (see below) also carry the goods.

TVE1: Features dubbed American series and a good selection of late-night movies.

TVE2: News and some documentaries along with made-for-TV movies, Spanish style.

TV3 and Canal 33: All Catalan programming, all the time.

Tele 5: Dubbed American programming from *Club Disney* to *The Simpsons* to *Melrose Place*.

Antena 3: Regional news, and dubbed and original series. Heavy on family programming.

BTV: City station with local news and some offbeat programming.

Canal Plus: A paid channel, much like the US's HBO, with original television programs, music specials, and movies. Programming is almost entirely in Spanish.

LEISURE READING

If you know any Spanish, your first purchase in Barcelona should be the Spanish-language **Guía del Ocio** (Guide to Leisure), a weekly booklet that lists anything and everything happening in Barcelona in the coming week: concerts, restaurant events, nightlife, galleries, games, free events, theater and dance performances, movie listings, and more. The guide comes out on Thursday or Friday, so be sure you're picking up the current one. The guide is published in Spanish, but even those who don't speak Spanish well will be able to understand easily enough the listings and advertisements. The *Guía del Ocio* is available at newsstands all over the city for the very economical price of €0.90.

Flaix TV (Channel 9): Catalunya's version of MTV with plenty of British and American videos in heavy rotation.

RADIO

When you turn on the radio in Barcelona, expect to hear lots of Catalan—nearly all the DJs prefer to speak in the mother tongue rather than Spanish. Many also have the irritating habit of jabbering over at least half of the song being played. Categorizing stations is a challenge, since most change genre according to the time of day.

95.5 The dependable "Radio Club 25" can always be counted on not to stray too far from top-40 pop. The station where you'll hear the song of the moment at least hourly.

96.6 Independent radio, can shift from house to jazz to metal in a matter of moments.

100.8 Dance, you fool, dance! *Con el ritmo latino.*

101.5 Catalunya Música; soothing classical and opera sounds.

102.0 Catalunya Radio; all the latest news—in Catalan, but they'll throw some Spanish in there, too.

105.0 Soft rock, except for when it's rocking out with dance pop.

105.7 The most popular choice of the young set—all house music, all the time. Afternoon dance party, anyone?

106.6 Oldies ranging from the 50s to the 80s, depending on their mood.

NEWSPAPERS & MAGAZINES

Barceloneses read more than their fellow Spaniards, but the newspapers they choose to buy vary widely by postal code. Two Catalunya-published papers dominate shelf space in the bourgeois l'Eixample: **El Periódico,** a left-leaning publication available in Catalan and Spanish, and **La VanGuardia,** a more conservative paper published in Spanish. For the more radical Catalanists, there's the **Abui,** a nationalist paper produced in Catalan only, and for the far left there's **El País,** based in Madrid but popular among Barcelona's immigrant and working class population. Also from Madrid are the arch-conservative **ABC** and the more mildly rightist **La Razón.** Not surprisingly, none of the Madrid papers make it into Catalunya without a special section dedicated to affairs of the fair northeastern province.

Of course, Spain would not be Spain (and Barcelona has to count itself in here) without a thriving *prensa rosa*, or tabloid press. By far the most popular magazines are **Hola!,** a sensationalist gossip magazine splashed with up-close pictures and details on the lives of the rich and famous, and **Lecturas,** an equally sensationalist but less picture-heavy review that's ever-so-slightly more in touch with the non-jetset crowd. For movie buffs there's **Fotogramas,** and for science, ecology, and technology nerds, **Muy Interesante** keeps up to date on all of the latest breakthroughs. **Quo,** meanwhile, has a better-rounded selection of writing on health, nature, and news.

For **English-speaking** expats, the English monthly **Barcelona Metropolitan** is full of personal experience stories, advice, and news about the city, while the **Broadsheet** covers Spain as a whole with more long feature articles on history, culture, and news. For all of you burgeoning young Hemingways, the semi-literature magazine **Outsider** just might give you a chance to be featured in print.

And of course, last but far from least, there's the indispensable **Guía del Ocio,** Barcelona's comprehensive guide on how to have fun every single weekend; it includes restaurant, nightlife, and theater listings, as well as info on the week's cultural events and performances. The guide is in Spanish, but listings are easy enough to understand even for the non-speaker (what about *Harry Potter* 9pm isn't clear?). Directions to venues are often lacking, but may be available in the **Entertainment** chapter (see p. 171) of this guide. Do not miss your copy, available at the kiosk nearest you.

Life and Times

The city of Barcelona lies within the country of Spain, but to equate Barcelona with Spain is not entirely accurate. Barcelona is shaped by politics and events that influence all of Spain, and so the history of the city often converges with the history of the modern nation. Spain, however, is a recent creation, and a combination of many older, formerly independent cultures and nations. Consequently, when Barcelona expresses patriotism, it is often to an alternate homeland: **Catalunya** (Catalonia or *Cataluña* in Spanish).

Barceloneses have long been the privileged class of Spain. During the Middle Ages, the city was the commercial center of a vast Mediterranean empire. Barcelona suffered financial decline in the 15th century as both the "discovery" of America and Sevilla's trade monopoly shifted commercial routes away from the Mediterranean. The Industrial Revolution's textile mills, however, propelled a turn-of-the-century economic boom, and the aristocracy grew in status and power. As the twentieth century approached, Josep Batlló, Eusebi Güell, and their compatriots commissioned architects like Domènech i Montaner, Puig i Cadafalch, and the legendary Antoni Gaudí to build private residences in l'Eixample, a spacious, gridded "upper" Barcelona district, higher in elevation and status than the tangled, lower-class Barri Gòtic. The result of these architectural pursuits was **Modernisme,** an artistic movement drawing its inspiration from nature. Even the suffocating years of Francisco Franco's Fascist regime could not dampen Barcelona's stature as the world's premier showcase of avant-garde architecture. Today, brilliantly daring buildings and parks stud the cityscape, battling for attention. Only the people themselves, with their trend-setting fashion sense and dynamic lifestyles, offer any real competition.

Today Catalunya is a region in Spain; in medieval times it was its own nation, and Barcelona was its capital. Catalunya has its own distinct history and language, and as a result, modern Barcelona has a strong sense of identity, a distinctive political sensibility, a living language, a novel approach to art, and a healthy secession movement. To appreciate the diversity of Spain, one has to visit Barcelona; to appreciate Barcelona, one has to consider it separate from Spain.

HISTORY

ROMAN TIMES

In an effort to subdue the North African powers in Carthage, the Romans ripped through Spain with a vengeance in the third century BC. They subjugated Barcelona's ancient residents, the **Laietani,** and settled next to Montjuïc in 210 BC. In honor of Augustine's rule in 15 BC, the Romans gave the small town the unwieldy name of Colonia Julia Augusta Faventia Paterna Barcino. **Barcino**—Roman Barcelona—lies mostly underneath the modern day Barri Gòtic, although Roman walls and columns occasionally poke above the ground.

Modern Barcelona is a swinging metropolis, but Barcino was anything but interesting. She was an unimportant provincial town, dwarfed in importance by her southern neighbor, **Tarragona,** the Roman provincial capital, now home to better beaches and ruins (see p. 245).

In close to seven centuries, the Romans drastically altered the face and character of Spain, introducing Rome's language, architecture, roads, irrigation techniques, grapes, olives, and wheat. Constantine declared **Christianity** the official religion of the region in AD 312. As in the rest of the Roman Empire, Roman power in Catalunya declined after Constantine's rule.

VANDALS, VISIGOTHS, MOORS, & FRANKS

A slew of Germanic tribes, including Swabians and Vandals, swept over Iberia in the early fifth century, but the **Visigoths,** under newly converted Christian Ataülf, emerged above the rest. The Visigoths established their court at Barcelona in 415 and laid the foundations of the Catalan feudal society of later centuries. The Visigoths effectively ruled Spain for the next 300 years, although more as a collection of politically disorganized and rather fragmented tribes than as a unified whole.

The Visigoths's disorganization paved the way for the next wave of invaders, this time from the south. Following Muslim unification, a small force of Arabs, Berbers, and Syrians invaded Spain in 711. Practically welcomed by the divided Visigoths, the **Moors** encountered little resistance, and the peninsula soon fell under the control of the caliphate of Damascus.

The Moorish presence in Catalunya was short lived. Charlemagne undermined Moorish power in the late 700s, and his son, Louis the Pious, defeated the Moors in Catalunya in 801. The government Louis the Pious left behind dominated the Catalan Middle Ages. While most of Spain spent centuries under Islamic rule, the Franks reinstated Christian power so promptly that Catalunya enjoyed almost continuous Christian rule since Constantine.

THE MIDDLE & GOLDEN AGES

The common Christianity of the Frankish counts and the Catalans they ruled made the Catalan Middle Ages a relatively cooperative time, with a couple of notable characters. The popular favorite is **Guifré el Pilós,** or Wilfred the Hairy (d. 898); according to legend, he was born hairy as a mountain troll, with hair on the soles of his feet. The Frankish king, **Charles the Bald** (oh, the irony), installed Wilfred the Hairy as count of the region in 874. Guifré spent his life defending his monarch, endowing religious institutions, moving power and importance from Tarragona to Barcelona, unifying various parts of Catalunya, and growing more hair every day. His house held power in Catalunya until 1410.

The Moorish return to Barcelona in 985 marked the beginning of Catalan independence. Guifré's descendant, **Count Borrell,** a man with unknown quantities of bodily hair, asked the Frankish king for aid in the form of military defense from Moorish invasion. When the king ignored this request, Barcelona ceased to acknowledge his sovereignty. Catalunya became independent of Frankish control, and after defeating the Moors on their own in 989, Catalunya was totally independent.

Barcelona grew wealthy at the start of the new millennium under the successive power of four counts by the same name of **Ramon Berenguer,** all of whom expanded the geographical boundaries of Catalunya. Ramon Berenguer III married Princess Dolça of Provence and so extended Catalan power into modern-day France. **Ramon Berenguer IV** is of particular historical relevance because of his 1137 marriage to the distastefully underage **Petronella of Aragón,** the daughter of the king of Aragón (a neighboring province). As the toddler bride enjoyed her terrible twos, Catalunya grew even more powerful through solidarity with Aragón. In the long term, the union of these two regions doomed Catalunya to Madrid's dominance, but in the short term, this cooperation with Aragón meant that Catalunya could comfortably look toward the Mediterranean and focus on more commercial affairs.

Catalunya's most lucrative exports at this time were iron and wool. As **Jaume I** (1213-76) expanded the waterfront under Catalan control by conquering Valencia and the Balearic Islands, Barcelona surfed the maritime wave of commercial success into the Catalan **Golden Age** of painting and literature that accompanied such prosperity. Oceanfront expansion aside, Jaume I also gave the city the government infrastructures of **Les Corts** and the **Generalitat**—the modern regional government—but finally renounced Catalan power over the Pyrenees in France.

The fourteenth century saw the success of Catalunya's brief-yet-glorious designs at an empire. With so much seafront property, Barcelona was one of the wealthiest ports in the Mediterranean; it was also very desirable to the rest of Spain. A series of events left Barcelona open to a takeover. As in the rest of Europe, the **Black Death** killed a substantial portion of the population in the 1340s, leaving the city noticeably weakened. When the last of Guifré's ruling descendants, Martí I, died childless in 1410, power in Catalunya was again up for grabs.

Columbus Comes Down From His Tower

Pl. Reial

On the Steps to Palau d'Art Catalana

CASTILIANISATION

CATHOLIC MONARCHS

In 1469, the marriage of **Los Reyes Católicos** (the Catholic Monarchs), **Fernando de Aragón** and **Isabel de Castilla,** joined Iberia's two mightiest Christian kingdoms, Castilla and Aragón. Since Aragón was already loosely united with Catalunya, Fernando inherited Catalunya in 1479. By 1492, the dynamic duo had captured Granada (the last Moorish stronghold) and shuttled off **Columbus** to explore the New World. The Catholic Monarchs introduced the **Inquisition** in 1478, executing and then burning heretics, principally Jews. The Inquisition had two aims: to strengthen the authority of the Church and to unify Spain. Because Barcelona and other cities in Catalunya had a significant Jewish population, the Inquisition hit Catalunya with the same destructive force as it did the rest of Spain.

Barcelona now took orders from the court at Segovia, in the distant region of Castilla y Leon. With the world's attention on the New World, the Mediterranean was no longer a fashionable place for trade, and Catalunya was officially banned from trade in the New World by the Catholic Monarchs. In approximately 50 years of rule, the Catholic Monarchs heightened Spain's position as a world economic, political, and cultural power (made all the more enduring by lucrative conquests in the Americas). Prosperity for a newly united Spain did not mean prosperity for Catalunya, which lost its autonomy and faced a crippling economic recession.

THE HABSBURG DYNASTY

The daughter of Fernando and Isabel, **Juana la Loca** (the Mad), married **Felipe el Hermoso** (the Fair) of the powerful Hapsburg dynasty. Their son, **Carlos I** (1516-1556), who reigned as the last Roman Emperor over an immense empire comprising modern-day Holland, Belgium, Austria, Spain, parts of Germany, and Italy, and the massive American colonies. Spain was arguably the most powerful empire in the world under the Habsburgs, even as subsequent Habsburg monarchs began to lose some of their territory; this period of virtual world domination led to Spain's own **Golden Age** of painting and literature.

However, as most of Spain enjoyed the Golden Age, Catalunya found herself more and more marginalized, economically and culturally. While central Spain mass produced revolutionary painters like Velázquez and El Greco, the main product of Catalunya at this time was rebellion. Barcelona had lost her importance as a trade city, and Catalunya was inconveniently in the midst of numerous battles between the French and Spanish, beginning in 1635. The result of these constraints was the **Guerra dels Segadors** (Reapers' War) in 1640.

The Guerra dels Segadors—a title which later became the Catalan national anthem—was a Catalan attempt at independence originating from within the oppressed masses. The 12 years of war began with civil disobedience, not a plan; disgruntled Catalan workers happened across a Spanish viceroy and worked out their tensions on him until there were only pieces left. In the ensuing confusion, Catalunya used the tense Franco-Iberian relations to her advantage by siding with France, hoping that France would support the Catalan cry for independence. France did: **Louis XIII** of France even went so far as to send troops to help the Catalans defend themselves. However, the war was administrated badly on the Catalan side, and the French eventually betrayed Catalunya and created an alliance with Spain. When the war ended in 1652, these two nations divided the spoils. A treaty returned Catalunya to Habsburg control, with the exception of the northeastern corner, which was ceded to France.

WAR OF SPANISH SUCCESSION

The War of Spanish Succession, a.k.a. the Next Big Disaster, came when Habsburg king **Carlos II** died before producing an heir. Europe was generally very excited at Carlos's oversight, as it presented the opportunity for some lucky European nation X to install an X-friendly ruler on the Spanish throne. There were two main candidates for the position of Spanish monarch: the **Archduke Carlos,** from Austria, and **Felipe V,** a Bourbon from France and grandson of Louis XIV. Still bitter with France about their betrayal in the Guerra dels Segadors, Catalunya chose to support the Austrian candidate, while Spain and France chose the French contender. In 1713, it was clear Catalunya had backed the wrong horse. The **Treaty of Utrecht** made Felipe V the new monarch; his rule started a legacy of Catalan oppression that would continue through Franco.

BOURBON ON THE ROCKS

Felipe V (1713-1746) came down with an iron fist on Catalunya, punishing the region for her ill-fated political preferences. In an attempt to Castilianize the region and break its spirit, Felipe V attacked and restricted the Catalan language. Felipe also built the infamous **Ciutadella** (citadel), now a park, in 1718 (see p. 72); this oppressive new addition to the city boundaries left a visible military presence, a reminder to Barcelona not to cross Felipe again.

Communications Tower on Montjuïc

Luckily for Catalunya, the Bourbons who followed Felipe were able administrators who lightened the restrictions on Catalunya and improved the region's infrastructure. New canals, roads, organized settlements, agricultural reforms, and industrial expansion encouraged Barcelona's natural inclination to trade. **Carlos III** (1759-1788) lifted the ban on Catalan trade with the Americas in 1778, which led Barcelona to another economic boom.

These good times didn't last. **Napoleon** rained on Catalunya's parade when he invaded Spain in 1808 as part of his quest for world domination. Napoleon tempted Catalunya with promises of independence, but Catalunya's decision to side with Madrid in an effort to oust the French is one of the rare times that Catalunya showed total solidarity with Spain. The cooperation worked: the French were expelled in 1814. Industry and trade picked up again as a result. Unfortunately, at this point, under **Fernando VII** (1814-1833), Spain started losing her empire. Galvanized by Fernando's ineptitude and inspired by liberal ideas in the brand-spanking new Spanish **constitution,** most of Spain's Latin American empire soon attained independence. Domestically, parliamentary liberalism was restored in 1833 upon Fernando VII's death and survived the conservative challenge of the **Carlist Wars** (1833-1840); it would dominate Spanish politics until **Primo de Rivera's** comparatively mild and brief dictatorship in the 1920s.

Tàpies Foundations

Barceloneta

EXPANSION, THE RENAIXENÇA, & ANARCHY

Rapid industrialization and prosperity marked 19th-century Spain. A messy yet productive series of riots, demonstrations, and revolts protested the deplorable living circumstances of the working classes, even as a bourgeois class grew. As walled Barcelona's population increased too quickly for the two classes to live so close together, the **old walls** were finally torn down in 1854; this monumental bit of urban planning led to the expansion of Barcelona, in the form of **l'Eixample** (the Enlargement). For more on the planning of l'Eixample see p. 45).

The late 19th and early 20th centuries yielded Catalunya's industrial-inspired **Renaixença** (Renaissance), one of the most creative artistic periods in Catalan and Spanish history. The gridded blocks of l'Eixample were slowly filled in with bourgeois and buildings from Barcelona's **Modernisme** movement in architecture and design (see p. 53); artists like Picasso and Ramon Casas swapped techniques at the swanky underground cafe Els Quatre Gats (see p. 128). The Renaixença also saw the return of Catalan nationalism: the Catalan language was standardized and reaffirmed, and Catalan literature boomed.

The liberal mayor **Francesc de Paula Rius i Taulet** was a defining force in Barcelona at this time. In 1888, Rius i Taulet hosted the **Universal Exposition** in Barcelona, an event which introduced Catalan Modernisme to the world and transformed the face of the city. In a master stroke of symbolism, Rius i Taulet held the exposition in a formerly hated location: the site of Felipe V's oppressive Ciutadella, now transformed into a park. The event was an excuse to revamp and develop the city, as well as an opportunity to showcase Barcelona's artistic developments to the world. Despite the debt it left on the city, the Universal Exposition was a crucial moment for the rejuvenation Barcelona.

The last half of the 19th century also saw the rise of **anarchy** in Barcelona, primarily among the impoverished working class. In the 1890s, a series of bombings announced Barcelona's unlikely status as anarchy world headquarters. The most notable of these was the 1891 bombing of the Liceu opera house (now restored, see p. 61), designed to attack the wealthy and the system of centralized authority.

True anarchy hit the city in 1909 with the **Setmana Trágica (Tragic Week).** Protests against an unpopular imperialist war with Morocco drew support from Socialists and anarchists. Protests turned into organized strikes, which in turn morphed into unorganized revolts, riots, and violence. The week ended in the destruction of almost 100 buildings, most of them religious, and over 100 dead citizens.

DICTATORSHIPS & DRAMA

THE FIRST DICTATOR & THE SECOND REPUBLIC

Spain was deeply affected by **World War I,** although she did not participate. Europe's wartime economy brought waves of rural Catalans and impoverished Andalucian southerners to Barcelona. The influx of people looking for work rocked labor standards, invited chaos, and led Barcelona's Castilian Captain General **Miguel Primo de Rivera** to shut down Parliament and ascend to dictatorship in 1923, with the permission of **King Alfonso XIII** (1902-1931).

Primo de Rivera's years in power are often quickly passed over in history books because they pale in comparison to the dictatorship that would follow; however, the dictatorship was no treat for Catalunya. Once again, Catalunya's language and culture were repressed. In 1929, Primo de Rivera put on Barcelona's **International Exhibition** in an attempt to demonstrate that Barcelona was still thriving; the resulting tourist-trap **Poble Espanyol** may or may not have achieved this goal (see p. 90).

In the 1920s, Spain had both a dictator and a monarch; by 1931, it had neither. Primo de Rivera retired in 1930, and King Alfonso XIII, disgraced by his support for Primo de Rivera's dictatorship, fled Spain the next year. His departure gave rise to the **Second Republic** (1931-1936), beloved by liberals and intellectuals everywhere. During this short time, Republican liberals and Socialists established safeguards for

BARCELONA PLANNED
The Expansion from the Old City into l'Eixample

Barcelona radiates style. Everyone is stylish: the elderly couples promenading the Passeig de Gràcia in shades of distinguished gray and beige, the hipsters slinking by in engineered Levi's in the Barri Gòtic, the slow circle of people dancing the *sardanas* in front of the *Catedral* on Sunday afternoons, the young businessmen in their tailored suits crowding the metro. But style in Barcelona is hardly limited to the people; it includes almost everything, from the mundane to the actual layout of the city.

Barcelona is a city of, by, and for designers. In many ways what most enabled Barcelona to become a city of architectural gems was the planning of the new city, l'Eixample, or the Extension (*Ensanche* in Castilian). The first stone was laid in the Eixample in 1860, but the historical groundwork for this radical creation of a city began much earlier.

In the early 1800s, Barcelona hardly resembled the ample city that tourists gush over today. Barcelona proper was cramped within the walled-in Barri Gòtic. As Robert Hughes wrote in his seminal work, *Barcelona*, "mid-century Barcelona made Dickensian London look almost tolerable." The city walls had stood for over 100 years, since the Bourbons conquered the city in the early 1700s, and despite the promising construction of the new Passeig de Gràcia in 1927 connecting Barcelona from the towns of Gràcia, Sants, and Sant Gervasi across open fields, nothing was built.

After much political wrangling between civil and military authorities, in 1854 the go-ahead for demolition was given. Now faced with the necessity to build a city beyond the Barri Gòtic, some crucial decisions were made that ultimately created the long avenues that help make beloved Barcelona so stylish today. The Ajuntament of Barcelona held a competition for a new city plan in 1859. While cities were being redesigned throughout Europe (most notably Paris beginning in 1848), Barcelona was particularly unique in that there was no old city to demolish to make space for the new. Barcelona was a blank slate for the architect, an expanse of fields dotted only by a few scattered buildings.

Two plans came forward. One was by Antoni Rovira i Trias, the Ajuntament's resident architect. He proposed a plan similar to that of the new Paris, a fan-like radial layout extending out from what presumably would remain the heart of the new city, the Barri Gòtic. The other plan was by Ildefons Cerdà. Cerdà was an ideological socialist. He had researched worker conditions within the old city and had a vision of a new egalitarian city. His plan covered nine square kilometers with a carefully calculated grid with planned services. Among its specifications were that every 400 blocks would have a hospital and park. Every 100 blocks would have a market. Every 25 blocks would have a school. Of each block only a third of the area would be covered by buildings. The rest would be trees and gardens in the interior of the block. Some blocks were to be undeveloped park space. Buildings were to be 57 feet high, or around three stories.

Conservative Catalans were not interested in Cerdà's radical idealized city and Rovira i Trais's plan was selected in late 1859. But inexplicably Madrid reversed the decision eight months later and awarded the commission to Cerdà. Many Catalans were adamantly against the plan, but gradually the Eixample was built. As anyone who visits Barcelona knows, Cerdà's plan was hardly followed to the letter. There is a grid and angled corners, but buildings tower above the three-story limit and there is limited green space. Developers ignored the details of Cerdà's plan and the Ajuntament turned a blind eye.

But Cerdà's plan left a legacy for the Modernisme architects who have left such a deep imprint on the fabric of Barcelona's style. The rigid street plan let the fantastical and colorful deigns of the *modernistas* truly flourish. Passeig de Gràcia is lined with Modernista buildings. The glorious buildings of Lluis Domènech i Montaner, Josep Puig i Cadaflach, and Antoni Gaudí, just to mention the superstars, shine in l'Eixample. Gems also nestle in the side streets of l'Eixample, great *modernista* details rising above the tree-lined streets that Cerdà envisioned, creating a glamorous background for the stylish folks of Barcelona.

Sarah Jacoby was a Let's Go Managing Editor, a Researcher-Writer for India & Nepal 2001 and Spain & Portugal 1999, and an editor for Europe 2000. While living in Barcelona she worked for an Internet consulting company.

Gaudí's Deathmask

Palau Güell

Park Güell Structures

farmers and industrial workers, granted women suffrage, assured religious tolerance, and chipped away at traditional military dominance.

National euphoria faded quickly. The 1933 elections split the Republican-Socialist coalition, in the process increasing the power of right wing and Catholic parties. Military dissatisfaction led to a heightened profile of the Fascist party **Falange** (founded by Primo de Rivera's son José), which further polarized national politics. By 1936, radicals, anarchists, Socialists, and Republicans had formed a loose, federated alliance to win the next elections; since the Republic was weak, victory was short-lived. Once **Generalísimo Francisco Franco** snatched control of the Spanish army, militarist uprisings ensued, and the nation plunged into war.

THE CIVIL WAR

The three-year **Civil War** (1936-1939) ignited worldwide ideological passions; the causes and effects of the Civil War touch every aspect of 20th century Spain. Germany and Italy dropped troops, supplies, and munitions into Franco's lap, while the stubbornly isolationist US and the liberal European states were slow to aid the Republicans. Although Franco and the National-ists enjoyed popular support in Andalucía, Gali-cia, Navarra, and parts of Castilla, the Republicans controlled population and indus-trial centers. Barcelona was actually the Repub-lican capital from 1937 until Franco finally won the Civil War in 1939. The Soviet Union, some-what indirectly, called for a **Popular Front** of Com-munists, Socialists, and other leftist sympathizers to battle Franco's Fascism. But soon after, the West abandoned the coalition, and aid from the Soviet Union waned as Stalin began to see the benefits of an alliance with Hit-ler. Without international aid, Republican forces found themselves cut off from supplies and food, and began to surrender to the Nationalists. All told, bombings, executions, combat, starva-tion, and disease took nearly 600,000 lives nationwide, and in 1939 Franco's forces marched into Madrid and ended the war.

FRANCO

By the time the Civil War ended, **World War II** was already in full swing. With so many dead and such overwhelming debt in the wake of their own war, it was impossible for Spain to participate. Franco is generally regarded as a Bad Guy by the outside world and Catalunya, but he did make one positive contribution to World War II, helping Jews out of France as the situation there declined.

Brain-drain (as leading intellectuals emigrated or were assassinated), worker dissatisfaction, student unrest, regional discontent, and international isolation characterized the first decades of Franco's dictatorship. Barcelona lost virtually all of her innovative painters, artists, and writers to intimidation and exile (with the exception of Dalí, who suddenly became very controversial without producing any art of consequence). With intellectual and artistic growth thus stunted, Franco moved on to old-fashioned oppression: the Catalan language was again outlawed and dubbed an inferior dialect. Although Barcelona was, as usual, one of the wealthiest places in Spain, money was constantly drained out of Catalunya and redistributed where Franco saw fit; as a result, Barcelona was a constant source of protest. In 1960, **Jordi Pujol**, the future leader of Catalunya, even went so far as to sing the decidedly illegal Catalan national anthem in front of Franco at a concert on one of the dictator's visits, for which he spent three years in jail.

In his old age, Franco tried to smooth international relations by joining NATO and encouraging tourism, but the "national tragedy" (as the war and dictatorship were later called) did not officially end until Franco's death in 1975. Shortly before his own death, Franco reinstated **King Juan Carlos I** (1975-), grandson of Alfonso XIII. Juan Carlos I carefully set out to undo Franco's damage; he is idolized in all of Spain for reinstituting democracy when he could have conceivably continued the cycle of political oppression. In 1978, under premier **Adolfo Suárez,** Spain adopted a new constitution in a national referendum that led to the restoration of parliamentary government. This assured a comfortable degree of regional autonomy for Catalunya.

(POST)MODERNITY

DEMOCRACY AND THE CATALAN GENERALITAT

The post-Franco years have been marked by progressive social change. Divorce was legalized; women regained suffrage and educational opportunities. In 1978 the Catalan Generalitat, a regional semi-autonomous government, was created. **Jordi Pujol** became president in 1980, and continues to lead the region today. Catalunya still has a secession movement, but it is not violent. The region is generally comfortable with the degree of autonomy it has, which celebrates the Catalan language in public schools and allows Catalan control over all major Catalan resources.

Charismatic **Felipe González** led the PSOE (Spanish Socialist Worker's Party) to victory in the 1982 elections. In 1986, González opened the Spanish economy and championed consensus policies, overseeing Spain's integration into what was then the European Community (EC) and is now known by the dramatically different title of **European Union (EU).** Despite unpopular economic stands, González was reelected in 1986 and continued a program of massive public investment. The years 1986 to 1990 were outstanding for Spain's economy, but by the end of 1993, recession set in. In 1993, González and the PSOE barely maintained a majority in Parliament over the conservative **Partido Popular (PP).** **José Maria Aznar** led the PP into power after González's support eroded and has maintained a delicately balanced coalition with the support of the Catalan regional party.

THE OLYMPICS

From 1982 to 1997, the industrious Socialist **Pasqual Maragall** was the mayor of Barcelona; through his efforts, the **1992 Summer Olympics** were held in Barcelona. Maragall used the pressure of the international spotlight as an opportunity to completely revamp the city. New athletic arenas and apartment complexes were built; the beaches were cleaned up, the waterfront was remodeled into party central, and the prostitutes were (very temporarily) shuffled into less visible neighborhoods. **Poble Nou** (see p. 13) and **Montjuïc** (see p. 16) were visibly transformed in this process. Rejuvenated, Barcelona greeted the athletes, hospitably hosted the games, and remains cleaned up and built up from the experience.

Barcelona Fine Arts

For a city where movie-going is a big business and lovers exchange books on the most romantic day of the year (Día de Sant Jordi, p. 20), Barcelona has produced surprisingly little literature or cinema of lasting merit. Much of this has to do with the repression of the Catalan language and culture by the ruling Castilians. Still, here are a few highlights from the literary and cinematic tradition.

L'Atlantida, by Catalunya's most beloved poet, Jacint Verdaguer, is to the Catalans what *The Iliad* is to the Greeks. Jacinct won first prize in the 1879 *Jocs Florals* poetry competition with this entry.

Nada, the first novel by 23-year-old Barcelona native Carmen Laforet, exploded onto the scene in 1944 and won the Premio Nadal, the highest literary honor Iberia has to offer. *Nada* details the coming of age of a young girl in an eccentric family and is a virtual tour of Barcelona.

All About my Mother, Pedro Almodóvar's Oscar-winning hit movie about a single mother and the transvestite father of her son took the world by storm. This story of love, friendship, and grief is set in Barcelona.

Barcelona, Whit Stillman's movie about an uptight American working in Barcelona who is paid a sudden visit by his free-spirited brother, is a one-eyed ride through the city.

TODAY

The last decade has seen mixed progress in one of Spain's most pressing areas of concern—Basque nationalism and terrorism, carried out by the Basque separatist group, **ETA.** This issue concerns the whole country; while Basque hostility is traditionally directed at Madrid, there has been hostility toward Catalunya and the east coast in recent times. Basque violence generally occurs in the form of assassinations of political figures and terrorist bombings. Between September and December of 2000, two politicians and one police officer were shot within Barcelona's city limits; two bomb attacks during the same months injured others. The most recent attacks in Catalunya occurred in March 2001, when a police officer was killed in Rosas, north of Barcelona; in the same month, a car bomb was successfully diffused in Valencia.

On a brighter national note, the Spanish economy is currently in good and improving shape, and Barcelona is one of the wealthiest cities in Spain. Aznar describes visions of "a new Spain" and plans to reduce unemployment even further, draw more women into the workforce, and improve the faltering birthrate by restructuring family and work arrangements. Though the work reforms implemented have reduced the unemployment rate, they are not without controversy. For more on the state of workers in Spain, see **Workers of the World,** p. 34.

Despite some odd scenarios during election times, Catalan regional politics is also in good shape. In a sticky race, former mayor Joan Maragall ran against Catalan hero Jordi Pujol for control of the regional government, the **Generalitat.** The immense popularity of both men made the race a close one, but in the end, Pujol remains in power. Maragall has vacated the mayor's office, the **Ajuntament;** the current mayor of Barcelona is Socialist **Joan Clos,** who does justice to Maragall's legacy by continuing to look ahead to improve the city.

LANGUAGE

Catalunya, like many other regions of Spain, is bilingual. **Castellano** (Castilian or *Castellà* in Catalan), a.k.a. **Spanish,** spoken by almost everyone with varying degrees of ease, is Spain's official language. **Català (Catalan)** is spoken in all of Catalunya and has given rise through permutations to *Valencià,* the language of Valencia, *Mallorquín* of Mallorica, *Menorquín* of Menorca, and *Evissinc* of Ibiza.

Despite politically fueled rumors to the contrary, Catalan is not a dialect of Spanish or a combination of French and Spanish, but a full-fledged Romance language. Catalans will get insulted if a tourist—or a Spaniard—refers to their language as a dialect. Catalan and Castilian both have standardized grammars and literary traditions, both oral and written. Regional television broadcasts, strong political associations, the use of Catalan as vernacular and in church, and extensive schooling have saved Catalan from extinction.

City and provincial names in this book are usually listed in Catalan, and Castilian where appropriate. Information within cities (i.e. street or plaza names) are also listed in Catalan. Generally, when traveling throughout Spain, Castilian names are understood; however, it is polite to show respect towards Catalan; particularly in restaurants, the use of Catalan may get you better service.

On the Beach

ART

PAINTING & SCULPTURE

Over its long history, Catalan painting has seen a series of luminaries separated by several lulls. Flemish, French, and Italian techniques influenced the Middle Ages and the Renaissance; in recent history, the Surrealists have forged a dazzling, distinctive, and influential body of work.

EARLY, GOTHIC, & RENAISSANCE

As Catalunya's economy was separate from Spain's for so many centuries, the **Spanish Golden Age** and the **Catalan Golden Age** occurred at two different times. The 16th century produced such giants as El Greco and Velázquez in central Spain, but the most productive time for Catalan painting came much earlier, when Catalunya was independent. In the 11th and 12th centuries, through the Renaissance (not to be confused with the 19th century Catalan Renaixença, see p. 44), the most significant paintings were frescoes that decorated churches and their libraries. Fourteenth-century **Ferrer Bassa** is the most renowned painter of this sort; his frescoes can be seen in the Monestir de Pedralbes (see p. 96). The works of some of the most famous painters from this period, such as 15th-century **Jaume Huguet** and Flemish-influenced **Bartolomé Bermejo**, are on display in the MNAC (see p. 120); Huguet also has an important work in the Museu d'Història de Catalunya (see p. 116).

Gay Pride Parade

Bull Fighting Arena

I Dream of Dalí

As an adult, Dalí always appeared to be confident in his talents, but he was not always so confident in every aspect of his life. From an early age, Salvador Dalí was plagued by nightmares and insecurities. Sexually inexperienced until a late age, Dalí was sexually ambiguous and had a fear of sexual contact and impotence.

The defining moment in Dalí's artistic and personal development came when he moved to Madrid in the 1920s. Dalí arrived a terrified, inexperienced boy who could not cross the street on his own; the friendships he made in Madrid—with such artistic giants as Federico García Lorca, Pablo Neruda, and Luís Buñuel—dragged him out of his shell.

Even as he grew into the extroverted spectacle the world came to know, Dalí's fears were one of the two central subjects of his work; the other was landscapes—themes which he often combined. Dalí, influenced by Sigmund Freud, created his own brand of Surrealism. With it, he sought to connect the unconscious with the conscious by exploring the dreams of the unconscious in his paintings of the conscious, waking world.

BIRTH OF MODERNISM

Catalan painting experienced a lull under the Habsburgs until the 1800s, when Impressionist-inspired **Marià Fortuny** started to gain recognition; his paintings can be seen in the Museu d'Art Modern (see p. 111). His appearance reenergized Catalan art and began a long line of talented painters that would emerge in the nineteenth and twentieth centuries.

MODERNISME

Although Catalan Modernist painting, which mostly just followed the latest trends in Paris, is not as internationally recognized as Catalan Modernist architecture (see p. 53), it still produced some memorable characters and admirable works. One such fellow is **Ramon Casas** (1866-1932), a patron of the ever-famous **Els Quatre Gats** cafe (see p. 130), illustrator of the popular literary magazine **Pel i Plom,** owner of the first car in Barcelona, hot commodity in the advertising industry, and painter extraordinaire. His contemporary, **Santiago Rusinyol** (1861-1931), was another significant figure on the Modernist scene; despite his addiction to morphine and his literary aspirations, his novel use of color in his representations of nature produced a number of memorable works. Both artists are represented in the Museu d'Art Modern (see p. 111).

◪ SURREALISM

Surrealism explores the experience of the subconscious through various approaches: the world of childhood, the world of dreams, the world of madness. While this movement was started in France by **André Breton** with his avant-garde literary homage to a madwoman, *Nadja,* Catalunya produced three of the most innovative artists of the movement. Painter and sculptor **Joan Miró** (1893-1983) approached the subconscious from the perspective of childhood (see p. 117). His cryptic and symbolic squiggles became a statement against the authoritarian society of the post-Civil War years; indeed, his works are so closely tied to the events of 20th-century Spain that one can date them simply by observing the colors and images used. By contrast, fellow Catalan **Salvador Dalí** (1904-1989) scandalized high society and leftist intellectuals in France and Spain by reportedly supporting the Fascists; in reality, Dalí knew nothing about politics and he probably only encouraged such rumors to keep the spotlight on himself. The wildly mustached painter tapped into dreams and the unconscious for odd images like soft faces, bureau-women, and rotting donkeys, as well as repetitive images like melting clocks, his wife Gala, and praying peasants. A self-congratulatory fellow, Dalí founded the Teatre-Museu Dalí in Figueres (see p. 216). **Picasso** also dabbled in Surrealism, but his main contribution to the artistic world came in quite another form.

CUBISM

It is hard to imagine an artist who has had as profound an effect upon 20th-century painting as Andalucian-born **Pablo Ruíz Picasso** (1881-1973). As a child prodigy, Picasso headed for Barcelona, a hothouse for Modernist architecture and political activism. Bouncing back and forth between Barcelona and Paris, Picasso in 1900 inaugurated his Blue Period, characterized by somber depictions of society's outcasts. His permanent move to Paris in 1904 initiated his Rose Period, during which he probed into the curiously engrossing lives of clowns and acrobats. This thematic and stylistic evolution led Picasso through his own revolutionary style.

With his French colleague Georges Braque, Picasso founded Cubism, a method of painting objects simultaneously from multiple perspectives. Cubism evolved slowly, but the first Cubist painting is commonly recognized as **Las Señoritas de Avignon (the Ladies of Avignon)** in 1907. His most famous Cubist work, the gigantic 1937 mural *Guernica*, portrays the bombing of that Basque city by Nazi planes in cahoots with Fascist forces during the Spanish Civil War. A vehement protest against violence and fascism, *Guernica* now resides in the Centro de Arte Reina Sofía in Madrid. Barcelona's Museu Picasso has a commendable chronological spread of Picasso's work, from his earliest paintings to his Cubist engravings (see p. 109).

ABSTRACT

Since Franco's death in 1975, a new generation of artists has thrived. Catalan **Antoni Tàpies** constructs definition-defying works (painting? sculptures? collages?) out of unusual and unorthodox materials most would refer to as trash. Tàpies is a founding member of the self-proclaimed "Abstract Generation," which sponsored the magazine **Dau al Set**. Tàpies work is commonly interpreted as an expression of urban alienation and decay in the wake of Franco's oppression. The Fundació Tàpies showcases his postmodern angst (see p. 113).

MAY I HAVE THIS DANCE?

Those expecting to see flowing dresses and castanets will be disappointed: Catalunya does not have a tradition of flamenco dance. Instead, Catalans hold the **sardana** dear to their heart. The *sardana* is dance done in the round where young and old, male and female dance together. The dancers perform a variety of complicated skips and jumps. The dance is dependent on the cooperation of the entire group, symbolizing the unity of the village.

Unlike the flamenco, the *sardana* is a somber dance and is taken seriously by both the dancers and the viewers; while the rest of Spain, and most foreign viewers, mock the *sardana* and for its nearly comatose pace, the Catalan take pride in their traditional dance and consider it an integral part of their culture. A good place to catch the *sardana* is in front of the cathedral after mass on Sunday morning (see p. 63).

GET sm**art**

Gaudí

Revered by many as the "father of Barcelona," architect **Antoni Gaudí** was a brilliant eccentric who spent most of his life alone and far from the limelight. Born in Reus, Spain in 1852, he read incessantly as a student, soaking up the theories which would influence his work. Religion and nature were his main inspirations, and he was known to sit in front of the sea for hours at a time, proclaiming that each wave was telling him something. He never married (though it is said he did have one great love) and agreed to pose for a photograph only once.

The last 11 years of his life, Gaudí lived in a makeshift house near **La Sagrada Família,** hardly interacting with anyone; in 1926, he was killed by a streetcar while leaving the church. Taken to a pauper's morgue because of his shabby clothing, he remained unidentified for weeks.

Barcelona recently petitioned the Vatican to honor Gaudí as a saint. In addition to his devout and almost supernatural buildings (**Casa Milà** was conceived as a monument of the Immaculate Conception), Gaudí's miracles include inspiring unlikely converts to Catholicism, and generally reenergizing Spain's spirituality. The Pope is investigating the beatification.

ARCHITECTURE

As a reflection of its distinct political and social history, Barcelona lacks the "typically" Spanish, Arab-influenced style. Instead, the city boasts some of the most innovative and exciting architecture in the world as a result of the **Modernisme** movement.

ENTER THE ROMANS

The numerous **Roman ruins** that sprinkle the Spanish countryside testify to six centuries of colonization. While Barcelona holds a few remnants of the Romans' inhabitation (in the form of columns, walls, and sewers), the ruins in **Tarragona** are much more extensive (see p. 244). Arguably the greatest contribution of the Romans is their use of the invincible **arch** as a central element to the structure of their buildings.

ROMANESQUE

Little architecture remains from the Visigoths, who inhabited the area from 415 AD until the eighth century. Until the 12th century, the **Romanesque** style prevailed in Iberia. The Romanesque style is characterized by its extreme simplicity. The **Monestir Sant Pau del Camp** is Barcelona's one modest example of Romanesque architecture (see p. 75). North of the city in Ripoll, **Santa Maria de Ripoll** is a better example (see p. 236).

GOTHIC STYLE

The **Spanish Gothic** style, like Gothic elsewhere in Europe, brought experimentation with pointed arches, flying buttresses, slender walls, airy spaces, and stained-glass windows. In keeping with their patriotic love of deviation, the Catalan developed their own style by employing internal wall supports rather than external buttresses. The **Catalan Gothic** movement, dominant from the 13th to the 15th century, differs in that it is not as ornate and flamboyant as the rest of the world's take on the Gothic style, but is more plain and simple in decoration and style. Rather than high pointy towers, the Catalans created hexagonal towers. Instead of trying to surpass other buildings in vertical height, the Barcelona architects tested the use of horizontal planes in their surprisingly flat Gothic buildings. Using materials such as iron and stone, they created huge facades protecting beautiful gardens inside. Other Spanish riffs on the French original include centrally placed *coros* (choirs) and oversized *retablos* (brightly colored carved pieces placed above the high altar). **Santa Maria del Mar** and **Santa Maria del Pi** are two churches that exemplify this style (see p. 69). Barcelona's main Cathedral, **Església Catedral de la Santa Creu,** is the city's most traditional and most impressive building from this period (see p. 63).

RENAISSANCE & BAROQUE

New World riches inspired the **Plateresque** ("in the manner of a silversmith") style, a flashy extreme of Gothic that transformed wealthier parts of Spain, such as southern Andalucia. Intricate stonework and extravagant use of gold and silver splashed 15th- and 16th-century buildings. In the late 16th century, **Italian Renaissance** innovations in perspective and symmetry arrived in Spain to sober up the Plateresque style.

Opulence seized center stage once again in 17th- and 18th-century **Baroque** Spain, which came in the form of renovations to Gothic structures. The Baroque movement is responsible for the **Església de la Mercè** (see p. 84) and the **Palau Dalmases** (see p. 123).

MODERNISME

The Modernisme movement was born out of a growing sense of Catalan pride and nationalism; it became a symbolic and creative outlet for the province's increasing political autonomy. While Modernisme was not limited to Barcelona (known as *art nouveau* in France and *Jugendstil* in Germany), **Catalan Modernisme** has a unique flavor all its own. While the Modernisme movement included literature, visual arts, and other artistic forms, Catalan Modernisme is best known for its innovative and intriguing architecture. The movement exploded onto the European architecture scene at the **1888 Universal Exposition** and remained at its height through the first decade of the 20th century.

Modernisme rebelled against the realism of the 19th century. Where realism employed such conventional techniques as straight lines, rigidity, and order in form, Modernisme instead combined Nordic Gothic architecture with natural influences and imaginative materials, shapes, and designs. While some critics have dismissed the Modernisme movement as pretentious, the popularity of Barcelona's **Ruta del Modernisme** and support from the Surrealist movement is evidence for its overwhelming intrigue (see p. 57).

Antoni Gaudí i Comet (see p. 52), the most famous of the Modernisme architects, constructed the two most touristed sites in Barcelona, **La Casa Milà** (Milà House) and **La Sagrada Família** (The Sacred Family). Gaudí's genius comes in his understanding of space and his personal vision of the finished project. Combining Gothic influences with inspiration from nature and innovative materials, Gaudí created such marvels as **Casa Batlló** and **Park Güell** (see p. 91 and p. 75). The colorful infusion of history and nature are his defining characteristics. Gaudí's chimneys are known for their bold departure from the standard and for their intricate design. He frequently included reptiles and amphibians in his works, such as the tortoises found on the columns for the Nativity facade on La Sagrada Família, and the Park Güell's salamander fountain. Gaudí's ideas were so unprecedented that he worked alongside the craftsmen to execute his vision. His work is typically separated into four stages, culminating in his work on La Sagrada Família, a building he spent over 40 years creating and which remains unfinished.

While Gaudí is the most famous of the Modernisme architects, two others, Lluís Domènech i Montaner and Josep Puig i Cadafalch, deserve mention. As the director of Barcelona's School of Architecture, **Montaner** was in the position to influence not only Barcelona's architecture, but also its future architects. At the Universal Exposition of 1888 he presented his **Castell de Tres Dragones** (Castle of Three Dragons), designed as a restaurant for the Exposition. It was a huge success and marked the official beginning of the Modernisme movement. Domènech was especially innovative in his choice of building materials. He used stucco to imitate stone and also ignored the contemporary disdain for brick, as he was drawn to its organic quality and its connection to the earth. Like other architects of the Modernisme movement, he combined history with the Catalan culture to create his works, but he alone

MORE THAN A RIVALRY

When Franco came to power in 1936, he tried to destroy regionalism by creating a centralized Spain, controlled by Madrid, and dominated by Castilian culture. The Catalan flag and language were banned and the **Fútbol Club Barcelona,** which had already established a following, became the only outlet for Catalan nationalism. The team's logo bears the Catalan coat of arms, with a red cross and red and gold stripes above the blue and burgundy stripes of Barça.

Because Catalan nationalism was so oppressed, **Real Madrid,** Franco's team, became a hated rival, both for its excellence on the field and the fascism it represented. In 1941, the FCB was told they had to lose a cup match against Madrid. The team protested the fix by allowing Madrid to win 11-1; Barça's goalie was suspended for life for his flagrant nonchalance. When Barça became a powerhouse in the 1950s, Franco forced the team to give up one of its star players to Madrid. In protest, the entire Barça board of directors resigned.

Though the rivalry no longer holds the same political implications, it remains every bit as intense. The two teams, both with enormous financial resources and fiercely loyal fans, regularly battle for the championship of the Spanish First Division.

allowed Moorish influences to creep into his work. His most renowned works are the **Hospital de la Santa Creu i Sant Pau** and the **Palau de la Música Catalana** (see p. 83 and p. 70).

Josep Puig i Cadafalch is the youngest of the main Modernisme architects of Barcelona. He resented his works being labeled as Modernisme, as he felt that his and his peers' works exhibited more local flare than the beginnings of an international architectural movement. His use of spatial effects are especially notable, as is his attention to surfaces and materials. Puig was more of a planner than Gaudí or Domènech, and his works are clearly influenced by 15th-century Gothic architecture; his most well-known building is **Casa Amatler** (see p. 80).

NOUCENTISME

Noucentisme—a movement which covered all spheres of visual arts—is often overshadowed by other movements; indeed the movement pales in comparison to her Modernist architectural counterpart. A reaction to the disorder brought by Modernisme and World War I, Noucentisme is a Neoclassical revival that focused on order and simplicity. Puig i Cadafalch, reborn as a Noucentisme architect, was responsible for the redesign of Pl. de Catalunya. For examples of this movement, check out the area surrounding the **plaça,** the **Estació França,** and the **Museu Arqueològic.** The latter two were both built for the 1929 International Exhibition (see p. 44).

FROM FASCISM TO THE PRESENT

For the 1929 International Exposition, dictator Primo de Rivera commissioned **Poble Espanyol** to illustrate different types of Spanish architecture through the work of respected architects and designers **Ramon Reventós, Francesc Folguera,** and **Miquel Utrillo** (see p. 90). While arguably lame, this mini-town offers a compact walking tour of the different kinds of architecture found throughout Spain. So while the Arab influence never reached Barcelona, those visiting Spain will be comforted by the watered-down grandeur of Andalucia right in Barcelona.

After the Civil War destroyed Spain's economy and Franco entered the scene, growth and development of Barcelona's once prospering architectural innovations came to a halt. Few noteworthy architectural developments occurred during this era. Franco did sponsor the building of the university, although construction stopped a few years later due to a lack of funding. The building of **Camp Nou,** the soccer stadium, was funded by the people of Barcelona.

Today, while a significant style is not currently noticeable, the city is going through rapid urban development. After Franco's death, there has been a movement toward eliminating the changes he had made to Barcelona as well as a focus on beautifying the city. Mayor **Pasqual Maragall** was the key player in this endeavor; after managing to secure the **1992 Summer Olympics** for the city, he brought modern high-rises to Barcelona's beachfront property and turned the waterfront into Nightlife Central.

SPORTS

Barcelona's proximity to the ocean and the mountains lends the city to outdoor activities; while windsurfing, swimming, and boating prevail in seaside towns, hiking, biking, and winter sports dominate the mountains. Skiing is popular in the Pyrenees; everyone from the Spanish crown prince to French tourists cover the slopes in the winter.

In terms of organized competitive sports, the most popular is, of course, **fútbol** (soccer or football, as you prefer). *Fútbol* is a uniting passion for Spaniards; championship wins send fans into the streets for hours, even days, with painted faces, flags waving from cars, special horn-honks, and extended disco hours. Their pride is wellwarranted: the Spanish national team ranks with the finest in Europe, and reached the quarterfinals in the 2002 World Cup.

Barcelona's blue- and red-clad team, affectionately called **el Barça,** more formally known as **Fútbol Club Barcelona,** is among the best in Europe; hard-core fans follow the soccer team with an almost cultish fervor. The stadium, **Camp Nou,** is a nonstop party when an important game is in town (see p. 173). El Barça has participated in every European cup tournament since the first, in 1955. They won in the 1991-1992 season, and the team is very proud of their numerous trophies from various competitions. **Vítor Borba Ferreira Rivaldo,** a Brazilian forward, is a popular favorite, having been chosen as third world player in 2000 by **FIFA.**

Visitors to Spain are often eager to see a **bullfight,** or *corrida de toros.* Bullfighting is not native to Catalunya, but it has crept its way up to this corner of the peninsula, although it enjoys only modest popularity among the locals (see p. 177).

Sights

TOURS

RUTA DEL MODERNISME

For those with a few days in the city and an interest in seeing all the biggest sights, the Ruta del Modernisme is the cheapest and most flexible option. The Ruta del Modernisme isn't a tour precisely, in the sense that it doesn't offer a guide or organized transportation; it's a ticket which gives discounted entrance to Modernist sites, to be used at the owner's discretion. Passes (€3; students, over 65, and groups over 10 people €2) are good for a month and give holders a 25 to 30% discount on entrance to Palau Güell (see p. 75), La Sagrada Família (see p. 76), Casa Milà (La Pedrera; see p. 78), Palau de la Música Catalana (see p. 70), Casa-Museu Gaudí (see p. 121), Fundació Antoni Tàpies (see p. 113), the Museu d'Art Modern (see p. 111), the Museu de Zoologia (see p. 111), a tour of El Hospital de la Santa Creu i Sant Pau (see p. 83), tours of the facades of La Manzana de la Discòrdia (Casas Amatller, Lleó Morera, and Batlló; see p. 79), and other attractions. The pass also comes with a map and a pamphlet that gives a history of the movement and prioritize the sites. Purchase passes at **Casa Amatller,** Pg. Gràcia, 41 (☎ 93 488 01 39; www.rutamodern-isme.com. M: Pg. de Gràcia; see p. 80) near the intersection with C. Aragó. As many of these sights have mandatory hour-long tours or tours that only leave on the half-hour or hour, visiting all of them on the same day is virtually impossible.

THE STATUES OF LAS RAMBLAS

In a city as rich in artistic heritage as Barcelona, it is not surprising to find a series of sculptures lining Las Ramblas. What's surprising is when one of these suspiciously life-like statues begins to shimmy and shake. Hopefully you would have figured this out on your own, but these "statues" are in fact real people, putting in a hard day's work for tourist euros. Living statues are Las Ramblas's signature tourist attraction, drawing daily crowds of fascinated gawkers. Men and women dress in costumes and paint themselves head to toe in a solid color, then stand dead still on a platform for hours at a time. The best ones shift positions only when a coin is dropped into their jar, at which point they come alive in jerky motions, posing for pictures or thanking the donor. During a typical day, one might find silver mermaids, marble nuns, bronze Roman soldiers, and golden sax players. Toss them a euro and watch them stand and deliver.

BUS TURÍSTIC

If you don't feel like deciphering subway or bus routes and your boots *ain't* made for walkin', the clearly marked Bus Turístic stops at 27 points of interest along 2 different routes (red for the north-bound buses, blue for the south-bound); a ticket comes with a comprehensive info guide in six languages about each important sight. A full ride on both routes takes about 3½ hours, but you can get on and off as often as you wish. The easiest place to hop on the Bus Turístic is **Pl. de Catalunya,** in front of El Corte Inglés (see **Shopping,** p. 190). Many of the museums and sights covered by the tour bus offer discounts with bus ticket and are closed on Mondays. Purchase tickets on the bus, at the Pl. de Catalunya tourist office, at Estació Barcelona-Sants, or outside many of the major sights. All in all, the bus is a good idea if you want to see the whole city quickly, as it cuts transportation time, but not really necessary for a more leisurely take on the city. (Daily except Dec. 25 and Jan. 1; every 10-30min. 9am-9:30pm; 1-day pass €14, children aged 4-12 €8, 2-day pass €18.)

LAS RAMBLAS

see map p. 338-339

⁊ *M: Catalunya, Liceu, or Drassanes. Addresses with low numbers lie toward the port, while higher numbers climb toward the Pl. de Catalunya.*

Las Ramblas's pedestrian-only median strip is a veritable urban carnival, where street performers dance, fortune-tellers survey palms, human statues shift poses, vendors peddle animals and flowers, and artists draft caricatures and their own renditions of Barcelona—all for the benefit of droves of tourists and all, of course, for a small fee. A stroll along this bustling avenue can be an adventure at any hour, day or night. The wide, tree-lined thoroughfare dubbed Las Ramblas is actually composed of five distinct *ramblas* (promenades) that together form one long boulevard, about 1km long; however what follows is a description of the different segments of Las Ramblas and the sights along the way, beginning with Pl. de Catalunya in the north and heading towards the port in the south. People generally refer to the streets as one single entity, Las Ramblas, and not by their individual names.

La Rambla de les Canaletes and La Rambla dels Estudis are both accessible from M: Catalunya; La Rambla de Sant Josep and ◧La Rambla dels Caputxins are accessible from M: Liceu; La Rambla de Santa Monica is accessible from M: Drassanes.

LA RAMBLA DE LES CANALETES

The port-ward journey begins at the **Font de les Canaletes,** more of a pump than a fountain, recognizable by the four faucets and the Catalan crests (red crosses next to red and yellow stripes) that adorn it; this section of Las Ramblas is named for the fountain. Legend has it that visitors who sample the water will fall in love with the city (if they haven't already) and are bound to return to Barcelona someday. Stationed around here are the first of many **living statues** (see **Stand in the Place Where You Are,** p. 58) that line the walkway during the day. Because of its symbolic position on the Pl. de Catalunya and its central location, La Rambla de les Canaletes also sees a fair number of political demonstrations.

Chicks for Sale on Las Ramblas

LA RAMBLA DELS ESTUDIS

You'll hear the squawking of the caged residents of the next section of Las Ramblas before you see them. The next stretch of Las Ramblas, which extends to C. Carme and C. Portaferrissa, is often referred to as La Rambla dels Ocells—the **Promenade of the Birds.** A number of stalls here hawk birds of nearly every kind: roosters, parrots, doves, and even baby emus (good luck trying to sneak these cute and fuzzy souvenirs through customs). Rabbits, fish, gerbils, turtles, and other caged critters are also for sale. The official name of this stretch of *rambla* comes from the university that used to be located here; "*estudis*" is Catalan for "studies."

Portraitist on Las Ramblas

LA RAMBLA DE SANT JOSEP

While still in earshot of the birds, you'll start to smell the roses. A block later, the screeching bird stalls give way to the sunflowers, roses, and irises of *La Rambla de les Flors* (the Promenade of the Flowers). Vendors here have offered a good variety of bouquets since the mid 1800s. In April, the flower stands are joined by book vendors in preparation for the **Día de Sant Jordi,** a Catalan variance on Valentine's Day. On April 23, couples exchange gifts: women and girls receive flowers and men and boys receive books. The hulking stone building at the corner of C. Carme is the Església de Betlem, a Baroque church whose interior never recovered

Miró Mosaic

59

the local story

MARATHON MAN

If you think that street performers are just glorified beggars, think again. In Barcelona, street performance, especially on Las Ramblas, is a respected profession, carried out by some of the most talented of Barcelona's residents. Juan Sabate, known as "the marathon man of Las Ramblas," specializes in soccer-ball marvels and shares some thoughts here.

Q: How long have you been working here?

A: Here, in Barcelona, on Las Ramblas, about 10 years.

Q: And what do you do exactly?

A: I perform *marvel*, or tricks, with a soccer ball. I come from the world of soccer, so I have some skill with the ball. And when I retired, I turned that skill into marvel. I even have some world records. I hold the world's record for the greatest number of consecutive taps of the ball against my head while seated: 26,000. I also hold the world's record for the greatest number of taps while seated in a single hour: 8,700. I also give skill class for young kids. And I come here as often as I can, pretty much every day.

from an anarchist torching during the Civil War. A bit farther down is the famous traditional Catalan market, **Mercat de la Boqueria** (see p. 62), the oldest of the city's 40 markets. The Boqueria market is officially named **El Mercat de Sant Josep;** the market and the *rambla* are named for the same saint. At Pl. Boqueria, just before the Metro station, you'll walk across Joan Miró's circular pavement mosaic, created for the city in 1976 and now a popular meeting point. Last but certainly not least, this part of Las Ramblas is home to the infamous **Museu de l'Eròtica** (see **Museums,** p. 106).

LA BOQUERIA (MERCAT DE SANT JOSEP)

◪ *Las Ramblas, 95. M: Liceu, outside the Mercat exit. Open M-Sa 8am-8pm.*

Besides being one of the cheapest ways to get food in the city, La Boqueria is a sight in itself: a traditional (and relatively clean) Catalan market located right on Las Ramblas. Specialized vendors sell delicious-looking produce, fish, and meat from independent stands inside the market complex, which is an all-steel Modernist structure. This wonderland offers wholesale prices for fruit, cheese, meat, bread, wine, and more. There are even a couple of bars inside, like **Barcentral La Boquería,** where you can sit down and treat yourself to a delicious lunch of fresh fish (€5.50-16.80) or meat (€4-10.50). Some of the butcher displays can be gory, showcasing everything from freshly gutted fish to sheep's brains.

PALAU DE LA VIRREINA

◪ *Las Ramblas, 99, at C. Carme. M: Liceu. ☎93 316 10 00. Open Tu-Sa 11am-8:30pm; Su 11am-3pm. Free.*

Once the residence of a Peruvian viceroy, this 18th-century palace houses temporary photography, music, and graphics exhibits. Also on display are the latest incarnations of the 10-15 foot tall giant dolls who have taken part in the city's Carnival celebrations since as far back as 1320. The imposing couple Jaume and Violant, dressed in long, regal robes, are the undisputed king and queen of the Carnival parade. The cultural institute here, **ICUB,** serves as information headquarters for Barcelona's cultural festivals. Be sure to check out the famous rainbow stained-glass facade of the Casa Beethoven next door at Las Ramblas 97, now a well-stocked music store (see **Shopping,** p. 192).

LA RAMBLA DELS CAPUTXINS

Miró's street mosaic marks the beginning of La Rambla dels Caputxins, the most user-friendly of the five Rambla sisters and the first of Las Ramblas to be converted into an actual promenade. The pedestrian area widens, and the majestic trees provide a blanket of shade. Across from the recently renovated opera house (the **Liceu**; see below), a strip of restaurants with outdoor seating vie for tourist euros, offering unremarkable and fairly expensive food and prime people-watching perches. When you're in the area, go to the Miró mosaic *plaça* (intersection of La Rambla dels Caputxins and C. Boqueria) and look up: if you see umbrellas sticking out of one of the buildings, that's no accident, but a former umbrella store of some acclaim.

GRAN TEATRE DEL LICEU

🔀 *Las Ramblas, 51-59, on the corner of C. Sant Pau. ☎ 93 485 99 00. Information office open M-F 2-8:30pm and 1hr. before performances. Tours 10am M-F. €5.*

The Gran Teatre del Liceu has been Barcelona's opera house for over a century. It was once one of Europe's leading stages, playing host to the likes of José Carreras in his early years. Ravaged by a fire in January 1994, it reopened for performances in 1999 (see **Smooth Opera-ater**, p. 61). It is adorned with palatial ornamentation, gold facades, sculptures, grand circular side rooms, and a Spanish hall of mirrors.

🔳 LA RAMBLA DE SANTA MONICA

Following the tradition of nicknaming the parts of Las Ramblas after the goods sold there, this stretch would most likely be nicknamed *La Rambla de las Prostitutas*. After nightfall, women of the night patrol this wide area leading up to the port, beckoning passers by with loud kissing noises. During the day, however, the street distinguishes itself with some of the city's most skilled practitioners of a different fine art. These wizards can whip up dead-on caricatures in just five minutes, or invest hours on startlingly life-like portraits of their paying customers. Roving galleries sell landscapes and colorful psychedelic pieces worthy of a Pink Floyd album cover. La Rambla de Santa Monica is also home to the **Centre d'Art de Santa Monica** and the **Museu de Cera** (see p. 104). On some days (usually weekends), vendors also set up small stands and sell

SMOOTH OPERA-ATOR

The grand old dame of Barcelona high culture, the **Gran Teatre de Liceu**, has been a leading European opera house since its founding in 1847. But beneath this spectacularly restored theater is a tumultuous history. Not long after its opening as Europe's largest theater, an 1861 fire ravaged the Liceu, destroying its interior. The theater was rebuilt practically from scratch, but soon reopened. In 1868, an angry mob of commoners stormed the Liceu, a favorite bourgeoisie bastion. They snatched the marble bust of Queen Isabel II from the lobby, paraded it down Las Ramblas, and tossed it into the sea.

The social unrest became more dangerous in 1893; on opening night, a packed house of Barcelona bourgeoisie was enjoying Rossini's "William Tell." During the second act, an anarchist named Santiago Salvador threw a bomb into the crowd from an upper balcony, killing 20 and wounding many others. Salvador was executed, and the theater reopened the following season, but for years tickets were not sold for the seats of the tragedy's victims. One-hundred years later, in 1994, disaster struck again, when fire consumed the ill-fated interior for a second time. A multi-billion *peseta* restoration project has returned the Liceu to its former grandeur while allowing modernization of the facilities.

crafts. Although the area's nighttime reputation is notorious, La Rambla de Santa Monica is not particularly unsafe; nonetheless, group travel is always a good idea. Las Ramblas ends at the seafront-end of La Rambla de Santa Monica with one very visible statue.

MONUMENT A COLOM

 Portal de la Pau. M: Drassanes. Elevator open June-Sept. 9am-8:30pm; Oct.-Mar. M-F 10am-1:30pm and 3:30-6:30pm, Sa-Su 10am-6:30pm; Apr.-May 10am-2pm and 3:30-7:30pm, Sa-Su 10am-7:30pm. €1.80, children and over 65 €1.20, groups of more than 15 €1.50 per person.

At the port end of Las Ramblas, Ruis i Taulet's Monument a Colom towers 60m above the city. During the late 19th-century Renaixenca (Renaissance) movement in Barcelona, Catalan enthusiasts went a little overboard in their regional pride and decided to adopt Columbus as one of their own. Columbus, they claimed, was in fact from a northern town near Girona, and so in 1887-8 they built this statue in his honor. The fact that the statue points proudly toward Libya, not the Americas, doesn't help their claim; historians now agree that Columbus was actually from Genoa, Italy. At night, spotlights turn the statue, renovated in 1982, into a firebrand. Take the **elevator** up to the top and get a stunning, albeit somewhat obstructed, view of Barcelona.

see map p. 338-339

BARRI GÒTIC

 Walking tours of the Barri Gótic offered by the Tourism Office in Pl. Catalunya Sa-Su 10am in English; noon in Catalan and Spanish. Spaces are limited; buy tickets at the office or the Ajuntament (see p. 67) in advance. €7, children 4-12 €3. Visit www.bgb.es or www.barcelonaturisme.com.

The Barri Gòtic offers everything that Barcelona's Modernist architecture and l'Eixample do not. Its narrow, winding streets are not the products of careful planning and rapid execution, but have developed out of centuries of architectural and cultural mixing, from early Roman through the medieval Romanesque and Gothic periods. This area is best enjoyed by wandering slowly and paying close attention to your surroundings; nearly every street has at least a few interesting historical sights and an endless array of shops, eateries, and cafes.

PLAÇA DE L'ANGEL

M: Jaume I.

The Jaume I Metro stop lets out at the Plaça de l'Angel, where the main gate into Roman Barcino was once located. The *plaça* gets its name from the legend surrounding the moving of St. Eulalia's remains from Santa Maria del Mar to the cathedral: supposedly the martyred saint's body suddenly became too heavy to carry, and an angel appeared in the *plaça* pointing a finger at one of the church officials, who, it turned out, had secretly stolen one of Eulalia's toes. The angel statue placed in the *plaça* in the 17th century to commemorate the event is now in the **Museu d'Història de la Ciutat** (see p. 104).

ROMAN WALLS

M: Jaume I.

Several sections of the northeastern walls of Roman Barcino are still standing near the cathedral. C. Tapineria, which runs from Pl. de l'Angel (to your right with your back facing Via Laietana) to **Pl. Ramon Berenguer,** does double duty as a parking space for motorcycles and as a viewing space from which you can see a large stretch of a 4th-century defense wall under the Palau Reial Major. Continuing along C. Tapineria and making a left onto Av. de la Catedral lands you in Pl. Seu (in front of the

Cathedral), where you can see the only intact octagonal corner tower left today, part of the **Museu Diocesà** (see **Museums,** p. 107). To the right of the cathedral are several more Roman towers and a reconstruction of one of the two aqueducts which ran through here to supply water to Barcino.

CATHEDRAL & ENVIRONS

🚩 *M: Jaume I.*

In the cathedral's *plaça*, seven stylized letters crafted by Joan Brossa spell out "Barcino," commemorating the original Roman city settled on what is now Barcelona. The Romans first ripped through Spain in the 3rd century BC in an effort to subdue North African powers in Carthage. They subjugated the resident Laietani and settled next to Montjuïc in 210 BC. In 15 BC, in honor of Augustus's rule, the Romans gave the small town the unwieldy name of Colonia Julia Augusta Faventia Paterna Barcino.

■ ESGLÉSIA CATEDRAL DE LA SANTA CREU

🚩 *In Pl. Seu, up C. Bisbe from Pl. St. Jaume. Cathedral open daily 8am-1:30pm and 4-7:30pm. Cloister open 9am-1:15pm and 4-7pm. Elevator to the roof open M-Sa 10:30am-12:30pm and 4:30-6pm; €1.35. Choir area open M-F 9am-1pm and 4-7pm, Sa-Su 9am-1pm; €0.90. History recording (in English) €1.*

La Catedral de la Santa Creu (the Cathedral of the Holy Cross) is one of Barcelona's most popular historical monuments. More than 3 million people visit it every year, and it still serves as the active center of the archbishopric of Barcelona, with daily masses taking place in Catalan and Spanish. Three separate buildings have actually existed on the site: a 4th-century basilica, an 11th-century Romanesque church, and finally the present Gothic Cathedral, begun in 1298. The much-photographed main facade comes from yet another era (1882), when it was tacked on to the main structure by architect Josep Mestres. Adding to the architectural mix, it appears that Mestres worked from a plan drawn up by Frenchman Carles Galtés de Ruán in 1408.

As you first enter the church, directly to your right is the **Chapel of El Santo Cristo de Lepanto.** This chapel is usually reserved for prayer, but if you do get a look inside you will see the remains of **Saint Olegario,** who died in 1137 after serving as archbishop of Tarragona. Still standing at the

La Rambla del Mar

Cheese at La Boqueria

Entertainer on Las Ramblas

THE GUILD-ED AGE

One of the most defining features of medieval Barcelona was its workers' guilds; but these were not the quaint, mildly cooperative operations that history sometimes paints them to be. A member was not allowed to practice a trade without guild approval, and once you were a member your economic and social survival was utterly dependent upon your obeying all price fixings, quality controls, and production rules. The guilds had close connections to both the government and the Church (most maintained their own chapels, many of which are still visible in the Cathedral cloister), and when war broke out, they were often the first source of organized fighters. Naturally, the guilds tended to set up shop near one another for the purpose of sharing resources, and it is from their geographic concentrations that many of the streets in the Barri Gòtic get their names: needle-makers worked in C. Agullers, rope-weavers in C. Corders, cotton-sewers in C. Cotoners, shield-makers in C. Escudellers, glass-makers in C. Vidre, knife-molders in C. Dagueria, and so on and so forth.

front doors, you will see the cathedral **choir** directly in front of you. The backs of the stalls are painted with 46 coats of arms commemorating the Chapter of the Order of the Golden Fleece, an early United Nations meeting of sorts, held in Barcelona in 1519. The area below the choir seats is decorated with detailed sculptures of hunting and game-playing scenes. Walk around the choir, passing several of the Cathedral's small chapels (on the left and the right), and you will find the most important liturgical elements of the Cathedral, including the marble **cathedra** (bishop's throne; the origin of the word "cathedral"), the altar with the bronze **cross** designed by Frederic Marès in 1976, and most famous of all, the sunken **Crypt of Santa Eulalia**, one of Barcelona's patron saints. Completed in 1334, the crypt holds a white marble sarcophagus that depicts scenes from the saint's martyrdom at age 13. Discovered in the Santa Maria del Mar in 877, her remains were not transported here until 1339. You can descend the stairs and view the barred-off crypt.

Behind the altar, the Chapel of St. Joan Baptista i St. Josep features one of the most famous pieces of artwork in the Cathedral, the *Transfiguration of the Lord* altarpiece created by Bernat Martorell in 1450. The **elevator** to the roof is to the left of the altar, through the **Capella de les Animes del Purgatori;** it will give you a close-up view of the Cathedral's spires, as well as a pigeon's-eye view of Barcelona. The Cathedral **treasury** is to the right, behind the sacristy door. The treasury is not always open, but when it is, it is worth going inside to see the famous **monstrance** (the receptacle used for holding the Host, the holy bread of the Catholic religion), made of gold and silver and dripping with precious jewels. Once used for Corpus Christi processions, legend has it that the monstrance was given to the cathedral by the last Catalan king, Martí, before he died childless in 1410. Right outside of the sacristy you will see on the wall the **tombs** of Ramon Berenguer I and his wife, founders of the Romanesque cathedral, the second building that occupied this site.

Just to the right of the tombs is the exit into the peaceful **cloister,** home to the **Fountain of St. Jordi,** which is located directly across from the votive candle vending machines (€1 for a small votive, €2 for a large one). A sign at the Fountain of St. Jordi claims that the water flowing from it is safe for drinking, although *Let's Go* remains skeptical. Thirteen white geese occupy the cloister, serving as a reminder of St. Eulalia's age at the time of her death. They are joined by a less aesthetically pleasing group of uninvited pigeons. The chapels in the cloister were once dedicated to the various guilds of Barcelona, and a few of them are still maintained today (including the shoe-makers' and electricians'; see **The Guilded Age,** p. 64). The coats of arms of private families as well as the guilds adorn the cloister walkways, and if you look back toward the Cathedral interior, you can see the only remaining piece of the Romanesque structure, the large arched doorway leading back inside. The earlier 4th-century building was almost entirely destroyed by Muslim invaders in 985; what little is left is visible underground in the **Museu d'Història de la Ciutat** (see p. 104). Coming from the Cathedral, at the near right corner of the cloister you will find the **Cathedral museum,** whose most notable holding is Bartolomé Bermejo's renowned oil painting of a *pietà,* the image of Christ dying in the arms of his mother (in the Sala Capitular, to the left up on entrance).

Barri Gòtic

The front of the Cathedral is also the place to catch an impromptu performance of the **sardana,** the traditional Catalan dance (see p. 9). Performances generally occur Sunday mornings and afternoons after mass (at noon and 6:30 pm).

CARRER DEL BISBE

🚩 *M: Jaume I. Make a sharp left when you exit the main door of the Cathedral. Walk to the end of C. de Santa Llúcia, and you will intersect Carrer del Bisbe.*

In Roman times, C. del Bisbe served as the city's main north-south thoroughfare. Today it is lined with various official buildings. As you are walking from the Cathedral to C. del Bisbe, on the right is the entrance to the medieval **Casa de l'Ardiaca,** once home to the archdeacon and now the location of Barcelona's newspaper archives.

Holding Hands at the Pier

Stop and check out the mailslot designed by Domènech i Montaner in 1902, which juxtaposes a sculpted tortoise with several swallows—according to one theory, an expression of his opinion of the postal service (supposedly quick as a bird but actually slow as a turtle).

Directly across from the Casa de l'Ardiaca is the **Capella de Santa Llúcia;** it is not well labeled, but you can enter through one of two small metal doors. The chapel was built in 1268 and is one of only a few remaining Romanesque churches in the entire city. Every December 13, the Day of Santa Llúcia, locals pay their respects to the saint and the Fair of Sant Llúcia begins around the Cathedral.

Once you exit the chapel, make a left onto C. Bisbe. Walking down the street will take you past the **Palau de la Generalitat** on the right (see p. 4) and the **Casa de los Canónigos** on the left,

Palau Güell Façade

kids
IN THE CITY

Kid-Friendly Sights

If your kids are getting pooped with Modernisme and Picasso, check out some of the following sights, which should have something to entertain everyone:

Barcelona Aquarium: see p. 87.

Barcelona Zoo: see p. 74.

The Cascade Fountain and Lake: see p. 73.

La Rambla dels Estudis: p. 59.

La Rambla de Santa Monica: see p. 61.

Parc d'Attracions: p. 99.

Parc de la Creuta del Coll: p. 96.

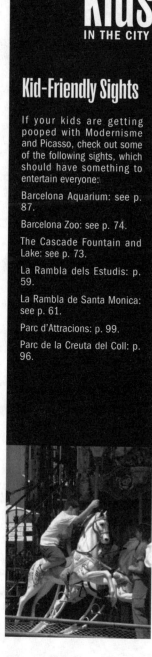

once home to the religious canons and now the office of the Catalan president. The two are connected by an elaborate neo-Gothic bridge built in 1929 as part of the restoration of the Barri Gòtic.

ROMAN TOMBS

🚶 *From Las Ramblas, turn onto C. Portaferrissa and take the first left; it will lead directly to the Pl. de la Vila de Madrid.*

In the Upper Barri Gòtic, between C. Portaferrissa and C. Canuda, the **Plaça de la Vila de Madrid** contains one final Roman site worth visiting: a row of 2nd- to 4th-century Roman tombs, lined up just as they originally were along a road leading out of Barcino (Roman law forbade burial within the city walls). The recently restored tombs are significantly lower than the rest of the *plaça*, proof of how much the physical terrain of Barcelona has changed over the past 2000 years.

PLAÇA DE SANT JAUME & AROUND

🚶 *M: Jaume I. From the Metro, walk to the Pl. de l'Angel, on the Via Laietana, and then down either C. Jaume I or C. Llibreteria to the plaça.*

When Roman colonizers constructed new outpost towns, they always followed the same basic plan, laying down two main streets that intersected in the shape of a short cross (in Barcino, the longer C. Bisbe ran north-south and the shorter C. Llibreteria east-west). At the central intersection they would build their forum, the center of civic and political life. (Under Augustus's rule, the forum also had to include a temple to the emperor.) The site of Barcino's original forum has never ceased serving as the seat of power in Barcelona, and today the city government and provincial government face off across the broad square, with the **Ajuntament** on the C. Jaume I side, and the **Generalitat** on the C. Llibreteria side. *Sardanas* are frequently danced here (see **May I Have This Dance,** p. 51), and the *plaça* always fills with merrymaking crowds on Catalan holidays. Just off the *plaça*, the Gothic **Església de Sants Just i Pastor** (1342) occupies a small square just off C. Ciutat. This is the only remaining church in the city which honors living wills: someone about to die can make a will to a friend, who can then repeat his last words at this altar, whereupon they become legally binding. The Pl. de Sant Jaume also houses the **Museu d'Història de la Ciutat** (see p. 104).

PALAU DE LA GENERALITAT

🏠 *Pl. St. Jaume. Enter to the right on C. Bisbe. M: Jaume I. ☎93 402 46 16. Open the 2nd and 4th Su of every month 10:30am-1:30pm. Closed Aug. Mandatory tours in Catalan, Spanish, or English every 30min. starting at 10:30am (in English usually 11:00 and 11:30, but call to be sure). Tours are limited, so come early, and bring ID. Free. Limited wheelchair accessibility. The first Su of every month the Palace hosts a free bell concert at noon.*

Located in the same place as the original Roman forum, the Palace of the Generalitat is the center of Catalunya's regional government. It has served as the seat of power for 115 presidents of Catalunya, from Berenguer de Cruïlles in 1359 to current president, Jordi Pujol. The oldest part of the building is the Gothic facade in C. Bisbe, site of the original entrance; the government officials who commissioned it in 1416 were so happy with the St. Jordi medallion designed by Marc Safont that they paid him double what they had originally promised. Most of the center of the palace was added in the 16th and 17th centuries, including the beautiful **Pati dels Tarongers** (Patio of Oranges) and the **Salón Dorado** (Gold Room), a hall with an ornate gold ceiling and tapestries inspired by Petrarch depicting the triumph of honor over death, and of time over honor. Also notable is the **Salón de Sant Jordi,** whose cupola is visible from the Pl. St. Jaume. Part of the 17th-century additions, this extravagant room features a St. Jordi statue by Frederic Marès and is covered in allegorical paintings delineating the history of Catalunya.

AJUNTAMENT

🏠 *Pl. St. Jaume. Open Su 10am-1:45pm. Tours at 10:30, 11:30am, and 12:30pm or as needed by large groups, usually in Catalan or Spanish. For English or French call ☎93 268 24 44. Self-guided tours also allowed; pamphlet guides are available in Catalan, Spanish, English, and French. Free.*

The Ajuntament is Barcelona's city hall and the office of Socialist Mayor Joan Clos. In the late 14th century, Barcelona's elite Consell de Cent (Council of One Hundred) decided to build their meeting house on the site of the original Roman forum. The most impressive room in the building, the **Saló de Cent,** was completed in 1369; King Pere III had his first meeting with the Consell de Cent there in 1373. With red-and-gold-brocaded walls, high arches, and a profusion of crystal chandeliers, it practically glows with Catalan pride. Smaller but equally stunning is the **Saló de la Reina Regente,** which was designed in 1860 for plenary meetings and boasts a half-dome stained glass skylight. The **Saló de las**

Palau Güell Roof Terrace

Sta. Maria del Mar

Sant Pau in El Raval

67

CATALAN JEWS

The history of Jews in Spain has been nothing short of contradictory; they have been the most persecuted people in the land but they also make up a substantial percentage of the country's most culturally accomplished, financially successful, and intellectually renowned historical figures. The paradox inherent in this situation loomed particularly large during Christopher Columbus's voyages to the New World. The sailor's first trip was financed mainly by King Fernando's treasurer Lluís Santagel, a converted Jew from Valencia, and the news of Columbus's shocking discoveries was spread throughout Europe by another converted Jew, publisher Leandre de Coscó. Meanwhile, Fernando and Isabel were busy recapturing Granada from the Muslims, and Santagel ended up financing Columbus's second trip predominantly with confiscated goods...from all of the Jews expelled from Spain in 1492. Even as the centralized Spanish government tried to oppress Catalanism, displaced Catalan Jews kept it alive. Today, there are still Jews in parts of the Middle East who speak a form a Catalan and cook decidedly Catalan food. These men and women are descendants of the Jews expelled from Barcelona in the 1400s.

Crónicas is lined with wall decorations by Josep Marià Sert, depicting episodes from Roger de Flor's expedition to the Far East in the 14th century. The entrance **courtyard,** meanwhile, serves as a display space for sculptures by some of Barcelona's most famous artists, including Josep Llimona, Josep Subirachs, and Joan Miró.

TEMPLE OF AUGUSTUS

🚩 Inside the Centre Excursionista de Catalunya building. The protective gate opens Tu-Su 10am-2pm, but the remains are visible through the gate as well.

Upon entering Pl. St. Jaume from C. Bisbe, make an immediate sharp left (basically a U-turn) into tiny C. Paradís. Follow this street around the corner, and at the end you will find a plaque marking **Mont Tàber,** the highest point of Roman Barcino, all of 16.9m above sea level. Right behind the plaque, inside the protective walls of the **Centre Excursionista Catalunya,** a local outdoors club, are the four columns from the original Roman **Temple of Augustus.** If the size of the columns bear any relationship to the size of the emperor's ego, then these remains should give you a pretty good idea of just how much Augustus liked himself. Built on the formerly towering summit of Mont Tàber over 2000 years ago, the now eye-level columns have not moved from their original position.

SOUTHERN ROMAN WALLS

🚩 C. Regomir, 3. M: Jaume I. From Pl. St. Jaume, take C. Ciutat; just as the street turns into C. Regomir, the Centre Pati Llimona will be on your left. ☎ 93 268 21 70. Centre Pati Llimona open M-F 9am-10pm and Sa-Su 10am-2pm.

In case you haven't had your fill of ancient walls yet, the second concentrated stretch of Roman walls is located in what was the southeastern corner of the original city, near present-day Pl. Regomir and Pl. Traginers. This civic center hosts free art exhibitions in its front room (usually photography) and also showcases a substantial piece of first-century Roman wall. The wall is visible from the street through a glass window but is also accessible for free via a ramp inside the building.

Soon after passing the civic center, turn left on C. Correu Vell. A tiny alley, C. de Groch, branches off to the left into a space where you can see a stretch of 4th-century wall and two square towers. If you then go back and take C. Correu Vell to its end, you will find yourself in small, quiet **Plaça Traginers,** which hosts yet another substantial segment of 4th-century walls.

EL CALL (JEWISH QUARTER)

🔏 *M: Jaume I.*

Records indicate that Jewish families started moving to Roman Barcino as early as the 2nd century. They tended to congregate near one another and intermarry, and soon El Call, or the Jewish quarter, sprang to life near the center of town, between present-day Pl. St. Jaume, C. Ferran, C. Banys Nous, and the Església Santa Maria del Pi. Although today there is little indicating the Jewish heritage of this area, for centuries El Call was the most vibrant center of intellectual and financial activity in all of Barcelona; Jews even received a certain amount of governmental support and protection in return for their substantial financial and cultural contributions to the city. Anti-Semitism spread throughout Europe in the thirteenth century, however, and Spain was no exception. In 1243, Jaume I ordered the complete isolation of the Jewish quarter from the rest of the city, and he forced all Jews to wear identifying red-and-yellow buttons. Anti-Semitism increased even more as citizens looked for scapegoats for the growing plagues and poverty of the 14th century, and in 1348, hundreds of Jews were blamed for the Black Death and tortured mercilessly until they "confessed" to their crime. In 1391, as harassment of Jews spread throughout Spain, a riot ended in the murder of nearly 1000 Jews in Barcelona's Call. By 1401, every single synagogue and Jewish cemetery was demolished, making the forced conversion law of 1492 an easy next step (see **Catalan Jews,** p. 68).

One Jewish synagogue was turned into a church which is still in use today, the **Església de Sant Jaume** (C. Ferran, 28). However, the only remaining tangible evidence of Jewish inhabitants in El Call is the ancient **Hebrew plaque** in tiny C. Marlet. To see it, from Pl. St. Jaume take C. Call and turn right onto C. Sant Domènech de Call and then left onto C. Marlet; it will be at the end on the right.

One of the best-known alleys in El Call actually has nothing to do with Jews: to the left off the end of C. Sant Domènech de Call (coming from C. Call) is the **Baixada de Sta. Eulalia,** said be the place where the city's patron saint was tortured to death and turned into a Christian martyr. On the wall at the start of the street a plaque written by a Catalan poet named Jacint Verdaguer, commemorating the legend.

SANTA MARIA DEL PI

🔏 *M: Liceu. Take C. Cardenal Casañas from Las Ramblas. Open M-F 8:30am-1pm and 4:30-8:30pm, Sa 8:30am-1pm and 4-9pm, Su 9am-2pm and 5-9pm. Be sure to observe proper church etiquette (see Once in Barcelona, p. 30).*

As far as religious buildings go, the Catedral de la Santa Creu tends to usurp tourist attention in the Barri Gòtic. However, the most popular among locals is the Església de Santa Maria del Pi, a small 14th-century church with Gothic stained-glass windows. The three *plaças* surrounding the church (Pl. del Pi, Placeta del Pi, and Pl. de St. Oriol) are some of the most pleasant places for relaxing in the entire Barri Gòtic.

PLAÇA REIAL

🔏 *M: Liceu or Drassanes. Be careful at night.*

The most crowded, happening *plaça* in the entire Barri Gòtic is the **Pl. Reial,** where tourists and locals alike congregate to eat and drink at night, and to sell stamps and coins at the Sunday morning flea market. Francesc Daniel Milona designed the *plaça* in one of Barcelona's first spurts of constructive (rather than oppressive) urban planning, replacing decrepit Barri Gòtic streets with a large, architecturally cohesive *plaça* in the 1850s. Near the fountain in the center of the square there are two street lamps designed by Antoni Gaudí at the very beginning of his architectural career. The *plaça* is a great place to grab a drink, whether it's a midday coffee or an early evening pint. It also hosts some of Barri Gòtic's more happening nightspots.

69

BORN AGAIN

The old Born market which sits at the head of Pg. del Born in La Ribera has a long and sordid past. In the 14th century, jousting tournaments were held in the Pl. del Born underneath the current market site. In fact, the word "born" originates from the name of the tips of the jousting spears used in these tournaments, which continued through the 17th century. Carrying on its violent tradition, the *plaça* was briefly used as a site for the *autos-da-fé* during the Inquisition later that century. From the late 19th century, however, the *plaça's* bloody legacy was present only in the meat stalls in the Mercat del Born.

Josep Fontseré was commissioned to design the market along with his work in the nearby Parc de la Ciutadella (see p. 72). His creation, a marvel of steel and glass that allowed for plenty of natural light, served as the city's major wholesale market for almost 100 years. When the market was moved out of the city in 1976, the building stood unused for many years. Finally, a joint project between the Ajuntament, the Ministry of Education and Culture, and the Generalitat was launched to convert the old market into a provincial library for Barcelona, slated to be open in 2005 with as much of Fontseré's original design preserved as possible. Meanwhile, a team of archaeologists from the Museu d'Història de la Ciutat (see p. 104) is working hard to uncover any medieval relics.

OTHER PLAÇAS IN THE BARRI GÒTIC

🚇 *M: Liceu or Jaume I.*

Farther toward the water, off C. Ample, the much newer **Pl. Mercé** is a popular spot for weddings, as well as for Barcelona's soccer team: the **Església de la Mercé** (see **Life & Times**, p. 53) on one side holds the image of the mother of God to which FCB players dedicate all of their successful games. One last *plaça* worth seeing is the **Pl. de Sant Felip Neri**, a right off C. Bisbe coming from the Cathedral. It is peaceful and pretty today, but has a rather morbid past: it was once the site of a Jewish cemetery, and in January 1938 a Civil War bomb exploded here, killing 20 children. The shrapnel marks are still visible on the facade of the Església de Sant Felip Neri.

LA RIBERA

see map p. 341

◼ PALAU DE LA MÚSICA CATALANA

🚇 *C. Sant Francesc de Paula, 2. M: Jaume I. Off Via Laietana near Pl. Urquinaona. Head up Via Laietana to the intersection of C. Ionqueres. ☎ 93 295 72 00; www.palaumusica.org. Entrance only with tour; in English on the hr., in Spanish on the half-hr. During high season it is wise to reserve 1 day in advance. Purchase tickets inside the Palau. Open daily Aug. 10am-6pm, Sept.-July 10am-3:30pm. Box office open M-Sa 9:45am-3pm, Su from 1hr. prior to the concert. No concerts in Aug.; check the Guía del Ocio for listings. €5, students and seniors €4; with Ruta del Modernisme pass €2.50. Concert tickets €9-125. MC/V.*

Flowers, flowers, and more flowers sprout and bloom in every crevice of this inspired masterpiece of a music hall. Commissioned in 1905 to house the growing and massively popular Orfeó Catalan, Modernist master Luis Domènech i Montaner colorfully harmonized nature and architecture in a this must-see concert hall. In 1997, UNESCO declared this magical palace a World Heritage Site. Debate continues over the political message of the inverted dome (weighing in, incidentally, at one ton of glass and iron), which is painted with 40 women dressed as angels. Some believe that Montaner was implying that women sing like angels and should have been allowed in the choir (at that time it was exclusively male). Others argue he was depicting women's fickleness by painting them with 40 different faces. The 2073-seat concert hall is also home to a 4000-pipe-tubed organ which has been broken since 1970 but is slated to be tooting away again in 2003.

SANTA MARIA DEL MAR

🚩 *Pl. Santa Maria, 1 M: Jaume 1. From the Metro, walk down C. de la Argentina to Pl. Santa Maria. ☎ 93 310 23 90. Open M-Sa 9am-1:30pm and 4:30-8pm, Su 9am-2pm and 5-8:30pm. Free. Concert information ☎ 93 319 05 16.*

Parc de la Ciutadella

La Ribera's streets come together in prayer, literally, at the foot of the Església Santa Maria del Mar's octagonal towers. The 14th-century structure, built over the course of 55 years with stone extracted from Montjuïc, owes its name (Mary of the Sea) to the many sailors that then populated La Ribera. Statues of Saint Peter and Saint Paul, flanking the austere front portal, beckon visitors into the surprisingly low, wide, open interior, the result of a fire 200 years ago that destroyed the church's interior and left it in its present state of somber majesty (with great acoustics). At 13m apart, the supporting columns span a width greater than any other medieval building in the world. This church is also a fascinating example of the limits of Gothic architecture—if it were 2 ft. higher it would collapse from structural instability.

EL FOSSAR DE LES MORERES

🚩 *Off C. de Santa Maria and next to the church's back entrance.*

Penguin at the Zoo

Though today it is nothing more than a brick-covered depression in the ground, the Fossar de les Moreres (Mulberry Cemetery) carries great significance as a reminder of Barcelona's past and of the Catalan struggle for cultural autonomy. The Catalans who resisted Felipe V's conquering troops in 1714 (see p. 42) were buried here in a mass grave, commemorated by mulberry trees *(les moreres)* and a plaque with a verse by the poet Sefari Pitarra: "In the Mulberry Cemetery no traitors are buried. Even though we lose our flags, this will be the urn of honor." The monument is sunken to recall the sinking of the grave as the bodies decomposed, and an eternal flame burns so that the light of their memory will never be extinguished. Demonstrators and patriots converge on Catalan National Day, Sept. 11th, to commemorate the siege of Barcelona and the subsequent ban on displays of Catalan nationalism.

Cascada Fountain

Façade of Sagrada Família

Spiral Staircase at Sagrada Família

MERCAT DE SANTA CATERINE

🚺 *M: Arc de Triomf. Just beyond the arch in Pg. Lluís Companys. Open July-Sept. Sa-Th 8am-2:30pm and 5-8pm, F 8am-8:30pm; Sept.-July Tu and Th 8am-2:30pm and 5-8pm.*

Across from the elaborate Palacio de Justicia, the Mercat de Santa Caterine occupies the same ranks as other traditional markets and is a great, cheap place to pick up food before entering the park or ingredients for dinner on your way back from sightseeing. Dozens of vendors sell produce, flowers, meats, and fish.

OTHER SIGHTS IN LA RIBERA

Carrer de Montcada, beginning behind Santa Maria de Mar, validates Barcelona's reputation as *"la ciudad del diseño"* (the city of design). Museums, art galleries, workshops, and Baroque palaces that once housed Barcelona's 16th-century bureaucrats are packed into just two blocks. The **Museu Picasso** (see p. 109) inhabits several such mansions, and the **Galería Maeght** (C. de Montcada 26; see p. 123), now a prestigious art gallery, was once an equally prestigious medieval aristocrat's manor (see p. 123). Off the Placeta de Montcada at the Pg. del Born end is the city's narrowest street, **C. de les Mosques** (Street of Flies), which was finally closed off in 1991 after residents complained that the narrow alley was being used far too frequently as a public urinal. Also worth a look is Antoni Tàpies' **Homenatge a Picasso,** a glass-enclosed sculpture on Pg. Picasso in front of the Museu Geologia. Installed in 1983, the jumble of wood furniture and steel beams was inspired by Picasso's comment that "A picture is not something to decorate a sitting room, but a weapon of attack and of defense against the enemy."

PARC DE LA CIUTADELLA

🚺 *Orientation and Transportation: M: Ciutadella-Vila Olímpica for zoo and rear entrance; M: Arc de Triomf for main entrance and the walking tour (see p. 8). Bus #14 runs from Pl. de Catalunya and stops at the Pg. Picasso/ Av. Marqués de l'Argentera entrance. ☎ 62 900 39 96. The park is bordered by Pg. Pujades to the west, Pg. Cicumvallació to the east, C. Wellington to the north, and Pg. Picasso to the south. The **Museu de Zoologia** (see **Museums,** p. 111), **Hivernacle, Museu de Geologia** (see **Museums,** p. 111), and **Umbracle** all line the Pg.*

Looking Down from Sagrada Família

Picasso side, while the **Museu d'Art Modern** (see **Museums**, p. 111) and the **Pl. D'Armes** are on the side of the park closer to C. Wellington. The **Cascada fountain** (see p. 73) is at the corner of C. Wellington and Pg. Pujades and faces the small lake. The **zoo** (see p. 74) has an entrance on C. Wellington. **Bike rental** is available from Los Paticletos, (☎ 93 319 78 85) Pg. Picasso, 44 (from €2.40 per hr.). Park gates open daily from 7:30am-10pm.

Sandwiched between La Ribera and Poble Nou, and a quick walk from Barceloneta and Barri Gòtic, Parc de la Ciutadella can be described as a touristic strawberry daiquiri: cool, refreshing relaxation with a kick of excitement, blended perfectly together. Barcelonese birds flock here to nibble at fruit dropped from the park's orange trees, while a good number of couples, lounging beneath the 30 acres of well-labeled fauna, nibble at each other. And even besides the feedin' and the lovin', there is a sea of things to do and see in the Parc.

Barcelona's military resistance to the Bourbon monarchy in the early 18th century convinced Felipe V to quarantine the city's influential citizens in the Ciutadella, a large citadel on the site of what is now Pg. Picasso. An entire neighborhood was razed and its citizens evacuated to make room for the citadel, which lorded threateningly over Barcelona. In a popular move, the city demolished the fortress in 1878, under the direction of **General Joan Prim** (honored with a statue at the end of Av. dels TilLers), and replaced it with the peaceful promenades of Parc de la Ciutadella. Architect Josep Fontseré won the competition to design the new park, and brought with him newcomers Domènech i Montaner (of Palau de la Música Catalana fame, see p. 70) and **Antoni Gaudí**. Several Modernist buildings went up years later when Ciutadella hosted the Universal Exposition in 1888 (see Life & Times, p. 50), including Montaner's stately **Castell dels Tres Dragons** (now **Museu de Zoologia**). Expo '88 also inspired the **Arc de Triomf**, just across Pg. Pujades and Passeig Lluis Companys from the park.

ARC DE TRIOMF

🚩 M: Arc de Triomf.

Rather than commemorating a military triumph, Barcelona's own Arc de Triomf was designed as the entrance to the **1888 Universal Exposition**. A stylistic nod to the Spanish Moors, the red bricks embrace green and yellow ceramic tiles and sculpted bats, angels, and lions. The main facade is a friendly face smiling down at you, dear tourist—it depicts the welcoming of foreign visitors to Barcelona.

█ HIVERNACLE

🚩 On Pg. Picasso, behind the Museu de Zoologia. M: Arc de Triomf. Cafe (☎ 93 295 40 17) menú del día (€12), bocadillos (€5-9), tapas (€3-9). Open 10am-1am. MC/V.

Originally built to showcase unusual tropical plants not sturdy enough for the climate of Barcelona, Josep Amergós's iron and glass Hivernacle (greenhouse) now adds white-clothed tables and bow-tied waiters to exotic fauna for a tropical afternoon meal or drink. The park's **public restrooms** also lurk amongst the greenery. On Wednesday evenings from May through July, the Hivernacle holds jazz concerts (10:30pm, €2.40), and Thursday nights in July free classical music concerts begin at 10:15pm.

Farther down the Pg. Picasso on the other side of the Museu Geologia, the **Umbracle** offers a cooler, shadier escape than its brother greenhouse.

CASCADA FOUNTAIN & LAKE

🚩 In the northeast corner of the park, directly accessible from the Pg. Pujades/C. Wellington entrance. Open M-F noon-7pm, Sa-Su 11am-8:30pm. The small lake rents paddle boats (€1.80 per 30min.).

The grandiose, often excessive details of Ciutadella's Cascada Fountain are, not surprisingly, the work of Fontseré's young assistant Antoni Gaudí. Eye-catching even from the other side of the park, the structure is adorned with grecian statues, drag-

MATING GAME

You've seen him in your dreams for months now. Walking around the city, you can feel his presence. Finally, its time for a private audience. Though some call him Snowflake, in his native Catalan he's Floquet de Neu (Floquet to his friends), the world's only white gorilla, who bears more than a passing resemblance to Willie Nelson. Taken from the forest in west Africa in the 60s, Floquet has been the toast of Barcelona ever since.

Spend some time with him at the zoo (see p. 74), and you may be lucky enough to observe a behavior common to both captive and wild gorillas—coprophagy, or eating ones own excrement. Vitamin D is not available in the gorillas' natural habitat, but is produced by bacteria in their hind gut; eating everything twice helps satisfy their nutritional needs. Floquet has made an art form of the practice.

ons, and a Venus on the half shell, while double staircases lead to the upper levels. The front of the fountain faces a small but stacked snack bar and a full-scale statue of a Mammoth, the large beasts whose remains have been discovered near Les Corts.

▧ PARC ZOOLÒGIC

🛈 *M: Ciutadella. Follow C. Wellington out of the Metro. The zoo is accessible from a separate entrance on C. Wellington. From inside the park, the zoo entrance is next to the Museu d'Art Modern/Parliament building.* ☎ *93 225 67 80. Open Nov.-Feb. 10am-5pm; Mar and Oct. 10am-6pm; Apr. and Sept. 10am-7pm; May-Aug. 9:30am-7:30pm. Two-person motorcarts (€11 per hr.) are available near the parkside entrance. The zoo has its own restaurants and snack bars. Wheelchair accessible. €10; children ages 3-12 €6.50; seniors over 65 €5.80. May-Sept. after 5pm entrance €6.50, children €4, and seniors €3.60. AmEx/D/MC/V.*

Animal rights activists be prepared: standards for zoos and animal treatment in Spain may be different than those in other countries. Though the quarters are cramped for the zoo's residents, the zoo still draws park-goers young and old. Charismatic ▧**Floquet de Neu** (Snowflake), the world's only albino gorilla, is the zoo's main attraction, although the elephants, hippos, seals, and other residents also amuse. The zoo also features an aquarium, petting zoo, and the famous **Senyoreta del Paraigua** sculpture, located at the south of the park by the aquarium. An enduring symbol from the 1888 Exposition, the sculpture and fountain have become emblems of Barcelona. *Senyoreta del Paraigua* (Lady with the Umbrella; 1885) was designed by the sculptor Joan Roig i Solé, who was a founder of the Sitges school and painted seascapes in an impressionistic style. The *senyoreta*, who shoots water from the top of her umbrella, was modeled after the Catalan painter Pepita Teixidor and is known informally to many Barceloneses simply as "Pepita."

PLAÇA D'ARMES

🛈 *Situated in front of the Museu d'Art Modern and the Parliament of Catalunya. Enter through the gate at Pg. Picasso/Av. Marqués de L'Argentera and continue straight past the statue of General Prim.*

Despite its macho name, this *plaça*, laid out by French landscape artist Jean Forestier, is less about military demonstrations and more in the vein of contemplative tranquility. The tall, squared hedges of the *plaça's* inner boundaries enclose a copy of Josep Llimona's sculpture

Desconsol (1907); a woman collapsed in despair, centered in a glass-like pond. This is a perfect place for a quiet break before or after attacking the modern marvels of the nearby museum.

EL RAVAL

see map p. 340

▓ PALAU GÜELL

🖪 *C. Nou de La Rambla, 3-5. M: Liceu, 2 blocks from the Opera Liceu, off Las Ramblas. ☎ 93 317 39 74; fax 93 317 37 79. Open Mar.-Oct. Su 10am-2pm, M-Sa 10am-8pm, last tour at 6:15pm; Nov.-Dec. M-Sa 10am-6pm. €3, students €1.50. Visits by guided tour only, departing every 15min. Often sells out for the day in the afternoon; get your tickets early.*

Antoni Gaudí's Palau Güell (1886)—a dark, haunting Modernist residence built for patron Eusebi Güell (of Park Güell fame) and declared a UN World Heritage Site in 1999—has one of Barcelona's most spectacular interiors. Güell and Gaudí spared no expense in the construction of this sumptuous, dream-like home, with which some say Gaudí truly came into his own as a premier architect. Note the brilliant equation of function and design, as well as the various psychedelic ceilings; legend has it that Güell was able to spy on his guests through the ceiling in the Visitor's Room. The 20 unique rooftop chimneys display Gaudí's first use of the *trencadis*—the covering of surfaces with irregular shards of ceramic or glass, a technique often seen in his later work.

ESGLÉSIA DE SANT PAU DEL CAMP

🖪 *M: Parallel, at the intersection of C. Sant Pau and C. Carretes, 2 blocks off Av. Parallel. Open W-M 5-8pm.*

Although this small, ancient stone church may not impress at first glance, art and design students will note the decorated columns, vaulted ceilings, and tiny, intricately detailed stained-glass windows that together make this medieval marvel one of the most important examples of Romanesque architecture in the city of Barcelona. When first founded in 912, the church stood in the country, well outside the city walls. However, the current church building, constructed in the 12th century, is very much a part of the city. Guifré Borrell, the church's founder and the son of Wilfred the Hairy (see **Life & Times,** p. 40), was buried here in 911.

With gorillas and other apes in endangered species status (in danger of extinction in the wild in the next 20 years), zoos all over the world are making concerted efforts to aid reproduction. Because of Floquet's dashing good looks, special measures are being taken in his case. In an effort to breed another white gorilla (Floquet's blue eyes mean he is not, in fact, an albino, but lucistic, an even rarer genetic abnormality), he has been encouraged to breed with his daughters. With over a dozen offspring to date, there is still no Floquet Jr.; Floquet de Neu may be the last of his kind (although a gorilla with white fingertips was once found in the forest where Floquet is from). Floquet's uniqueness is all the more reason for a pilgrimage to Barcelona.

Gaze deep into Floquet's blue eyes. Does he know the extent of his fame? Does he recognize the god-like reverence he commands, the important duty he performs by being a spokesman for his wild cousins? Probably. He's a pretty cool ape.

Far-out Facade

Gaudí was a religious man, and his plans for La Sagrada Família called for elaborate and deliberate symbolism in almost every single decorative element of the church. The cypress tree on the **Nativity Facade,** according to one theory, symbolizes the stairway to heaven (cypress trees do not put down deeper roots with time but only grow increasingly taller); the tree is crowned with the word "Tau," the Greek for God. Similarly, the top of each of the eight finished towers carries the first letter of one of the names of the apostles (and the words "Hosanna" and "Excelsis" are written in a spiral up the sides of the towers). Inside, on the **Portal of the Rosary,** overt references to modern life lurk amongst more traditional religious imagery: the Temptation of Man is represented in one carving by the devil handing a bomb to a terrorist and in another by his waving a purse at a prostitute.

Suberachs, Gaudí's successor, continued the religious symbolism in his **Passion Facade.** To the left a snake lurks behind Judas, symbolizing the disciple's betrayal of Jesus. The 4x4 box of numbers next to Him contains 310 possible combinations of four numbers, each of which adds up to 33, Christ's age when He died. The faceless woman in the center of the facade, **Veronica,** represents the Biblical woman with the same name and the miraculous appearance of Christ's face on the cloth she compassionately wiped His face with.

UNIVERSITAT DE BARCELONA

🔝 *Pl. Universitat. M: Universitat. Open M-F 9am-10pm.*

Overlooking Gran Vía, this palatial 19th-century building housed the University of Barcelona until much of its campus moved north to Pedralbes in the 1950s. Today, the religion, mathematics, and language departments remain, along with regal hallways and several beautiful, shady courtyards lined by arches and columns and filled with trees, ponds, and fountains.

see map p. 344-345

L'EIXAMPLE

As Barcelona's bourgeoisie have increasingly moved uptown, the earliest residential districts in l'Eixample, around Pg. de Gràcia, have been filling with offices, services, and shops. But despite the gentrification, the original Modernist architecture that draws visitors to this vast part of Barcelona remains intact. The buildings on Pg. de Gràcia (such as Casa Milà, p. 78, and La Manzana de la Discòrdia, p. 79), Gaudí's Sagrada Família, and Domènech i Montaner's Hospital de la Santa Creu i Sant Pau are the landmark attractions, but more dedicated architecture lovers wander the streets of the so-called *Quadrant d'Or*, the area bounded by Av. Diagonal, C. Aribau, Pg. St. Joan, and the lower Rondas (Rda. Universitat and Rda. St. Pere). This neighborhood cradles the majority of expensive homes first built when the walls of the old city were torn down. If you plan on seeing a lot of the sights in l'Eixample, be sure to get a **Ruta del Modernisme** pass (see p. 57) and allow more than just an afternoon as two days can easily be consumed with sightseeing here.

🏛 LA SAGRADA FAMÍLIA

🔝 *C. Mallorca, 401; main entrance on C. Sardenya between C. Provença and C. Mallorca. M: Sagrada Família.* ☎ *93 207 30 31 or 93 208 04 14. Open Oct.-Mar. daily 9am-6pm, elevator open 9:30am-5:45pm; Apr.-Sept. 9am-8pm, elevator open 9:30am-7:45pm.* 🏛 *Guided tours Apr.-Sept. daily 11am, 1pm, 3pm, and 5:30pm; Oct. 11am, 1, and 3pm; Nov.-Mar. F-M 11am and 1pm. €3 (buy tickets right inside the Sardenya entrance). Elevator €1.50. Audio guides available in English, €3. Combined ticket for the Sagrada Família and Casa-Museu Gaudí (in Parc Güell, see p. 91) €7. Just La Sagrada Família and its museum €6, students and those with the Ruta pass, €4. Cash only.*

Although Gaudí's unfinished masterpiece is barely a shell of the intended finished product, La Sagrada Família is without a doubt the world's most visited construction site. Despite the fact that only eight of the church's 18 planned towers have been completed (and those the shortest, at that) and the church still doesn't have an "interior," millions of people make the turístic pilgrimage to witness its work-in-progress majesty. As it is an expatriatory church, its construction is entirely funded by popular donations (as opposed to the state or the Vatican); in the past, the donors were then guaranteed a place in heaven. Lucky for visitors that their entrance fee is considered just such a "popular donation." But while it is questionable whether the price of admission will get you through the pearly gates, it will get you into an awe-inspiring world of nature, spirituality, and art. Finished or not, La Sagrada Família has become tightly intertwined with the image of Barcelona.

La Sagrada Família was commissioned not by the Roman Catholic Church, but by an extremely pious right-wing organization called the Spiritual Association for Devotion to St. Joseph, or the Josephines. Founded in 1866 in reaction to the liberal ideas spreading throughout Europe, the group was determined to build an Expiatory Temple for Barcelona, where the city could reaffirm its faith to the Holy Family of Jesus, Mary, and Joseph, hence the building's full name, **Templo Expiatori de la Sagrada Família.** The first architect they chose quit almost immediately when his ideas for the church swayed from those of the project's commissar, and they replaced him with Gaudí in 1884, when he was only 31 years old. For the first 15 or 20 years, private contributions kept the building process going, but as the mood and culture of the city changed with the onset of the modern age, construction slowed drastically, and the Civil War (see p. 46) brought it to a complete halt. The years of the war proved tragic for the temple. First Gaudí died after being hit by a tram just outside the church's walls in 1926, having overseen the completion of only the **Nativity Facade.** To make matters worse, in 1936, arsonists on the revolutionary side of the Civil War broke into the crypt, opened Gaudí's tomb, smashed his plaster models, and burned every single document in the workshop in a display of anti-establishment fury.

Today, the building remains under the auspices of the Josephines; architect Jordi Bonet, whose father worked directly with Gaudí, is heading up the project with sculptor Josep Marià Subirachs, who finished the Passion Facade in 1998. Hampered by the lack of Gaudí's exact calculations, they are working from ongoing reconstructions of his original plaster models. The computer models that engineers are using to recreate his underlying mathematical logic are so complicated that only three people in the world know how to use them. As today's workers slowly put into form what they think Gaudí had in mind, they are doing things, architecturally, that have literally never been done before. Until now, it was nearly impossible to set a completion date because of the intricacies of the reconstructed models, new building, and the unsteady flow of donations. However, in 2001 Bonet announced that La Sagrada Família is expected to be finished by 2022.

The continuation of Gaudí's greatest obsession has been fraught with fierce controversy. Some, like Salvador Dalí, have argued that the church should have been left incomplete as a monument to the architect. Others believe that La Sagrada Família should be finished, but in a more "authentic" manner than has thus been the case. Critics usually attack most vehemently Subirachs's Passion Facade. The abstract, Cubist design contrasts starkly with the more traditional Nativity Facade, which depicts Christ's birth and faces the Pl. de Gaudí. The controversial **Passion Facade,** which faces the Pl. de la Sagrada Família, portrays Christ's Passion—Catholic lingo for his crucifixion, death, and resurrection. When completed, the front of the temple—the Glory Facade—will feature four more bell towers like those that already exist; together the 12 towers will represent the 12 apostles. Above the center of the church will rise a massive 170m Tower of Jesus, with a shorter spire just behind dedicated to Mary. The Jesus tower will in turn be surrounded by four more towers symbolizing the four Evangelists (the authors of the four gospels). As finishing touches, Gaudí envisioned an extravagant spouting fountain in front of the main Glory Facade and a tall purifying flame at the back. Gaudí's dedication to religious

I Get By With a Little Help from my Friends

The name of Antoni Gaudí has gained such international fame that he tends to be unilaterally associated with his greatest works. In reality, though, Gaudí usually operated more as a loose coordinator of a host of extremely skilled sculptors, iron-workers, and painters, some of whom he gave huge creative leeway. This was particularly true of his collaborative relationship with a man named **Josep Marià Jujol**. Some critics actually consider Jujol to be directly responsible for Gaudí's shift, between 1904 and 1908, from his earlier, heavier designs to the much more fluid, almost magical ones of his later years. Jujol designed the furniture for Casa Batlló, had complete control over the construction of the La Pedrera roof while Gaudí was away on other projects, and even created the famous ceramic-clad, winding bench at the Park Güell. So with such an intense and talented relationship, why didn't Jujol gain control of La Sagrada Família after Gaudí's untimely death? Many are upset about this oversight, but it remains a mystery of architectural intrigue.

themes in his work on La Sagrada Família (see **Far-Out Facade**, p. 76) has even earned the attention of the Vatican (see **Gaudí**, p. 52).

Visitors today can see detailed paintings of the projected church in the **Museu Gaudí**. Also on display are numerous pictures from the early years of the project, sketches by Gaudí, the glass-walled workshop where his models are still being restored, and various sculptures and decorative pieces from the temple. For a more somber experience, you can gaze down on Gaudí's crypt, where roses and tea lights line the grave as a statue of Mary watches lovingly over the man that lived (and arguably died) for this church.

■ CASA MILÀ (LA PEDRERA)

🏠 *Pg. de Gràcia, 92. M: Pg. de Gràcia. Enter around the corner on C. Provença. ☎93 484 59 95. Open daily 10am-8pm; last entry 7:30pm. €6; students and over 65 €3, with Ruta del Modernisme pass €4.20. Free guided tours M-F 4pm (English) and 6pm (Spanish and Catalan), Sa-Su 11am (English) and 11:30pm (Spanish and Catalan); you can also reserve a private group tour (€24 total). Tour times change frequently depending on the season; call ahead to check the current schedule.*

Although innovative, Gaudí's unusual designs for Casa Milà were not all admired 100 years ago. The building's namesake, wealthy businessman Pere Milà, hired Gaudí because he liked his work on neighboring Casa Batlló (see p. 81), but as the project progressed between 1906 and 1910, Milà's wife, Roser Segimon, became increasingly unhappy with both the aesthetics and the excessive cost of the building. Gaudí eventually filed a lawsuit against the couple over his fees, and the Casa Milà ended up being the only residence he designed for which he did not also craft the furniture (incidentally, Gaudí won the lawsuit, and promptly gave all of the money to the poor). Gaudí also originally intended to place a massive sculpture of the Virgin and Child in the most prominent corner of the rooftop, as the edifice purported to be a tribute to the Immaculate Conception. Either the Milàs didn't like the idea, or they were afraid to boast such a display of faith after the horrific violence of the Setmana Trágica in 1909 (see p. 44); in any case, Gaudí was denied this final touch.

Today, visitors have access to the main and top floors of the building. The rest of Casa Milà is inhabited by the lucky yet patient (and wealthy) people who waited more than 20 years on the waiting list for an apartment. The top floor is filled with displays about the construction of this and other Gaudí works in four different languages. Casa Milà in particular is built around two central courtyards, with an underground park in the basement and not a single flat wall in the entire space. For a great photo-op, climb to the roof of Casa Milà to take a picture of **La Sagrada Família** (see p. 76) framed by an arch.

█ LA MANZANA DE LA DISCÒRDIA

La Pedrera

█ Pg. de Gràcia, 35 (Casa Lleó Morera), 41 (Casa Amatller), and 43 (Casa Batlló). M: Pg. de Gràcia. ☎ 93 488 01 39. 1st fl. of Casa Amatller, where Ruta del Modernisme passes are sold (see p. 57), open M-Sa 10am-7pm, Su and holidays 10am-2pm. With the Ruta pass, free tours of all 3 facades available daily 10am-6pm on the hr. (10am, noon, 1, 3, 4, and 6pm in English); bring your Ruta pass to the desk at Casa Amatller.

According to Greek myth, a piece of fruit was responsible for the Trojan War: the goddess of Discord created a golden apple as a prize for the most beautiful goddess, and divine disharmony ensued (see **The Battle of the Apple**, p. 80). Barcelona has its own competition for the golden apple on the block of Pg. de Gràcia between C. Consell de Cent and C.'Aragó, where trademark houses by the three most important architects of Modernism tower side by side in proud competition: the **Casa Lleó Morera** by Domènech i Montaner, the **Casa Amatller** by Puig i Cadafalch, and the **Casa Batlló** by Gaudí. Even the strongest Catalanists haven't wanted to give up the pun in the old name *"la manzana,"* which in Castilian means both "block" and "apple." All of these creations are renovations of older, pre-existing edifices. To see the architectural contrast most clearly, take a look from the other side of Pg. de Gràcia.

Façade of La Pedrera

CASA LLEÓ MORERA

In 1902, textile tycoon Albert Lleó Morera hired Domènech i Montaner to add some pizzazz to his boring 1864 home on the corner of Pg. de Gràcia and C. Consell de Cent. Montaner responded by creating one of the most lavish examples of decorative architecture in Barcelona. Much of the street-level exterior was destroyed by the Loewe leather shop that now occupies the entry, but if you look up at the second-floor balconies on either side of the corner tribune, you can see two nymphs on each balcony, holding (from left to right) a gramophone, an electric lightbulb, a telephone, and a camera: symbols of the new leisure

Courtyard of Casa Milà

BATTLE OF THE APPLE

Note to self: *invite the Goddess of Discord to your wedding*. Last time she was passed over, she interrupted the VIP-filled celebration by flinging a golden apple through the window labeled "for the most beautiful goddess of all." Hera, Athena, and Aphrodite immediately began claiming it as their own, and Zeus was faced with the impossible task of making peace between his own wife and daughters. Like most head honchos, he decided to pass the buck and chose the young Trojan prince Paris to make the choice for him. Hera bribed the boy with all of the riches in the land, Athena offered him supreme wisdom, and Aphrodite promised him Helen, the most beautiful woman in the world. Apparently Paris let his second brain do the thinking, and Helen's husband (yup, she was taken) responded by sending battleships to Troy.

So what does this have to do with 21st-century Barcelona? The answer lies along Passeig de Gràcia, where three gorgeous Modernista facades designed by rival architectural gods vie for the title of most beautiful of them all. Want to play Paris? Head down and judge for yourself. For Barcelona's own version of this mythical battle, see **La Manzana de la Discòrdia,** p. 79.

technology available to the bourgeoisie of the early 1900s. On the wall of the balcony above the tribune itself you can see carved lions; mulberry leaves lace around the tops of the tribune's vertical columns. Together these refer to the family name: *lleó* in Catalan means "lion," and *morera* means "mulberry tree".

The mezzanine level of the interior, unfortunately closed to the public, boasts a stunning dining room with glimmering stained-glass windows and detailed ceramic mosaics of the Lleó Morera family picnicking outdoors. The famous furniture that Gaspar Homar originally designed for this room is now on display at the Museu d'Art Modern (see **Museums,** p. 111), and the Ruta del Modernisme booklet guide has a decent picture of the gorgeous stained-glass wall (as do most coffee-table books on Barcelona architecture).

CASA AMATLLER

Chocolate mogul Antoni Amatller laid the first seed for La Manzana de la Discòrdia in 1898, when he commissioned Puig i Cadafalch to redo the facade of his prominent home. Cadafalch turned out a mix of neo-Gothic, Islamic, and Dutch architecture best known for its stylized, geometric, pink, blue, and cream upper facade. The lower exterior of the house is also noteworthy; look carefully and you can see various facets of the owner's personality inscribed in sculpture. Above the main door, the prominent carving of Catalan hero St. Jordi battling the dragon demonstrates Amatller's Catalan nationalism and the four figures engaged in painting, sculpture, architecture, and music represent Amatller's broad cultural interests. On either side of the main second-floor windows, there are caricatures of Amatller's favorite pastimes. On the left, small monkeys and rabbits busily mold iron (the main Catalan industry of Amatller's time), and a donkey with glasses reads a book while another plays with a camera; on the right side, frogs and pigs hold glass vases and pottery, a reference to Amatller's passion for vase-collecting. A huge "A" for Amatller adorns the outside of the entrance, intertwined with almond leaves (*amatller* means "almond" in Catalan).

The building's facade resembles Flemish architecture, which some argue is a reference to the fact that Amatller traded chocolate in Flanders, a spanish colony. Others suggest that the resemblance to this style was a political statement by Puig i Cadafalch, a protest against Catalunya's own near-colonial relationship with the central government in Madrid. Still others believe that it was simply the best shape to cover the photography studio on the top floor.

Inside, the entrance foyer still has fascinating iron and glass lamps, bright decorative tiles, and a stained-glass skylight just to the right off the main hallway. When the Ruta del Modernisme office on the first floor is open, you can wander the small temporary art exhibit in the back room and buy some Amatller chocolate to see for yourself whether he deserved his fortune. The apartment where the millionaire lived with his daughter is now home to the **Institut Amatller d'Art Hispànic,** open to students of the institute.

The **Joieria Bagués,** which holds a well-known collection of Modernist pieces from the Masriera tradition, occupies the right side of the entrance level. A tour of the store's sparkling dragonflies, nymphs, and flowers is allowed with the Ruta pass.

CASA BATLLÓ

Eager to sow his wild oats with fair-faced Helen, young Paris could not help but give the golden apple to Aphrodite, Goddess of Beauty. Today most visitors choose to bestow the same honor upon the most fantastical member of the Block of Discord, Gaudí's Casa Batlló. Shimmering and curving in shades of blue and green, the house looks slightly different at every hour of the day. Every visitor has their favorite time of day to see Casa Batlló; perhaps the evening light best flatters its creepy lines and squiggles. Most see the building as a depiction of the legend of St. Jordi and the dragon. This interpretation incorporates all the major facets of the building: the tall pinnacle on the left symbolizes the knight's lance after it has pierced the dragon's scaly back, represented by the warped, multi-colored, ceramic roof. The stairwell inside has been interpreted as the winding of the dragon's tail or the curves of his vertebrae, the outside balconies as skulls, and the molded columns as the bones of his unfortunate victims.

Like the other two houses on the block, Casa Batlló was the result of a remodeling job on an older, ordinary building, this one requested in 1904 by Josep Batlló, a wealthy beneficiary of the Industrial Revolution's textile boom. Gaudí did away with straight lines altogether, even in the furniture. Particularly interesting is the way he tiled the central inner patio, dark blue on the top and lighter on the bottom, in order to distribute the light from above as evenly as possible.

Apparently candy manufacturers have a sweet-tooth for Modernism: the Chupa-Chups lollipop company now owns the Casa Batlló and it is usually closed to the public unless you want to rent it for a night for a cool €6025. Fortunately, the Espai Gaudí in Casa Milà has a good video presentation which allows you to see the tiled walls, colorful mosaics, and sensuous curves of the inside of the house as well as some interesting details on the exterior.

MORE MODERNISM ON PG. DE GRÀCIA

🖪 M: Catalunya, or bus #24.

If you want to prolong the magical mystery tour of Modernisme, a jaunt down the Pg. de Gràcia acquaints you with equally interesting though less famous modernist facades. Start at M: Catalunya and make your way up the Pg. de Gràcia. On the right at no. 18, you will see the **Joieria Roca;** though today it is reminiscent of retro-cool Art Deco, this glass-block, curving building was way ahead of its time in 1934, when architect Josep Lluís Sert sparked a serious conservative backlash with his unconventional design for the facade. **Casa Olano,** at no. 60, was used as headquarters for the Basque government during the Spanish Civil War; a plaque to this effect still hangs above the doorway. The building earned its nickname "Pirate House" from the rendition of sailor Juan Sebastian Elcano on the front wall that glares menacingly down at passersby. Up a little farther at no. 66 is one of the most attractive corner facades on the Pg. de Gràcia, part of the **Casa Vidua Marfà,** built by Manual

Gaudí's Casa Batlló

Casa Amatller, Saint Jordi Detail

Casa Lleo Morera

Comas Thos in 1905. Today it houses Barcelona's School of Tourism, but you can walk into the entrance foyer and look up at the multi-colored skylight.

A few blocks further at no. 96, the **Casa Casas** shares the limelight with Casa Milà. Notable mainly for its previous inhabitant, the Catalan painter Ramon Casas, the first two floors are now occupied by the **Vinçon** furniture and knick-knack stores (see **Shopping,** p. 191). Walk inside to view the house's original stone entry, stairwell, and an imposing carved fireplace, or outside to the back patio, where you can see the reddish-colored back side of La Pedrera.

One block over, at the intersection of Diagonal and Rambla de Catalunya (no. 126), the literally two-faced **Can Serra** is worth a look as well. The original turreted pink-and-peach stone building, in French Gothic style, was built by Puig i Cadafalch in 1908 and is adorned with a sculpture by Eusebi Arnau of St. Jordi, the dragon, the princess, and some strangely entangled centaurs. The bulk of the house was razed in 1981, and now the old Gothic facade wraps around a smooth, black, glossy structure home to the Disputació of Barcelona.

& EVEN MORE WITHIN A FEW BLOCKS...

Still want more? Then go back to Pl. de Catalunya and walk up the Pg. de Gràcia only one block to C. Casp, where you will turn right and continue for a few blocks to no. 48, **Casa Calvet.** This house was Gaudí's first apartment building. It was also, in fact, the only thing he ever won an award for during his lifetime: the Ajuntament's first annual prize for Best Building of the Year, given out in 1900. Now the building houses an upscale restaurant with a gorgeous interior colored by stained glass. (Entrees €17.50-26.71; open M-Sa 1-3:30pm and 8:30-11pm.) From Casa Calvet, backtrack half a block to C. Roger de Llúria, turn right, and walk up 2½ blocks. On your right, at no. 56, will be a small passageway leading to the **Torre de les Aigües,** the water tower built by Josep Oriol Mestres in 1879 to supply water to the first houses of l'Eixample. Today it overlooks a small summertime pool for neighborhood children. A half-block farther up, at the intersection of C. Roger de Llúria and C. Consell de Cent, you will see the pink-and-peach painted exterior of the oldest house in l'Eixample, built in 1864. Four houses were actually built here at once, one on each corner, for landowner Josep Cerdà, but only this one remains today.

HOSPITAL DE LA SANTA CREU I SANT PAU

🢪 *Sant Antoni M. Claret, 167. Entrance at corner of C. Cartagena and C. St. Antonia Maria Claret. M: Hospital de St. Pau, C. Cartagena exit. ☎ 93 488 20 78; www.santpau.es. Hospital grounds open 24hr. 50min. guided tours Sa-Su 10am-2pm every 30min., in Catalan, Spanish, or English as needed. Last tour leaves 1:30pm. €4.21, students and over 65 €3.01. Cash only. Free map of grounds in foyer.*

Designated a UNESCO monument in 1997, the brilliant Modernist Hospital de la Santa Creu i Sant Pau was Domènech i Montaner's (of Palau fame) lifetime masterpiece. The entire complex covers nine full L'Eixample blocks, or 320 acres, and the pavilions designed by Domènech i Montaner are so colorful and whimsically decorated that they almost resemble gingerbread houses. Meanwhile, the outdoor spaces are often compared to an oasis or garden city in a sea of monotonous urban gridding; they once included a small forest and still boast more than 300 different types of plants, as well as plenty of wide, shaded paths.

Detail on Palau de la Música Catalana

Begun in 1905, this unusual hospital owes its existence to a wealthy Catalan banker named Pau Gil who spent his entire adult life in Paris. While there, he was influenced by new French theories on proper hygiene and therapeutic hospital designs, and he endowed Barcelona with three million pesetas to build a new type of city hospital: not only sanitary, but also aesthetically pleasing, a more complete healing experience. A design by architect Domènech i Estapa was originally chosen for the building, but he was soon dropped in favor of Domènech i Montaner, who more skillfully incorporated medical and sanitary concerns. Domènech i Montaner designed a set of 12 pavilions, each of which would be no more than one or two stories and would serve only 28 patients. The interior of each pavilion was painted various shades of green, and each room had plenty of natural light. Domènech i Montaner took note of wind patterns and put the most infectious wards at the back of the hospital, at the "end" of the current.

Modernist and Modern

The money for Domènech i Montaner's design ran out just as he finished up in 1910, and construction on the hospital was not continued until 1915, when it gained further financial backing by merging with the city's ancient Hospital de la Santa Creu (founded 1401). Domènech i Montaner's son undertook the expansion of his father's work, though in a completely different style (Modernism fell out of fashion as soon as

Casa de las Punxes

he began working), and the completed joint complex, with 48 pavilions, was officially opened in 1930 by King Alfonso XIII. Even with the vast additions to Montaner's pavilions, the Hospital de la Santa Creu i Sant Pau still has one of the highest space-to-patient ratios in all of Europe, with 140 sq. m for each of the 600 patients.

The most interesting attraction for most tourists is the main administrative building, which is steeped in decorative symbolism. The letters P and G, a tribute to Pau Gil, recur over and over in various surprising motifs. The four sculptured figures on the front facade represent faith, hope, charity, and work; the multi-domed ceiling of the entrance foyer is covered with the symbols of Catalunya, Barcelona, St. Jordi (the patron saint of Barcelona), the city of Paris, the bankers' association (a nod to P. G. again), and the years in which the Modernist portion of the building was begun and finished.

The hospital is actually slated to close in the year 2004, when the medical services will be relocated to more modern facilities nearby. The future fate of the complex has not yet been set in stone, but rumor has it that it may become a stunning university.

ESGLÉSIA DE LES SALESES

🚩 *Pg. de St. Joan, M: Verdaguer.*

The Església de les Saleses stands out as one of the prettiest churches in the entire city of Barcelona. Built in 1885 by Joan Martorell i Montells, one of Gaudí's mentors, it originally served as a nun's convent and was severely damaged during the 1909 *Setmana Trágica* (Tragic Week; see **Life & Times,** p. 44). It became a school and finally a Catholic parish in 1945, after it was repaired. It is generally considered a direct precursor to the Modernist movement, with its detailed, almost coquettish brick, stone, and glass exterior decorations.

PLAÇA GLÒRIES

🚩 *M: Glòries.*

The two most prominent *plaças* in L'Eixample Dreta (east of the Pg. de Gràcia) are **Pl. Glòries** and **Pl. Tetuán,** both of which are home to weighty city monuments. The Pl. Glòries is by far the biggest in l'Eixample; at the intersection of Av. Meridiana and Av. Diagonal, its small central park is entirely circled by a wide roadway packed with fast-moving cars. The bizarre **Monument to the Metre** crosses the length of the park in a bronze cross section of the earth's surface that is disturbingly reminiscent of a jagged razor; donated by the Dunkirk (Ireland) City Council in 1992, it commemorates the 200th anniversary of the measuring of the Prime Meridian between Barcelona and Dunkirk, marking where the master of all longitudinal lines slices through the city. The 12 black plaques around the *plaça* use famous quotations or excerpts to memorialize 12 "glorious" elements of Catalan history, including Romanesque art, Gothic architecture, industrialization, science and technology contributions, Catalan law, self-government, and more. But biggest doesn't necessarily mean best; the space is more dustbowl than "park" and the lack of proximity to other sights may make this an area to keep off a tight itinerary.

PLAÇA TETUÁN

🚩 *M: Tetuán*

The centerpiece of the Pl. Tetuán is a hefty **monument to Bartomeu Robert,** done by Josep Llimona in 1910 in honor of the former city mayor. It was torn down under Franco because of its excessive nationalistic symbolism, but was finally replaced and recognized by King Juan Carlos and Queen Sofia in 1985.

MONUMENTS IN L'EIXAMPLE DRETA

🚩 *M: Verdaguer, which is at the intersection of Av. Diagonal and Pg. de St. Joan*

A good number of Barcelona's more than 400 monuments adorn l'Eixample, where wide streets and open corners lend them plenty of visibility. Some of the better-known include the submarine sculpture in honor of inventor **Narcis Monturiol** (C. Girona and Av. Diagonal, M: Verdaguer), the monument to **Anton Clavé,** founder of many popular choral societies (Pg. de St. Joan and Trav. de Gràcia; also accessible from M: Joanic), and the monument to Catalan poet **Jacint Verdaguer** (Pg. St. Joan and Av. Diagonal).

Festival Time in Barceloneta

OTHER SIGHTS IN L'EIXAMPLE DRETA

🚩 *M: Diagonal.*

One of the most famous Modernist houses in the city sits near the intersection of Av. Diagonal and C. Roger de Llúria, at Av. Diagonal 416-420 (also accessible from M: Joanic). Designed by Puig i Cadafalch in 1905, it is called the **Casa de las Punxes (House of Spikes)** for its distinctively pointy medieval turrets, and deftly combines Modernista flair with Gothic overtones. On the same block, Salvador Valeri's **Casa Comalat** (Av. Diagonal 442) has two facades; the one facing Av. Diagonal is well-decorated with subtle stone textures. Nearby, Puig i Cadafalch's **Palau del Baló de Quadras,** Av. Diagonal, 373, has an even more ornate facade, almost entirely covered with varied sculptures.

Barceloneta Clocktower

L'EIXAMPLE ESQUERRA

MEDITATION

🚩 *M: Catalunya. From Pl. de Catalunya, walk up La Rambla de Catalunya one block to Gran Via; the statue is in the middle of La Rambla, across from Comme-Bio.*

At the bottom of La Rambla de Catalunya near Gran Via sits one of those things a slight alteration of consciousness might help you to appreciate to its fullest: a bull lost in deep contemplation. Officially titled *Meditation*, this thoughtful bull's pose mimics that of Rodin's *The Thinker*. Easy to miss, but impossible to forget, his brooding countenance will

Circular Sharktank at the Aquarium

be forever emblazoned on your memory. At the opposite end of the avenue, his cousin *Coquette*, a flirtatious giraffe of questionable virtue, seduces passersby on Av. Diagonal.

OTHER SIGHTS IN L'EIXAMPLE ESQUERRA

◪ M: Urgell and M: Hospital Clínic.

L'Eixample Esquerra is home to several Modernist masterpieces. **Casa Golferichs,** Gran Via, 491, at the intersection with C. Viladomat (M: Urgell), a brown brick structure with Moorish influences, was designed by one of Gaudí's collaborators, Joan Rubió, in 1901. Concerts are often held in the courtyard during the summer, and the interior hosts art exhibitions and conferences. (☎93 323 77 90. Open M-F 10am-2pm and 4-10pm, Sa 10am-2pm and 5-9pm. Wheelchair accessible. Free.) Further down the Gran Via at number 475, Pere Falqués and Antoni de Flaguerra's **Casa de Lactància** (M: Urgell) is now a nursing home. Stone carvings by Eusebi Arnau and a mosaic flag of Barcelona can be viewed from outside, but step inside the foyer to see the equally impressive wrought iron interior balcony and delicate stained glass windows.

At the other end of l'Eixample, **Casa Company,** C. Buenos Aires, 56-58, at the intersection with C. Casanova (M: Hospital Clinic), was constructed in 1911 by Puig i Cadafalch for a local family. The creamy white Art Deco building with painted decorations was converted into Dr. Melcior Colet's gynecology practice in 1940, and later donated to the government of Catalunya. Today, it houses the Museu i Centre d'Estudis de l'Esport Dr. Melcior Colet (see p. 114), a small museum devoted to Catalan sports history (☎93 419 22 32. Open M-F 10am-2pm and 4-8pm).

see map p. 349

POBLE NOU & PORT OLÍMPIC

WALKING TOUR

The **Vila Olímpica** and **Port Olímpic** are best viewed in an easy loop (45 min.) beginning and ending at M: Ciutadella/Vila Olímpica. Come out of the Metro with the twin skyscrapers to your right and cross C. Ramon Trias Fargos to get to the intersection of C. de Marina and **Avinguda d'Icària.** Follow Av. Icària for three blocks or so. As you walk, the **Parc de Carles I** will be on your left, with its tall, infamous **Culo de Urculo** statue (Hercules's, um, posterior). The huge metal sculptures down the center of the street, something slinking like a mix of thatched roofs and telephone poles, were named **Pergolas** by architect Enric Miralles; they are an ultramodern take on the original latticed rooftop gardens with climbing plants common in ancient Egypt. To the right on the second block of Av. Icària is the **Centre de la Vila,** a two-story shopping mall, lacking most of the major store names scattered throughout the rest of Barcelona but boasting, nonetheless, a 15-screen cinema and several decent restaurants.

At the intersection with Av. Bogatell and C. Frederic Mompau, take the red-brick ramp to the right leading upward to an apartment complex. At the end of the ramp is the Pl. Tirant lo Blanc, the center of the athlete housing, and the perfect place to sit and imagine what it must have been like to live in the Vila Olímpica in 1992. A statue of an athlete staring wistfully into a stream commemorates the site. In classic Barcelona style, even the curbs of the sidewalks curve in long wavy lines. From here, facing the sea, cross one of the four wooden bridges over the highway and waterway, into the Parc dels Ponts, then turn right onto the sandy path. This path leads to the **Pl. dels Champions,** site of the tiered platform used to honor gold, silver, and bronze medal-winners; you can steal a moment of imagined glory in the quiet square by standing on the now rusting platform. Names of the actual Olympic winners are set in plaques in the ground. Continuing onward brings you to the **Parc del Port Olímpic,** a long, triumphant sand walkway lined by tall white spires and culminating in Robert

Llimos's Marc statue, an apt symbol for a city known for muscling past both physical boundaries and architectural norms; you can walk between the spires, or on the shaded pathway next to them. Across the fountain lies the Parc de Cascades, home to Antoni Llena's Dalí-esque **David and Goliath.** Finally, to get from here to Frank Gehry's copper **Peix (Fish)** and the **Port Olímpic,** return to the fountain, turn right toward the water, and go left at the beach.

Poble Nou's own small Rambla makes for a pleasant afternoon walk free of the hordes of people in the city center, and it offers a glimpse of real Catalan life, unaffected by tourism. Otherwise, Poble Nou offers **beaches** (see p. 171), a small **hearse museum** (see p. 116), and some other novel attractions.

OTHER SIGHTS

CEMENTIRI DE L'EST

🔢 *At the dead-end of Av. Icària. M: Llacuna. From the Metro, walk down C. Ciutat de Granada toward the waterfront towers; at the T-intersection with C. Taulat, turn right and follow the white walls of the cemetery to the gated opening. Open daily 8am-6pm.*

Pre-l'Eixample Barcelona desperately needed every inch inside city walls for living space, so in 1773 this cemetery was built outside the walls to safely house some of Barcelona's most important dead. Crumbling monuments and miniature churches crowd the back of the plot; towards the front of the cemetery, in the center aisle, there is also a statue erected in memory of the thousands of people in Barcelona who died during the yellow fever epidemic of 1821.

BARCELONETA

see map p. 350

🔳 TORRE SAN SEBASTIÀ

🔢 *Pg. Joan de Borbo. M: Barceloneta. In Port Vell, as you walk down Joan de Borbo and see the beaches to the left, stay right and look for the obvious high tower. ☎ 93 441 48 20. To Jaume I one-way or round-trip €7.50, to Montjuïc one-way €7.50, round-trip €9.50. Also accessible from Montjuïc (see the **Jardins Verdaguer,** p. 90). Open daily 11am-8pm.*

One of the easiest and best ways to view the city is on these cable cars, which span the entire Port Vell, connecting beachy Barceloneta with mountainous Montjuïc. The full ride, which takes about 10min. each way and offers an intermediate stop at the Jaume I tower near Colom, gives an aerial perspective of the entire city. Bring your camera to get some postcard-perfect shots of Barcelona. If you're looking to splurge, there's also a fancy restaurant at the top of the San Sebastià tower.

PORT VELL

see map p. 350

🔳 L'AQUÀRIUM DE BARCELONA

🔢 *On the Moll d'Espanya, next to Maremàgnum and the cinema. M: Drassanes or Barceloneta. ☎ 93 221 74 74. Open daily July-Aug. 9:30am-11pm; Sept.-June 9:30am-9pm. Last entrance 1hr. before closing. €11, under 12 and seniors €7.70, students 10% off. Wheelchair accessible.*

Barcelona's new aquarium—the largest in Europe—is a state-of-the-art aquatic wonder. The museum features over 20 tanks that focus on the sealife of the Mediterranean, with nods to the Great Barrier Reef and other climates, copious amounts of octopi, and a plethora of penguins. The museum's layout is as fascinating as the best snorkeling dives, minus the wetness and jellyfish stings. For those not still terrified by the *Jaws* movies, the visit's highlight is an 80m-long glass tunnel (with moving walkway) through an ocean tank of sharks, sting rays, and one two-dimen-

SANT JORDI

English speakers usually know the legend of Saint George and the Dragon from the British religious and folkloric tradition; Saint George is, after all, the patron saint of Britain, renowned for battling a dragon and saving the Christians. However, the English are not the only people with a claim to Saint George, known in Barcelona by his Catalan name, Sant Jordi. In the 13th century, King Jaume I had a vision of Sant Jordi aiding him in battle against Mallorca, and this historic hallucination started Catalunya's long-founded obsession with the saint. Names and images of him are everywhere: the Olympic Palau d'Esports Sant Jordi, April 24th's romantic Día de Sant Jordi, and Casa Batlló's scaly, dragonesque rooftop. Jordi is also one of the most popular Catalan first names, as it symbolizes heroism and high moral caliber.

sional fish with no fins. Just four inches of glass separate the crowds from the water, filled with thousands of fish and over a million gallons of Mediterranean water. The tour ends with a series of 50 interactive exhibits about the ocean and its inhabitants, which kids (and playful adults) will adore.

OTHER SIGHTS AROUND PORT VELL

🚇 *M: Drassanes or Barceloneta.*

Ever-ambitious Barcelona wishes to become known as the greatest port on the Mediterranean, and has made amazing progress toward achieving that goal in just over a decade. The newest addition to the waterfront is the new **World Trade Center,** built in 1999 and designed by the renowned architect I. M. Pei (who also built the glass pyramid in front of Paris's Louvre Museum). The design reminds many of a cruise ship, only fitting considering its proximity to the cruise-ship docks of the port, which have room for eight full-size liners in all. The ultra-modern complex includes the luxurious Grand Marina Hotel (just completed in 2002), office space, restaurants and cafes, and a convention center. At the other end of Pg. Colom in front of the post office (a sight in and of itself—a postal palace created for the 1929 International Exhibition; see p. 54) is **Cap de Barcelona,** also known as Barcelona Head. This 60 foot-plus sculpture, a bright, cartoonish woman's face, was created by the late American pop artist Roy Lichtenstein for the 1992 Olympics.

MONTJUÏC

CASTELL DE MONTJUÏC

see map p. 348

🚇 *From M: Parallel, take the funicular (every 10min.) to Av. Miramar and then the Teleféric de Montjuïc cable car to the castle. Teleféric open M-Sa 11:15am-9pm. One-way €3.20, round-trip €4.50. Alternatively, walk up the steep slope on C. Foc, next to the funicular station. Castle open Mar. 21-Nov. 14 Tu-Su 9:30am-7:30pm; Nov. 15-Mar. 20 Tu-Su 9:30am-5pm.*

The first section of this massive castle was built in 1640 in just 30 days. Fifty-four years later the main castle which today dominates the top of the mountain was constructed. It was added to until 1799, when it could accommodate over 3000 people. In 1960, the fortress was given to the city, which eventually converted it into a military museum. A visit to this historic fortress and its **Museu Militar** (see **Museums,** p. 120) is a great way to get an overview of the city—both of its layout and its history. The castle's exterior *mirador* offers spectacular views of the bay and the city. Enjoy a sandwich and coffee at the outdoor **cafe** while 19th-century cannons stare you down.

FONTS LUMINOSES

🔏 *On Av. Reina María Cristina. Shows June-Sept. Th-Su every 30min. 9:30pm-12:30am; Oct.-May F-Sa 7-8:30pm. Free.*

The Fonts Luminoses (Illuminated Fountains) run alongside Av. Reina Maria Cristina and are dominated by the huge central **Font Mágica** (Magic Fountain). The fountains are visible from Pl. d'Espanya, in front of the **Palau Nacional** (see **Museums,** p. 120). During the weekends, colored lights and dramatic music bring the fountains to life in a spectacular display not to be missed.

PAVELLÓ MIES VAN DER ROHE

🔏 *From M: Espanya, follow Av. Reina Maria Cristina until the Font Mágica. Face the Palau Nacional and the Font Mágica; the Pavelló is to the right. ☎ 93 423 40 16; www.miesbcn.com. Open daily 10am-8pm. €3, students €1.50, under 12 free.*

Renowned as one of the most original works of the famous German architect Mies van der Rohe, this aesthetically provocative pavilion—also known as the **Pavelló Barcelona**—is an exemplar of spatial serenity far ahead of its time. Van der Rohe built a pavilion for the 1929 International Exhibition, but his contribution—a minimalist marvel of glass, stone, marble, and steel—was demolished in 1930 when no one bought it. The pavilion standing in its place today is a replica commissioned by the Barcelona city government. The open-air courtyards are also home to Georg Kolbe's graceful statue, 🖼*Morning*, and several copies of van der Rohe's famous *Barcelona chair*, one of the first designs of a tubular steel chair.

ANELLA OLÍMPICA

🔏 *The easiest way to get to the Olympic Area is to take the funicular from inside the M: Parallel station at Av. Parallel and Nou de la Rambla. Wheelchair accessible. Turn left out of the funicular station on to Av. Miramar and follow it past the Fundació Miró. The road turns into Av. de l'Estadi; the stadium is on your left. Alternatively, take bus #50 from la Plaça d'Espanya and ask to be let off when you see the stadium on your right.*

In 1929, Barcelona inaugurated the Estadi Olímpic de Montjuïc (Olympic Stadium) in its bid for the 1932 Olympic games. Over 50 years later, Catalan architects Federic Correa and Alfons Milà, designers of the *Anella Olímpica* (Olympic Ring) esplanade, completed the facilities in time for the '92 Games, with the help of Italian architect Vittorio Gregotti. Eleven years later, Montjuïc's Olympic area is still a major tourist draw. The **Torre de Telefónica,** designed by Valencian Santiago Calatrava, commands the Olympic skyline at 394ft. In addition to commemorating Barcelona's role as host in '92, the *Anella Olímpica* lives on as a well-equipped arena serving the sporting needs of professionals, amateurs, and tourists alike. Today, you can catch a soccer game at the **Estadi Olímpic** (see **Entertainment,** p. 173) or swim in the Piscines Bernat Picorne II (see p. 174).

PALAU D'ESPORTS SANT JORDI

🔏 *☎ 93 426 20 89. Call in advance to visit. For concert information, check www.agendabcn.com or the Guía del Ocio, available at any newsstand.*

Designed by Japanese architect Arata Isozaki, the Palau Sant Jordi is the most technologically sophisticated of the Olympic structures. It currently serves as one of the city's biggest sports and concert venues, playing host to big-name superstars like

Madonna, who kicked off her 2001 world tour here. The roof was built on the ground and then lifted and secured into its present position over the course of 10 days. Standing in front of the palace are *utsuroshi*—minimalist concrete and metal tree-like structures designed by Isozaki's wife, Aiko Miyawaki.

GALERÍA OLÍMPICA

🚩 *At the far end of the Estadi Olímpic, toward Palau Sant Jordi.* ☎ *93 426 06 60. Open M-F 10am-2pm and 4-6pm. €2.40, students €2.10, seniors €1.10.*

Video segments, colorful costumes, sports equipment, plenty of merchandise, and giant photos displayed everywhere try to tell the story of the 25th Olympic Games at this small permanent exhibition. But if you're in a pinch and can't visit, don't worry about missing anything substantial.

POBLE ESPANYOL

🚩 *On Av. Marqués de Comillas, to the right when facing the Palau Nacional. From M: Espanya, go up the outdoor escalators or catch bus #50 at Pl. d'Espanya and ask to be let off at Poble Espanyol.* ☎ *93 508 63 00; www.poble-espanyol.com. Open M 9am-8pm, Tu-Th 9am-2am, F-Sa 9am-4am, Su 9am-midnight. €7, students €4.40, seniors €4.40, children 7-12 €3.60. Guided tours in English daily 1:30 and 3:30pm; €3 plus admission. MC/V.*

If Spain built an Epcot Center, it would look like Poble Espanyol. Created for the International Exhibition in 1929 (see **Life & Times,** p. 54), this tourist-oriented "town" features replicas of famous buildings and sights from every region of Spain and swarms with school children and tourists. Shops and artists' workshops sell everything from tacky souvenirs to gallery pieces, and the large open-air courtyard occasionally serves as a concert or theater venue. Smack-dab in the center of this souvenir bazaar catering to tourists, there is also a small but fascinating contemporary art museum. During daylight hours, Poble Espanyol is not much more than an outdoor shopping mall dressed up in the architecture of Old Spain and crammed with restaurants. But once night falls, the disco scene here brings new meaning to the word "party."

JARDINS VERDAGUER

🚩 *Av. Miramar. Between the Fundació Miró and the Castell de Montjuïc. From M: Parallel, take the funicular to Av. Miramar. Turn right out of the funicular and walk along Av. Miramar, then uphill on C. Montjuïc. Open Nov.-Feb. daily 10am-6pm; Mar. and Oct. daily 10am-7pm; Apr. and Sept. daily 10am-8pm; May-Aug. daily 10am-9pm. Free.*

Named after the Catalan poet Mossén Jacint Verdaguer, these expansive gardens merit a visit on a leisurely day when they will charm you with their quiet walkways, rolling green hills, multi-hued pottery and bottle mosaics, and enchanting views of the sea. Perhaps most enchanting is the glistening water trickling from a pond at the top of the hill down a descending series of pools.

Outside the gardens, in a small island in the middle of C. Montjuïc, the **Sardana** statue (see **May I Have This Dance,** p. 51), crafted by Josep Cañas in 1966, commemorates this traditional Catalan dance. Farther downhill, where C. Montjuïc meets Av. Miramar, the Miramar lookout hosts a restaurant and bar with fine views of the city and sea. The *teléféric* cable car to Barceloneta leaves from here (see p. 87).

PARC JOAN MIRÓ

🚩 *C. Tarragona. M: Espanya or Tarragona. A 5min. walk down C. Tarragona from Pl. de Espanya.*

Miró's giant *Dona i Ocell (Woman and Bird,* 1982) holds court in the center of a park dedicated to the artist. This colorful (if slightly scandalous) sculpture rises 22m (72ft.) into the air, a mosaic of glazed greens, yellows, reds, and blues in homage to Gaudí. Miró changed the name from *Le Coq* after city planners objected.

CEMENTIRI DEL SUD-OEST

Bus #38 from Pl. de Catalunya will drop you off across from the main entrance. Or, from inside Montjuïc, follow Av. del Castell to the left with your back to the Castle. The back entrance to the cemetery is a 20min. walk downhill and will be on your left. To get to Fossar de la Pedrera, turn left on Via Santa Eulalia by the cemetery's main entrance, and then take the 2nd right onto Sant Josep. Follow this paved path and look for signs directing you to Fossar. A helpful cemetery map is available from the administration offices at the main entrance, across from the bus stop. Open daily 8am-5:30pm. Free.

Cannon Café at Montjuïc Castle

The dead have never had it so good. Just as we are today mesmerized by the great pyramids of Egypt or the ancient Roman catacombs, one day far in the future, people will be similarly awed—if they are not already—by this gigantic Modernist cemetery built on the slopes of Montjuïc. The amazing complex of stone, brick, sculpture, and stained glass, which dates from 1883, is arguably the most stylish place to spend eternity in all of Spain. Watch out for the flocks of black Mercedes speeding through on weekends as part of funeral processions. Of special note are the **Amatller family tomb** designed by Puig i Cadafalch (who also designed their house in l'Eixample; see p. 80) and the statuary-topped Batlló family resting place (of Casa Batlló fame; see p. 81). Winding paths curve up along a terraced cliff and provide lovely views of the sea.

Montjuïc Steps

In the cemetery's northeast corner, the **Fossar de la Pedrera** commemorates the site where many Republican heroes of the Civil War (see **Life & Times**, p. 46), were rounded up and shot immediately following the war. Stone pillars are engraved with the names of the victims, and an arched statue set in a small pond honors Catalan President Lluís Companys, who was assassinated by Franco on this very spot in 1940.

ZONA ALTA

GRÀCIA

see map p. 346

PARK GÜELL

Park Güell is located in the upper limits of Gràcia, several blocks west of the major thoroughfare Trav. de Dalt. The park's main entrance faces C. Olot, though there are other entrances on Av. Sant Josep de la Muntanya, Carretera del Carmel, and Av. del Coll del Portell. The easiest way to reach the park is by bus #24 from Pl. de Catalunya, which runs up Pg. de Gràcia and stops at the upper park entrance toward the end of its route. Bus #25 con-

Architecture at Poble Espanyol

Park Güell Structures

Lizard at Park Güelll

Serpentine Bench

nects the park to the Sagrada Família. The most scenic way to enter the park is a 5-10min. uphill hike; take the Metro to Vallarca, walk straight out of the Metro down Av. l'Hospital Militar for 4 blocks, turn left onto Baixada de la Gloria, and take the outdoor escalators uphill to the park's back entrance. There are 2 cafes in the park, though prices are relatively high and during busy times it can be difficult to find an open table. For cheaper eating, a small grocery store at C. Laddard, 57 is open daily 10am-8pm and offers the classic picnic staples. Park ☎ 93 219 38 11. Free. Open daily May-Sept. 10am-9pm; Mar.-Apr. and Oct. 10am-7pm; Nov.-Feb. 10am-6pm.

On a hill at the northern edge of Gràcia lies one of Barcelona's greatest treasures and the world's most enchanting public park. The park was designed entirely by Gaudí, and—in typical Gaudí fashion—was not completed until after his death. Eusebi Güell, a Catalan industrialist and arts patron, commissioned the renowned Gaudí (having so liked the results of their collaboration on Güell's Palau) to fashion a garden city in the tradition of Hampstead Heath and other parks in England, where Güell had spent many years. Güell was a bit obsessed with rank and power (he longed to be granted a title by the king), and he envisioned a utopic community devoid of the lower classes (the turn-of-the-century take on the gated community), with 60 houses. But when Güell died in 1918 and WWI descended, construction slowed to a halt and only three houses went up before Gaudí passed away. Barceloneses at the turn of the century tended to be put off by Gaudí's shockingly bold designs and disparaged the park's then great distance from the city, and as a result, only two aristocrats signed on. As a housing development, Park Güell was considered a failure.

As a park, it is fantastic. In 1922, the Barcelona city council bought Park Güell and opened up its multicolored dwarfish buildings and sparkling ceramic-mosaic stairways to the public. The park has since been honored by being named a UNESCO World Heritage Site. Combining natural influences, Catalan themes, and religious symbolism, Gaudí's Park Güell is a symphony of color and form. It is at once dreamy and whimsical, organic and tactile. The most eye-catching elements of the park—the surreal mosaics and fairy tale fountains—are clustered around the main entrance on C. Olot. The entrance's **Palmetto Gate,** a replica of the iron work on Gaudí's Casa Vicens, is flanked by two dwarfish buildings originally meant to house the community's administration offices and the porter. Visitors today can stop by the **LAIE** book and gift shop in the house on the left as you face the park (☎ 93 284 62 00. Open during park hours). These otherworldly houses were inspired by a Catalan production of *Hansel and Gretel*; the spire-topped construction belongs to the children and the other, crowned with a bright red poisonous mushroom, belongs to the witch. Lavishly decorated with fan-shaped mosaics, the roofs almost resemble edible gingerbread and cream frosting. Behind Hansel and Gretel's house, you will find the park's restrooms and a popular cafe. (Coffee €2; tapas €2-3; *bocadillos* €3-4. Open during park hours.)

Facing the majestic double staircase, a cavernous stone area to the right was originally meant to house the carriages of park residents. It now serves as a shaded rest area for visitors. If looked at the right way, it resembles an elephant. The staircase itself is divided into three sections, each with its own mosaic, including a jumble of roots and plants overseen by a snake which peers out from the shield of Catalunya, and up the stairs. Tourists jostle to take pictures of their loved ones with Gaudí's gaping, multicolored **salamander fountain** as it drools into the basin below. A popular symbol of the park and the symbol for alchemy, the salamander's sleek body is covered with a tightly woven mosaic of green, orange, and blue. Some believe that the animal is a reference to the shield of the French city of Nîmes, the northern boundary of Old Catalunya. At the next level, a curvaceous red mosaic fountain, which holds a stone interpreted to be either an oracle or the philosopher's stone, sits in front of a mouth-like bench which is supposedly entirely protected from the wind, and remains in the shade for 3 seasons (winter is the sunny one).

The stairs lead up to the **Hall of One Hundred Columns (Teatro Griego),** a Modernist masterpiece of 86 Doric columns (but who's counting?). A spectacular open space meant for the community's market, the hall's columns support a ceiling constructed of white-tiled domes. Toward the center, where musicians often play classical music, multicolored medallions are interspersed among the ceiling domes. Josep Maria Jujol, Gaudí's right-hand man, created each medallion, using bits of mirror, plates, glasses, and even porcelain dolls.

Stairs on either side of the hall lead up to the **Pl. de la Naturalesa,** a barren open area partly supported by the columned hall below and surrounded by the **serpentine bench,** the longest park bench in the world. The shape of the bench is not only aesthetic, but is architecturally necessary given the position of the columns below. It is also designed to cradle visitor's buttocks and is consequently incredibly comfortable thanks to the rumored "creative methods" of Jujol (he is said to have made one of the workers sit bare-assed in the wet cement to add that extra anatomically correct touch). Pieced together from broken ceramic remnants from local pottery workshops, Gaudí and Jujol's multicolored bench is covered with brightly colored flowers, geometric patterns, and the odd religious image or two. During the park's restoration in 1995, workers discovered that the 21 distinct tones of white are cast-offs from the Casa Milà (see p. 78) which had been cemented in the bench. The bench's abstract collage later became a great inspiration for Joan Miró's Surrealist work. Overlooking the *plaça,* a self-service cafe offers outdoor tables. (Juice and water €2; beer and *sangria* €2-4; *bocadillos* €3.20-3.80. Open during park hours.)

From here, sweeping paths supported by columns (meant to resemble palm trees) swerve through hedges and ascend to the park's summit, which commands tremendous views of the city. A pleasant walk through the grounds begins at the path directly to right of the lizard fountain when walking up the stairs. Follow the wide path past the sunny flower beds and open grassy area and veer right toward the shaded benches. As the path twists uphill, the turreted, pink **Casa-Museu Gaudí** (see **Museums,** p. 121) appears on your left. Farther ahead, the **Pont dels Enamorats** offers views of the city all the way to the sea and Gaudí's **stone trees**—tall columns topped with agave plants—are interspersed with curved benches that seem to hang in mid-air. Around the next curve **Casa Trias** (1905), the park's third house, purchased by the lawyer Trías Domènech and still owned by his family, is surrounded by less-scenic walking paths that loop around to the left along Av. del Coll del Portell. Farther along the wide, main path, past a grassy area with a small playground and plenty of benches, an upward slope spirals up to **El Turo de Les Tres Creus.** Originally destined to be the park residents' church, the small tower is topped only with three crosses (one resembles an arrow) which appear to form one when you look toward the east. This peak is the park's highest point, and it offers a dazzling 360° view of the city below. To head back down, follow the twisting path that slopes down toward the sea. Check out the top-angle views of the Hansel and Gretel houses and other park structures. At the Av. Sant Josep de la Muntanya entrance, follow a narrow path to the right until it becomes **El Viaducte de la Bugadera** as it passes Güell's house (now a school) on the right. The irregularly shaped stone columns that support the covered passageway are each composed of fascinating, unusual shapes and configurations. You'll find the statue of **La Bugadera** (the washerwoman), one of the last columns in the passageway. Stairs ahead lead back to the Pl. de la Naturalesa.

CASAS

Aside from the Park Güell, the narrow, peaceful streets of Gràcia are home to several of Modernisme's lesser known, but not less grand, architectural masterpieces. Since these buildings truly are *casas* (private houses), their interiors are unfortunately closed to the public; however, the captivating external designs and details are incentive to take a peak.

■ CASA VICENS

🖬 *C. Carolines, 24-26. From M: Fontana, walk uphill on Gran de Gràcia and turn left on C. Carolines.*

One of Gaudí's earliest projects, Casa Vicens was designed for a local tile manufacturer, and as such, is fittingly decorated with blocks of cheerful white, green, and yellow ceramic tiles accented with red-painted brick. If you came here right after Casa Milà expecting the same fluid lines and curves, sorry. Gaudí studied Arabic design to come up with the colorful rigid angles that characterize this *casa*. However, the graceful, fluid ironwork that spills out of the windows as balconies and creeps up the facade as a palm-fronted gate foreshadows the architect's anti-angle ideals evident in later projects.

OTHER CASAS

🖬 *Throughout Gràcia. M: Lesseps for Casa Ramos; M: Diagonal for Casa Cama and Casa Fuster.*

Though not as well-preserved as the Modernisme landmarks in L'Eixample, a handful of *casas* spice up the landscape of Gràcia with a touch of class. Several blocks up the Gran de Gràcia at Pl. Lesseps, **Casa Ramos,** Pl. de Lesseps, 32, was completed by Jaume Torres in 1906 and is in fact three separate buildings which share a facade. Although the building is partially blocked by storefronts and a ramp, its Modernist floral motif and insect-patterned grilles still manage to stand out. Back toward Av. Diagonal, **Casa Cama,** Gran de Gràcia, 15, is one of Berenguer's designs, with delicately curved stained-glass windows. Across the street, at Pg. de Gràcia, 132, **Casa Fuster** marks the transition between Gran de Gràcia and the Pg. de Gràcia. Lluís Domènech i Montaner fashioned this impressive neo-Gothic marble building from 1908 to 1911, putting heavy emphasis on the cylindrical corner windows. Get up close to see the nesting birds sculpted at the top of the corner columns. **Casa Ferrer,** Pg. de Gràcia, 113, was completed in 1906 by Pere Falqués. Though its stone facade has been somewhat neglected, it finds beauty in simple lines and understated grandeur.

PLAÇAS IN GRÀCIA

🖬 *M: Diagonal or Fontana.*

Gràcia has several notable *plaças* where locals gather over long meals at outdoor tables, day and night; a quick stroll through them is a great way to get acquainted with the neighborhood. ■**Pl. Ruis i Taulet,** two blocks below Trav. de Gràcia near the Gran de Gràcia, is home to the **Torre del Reloj** (Clock Tower), an emblem of the Revolution of 1868. Facing the *plaça* is Gràcia's sky-blue town hall, a Modernist work designed by local architect Francesc Berenguer and adorned with Gràcia's town shield. Several blocks down C. Puigmartí, at the intersection of C. Quevado, is **Pl. de John Lennon,** which honors the rock legend with a record-shaped plaque engraved with "Give Peace a Chance" in Catalan. This is a favorite playground spot for local children and their parents. While the **Pl. del Poble Romaní,** one block down C. Siracusa, is not the loveliest of the group, it is the former site of the Puigmartí textile factory and now commemorates the local Gypsy community, as well as Gràcia's working-class roots, with a large brick tower. **Pl. del Diamante,** farther uphill on C. Astúries, was made famous by Catalan author Mercè Rodoreda's 1962 novel of the same title. The novel is commemorated by *La Colometa*, a dramatic bronze statue of Rodoreda's heroine, who deals with the trials of everyday living during and following the Spanish Civil War. Farther along C. Astúries, **Pl. Virreina** is bordered by tapas bars, pastel painted houses, and the grand Church of Sant Joan de Gràcia. Across C. L'Or, the pink and cream **Casa Rubina** at no.44 is one of Berenguer's most decorative works. Tiny but tantalizing, **Pl. del Sol,** one block above Trav. de Gràcia off C. Canó, is skirted by a fantastic selection of cafes and bars teeming with young (and often drunk) locals at night.

Gràcia Markets

MARKETS

🚇 *FCG: Gràcia.*

Gràcia's markets embody the multifaceted soul of this eclectic community, as older residents shop alongside hip young things. Two major markets offer inexpensive food options and great people-watching. Vegetarians beware: the meat and fish stands are not for the faint of heart. **Mercat de la Llibertat,** in the Pl. de la Llibertat, one block off Via Augusta from FGC: Gràcia, was originally designed as an open-air market by Berenguer in 1875 but was covered years later. The wrought iron gates and floral details are particularly impressive, as is the drinking fountain at the front of the market, which bears Gràcia's shield. Vendors offer everything from fresh eggs to dried fruit. (☎93 415 90 93. Open M 5-8pm, Tu-Th 8am-2pm and 5-8pm, F 8am-8pm, though some vendors close for the siesta, Sa 7am-3pm). **Mercat de L'Abaceria Central** is conveniently located in the heart of Gràcia at the intersection of Trav. de Gràcia and C. Torrijos. Hundreds of produce stalls congregate inside, while outside vendors sell flowers, clothing, and trinkets. (M: Joanic. Open M-Th 7am-2:30pm and 5:30-8:30pm, F-Sa 6am-3pm and 5-8:30pm.)

Monastery of Pedralbes

Tomb at Monastery of Pedralbes

HORTA & VALL D'HEBRON

Horta is less a sightseeing mecca than a great place to plunk down for the afternoon in a park somewhere or work up a sweat at one of the sports facilities.

◼ JARDINS DEL LABERINT D'HORTA

🏛 *C. dels Germans Desvalts, directly behind the Velodróm, up the steep steps. M: Mundet. From the Montbau exit, facing the Jardins Pedro Muñez Seca, turn right and follow Pg. de Vall d'Hebron for about 20min., turning right at the Velodróm cycling facility.* ☎93 428 39 34. *Guided tours leave at 11am on the first Su of some months, particularly in summer (€1.20). To arrange a private group tour call* ☎93 413 24 22. *For a mobile phone walking tour, call* ☎62 900 39 97. *Open daily Nov.-Feb. 10am-6pm; Mar. and Oct. 10am-7pm; Apr. and Sept. 10am-8pm; May-Aug. 10am-9pm. Entrance M-Tu and Th-Sa €1.65, with a camet joven €1.05, under 5 free. Su and W free.*

Once the private grounds of a wealthy marquis, this pristine 17-acre garden—complete with manicured walkways, a love canal, a romantic garden, a cascade, and, of course, the labyrinth—warrants the trip from town. A hot summer afternoon can in an instant become a cool, refreshing bit of paradise when enjoying the shade of the green fronds and the tinkle of water that pervades every inch of this fairy-tale park.

PARC DE LA CREUTA DEL COLL

🏛 *Pg. Mare de Déu del Coll, 93. M: Vallcarca or bus #25, 28, or 87. Exit metro onto Av. L'Hospital Militar. From the exit, walk down C. La Argentina and take a left onto C. Cambrils, which turns into C. Gustavo Bécquer, which soon makes a sharp right turn up a ramp to a bridge without changing name. At the head of the bridge, take a left onto Pg. Mare de Déu del Coll, which you will follow for about 15min., mostly uphill; the park entrance lies above an obvious set of sandstone steps.* ☎93 459 24 27. *Beach chairs €2.50. Swimming M-F €2.70, Sa-Su and holidays €3. Pool open late June-Aug. M-F 10am-4pm, Sa-Su 10am-7pm. Park gates open daily Nov.-Feb. 10am-6pm; Mar. and Oct. 10am-7pm; Apr. and Sept. 10am-8pm; May-Aug. 10am-9pm. Wheelchair accessible, but the entrance is steep, and there is a lot of sand inside.*

This park is like a small, arid, man-made valley basin, carved out of a steep hillside and complete with a long, shallow pool. The pool, tennis tables and playground packed with families make this a good place to bring young children on a hot day.

PEDRALBES & LES CORTS

◼ MONESTIR DE PEDRALBES

🏛 *Baixada del Monestir, 9. FGC: Reina Elisenda. A 10min. walk down Pg. Reina Elisenda. If you go to M: Palau Reial, go north on Av. Pedrables from Pl. Pius XII (street is not well labeled, but it is the major roadway) and follow road signs to the monastery. Also accessible by buses #22, 63, 64, 75 (only during the school year), 78, and 114.* ☎93 203 92 82 or 93 203 91 16. *€3.50, students 16-25 €2, under 16 free. Combined ticket with art collection €4.80, students 16-25 €3, under 16 free; combined ticket also good for the Museu d'Història de la Ciutat (see p. 104) and Museu-Casa Verdaguer (see p. 123). Open daily 10am-2pm. Church open M-Sa 11am-1pm, Su 11am-12:30pm.*

The devout Queen Elisenda founded this monastery in 1327 to atone for her earthly sins, and it has housed the Poor Clares order ever since. Today, visitors can peek into the lives these women led centuries ago: their courtyard, infirmary, kitchen, and dining hall are all open to the public. The tiny cells where the nuns spent their days in prayer will make visitors appreciate their own cramped hostels. Set amidst the low-rise apartments of Zona Alta, the monastery makes a refreshing and historically interesting break for those with the time to leave the chaos of downtown Barcelona. The monastery also has a large collection of furniture and manuscripts from the Middle Ages. The artistic highlight of the cloister is the Capella St. Miguel, where a set of frescoes by the Italian artist Ferrer Bassa depict the seven joys of the Blessed Virgin on the bottom level, and scenes from the Passion of Christ on the top level. The monastery also received part of the **Thyssen Bornemisza** collection (see p. 122).

PALAU REIAL DE PEDRALBES

🚩 Av. Diagonal, 686, recognizable by its distinctive pale orange entrance. M: Palau Reial. For an audio tour of the park and its points of interest, cell phone users can call ☎ 629 003 998 to hear descriptions in English, Spanish, or Catalan; simply press the number corresponding to the area to hear a short history and explanation. At the far end of the park is the Palau Real de Pedralbes.

Stone Fox Architectural Detail

Chirping birds almost manage to drown out the blaring traffic of Av. Diagonal in this green and shady park laid out in classical style. The park makes a quiet, excluded getaway from the rest of the city. Gaudí enthusiasts will want to check out the drinking fountain, designed in his early years, although it pales in comparison to his other more grandiose works and was promptly ignored by the city after he finished it. The fountain lies off the main path, to the left as you approach the palace, in a small forest of bamboo shoots; the simple design is a rather small twisting iron dragon that spouts water over a Catalan shield. Above, a bust of Hercules surveys the proceedings. "Rediscovered" in 1983 after decades of neglect, the fountain was restored, and now provides perfectly drinkable water to visitors of the park.

When the Güell family wanted to thank the King of Spain for making their father **Eusebi Güell** a count, they didn't say it with flowers—they said it with a royal palace, given to Spain at the International Exposition of 1929. The pale orange mansion, with its uninspiring design and painted-on facade, borders on tacky, but conceals an elegant interior; nonetheless, it is really only worth visiting if you are going to see its two main attractions: the **Museu de les Arts Decoratives** and the **Museu de Cerámica** (see p. 122).

Parc d'Attractions

FINCA GÜELL

🚩 Av. Pedralbes, 7. M: Palau Reial. A 5min. walk from Av. Diagonal, on the left. Private residence, closed to the public.

Those disappointed with the relatively unimposing Gaudí iron dragon in the Parc del Palau Reial should head up Av. Pedralbes to see the beast Gaudí created for this estate's gate—now *that's* a dragon. The ferocious 4½m dragon guards the front fence of the *finca* (farm), flashing fearsome fangs. Visitors can only see as far as the twisted wrought iron dragon, but it's worth the short walk up from the park.

El Sagrat Cor

Sardena Statue on Montjuïc

Poble Espagnol

Views from the Montjuïc Cablecar

SARRIÀ

🚩 *FGC: Sarrià. Exit the FGC station at the "Sortida Mare de Déu de Núria," then make a right, then make the first left (down a very short street), and then a left onto C. Mare de Déu de Núria. Then make a right onto C. Canet and follow Canet to the end and turn onto C. Major Sarrià. Most of the sights will be off this main road.*

In the sea of tourist literature on Gaudí and his frenetic genius, the architect's two works in Sarrià are often completely ignored. Lest you follow the Sarrià-hating ways of tourist dogma, a visit to Casa Bellesguard and the Collegi de les Teresianes is in order.

CASA BELLESGUARD

🚩 *C. Bellesguard, 16-20. FCG: Sarrià or Av. Tibidabo. Take buses #14, 30, 66, 70, or 72 to Pg. Bonanova, then take C. Escoles Pies up the steep hill to where it dead-ends at C. Immaculada, and make a right. Walk for several long blocks until C. Immaculada dead-ends at C. Bellesguard and make a left up the hill; Casa Bellesguard is on your right.*

Casa Bellesguard's striking design merits a look, even if your thighs burn all the way up Sarrià's steep incline. The building, now a private home, is closed to the public, but for true Gaudí fanatics, even a peek from the street is worth the walk. Built by Gaudí in 1902, Casa Bellesguard is one of the architect's neo-Gothic designs; the building looks like something out of a medieval fairy tale. Fans of Gaudí's trademark colorful mosaic details need not despair, though, as he worked in some of those as well. Tall and fairly compact, with one sculpture-topped spire, Casa Bellesguard is adorned with metal grillwork, tiled benches resplendent with blue and red fish, and three Rapunzel-esque balconies. A stone staircase and landing to the left of the entrance gate provide a picturesque view of the building and the surrounding hills.

COLLEGI DE LES TERESIANES

🚩 *C. Ganduxer, 85-105. FGC: Bonanova. Buses #14, 16, 72, or 74. ☎ 93 212 33 54. Call in advance to schedule a tour, offered Sept.-June Sa 11am-1pm. Free.*

Built from 1888 to 1889, the stately neo-Gothic building now serves as a Catholic school dedicated to Saint Teresa. Gaudí designed the wing to the right as you enter the gate, and while he was constrained by a low budget, he managed to pull together some innovative features. On the building's facade, a row of a repeating symbols—JSH, for *Jesú Salvate Hombres* (Jesus Saves Men)—adorns the space between two rows of windows. The arcs of the lower windows recall the shape of hands in prayer, while the pineapple shape which tops a tower on the left symbolizes strength. Though Gaudí was content to supervise most of the wing's construction, he fashioned the iron gate himself, repeating symbols of Saint Teresa. While these details can be appreciated from outside, it is the school's main internal hallways which are admired by architects worldwide for their perfect parabolic arches.

RESIDENTIAL SARRIÀ

🚪 *Jardins Villa Cecilia open Dec.-Feb. 10am-6pm; Mar. and Oct. 10am-7pm; Apr. and Sept. 10am-8pm; May-Aug. 10am-9pm.*

A visit to the Sarrià is a pleasant way to see the traditional home of the Catalan bourgeois and a more suburban side of Barcelona. The upper part of Sarrià, closer to the Collserola hills, is the place to stroll and gawk at the lavish gated mansions and private schools; **C. Iradier** and **C. Escoles Pies** are particularly well-endowed. The lower, older area of Sarrià is concentrated around the **Pl. Sarrià,** notable for the Neoclassical **Sant Vicenç de Sarrià Church** (1816). The front entrance of the church faces **C. Major de Sarrià,** the area's main street, full of restaurants and cafes. Pl. Sarrià also has an antique flea market during the summer on Tuesdays (9am-8pm) and a small used-book flea market on Fridays (9am-8pm).

In the middle of Sarrià's car-width streets, the low-traffic **Pl. Sant Vicenç** serves as a shaded stop for locals meandering off C. Major de Sarrià. The *plaça* is bordered by a mix of classic, older homes, and brightly colored new ones. In the *plaça's* center, **Sant Vicenç** himself stands guard, despite the gradual loss of his nose due to statuary wear and tear. Once a year, on May 11, Plaça Sant Vicenç hosts **La Fira de Sant Ponç,** a festival honoring the patron saint of herbalists and beekeepers; various herbs, medicinal plants, honey products, and cheeses are put out for the occasion.

Sarrià also boasts some of the most relaxing and well-manicured public spaces in the city. More like a park than a formal garden, the **Jardins de la Villa Amelia** attract dog-walkers and mid-afternoon loungers to its orderly, well-kept grounds. Palm tree- and eucalyptus-lined paths radiate out from a central fountain, and there is plenty of bench space to go around. A pleasant yet unobtrusive cafe lies between the park's restrooms and the playground area. Across C. Sant Amelia, the **Jardins Villa Cecilia** are not quite as lush, but they do boast an impressive hedge maze.

TIBIDABO

Tibidabo is named for the phrase the devil used to tempt Job: "Haec omnia tibidabo si cadens adoraveris me." ("All of this I will give to you if you worship me.") "All of this" is a gloriously high view of massive Barcelona reduced to miniature, spilling into the seemingly endless aquamarine Mediterranean. Besides the view, pleasure-seekers and those seeking God can both be satisfied with the rather incongruous duo of an adjacent amusement park and church. On the way up the mountain, the colorful **La Rotonda** in Pl. JFK and **Casa Roviralta** (Av. Tibidabo, 31, on the way up to Pl. Dr. Andreu), a stunning Modernist edifice and a National Historic and Artistic monument, both evoke the aristocracy's penchant for beautiful buildings. At the base of the Tibidabo mountain lies the distinctive silver-domed **Observatori Fabra,** built in 1904; piercing the skyline next to El Sagrat Cor is the highly-ornamented **Dos Rius** water tower, built in 1902 by Josep Amargós i Samaranch. Tibidabo is also home to several museums (see p. 122), though in truth, nothing compares to the temptingly grandiose view.

PARC D'ATTRACIONS

🚪 *Pl. Tibidabo. ☎ 93 211 79 42. Open Jan.-Apr. Sa-Su noon-7pm; May F 10am-5pm, Sa-Su noon-7pm; June Th-F 10am-5pm, Sa-Su and holidays noon-8pm; July M-Th noon-9pm, F and Su noon-1am, Sa noon-11pm; Aug. M-Th and Su noon-10pm, F noon-11pm, Sa noon-midnight; early Sept. M-F noon-10pm, Sa-Su noon-9pm; late Sept. Sa-Su noon-9pm; Oct. Sa-Su noon-8pm; Nov.-Dec. Sa-*

Su and holidays noon-6pm; closed Dec. 25. €20 for unlimited ride access, over 60 €8, under 110cm tall €8, disabled visitors €5; €10 for the 6 most popular rides only. Most attractions wheel-chair accessible.

Opened in 1899, this colorful amusement park may be more weekend carnival than Disney World, but the rides use the mountain to its full advantage—some flinging the riders far out into the air. The park also has marionette and haunted house shows, miradors with pay-per-use binoculars (€0.50), the **Museu de Autòmats** (Robot museum; see p. 122), and 13 different restaurants and cafes.

EL SAGRAT COR

🚩 *Pl. Tibidabo. ☎ 93 417 56 86. Lower stairs, which offer decent views, open 10am-7pm. Elevator to the top open daily 10am-2pm and 3-7pm, €1.50. Wheelchair accessible at the lower levels.*

This neo-Gothic church of the Sacred Heart immediately recalls Paris's own Sacre Coeur in Montmartre, albeit on a more modern and less exquisite scale. Founded in 1886 by St. John Bosco, the current building is celebrating its 100th year until June 29, 2003. At its peak of 575.07m, the church has one of the best views in Catalunya.

TORRE DE COLLSEROLA

🚩 *Bus #211 from Pl. Tibidabo or a short walk from Vallvidrera or Tibidabo (when facing the funicu-lar station, follow path to the right). ☎ 93 406 93 54. Open Nov.-Mar. M-F 11am-2:30pm and 3:30-6pm, Sa-Su 11am-6pm; Apr. M-F 11am-2:30pm and 3:30-6pm, Sa-Su 11am-7pm; May M-F 11am-2:30pm and 3:30-7pm, Sa-Su 11am-7pm; June M-F 11am-2:30pm and 3:30-7pm, Sa-Su 11am-8pm; July-Sept. M-F 11am-2:30pm and 3:30-8pm, Sa-Su 11am-8pm; Oct. M-F 11am-2:30pm and 3:30-7pm, Sa-Su 11am-7pm. €4.40, groups of 15+ €3.10 per person, under 7 free. MC/V.*

Over 288m above ground and 560m above sea level, Barcelona's main communica-tions tower soars (quite controversially) into the skyline. Built to transmit TV and radio signals for the 1992 Olympics, the tower allows visitors up to the 10th platform in an external glass elevator (2½min.), where captioned pictures of the city help explain the seemingly unending views. While interesting, the view from Sagrat Cor is higher and a bit more majestic (not to mention closer to the funicular station).

PARC DE COLLSEROLA

🚩 *Take the FGC train to Baixador de Vallvidrera and follow the steps at the top of the stop for 10min. Tourist office: Carretera de l'Església, 92. ☎ 93 280 35 52. Open daily 9:30am-3pm except Dec. 25-26 and Jan. 1 and 6.*

Created in its present form by Barcelona's 1976 General Metropolitan Plan, the Parc de Collserola encompasses 16,000 acres of greenery within minutes of the city cen-ter. People come here to hike, bike, horseback ride, and drive on designated routes through the forest. There are more than two dozen restaurants, snack bars, and pic-nic places scattered throughout the hills. Before exploring the park, it is extremely useful to stop at the **Centre d'Informació.** There is a permanent exhibit in the center, on birds and the park itself, and the helpful staff sells numerous guides and maps and gives out free pamphlets, available upon request. For those planning to make extended or repeat visits, invest in the hefty, trilingual Parc de Collserola Guide Book (€18.03) at the info center; it comes with color photos and a keyed map locat-ing every picture in the book (as well as suggesting hiking/biking route you can use to get there). The smaller, cheaper Peu Per Collserola (€11.42) also has pictures and locator maps, but is only available in Catalan. The main map (€6; available in English) is by far the most useful, as it plots every major road and service in the park. The center also has bathrooms, a snack bar, a public telephone, and a brief informational video about the park, on request.

Parc de Collserola is full of enough natural and man-made sights to pack a long afternoon escape from the city. Most accessible is the **Museu-Casa Verdaguer** (see **Museums,** p. 123). Numerous lookout points in the park offer good views of the city and surrounding hills, especially the ▓**Mirador de Vila Paula** (also known as the Mirador de Sarrià). Take the FGC train from Pl. de Catalunya to the Peu del Funicular stop, walk up the hill from the station on Av. de Vallvidrera, follow it along the tight, immediate left turn, then a right turn, and then a few smaller twists and curves (about 10-15min.); it will be up the hill a bit on your right. If you've got a car, this is the place to bring your date for some romantic parking; if not, be very careful walking along the narrow, twisting highway, especially at dusk.

Also inside the park are more than 50 notable archaeological finds and ruins. The **Cova de l'Or**, the oldest cave dwelling in the park, dates back to the Neolithic period, 6000 BC (although it could not be visited at the time of publication). The terraced remains of a 4th-to 6th-century BC Laietana dwelling can be seen on La Penya del Moro hillside. **Castellciuró,** a castle built in the 14th century over 12th-century remains, serves as a particularly good lookout point. Interesting remains from the last two centuries include the Modernist, turreted washing and disinfection pavilion "El Castell," begun as a tuberculosis hospital on Tibidabo but never completed, and the remains of Dr. Salvador Andreu's Arrabassada **Casino.** Opened in 1911 with a proud exterior staircase reminiscent of the Paris Opera, the building was closed down by municipal authorities in 1912 and is now in an advanced state of ruin. Legend has it that its closing was related to its popularity as a place to play roulette—Russian roulette, with suicide room included.

Museums

Barcelona has always been on the cutting edge of defining what can be included in the category of "art;" if it can fit in a museum, you can bet a museum has been built in Barcelona to accommodate it. The city's museums range from Surrealist art and classical masterpieces to historical exhibits and one-of-a-kind curiosities, such as a shoe museum, an erotica museum, and even a hearse museum. It's impossible to rank these different institutions with respect to each other, so museums below are listed alphabetically by neighborhood, with a handy chart on p. 105 to search by type.

Serious culture vultures should consider investing in the **Articket** which gives half-price admission to six of Barcelona's premier art centers. It offers half-price admission to the Museu Nacional d'Art de Catalunya (MNAC; see p. 120), the Fundació Joan Miró (see p. 118), the Fundació Antoni Tàpies (see p. 113), the Centre de Cultura Contemporània de Barcelona (CCCB; see p. 112), the Centre Cultural Caixa Catalunya (in la Pedrera; see p. 78), and the Museu d'Art Contemporani de Barcelona (MACBA; see p. 112). The ticket, available at tourist offices (see **Service Directory,** p. 317) and the ticket offices of the museums, goes for €15, and is valid for up to three months.

the hidden deal

see map p. 338-339

BARRI GÒTIC & LAS RAMBLAS

Free Time

Most museums in the city offer free entrance on certain days.

Fundació Francisco Godia: Free tours Sa-Su at noon (see p. 113).

Museu d'Art Modern: Free first Th of the month (see p. 111).

Museu de Geologia: Free first Su of the month (see p. 111).

Museu de Zoologia: Free first Su of the month (see p. 111).

Museu Etnològic: Free first Su of the month (see p. 120).

Museu Frederic Marès: Free W 3-7pm and first Su of the month (see p. 106).

Museu Picasso: Free first Su of the month (see p. 109).

Museu Tèxtil i d'Indumentària: Free first Sa of the month after 3pm (see p. 110).

⬛ CENTRE D'ART DE SANTA MONICA

🛈 *Las Ramblas, 7, on the right as you approach the port. M: Drassanes. ☎ 93 316 27 27. Cultural center open M-F 9:30am-2pm and 3:30-7:30pm, Sa 10am-2pm. Gallery open M-F 11am–2pm, and 5-8pm, holidays 11am-3pm. Call for info on exhibitions. Free.*

One can only imagine what the nuns of this former convent would have thought of the edgy art installations (recently "How Difficult it is to Sleep Alone" and "Transsexual Express") that rotate through this free gallery, which is definitely worth a visit for modern art fans. The site also houses a cultural information center, with info on museums and festivals throughout the city, and a museum of temporary contemporary art exhibits.

MUSEU DE CERA (WAX MUSEUM)

🛈 *Las Ramblas, 4, on the left as you face the port. M: Drassanes. ☎ 93 317 26 49. Open M-F 10am-2pm and 4-8pm, Sa 11am-2:30pm, Su and holidays 4:30-9pm. €6.65, children 5-11 €3.75. On Saturday nights in April, May, and June, special shows at 8:30 and 9:30pm with actors and special effects €12 (including a cup of cava).*

Close to 300 wax celebrities and legends will keep visitors guessing which figures are wax and which are just creepy-looking tourists. Imagine what kinds of conversation would be taking place as Adolph Hitler, Winston Churchill, and Bill Clinton rub elbows in the throne room. Catalunya buffs will appreciate historical figures such as Jaume I and the architectural tag-team of Güell and Gaudí. Everyone else will enjoy the horror room, filled with monsters, infamous villains, and gruesome scenes of death. Look out for a new model of Claudia Schiffer, strutting her stuff on the runway.

MUSEU D'HISTÒRIA DE LA CIUTAT

🛈 *In Pl. del Rei. M: Jaume I. Walk up C. Jaume I and take the first right. Enter on C. Verguer. ☎ 93 315 11 11. Open June-Sept. Tu-Sa 10am-8pm, Su 10am-2pm; Oct.-May Tu-Sa 10am-2pm and 4-8pm, Su 10am-2pm. Closed Jan. 1,*

May 1, June 24, and Dec. 25-26. Museum €3.50, students €2; exhibition €3, students €1.50; combined museum and exhibition €5.50, students €3.50. Your ticket can be used again if you ask them to issue you another access card on the way out. Most displays are in Spanish and Catalan, but pamphlets are available in English.

There are two components to Barcelona's city history museum: the Palau Reial Major and the underground Roman archaeological excavations. Built on top of the fourth-century city walls, the **Palau Reial Major** served as the residence of the Catalan-Aragonese monarchs from the end of the 10th century through the 15th century. After the last Catalan king died in 1410, it began to deteriorate and was finally abandoned by royalty in the 16th century, and was put to use as a seat for royal scribes and the Inquisition. In 1718, it was given to the Sisters of Santa Clara as a convent when Felipe's construction of the Ciutadella (see p. 72) forced them out of their original location. The nuns left at the start of the Spanish Civil War, and as restoration was begun on the building, the **Saló de Tinell** (Throne Room) was discovered wholly intact under a baroque chapel. Finished in 1370, the huge Gothic room is believed to have been the place where Columbus was received by Fernando and Isabel after his journey to America. Today, it houses year-long temporary exhibitions; 2003 will begin with an exhibition on the role of the bull in Mediterranean culture, which will run through February. The museum itself is an interesting look at the history of ancient Barcelona.

Next to the Saló de Tinell you will find the **Capella de Santa Agata** (Chapel of St. Agatha), begun in 1302 during the reign of Jaume II and now considered one of the most beautiful works of medieval architecture in Barcelona. Its star attraction is the *Epiphany* altarpiece done by Jaume Huguet in 1465; resplendent in gold, with highly realistic portrayals of the most important scenes in the life of Jesus, this *retablo* is in turn considered one of the best examples of Catalan Gothic painting in existence. From the chapel you can access the **Mirador del Rei Martí**, a watchtower built in 1557 but named for the last Catalan king; from here you can see the **Pl. del Rei**, the *plaça* formed by the Palau Reial Major, the Chapel of St. Agatha, and the **Palau de Lloctinent,** a 16th-century modification of the royal palace which until 1994 housed the archives of the Crown of Aragó.

The second part of the museum lies underground, in an area discovered when space was being cleared for the Via Laietana. The largest underground excavation of any ancient city in Europe, this **archeological exhibit** allows visi-

MUSEUMS BY TYPE

ART & ARCHITECTURE

Centre d'Art de St. Monica (p. 104)

Centre de Cultura Contemporània de Barcelona (p. 112)

Col·lecció Thyssen Bornemisza (p. 122)

Fundació Antoni Tàpies (p. 113)

Fundació Francisco Godia (p. 113)

Fundació Joan Miró (p. 118)

Galleries (p. 123)

Museu d'Art Contemporani (p. 112)

Museu d'Art Modern (p. 111)

Museu Nacional d'Art de Catalunya (p. 120)

Museu Picasso (p. 109)

DECORATIVE ARTS

Museu de Ceràmica (p. 122)

Museu de les Arts Decoratives (p. 122)

Museu Tèxtil i d'Indumentària (p. 110)

HISTORY, CULTURE, & ARCHEOLOGY

Casa-Museu Gaudí (p. 121)

Casa-Museu Verdaguer (p. 123)

Museu Arqueològic de Catalunya (p. 119)

Museu Dioscesà (p. 107)

Museu Egipci (p. 115)

Museu Etnològic (p. 120)

Museu d'Història de Catalunya (p. 116)

Museu d'Història de la Ciutat (p. 104)

Museu Frederic Marès (p. 106)

Museu Marítim (p. 118)

Museu Militar (120)

(Continued on p. 107)

the hidden deal

Free All the Time

Some museums in Barcelona offer the best deal of all: no admission ever. If you're looking for some low-budget culture, check out these spots anytime:

Centre d'Art de Santa Monica: see **p. 104**.

Museu-Casa Verdaguer: see p. 123.

Museu d'Autòmats: (free with Parc d'Attracions admission) see **p. 122**.

Museu de Carrosses Fúnebres: see **p. 116**.

Museu de l'Esport: see **p. 114**.

Museu del Perfum: see **p. 115**.

tors to walk through incredibly intact remains of an entire corner of the Roman town of Barcino. You can see the original city boundary wall and walking paths, a dye-shop, and laundry shop which still has faintly visible soap residues, a fish product factory, and a fascinating wine production facility which has intact ceramic wine containers. You can also walk through a large portion of the sprawling Episcopal palace and see a mosaic floor from the home of a wealthy second-century Roman.

MUSEU DE L'ERÒTICA

🔊 *Las Ramblas, 96, on the left as you face the port.* ☎ *93 318 98 65; www.eroticamuseum.com. Open June-Sept. 10am-midnight; Oct.-May 11am-9pm. €7, students €6.*

Barcelona's unique museum examines the history of eroticism, from ancient Greece, Asia, and Africa to modern times. Of particular interest are the anthropological and sociological insights which can be gleaned from a careful examination of these societies' erotica. Um, yeah, okay. Just show us the fly honeys! Barcelona's only erotica museum attracts many of Barcelona's most intrepid tourists. The random assortment (part of one man's private collection) unevenly spans human history and depicts more sexual acrobatics than even you thought possible. Check out a porn flick commissioned by Spain's very own King Alfonso XIII and listen to dirty talk in English, German, Spanish, and French. The giant wooden phallus overlooking the Boqueria market (see p. 60) is an irresistible photo op. The museum also displays current erotic works for sale. In the end, the museum's greatest historical revelation may be that, indeed, little has changed.

MUSEU FREDERIC MARÈS

🔊 *Pl. Sant Iu, 5-6, in the Palau Reial. From M: Jaume I, walk down C. Llibreteria and turn right on C. Freneria, which will lead you to the museum.* ☎ *93 310 58 00; museumares@mail.bcn.es. Open Tu-Sa 10am-7pm, Su and holidays 10am-3pm. Museum cafe open Apr. 1-Sept. 30 10am-10pm. €3, groups of ten or more €1.80, students under 25 €1.50, under 16 free. Free guided tours in Catalan and Spanish every Sunday at 11:30am; for private tours or tours in English, call ahead. The free floorplan pamphlet and one-page descriptions located in each major room are available in English. Free W afternoons and first Su of the month. Cash only. Wheelchair accessible.*

This museum is the answer to the question, "What happens when you give an eccentric collector with a keen interest in art a lot of money and tons of travel time?" Marès (1893-1991) was one of Spain's better-known sculptors and an avid collector of just about everything. In 1946, in a classic example of the individualized bourgeois patronage of the arts so common in Catalunya, he founded this museum and donated his entire private collection, as well as some of his own sculptures. The building itself was originally part of the Palau Reial Major, home to the monarchs of the Catalan-Aragonese dynasty (see p. 62) from the end of the 10th century through the 15th century. The Renaissance-style entrance door to the museum still has the original 16th-century royal sign above it, and the entrance courtyard dates from the 13th century (ground floor) and 15th century (upper galleries).

Inside the museum, the lower floors house a huge collection of Spanish and Hispanic sculpture, from pre-Roman times (including tiny Iberian religious figurines) through the 20th century. Of particular note is the collection of Marès's own sculptures in his private library on the second floor. The upper floors contain Marès's "Sentimental Museum;" an overwhelming collection of middle-class daily life objects from the Romantic era, from fans, jewelry, hair combs, and purses to watches, canes, pipes, and eyeglasses. In addition to Marès's collection, the entrance floor has a small temporary exhibition space to the left of the reception. The museum can be overwhelming and repetitive to even the most dedicated of art history students, but any average tourist will enjoy a quick look at the bizzare and unique collection.

MUSEU DIOCESÀ

🚩 *Av. de la Catedral, 4, next to the cathedral. ☎ 93 315 22 13. Open Tu-Sa 10am-2pm and 5-8pm, Su 10am-2pm. €1.80. Descriptions and free pamphlet guide are in Catalan, but the staff is extremely friendly and speaks Spanish whether you have questions or not. Wheelchair accessible.*

This small museum tends to be overshadowed by the cathedral next door, both literally and figuratively, but it is a treasure trove for history buffs, as it contains the city's only intact octagonal defense tower from Roman Barcino. As you walk up the floors of the museum, a wire with flags on it marks off the additions from each era of the tower's life: the round base at the bottom from the first century AD, the octagonal base on top of that from the 4th century, the next section

MORE MUSEUMS BY TYPE

(Continued from p. 105)

from medieval times (look for uniform windows), and the fourth from the Gothic period (14th and 15th centuries; look for the higher, more delicate row of windows). From the top floor gallery, you can even see blackened stones from fires started by invading Muslim armies in the Middle Ages. The entrance to the museum galleries leads through the original wall and into a Gothic building that was originally (around 1000) the city's oldest homeless shelter/soup kitchen, the **Pia Almoina.** During the 18th century, under the dreaded Felipe V, the building was converted into a prison—you can see wall etchings by prisoners at the top of the stairs leading to the top floor. Most believe that the old graffiti includes a camping/outdoors scene and a long line of tally marks counting the passing days.

The museum's collection of religious artifacts covers two main periods, the Romanesque (12th and 13th centuries), and the Gothic (14th and 15th centuries). Highlights include an almost entirely intact church fresco from 1122, varied wood and marble Virgin sculptures, and a beautifully handwritten Latin document by Felipe II. The museum's crown jewel, though, is the stunning, gold, diamond-adorned **Custodià del Pi,** made in 1587 and originally used in the nearby Santa Maria del Pi church. In the Catholic religion, the *custodià* is used to store the Host, or holy bread, before and after the rite of communion. Still in perfect condition today, it drips with ornate detail and delicate religious symbolism. Equally breathtaking is the view of the cathedral from the museum's top-floor gallery. The museum also hosts a series of rotating historical exhibits, and part of its space is frequently rented out for modern art displays.

MUSEU DEL CALÇAT (SHOE MUSEUM)

🚩 *Pl. Sant Felip Neri, 5.* ☎ *93 301 45 33. M: Jaume I. Open Tu-Su 11am-2pm. €2. Only 1½ rooms, but you can call for guided tours. Pamphlet on the history of the museum €2.*

This bizarre collection of footwear throughout history is a tribute to the ancient guilds of Barcelona, tracing the existence of master shoemakers to an official document signed by the Bishop of Barcelona in 1203 (even today a few faithful members tend to the guild's chapel in the Cathedral de la Sant Creu; see **The Guilded Age,** p. 64). The tiny and unremarkable museum will probably interest only the most dedicated of shoe fans. The exhibit, tucked obscurely away in the *Plaça* Sant Felip Neri, spans much of the past three centuries including everything from eighteenth-century men's sandals to track spikes from the 1940s and the boots which Carles Vallés wore to the top of Mt. Everest to plant the Catalan flag. Modern-day men can leave their twentieth century machismo at the door and admire some of the pointed-toe, high-heeled men's boots of years past while women can say their thanks that pricey, silver-plated dress shoes aren't quite the rage they once were.

see map p. 341

LA RIBERA

MUSEU BARBIER-MUELLER

🚩 *C. Montcada, 12-14.* ☎ *93 310 45 16. M: Jaume I. Open Tu-Sa 10am-6pm, Su 10am-3pm. Combined admission with Museu Tèxtil i d'Indumentària next door; see below. €3, students and seniors €1.50. Free 1st Su of the month. Wheelchair accessible.*

Eerily illuminated relics from the pre-Columbian Americas line darkened rooms in this small museum devoted to the conquistadors' booty. Tapestries, carvings, ornaments, vases, sculptures, and jewelry which date from 200 BC and were taken from the sites of the Olmecs, Mayas, Aztecs, Coclé, Mochicas, and Incas. You may want to pass up the meager museum (only 3 rooms), which does not even discuss Spain or Catalunya, in favor of the larger museums that abound in the area.

◼ MUSEU PICASSO

> When I was a child, my mother said to me, "If you become a soldier, you'll be a general. If you become a monk, you'll end up as the Pope." Instead, I became a painter and wound up as Picasso.
> —Pablo Picasso

🏠 C. Montcada, 15-19. ☎ 93 319 63 10. M: Jaume I. Go down C. Princesa from the Metro, and turn right on C. Montcada. Open Tu-Sa 10am-8pm, Su 10am-3pm. €4.80, students and seniors €2.40, under 16 free. Special exhibits €4.80, students and seniors €2.40. First Su of each month free. Wheelchair accessible.

This incredible museum traces the development of Picasso as an artist, with a chronologically organized collection of his early works that weaves through five connected mansions once occupied by Barcelona's nobility. Although the museum offers little from Picasso's more well-known middle years, it boasts the world's best collection of work from his formative period in Barcelona. The museum showcases each of Picasso's re-inventions of himself, from his deeply personal, tormented Blue Period, to his form-fascinated Rose Period, to his reign as master of Cubism. Like the Fundació Miró (see p. 118), the museum is practically an autobiography of the artist's life, depicting his many (many) lovers, his emotional ups and downs, his obsessions with the bull and the taurine, his family, and the politics around him. The collection was started in 1963 with a donation from Picasso's friend Jaume Sabartés; it was later expanded by Picasso himself and by relatives after his death.

Most impressive of all the work in the museum is the display of the artist's 58 Cubist interpretations of Velázquez's *Las Meninas* (translated to *Ladies in Waiting*, which hangs in the Museu del Prado in Madrid). The original *Las Meninas* is a breathtaking, 7ft. masterpiece: a group painting of a familiar royal scene. Rather than the typical posed painting, Velázquez captured an instantaneous moment on canvas. Generally agreed to be the finest Spanish—if not international—painting, Spanish painters have created their own interpretations of *Las Meninas*, a sort of rite of passage into greatness. Francisco Goya considered himself the inheritor of Velázquez's position as the best Spanish painter and hence etched the master's famous painting.

This pattern continued with Picasso, who considered himself the next in line for this title. What is most remarkable about Picasso is that instead of recreating the painting in its original

An Hour In the Picasso Museum

Though some students of art history spend their entire lives analyzing the stylistics and innovations of the man who some have called the father of modern art, an hour in the Museu Picasso can easily leave you with enough knowledge to impress your friends. To help along the learned image, be sure to tilt your head and put on a look of extreme concentration at these key works.

The First Communion (1896) was the young master's first major work.

Portrait of my Aunt Pepa (1896) was the artist's first attempt at portraiture.

Caballo Corneado (1917) depicts a horse falling on a knife or bull's horn, recalling Picasso's obsession with horses and bullfights that inspired his painting *Guernica*.

The **Las Meninas studies** in Sala 11 are based on Velasquez's celebrated 1656 work; don't miss **Las Meninas (conjunto);** (1957), where, rather than focusing on isolated parts of the original, Picasso reinterprets the entire work.

Desamparados (1903) is one of the museum's few pieces from the **Blue Period** (1901-1904; brought on by the suicide of the artist's friend Casagemas, whose lover Picasso had wooed away), during which Picasso used blue tones and sordid subject matter to express sadness.

El Retrato de la Señora Canals is from Picasso's brief **Rose Period** (1904-5), during which he sent the blues (hues and otherwise) packing and embraced with bright colors and more optimistic subjects.

grandeur, as Goya did, he chose to apply his own, unique styles as a way of interpreting Velázquez's mysterious work. He shows all of the main characters from the original painting, but rearranges them to emphasize different parts. *Las Meninas* is exalted for its rigid linearity and the mystery behind what Velázquez (who painted himself into the original) is painting on the canvas he is working on within the painting itself. Because of the linear construction and multiple focal points in the original, the subject of his painting within the painting is a mystery. However, this mystery is lost in Picasso's focused, cubist recreations, as Velázquez's unique usage of space is eliminated and the trick that Velázquez is playing on the spectator is lost. Picasso reinvents the many vantage points of the original in his Cubist reinterpretation of multiple angles and lines of vision, along his own terms. The reinterpretation of *La Meninas* was a very controversial move for Picasso, as he destroyed the magic of a historical painting in which Spaniards take a great deal of national pride.

Easily Barcelona's most popular museum, lines at the Museu Picasso often snake a good way down C. Montcada. The best times to avoid the museum-going masses are mornings and early evenings when the crowd thins out.

MUSEU TÉXTIL I D'INDUMENTÀRIA

🚺 *C. Montcada 12. M: Jaume I. ☎93 310 45 16. Open Tu-Sa 10am-6pm, Su 10am-3pm. Combined admission with Museu Barbier-Mueller, buy tickets there (see above). One ticket gets you into this museum, the Museu de les Arts Decoratives (see p. 122), and the Museu de Ceràmica (see p. 122) up to one month after purchase. €3, students and seniors €1.50. 1st Sa of the month after 3pm free. Wheelchair accessible.*

Still trying to figure out what Spanish lace is? The Museu Téxtil I D'Indumentaràrria offers not only a lesson in lace, but also a quick tour of the history of European fashion, from bustles and sadistic-looking corsets to V-necks and miniskirts. While the visual history of clothing can be titillating to the true fashionista, all signs are (sigh) in Catalan, prohibiting the average tourist from gleaning much historical info about the garb. For those not feeling stylish enough, the swank cafe and "gift shop" (more of a clothing stop than a tourist trove) can add a touch of class to almost anyone who thinks an "accessory" is a fanny pack.

🍫MUSEU DE LA XOCOLATA (CHOCOLATE MUSEUM)

🚺 *Pl. Pons i Clerch, corner of C. Comerç. M: Jaume I. Follow C. Princesa and turn left on C. Comerç. ☎93 268 78 78. Open M and W-Sa 10am-7pm, Su 10am-3pm. €3, students and seniors €2.50. Workshops €6. Wheelchair accessible.*

Arguably the most delectable museum in Spain. If you can halt the inevitable excessive salivation for a few moments, the multilingual signs spew gobs of information about the history, production, and ingestion of this sensual treat. But perhaps more interesting are the exquisite chocolate sculptures, particularly the edible versions of La Sagrada Família and the Arc de Triomf. Still not satisfied? Do some hands-on training at the small cafe and indulge in a workshop on cake baking, the history of chocolate, or chocolate tasting; call for information.

see map
p. 350

PARC DE LA CIUTADELLA

The following museums are all located in the Parc de la Ciutadella (see **Sights**, p. 72).

▨ MUSEU D'ART MODERN

🗹 *In Pl. D'Armes. M: Arc de Triomf. Follow Pg. Tilles to the statue of General Prim at the roundabout and turn left toward Pl. D'Armes; signs point the way to the museum. ☎ 93 319 57 28. Open Tu-Sa 10am-7pm, Su 10am-2:30pm. €3, students and children €2. Free entrance first Th of every month. Wheelchair accessible.*

Modernism is Barcelona's claim to fame, and this is the place to learn all about its multifaceted, quirky character. Easily manageable in about an hour, the museum simultaneously offers a quick lesson in Catalan art and a glimpse into the city at the turn of the century. Check out noteworthy works like Francesc Lacoma's *La Familia del Pintor* (see his mom looking over his shoulder?), Ramon Casas's *Plein Air*, Josep Llimona's *Desconsol* (the original of the sculpture in the Placa d'Armes), Homar's surprisingly Japanese-like works, and Isidre Nonell's paintings of Gypsy women. Don't miss the room of Josep Clará's *Noucentist* sculptures, reminiscent of French scultptor Rodin. Noucentism, a derivative of Modernism, sought to reinsert classical beauty into art by adding motion and emotion without adhering to formal techniques. The museum also displays furniture designed by Antoni Gaudí for Casa Battló (see **Sights,** p. 81), as well as several fixtures from Puig i Cadalfach's Casa Amatller (see **Sights,** p. 80). Don't get too excited for the two Dalí paintings in the collection; they are from his formative stages and, therefore, differ greatly from the surrealist puzzles for which he is known.

MUSEU DE GEOLOGIA

🗹 *On Pg. Picasso, 2 buildings behind the Museu Zoologia. M: Arc de Triomf. Entrance faces inside of park. ☎ 93 319 68 95. Open Tu-Sa 10am-2pm and Th 10am-6:30pm. €3, students and seniors €1.50, free first Su of each month. Combined entrance with Museu de Zoologia (see below). Wheelchair accessible.*

Another park structure designed by Fontseré (with the help of Antoni Rovira i Trias), the Museu de Geologia opened in 1882 as the first public museum in the city. Perhaps a geological craze had swept through Catalonia in that era, but in more modern times, the "chock-full-o' rocks" museum, lacking much explanation in any language other than the scientific names and places of origin, may be a bit tedious for the average tourist.

MUSEU DE ZOOLOGIA (CASTELL DELS TRES DRAGONS)

🗹 *Entrances on Pg. Pujades/Pg. de Lluís Companys and Pg. Picasso/C. Princesa. At the corner of Pg. Picasso and Pg. Pujades. M: Arc de Triomf. ☎ 93 319 69 12. Open Tu-Su 10am-2pm and Th 10am-6:30pm. €3, students and seniors €1.50. Combined entrance with Museu de Geologia. Free first Su of every month. Wheelchair accessible.*

Designed as a restaurant for Expo '88 and taking its name from a then-popular Frederic Soler play, Montaner's Castell dels Tres Dragons (Castle of Three Dragons) was later used by the architect as a Modernist workshop. The splendor of the building's blue and white tile work and brick turrets can be best appreciated from outside. Inside, besides an impressively large whale skeleton on the first floor, an unremarkable collection of taxidermy and fauna samples fills the majority of the museum. However, the fact that most informational placards are in English may be enough to attract Catalan-weary visitors.

EL RAVAL

see map p. 340

Both museums in El Raval are covered by the **Articket,** a worthwhile investment for those planning to hit a lot of the city's museums; see p. 103 for details.

kids
IN THE CITY

KIDDING AROUND IN BARCELONA

If you're looking for a place to bring the kids for an afternoon, try out some of the following:

Park Güell. Gaudí seems to have designed this colorful park with his inner-child in mind; see **p. 91**.

Fundació Miró. Sometimes kids understand this stuff better than adults; see p. 118.

L'Aquàrium de Barcelona. Fishy fun for the whole family; see p. 87.

Museu d'Autòmats. Let the kids press some buttons that aren't your own; see p. 122.

Parc d'Attracions. Kid-friendly amusement rides and plenty of places for adults to rest; see p. 99.

Museu de Cera. A gorey wax museum that will entertain older children; see p. 104.

Museu Egipci. Kids love mummies; see **p. 115**.

Museu de Xocolata. Luckily, all of the exhibits are "look but don't eat"; see **p. 110**.

Museu FCB. More oriented towards sports-crazed little boys and their sports-crazed dads; see p. 122.

Museu de Zoologia. Animals from everywhere, stuffed and startling; see p. 111.

CENTRE DE CULTURA CONTEMPORÀNIA DE BARCELONA (CCCB)

🛊 *Casa de Caritat. C. Montalegre, 5. M: Catalunya or Universitat, next to the MACBA (see above).* ☎ *93 306 41 00. Open Tu-Su 10am-8pm. €4, students €3, children free.*

At first glance, the center stands out for its jarring mixture of architectural styles, consisting of an unassuming early 20th-century theater, and its 1994 addition, an enormous and very sleek wing constructed of black glass. The institution itself stands out as well, with a wonderful variety of temporary photo and art exhibits, film screenings, and music and dance performances. In 2002 the 7th International Gay and Lesbian Film Festival came to Barcelona, including an exhibition exploring the artistic influences and legacy of Gaudí and his work. Check the *Guía del Ocio* for scheduled events.

🛋 MUSEU D'ART CONTEMPORANI (MACBA)

🛊 *Pl. dels Angels, 1. M: Universitat or Catalunya. From Pl. de Catalunya, take a right onto C. Elisabets and follow it to Pl. dels Angels.* ☎ *93 412 08 10; www.macba.es. Open July-Sept. M, W, and F 11am-8pm; Th 11am-9:30pm; Sa 10am-8pm; Su 10am-3pm. Oct.-June M and W-F 11am-7:30pm, Sa 10am-8pm, Su 10am-3pm. €6, students €4, 16 and under free.*

Inaugurated in 1995, the construction of the gleaming white MACBA, designed by American architect Richard Meier, was the final product of a collaboration between Barcelona's mayor and the Catalan government to restore El Raval by turning the neighborhood into a regional artistic and cultural focal point. The museum's modernity and scale, as well as sheer brightness, are a startling contrast with the narrow alleys and aging cobblestone streets of the neighborhood where it sits. The building's sparse decor was designed to allow the art to speak for itself, which it has—the MACBA has received worldwide acclaim for its focus on avant-garde art between the two world wars. Eclectic, often interactive, and always experimental exhibits focus on three-dimensional art, photography, video, and graphic work from the past 40 years and regularly rotate. Exhibits in 2002 included "Sonic Process: A New Geography of Sounds," an impressive exploration of the hybridization of music and the visual arts, and "Fauna," a reconceptualization of evolution and taxidermy featuring a stuffed, four-winged bird with a turtle shell, among other spectacular things.

L'EIXAMPLE

FUNDACIÓ ANTONI TÀPIES

⛰ C. Aragó, 255. M: Pg. de Gràcia. Around the corner from the Manzana de la Discòrdia, and between Pg. de Gràcia and La Rambla de Catalunya. ☎ 93 487 03 15; www.fundaciotapies.org. Museum open Tu-Su 10am-8pm. Library upstairs open by appointment only, Tu-F 11am-8pm. €4.20, students and seniors €2.10. Wheelchair accessible

Tàpies's massive and bizarre wire sculpture *(Cloud with Chair)* atop Domènech i Montaner's red brick building announces this collection of contemporary, abstract art by Antoni Tàpies and many other contemporary artists from around the world. The top floor of the foundation is dedicated to famous Catalan artists, including Tàpies, while the other two floors feature special exhibits of other popular modern artists.

The Pope at the Wax Museum

Tàpies is one of Catalunya's best-known artists; his art often defies definition, springing out of the traditions of Surrealism and Magicism and drawing inspiration from Picasso and Miró. His works are often a mixture of painting and sculpture, generally referred to as collage, although he is the creator of a number of abstract sculptures as well. Most of his paintings include a "T" in some form, a symbol that has been variously interpreted and misinterpreted as a religious cross, as sexual penetration, and as the artist's own signature. In truth, no one knows the real meaning, if there even is one.

Tàpies's use of unorthodox materials—including objects found in the trash—and his dark, dirty colors are often interpreted as a protest against the dictatorship he grew up under and the subsequent urban alienation he felt pervading Spain's cities. Tàpies's works use everyday materials, like sand, glue, wood, marble powder, dirt, and wire, to show the eloquence inherent in simplicity. Many pieces have been compared to graffiti on city walls: silent, sometimes hideous expressions of protest that are somehow also an expression of art by the way they reflect the closed state of Spain during the time they were created.

The Fundació Tàpies is known for showcasing avant garde contemporary art, from kinetic sculptures to performance art and from globally famous masters to relative unknowns. An exhibit entitled "Tàpies and his books" is slated for the beginning of 2003. The library, reflecting Tàpies's own interests in Asia, is stocked with books on non-Western art and artifacts.

Erotica Museum

Museum of Contemporary Art

FUNDACIÓ FRANCISCO GODIA

∄ *C. València, 284. Go to third floor and ring bell for entrance.* ☎ *93 272 31 80; www.fundacionf-godia.org. Open W-M 10am-8pm. Free guided tours Sa-Su at noon (no English); otherwise call ahead for a guided tour (€6 per person). Wall descriptions and printed guides in English, Spanish, and Catalan. €4.50; students, over 65, and disabled €2.10. Joint ticket with the Museu Egipci (see p. 115) €8.50; students, over 65, and disabled €6.50. MC/V. Wheelchair accessible.*

The Fundació Francisco Godia was created in 1998 by the namesake's daughter in order to open his private art collection for public viewing. Francisco Godia (1921-1990) was a bizarre mix of astute businessman, Spain's best Formula One race car driver, and passionate supporter of the arts. His collection, which fills 10 small rooms, runs from the 12th to the 20th century, with a heavy emphasis on medieval sculpture and painting, Spanish ceramics of the last 500 years, and modern paintings by Spanish artists like Ramon Casas, Isidre Nonell, and José Gutiérrez Solana. Highlights include Solana's bold, dark-lined *Bullfight at Ronda* (1927), Isidre Nonell's dark *Gypsy Woman* (1905), Francesc Gimeno's life-like *Mother and Daughter* (1898), and the popular piece *At the Racecourse* (1905), by Ramon Casas. Be sure to check out the front room filled with Godia's racing trophies, proof that NASCAR and art are not mutually exclusive.

MUSEU DE CLAVEGUERAM (SEWER MUSEUM)

∄ *Pg. de St. Joan, 98. M: Verdaguer.* ☎ *93 457 65 50. Open Tu-Su 9am-2pm. €1.20.*

The Teenage Mutant Ninja Turtles would have approved of Barcelona's openness to quirky museum collections. This one, a documentary on the development of Barcelona's sewers, was inspired by the major infrastructure renovations required for the 1992 Olympics (see p. 47). With a proliferation of pictures and little-known historical information, it traces the city's waste plumbing from Roman times to modern. Unfortunately for curious tourists who have spent many precious euros on water to accompany their restaurant meals, it does not explain Barceloneses' refusal to serve the city's tap water. Kowabunga, dude!

MUSEU DEL CÒMIC I DE LA ILLUSTRACIÓ

∄ *C. Santa Carolina, 25. M: Alfons X. Walk down Trav. de Gràcia and take a right on C. Padilla; C. Santa Carolina is on the left. Knock on the metal door to enter.* ☎ *93 348 15 13; www.inter-ars.com. Open M-Sa 10am-2pm and 5-8pm. €3, under 14 and over 65 €2.10.*

Comic strip artists in Spain have not had an easy time, between the Civil War, the economic difficulties of the postwar years, Franco's censorship, and the overwhelming competition from Japanese animation. This small private collection was carefully put together to serve as a representative sampling of some of the best comics done in Spain between 1915 and the 1970s. For the politically minded, the Franco propaganda aimed directly at children is particularly interesting to see; look for the January 30, 1938 and July 18, 1939 editions of *Flecha*, the *"semanario nacional infantil"* of the time, in order to see proud soldiers grasping the Spanish flag and cheering, "Franco! Franco! Franco!" While the avid comic enthusiast may be drooling at the displays, the one room collection may be a bit tiny and disappointing for those with a taste for bigger bangs for the bucks, especially since the majority of work is in Spanish or Catalan.

MUSEU DE L'ESPORT

∄ *C. Buenos Aires, 56-8. Walk north on C. Villarroel and turn left onto C. Buenos Aires.* ☎ *93 419 22 32. M: Hospital Clinic. Open M-F 10am-2pm and 4-8pm. Free.*

Yup, there are more sports in Spain than soccer, and this museum sets out to prove it. Here, Puig i Cadafalch's Casa Company houses the Museu de l'Esport, a collection focused on Catalan sports.

MUSEU EGIPCI

🚩 *C. València, 284, just to the left off Pg. de Gràcia when facing Pl. de Catalunya. M: Pg. de Gràcia. ☎ 93 488 01 88; www.fundclos.com. Open M-Sa 10am-8pm, Su 10am-2pm. Closed Dec. 25-26 and Jan. 1. Descriptions in Spanish and Catalan. €5.50; students, over 65, and disabled €4.50. Joint admission with the Fundació Godia (next door; see p. 114) €8.50; students, over 65, and handicapped €6.50. Free tours in Spanish and Catalan Sa 11am and 5pm; call ahead to hire an English guide (€8.50). MC/V. Wheelchair accessible.*

In 1993, wealthy Barcelonese Jordi Clos decided to turn a private passion into Spain's only museum dedicated entirely to Pharaonic Egypt. More than 500 Egyptian artifacts, including jewelry, pottery, and several displays focused on tombs, mummies, and the beliefs surrounding death in ancient Egypt pack two floors as tightly as a Pharaoh's tomb. The museum is extremely well-organized (displays are arranged by themes) and accessible; ask for an English guide and receive a 30-page booklet with detailed descriptions of each artifact. Catch the dramatic reenactment of Egyptian legends Friday nights from 9:30 to 11pm, complete with a tour and a cup of *cava* (€12, students 10.50; reservations required).

MUSEU DEL PERFUM

🚩 *Pg. de Gràcia, 39. ☎ 93 216 01 46; www.perfum-museum.com. M: Pg. de Gràcia. Open M-F 11am-1:30pm and 4-8pm. Free.*

The Museu del Perfum is easy to miss, located at the back of a perfectly ordinary-looking perfume store in an inconspicuous building between some of the city's most-admired houses. The collection inside, however, should not be overlooked, with nearly a thousand quirky, varied perfume containers, from second-century BC Roman vials to 14th-century Arab pieces to miniatures from pre-Columbian Ecuador. Some of the more original designs include a mouse, a lightbulb, the Eiffel Tower, and a suicidal bottle with a knife-shaped throat applicator. Even Salvador Dalí took a crack at this little-known art form, with a huge bottle titled "The Sun King."

MUSEU TAURÍ

🚩 *Gran Via de les Corts Catalanes, 749. M: Monumental. ☎ 93 245 58 04. Open M-Sa 11am-2pm and 4-8pm, Su 11am-2pm, fight days 10:30am-1pm. Admission includes entrance to the museum, the bullring, and the bullpens. Museum descriptions in English, Spanish, German, and Italian. €4, children €3.*

This dense, two-room collection proudly commemorates the tradition of bullfighting, with pictures of major fights and fighters, old posters and stamps, a colorful exhibit on the evolution of the bullfighter's costume throughout time, and a good number of stuffed bulls' heads on the walls (minus, of course, however many ears their human opponents earned in completing the kill). You can also see a picture display on one much luckier beast, the first bull to be spared in the Plaza Monumental by unanimous public request (a remarkable feat, after more than 50 years of fights in the ring). Even he lost his ears, though, to reward the efforts of *matador* Andrés Hernando. For tickets to a bullfight (which is a less common form of entertainment in Barcelona than it is in the rest of Spain), see **Entertainment,** p. 177; for some perspective on the sport, see **No Bull,** p. 176. While a bullfight can be off-putting for even the most sturdy stomach, a trip to this museum will satisfy curiosity without the violent repercussions.

GET sm**art**

Miró's Obsessions

Like Dalí, Joan Miró had a repertoire of symbols he employed in his paintings and sculptures to convey certain themes. Calling them his "obsessions," Miró developed this language during WWII when he was living in Normandy. Miró aimed "to express precisely all the golden sparks of our soul." He most frequently painted women and birds. Other obsessions include a **net** (the earth), **stars** (the unattainable heavens), and birds (connecting the two). His symbols are not all so lofty; don't confuse the stars with Miró's infamous **asterisk,** a symbol for the anus.

The colors and images Miró uses in his paintings also serve as a measure of his emotional state and the politics of the time. Paintings with dark backgrounds and brown tones that depict creatures with teeth are generally from the Civil War and dictatorship period (see p. 44), when Miró went into a self-induced exile and subsequent depression; tormented, nightmarish paintings from this time are his form of silent protest. Works with white backgrounds and bright primary colors were created as the dictatorship relaxed and democracy began. The visual optimism of these works reflects Miró's own greatly improved emotional health and hopes for Spain.

see map p. 349

POBLE NOU & PORT OLÍMPIC

MUSEU DE CARROSSES FÚNEBRES (HEARSE MUSEUM)

🏛 *C. Sancho de Ávila, 2. M: Marina. From the Metro, follow Av. Meridiana away from C. Marina until its intersection with C. Sancho de Ávila.* ☎ *93 484 17 00; www.funerariabarcelona.com. Open M-F 10am-1pm and 4-6pm, Sa-Su 10am-1pm. Free, includes a guided tour.*

Enter the gray office building right on the corner (there is no sign for the museum outside, and no apparent street number, but the building is labeled **Serveis Funeraris de Barcelona, S.A.**) and ask at the information desk inside for a tour of the Museu de Carrosses. The museum gets few visitors, so your interest will not go unappreciated by the tour guides, who are happy to talk to anyone alive. This small collection of 22 plush 19th- and early 20th-century horse-drawn hearses may be morbid, but it is also surprisingly intriguing. Only virgins could ride to their grave in white carriages, and only the richest families could afford brocades.

BARCELONETA

see map p. 350

MUSEU D'HISTÒRIA DE CATALUNYA

🏛 *Palau de Mar, Pl. Pau Vila, 3, on the waterfront.* ☎ *93 225 47 00; www.cultura.gencat.es/museus/mhc. €3, students, seniors, and children €2.10. Mandatory bag check €0.50. There is a cafe located on the 4th fl. Open Tu-Sa 10am-7pm, W 10am-8pm, Su 10am-2:30pm. Ask at the front desk to borrow an English or Spanish text guide for free.*

This museum sits in the recently renovated Palau de Mar (Palace of the Sea) building. Although originally constructed in 1900 as a decidedly un-palatial port warehouse, the palace is now one of the most beautiful buildings on the Port Vell waterfront. The two floors of the museum take you on an interactive journey through Catalan history, from its prehistoric roots to the 20th century. The first floor houses temporary exhibits on selected topics in Catalan history. Major displays are in Catalan, English, and Spanish; most secondary displays are in

THE WONDERFUL WORLD OF JOAN MIRÓ

Tourists on the Spanish art circuit tend to run into each other frequently because they are all clamoring to see the same great Spanish masters in two weeks or less. Somehow, between mad dashes to the Prado, the Picasso Museum, and the Teatre-Museu Dalí, not everyone pauses to take note of the works of one of the most innovative artists and endearing characters of 20th-century Spain—Joan Miró.

Miró is often overlooked by travelers, written off as eccentric and inaccessible; his popularity in Spain and his native Catalunya is regarded as peculiar rather than intriguing. Yet commanding an appreciation of his life and of his works is one of the most enriching ways to experience Barcelona, Catalunya, and Spain, for his works chronicle the region's recent turbulent history, and look forward from Franco with a generous, yet distinctly Catalan optimism.

Born in Barcelona in 1893, Joan Miró displayed a strong sense of Catalan nationalism his whole life. In Paris he was exposed to Cubist art but rejected its emphasis on the visual and spatial elements; he made a conscious decision to try to go beyond these plastic elements of painting and sculpture. On returning to Barcelona, Miró produced a series of works that treated everyday Catalan life as subjects. Throughout the 1920s and early 1930s, Miró's works became increasingly intuitive; while his paintings always represent objects and are therefore never abstract (as they are so often mislabeled; for more info on reading Miró's code of objects, see **Miró's Obsessions,** p. 116), the spaces he represents become increasingly simplified and free of gravity, and as the object he paints float away, some of them become difficult to recognize on the simply colored background. His paintings from this world invoke the intuitive world of childhood, not quite yet part of reality or reason.

With Franco's rise to power in 1936, Spain became a dangerous place for artists and intellectuals; Republican Miró retreated into a deep depression and a self-imposed exile on the Balearic islands. His works from the 1940s are moving in the way that they detail not only his depression, but the depression of Catalunya. The backgrounds of his works turned a dark brown, and the focus of his painting became nightmarish creatures with gaping maws, or deformed and perverse characters. *A Man and a Woman in front of a pile of Excrement*, which represents a deformed man and woman celebrating their recent bowel movement (a distinctly Catalan theme; see **Waste with Taste,** p. 144), is one such work from this period that clearly provides a dark, satiric commentary on the state of Catalunya under Franco.

Although Miró refused to sign the Surrealist manifesto, he is Spain's first Surrealist painter, for appreciation of his art depends not on how well he copies objects in the "real world," but on how the observer responds to his infantile interpretation. Although he was not appreciated in his native Spain until the 1970s, he was lauded in Paris throughout the Franco era. As the dictatorship weakened and eventually ended, Miró returned to a brighter and more joyful style of painting in his old age, using white backgrounds and primary colors. He also, for the first time, displayed a sense of Spanish nationalism, which he no longer saw as necessarily in conflict with his Catalan nationalism; his *España* is famous for its bright colors, playful style, and proud declaration of nationalism. It is a forceful and optimistic commentary on his hopes for post-Franco Spain.

Apart from appreciating Miró's art, one also has to admire his activist spirit and presence in Barcelona and Spain. After the fall of the dictatorship, Miró sprinkled every corner of Barcelona with public works of art to try to beautify and re-energize his then-battered city. His mural at the airport is a welcome homecoming for Catalan residents, and his ceramic mural in the center of Las Ramblas is one of the most popular meeting places in the city. His greatest donation to Barcelona is, of course, the Fundació Miró. Rather than creating a museum that was a self-aggrandizing monument to himself (see the **Teatre-Museu Dalí,** p. 216), Miró created this foundation to foster interest in and appreciation of modern art, which had never had a space to display itself safely under Franco. Miró died on Mallorca in 1983, but he is one of the most present artists in Barcelona; his art reaches outside museums and self-referential buildings and lives alongside residents and travelers, in the city itself.

Sarah Kenney was editor of Let's Go: Barcelona 2002. She lived in Barcelona for a year, where she learned to speak Spanish and Catalan. She is currently editing for a spanish-language publishing company in Boston and teaching English for a non-profit organization. She is an avid fan of Floquet de Neu.

GET sm art

An Hour In the Fundació Miró

Room 11: The first room of the permanent collection features **Tapestry of the Foundation**, an enormous work of manifold textures and primary and secondary colors portraying a woman. Note the 8-pointed star and blue moon which signify the heavens.

Between rooms 11 and 12: Look to the left outside of the window at **Mercury Fountain,** created by Miró's close friend Alexander Calder for the 1937 World's Fair and in commemoration of the Civil War-torn town of Almáden. The fountain represents Calder's attempt to embody movement in sculpture.

Room 16: Two of Miró's early paintings, **The Beach of Mont-roig** and **Street in Pedralbes**, show the avant-garde influences of Impressionism, Cubism, and Futurism in his development. The emptiness and total absence of detail in Miró's **Dream Paintings** (1925-1927), portray an eerie dream world that no longer shows "the pull of gravity."

Room 17: In **Self-portrait**, Miró used two amplifying mirrors to evoke the image of his face as a fertile landscape. The adjoining space holds Miró's **Constellation Series** in which, in his attempt to create poetry though visual

(fairly basic) Catalan. One interactive exhibit allows you to try on a full suit of medieval armor while another lets you take a load off at a replica of a 1950s Barcelona soda shoppe.

PORT VELL

see map p. 350

MUSEU MARÍTIM

⊠ *Av. Drassanes, off the rotary around the Monument a Colom, the street to Columbus's back. M: Drassanes.* ☎ *93 342 99 20. Open daily 10am-7pm. €5.40; under 16, students, and seniors €2.70. Wheelchair accessible.*

The *Drassanes Reiales de Barcelona* (Royal Shipyards of Barcelona) began constructing ships for the Catalan-Aragonese empire in the 13th century. Still amazingly well preserved today, the shipyards are considered the world's greatest standing example of Civil (i.e., non-religious) Gothic architecture and are currently awaiting nomination as a UNESCO World Heritage Site. The complex consists of a series of huge indoor bays with slender pillars where entire ships could be constructed at a time and stored over the winter. Since 1941, the building has housed the Maritime Museum, which traces the evolution of shipbuilding and life on the high seas. Surprisingly high-tech and modern, the museum provides detailed and sleekly produced audio guides to the exhibits in English, Spanish, German, and French. Model ships, medieval maps, and detailed dioramas illuminate the maritime history of man from the raft to the submarine. The visit ends with **The Great Adventure of the Sea,** a Disney-like journey through life-size maritime reconstructions. In the galley of an actual 16th-century warship one can watch virtual slaves rowing, or later, under the stars, feel the strong breeze on the deck of a passenger steamship.

MONTJUÏC

see map p. 348

✴ FUNDACIÓ JOAN MIRÓ

⊠ *Av. Miramar, 71-75.* ☎ *93 443 94 70; www.bcn.fjmiro.es. Take the funicular from M: Parallel. Turn left out of the funicular station; the museum is a 5min. walk up on the right. Open July-Aug. Tu-W and F-Sa 10am-8pm, Th 10am-9:30pm, Su 10am-2:30pm; Oct.-June Tu-W and F-Sa 10am-7pm, Th 10am-9:30pm, Su 10am-2:30pm. €7.20, students and seniors €3.90. Wheelchair accessible. In addition to exhibits, the Fundació has a cafe, bookstore, and giftshop.*

Catalunya's Joan Miró was one of the world's greatest Surrealist artists and his thousands of paintings and sculptures represent a never-ending quest to transcend conventional perspectives of the world through the invention of alternative ones. Miró's work is often incorrectly referred to as "abstract" by confused tourists who do not know how to read his paintings; be sure to pick up a free headphone set from the ticket desk to guide you through some of the most famous pieces in the foundation (see **Miró's Obsessions**, p. 116). Miró's works embody an intriguing private world of concrete meanings, and deciphering his imaginative interpretations of the world around him can be remarkably satisfying. For information on individual pieces, see **An Hour In Funació Miró**, p. 118.

Miró's works are a personal and poignant tour through 20th-century Spanish history; his fundamental optimism and generosity have made him one of Spain's—not just Catalunya's—most beloved artists. More than a museum, the Fundació Miró is a rotating collection of 10,000 of the artist's works, pieces by other artists inspired by Miró's unique style, and a foundation to support contemporary art and young Catalan artists. Designed by Miró's friend Josep Luís Sert, the Fundació links interior and exterior spaces with massive windows and outdoor patios. Skylights illuminate an extensive collection of statues, paintings, and *sobreteixims* (multimedia tapestries) from Miró's career. The Fundació also sponsors music recitals in the summer months on Thursdays at 8:30pm (€5), and occasionally hosts film festivals (check the website for listings).

MUSEU ARQUEOLÒGIC DE CATALUNYA

🏛 *Pg. Santa Madrona, 39-41.* ☎ *93 423 21 49; www.mac.es. From M: Espanya, take bus #55 up the hill to the Palau Nacional. When facing the Palau Nacional, the museum is to the left. Open Tu-Sa 9:30am-7pm, Su 10am-2:30pm. €2.40, students and seniors €1.80.*

A vast array of jewelry, earthenware, sculptures, mosaics, and countless other artifacts recovered from Catalonia and the Balearic Islands tries to illustrate the region's dramatic evolution from prehistoric times to the High Middle Ages, but leaves much to the imagination without helpful historical context and explanations. Several rooms feature a collection of Carthaginian art from Ibiza, fascinating models of huge Megalithic funeral monuments, and excavated relics from the Greco-Roman city of Empúries in surrounding Catalunya.

means, he began to develop his own personal language of women, birds, the sun, the moon, and the stars.

Room 18 (upstairs): Figure in front of the Sun is an ambitious work trying to achieve a certain harmony among its disparate elements: a white monochrome background, dramatic black brushstrokes, and vibrant blue, red, and yellow shapes.

Room 19: Sun Bird is an enlarged marble version of a sculpture Miró had been working on in bronze since his youth. Note how the bird mediates between heaven and earth: the fallen moon shape connects the bird to the celestial world while the solid base ties the bird to the terrestrial world.

Room 20: The hope of the man condemned to death, Fireworks, and **Painting on a white ground for the solitary man**, each a three-part work, are products of Miró's experimentation with space, color, and Jackson Pollack's infamous dripping technique.

Room 22: The lark's wing ringed in the blue of gold meets the heart of the poppy asleep in the field of diamonds, with its strongly contrasting colors, epitomizes Miró's desire "to achieve the maximum intensity with the minimum of means." First conceived of as a pair, **Hair pursued by two planets** and **Drop of water on pink snow** were only recently united in the Fundació collection. Note how the two paintings communicate with each other in a sort of natural dialogue through their contrasting colors, shapes, and motifs.

MUSEU ETNOLÒGIC

🛈 *Pg. Santa Madrona, uphill from Museu Arqueològic (see above).* ☎*93 424 68 07; www.museuetnologic.bcn.es. Open W and F-Su 10am-2pm, Tu and Th 10am-7pm. €3, students and seniors €1.50. Free 1st Su of every month.*

Regularly changing exhibits focus on specialized aspects of individual cultures and countries using carefully selected displays of documentary photographs, crafts, and artifacts. Recent exhibits have concerned food in Japan, whistles and flutes of the hispanic world, and the artists of New Mexico who create devotional images of saints. Call ahead for information on current exhibits.

MUSEU MILITAR

🛈 *Inside the **Castell de Montjuïc** (see p. 88). From M: Parallel, take the funicular (every 10min.) to Av. Miramar and then the Teleféric de Montjuïc cable car (open M-Sa 11:15am-9pm) from Av. Miramar to the castle (one-way €3.20, round-trip €4.50). Or, walk up the steep slope on C. Foc, next to the funicular station.* ☎*93 329 86 13. Open Mar. 21-Nov. 14 Tu-Su 9:30am-8pm; Nov. 15-Mar. 20 Tu-Su 9:30am-5pm. Museum entrance €2.50.*

Within its more than twenty rooms, the Museu Militar displays just about every kind of weapon you could imagine a soldier might have carried over the last millennium, as well as countless other Montjuïc relics—it is a particularly fascinating collection due to the castle's rich and sordid history. Keep a close eye out for the impressive miniature models of the fortresses of Catalunya, a series of oil paintings showing leaders of Catalunya beginning from Charlemagne, the eleventh-century tombstones excavated from Montjuïc's Jewish cemetery, Barcelona's only remaining statue of Franco, and the second-largest sword collection in Spain.

MUSEU NACIONAL D'ART DE CATALUNYA (PALAU NACIONAL)

🛈 *From M: Espanya, walk up Av. Reina María Cristina, away from the twin brick towers, and take the escalators to the top.* ☎*93 622 03 60; www.mnac.es. Open Tu-Sa 10am-7pm, Su 10am-2:30pm. €4.80, €6 with temporary exhibits; students and seniors €3.30/€4.20. Free first Th of every month. Wheelchair accessible.*

Designed by Enric Catá, Pedro Cendoya, and Pere Domènech for the 1929 International Exposition (see **Life & Times,** p. 54), the beautifully august Palau Nacional has housed the Museu Nacional d'Art de Catalunya since 1934. The view from the Palau is one of the best in all of Barcelona. Its main hall is often used for public events, while the wings are home to the world's finest collection of Catalan Romanesque art and a wide variety of Gothic pieces. The Romanesque frescoes, now integrated as murals into dummy chapels, were salvaged from their original, less protected locations in northern Catalunya's churches in the 1920s by Barcelona's city government. The result is a surprisingly spiritual tour through some of Catalunya's medieval masterpeices. The museum's Gothic art corridor displays murals from stately homes and religious buildings in Mallorca and its paintings evoke the Gothic preoccupation with the gruesome martyrings of saints. The images of beheadings, impalings, burnings, buryings, and crucifixions are not for the faint of heart. The corridor features painters Jaume Huguet and Bartolomé Bermejo.

In the midst of these displays, the MNAC is constructing and renovating separate areas of the building to house the Museu d'Art Modern collection, which will be displayed here beginning sometime in 2003, allowing the museum to display an even broader collection of Catalan art. The museum also hosts temporary exhibits; 2002 showcased a breathtaking photo display of the concentration camps of the Holocaust.

ZONA ALTA

GRÀCIA

see map p. 346

CASA-MUSEU GAUDÍ

🏠 *Inside Park Güell (see **Sights,** p. 91), to the right of the Hall of One Hundred Columns when facing away from the sea. Closest direct park entrance is Carretera del Carmel.* ☎ *93 219 38 11. Open daily Nov.-Feb. 10am-6pm; Mar.-Apr. and Oct. 10am-7pm; May-Sept. 10am-8pm. Last entrance is 15min. before closing. €2.40.*

Ironically designed not by Gaudí but by his friend and colleague, Fransesc Berenguer, the Casa-Museu Gaudí was the celebrated architect's home from 1906 to 1926 until he moved into the Sagrada Família several months before his death. Gaudí's leftover fence work from other projects was used to create the garden of metallic plant sculptures in front of the museum. The three-story house is a great place to examine close-up Gaudí's anatomical furniture designs from the Casa Batlló, paintings of several of his works by notable artists, and the master's own austere bedroom, where the bronze cast of his death mask keeps an eye on visitors. The third floor displays several pieces by the sculptor Carlos Mani, who collaborated with Gaudí on La Sagrada Família. Before leaving, peek into the Modernist bathroom where the toilet seat curves in Gaudí's trademark saddle-shape.

PEDRALBES & LES CORTS

🏟 MUSEU DEL FÚTBOL CLUB BARCELONA

🏛 *C. Aristides Maillol, next to the stadium. M: Collblanc. Enter through access gates 7 or 9.* ☎ *93 496 36 08. Museum entrance €4.80, children under 13 €3.50; with 45min. stadium tour €8.90, children under 13 €3.50. Tours run every 15 min. Open M-Sa 10am-6:30pm, Su 10am-2pm.*

Busloads of tour groups from all over the world pour into this museum, making it a close second to the Picasso Museum as Barcelona's most visited. The museum merits all the attention it gets, as it has created a fitting homage to one of soccer's greatest clubs. Any sports fan will appreciate the storied history of the team, which began in 1899 when a Swiss soccer star, Hans Gamper, moved to Barcelona and gathered together a group interested in playing soccer. Recent greats

Museu del Perfum

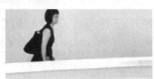

Fundació Miró

At the Fundació Miró

on the team include Maradona, Ronaldo, Luis Figo, and current stars Kluivert and Rivaldo. Room after room displays countless cups the team has won, including the coveted European Cup won in 1992. Other areas exhibit art related to the sport of soccer and photos of past teams; check out some of the funky uniform variations on the familiar blue and burgundy team colors. The high point, especially if you can't get to an actual match, is the chance to enter the stadium itself, sit down on the second level, and take in the enormity of the stadium, **Camp Nou** (see p. 175). In addition, the tour shows you the museum, dressing rooms, a tunnel to the playing field, and players' benches. In the same complex, a gift shop sells all varieties of official FCB merchandise, and stands outside offer hamburgers, hot dogs, and drinks.

COLLECIÓ THYSSEN-BORNEMISZA

🚩 *Baixada del Monestir, 9, in the Monestir de Pedralbes (see p. 96). FCG: Reina Elisenda. ☎ 93 481 10 41; www.museothyssen.org. Same hours as the monastery. €3, students and over 65 €1.80, under 16 free. Combined ticket with monastery €4.80, students €3, children free.*

The former dormitory of the St. Clare nuns now houses a small but impressive collection of medieval, Renaissance, and Baroque art, consisting almost entirely of religious paintings from the larger collection in Madrid. Highlights include works by Velázquez, Rubens, and Fra Angelico. A must-see for art-history buffs.

MUSEU DE CERÀMICA

🚩 *Av. Diagonal, 686, 2nd and 3rd floors of the Palau Reial. M: Palau Reial. ☎ 93 280 16 21; fax 93 205 45 18; www.museuceramica.bcn.es. One ticket gets you into both this museum and the Museu de les Arts Decoratives (see below). Keep your receipt for entrance into La Ribera's Museu Tèxtil i d'Indumentària (see p. 110), the 3rd of Catalunya's "Museums of Applied Arts," up to one month after purchase. Open Tu-Sa 10am-6pm, Su and holidays 10am-3pm. €3.50, students under 25 €2.50, under 16 free.*

Everything you ever wanted to know about Spain's tradition of ceramics is on display in the Museu de Ceràmica, which traces the evolution of Spanish ceramic sculpture from the 11th century to the present. The displays show off skillfully crafted plates, tiles, jars, and bowls gathered from all regions of Spain. The true highlight is found upstairs in the more abstract 20th-century collection, which contains a room featuring a small collection of ceramic works by Picasso and Miró; imagine drinking *sangria* out of a pitcher designed by the master of Cubism. One of Barcelona's three museums of "applied arts" (the other two are the Museu de les Arts Decoratives, below, and the Museu Tèxtil i d'Indumentària on p. 110), it may only be worth the visit if you are a true art history lover.

MUSEU DE LES ARTS DECORATIVES

🚩 *Av. Diagonal, 686. M: Palau Reial, on the 2nd floor of the Palau Reial (see p. 96) opposite the Museu de Ceràmica. ☎ 93 280 50 24; fax 93 280 18 74; www.museuartsdecoratives.bcn.es. Same ticket at Museu de Ceràmica; see above.*

Recognizing the artistic value of items often taken for granted in daily life, the Museum of Decorative Arts displays home furnishings from as far back as the Middle Ages. Take a walk through history and appreciate (or regret) how far we've come. A large collection of 19th-century furniture shows how the Catalan bourgeoisie lived. The eclectic collection also contains such items as a mop and bucket from the 1950s and an extensive display of industrial furniture from the 20th century.

TIBIDABO

🖼 MUSEU D'AUTÒMATS

🚩 *Located inside the Parc d'Attracions. Same hours as the park (see p. 99). Free with park admission.*

A remarkably entertaining collection of 19th- and 20th-century automated displays, from models of ski hills and the park itself to full-fledged jazz bands, dancers in ballrooms, and a winking gypsy. Just press the green buttons and watch 'em go. Be sure to catch the morbid recreation of an automated beheading and hanging, all in miniature dimensions.

MUSEU-CASA VERDAGUER

🏛 *Carretera de les Planes. ☎ 93 204 78 05; call ☎ 93 315 11 11 for a guided tour. FGC: Baixador de Vallvidrera. Follow signs from the train station. Open Sa-Su 10am-2pm. Free.*

Jacint Verdaguer, the most important poet of the Catalan literary Renaissance, lived in this 16th-century house for 24 days before dying on June 10, 1902. Verdaguer is known for winning the Catalan poetry contest, *Jocs Florals*, with his epic poem *L'Atlantida*. The rooms have been preserved as they were before his death, and detailed explanations of the artist's life and works fill the house; unfortunately for many visitors, all the explanations are in Catalan. The path up to the museum is peppered with his poetry, also in Catalan.

MUSEU DE LA CIÈNCIA

🏛 *C. Teodor Roviralta, 55. ☎ 93 212 60 50.*

Located at the halfway stop on the bus or tram from Pl. JFK to Pl. Dr. Andreu, the recently renovated science museum offers extremely well-organized, hands-on exhibits great for kids.

GALLERIES

One of the capitals of cutting-edge art, Barcelona showcases many of the latest artistic trends. Many private showings display the works of both budding artists and renowned masters, but don't expect cheap finds on either count. Most of Barcelona's galleries are located in **La Ribera** around **C. Montcada.** The following galleries all welcome visitors and carry museum-quality works.

Galería Maeght, C. Montcada, 25 (☎93 310 42 45; www.maeght.com). M: Jaume I, in **La Ribera.** Two floors of display including pieces from Miró, Tàpies, Calder, and Giacometti enhanced by the architecture of the authentic *palau* it inhabits. Shop carries a wide selection of art books (€22+), prints, posters, and postcards. Open Tu-Sa 10am-2pm and 4-8pm.

Galería Surrealista, C. Montcada, 19 (☎93 310 33 11; fax 93 310 68 15). M: Jaume I, in **La Ribera.** Next to the Museu Picasso, and just as well-stocked. Specializes entirely in the work of Dalí, Miró, and Picasso, featuring limited editions, lithographs, and ceramics. Picasso's *Guernica* sketches are a steal at a mere €901.50 each. A couch of hot pink lips spices up the scene. Open M-Sa 10am-8pm.

ARTquitect, C. Comerc, 31 (☎93 844 40 71; fax 93 844 40 71). M: Barceloneta, in **La Ribera.** Finding beauty in the art of bathroom design, a quirky gallery for those tired of traditional art. Eccentricity and function combine in the well-lighted displays of bowls and baths. Who knew a plunger could be art? Open M-F 10am-2pm and 4-8pm, Sa 11am-8pm.

Galería Montcada, C. Montcada, 20 (☎93 268 00 14; fax 93 415 46 94; www.galeria-montcada.com). M: Jaume I, in **La Ribera.** Small gallery in the historic Palau Dalmases. Rotating, month-long exhibits generally spotlight Catalan artists. Best bet for (possibly) affordable art. Open Tu-Su 11am-2pm and 4-8pm.

Círculo del Arte, C. Princesa, 52 (☎93 268 88 20; fax 93 319 26 51), in **La Ribera.** M: Jaume I. Spacious modern gallery with seasonal exhibits. Showcases mainly Spanish artists, with a sprinkling of Germans and Americans. Regular offerings of Miró, Calder, Keith Haring, and Claes Oldenburg. Open M-Sa 11am-2pm and 4:30-8pm, Su 11am-2pm.

Food & Drink

You can't turn a corner in Barcelona without encountering a restaurant, cafe, *cafetería*, or sidewalk food vendor. Food in Barcelona is delicious, of course, and more diverse than you'll find in the rest of Spain. Almost everywhere that sells food also sells alcohol, even McDonald's. Below are listings of restaurants ranked by neighborhood; for a table of food by type, see p. 127. For a Spanish-language menu reader, see p. 133; for a brief synopsis of some Catalan specialties, see p. 140.

see map p. 338-339

BARRI GÒTIC & LAS RAMBLAS

The Barri Gòtic is a gold mine of eclectic restaurants, from typical Catalan to Indian, Basque, vegetarian, Middle-Eastern, and more. Most food spots are unpretentious and intimate by default (not much space in these old, old buildings). Between meals, the best places for coffee, drinks, and just hanging out are the Pl. Reial and the *plaças* surrounding the Església Santa Maria del Pi. For late-night munchies or to keep to a super-tight budget, head to the popular falafel and schwarma stands; the best options in price and taste are **Maoz Falafel** (C. Ferran 13; falafel €3.50; open Su-Th 11am-2am, F-Sa 11am-3am) and **Buen Bocado** (C. Escudellers 31; falafel €2, schwarma €3; open Su-Th 1pm-2am, F-Sa 1pm-2:30am).

FOOD BY TYPE

AMERICANESQUE
Chicago Pizza Pie Factory (137)	EIX
Hard Rock Café (149)	EIX
Vips (149)	EIX

BASQUE
Euskal Etxea (133)	LR
Irati (128)	BG
Txapela (136)	EIX
Txirimiri (133)	LR

BREAKFAST
Bar Estudiantil (142)	EIX
Cafeteria Estació de França (142)	LR
La Table Du Pain (135)	ER
Sechi Caffé Italiano (142)	GR
The Bagel Shop (131)	BG

BUFFET
A-Tipic (139)	EIX
El Club dels Aventurers (147)	TI
El Rodizio Grill (138)	EIX
FresCo (148)	EIX
Restaurante Biocenter (136)	ER
Restaurante Self Naturista (131)	BG
Terrablava (131)	BG

CAFÉS
Aroma (149)	CH
Arc Café (130)	BG
Café del Born (134)	LR
Café Torino (137)	EIX
Carmelitas (135)	ER
Cullera de Boix (139)	EIX
Escribà (127)	Rmbl
Foix de Sarrià (146)	SAR
Il Caffe di Roma (149)	CH
Jamaica (149)	CH
La Colmena (131)	BG
Laie Llibreria Café (138)	EIX
Suborn (133)	LR
Tèxtil Café (133)	LR

CATALAN
A'Rogueira (146)	SAR
Bar Restaurante Romesco (136)	ER
Can Cargol (138)	EIX
Can Cortada (145)	HO
Can Travi Nou (145)	HO
Casa Joana (146)	SAR
Colibrí (132)	ER
El Asador de Aranda (147)	TI
El Cargolet Picant (146)	LC
El Raconet (140)	EIX
El Tastavins (144)	GR
Els Quatre Gats (130)	BG
Enng (141)	PN
Font de Les Planes (147)	TI
L'Ancora (146)	LC

La Font de Prades (143)	MJ
La Parra (146)	ST
La Pérgola (143)	MJ
La Venta (147)	TI
Les Quinze Nits (128)	BG
Los Caracoles (128)	BG
Madrid-Barcelona (136)	EIX
Merendero de la Mari (142)	PV
Restaurante Bar Marcelino (143)	MJ
Restaurante Can Lluís (134)	ER
Restaurante Casa Dario (132)	EIX
Restaurante Maravillas (146)	SAR
Restaurante Riera (134)	ER
Restaurante Terrani (139)	EIX
Via Veneto (146)	SAR

CHINESE
Wok & Bol (138)	EIX

CRÊPES
Xavi Petit (145)	GR

CUBAN
La Habana Vieja (131)	LR

GALICIAN
Botafumeiro (143)	GR

HEALTH FOOD
Hostal de Rita (136)	EIX
Kamasawa (130)	BG
Mamacafé (135)	ER
Restaurante Casa Regina (144)	GR
Restaurante Illa de Gràcia (144)	GR

ICE CREAM
Italiano's (128)	Rmbl

INDIAN
Govinda (131)	BG
Shalimar (135)	ER

INDONESIAN
Betawi (131)	BG

INTERNATIONAL
Bar Ra (134)	ER
El Criollo (140)	EIX
El Racó d'en Baltá (139)	EIX
Gades (131)	LR
Harmony (140)	EIX
La Cocotte (132)	LR
Oolong (130)	BG
Silenus (135)	ER
Pla dels Angels (134)	ER

ITALIAN
Buenas Migas (134)	ER
Calero's Pizzeria (146)	ST
Giorgio (137)	EIX
Il Mercante di Venezia (129)	BG
El Salón (129)	BG
La Gavina (144)	GR
PastaFiore (148)	CH

MORE FOOD BY TYPE

JAPANESE
Ginza (140) — EIX
Taira (132) — LR

MIDDLE EASTERN & AFRICAN
dahabi (140) — EIX
Equinox Sol (145) — GR
NUT (144) — GR
Thiossan (130) — BG

MEDITERRANEAN
Agua (141) — PO
Café Miranda (138) — EIX
La Provença (140) — EIX
Mandongo (142) — PV

PAN-ASIAN
Mandalay Café (138) — EIX
Mandongo (142) — PV

SANDWICH SHOPS
Bocatta (149) — CH
Fresh & Ready (148) — CH
La Baguetina Catalana (148) — BG
Mauri (137) — EIX
Pans & Co. (147) — CH
Sandwich & Friends (132) — LR
Venus Delicatessen (129) — BG
Xaloc (131) — BG

SEAFOOD
Agua (141) — PO
Café L'Imma (142) — BAR
La Mar Salada (142) — BAR
La Muscleria (138) — EIX
La Oca Mar (141) — PO
La Taverna d'en Pep (142) — BAR
Merendero de la Mari (142) — PV
Restaurante Salamanca (143) — BAR

SPANISH
Bar Restautante Los Toreros (135) — ER
Café de l'Opera (127) — Rmbl
Campechano (139) — EIX
L'Antic Bocoi del Gòtic (129) — BG
La Bodegueta (139) — EIX
Mi Burrito y Yo (128) — BG

TAPAS BARS
ba-ba-reeba (136) — EIX
Barcelónia (133) — LR
Cal Pep (133) — LR
Euskal Etxea (133) — LR
Irati (128) — BG
La Flauta (140) — EIX
TapasBar (148) — PV
Txapela (136) — EIX
Txirimiri (133) — LR
Va de Vi (132) — LR
Xampanyet (132) — LR

THAI
Thai Gardens (136) — EIX

VEGETARIAN/VEGAN
Comme-Bio (137) — EIX
Govinda (131) — BG
Juicy Jones (128) — BG
La Buena Tierra (144) — GR
L'Hortet (135) — ER
Restaurante Illa de Gràcia (144) — GR
Restaurante Self Naturista (131) — BG

LEGEND
BAR=Barceloneta	MJ=Montjuïc
BG=Barri Gòtic	PN=Poble Nou
CH=Chains	PO=Port Olímpic
EIX=Eixample	PV=Port Vell
ER=El Raval	Rmbl=Las Ramblas
GR=Gràcia	SAR=Sarrià
HO=Horts	ST=Sants
LC=Les Corts	TI=Tibidabo
LR=La Ribera	

LAS RAMBLAS

Food on Las Ramblas is everywhere and generally unremarkable; people eat at the restaurants here, which are mostly carbon copies of each other, more for the experience and convenience than the delicacies.

Escribà, Las Ramblas, 83 (☎93 301 60 27). M: Liceu. Delight in one of their tempting pastries while watching the world go by on La Rambla de les Flores. This small, classy cafe recalls the Barcelona of 1906, when the cafe was founded. There's no menu; just choose a pastry from the case at the front counter and they'll bring it to your table. Outside seating is available. Coffee €1.20, pastries €2-3. Open daily 8:30am-9pm. ❶

Café de l'Opera, Las Ramblas, 74 (☎93 317 75 85). M: Liceu. A drink at this Barcelona institution was typically a post-opera tradition for bourgeois Barcelonese. Today, the cafe caters to a mostly middle-aged crowd of many classes. Outdoor seating is available. Hot chocolate €1.70, *churros* €1.20, Tapas €2.20-6.60. Open M-Sa 9am-2:30am, Su 9am-3pm. ❶

TAPAS 101

Hopping from one tapas bar to another is a fun and cheap way to pass the evening. Don't wait to be seated and don't look for a waiter to serve you; most tapas bars are self-serve and standing room only. Take a plate and help yourself to the toothpick-skewered goodies that line the bars. Keep your toothpicks—they'll be tallied up on your way out to determine your bill. If you're tired of standing at the bar, most places offer more expensive sit-down menus as well. Barcelona's many tapas (sometimes called *pintxos*) bars, concentrated in La Ribera and Gràcia, often serve *montaditos*, thick slices of bread topped with all sorts of delectables from sausage to tortillas to anchovies. Vegetarian tapas are rare—be forewarned, for example, that slender white strands on some *montaditos* are actually eels masquerading as noodles. Generally served around lunchtime and dinnertime, *montaditos* are presented on platters at the bar. *Montaditos* go well with a glass of *cava*, bubbly Spanish champagne, or even a cup of *sidra*, a sour alcoholic cider generally poured from several feet above your glass.

Italiano's, Las Ramblas, 78. Nothing goes better with ice cream on a hot summer day than a half-liter of beer, right? Test it out for yourself at this popular *heladería/cervecería*. Try the *gofres* (Belgian waffles; €1.75). Single scoop €1,50, triple €2.70. Beers €3. Coffee, tea, or *horchata* €1.60-3.60. Open daily 10am-2am. ❶

LOWER BARRI GÒTIC

Les Quinze Nits, Pl. Reial, 6 (☎ 93 317 30 75). M: Liceu. In the back left corner of the plaza coming from Las Ramblas through Pl. Reial. Without a doubt, one of the most popular restaurants in Barcelona, with nightly lines of up to 50 people waiting to get in (don't be afraid—they move quickly). Stylish white-linen decor with minimalist, ambient lighting. Delicious Catalan entrees at unbelievable prices (€3-7). Come at lunch time to avoid the crowds and take advantage of the daily lunch *menú* (€6-7). No reservations. Open daily 1-3:45pm and 8:30-11:30pm. MC/V. ❶

Irati, C. Cardenal Casañas, 17 (☎93 302 30 84). M: Liceu. An excellent Basque restaurant that attracts droves of hungry tapas-seekers. Ask for a plate, fill it with creative nibblers from the long bar covered in serving platters, and they'll count the toothpicks at the end to figure out your bill (€1 apiece). Bartenders also pour Basque *sidra* (cider) behind their backs—with the bottle high above your glass. Starters around €9. Entrees €15-18. Open daily noon-1am. AmEx/MC/V. ❷

Los Caracoles, C. Escudellers, 14 (☎93 301 20 41). M: Drassanes. What started as a snail shop in 1835 is now a presumably more lucrative Catalan restaurant with mouth-watering decor: chickens roasting over open flames, walls and ceilings covered with oversized veggies and utensils, and your food sizzling in front of you in the walk-through kitchen. Dishes taste as good as they look; specialties include, of course, the *caracoles* (snails; €7.21), half of a rabbit (€10.22), and chicken (€9.02). Expect a wait for dinner. Open daily 1pm-midnight. AmEx/MC/V. ❸

Mi Burrito y Yo, Paso de la Enseñanza, 2 (☎93 318 27 42). M: Jaume I, in the Barri Gòtic. To the left off C. Ferran immediately after Pl. St. Jaume. Not a touristy Mexican joint (burrito here means "little donkey"), but one of the most inviting, lively grill-restaurant/*bodegas* in the city. The basement room is warm, with red plaid decor and nightly live music starting at 9:30pm. Specialties include grilled meat *(carne a la brasa)*. Starters around €8. Most entrees €10-20. Open daily 1-4pm and 6:30-11:30pm. AmEx/MC/V. ❹

Juicy Jones, Cardenal Casañas, 7 (☎93 302 43 30; group dinner reservations ☎606 20 49 06). M: Liceu. A touch of psychedelic flower-power in Barcelona, with wildly decorated walls and a long bar spilling over with fresh fruit. The creative vegan *Menú* (€7) features rice, veggies, soups, and salad (after 1pm only). Plethora of fresh juices in creative combinations €2-3.50. Dining room in the back with low ceiling and limited seating. Open daily 10am-11:30pm. Cash only. ❷

L'Antic Bocoi del Gòtic, Baixada de Viladecols, 3 (☎93 310 50 67). M: Jaume I. At the end of the street that starts as C. Dagueria, a left off C. Jaume I coming from Pl. del Angel (it changes names 3 times en route). For the most part, the only tourists who come to this small, intimate restaurant/*bodega* are those invited by local friends; formed in part by a first-century Roman wall, it's precisely the kind of tiny, romantic, and hard-to-find place one imagines stumbling upon in the "Gothic Quarter." Salads, pâtés, and sausages around €6; gourmet cheeses €9-11. Wine €9-18 per bottle. Open M-Sa 8:30pm-midnight. AmEx/MC/V. ❷

Café de l'Opera

Il Mercante di Venezia, C. Jose Anselmo Clavé, 11 (☎93 317 18 28). M: Drassanes. Gold drapes, dim lighting, and a lengthy menu of Italian food make this perfect for a romantic meal. Gnocchi is their specialty, and they offer a wide range of creative dishes featuring the small potato dumplings. Pasta €6; pizza €5.75-8.75; meat and fish dishes €7-12. Reservations recommended, and are necessary on Friday and Saturday nights (people are reserved in one of two seatings, either at 8:30 or 11pm; 11pm seating is less rushed). Open Tu-Sa 11am-2:45pm and 8:30pm-midnight (a bit later on F and Sa), Su 8:30pm-midnight. MC/V. Just a few minutes farther along C. Clavé, in Pl. Duc de Medinaceli, sister restaurant **Le Tre Venezie** (☎93 342 42 52) serves similar food in a sharper, cooler atmosphere, better for larger parties. Open W-Sa 1:30-4pm and 8:30pm-midnight, Su 1:30-3:30pm. ❷

Les Quinze Nits

Venus Delicatessen, C. Avinyó, 25 (☎93 301 15 85). M: Liceu. Take a right off C. Ferran coming from Las Ramblas. With a black-and-white tiled floor and monthly local art shows on the stucco walls, this Mediterranean cafe fits in well with the funky scene on C. Avinyó. All of their food is made with "mucho amor," and includes a variety of creative salads. Try the *ensalada erótica* with lasagna, hummus, or an omelette and a glass of wine while you watch the street that inspired Picasso's *Mademoiselles d'Avignon*. Coffee, wine, pastries, and a large selection of vegetarian dishes (€6-8.50). Salads €5. Open M-Sa noon-midnight. Cash only. ❷

El Salón, C. l'Hostal d'en Sol, 6-8 (☎93 315 21 59). M: Jaume I. Follow Via Laietana toward the water, turn right on C. Gignàs, and then right on tiny l'Hostal d'en Sol. This mellow bar-bistro is the perfect place to unwind after a day spent jostling fellow tourists. The terrace, nestled against a large section of first-century Roman wall, offers a taste of relaxing *plaça* life in one of the least-touristed parts of the Barri Gòtic. Plates of

Pouring Sidra at Irati

Ham-ing It Up

Jamón. The word pervades every menu, butcher shop, and household not only Barcelona but in all of Spain. On tapas, on the plate, and in your mouth, avoiding this porcine obsession proves almost as difficult as successfully ordering tap water at a Barcelona restaurant. Frito-Lay even makes *Jamón! Jamón!* flavored chips. To say that Spaniards worship ham is not that far off the mark—the infamous obsequiousness of the meat has religious origins. During the Spanish Inquisition, when thousands of Jews and Muslims were being persecuted as heretics, Spaniards of all religious backgrounds would eat pork products as a way of showing their Christian allegiance and avoiding the wrath of the Church. The reasoning was, the more ham you ingested, the less likely you were to fall under suspicion. While the Inquisition eventually ended, the cult of *jamón* had caught on. Ham consumption transformed into a show of nationalism rather than religious affiliation. Nowadays, most Spaniards would probably not describe their ham as either pious or patriotic. To them, it's just plain yummy.

bruschetta, gnocchi, chicken, or fish €6-12. Wine €1.80-5.40, cocktails €4.50. Restaurant open M-Sa 2-5pm and 8:30pm-midnight. Bar open daily 2pm-2:30am. AmEx/MC/V. ❷

Oolong, C. Gignàs, 25 (☎93 315 12 59). M: Jaume I, a right off Via Laietana coming from the Metro. A small but hip hole-in-the-wall that serves self-described *"comida mundial divertida"* (fun international food). The menu includes everything from duck breast, tortellini, and chicken fajitas to veggies with mango sauce and Caribbean salad. Salads €4.40-7.90. Hot dishes €4.10-11. Open M-Sa 8pm-2am, Su 8pm-1am. Cash only. ❷

Kamasawa, C. Escudellers, 39 (☎658 33 30 30). M: Liceu or Drassanes. An alternative experience in every sense of the word, with dim lighting, wedding-like decor (including twisting faux-marble columns and draped white veils), and exotic, romantic twists on health food, using everything from fruit and veggies to rice, noodles, and tofu. Salads €6-9. *Menú* €12-15. Open daily 6pm-1am. Cash only. ❷

Arc Café, C. Carabassa, 19 (☎ 93 302 52 04). M: Drassanes. Turn onto C. Clavé (turns into C. Ample) from Las Ramblas and make the fifth left; restaurant will be on your right. If you're looking to get away from the crowded areas of Barri Gòtic, this gay-friendly cafe and bar serves creative soups and salads in a cozy, out-of-the-way niche. Watch them prepare your meal in the corner kitchen. Entrees €3.50-7, lunch *menú* €7. Open M-Th 9am-2am, F 9am-3am, Su 11am-2am. ❷

Thiossan, C. del Vidre, 3 (☎93 3317 10 31). M: Liceu. Just off Pl. Reial, in the left corner toward the waterfront. A small funky Senegalese restaurant/bar/chill-out room, with good reggae music, great wall hangings, very friendly staff, and a limited but unique menu: to drink, beer, ginger, or *bissap* (€2) and to eat, the daily African plate (€5.40). Open Su and Tu-Th 8:30pm-2am, F-Sa 8:30pm-3am. Cash only. ❶

UPPER BARRI GÒTIC

▨ **Els Quatre Gats,** C. Montsió, 3 (☎93 302 41 40). M: Catalunya. Take the 2nd left off Av. Portal de l'Angel. Usually translated as "the four cats," *Els Quatre Gats* is actually a figurative Catalan expression meaning "just a few guys," an ironically diminutive name considering the cafe's prestigious clientele. An old Modernist hangout of Picasso's with lots of Bohemian character; he loved it so much he designed a personalized menu (on display at Museu Picasso; see p. 109). Ramon Casas left his artistic mark as well, in the form of a self-portrait of himself and a fellow artist on a bicycle built for two (on display in the Museu d'Art Modern; see p. 111). Reproductions of these works and more adorn the walls. The restaurant tends to attract more tourists than locals, but it is definitely worth having one nice meal here. Food is expensive (entrees around €12-15), making tapas the best way to go (about €2-4). Coffee is also cheap (€1) and good. Live piano and violin 9pm-1am. Open M-Sa 9am-2am, Su 5pm-2am. Closed Aug. AmEx/MC/V. ❸

Betawi, C. Montsió, 6 (☎93 412 62 64). M: Catalunya. Take the 2nd left off Portal de l'Angel coming from the Metro. A peaceful, delicately decorated Indonesian restaurant with small tapestry-covered tables and woven place mats. The food verges on gourmet, both in taste and size. Menú €7.81. Most entrees €7-9. Open M 1-4pm, Tu-Sa 1-4pm and 8-11pm. AmEx/MC/V. ❷

Govinda, Pl. Vila de Madrid, 4 (☎93 318 77 29). M: Catalunya. Just to the right off Las Ramblas on C. Canuda. A flute-playing mural of Krishna greets happy vegetarian and vegan customers. A true child of globalization: vegetarian Indian food served a few feet from a row of Roman tombs that are nearly 2000 years old, in one of the world's most pork-crazed countries. Serves *thali* (traditional Indian "sampler" meals with a variety of dishes on one platter; €15.50-18.50), as well as spring rolls, crepes, rice, Indian bread, fruit *lassis*, and more. International salad bar €4-6. M-F menú €8. Most entrees around €7. Open daily 1-4pm, for dinner Tu-Th 8-11pm and F-Sa 8-11:45pm. AmEx/MC/V. ❷

Xaloc, C. de la Palla, 13-17 (☎93 301 19 90). M: Liceu. From Las Ramblas, turn onto C. Casanas, walk straight through Pl. del Pi onto C. de las Casanas; the restaurant is on your left. Tucked away on a small side street away from the chaos, this classy delicatessen has a restaurant right next to the butcher counter. Specialties include salads (€3.40-6), meat and poultry sandwiches on tasty baguettes (€2.90-7.30), a selection of *carpaccios*, and an extensive wine list. Tapas €.80-60. Open daily 9am-midnight. MC/V. ❶

La Colmena, Pl. de l'Angel, 12 (☎93 315 13 56). M: Jaume I. After more than 120 years in the Pl. de l'Angel, this absolutely divine pastry and candy shop has more than earned its prime location. Don't walk in unless you're prepared to buy, because you *will*—no one's strong enough to resist. Most pastries €1-3. Open daily 9am-9pm. AmEx/MC/V. ❶

The Bagel Shop, C. Canuda, 25 (☎93 302 41 61). M: Catalunya. Walk down Las Ramblas and take the 1st left and then bear right onto C. Canuda. Barcelona meets New York City. Diverse bagel selection (€0.55 each), bagel sandwiches, and varied spreads, from cream cheese and peanut butter to caramel and chocolate (€3-6). Try a speciality Catalan bagel. M-Sa you can get a bagel or croissant and coffee or tea for €1.68. Sept.-June they serve a Su pancake and eggs brunch 11am-4pm (€4.80-5.10). Open M-Sa 9:30am-9:30pm, Su (Sept.-June only) 11am-4pm. Cash only. **Branch** at Pl. Rius i Taulet, 8. ❶

Terrablava, Via Laietana, 55 (☎93 322 15 85). An all-you-can-eat buffet of veggies, pasta, pizza, meat dishes, fruit, coffee, and probably the best salad bar in the area. Lunchtime brings a circus of famished locals. Food also available a la carte to go. Buffet €8.40 (includes tax and a drink). Open daily 12:30pm-1am. Cash only. ❷

Restaurante Self Naturista, C. Santa Anna, 11-17 (☎93 318 26 84). M: Catalunya, right off Las Ramblas. A self-service vegetarian cafeteria with enormous selection and enough dessert options to fill a bakery. Entrees under €3. Lunch menú €6.50. Open M-Sa 11:30am-10pm. Cash only. ❶

LA RIBERA

see map p. 341

East of Via Laietana, La Ribera is home to numerous bars and small restaurants. The neighborhood's narrow allies and luminous, old-fashioned street lamps make for romantic dinners.

RESTAURANTS

🛡 **La Habana Vieja,** Carrer dels Banys Vells, 2 (☎93 268 25 04). M: Jaume I. Banys Vells is parallel to C. Montcada. Pulsing Cuban music sets the mood in this family-style place. Large portions great for sharing among friends. Cuban rice €3.60-5.42; meat dishes €9.60-12. Open Tu-Su 10am-4:30pm and 8:30pm-1am, M 10am-4:30pm and 8:30-11pm. ❷

Gades, C. L'Esparteria, 10 (☎93 310 44 55). M: Jaume I Enter C. Vidreira across from C. Montcada off Pg. del Born, and first left onto C. L'Esparteria. Get your "dip" on in the romantic, dark stone walls of this fondue heaven. A wide range of cheese fondues (€10.60) are a

the BIG
$plurge

Colibri, C. Riera Alta, 33-35 (☎93 443 23 06). M: Sant Antoni. From the Metro, head down C. Riera Alta; it will be on your right at the intersection with C. Sant Vincenç. Every morning the chef at Colibri goes to the market to buy the freshest and finest ingredients available. In the evening he turns them into the most divinely flavored dishes you have ever tasted. Friendly, English-speaking staff complements the elegant but unpretentious atmosphere. The pistachio vinaigrette sea bass filet (€25.09) is unbelievable. Call ahead for reservations. Open M-F 1:30-3:30pm and 8:30-11:30pm. ❺

Restaurante Casa Dario, C. Consell de Cent, 256 (☎93 453 31 35). M: Universitat. From Pl. de la Universitat, walk 2 blocks up C. Aribau and turn right. Put a dent in your wallet with class at one of the nicest—and most expensive—restaurants in the city. Appetizers and salads €5.85-16.25. Meat and seafood entrees €7.80-101.60 but average €20. Open M-Sa 1-4pm and 8pm-midnight. AmEx/V. ❺

treat for those with a penchant for melted cheese, while interesting salads (€5.90-9.65) are offered for those with fondue-phobia. If the 'due doesn't do you, take home some of the surrealist art on the walls (€100+). Open M-Th 10:30pm-12:30am, F-Sa 10:30pm-1:30am. ❷

Taira, C. Comerc, 7 (☎93 310 24 97). From M: Jaume I, follow C. Princesa then turn left on C. Comerc. Paper lanterns appear suspended in midair while the "in" crowd of Barcelona chills on floor-level futons and funky, dark wood chairs at this swank sushi hot spot. Splurge on the sushi moriawase (€16.20) for 6 pieces of nigiri and 6 pieces of maki, and finish up with a sorbete de sake (€3.60). Open M-F 1pm-4pm and 9pm-1am, Sa-Su 9pm-1am. ❹

La Cocotte, Pg. del Born, 16 (☎93 319 17 34). M: Jaume I. Eclectic international menu offers mostly vegetarian food in a cozy, red-tabled interior. The effect of globalization on menus has never been more evident. Culinary offerings range from moussaka (€7.10) to vegetarian burritos (€6) to chicken curry (€6.15). Eat in or take out. Entrees €4.50-7.10. Open Tu-Su 9pm-midnight. ❷

Sandwich & Friends, Pg. del Born, 27 (☎93 310 07 86). From M: Jaume I, follow C. Princesa, and turn right on C. Comerç and right again on Pg. del Born. Sleek and super-trendy sandwich bar serves veggie or meat-filled goodies (€3.40-7) and salads (€4-5). Try the *Bim*—eggplant, gouda, zucchini, tomato, and onion on a baguette (€4.40), or the *Elena*—white rice, corn, pears, lettuce, and soy dressing (€3.75). Open Su-W noon-12:30am, Th-Sa noon-1am. ❶

TAPAS BARS

Xampanyet, C. Montcado, 22 (☎93 319 70 03). From M: Jaume I. From the Metro, cross Via Laietana, walk down C. Princesa, and turn right on C. Montcado. Xampanyet is on the right after the Museu Picasso. Juan Carlos, the 3rd-generation proprietor, treats everyone like family. The house special—*cava* (choose from 17 varieties)—is served with anchovies at the colorful bar. Glasses €0.80 and up. Bottles €5.40 and up. Open Tu-Sa noon-4pm and 7-11:30pm, Su noon-4pm. Closed in Aug. ❶

Va de Vi, C. Banys Vells, 16 (☎93 319 29 00). From M: Jaume I, walk down C. Princesa, turn right on C. Montcada, right again on C. Barra de Ferro, and finally left on C. Banys Vells. Possibly the most romantic restaurant in La Ribera. Cavernous, medieval wine bar in a 16th-century stone building, softly illumined by candles and delicate lamps. Choose from over 170 varieties of wine (glasses from €1.60-4), a wide selection of cheeses (€3-7.20), and tapas (€2.70-5.40). Open Su-W 6pm-1am, Th 6pm-2am, F-Sa 6pm-3am. ❷

Cal Pep, Pl. de les Olles, 8 (☎93 310 79 61). From M: Barceloneta, follow Pg. Joan de Borbó, then turn right on Av. Marqués de l'Argentera, and left on C. Palau. During peak hours it can be difficult to even find standing room in the small bar, but the fresh, unusual tapas—like sauteed spinach with garbanzo beans and smoked ham (€4)—make it all worthwhile. Country-style sit-down restaurant in rear (entrees €4-9). Beer €1.20. Drinks €3-6. Open Tu-Sa 1-4:30pm and 8-11:45pm. Closed in Aug. ❷

Euskal Etxea, Placeta Montcada, 1-3 (☎93 315 14 47). M: Jaume I, at the end of C. Montcada by Pg. del Born. Locals cram into the often standing-room only bar to greet the endless trays of delectable tapas that are brought out 12:30-2:30pm and 7:30-10pm. Sit-down restaurant in back serves Basque cuisine (entrees €9.10-24). Tapas €1; beer €1.40, mixed drinks €1-2. Open Tu-Sa 12:30-11:30pm, Su 1-3:30pm. ❹

Barcelónia, Pl. Comercial, 11 (☎93 268 70 21). From M: Jaume I, follow C. Princesa almost to its end and turn right on C. Comerç; the *plaça* is ahead on the right. Young neighborhood trendoids gather to feast on a traditional selection of tapas (€0.90). Innovative sit-down menu includes dishes like *bacalao* (cod) with honey, pine nuts, and feta (€10.30). 3-course lunch *menú* €7.20. Beer and wine from €1. Open Su-Th 1pm-midnight, F-Sa 1pm-1am. ❷

Txirimiri, C. Princesa, 11 (☎93 310 18 05). Enough tapas to feed a small village (€0.90 each). Sit at the long wooden bar and try *la gula,* a seafood and veggie specialty from the Basque region. Tapas outshine the small lunch and dinner menu. Beer €1.50, *cava* and wine €1.80. Open Tu-Su noon-midnight. MC/V. ❶

CAFES

Tèxtil Café, C. Montcada, 12 (☎93 268 25 98). M: Jaume I. Set in the picturesque courtyard of the Museu Tèxtil i d'Indumentària (see **Museums,** p. 110), in one of C. Montcada's Gothic masterpieces. Elegant but relaxed cafe for a post-museum coffee or meal. Weekday lunch *menú* €8.75. Wine and *cava* €1.50-2.10 per glass. Hot and cold sandwiches €2-5. Open Tu-Su 10am-midnight. Wheelchair accessible. ❶

Suborn, Pg. Picasso, 42 (☎93 310 11 10). M: Barceloneta, across from Parc de la Ciutadella. Eclectic restaurant with plenty of vegetarian options by day; popular, bass-thumping bar by night. Entrees like salmon teriyaki and pasta with mascarpone, ricotta, lemon, and pesto from €4.50-13. Lunch *menú* €12. Beer €1.80. Drinks €5. Open Tu-Th and Su 12:30-4:30pm and 9pm-2:30am, F-Sa 12:30-4:30pm and 9pm-3am. ❷

MENU READER

Before traveling to Barcelona, you will want to consider any specific dietary needs you require to make sure they can be met during your visit. Below is a glossary of common Spanish words that you will encounter on menus during your stay. ¡Buen provecho!

aceitunas: olives.

aceite y vinagre: olive oil and vinegar; typically used as a salad dressing.

agua: water.

arroz: rice.

batido: milk shake.

bocadillo: baguette sandwich.

calamares: calamari (squid).

chorizo: Spanish-style sausage; can be eaten in a sandwich with bread or as an appetizer.

churros: a rich, donut-like pastry eaten for breakfast with coffee or *chocolate,* a thick hot chocolate.

cerveza: beer.

cocido: stew. Varieties include *cocido madrileño* and *cocido gallego.* Both are meat- and bean-heavy.

cordero asado: roasted lamb with garlic.

ensalada: salad.

fideua: like *paella,* but uses noodles instead of rice.

fruta: fruit; generally eaten for breakfast or dessert.

galletas: cookies.

gambas: shrimp.

gazpacho: cold tomato soup.

granizado: slushie drink.

infusión: herbal tea.

jamón serrano: serrano ham.

lomo: cured ham.

(Continued on p. 135.)

the hidden deal

El Raval

Restaurante Riera, C. Joaquim Costa, 30 (☎93 443 32 93). M: Liceu or Universitat. Off C. Carme coming from Liceu; off Ronda de Sant Antoni from Universitat, 1 block from the MACBA. If you're tired of tapas-sized portions and want to eat heartily without breaking the bank, the Riera family provides a feast fit for a very hungry king, complete with dessert (€5.50-6)–one of the best deals in town. Open daily 1-4pm and 8-11pm. ❶

Buenas Migas, Pl. Bonsuccés, 6 (☎93 318 37 08). M: Catalunya, off Las Ramblas. This *focacceria* on the Pl. Bonsuccés offers one of the neighborhood's most pleasant outdoor eating experiences. Enjoy coffee or tea (€0.85-1.20) at one of the shaded tables across the street, or stay indoors with your *focaccia* (thick Italian bread; €2.30-3.70) in the rustic-feeling interior. The rich cakes, which can be topped with almost anything–from bacon to brie–are definitely worth a try. Open Su-W 10am-10pm, Th-Sa 10am-midnight. ❶

Café del Born, Pl. Comercial, 10 (☎93 268 32 72). M: Jaume I. Bistro-style cafe with more leg room than its neighbors. Vegetarian selections like four-cheese spaghetti with asparagus (€6.85), as well as traditional meat-filled Catalan dishes (entrees €3.80-9). Tasty lunch *menú* €7.45. Open M-Th 9am-1am, F-Sa 9am-3am, Su 10am-1am. Wheelchair accessible. ❷

EL RAVAL

see map p. 340

The area west of Las Ramblas is filled with more than its share of good restaurants. Numerous tiny local places have long reflected the ethnic diversity of the neighborhood, but as the government continues its efforts to clean up and revitalize El Raval, trendier gourmet places have started to move into the area as well. Perhaps best of all, because of the enormous range of clientele to which these restaurants cater—students, tourists, blue-collar workers, yuppies, recent immigrants, and businessmen alike—great food comes for fairly inexpensive prices.

▨ Bar Ra, Pl. de la Garduña (☎93 301 41 63). M: Liceu, just behind Las Ramblas's Boquería market. Everything about Ra exudes cool, from its erotic Hindu mural, bursting with color, to the individually painted tablecloths at each outdoor table–to the waiters themselves. The artfully prepared international offerings, a creative mixture of traditional Spanish and trendy California, like the excellent vegetarian lasagna (€7.25) and duck magret with mango and pumpkin sauce (€9.50), seldom disappoint. Entrees €6.50-12.75. Open M-Sa 9am-midnight. Dinner by reservation only. ❷

Restaurante Can Lluís, C. Cera, 49 (☎93 441 11 87). M: Sant Antoni. From the Metro, head down Ronda S. Pau and take the 2nd left on C. Cera. For over 100 years, under the ownership of the same family for 3 generations, Can Lluís has been a defining force in Catalan cuisine. Eschewing trendiness, the menu is filled with traditional Catalan favorites prepared home-style and always bursting with flavor, among them succulent baby goat ribs (€9.80), grilled squid (€8.90), and fresh-grilled asparagus (€5.40). Dinner *menú* (with good wine selection) €19.90. Entrees €8.90-18.60. Open M-Sa 1:30-4pm and 8:30-11:30pm. V. ❸

Pla dels Angels, C. Ferlandina, 23 (☎93 443 31 03). Directly in front of the MACBA (see **Museums,** p. 112). The funky decor of this colorful, inexpensive eatery is fitting for its proximity to Barcelona's contemporary art museum. Sit outside and check out the museum or get a table indoors while indulging in gnocchi with goat cheese sauce and red peppers (€3.20) or leg of duck in asparagus and carmelized *cava* sauce (€5.75). Lunchtime pastas €3.20, entrees €5.55-5.75. Open M-Th 1-3:30pm and 9-11:30pm, F-Sa 9-11:30pm. ❷

Silenus, C. Angels, 8 (☎93 302 26 80). From M: Catalunya, a right off C. Carme. Almost as much art gallery as restaurant, softly elegant Silenus is the place for good meals and quiet conversation. Art expositions on the walls, featuring local artists, change every couple of months. Fish and meat entrees from the menu, unforgettably entitled "A Short Treatise on the Passions of Flavors," include duck and tuna (€10.85-18.10), as well as the exotic *filete de kangoo* in licorice sauce: yep, kangaroo (€16.20). Menu changes daily. Open M-Th 11am-11:30pm, F 11am-midnight, Sa 1pm-midnight. MC/V. ❹

Mamacafé, C. Doctor Dou, 10 (☎93 301 29 40), a right off C. Pintor Fortuny. A great place to find healthy, fresh vegetarian and meat options with an exotic twist. The ambience manages to be casual without being shabby, artsy without being pretentious. Options include ravioli stuffed with brie (€7.70) and salmon in lemon-rosemary oil (€10.10). *Menú* €7.50. Open M 1-5pm, Tu-Sa 1pm-1am.❷

Carmelitas, C. Carme, 42 (☎93 329 34 96), a few blocks off Las Ramblas. Sunshine brightens the simple and stylish interior of this new, airy restaurant during the day, and a red glow illuminates it at night. Lunch *menú* €8.50. Rotating fish and meat entrees €9-15. Open M-Sa 1:30-4pm and 9-midnight. ❸

La Table Du Pain, Ronda Universitat, 20 (☎93 318 67 80). M: Catalunya. Near Pl. Catalunya. Orange-yellow pastel-colored walls, wooden tables, and high ceilings offer a refreshing setting in which to enjoy the delicious, inexpensive food. Breakfasts €1.68-6. Salads, pastas, and specialities €5-6.50. Open M-Th 9am-9pm, F-Sa 9am-10:30pm. ❶

L'Hortet, C. del Pintor Fortuny, 32 (☎93 317 61 89). M: Catalunya. Off Las Ramblas. Gorgeous landscape paintings complement freshly prepared vegetarian options. Lunch *menú* €7.75, dinner *menú* €9.75. Light entrees feature pastas, pizzas, and couscous. Open daily 1:15-4pm and 8:30-11pm. ❷

Shalimar, C. Carme, 71 (☎93 329 34 96). For some South Asian spice, look to the tasty and relatively inexpensive Pakistani and Indian favorites offered at this small, simply decorated restaurant. Chicken, lamb, and seafood curries €6.50-8.70. Chicken tandoori €6.50. Open W-M 1-4pm and 8-11:30pm, Tu 8-11:30pm. ❷

Bar Restaurante Los Toreros, C. Xuclá, 3-5 (☎93 318 23 25). M: Catalunya. On a narrow alley between C. Pintor Fortuny and C. Carme, both off Las Ramblas. Decorated with a bull's head and pictures celebrating bullfighting, the popular Los Toreros specializes in group meals—come with friends and order from one of

MENU READER

(continued from p. 133)

magdalena: muffin.

mantequilla: butter.

mazapán: marzipan.

menú: A daily set menu, served at lunch and dinner. Generally two courses, bread, dessert, a drink; and a very good deal.

orchata: tiger-nut milk; tastes like almond.

paella: a family-size rice dish typically filled with seafood or meat.

pan: bread; Spaniards typically eat the baguette kind. *Pan integral* is wheat bread; *pan de molde* is sliced bread.

pasteles: pastries.

patatas: potatoes. *Patatas bravas* are a popular tapa consisting of potatoes in a spicy sauce.

pavo: turkey.

pescado: fish. Varieties include *salmon* (salmon), *trucha* (trout), *bacalao* (cod), *atún* (tuna), *ángilas* (eel), and more.

pollo: chicken.

polvorones: a holiday sweet made from crushed almonds and sugar.

postre: dessert.

puerco: pork.

queso: cheese; varieties include Manchego and *fresco.*

Raciones: larger portions of tapas.

sopa: soup.

tarta: cake.

tortilla española: a potato omelette.

turrón: a chocolate-like holiday treat that can include goodies such as almonds and coconut.

zumo de naranja: orange juice.

the many *menús para grupos*, which feed at least 6 people (€13-20 per person). A tasty solo lunch *menú* (€7.30) and a nighttime tapas menu, both favorites among locals, are also offered. Open Tu-Sa 1-4pm and 8pm-midnight, Su noon-5pm. ❷

Restaurante Biocenter, C. del Pintor Fortuny, 25 (☎93 301 45 83). M: Catalunya. Off Las Ramblas. Stuff yourself full with wholesome vegetarian foods at the large buffet. *Menú* M-F €7.50, Sa €10.50. Open M-Sa 1-5pm. ❷

Bar Restaurante Romesco, C. Sant Pau, 28 (☎93 318 93 81). M: Liceu. From the Metro, walk up Las Ramblas and turn left onto C. Sant Pau. Take the 1st right; Romesco is immediately on the left. This small diner serves simple, dirt-cheap food. *Frijoles negros* (black beans; €3.75) and *crema catalana* (€1.65) are their specialties; their fries are among the best in Barcelona. Fish, chicken, and meat dishes €2.55-5.80. Open M-Sa 1pm-midnight. ❷

L'EIXAMPLE

see map p. 344-345

With sidewalk cafes serving the multi-ethnic to the super authentic, wandering in l'Eixample can easily induce watering mouths and rumbling tummies. These upper neighborhoods are full of good places to spend a long, enjoyable dinner (especially l'Eixample Esquerra), but they are spread out widely and interspersed with plenty of nondescript corner bars serving the endless apartment buildings in the area. If you want to sample one of l'Eixample's trendy, high-quality restaurants, you are best off picking one ahead of time and walking with blinders on past all the tempting but, in truth, carbon-copied eateries. Expect to make reservations on weekends, and with some exceptions, be prepared to pay well for the food and atmosphere.

AROUND PG. DE GRÀCIA

Pg. de Gràcia is lined with nearly as many tapas bars and cafes as shops and Modernist architecture. Most are tourist-oriented, have sidewalk tables, and are on the expensive side, especially to eat outside (many charge up to 15% extra for this privilege). On Friday and Saturday almost all of them stay open until 2am (during the week until 1 or 1:30am), making them a good place for late-night food.

⚐ **Thai Gardens,** C. Diputació, 273 (☎93 487 98 98). M: Catalunya. Extravagant decor, complete with a wooden bridge entrance, lush greenery, and colorful pillows, fill Thai Gardens with the aroma of amor (and sweetly spiced incense). Call ahead to reserve a traditional *kantok* table (cushions on the ground). Weekday lunch *menú* €10.80; regular *menú* €23.50. Pad thai €6. Entrees €9-13.50. Open Su-Th 1:30-4pm and 8:30pm-midnight, F-Sa 1:30-4pm and 8:30pm-1am. Wheelchair accessible. ❸

Txapela (Euskal Taberna), Pg. de Gràcia, 8-10 (☎93 412 02 89). M: Catalunya. This Basque restaurant is a godsend for the tapas-clueless traveler who wants to learn: the placemats have pictures with the name and description of each tapa, and you can order by number. About half the size of most normal tapas, each costs only €1.05. Open M-Th 8am-1:30am, F-Su 10am-2am. Wheelchair accessible. ❷

Hostal de Rita, C. Aragó, 279 (☎93 487 23 76). M: Pg. de Gràcia. To the right off Pg. de Gràcia, coming from Pl. de Catalunya. Lines of up to 20 locals waiting to eat lunch here are not uncommon; the food is just as tasty and elegant as it is cheap. A fish- and chicken-based menu section is dedicated to low-calorie dishes. Weekday lunch *menú* €6.61. Entrees €4-9.50. Open daily 1-3:45pm and 8:30-11:30pm. Wheelchair accessible. ❷

Madrid-Barcelona (Pa Amb Tomàquet), C. Aragó, 282, (☎93 215 70 26). M: Pg. de Gràcia, on the corner with Pg. de Gràcia. Named for the railroad line that used to run here, this classy but cheap lunchtime hotspot attracts hordes of native businessmen and shoppers. Waiters ladle soup and rice at your table, straight from the stove. Entrees €4.20-6.60. Open M-Sa 1-4pm and 8:30-midnight. MC/V. Wheelchair accessible. ❶

ba-ba-reeba, Pg. de Gràcia, 28 (☎93 301 43 02). M: Pg. de Gràcia. One of the most obvious spots on the Passeig, the tapas here—bigger and glossier than usual—have definitely been

Americanized, but if that's what you want, they taste good, especially the *pa amb tomaquet*. Entrees €4.30-15.20. Most tapas €2.35-4, some €6-12.50. Sidewalk seating 15% extra. Take-out available. Open M-Th 7:30am-1:30am, F 7:30am-2am, Sa 8am-2am, Su 8am-1:30am. Wheelchair accessible. ❷

Giorgio, C. Aragó, 277 (☎93 487 42 31). M: Pg. de Gràcia. To the right off Pg. de Gràcia, coming from Pl. de Catalunya. Known for its rich *risotto* (€7.75-9.45), Giorgio serves affordable Italian food in a blue-and-yellow dining room that feels much more expensive than it is. The wines are all Italian and easy on the wallet. Pizzas and pastas €6.45-8.65. Weekday *menú* €10.34. Take-out available for pizzas. Open daily 1-4pm and 8pm-midnight. Wheelchair accessible. ❷

Café Torino, Pg. de Gràcia, 59 (☎93 487 75 11). M: Pg. de Gràcia. Originally designed by the likes of Gaudí, Puig i Cadafalch, and Falqués as a spot for sampling vermouth, at that time a drink novelty, this Modernist coffee spot celebrated its 100th anniversary in 2002. The outdoor tables are blissfully cool and shaded in the morning. Coffee and tea €1-2.10. Hot cocoa €1.95. Open Su-Th 8am-11:30pm, F-Sa 9am-1am. Cash only. Wheelchair accessible. ❶

Chicago Pizza Pie Factory, C. Provença, 300 (☎93 215 94 15). M: Diagonal. Near the corner with C. Pau Claris, within sight of La Pedrera. The windy city comes to the Mediterranean with tasty deep dish pizzas that make diners lose themselves to American nostalgia. Starters (onion rings, nachos, chicken caesar salad) €4.65-5.75. Individual deep-dish or thin-crust pizzas €8.90. Take-out available. Happy Hour with drink and food discounts 5-8pm. Open M-Th 1-4:30pm and 8pm-12:30am, F-Sa 1pm-1:30am, Su 1pm-12:30am. ❷

Mauri, Rambla de Catalunya, 102 (☎93 215 10 20). M: Diagonal. This *pastisseria* has been turning out delicate sweets, mouth-watering bonbons, and gourmet sandwiches since 1929. Come to buy delectable gifts, to have lunch in the restaurant, or simply to admire the cake decorations. A second location across the street, at no. 103, specializes in candy and gift baskets (☎93 215 81 46). Open M-F 8am-9pm, Sa 9am-9pm, Su and holidays 9am-3pm. ❶

L'EIXAMPLE DRETA

🖾 **Comme-Bio,** C. Gran Via, 603 (☎93 301 03 76). M: Catalunya or Universitat. On the corner of Gran Via and Rambla de Catalunya. If you've started to wonder if vegetable harvests actually make it to Spain, come here for fresh salad, hummus, tofu, yogurt, or juice. While you're at it, read up on local yoga lessons and try on organic makeup. Restaurant, food-to-go, and small grocery store all in one. Pasta, rice, and veggie

Juicy Jones

Els Quatre Gats

Lunch at Ra

LGB ▼
BARCELONA

What a Drag

Café Miranda, C. Casanova, 30 (☎93 453 52 49). M: Universitat, in **l'Eixample.** Lavishly decked out in faux leopard fur and palm trees, this gay restaurant features male and female drag performers who serenade diners at regular half-hour intervals after 10:30pm. Seasonal menu includes Mediterranean delicacies like marinated calamari salad in black vinegar and spring rolls stuffed with goat cheese and spinach. The friendly waitstaff and mixed crowd make it a very popular place; reservations are recommended. Don't leave without taking a peek at the hot-pink and electric-blue (gender designated) bathrooms. Three-course *menú* €19.83. Wine from €5.86 per bottle. Open daily 9pm-1am. MC/V.

pizzas around €6. Salads €5-6. Open daily 9am-11:30pm; dinner service starts at 8pm. Another **branch** a few blocks away (Via Laietana, 28; ☎93 319 89 68). ❶

🔲 **Mandalay Café**, C. Provença, 330 (☎93 458 60 17), between C. Roger de Llúria and C. Bruc. M: Verdaguer. Exotic international cuisine (mostly pan-Asian), including gourmet dim sum, Vietnamese noodles, seared tuna, and salads, served in a room so draped in color and sultanesque luxury (you can eat on a bed!) it's been featured in books on interior decorating. F-Sa night trapeze artist around 11pm; variable extra cover charge for show. Entrees €10-18. English-speaking host. Open Tu-Sa 9-11pm. MC/V. ❸

🔲 **Laie Llibreria Café**, C. Pau Claris, 85 (☎93 318 17 39; www.laie.es). M: Urquinaona. An ultra-cool lunch spot for more than just bookworms, this urban oasis offers a cheap, fresh and plentiful all-you-can-eat buffet lunch (€8.90) in an open, bamboo-draped lunch room well lighted by a glass ceiling. Grab a praline capuccino (€2.30) at the bar on the way out. Vegetarian dinner *menú* €14.90. Open M-F 9am-1am, Sa 10am-1am. AmEx/MC/V. ❷

Wok & Bol, C. Diputació, 294 (☎ 93 302 76 75), between C. Roger de Llúria and C. Bruc. M: Girona. An elegant, stand-out Chinese restaurant, serving dim sum (€3-5 per small dish), whole Peking ducks (€16.20 per person), and Chinese fondue (€18), in addition to more common dishes like chow mein and veggie stir fries (€4.20). Make reservations and then ponder the slightly eerie Chinese mannequins having tea in the window. Open M-F 1:30-3:30pm and 9:15-11:30pm, Sa 1:30-11:30pm. ❸

La Muscleria, C. Mallorca, 290 (☎93 458 98 44), on the corner with C. Bruc. M: Verdaguer. Mussels of every size, shape, and flavor, culled from Catalunya, France, Galicia, and The Netherlands served in a bustling basement or on outdoor tables. Main plates (a huge bowl of mussels for €8) come with French fries. Lots of salads (€4.50-5.50) and *cocas* (like pizza; €5.25-6). Make reservations W-Sa. Open M-Th 1-4pm and 8:30pm-midnight, F-Sa 1-4pm and 8:30pm-1am. No Sa lunch July-Aug. ❷

Can Cargol, C. València, 324 (☎93 458 00 17), on the corner with C. Bruc. M: Girona. Extremely popular Catalan restaurant with make-your-own *pan con tomate* and lots of snail options. Snails €7. Fish and meat dishes €4-5.50, some €9-12. Make reservations on weekends. Open 1:30-4pm and 8:30pm-midnight. ❷

El Rodizio Grill, C. Consell de Cent, 403 (☎93 265 51 12), right next to M: Girona. All-you-can-eat Brazilian and Mediterranean buffet, featuring 10 grilled shish kebab-style meats plus chicken, salmon, and cod. Cold dishes include sushi, pasta, and salads.

Lunch €7.75. Dinner €11.50. Desserts €2.44. Open M-Th 1-4pm and 8:30pm-midnight, F-Sa 1-4pm and 8:30pm-1am, Su 1-4pm. ❷

Cullera de Boix, C. Ronda de St. Pere, 24 (☎93 268 13 36), between C. Bruc and Pl. Urquinaona. M: Urquinaona. With metal chairs, light wood tables, and sleek hanging lamps, this upscale cafe-restaurant could easily be in Manhattan. Specializes in rice (€5.89-17) and salads (€4.80). Midday *arroz del día* €5; *plato del día* €5.10. Reservations wise for weekend dinners. Open daily 1-4pm and 9pm-midnight. ❷

A-Tipic, C. Bruc, 79 (☎93 215 51 06), between C. Aragó and C. Consell de Cent. A lunchtime gem for vegetarians. A simple buffet (€7.80) that tastes more like home than a cafeteria, served in a relaxing blue-and-yellow dining room. Salad, rice, pasta, veggie calzones, and sometimes chicken. Open Sept.-July M-F 1-4pm. MC/V. ❷

La Bodegueta, Rambla de Catalunya, 100 (☎93 215 48 94), near C. Provença. M: Diagonal. An informal and affordable spot for Spanish wine, big tapas platters (especially good Iberian meats), and pleasant terrace seats on the Rambla. A good place to unwind with a drink before starting the evening. *Menú* served M-F 1-4pm (€7.80). Open M-F 7am-1:50am, Sa 8am-1:50am, Su 7am-1:15am. Cash only. ❷

Campechano, C. València, 286 (☎93 215 62 33). M: Catalunya. Just to the right of Pg. de Gràcia coming from Pl. de Catalunya. This restaurant goes all out to recreate the atmosphere of a 1940s *merendero* (BBQ/picnic area) on the Barcelona mountainside, from a few live trees and a painted forest wall to train-stop signs marking your progress "toward the mountain." Choose your favorite meat or poultry from their huge list and they'll grill it; french fries, salad, and a few other dishes serve as sides. Salads €5-6. Grilled entrees €5-14.50. Open daily 1-4pm and 8:30-midnight. ❷

L'EIXAMPLE ESQUERRA

🏴 **El Racó d'en Baltá,** C. Aribau, 125 (☎93 453 10 44), at the intersection with C. Rosselló. M: Hospital Clínic. Eccentric, colorful restaurant offers incredibly creative and flavorful Mediterranean-style dishes inspired by ingredients from all over the world, like the orgasmic duck magret with pumpkin and pears (€11.75) and the salted ice cream (€3.85). F-Sa nights, the funky top floor with hanging sculptures is opened up for your dining pleasure. Fish and meat entrees €9.90-15.50. Bottles of wine and *cava* €3.85-15.45. Open M 9-10:45pm, Tu-Sa 1-3:45pm and 9-10:45pm. AmEx/D/MC/V. ❸

Restaurante Terrani, C. Londres, 89 (☎93 321 15 22). M: Hospital Clínic. Take the Villarroel exit, walk 3 blocks up Villarroel, and turn right on Londres; it's 1½ blocks down on your left. An über-stylish restaurant

Sangria at ba-ba-reeba

Thai Garden

Gazpacho at La Provença

CATALAN CUISINE

Pa amb tomaquet/Pan con tomate: toasted bread served with tomato and garlic. Sometimes comes prepared, but more authentic places let you do it yourself. Cut the tomato in half and rub it generously over the toast. Then cut the garlic in half and rub it on the toast. Be careful with the garlic, or you'll be reeking of it for days to come.

Crema catalana: The definitive Catalan dessert. A light custard with a caramelized top, very similar to *crème brulée*. So popular that ice cream stores sell *crema catalana* ice cream and Dunkin' Donuts offers a *crema catalana*-filled donut. Especially delicious is the *crema catalana* liqueur, with the consistency of Kahlua or Bailey's and a nutmeg flavor similar to egg nog.

Espinacs a la catalana: spinach sautéed with pine nuts, raisins, and sometimes anchovies.

Romesco de peix: a seafood medley in a *romesco* sauce of tomatoes, garlic, peppers, and nuts.

Fideus: like a *paella*, but prepared with thin noodles instead of rice.

Esqueixada: a shredded cod, olive, vinegar, tomato, bean, and red pepper salad.

Mel i Mató: a dessert of honey and curd cheese.

where vibrant blues and oranges splash the walls and a light, jazzy mix complements the delicious chef's specialties (€11.40-14.10). Dinner *menú* €16 and up. Reservations suggested. Open daily 1:30-4pm and 9pm-midnight. AmEx/D/MC/V. ❸

El Criollo, C. Aribau, 85 (☎93 454 23 28). M: Hospital Clínic. A Peruvian oasis in l'Eixample. Choose from hearty dishes like *ají de gallina*—shredded chicken in a thick, spicy nut sauce (€6.60). Weekday lunch *menú* €7.50. Entrees €5.70-8. Open M 9pm-midnight, Tu-Sa 1-4pm and 9pm-midnight. ❷

Harmony, C. Fontanella, 14 (☎93 412 77 02; www.harmony.es). M: Catalunya. When you don't know if you want Italian, Spanish, Japanese or Mexican for dinner, you now have a place to go. Collaborating with UNICEF, Harmony suggests that globalization can be a wonderfully tasty thing. Portions on the small side, but hey, it's a small world after all. Nachos €6.80; duck ham salad with fresh mint dressing €8.90; entrees €8.90-13.80. Open daily 8am-1am.

Ginza, C. Provença, 205 (☎93 451 71 93), between Balmes and Enric Granados. M: Diagonal or FGC: Provença. Sleek, bamboo- and wood-filled restaurant serves delectable, affordable Japanese food. Eat in or take out. Sushi €5.10-13.25. Weekday four-course lunch *menú* €7.20. Daily dinner *menús* M-Th €9.35, F-Su €11.15. Open M-Sa 1-4pm and 8pm-midnight, Su 1-4pm. MC/V. ❷

La Provença, C. Provença, 242 (☎93 323 23 67). M: Diagonal. Enter through a hall of lanterns to a quiet banquet room with chandeliers and pastel tablecloths. Dishes lean toward a Mediterranean influence. Specialties include carpaccio, fresh fish, and vegetables. Entrees €8.40-11. Dress well. Reservations recommended, especially on weekends. Open daily 1-4:30pm and 9pm-midnight. AmEx/D/MC/V. ❸

El Raconet, C. Enrique Granados, 95 (☎93 218 10 57). M: Diagonal. Family-run corner eatery with sidewalk tables. Plenty of Catalan mainstays, including a wide selection of *bacalao* (cod), and vegetarian options. Small offering of bagels topped with cheeses or meats €4.50. Meat and fish entrees €6.60-13.50. M 1-4:30pm, Tu-Sa 1-4:30pm and 9-11:30pm. AmEx/MC/V. ❸

dahabi, Pl. Universitat, 1 (☎93 451 43 39). M: Universitat. A spiritual aura hangs amidst the waiters in long black robes, the gold crushed-velvet benches, and the elegantly presented Syrian-Lebanese cuisine. Huge sampler includes 3 courses plus dessert (€27 per person). Entrees €9-19. Open M-Sa 1-4pm and 8:30pm-midnight. ❸

La Flauta, C. Aribau, 23 (☎93 323 70 38). M: Pg. de Gràcia. The house specialties, reasonably enough, are hot or cold *flautas*—skinny, crusty bread sandwiches stuffed with veggies, cheeses, and meats (half €2.50-5.38; whole €3.10-7.50). Plenty of vegetarian options and a large selection of *tapas del día*. Weekday 3-course lunch *menú* €9. Salads €2.98-5.38. Open M-F 7am-1:30am, Sa 7am-1am. MC/V. **Branch** at C. Balmes, 164-166. ❷

POBLE NOU & PORT OLÍMPIC

see map p. 349

POBLE NOU

Cheap, local food is readily available in Poble Nou, although you'll stick out as a tourist if you eat in the neighborhood watering holes. If you don't mind being the odd non-Catalan speaker, the food at **Enng ❶,** C. Ramon Turró, 120, is cheap and tasty and you can still expect good service. (From M: Bogatell, walk east on C. Pujades and then make a right onto C. Avila; the restaurant is on the corner of C. Avila and C. Ramon Turró. ☎93 225 00 12. Entrees €2-8. Open daily 5am-10pm.)

PORT OLÍMPIC

Food in the Port Olímpic area is not cheap, even in the fast-food restaurants that are starting to move in. For a budget day at the beach or walking the Olympic parks, pack a picnic lunch from the **supermarkets** listed on p. 316 and bring it with you. If you want to eat in the port itself, there are more than 20 restaurants, mostly seafood-based, to choose from. In most, a full three-course dinner meal will cost €30-50. The following listings are standouts among the waterfront restaurants, which are always best in good weather.

▨ **Agua,** Pg. Marítim de la Barceloneta, 30 (☎93 225 12 72; fax 93 335 18 61), the farthest establishment to the right of the copper fish. This upscale restaurant, which appeared in *Town and Country* in 2002, attracts large numbers of tourists and trendy Barceloneses alike. Don't be scared off by the fancy Art Deco interior; the prices are actually quite reasonable. Stare at the Picasso wannabes that dot the walls as you enjoy their specialties, seafood and rice dishes. Getting a table on the terrace is difficult, but worth the trouble. Reservations recommended. Tapas €1.20-7.85; starters €4-5.90; pastas €5.75-8.40; entrees €5.45-13.85. Open daily noon-5pm and 8pm-1am. AmEx/MC/V. Wheelchair accessible. ❷

La Oca Mar (☎93 225 01 00, www.restaurantelaoca.com), on Platja Nova Marbella, a 20min. walk up the beach from the Port Olímpic, keeping the water on your right, next to the Platja Mar Bella. A bit of a hike without a car, but it may be unusual enough to be worth it: the entire restaurant is built like a large

Horse Meat

Churros con Chocolate

Sampling Tapas

BREAKFAST OF CHAM-PIONS

Several brave establishments open their doors for the city that keeps going until the early morning. If you find yourself winding down after an evening out, or up at dawn on your way out of town, try these early-bird breakfast options.

Bar Estudiantil, Pl. Universitat, 12, serves regular cafe-bar fare and hardly ever closes. (☎93 302 31 25. Open daily 6am-3am.)

For pry-your-eyes-open coffee, try the delightful, family-run **Sechi Caffé Italiano** at the bottom of Gràcia on Trav. de Gràcia, 34. (☎93 200 56 93. Open M-F 7am-8:30pm. Closed Aug.)

Or, luxuriate in the classy, high-ceilinged **Cafeteria Estació de França,** in the train station. (☎93 310 16 33. Open daily 7:30am-9pm.)

If you need help ordering your morning caffeine fix, check **Would You Like Coffee With That?** (p. 148).

ship, with a long "bow"/terrace extending far into the ocean for sunset-gazing. Best for large groups; small parties are seated inside, away from the panoramic views of the water. Entrees €9-17.75. Open daily 1pm-1am. AmEx/MC/V. Wheelchair accessible. ❸

BARCELONETA

As the historic home of sailors and fishermen, Barceloneta houses a number of good seafood restaurants, with the same quality fish for lower prices than the waterfront or Port Olímpic areas.

La Mar Salada, Pg. Juan de Borbo, 58 (☎93 221 21 27). Toward the end of Juan de Borbo, near the beach. The friendly staff makes this bright and open restaurant with a view of the waterfront all the more pleasant. Penny pinchers should try the mussels (€4.81), while bigger spenders can opt for the huge 2-person shellfish platter, a crustacean overloaded with lobster, crab, shrimp, clams, and oysters €37.26. Seating for large groups available upstairs. *Menú* €7.50. Open W-M 1-4pm and 8pm-midnight. ❷

Café L'Imma, Pg. Joan de Borbo, 30 (☎93 221 40 03). This portside restaurant, nestled in among many catering to tourists along the Pg. Joan de Borbo, separates itself from the rest with its wide selection of fresh fish. Pull up under an umbrella outside and watch as foreigners and locals mingle along the busy street leading to the beach. *Menú* €8, fish dishes €15-28, other meat dishes €5.50-14.50. ❸

La Taverna d'en Pep, C. de La Manquista, 8 (☎93 331 89 12). If you're looking to get away from the crowded, touristy Pg. Joan de Borbo, turn down this side street and walk about a block to find this clean, cozy, and friendly restaurant on your right. Enjoy the extensive wine list and excellent range of meat and seafood dishes amid the nautical decor. Definitely worth the few extra euros. *Menú* €8.40, fish and meat dishes €7-18. Open M-Sa 1-3:30pm and 9-11:30pm for meals, 9pm-midnight for drinks and appetizers. ❷

PORT VELL

see map p. 350

Restaurants tend to group around two central areas: in the vicinities of the Palau de Mar and around Maremàgnum. The Port Vell side of the Palau de Mar, or "Palace of the Sea," (on Port Vell at the far end of Pg. Colom) houses several fancy harborside restaurants, where well-dressed waiters serve lunch to tourists in baseball caps and flip-flops. (Dinners, however, are considerably more formal.) The elegant **Merendero de la Mari** ❹ has an extensive seafood menu, including fresh lobster (€12.23), and perhaps the best *paella* in the city. Order it with rice (€15.75) or *fideos* (€17.32), a small, thin pasta—a Catalan specialty. (☎93 221 31 41. Open M-Sa 12:30-4pm and 8:30-11:30pm, Su 12:30-4pm. MC/V.)

Maremàgnum, Barcelona's glitzy leisure center, has a number of unsurprisingly seafood- and tourist-oriented restaurants, mostly chains. Fast food joints, ice-cream shops and pricey tapas places are in abundant supply. One exceptional choice, though slightly indulgent, is **Mandongo ❸**, on the second floor. The decor evokes a beachside bungalow, and the cuisine is a fusion of Asian and Mediterranean. Dishes include an outstanding salmon in banana leaf (€10.94), mouthwatering steaks (€12-20), and a specialty *paella* (€11.36), prepared to be eaten without a knife. The sushi (€8.47), however, leaves quite a bit to be desired. (☎93 225 81 43. Open M-F 1-4pm and 8pm-midnight, Sa-Su 1pm-midnight. MC/V.)

MONTJUÏC

see map p. 348

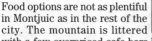

Food options are not as plentiful in Montjuic as in the rest of the city. The mountain is littered with a few overpriced cafe-bars like the popular **Bar Miramar** on the Miramar vista. The Fundació Miró, MNAC, Castell de Montjuïc, and Teatre Grec all have pleasant cafes, but to find more than drinks and sandwiches, one must turn to one of the restaurants listed below or enter the depths of Poble Espanyol, where *menús* serving food from all over Spain run €12. Some restaurants, bars, and grocery stores also line **Av. Parallel** in Poble Sec.

La Font de Prades (☎93 426 75 19), at the Plaça de la Font in Poble Espanyol. Set back in a quiet, less-trafficked area of Poble Espanyol, this elegantly romantic restaurant offers traditional Catalan cuisine in a tranquil atmosphere. Feast by the fountain on the *menú* (€12). Open Tu-Sa 1-4pm and 8:30-11pm. ❸

La Pérgola (☎93 325 20 08), at the corner of Av. Reina María Cristina and Av. del Marques de Comillas. 2 different restaurants at the same location. One offers a tasty buffet-style *menú* (€9.65) that is popular with international businessmen and tourists alike. (Open mid-June to Sept. Th-Su 1-4pm and 8-11pm, M-W 1-4pm; Oct. to mid-June daily 1-4pm.) ❷ The other offers a classic full-service dining room in which the tuxedoed staff will serve you such carefully prepared favorites as scallopini of suckling pig with Roquefort sauce (€10.80). Entrees €11-17.15; desserts €4.25-5.15. Open daily 1-3:30pm. ❹

Restaurante Bar Marcelino (☎93 441 10 79), on Av. Miramar right outside the funicular station. Refresh yourself at the bar or enjoy from the selection of combination plates (€5.41-6), pizzas (€5.40), and sandwiches on the outdoor patio. Open F-W 8am-9:30pm. ❷

the BIG $plurge

FRESH FISH

Restaurante Marisquería Salamanca, Almirante Cervera, 34 (☎93 221 50 33), set back from the beach toward the beginning of Pg. Marítim. If you're looking to splurge at the end of a long day at the beach, this is definitely the place to indulge your seafood cravings. With a shaded terrace right across from Platje Barceloneta, Salamanca has perhaps the best fish and the best view in Barceloneta. Grilled seafood appetizers come sizzling to your table, and the shellfish platter (€28) will keep you satisfied for days. Fish dishes €21-40. Open daily 1pm-midnight. ❺

Botafumeiro, C. Gran de Gràcia, 81 (☎93 218 42 30). M: Fontana, in **Gràcia**. Upscale and highly reputed Galician seafood restaurant serves large portions (entrees €13.25-34) in an elegant atmosphere where tuxedoed waiters sport huge smiles and tempt you with your every culinary fancy. Very popular, but less crowded at lunch. Reservations recommended. Open daily 1pm-1am. Closed first three weeks of Aug. AmEx/D/MC. Wheelchair accessible. ❺

143

WASTE WITH TASTE

Christmastime in Barcelona can look like a crappy way to spend the holiday. Why? You might be startled to see what appears to be feces in the windows of pastry shops and in the hands of young children. These marzipan cakes, called *tifas*, are a popular Christmas treat, disgustingly realistic, but actually pretty tasty.

The Catalan have an affinity for the scatological, which the Christmas season seems to bring to the forefront. On Christmas Eve, some Catalan families place under their tree a delightful little treat called the *Caga Tío*—the "Shit Log": a box filled with candies and goodies, covered by a blanket. The children then beat the shit out of it (pardon the pun) with sticks, chanting in Catalan: "Shit, log, shit, candies and nougat, and if you don't shit well, I'll bash you with my stick!" The log bursts open, rewarding the delighted children. For more on the Catalan affinity for Christmastime caga, see p. 214.

ZONA ALTA

GRÀCIA

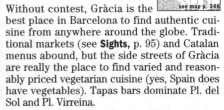
see map p. 346

Without contest, Gràcia is the best place in Barcelona to find authentic cuisine from anywhere around the globe. Traditional markets (see **Sights**, p. 95) and Catalan menus abound, but the side streets of Gràcia are really the place to find varied and reasonably priced vegetarian cuisine (yes, Spain does have vegetables). Tapas bars dominate Pl. del Sol and Pl. Virreina.

La Buena Tierra, C. Encarnació, 56 (☎93 219 82 13). M: Joanic. Follow C. Escorial for 2 blocks and turn left on C. Encarnació. Features vegetarian delicacies with a Catalan twist, but plenty of meat dishes too. Choose from a range of entrees like *moussaka* or *canelones de espinacas* (€4.51-6.85) and get back to nature on the backyard terrace. Open Tu-F 1-4pm and 8-11pm, F 1-4pm and 8pm-midnight, Su 1-4pm. D. ❷

La Gavina, C. Ros de Olano, 17 (☎93 415 74 50), at the corner of C. St. Joaquím. Funky Italian pizzeria complete with a life-size patron saint and confessional candles. Pizzas serving several people €7.50-16; try the *Catalana*—tomato, mozzarella, chorizo sausage, garlic, and artichokes (€16). Open Tu-Su 2pm-1am, F-Sa 2pm-2am. Wheelchair accessible. ❸

NUT, C. Verdi, 2 (☎93 210 86 40), at Pl. Revolució Setembre de 1868. M: Fontana. Don't walk like an Egyptian—eat like one! Cuisine from the land of the Pharoahs, like *kuchari* (rice with lentils and spices; €6.25), washed back with *carcade* (€3.50) in a stone-walled dining room bedecked by hieroglyphic tapestries. Entrees €4.60-9.85. Open daily 12:30-5pm and 8:30pm-1am. ❷

Restaurant Illa de Gràcia, C. Sant Domenec, 19 (☎93 238 02 29). M: Diagonal. Follow Gran de Gràcia for 5 blocks and make a right onto C. Sant Domenec. Huge vegetarian menu with tons of well-balanced options picked at by stylish young health-nuts. Excellent selection of fresh juices. *Menú* €5.41. Salads €3.31-4.21. Entrees €2.55-4.11. Open Tu-F 1-4pm and 9pm-midnight, Sa-Su noon-4pm and 9pm-midnight. Closed Aug. D/MC/V. ❶

Restaurante Casa Regina (El 19 De La Riera), C. Riera De Sant Miquel, 19 (☎93 237 86 01). M: Diagonal. Turn left on Diagonal, and C. Riera de Sant Miquel is the 1st right. Serves only organic food, including a salad bar and many vegetarian options. Plenty of magazines to browse through while eating. Lunch *menú* €6.50-9.50; dinner entrees €10.50-12. Open M-W noon-5pm, Th-Sa noon-5pm and 8-11pm. MC/V. ❸

El Tastavins, C. Ramón y Cajal, 12 (☎93 213 60 31), near Pl. Sol. M: Joanic. A small offering of satisfying Catalan mainstays. No English menu (or speakers), but waiters become masters of charades impersonating the dishes they wish to explain. *Menú* €7.45. Entrees €9.50-14.50. Open Tu-Sa 1:30-4pm and 9pm-midnight, Su 1:30-4pm. ❷

Equinox Sol, Pl. de Sol, 14 (☎ 93 415 79 76). FGC: Gràcia or M: Fontana. "The King of Shawarma & Falafel" boasts 3 family-run Lebanese restaurants; their Pl. del Sol branch is the busiest. Shawarma €2.70 for a sandwich, €4.50 for a meal; tabbouleh or falafel €3.35-4. Open daily 1pm-2am. ❶

Xavi Petit, C. Bonavista, 2 (☎93 237 88 26). M: Diagonal, off Gran de Gràcia. Cheese, meat, and chocolate-filled crêpes can be a hearty meal or just dessert at this friendly neighborhood cafe. Crêpes run €3.76. Crêpe-less afternoon *menú* €7.80. Tapas €1.05-3.76. Open M-Sa 8am-11:30pm. AmEx/V. ❷

HORTA

Horta's best-known restaurants are Can Cortada and Can Travi Nou. Neither is particularly cheap; nestled in spacious medieval dwellings, both are favorites of large tour groups, for good reason. The ▓**Can Cortada** ❹ was built in the 11th century as a feudal defense tower and converted into a farmhouse in the 15th century. On the way to the downstairs dining room you can still see the old underground dungeon tunnels and the horse feeding corner. Feast on their traditional Catalan staples. (Av. de l'Estatut de Catalunya. Exit left from M: Mundet and turn left onto Pg. de Vall d'Hebron; it is visible from Pg. de Vall d'Hebron. ☎93 427 23 15. Entrees €5.94-13.12. Three-course meal €18-27. Open daily 1:30-4pm and 8:30-11:30pm. Reservations recommended. AmEx/MC/V. Wheelchair accessible.) Five minutes down the street, 17th-century **Can Travi Nou** ❺ has a cozier, more residential atmosphere. (Exit M: Mundet to the left and turn right onto Pg. de Vall d'Hebron. Take a right at C. Jorge Manrique; it's at the end of the street. ☎93 428 03 01. Reservations recommended. Three-course meal €24-30. Open M-Sa 1:30-4pm and 8:30-11pm, Su 1:30-4pm. AmEx/MC/V. Wheelchair accessible.)

LES CORTS

Dining in Les Corts doesn't get too fancy. The neighborhood's small bars and cafes feed hordes of soccer fans on game days, but the area is not known for its cuisine.

El Cargolet Picant, Riera Blanca, 7 (☎93 334 04 54). M: Collblanc. At the corner of Trav. de Les Corts and C. Aristides Maillol. Busy even on non-game days, "The Spicy Snail" specializes in, of course, 9 snail dishes (about €9 each). Less adventurous visitors can choose from a number of meat entrees (about €4-8). *Menú* €7.36. Open daily 7am-2am. ❷

Interesting Seafood

Bakery

Brains

L'Ancora, Passatge Costa, 6 (☎93 440 00 07). M: Collblanc. Off C. de Collblanc, across the street from the Metro station. A convenient *cervecería* (beer cafe) that also sells ice cream and sandwiches. Start a debate over the latest Barça controversy while munching on *bocadillos* (€2.40) or Catalan entrees (€6). Open M-Sa 7am-8pm. ❷

SANTS

Sants boasts at least one phenomenal restaurant and several places worth leaving the station for a pre-train meal. For travelers shamelessly craving American fast-food sweets, there is a Dunkin' Donuts in Pl. Sants, behind the station.

🔳 **La Parra,** C. Joanot Martorall, 3 (☎93 332 51 34), a steep alley right of C. Sants, 2 blocks before M: Hostafrancs. An authentic experience if ever there was one. This hidden gem has been serving fresh Mediterranean fare in the same house for 2 centuries; when C. Sants was the main road into Barcelona, travelers would rest their horses here and eat before entering the city. Huge appetizers €9-13. Entrees €7-12. Open Tu-F 8:30pm-midnight, Sa-Su noon-4pm. MC/V. Wheelchair accessible only with difficulty. ❷

Calero's Pizzeria (☎93 411 04 13), at the corner of C. Galileo, on the right side of Pl. Sants coming from the back of the station. An Italian haven for lovers of pizza (€4.65-6.05) and pasta (€4.25-9.25) that draws nightly crowds of Catalan-speaking locals. Open M-Th 8:30-11:45pm, F-Su 2-4pm and 8:30-11:45pm. AmEx/MC/V. Wheelchair accessible. ❷

SARRIÀ

Sarrià is an excellent area for no-frills Catalan fare; most restaurants are on or very near C. Major de Sarrià. Come armed with your Catalan dictionary or just a sense of culinary adventure—most menus and waiters do not provide English translations. All restaurants are near M: Sarrià or Reina Elisenda.

Casa Joana, C. Major de Sarrià, 59 (☎93 203 10 36; fax 93 203 23 06). Traditional, tasty Catalan dishes are served in big portions at reasonable prices in this 4th-generation run restaurant. *Menú* (€11.50) includes an appetizer, entree, drink, and dessert. Open M-S 1-4pm and 9-11pm. D/MC/V. ❸

Caffe San Marco, C. Pedro de la Creu, 15, on the corner of C. Major de Sarrià. A little taste of Venice right here in Barcelona, complete with elaborate glass chandeliers and tasteful pale green curtains. Coffees and teas €0.80-4. Open M-Sa 7:30am-9:30pm, Su 8am-9:30pm. ❶

Foix de Sarrià, C. Major de Sarrià, 57 (☎93 203 07 14; fax 93 280 65 56). Elegant local pastry institution founded in 1886 and named for Catalan poet J.V. Foix. Peruse the irresistible selection of homemade tarts and cream-filled delights (around €2) served in the gilded interior; defy temptation if you can. Also stocks *gelato*, wine, cheeses, chocolates, and meats. Open daily 8am-9pm. **Branch** right up the street in Pl. de Sarria, 12-13 (☎ 93 203 04 73). ❶

Restaurante Maravillas, C. Cornet i Mas, 38. From C. Major de Sarrià, turn onto C. Rocaberti and walk 1 short block. Three tasteful and romantic rooms with soft lighting and pastel walls. Vegetarian options. Three-course lunch *menú* during the week €10.22. Entrees €5.41-15. Open M-Sa 1:30-4pm and 9-11:30pm. MC/V. ❸

Via Veneto, C. Ganduxer, 10-12. FGC: Bonanova or bus #67 or 68 from Pl. de Catalunya to Av. Diagonal just past Pl. Francesco Macia. C. Ganduxer begins at Av. Diagonal; the restaurant is 1 block up on the right. Surrounded by the upscale shops and modern high-rise apartment buildings of lower Sarrià, Via Veneto is right at home. Swanky and pricey (most entrees €11-30)—complete with a doorman—Via Veneto serves Spanish, Catalan, and French dishes. Open M-F 1:30-4pm and 8:45-11:30pm, Sa 8:45-11:30pm. MC/V. ❺

A'Rogueira, Pl. d'Artos, 6. A popular bar and restaurant with plenty of outside tables on the busy Pl. d'Artos, at the bottom of C. Major de Sarrià. Popular among locals and more affordable than most options in Sarrià. Tapas €0.90-7.20; *bocadillos* €2.10-5.40; entrees €3.90-15. Open daily 7am-2am. ❷

TIBIDABO

Tibidabo has several options for food, but most of them require stretching your budget; thirty- and forty-something professionals dominate the crowds here. Inside the Parc de Collserola, mediocre food options abound; check with the info office for a location guide. For self-starters, *merenderos* are open-air spaces with picnic tables, grills, and all the utensils you will ever need available for rent. Try the one at **Font de Les Planes**, FGC: Les Planes, across the highway bridge. (Tables €4 each. Grills €3, plus €10 deposit. Bag of charcoal €3.80. Paella pans €3 for 6 people, €4.80 for 12 people; additional €3 deposit. Open W-M 9am-7pm).

🔖 **El Asador de Aranda,** Av. de Tibidabo, 31 (☎93 417 01 15; www.asadoraranda.com). FGC: Av. Tibidabo. Halfway up the hill from Pl. JFK. Medieval romance in a luxurious historic building with enough authentic Castilian fare to write home about. 3-course *menús* start at €29.50. Open M-Sa 1-4pm and 9pm-midnight, Su 1-4pm. AmEx/MC/V. ❺

Restaurant Font de Les Planes (☎93 280 59 49). From FGC: Les Planes, walk across the highway bridge and through the large lot on your left. Restaurant is right behind the *merendero*. Make-your-own *pan con tomate* complements the succulent paella and grilled meats in this shady, quiet retreat from the bustle of the urban landscape. Great for a mid-hike meal. Entrees €5.25-13.20. Reservations recommended on Sa/Su. Open Sept.-June M-F 9am-10pm, Sa 9am-midnight, Su 9am-9pm; July-Aug. daily 9am-midnight. MC/V. ❷

La Venta (☎93 212 64 55). Pl. Dr. Andreu, at the end of Av. de Tibidabo. Good Catalan cuisine in an enticingly tiled-and-latticed dining room or a breezy terrace. Upscale crowd. Entrees €9.50-27. Open M-Sa 11:30am-3:15pm and 9-10:15pm. AmEx/MC/V. ❹

El Club dels Aventurers (☎93 211 79 42). Pl. del Tibidabo, in front of Parc d'Attracions. Mostly families venture into this self-dubbed "magic restaurant" for a large, but pricey, buffet (€14, children €12). Open daily 1-4:30pm. ❸

CHAINS

RESTAURANT CHAINS

Pans & Company. Perhaps the most visible franchise in Spain, this fast-food *bocadillo* chain started up in 1991 right here in Barcelona, as its Catalan name attests. Since then, it has spread like a tasty virus. Hot and cold *bocadillos* of ham, chicken, tuna, or other fillings come with fries and a drink for €3.95-5.50. Pre-prepared vegetable and pasta salads €2.40. Learn to love Pans—it's inescapable. ❶

Ice Cream and Outdoor Elevator

Granizado

Café con Leche

CAN I GET COFFEE WITH THAT?

Spanish coffee is known for being tasty and strong. Don't expect a water-downed version of a cup of Joe, because you're about to get the real thing. Also don't expect to find coffees to go, as European custom demands drinking leisurely on the spot.

Azucar: sugar.

Café: coffee with hot milk and sugar on the side; the *camarero* (waiter) will ask you to be more specific.

Cortado: an espresso-like coffee served in a smaller mug. It is mostly coffee with a bit of milk; sugar is provided on the side.

Café con leche: half coffee and half milk with sugar on the side. You can request to have it in a mug or a glass; generally consumed only at breakfast.

Café americano: a shot of espresso lengthened with hot water; closely resembles American coffee.

Café sólo: black coffee (no milk or sugar).

Café con hielo: iced coffee served in a tall glass; sugar on the side.

Leche: milk.

Other options: You can also request to have a **doble de café** which means that the *camarero* will double the amount of coffee in your drink (and add some milk) and serve it in a tall glass.

TapasBar (☎93 225 81 80), Moll d'Espanya. In spite of its tacky name, TapasBar is a card-carrying member of the elite club of Grade A restaurant chains; their bright yellow logo is a stamp of quality of atmosphere as well as of food. They have nearly 30 locations in Spain and Portugal (6 of them in Barcelona) and specialize in, you guessed it, tapas! (Two popular locations include the Moll d'Espanya and near the Hotel Arts on Av. Litoral Mar.) For adventurous diners, they offer 2-person meals of 8 kinds of tapas (€24-32). Most tapas €2.61-7.36. Coffee, desserts, full meals available. Hours vary per store, but most open around M-F 11am-1am, Sa-Su 11am-2am. AmEx/MC/V. ❸

FresCo, Ronda Universitat, 29 (☎93 301 68 37) off Pl. de Catalunya. M: Catalunya. A hugely popular all-you-can-eat buffet extravaganza. 3 l'Eixample locations attract everyone from tiny female Spaniards picking delicately at their salads to packs of ravenous families gorging themselves on a good deal. Either way, the endlessly varied salad bar, pasta, pizza, frozen yogurt, coffee, and fruit are the perfect escape from meat and oil-heavy Catalan staples. Lunch buffet €6.60, dinner buffet €8.80; both include 1 drink. Also at Av. Diagonal, 449 and C. València, 263. Reservations necessary on weekends. Open daily 12:45pm-1am. MC/V. ❷

Fresh & Ready. This 7-store chain has rapidly become a crutch for busy Catalan career-minded types. They serve coffee, juice, and pastries like any cafe, but also offer a huge array of refrigerated, pre-packaged salads, sandwiches, and yogurts to-go, ranging from Thai chicken and smoked salmon to simple *tortilla española*. The food is indeed fresh, though a little pricey for the small portions. Sandwiches and salads €2.55-3.75, half-sandwiches €1.50. Open Su-Th 8am-11pm, F-Sa 8am-midnight. Cash only. ❶

La Baguetina Catalana (☎93 539 52 08). With more than 42 stores in Barcelona, La Baguetina is almost as ubiquitous as Pans & Co. Its main offerings include *bocadillos, palmeras, croissants,* and *cocas* (bread pizzas), but it is best known for its late hours in tourist-heavy areas like Las Ramblas, where stumbling revelers line up for bready snacks until 3am. *Bocadillos* €2.40-3. *Cocas* €4.80. Opening hours range from 6-8am, depending on location, and closing hours from midnight to 3am. Cash only. ❶

Pastafiore. Owned by the same company as Pans & Co., Pastafiore serves up quick Italian food, including spaghetti, lasagna, ravioli, and tortellini. The hot dishes aren't half bad, and the midday *menú* (€5.95-7.50) is a decent deal for pizza, salad, and a drink. Pasta dishes around €4.50. Salads €2.95. Personal pizzas €4.65-5.95. Open Su-Th noon-midnight, F-Sa noon-1am. Cash only. ❶

Bocatta. Virtually indistinguishable from the yellow Pans & Co. with which it competes, save the green decor, and a selection of vegetable *bocadillos* (€2.40-3.30). Hot and cold *bocadillos,* heavy on the ham. Value meals €3.90-5.10. Salad selection a bit more varied (€2-3.15). ❶

Vips, Rambla de Catalunya, 7-9 (☎93 317 48 05). M: Catalunya. Barcelona's only international franchise, perfect for homesick Americans. Spanish and American food served in the restaurant, including grilled chicken salads, veggie sandwiches, quesadillas, and hamburgers (most around €6). The store sells books, road maps, and magazines, as well as CDs, videos, snacks, drinks, gifts, and cards. 4 computers for pricey Internet use, but check for frequently offered "specials" (9am-4pm €1.50 per 30min., 4pm-3am €0.90 for 15min.). Open daily 9am-3am. AmEx/MC/V. Wheelchair accessible. ❷

Hard Rock Café, Pl. de Catalunya, 21 (☎93 270 23 05). M: Catalunya. For those that want to rock and roll all night and party every day, but need an occasional break to eat. The 2hr. wait on many nights can be a major bummer. Good burgers (€6.49-9.79, including veggie burgers) and "Really Big Sandwiches" (€7.79-8.29) dominate the menu. Open daily 12:30pm-1am. For t-shirt seekers, the gift shop opens at 10am. ❷

COFFEE CHAINS

Though you won't find a Starbucks, rest assured that Barcelona has its own coffeehouse chains. All are roughly similar in prices and design; all serve a range of coffees and a small selection of ice cream, pastries, teas, and *bocadillos*, and generally offer breakfast specials for €1.50-3. **Jamaica** and **Il Caffe di Roma** are nearly indistinguishable. **Aroma** is the classiest of the lot, with warmly lit, dark wood interiors that almost conceal its chain status. But for all those homesick for a good ole' styrofoam cup of Joe, **Dunkin Donuts** pops up seemingly everywhere. Ah, some things never change.

Nightlife

The nightlife in Barcelona needs no introduction: whether you're looking for psychedelic absinthe shots, a great place for grunge rock, a sunrise foam party, or just someplace quiet to sit back and enjoy a drink (surrounded by fake gnomes), this city has it all. Things don't get going until late (don't bother showing up before 1am at a club) and keep going for as long as you can handle it. Check the *Guia del Ocio*, available at newsstands, for even more up-to-date listings of nighttime fun.

BARRI GÒTIC & LAS RAMBLAS

Nightfall is the only thing that really distinguishes the upper from the lower Barri Gòtic. The area above C. Ferran, dominated by shops, restaurants, and hostels, virtually shuts down by midnight, while C. Ferran and below starts to look like a human river, with tourists and locals alike weaving their way from bar to bar. There are a few clubs and several pop-hybrid bar/clubs in and near Pl. Reial, but overall the Barri Gòtic is the place for drinking and hanging out rather than for wild and crazy dance parties of the type found at Maremàgnum or Montjuïc. Also be advised that while the Pl. Reial has some great nightlife spots and is not particularly dangerous, it is also a touristed area with a colorful reputation that includes drug dealing, pick-pocketing, and prostitution. Don't go to this area looking for that action; it's not as visible as rumors would have you believe, and it is generally well-policed. The Pl. Reial is a fun place to pass the night, but watch your wallet and travel with a buddy.

BARS

Schilling, C. Ferran, 23 (☎93 317 67 87). M: Liceu. Don't let the fancy exterior or interior fool you. Schilling is surprisingly diverse and is one of the more chill bars in the area, with a lot more breathing space than most bars in the Barri Gòtic. Mixed gay and straight crowd. Excellent *sangría* (pitcher €13.40). Mixed drinks €4.90. Wine €1.70. Beer €1.70. Open 10am-2:30am. Cash only.

Vildsvin, C. Ferran, 38 (☎93 317 94 07). M: Liceu. On your right as you go down C. Ferran from Las Ramblas. Oysters are the speciality of the house at this Norwegian bar; get them on their own (half dozen €7.20; one dozen €13.20), with beer, or with *cava* (two oysters and a beer or a glass of *cava* €4.50). If you're tired of all the Damm beer that everyone else is serving, Vildsvin offers a wide selection of international beers (€4-7.50). Mixed crowd of tourists and locals. Dinner served. Tapas €3-5, desserts €3.50-10, entrees €8-26.50. Open 9am-2am, F-Sa 9am-3am.

El Bosq de les Fades (☎93 317 26 49). M: Drassanes. Walk to the Wax Museum and then make a right. From the maniacal geniuses who brought you the wax museum, El Bosq de les Fades (the Forest of Fables) is a fairy-tale world, complete with gnarly trees, waterfalls, gnomes, a small bridge, and plush side rooms. Open M-Th until 1:30am, F-Sa until 2:30am.

Molly's Fair City, C. Ferran, 7 (☎93 342 40 26). M: Liceu. With blaring music, fast-flowing imported beer, and a prime location next to the Pl. Reial, Molly's is the place to go if you're looking to meet English-speaking tourists in the Barri Gòtic, although plenty of Spaniards squeeze in as well. Guinness on tap €4.90. Bottled beer €4.40. Mixed drinks €6. Open M-F 8pm-2:30am, Sa-Su 7pm-3am. Cash only.

Dot Light Club, C. Nou de Sant Francesc 7 (☎93 302 70 26). M: Drassanes. Take the second right off C. Escudellers. It's easy to miss, so watch for the sign that reads "DOT" above the door. The chic atmosphere in this futuristic 2-room bar/club is all about funky lighting and cutting edge DJ action every night, with a different theme for each night of the week: Wednesday "Deep Beats," Thursday "Phat Beats," Friday "Spacefunk," etc. Nightly indy films at 10:30pm. Beer €2.70. Drinks €5.40. Open Tu-Th and Su 10:30pm-2:30am, F-Sa 10:30pm-3am. Cash only.

Margarita Blue, C. J. A. Clavé, 6 (☎93 317 71 76). M: Drassanes. Off Las Ramblas, 1 block from the port. With blue margaritas and retro-80s pop tunes, this Mexican-themed bar draws a 20- and 30-something crowd of locals and tourists alike. Creative Mexican food accompanies the tequila; most dishes run €3.50-8. Blue margaritas €3. Beer €3.45. Other drinks €5.10. Tu night magic shows, W night drag queen performances (around 11:30pm/midnight) Open Su-W 7pm-2am, Th 7pm-2:30am, F-Sa 7pm-3am (kitchen closes Su-Th at 1am, F-Sa at 1:30am).

Fonfone, C. Escudellers, 24 (☎93 317 14 24). M: Liceu or Drassanes. Atmospheric lighting and good sounds draw 1am crowds to FonFone, another futuristic bar/club mix with plenty of green leather couches and a good-sized dance area. A different DJ every night, drawing from talent pools as far away as San Francisco, NYC, and London. Music includes lounge, house, free style, garage, and more. Beer €3. Mixeddrinks €6. Open Su-Th 9:30pm-2:30am, F-Sa 9:30pm-3am. Cash only.

La Verònica, C. Avinyò, 30 (☎93 412 12 22). M: Liceu. Also has an entrance and outside tables on Plaça George Orwell. This funky bar fits in well with its location, serving cheap beer (€1.60) to an alternative crowd overlooking Plaça "Trippy." The friendly staff will make you feel like family. Salads and pizza served on weekend afternoons, with lots of vegetarian options. Mixed gay and straight crowd. Open daily 7pm-2am. Mixed drinks €3.

Café Royale, C. Nou de Zurbano, 3 (☎93 412 14 33). M: Liceu. On the tiny street leading out of the corner of Pl. Reial occupied by Jamboree (it's the street on the right if you walk into the *plaça* from Las Ramblas). The self-proclaimed "only" place in the city to chill out to soul and funk. Arrive by midnight if you want one of the velveteen or leather seats; after that, chances are you'll wait up to 1hr. to get in. Mixed crowd of 20- and 30-somethings. Beer €3.50. Mixeddrinks €4.80-6. Open Sa-Th 8pm-2:30am, F 8pm-3am. V, min. charge €24.

Glaciar Bar, Pl. Reial, 3. M: Liceu. In the near left corner coming from Las Ramblas. A hidden treasure in a sea of indistinguishable tourist bars. With a fancy, spacious interior, laid-back atmosphere, lots of local patrons, plenty of outside tables, and free winter photo exhibits upstairs. Beer €1.50-2. Mixed drinks €4. Liter of *sangría* €10. Open M-Sa 4pm-2:30am, Su 8am-2:30am. Cash only.

Harlem Jazz Club, C. Comtesa de Sobradiel, 8 (☎93 310 07 55). M: Liceu. Between Pl. Reial and Via Laietana. Live music alternating between blues, jazz, reggae, flamenco, and acoustic rock attracts international musicians from as far away as Senegal, Kenya, Brazil, and Cuba. Two sessions per night: Tu-Th and Su 10:30pm and midnight, F-Sa 11:30pm and 1am. The second session is always much more crowded, especially on weekends. Advance tickets/ current play schedules available at tourist offices and www.atrapalo.com. F-Sa cover €5 (includes 1 drink); occasionally weekday shows charge cover as well. Open daily 10pm-4am. Closes once a week, either on M or Tu. Get a schedule for the month at the front door. Cash only.

Barcelona Pipa Club, Pl. Reial, 3 (☎93 302 47 32). M: Liceu. Decidedly unmarked; look for the small name plaque on the door to the left of Glacier bar (on your left as you enter the square from Las Ramblas) and ring the doorbell to be let in. This private smokers' club opens daily (albeit inconspicuously). The decor is 100% Sherlock Holmes, the music jazz and fusion, the people a mix of local bartenders, artists, and tourists in the know. Occasional activities like tango classes and poetry readings. Gets crowded after 2am, no entrance allowed after 4am. Cocktails €5.50. Beer €3. Cash only. Open daily 11pm-5am.

Hook Bar, C. Ample, 35 (☎92 442 09 84). M: Drassanes from Las Ramblas turn down C. J. A. Clavé, which will turn into C. Ample. The bar is near the end of the street. If Peter Pan ever does grow up, this is where he'll come to drink; pirate gizmos and sailing paraphernalia deck the walls, and the cocktail menu includes drinks with names like "Niños Perdidos" (Lost Boys). Mainstream tourist crowds tend not to make it this far from Las Ramblas, but it might be worth coming just to indulge in a little history: in 1809, Catalan revolutionaries plotting against the Bourbon monarchy were hanged here, and the hook is still visible in the ceiling. Beer €2.50-3.50. Cocktails €5. Tapas €3-5. Open Tu-Th and Su 7:30pm-2am, F-Sa 7:30pm-3am. Cash only.

Casa El Agüelo, C. Avinyó, 37 (☎93 310 23 25). M: Liceu. Take a right off C. Ferran, coming from Las Ramblas. A cozy tavern whose decor is somewhere between medieval Catalonia and the American West. Brick walls, fireplaces, long wooden tables, and a cav-

DRINKING LIKE A SPANIARD

Anís: anisette; a licorice flavored liquor.

Bosca: vodka and a citrus carbonated beverage.

Calimocho: cheap red wine and Coke.

Cacique: rum with coke and lemon or orange soda.

Cava: Catalunya's versions of champagne. Tasty and cheaper than the real stuff.

Cerveza: Beer! *Caña de cerveza* means draught beer. For more on beer, see p. 158.

Chupito: a shot, generally taken after dinner or at a club.

Creme Catalana: a sweet liquor, similar to Bailey's.

Cuba Libre: Generally a rum and coke, although if you specify *con ginebra,* it's with gin.

Mini: a liter of beer, usually in a large lk cup.

Mosto: sweet white wine.

Sangría: A changing recipe that depends on the taste of the maker. Generally, *sangría* is made up of very cheap wine, spiced up with hard liquor, fruit, fruit juice, and some form of citrus carbonated beverage. The wooden spoon is to keep the ice and the fruit OUT of your glass; don't dump it all in.

Sidra: Basque cider, poured from a height to aerate the cider.

Sol y Sombra: cognac and anisette.

Ponché: also known as the "silver bullet." A sweet liquer.

Rioja: a region in Spain famous for its red wine.

Tinto: red wine.

Don Simón: boxed wine; typically drunk with Casera.

LGB ▼
BARCELONA

LGB Nightlife

Barcelona (and the surrounding beach towns, like Sitges) have some of the best LGB nightlife around—everything from raging clubs to low-key bars. Check out these listings to find what suits your tastes. In particular, the part of the l'Eixample Esquerra between C. Urgell, C. Aragó, the Gran Via, and C. Aribau is a virtual mecca for gay partying.

ernous, dungeon-like basement. A good place for cheap beer with a big group of friends. Beer €5 per liter, pitcher of *sangría* €8. Open M-F 7pm-2am, Sa-Su 7pm-3am. Cash only.

PLAÇA "TRIPPY"

This is the kind of place your mom prays you'll never set foot. Officially named Plaça George Orwell, this is a popular hangout for Barcelona's alternative crowd. It is rumored that the government removed all of the benches here to dissuade loitering and drug dealing; how successful they were is highly debatable. Two popular bar restaurants in the *plaça* have outside seating: **La Verònica** (see p. 152) and grungier, more casual **Bar Ovisos,** which stays open until 1am, offering simple Catalan food and cheap beer (€1.20 during the day, €1.80 at night).

CLUBS

Jamboree, Pl. Reial, 17 (☎93 319 17 89). M: Liceu. In the corner immediately to your right coming from Las Ramblas. What was once a convent now serves as one of the city's most popular live music venues. At 1:30am, the brick basement area turns into a packed hip-hop dance club (open until 5am). Jazz or blues performances daily M-F €6 with one drink, Sa-Su €9-12; €1.20 discount if you buy ahead of time at a ServiCaixa machine. Open daily 11pm-1am. Upstairs, the attached club **Tarantos** hosts flamenco shows for the tourist set. (€25) Open M-Sa 9:30pm-midnight.

New York, C. Escudellers, 5 (☎93 318 87 30). M: Drassanes, right off Las Ramblas. Once a strip joint, now the biggest club in the Barri Gòtic, with plenty of drink tables overlooking the red-and-black, strobe-lit dance floor. Crowds don't arrive until well after 3am; music includes reggae and British pop. Cover 11:30pm-2am €5.40 (includes 1 beer); 2-5am €11.40, (includes any drink). Open Th-Sa midnight-5am. Cash only.

Karma, Pl. Reial, 10. M: Liceu. In the back right corner coming from Las Ramblas. A basement-level dance club with a long and narrow dance floor playing rock and pop to a touristy crowd in their late 20s or 30s. Bar upstairs has outdoor seating. Beer €3. Mixed drinks €6. Open Tu-Su midnight-5am. Cash only.

see map p. 341

LA RIBERA

Plàstic Café, Pg. del Born, 19 (☎93 310 25 96). M: Jaume I, follow C. Princesa, turn right on C. Comerç, and right again on Pg. del Born. "Café" is a misnomer for this jam-packed, hyper trendy bar, with a funky mix of international, house, and 80s pop spinning in the background. Watch friendly bartenders do fancy tricks with bottles or hit the small dance floor reserved for those who just can't help shaking their booty to the head-bobbing tunes. Beer €2.40-3. Mixed drinks €3 and up. Open Su-Th 10pm-2:30am, F-Sa 10pm-3am.

El Copetin, Pg. del Born, 19. M: Jaume I. Cuban rhythm infuses everything in this casual yet peppy nightspot. Grab a *mojito* (€4), the mint concoction that is the *copetin* (cocktail) of the house, and enjoy the live Cuban music that fills the air with tropical spirit. Open Su-Th 6pm-2am, F-Sa 6pm-3am.

Palau Dalmases, C. Montcada, 20 (☎93 310 06 73). A self-labeled "Baroque space" in a 17th-century palace fittingly decorated with lavish oil paintings, candelabras, and statues. Romantic candle-lit tables complete the atmosphere. Live opera performances Th at 11pm (€20, includes one drink). Mixed drinks €5.40-9. Fresh juice €7.20. Open Tu-Sa 10pm-2am, Su 6pm-10pm.

Pitin Bar, Pg. del Born, 34 (☎93 319 50 87). Chill beneath a starry sky of tiny blue lights, or people-watch from one of the intimate upstairs tables. Trippy lounge music will put you in the mood for absinthe (€2.10). Mixed drinks €4.50-8. Open daily 6pm-2am.

Mudanzas, C. Vidreira, 15 (☎93 319 11 37). M: Jaume I. Everything is black, even the suits. The only color comes from hundreds of illuminated bottles lining the wall behind the bar. A hip, young, professional crowd. Wide selection of rum, whiskey, and wines €1.20-5. Open Su- F 10am-2am, Sa 11am-2am.

EL RAVAL

see map p. 340

BARS

If glamorous clubs and all-night dancing are your scene, El Raval is not for you. El Raval is densely packed with a bar for every variety of bar-hopper: the Irish pubber, the American, the absinthe-abuser, the social drinker, the lounge lizard, and the foosball maniac.

La Oveja Negra, C. Sitges, 5 (☎93 317 10 87). M: Catalunya. From Pl. de Catalunya, go down Las Ramblas and take the 1st right onto C. Tallers; C. Sitges is the 1st left. The most touristed tavern in town. Gossip (in English) about your European backpacking romp over foosball and huge pitchers of beer or *sangría* (€6.90). Open M-Th 9am-3am, F 9am-3:30am, Sa 5pm-3:30am, Su 5pm-3am.

(El Café que pone) Muebles Navarro, Riera Alta, 4-6, a right off C. Carme. A mature local crowd is drawn here by the eclectic art decorating the walls, mellow

in recent news

Inside Voices

Pumping house beats might be the nighttime prowler's idea of a good time, but one man's pleasure is another man's pain. **The people of La Ribera**—or at least those whose clubbin' days belong to yesteryear—have recently decided they have had enough of being kept up by the vocal pyrotechnics of drunken tourists belting out their national anthem and Britney Spears moaning her latest tune. Frustrated that their complaints to the city have been ignored because the nightlife industry brings so much revenue to the city, the locals have organized themselves into an association, **El Fórum Veinal de la Ribera (FVR),** to demand that the city mandate a reduction in the late-night noise and come up with a plan for how to balance out the interests of nightlife entrepreneurs with the interests of those who hope to sleep at night. So far the house has not turned down its house music or stopped serving intoxicated tourists, but the battle is not over yet.

ABSINTHE MINDED

Step inside the old-fashioned bars of El Raval and you are likely to find daredevils sipping *absenta* (absinthe), the translucent golden firewater banned everywhere except Spain and the Czech Republic. This licorice-flavored alcohol comes from the ajenjo plant and is said to have hallucinogenic affects similar to peyote. Once France's national drink, 150-proof absinthe used to be all the rage among Impressionist painters and the Parisian bourgeoisie. Supposedly, the death of artist Paul Gauguin (and the discovery of more than 200 bottles of the stuff under his bed) prompted France to call for absinthe abstinence.

Spain chose not to follow suit, however, and the drink is still served in a safer 110-proof version (a more potent 140-proof version is also available). Served with a bottle of water, a sugar cube, and a spoon, there is a certain method to the madness. First, soak the sugar cube in the flammable alcohol. Then, holding the cube in the spoon, light the sugar on fire, repeating as necessary, until the sugar has melted and can be stirred into the drink. The water serves either to dilute the strong-tasting drink, or as a chaser if you choose to take it straight up. Though hardly hallucinogenic, the drink can still do a number on the drinker, creating a detached, spaced-out feeling and causing memory loss. Sage bartenders warn that even two absinthes may end your night early, and that three or more can be, as our humble Let's Go researchers discovered, "bad news."

ambience ideal for conversation, and huge, comfy conches on which friends get friendlier as they snuggle. Beer and wine €2-2.50, mixed drinks €3.60-9. Snacks (€1.35-5.10) served until 11:30pm. Open Tu-Th 6pm-2am, F-Sa 6pm-3am.

London Bar, C. Nou de la Rambla, 34 (☎93 318 52 61). M: Liceu. Off Las Ramblas. Rub shoulders with unruly, fun-loving expats at this smoky Modernist tavern, around since 1910. Live music starts at 12:30am nightly, usually rock or blues. Beer €3; wine €2; absinthe €3. Open Su and Tu-Th, 7:30pm-4:30am, F-Sa 7:30pm-5am.

Sant Pau 68, C. Sant Pau, 68 (☎93 441 31 15). M: Liceu. Follow C. Sant Pau off Las Ramblas past Marsella Bar. Popular among locals, Sant Pau 68 is one of the hippest, newest bars in El Raval. Party away in the club-like ground floor or chill in the calmer loft area upstairs with your beer (€1.80), wine (€1.20), or mixed drink (€4.20-6). Open Tu-Th 8pm-2:30am, F-Sa 8pm-3am.

Marsella Bar, C. Sant Pau, 65 (☎93 442 72 63). M: Liceu. Follow C. Sant Pau off Las Ramblas to the corner of Sant Ramon. Enjoying a drink in a 19th-century tavern must have felt a lot like this. Religious figurines grace the dark wood-paneled walls of this weathered watering hole packed with foreigners and locals alike; hopefully they're watching over the adventurous absinthe drinkers (€3.30) who frequent the place. Beer €2, mixed drinks €4.50. Open M-Th 10pm-2:30am, F-Sa 10pm-3:30am.

Lupino, C. Carme, 33 (☎93 412 36 97). M: Liceu. Ultra-chic restaurant and lounge right out of L.A. combines dynamic, articulate lighting and a cool aqua color scheme into a work of art that makes you want to go to design school. Restaurant offers such delights as lamb confit with peach medley sauce (€10.20). Cocktails €5.50. Restaurant open Su-W 8:30pm-midnight, Th-Sa 8:30pm-1am. Lounge open Su-Th noon-2:30am, F-Sa noon-3am.

Casa Almirall, C. Joaquim Costa, 33. M: Universitat. Take the C. Pelai Metro exit, turn left at the end of the block, and turn again at the 2nd left. The bar is down a few blocks at the corner of C. Ferlandina. A cavernous space with weathered couches and a dark, warm ambience. Laid-back Casa Almirall is Barcelona's oldest bar, founded in 1860. The staff will walk you through your first glass of *absenta* (absinthe; €4.50)—and cut you off after your second (see **Absinthe Minded,** p. 156). Beer €1.90, mixed drinks €5. Open Su-Th 7pm-2:30am, F-Sa 7pm-3am.

Rita Blue, Pl. Sant Agustí, 3, on C. Hospital (☎93 318 63 21), off Las Ramblas. It's not clear why Rita is blue, considering the excellent live music at her hip, colorful restaurant/bar/club. Live house music plays W-Su nights (11pm) downstairs. DJs, poetry slams, and other musical performances are scheduled regularly. Call ahead. Beer €2.20, mixed drinks €5-10. Open Th-Sa 1pm-3am, Su-W 1pm-2am.

The Quiet Man, Marqués Barbera, 11 (☎93 412 12 19). M: Liceu. Take C. Unió off Las Ramblas; after 2 blocks it becomes Marqués Barbera. As authentic an Irish pub as you'll find in Barcelona, with a homey decor, a good collection of Beleek (fine Irish china), and a friendly Irish staff. Live music (pop, hip-hop, and jazz) Th-Sa at midnight, Su at 8:30pm. Pints of imported drafts €4, bottles €3.40; mixed drinks €5.20. Open Su-W 6pm-2:30am, Th-Sa 6pm-3am.

Pastis, Santa Mónica, 4 (☎93 318 79 80), off Las Ramblas. Every square inch of this small, crowded, over 50-year old tavern is covered with something of interest: portraits, pictures, alcohol, a false woman suspended from the ceiling, and, most appealingly, people. Sept.-July live French music Su 11:30pm, live tango bands Th 11:30pm. Open Su-Th 7:30pm-2am, F-Sa 7:30pm-3:30am.

Jamboree, Pl. Reial

La Confiteria, Sant Pau, 128 (☎93 443 04 58). M: Parallel. At the corner of Rda. Sant Pau. At this former bakery, happily chatting customers from all over the world have replaced the cookies and cakes formerly on display in its large windows. Wood panels and soft frescoes decorate the classic, well-lit bar. Step into the back room for a decidedly more modern feel, with additional tables and rotating art and photography exhibits. Beer €1.50; wine €1.60; mixed drinks €4.75. Tapas (€3.10-8.45) served until midnight. Open M-Sa 6pm-3am, Su 6pm-2am.

Muy Buenas, C. Carme, 63 (☎93 442 50 53). M: Liceu. The bar area suggests a time-warp back to the early days of the last century, but the boldly painted walls put this cavernous 2-story tavern squarely in modern times. Serves Middle Eastern food daily 1-5pm and 8pm-12:30am. Poetry readings at 9pm on Su and W. Open Su-Th 9am-2am, F-Sa 9am-3am.

Pool at La Oveja Negra

Raval-Bar, C. Doctor Dou, 19 (☎93 302 41 33). No matter how tired or stressed they may be, locals come here to sit with friends, listen to music, and waste their night away on huge U-shaped couches, staring up at a 6m-tall woman with a beer. Beer €2.40; wine €1.80. Open Su-W 8pm-2:30am, F-Sa 8pm-3am.

Acido Oxido, C. Joaquim Costa, 61 (☎93 412 09 39). M: Universitat. Take the C. Pelai Metro exit, turn left at the end of the block, and turn again at the 2nd left. Caters to a gay clientele. Order mixed drinks (€6-9, 1 drink min.) from a briefs-clad bartender as you saddle up to the bar. Where some bars opt for sports or sitcoms on the TV, the Acido showcases hardcore gay porn videos, while patrons dance on the small dance floor in the back or hook up in the transparent bathrooms. Open daily 10pm-2:30am and 5-9:30am.

Beer at La Oveja Negra

BEER!

Barcelona beer-drinkers have been Dammed to an eternity of mediocre to sub-par beers, thanks to a near monopoly by the Damm brewing company. Barcelona's biggest brewery produces **Estrella Damm,** the default beer at nearly every bar in the city, often the only choice on tap. If you want to drink cheaply, get used to this somewhat bitter pilsner. Other less common variants include Voll-Damm, a 7.2% alcohol beast of a beer, and just plain Damm.

Of local beers, **San Miguel** is perhaps the best option, a bit smoother than its Damm counterparts. One can occasionally order southern Spanish beers such as **Cruzcampo,** which at least assure Barcelona drinkers that they're not missing much. **Heineken,** which has a brewery in Sevilla, is by far the most common import, with the Mexican **Corona** (here called *Coronita*) also a favorite. Perhaps spurred on by the uninspiring Spanish beer selection, the city has a surprising number of expat pubs, where one can always find a good pint of **Guinness.**

CLUBS

La Paloma, Tigre, 27 (☎93 301 68 97). M: Universitat. Take the C. Pelai Metro exit, turn left at the end of the block, and walk down Rda. Sant Antoni until you reach C. Tigre on your left. The club is a block down. One would never guess that this dance hall, with its ornate, theater-like interior, huge dance floor, and balcony seating, was a factory until 1903. Live salsa and popular Spanish music keeps a more mature clientele dancing throughout the night, but a younger crowd storms the place on Thursday when the club turns into "Bongo Lounge," a raging dance scene (midnight-5:30am), as well as late Friday and Saturday nights when live DJs take control of things. Drinks €5-8. Cover Th-Su 6-9:30pm €3.50; other times €6. Paloma open Th-Su 6-9:30pm, F 11:30pm-2:30am, Sa 11:3pm-3am. Bongo open F 2:30-6am, Sa 3-6am.

Moog, Arc del Teatre, 3 (☎93 301 72 82). M: Drassanes. Off Las Ramblas, down the alley next to the Easy Everything Internet center. One of the focal points of the emerging Barcelona techno scene. Serious fans pack this small club for a late-night dose of hard electronica. Regular appearances by major international DJs, especially on W nights. Upstairs, on a smaller dance floor, a gay-straight mixed crowd grooves to 70s and 80s disco music (open 2-5am). Cover and drink €12, before 2am (with flyer given out on Las Ramblas) €8. Beer €4, mixed drinks €8. Open nightly midnight-5am or later; most don't show up until 2 or 3am.

L'EIXAMPLE

see map p. 344-345

The wide variety of nightlife options in L'Eixample reflects the area's ideal of openness; there is a place for everyone here. Most of the biggest and best *discotecas* rock and bop it here outside the tourist-heavy Ramblas area—this is where most natives do their dancing. Most of the places worth trekking to are located in western l'Eixample Esquerra, although a few are scattered on the right side. The part of l'Eixample Esquerra (west of Pg. de Gràcia) between C. Urgell, C. Aragó, the Gran Via, and C. Aribau is dense with gay nightlife, hence its apropos nickname, "Gay-xiample."

BARS

▨ **La Fira,** C. Provença, 171 (☎658 84 04 15). M: Hospital Clinic or FGC: Provença. A bar like no other, La Fira is a hodgepodge collection of fun house and circus castaways. Bartenders pour drinks under the big top for a hip crowd reclining in red pleather booths or dangling from carousel swings. Creepy fun-house mirrors and laughing clowns complete the picture. DJs spin a mix of funk, disco, and oldies. Open M-Th 10pm-3am, F-Sa 10pm-4:30am, Su 6pm-1am.

Dietrich, C. Consell de Cent, 255 (☎93 451 77 07). M: Pg. de Gràcia. A rather unflattering painting of Marlene Dietrich in the semi-nude greets a mostly gay crowd. Bartenders are scantily clad, and at 1:30am you can see even more flesh and some incredible feats of flexibility when the nightly drag/strip/dance show begins. Trendy partiers crowd in to be part of the action. Beer €3.50. Drinks €5-8. Open Su-Th 10:30pm-2:30am, F-Sa 10:30pm-3am.

El Café que pone Muebles Navarro

Fuse, C. Roger de Llúria, 40 (☎93 301 74 99), between C. Gran Via and C. Diputació. M: Tetuán or Pg. de Gràcia. A cutting-edge Japanese-Mediterranean restaurant, cocktail bar, dance club, and Internet cafe all in one. Techno and electronic dance floor with riser seating for people-watching. Mixed gay and straight crowd in their 20s. Beer €2.40, mixed drinks €6. Restaurant open M-Sa 8:30pm-1am (3 courses with wine €24-30). Bar/club open Th-Sa 1-3am. MC/V.

Les Gens que J'Aime, C. València, 286 (☎93 215 68 79), just off Pg. de Gràcia. M: Pg. de Gràcia. Travel back to Gaudí's time in this intimate bar dripping with chandeliers, mirrors, old paintings, plush corner sofas, and arm chairs. Background soul, funk, and jazz sooths those looking for something a bit more chill. Beer €3, mixed drinks €5. Mini-bottles of wine €8.10. Open daily 7pm-2:30am. Cash only.

Casa Almirall

The Michael Collins Irish Pub, Pl. Sagrada Família, 4 (☎93 459 19 64). M: Sagrada Família. Directly across the *plaça* from the church. Popular among locals in their late 20s and 30s. 100% Irish, from the waitstaff to the smoky, wooden decor. American and European sports on the TV. Pub food Sept-June 1-8pm (sandwiches €3-5). Live music Th-Su after 11pm (Irish, local guitarists, covers of American rock). Pint of Guinness €3.80. Bottled beer €2.90, mixed drinks €5. Open daily 2pm-3am. Cash only.

berlin, C. Muntaner, 240 (☎93 200 65 42). M: Diagonal. A slice of streamlined German style in Barcelona. Corner bar with marble accents and huge, naked light bulbs attracts area hipsters and hordes of l'Eixample yuppies and Barcelona's most beautiful people. Beer €1.80-2.40, mixed drinks €3.61-4.80.

Raval Bar

domèstic, C. Diputació, 215 (☎93 453 16 61). M: Urgell. Multifaceted *bar-musical* with frequent poetry readings, art expositions, and live music. If all that seems too ambitious, it's also a fine place to just sit and have a drink. Artsy, too-cool-for-capital-letters crowd takes in funk, acid jazz, and soul rhythms on domèstic's overstuffed chairs. Small offering of eclectic Mediterranean food until midnight €3-7.80. Beer €2.50, mixed drinks €5. Open Tu-Th, Su 7pm-2:30am; F-Sa 8pm-3am.

from the
road

Sleepless in Barça

I consider myself an avid partygoer back in the US, so I was excited to get to Barcelona, a city famous for its hard-core nightlife. My first night in Barcelona, I followed my normal, U.S. routines: I had dinner at 7, came home, got dressed, and went with friends to a bar at 11.

We stood alone in the bar for an hour and wondered where everyone was. After visiting a few more similarly vacant bars, we hit up a club at 12:30am. The bouncer looked at us like we were crazy and let us in, no cover.

If you want to have an entire discotheque to yourself for free, head to a club at 12:30am. In Barcelona bars don't get started until about 1am, and the clubs until (at the *very* earliest) 2:30am or 3am. As we walked the streets to kill time, people were leisurely finishing dinner. When we finally made it back to the club at 2:30, we asked the age-old question that has occurred to tourists visiting Spain since the dawn of time: "How do Spaniards get up in the morning?"

If anyone in Barcelona *was* awake the next morning, we were too unconscious to know about it. If you want to make the most of Barcelona's nightlife, though, learn to make most of your siesta time, because when people in this country party, they mean business.

—Adam Weiss

Topxi, C. València, 358 (☎93 207 01 20), just off Pg. St. Joan. M: Verdaguer. A small, unpretentious bar/club that just happens to put on some of the most flamboyant drag queen shows in the city—in intimate quarters. Daily shows at 2am, plus a sit-down show Su at 8pm. Mostly gay crowd, but some women and straight couples as well. Cover €6 for men, €9 for women (includes 1 drink). Open M-Th 11pm-5am, F-Sa 11pm-6am, Su 7pm-5am. Cash only.

Caligula, C. Consell de Cent, 257 (☎93 451 48 92). M: Pg. de Gràcia. Gay bar invokes a romantic atmosphere with draped fabrics, tea lights, and massive floral arrangements. Chill crowd gathers around bar and sidewalk tables. Look out for a hot pink poodle! Beer €4, mixed drinks €5-7. Open daily 10pm-3am.

The Pop Bar, C. Aribau, 103 (☎93 451 29 58). M: Hospital Clinic or FGC: Provença. Groovy baby, yeah! Join a hip crowd and travel back in time to the early 60s, when orange and brown was a cool color combination. DJs spin house and pop, as well as the requisite 60s tunes. Beer €3-3.60, mixed drinks €4.80. Open Tu-Sa 10pm-3:30am.

Aloha, C. Provença, 159 (☎93 451 79 62). M: Hospital Clinic or FGC: Provença. Barcelona's Hawaiian paradise—complete with exotic caged birds, leis, and plenty of bamboo. 2 pool tables and a wide liquor selection. Cross the bridge by the waterfall to find the darkened, intimate tiki huts perfect for private parties for 2 to 20. Try the *coco loco,* coconut milk and rum (€6). Second drinks are half price. Open Su-Th 6pm-3am and F-Sa 6pm-4am.

La Filharmónica, C. Mallorca, 204 (☎93 451 11 53). M: Hospital Clinic, or FGC: Provença. English pub hosts live music (jazz, tango, blues, country) almost every night, and is a popular place for both young and old. Don't miss the country line dance classes Su and Tu nights, or quiz night (in Eng.) on Th. Daily *menú* €7.80. Sunday's special is roast beef and potatoes. Pint of Guinness €4.90, cocktails €4-5. Live music cover €3.75-6 (includes one drink). Open M-Th 9am-2:30am, F 9am-3:30am, Sa 11am-3:30am, Su 11am-2:30am.

Let's Go, Av. Diagonal, 337 (☎93 458 21 60), next to Pg. St. Joan. M: Verdaguer. Great minds think alike, no? Just like the guide your eyes are skimming, this local bar's specialty is doing things on the cheap, with beer a mere €2. Foosball, pool, and Spanish and English pop music. Drinks €4. Open daily 10pm-2am. Cash only.

CLUBS

▨ **Buenavista Salsoteca,** C. Rosselló, 217 (☎93 237 65 28). FGC: Provença. Appropriately, this over-the-top salsa club manages to attract a laid-back crowd. The music is irresistible and the dancers are not shy. Free salsa and merengue lessons W and Th at 10:30pm. Su-Th free; F-Sa cover €9 (includes 1 drink). Open W-Th 11pm-4am, F-Sa 11pm-5am, Su 8pm-1am.

Luz de Gas, C. Muntaner, 246 (☎93 209 77 11). M: Diagonal. Chandeliers, gilded mirrors, and deep red walls set the mood in this hip, uptown club. Live music every night including the occasional big-name jazz, blues, or soul performer like Branford Marsalis or Monica Green. After 1am, the chairs are folded up and the luxurious club becomes a high-class disco. Beer €5, mixed drinks €8. Live music concerts €15; check the *Guía del Ocio* for listings. Wheelchair accessible. Open M-Sa 11pm-5am.

Beer at Pl. Pi

Salvation, Ronda de St. Pere, 19-21, between C. Bruc and Pl. Urquinaona. M: Urquinaona. The place to come if you've sinned...and want to keep on sinning. A popular gay club with 2 huge dance floors and pounding house music. Su is a mixed crowd; F and Sa women have to have special passes, which they can request midnight-3am at Dietrich (see p. 159), Zeldas, or Medusa. Beer €5, mixed drinks €8. Cover €9 (includes 1 drink). Wheelchair accessible. Open F-Su midnight-6am.

La Boite, Av. Diagonal, 477 (☎93 419 59 50). M: Hospital Clinic, club is inside courtyard. Big names sometimes come to perform in this intimate disco setting. Live jazz, funk, and blues nightly midnight-2am. A smaller dance floor and plenty of bar room makes this a great place for people that shun the gyrating masses of larger venues. Drinks €4.20-7.20. Music cover Su-Th €6, F-Sa €9. Disco free entrance Su-Th after 2am, cover €12 F-Sa after 2am (includes one drink). Open Su-Th 11:30pm-5am, F-Sa 11:30pm-6am.

Cava at Xampanyet

Illusion, C. Lepanto, 408 (☎93 247 36 00), right below M: Alfons X. A favorite destination for students and local kids in their 20s, this club is more happening in the winter than summer. Two dance rooms: house music in the main and salsa in the smaller. Go-go shows every 15min. or so, starting around 3am. Beer €4, mixed drinks €6. Hosts a gay session ("T Dance") Su 7pm-midnight. 18+. Cover F €6, Sa €8, Su €7.50. Open F midnight-5am, Sa 6-10pm (for 16+) and 12:30-5:30am. Closed Aug. Cash only.

Aire (Sala Diana), C. València, 236. M: Pg. de Gràcia. One of Barcelona's biggest and most popular lesbian clubs. Throngs of women crowd the multicolored dance floor, grooving to pop, house, and 80s classics. Women-only strip show from 6-10pm first Su of every month. Cover Su-F €5, Sa €6 (includes one drink). Open Su-F 11pm-3am. Check out the Arena family's other **gay discos,** some of the most popular in the area: **Arena (Sala Classic)** at C. Diputació, 233 plays 80s tunes; **Arena (Sala Dandy)** at Gran

Absinthe

161

Via, 593 pumps techno beats. The popular **Arena (Sala Madre)** at C. Balmes, 32 is mostly for men, as is the more relaxed **Punto BCN** bar at C. Muntaner, 63.

Sol, C. Villarroel, 216 (☎93 237 86 58). M: Hospital Clinic or Diagonal. Barcelona's beautiful, uptown set hits the wooden, elegantly lighted dance floor or mingles upstairs on the chill cream couches. Downstairs disco plays pop and house; upstairs smaller, less intense disco. Mixed drinks €4.80-7.20. Cover €9 (includes one drink). Open Th-Sa midnight-5:30am.

see map p. 349

POBLE NOU

If you want to party in Poble Nou, trade in your skimpy clubbing outfit for something a little more grunge, brush up your foosball skills, and be prepared to indulge in some heavy metal with rebellious Spanish teens. This neighborhood is the place to be for hard rock and alternative music. Locals have put abandoned warehouses to good use in the blocks around M: Marina, and more than 20 bars and discos coexist within a few minutes of each other. The drinking here is remarkably cheap, and as the patrons are locals, not tourists, the crowd flow is the reverse of the rest of the city: packed during the school year and slower in the summer.

La Ovella Negra (Megataverna del Poble Nou), C. Zamora, 78 (☎93 309 59 38). From M: Marina, walk 2 blocks along C. Almogàvers and turn right on C. Zamora. This cavernous warehouse turned medieval tavern is the brother of La Oveja Negra in El Raval and is *the* place to come for the first few beers of the night. Foosball games on the 2nd floor are nearly as intense as the real-life FCB/Real Madrid rivalry. Filling tapas and *bocadillos* €2-4. Wheelchair accessible. Kitchen open until 12:30am. Open Th-Su 5pm-3am; disco open Sept.-May.

Razzmatazz, C. Pamplona, 88 (☎93 320 82 00), 2½ blocks from M: Marina following C. Almogàvers. Another huge warehouse turned entertainment complex, with huge, strobe-lit dance floors and a few lounge areas. A 2-in-1 club: choose the front entrance for 3 rooms *or* the back entrance for 2; the entrances are not connected. Cover €8, includes 1 drink. Open F, Sa, and holidays 1-5am. MC/V.

DIXI 724, C. Pallars, 97. Boasts cheap beer, a bizarre shark-turned-airplane hanging from the ceiling, and tons of space for college crowds. Open F-Su 6pm-3am.

Bar Coyote & Co., C. Pere IV, 68. Offers a Western twist on the typical Spanish bar, complete with a poster of the Coyote Ugly girls. Open F-Su 6pm-3am.

Q3, C. Pere IV, 49. Small heavy-metal haven blasts Marilyn Manson. Open F-Sa 6pm-6am.

Boveda, C. Pallars, 97. Boveda celebrates its impressive 10-year anniversary as a consistently popular club with loud, pounding dance beats. Open F-Sa 6pm-10pm and midnight-6am, Su 6pm-10pm.

Garatge Club, C. Pallars, 195. You'll feel right at home when this club rolls up its graffiti-covered garage door to serve as a venue for hard rock concerts.

see map p. 349

PORT OLÍMPIC

Cinderella and the Port Olímpic have one thing in common: after midnight they become entirely different creatures. In contrast to the rest of Poble Nou, the Port Olímpic caters to tourists with money to burn. A long strip of single-room, side-by-side glitzy clubs fling open their doors, and the once-peaceful walkway becomes a packed carnival of wild, skimpily dressed dance fiends and late-night eaters and drinkers (food options include McDonald's, Häagen-Daz, hotdog stands, and fish restaurants). Mixed drinks are expensive (€6-7.25), but people seem to get enough to start table-dancing almost as soon as the doors open. **Pachito** is the place to go for swanky clubbers; the **Kennedy Irish Sailing Club** (beer €4.21) is a popular haven for pubbers. There is no cover anywhere. If you don't like the music in one club, just shove your way outside and choose another; the range includes salsa, techno, hip-hop, and plenty of American pop. The entire complex is open 5pm-6am.

PASSEIG MARÍTIM

Just to the right of the port, facing the water, these establishments each have large buildings of their own and do charge cover.

Luna Mora (☎93 221 61 61). C. Ramón Trias Fargas, on the corner with Pg. Marítim. This lunar-themed, planetarium-like disco with a more mature crowd is one of the best places for late-night dancing on the beach. 2 huge dance floors, one for salsa and one for house, and plenty of long couches. The mostly local crowd doesn't arrive until 3am. Beer €5, mixed drinks €8. Cover (includes one drink) €12. Open F midnight-6am, Sa midnight-6:30am.

El El, Pg. Marítim, 36 (☎93 225 92 00). From the beach, hidden behind the Greek restaurant Dionisos; enter from above. Colored strobe lights, fog machines, and techno beats entrance the wild crowd at this lively dance club. Beer €4, mixed drinks €7. Cover (includes 2 drinks) Th-F and Su €12, Sa €15, free if you eat dinner at Dionisos. Open July-Aug. daily midnight-6am; Sept.-June Th-Su midnight-6am. MC/V.

Baja Beach Club, Pg. Marítim, 34 (☎93 225 91 00). If Baywatch were a club, this would be it. When not platform-dancing, bikini-clad waitresses and shirtless muscle men serve drinks from coolers as patrons get their groove on amidst fake palm trees and a decorative speedboat. Indoor/outdoor restaurant and an ATM. Food served until 12:30am; entrees €7.80-21.05. Beer €3.50, mixed drinks €7. Cover Th-Sa €14, Su €12; Su free for ladies, and free if you eat dinner. Open June-Sept. M-W noon-2am, Th and Su noon-5am, F-Sa noon-6am; Oct.-May M-W noon-5pm, Th-Sa noon-1am. Wheelchair accessible. MC/V.

El Gran Casino, C. Marina, 19 (☎93 225 78 78), under the fish. Minimum bets are quite low, despite the glam atmosphere. An older crowd, mostly over 40. Entrance fee €4.50. Minimum bets for blackjack, American roulette, French roulette, craps, slots, and *punto banco* hover around €3. No sneakers. Passport ID required. Open daily 1pm-5am. MC/V.

MAREMÀGNUM

see map p. 350

Like Dr. Jekyll, Barcelona's biggest mall has more than one personality. By night, the waterfront shopping center transforms into an overwhelming tri-level maze of dance clubs. Each club plays its own music, from pop to salsa to house, for crowds of international students, tourists, and the occasional Spaniard. Maremàgnum is not the most "authentic" experience to be had in Barcelona, but it certainly is an experience. On those

Beautiful Drag

Pl. del Sol

Van Gogh Bar

the local story

Feeling Lucky?

In his quest to give you a close-up look at Barcelona, LG researcher Adam Weiss had a tarot card reading by Vicente San Nicholas, a psychic in Plaça Catalunya. Love, money, and happiness lie ahead for this fearless research-writer, but are we to believe that San Nicholas has any special powers? Let's Go inquired further to find out more about the occult sciences.

Q: Do a lot of people believe in what you do?

A: Yes, although there was a program on TV and they put on people who were not professionals, and that was a strong blow to this science, but at any rate necessity makes it so that people look for a kind of life-saver in order to have some meaning in their lives. In many cases, I have consulted people who intended to commit suicide, and I opened the road to hope, because I showed them that life wasn't as bad as they thought.

Q: And if you see something bad, do you tell it?

A: Well, I will say it if I see the person is not too sensitive. If I see that they are not interested in these kinds of things, I don't say it.

slower weekday nights or after bars close at 3am, this is the spot to hit. No one charges cover; clubs make their money off exorbitant drink prices. Catching a cab home can be a nightmare for bleary-eyed revelers. The Nitbus is one option (see p. 28); other adventurous souls get some coffee and croissants or *churros con chocolate* and wait for the Metro to re-open at 6am. All clubs are accessible by M: Drassanes and can be reached by walking to the ocean end of Las Ramblas and continuing over the ocean on La Rambla del Mar footbridge. What follows is just a taste of the salty nightlife that awaits.

Nayandei (☎93 225 81 37), top floor. Actually 2 clubs side by side: **Disco,** with scantily-clad go-go dancers and an open-door policy, and **Boite,** which is slightly more exclusive, with a shoes/pants/decent shirt dress code. Whatever the outfit, both clubs play energetic dance-pop with a decidedly Latin flavor. Beer €5, mixed drinks €7.50-8; drinks 2-for-1. Open Su-Th 9pm-4:30am, F-Sa 9pm-5am.

Star Winds, top floor. Pumping bass and non-stop house make this the choice of clubbers unable to stomach the cheesy pop or golden oldies playing elsewhere. Beer €5, mixed drinks €7.50-8. Open Su-Th 10:30pm-4:30am, F-Sa 10:30pm-5am.

Mojito Bar (☎93 225 80 14), first floor. The windows of this *salsoteca* are often as crowded as the dance floor itself, as admirers gawk at the spectacular moves of dancers inside. The salsa and merengue music attracts both truly excellent dancers and novices who try valiantly to keep up. In the summer, salsa dance lessons every night at 9pm—call ahead for info and to sign up. Beer €4.50, mixed drinks €5.50. Open Su-Th 9pm-4:30am, F-Sa 9pm-5am.

Irish Winds (☎93 225 81 87), top floor. Live Irish music entertains a mellow crowd, relaxing with their pints in this wood-paneled pub...is this really Maremàgnum? A complete change out from the surrounding kooky club scene. Pints €3.50 and up. Live music Th-F 11:30pm-1:30am, Sa 10:30pm-2:30am, Su 8:30-10:30pm. Open Su 12:30pm-4:30am, M-Th 1pm-4:30am, F-Sa 1pm-5:30am.

Central Golf, top floor. The clubs upstairs surround this mini-golf course, a favorite drunken leisure activity. If you're seeing multiple holes, aim for the middle one. €5 per round. Open Su-Th noon-3am, F-Sa noon-4am.

Fiesta (☎93 225 81 38), first floor. A mixed bag of hip-hop, pop, and oldies keeps the full house dancing through the night. This place is as crowded as it gets, which can be a blessing on early weeknights and a pain on weekends. Beer €5, mixed drinks €8 and up. Open daily 10:30pm-5am.

MONTJUÏC

see map p. 348

BARS

Tinta Roja, C. Creu dels Molers, 17 (☎93 443 32 43). From M: Poble Sec, walk down Av. Parallel and turn right on C. Creu dels Molers; it will be on your left. An old factory that has been lovingly converted into a spectacle of Argentinian delights by owners and tango gurus Hugo and Carmen. Eclectically furnished with mirrors, deep red walls, and thrift-store leftovers, Tinta Roja is a multifaceted art space featuring tango dance and music shows (€3-8). Receive tango lessons from Hugo himself (Tu 9-10:30pm, €14 each or €96 for 2 months). Candlelit bar. Call ahead for show reservations. Open July-Aug. Tu-Th 7pm-1:30am, F-Sa 8pm-3am; Sept.-June Tu-Th and Su 7pm-1:30am, F-Sa 8pm-3am.

Fake Moustaches

Mau Mau, C. d'En Fontrodona, 33 (☎60 686 06 17). M: Parallel. Follow C. d'En Fontrodona as it bends right, past C. Blai. Look for a white door and ring the bell. Chill bar/lounge with its own distinctive style attracts a funky, young crowd who come to talk, relax, and take in the jazz, hip-hop, and funk beats. A mostly local crowd buys yearlong "membership" (€4), but out-of-towners need only sign in at the door. Drinks €3 and up. Open Th 11pm-2:30am, F-Sa 11pm-3am, Su 6-11pm.

Rouge, C. Poeta Cabanyes, 21 (☎93 442 49 85). M: Parallel. From Av. Parallel, turn onto C. Peeta Cabanyes. Look for the door on your left and ring the bell. Bathed in warm red light, Rouge is an über-hip bar/lounge with a clientele and a cocktail menu to match. Test the Rouge Punch—rum, cane sugar, and lime (€6.50)—while the DJ/owner spins hip-hop, electronica, jazz, and pop, giving new meaning to the idea of "swanky music." Drinks €3-8. Open Th-Sa 11pm-5am.

Maremàgnum at Night

CLUBS

La Terrrazza/Discothèque (☎93 423 12 85), on Av. Marqués de Comillas. M: Espanya, in Poble Espanyol. Enter to the right of the front gates of Poble Espanyol and shake it until the early morn in La Terrrazza's hip outdoor *plaça.* Barceloneses decked out in everything from Mango club wear to leather and chains groove to house beats and the occasional guest DJ. Same deal when the club heads inside from Oct.-May and becomes *Discothèque.* Drinks €4-8. Cover (includes 1 drink) Th and Su €12.15, F-Sa €15. Open Sept.-June Th-Su midnight-6am; July-Aug. Su only.

Torres de Ávila (☎93 424 93 09). M: Espanya. Next to the main entrance of Poble Espanyol. A million-peseta construction that was at the height of club

Poble Espanyol at Night

165

chic when it was built in the '80s, Torres is still going strong as one of the city's hottest night spots, complete with glass elevators, 7 different bars, and a summertime rooftop terrace with gorgeous views of the city. DJs spin house and techno. Drinks €5-10. Dress to impress. Cover €18, includes 1 drink. Open Th-Sa midnight-6:30am.

Club Apolo/Nitsaclub, C. Nou de la Rambla, 113 (☎93 301 00 90). M: Parallel. Old 1950s dance hall hosts live music shows, usually reggae, rock, or funk. F-Sa nights *Nitsaclub*, a hip-hop/pop/soul extravaganza, features a slew of international guest DJs. Smaller dance floor upstairs gets it going to house. Work it. Cover €12, includes 1 drink. Open 12:30-6:30am.

Candela, C. Mexic 7-9. M: Espanya. Parallel to Av. Reina María Cristina and close to Poble Espanyol. New warehouse-style club is an un-touristed find featuring merengue and salsa rhythms that will make you sweat. Occasionally has live music. Multi-racial clientele. Gets started late. Drinks €4-9. No sneakers. Cover €6. Open F-Su 11:30pm-5am.

ZONA ALTA

GRÀCIA

see map p. 346

After dark, local hipsters and alterna-kids are drawn to Gràcia like bees to honey. The scene is on the mellow side—groups and young couples converge on the area's many bars and crowd the *plaças* until well into the night, often accompanied by an amateur guitarist or two. **Pl. Virreina** and **Pl. de Rius i Taulet** have a variety of tapas bars and relaxed crowds. ▧**Pl. del Sol** is the busiest place to party—try **Sol Soler** (☎93 217 44 40), **Sol de Nit** (☎93 237 39 37), and **Cafe del Sol** (☎93 415 56 63). All three are open daily until 2 or 3am. If the bars are as packed, feel free to bring your drink or even a bottle of wine out to the *plaça*.

BARS

▧ **Gasterea,** C. Verdi, 39 (☎93 237 23 43). M: Fontana. Follow C. Astúries for several blocks and make a right on C. Verdi. Yellow walls cast a warm glow in this table-less bar. Grab a seat at one of the counters and dig in to Gasterea's selection of excellent, fresh tapas (€1.05) like eggplant with goat cheese. Su-Tu and Th 7:30pm-1am, F-Sa 7:30pm-2am.

Buda, C. Torrent de L'Olla, 134 (☎65 804 567). M: Fontana. Follow C. Astúries and turn right on C. Torrent de L'Olla. Exposed stone walls illuminate funky wall lamps at this chill bar with pool table and darts. Oh-so-good for relaxing. Beer €2.25-3, mixed drinks €4.50-4.80. Open M-Th 9pm-2:30am, F-Sa 9pm-3:30am.

Ikastola, C. La Perla, 22, off C. Verdi. M: Fontana. Does being a grown-up have you down? Then head back to Ikastola (the Basque word for "nursery school") without letting go of the perks of adulthood, like alcohol. Chalkboard-covered walls beckon would-be Picasso's and Verdaguer's to leave their childish mark. Beer €3, mixed drinks €5. Also serves nutritious yet delicious sandwiches and salads for lunch (€2.50-4). Open M-F noon-1am, Sa-Su 6pm-2am.

Flann O'Brien's, C. Casanova, 264 (☎93 201 16 06). M: Diagonal. Authentic Irish pub with barrels for tables and rugby shirts hanging from the ceiling. Popular with Barcelona's English-speaking expats. Top off your evening with a Guinness or a mixed drink (€3-6). Open daily 6pm-3am.

Casablanca, C. Bonavista, 6 (☎93 237 63 99). M: Diagonal. Images of Rick and Ilsa in this plush, black marble and mirrors bar beckon you to try one of Casablanca's *cava* (Catalan champagne) specialties, like the *Jalisco* with tequila and lemon juice (€5.50). Sophisticated crowd; dress accordingly. Open M-Th 1-3:45pm and 6:45pm-2:30am, F-Sa 1-3:45pm and 6:45pm-3:30am. MC/V.

Café de la Calle, C. Vic, 11 (☎93 218 38 63). M: Fontana. Follow Gran de Gràcia downhill and turn right on Trav. de Gràcia, then take a left on the next block, C. Vic. Intricate yet elegant touches flavor the maze of small rooms filled with quiet places to converse at this gay- and lesbian-friendly bar. A perfect place for those who need a break from the wild gay club scene. Rotating collection of art on the multicolored walls. Drinks €3-5.40. Open daily 6pm-3am.

Pirineus Bar, C. Bailen, 244 (☎93 219 27 71). M: Joanic. A local bar with soul. All ages grab late-night tapas here to watch Barça games or MTV on the LCD-screen, wall-mounted TV. Tapas around €3. *Menú* €6.60. Open daily 7am-3am.

Blues Café, C. Perla, 37 (☎93 416 09 65). M: Fontana. Follow C. Astúries to C. Verdi and turn right, walk 2 blocks to C. Perla, and turn left. Plastered with photos of blues legends. Plenty of cheap beer to go around (€1.50). Open Su-Th 6:30pm-2am, F-Sa 6:30pm-3am.

Bahía, C. Seneca, 12. From M: Diagonal, walk uphill on Pg. de Gràcia and turn left on C. Seneca. Popular and funky lesbian bar. All are welcome. Beer €2.50, mixed drinks €5-6. Open Tu-Th 10pm-3am, F-Sa 10pm-3am and 6am-10am.

CLUBS

Row, C. Rosselló, 208 (☎93 237 54 05). FGC: Provença. Trendy Spaniards and tourists alike converge on this multilevel club, grinding to house and techno beats. The door policy leans toward snooty, so dress to impress. Drinks €6-7. Cover €12. Open W-Sa 11pm-5:30am.

KGB, C. Alegre de Dalt, 55 (☎93 210 59 06). M: Joanic. From the Metro, walk along C. Pi i Maragall and take the 1st left; to get a cab home, come back to Pi i Maragall. Loud rock and techno delivered to a mixed crowd of students and Soviet secret agents. Occasional live concerts 10pm-1am. Beer €3-4, mixed drinks €6. Cover €9 with 1 drink, €11 with 2 drinks. Open F-Su 1-8am. Cash only.

Bamboleo, C. Topazi, 24 (☎93 217 32 60) M: Fontana. Above Pl. del Diamante. Cuban bar hosts salsa, techno, and rock DJs, and friendly, informal turns on the foosball table. Calimocho, mojitos, and piña coladas €4 each. Open M-Th 7pm-2:30am, F-Sa 7pm-3am.

SARRIÀ

A fairly tame neighborhood after dark, Sarrià lags behind its neighbors when it comes to nightlife. For low-key hangouts with just as much fun as downtown, try these spots near Major de Sarrià.

Versàtil, C. Major de Sarrià, 95 (☎93 203 11 10). Sparsely decorated bar/cafe caters to a hip, youngish crowd at night. Beer €1.25, mixed drinks €3.60-4.10. Open Su-Th 9:30am-midnight, F-Sa 9:30am-2:30am. Closed Sa in summer.

TIBIDABO

There isn't much nightlife in Tibidabo, but the few bars that do open their doors offer fabulous, shimmering night views of Barcelona from on high.

BARS

Mirabé (☎93 418 56 67), Pl. Dr. Andreu. A simple but elegant bar accented by a tiny illuminated pool opens up onto a romantic patio overlooking the luminous spanses of the Barcelonese Mediterranean shore. Drinks €6-7. Open M-Sa 7pm-3am, Su 5pm-3am.

Mirablau (☎93 418 58 79), Pl. Dr. Andreu. Next to Mirabé (see above). Mirablau's views are just as breathtaking, and its interior is a bit more conducive to tapas-munching. Tapas €1.50-4.10. Drinks €6-7. Open daily noon-5pm. AmEx/MC/V.

Meybeyé (☎93 417 92 79), Pl. Dr. Andreu. Set slightly back from the cliff, this is a better choice for those afraid of heights. A swank, dark, and sultry interior greets loungers for tapas and cocktails. Drinks €6 at night, €4 in the afternoon. Open daily noon-3am.

CLUBS

Partycular, Av. Tibidabo, 61 (☎93 211 62 61), halfway up the hill from Pl. JFK. An old mansion brims with a young crowd gyrating to pop, dance, and house hits. Drinks €7-8. Open M-Th 9pm-2am, F-Sa 9pm-4am.

On the Rooftop at Torres de Ávila

Torres de Ávila

Mas I Mas

☖ BETWEEN SARRIÀ AND GRÀCIA

Sick of expats and backpackers guzzling Guinness? Want to meet someone down the with local scene? The area around C. Marià Cubí is always a thumping, pumping, sure bet for some fun nightlife local-style, with its eclectic mix of late-night cafes, bars, and clubs. They are all a substantial walk from FCG: Muntaner, which doesn't even run past 9pm anyway (but hey, that's why taxis were invented). The following listings are some of this area's happenin' spots, but a jaunt down C. Marià Cubí between C. Muntaner and C. Calvet or C. d'Aribau below Travessera de Gràcia will turn up enough cool clubs and bars (and cool people that frequent them) to keep you partying until tomorrow and back.

☖ **Otto Zutz,** C. Lincoln, 15 (☎93 238 07 22; www.ottozutz.com; ozlistas@hotmail.com). FGC: Pl. Molina. Walk downhill on Via Augusta and take C. Lincoln when it splits off to the right. The place to see and be seen. Well-heeled Spaniards groove to house, hip-hop, funk, and rap beats while video installation lights up the indoor sky. 9 bars on 3 floors, with a floor for private parties and a lounge soaked in red light sporting bean bag chairs for those too cool to dance. Occasionally has live music. Beer €5, mixed drinks €8. Cover €15 (includes 1 drink), but look for discount cards at bars and upscale hotels all over the city, or email to get on the guest list for a discount. Open Tu-Sa midnight-6:30am.

☖ **D_Mer,** C. Plató, 13 (☎93 201 62 07). FCG: Muntaner. Walk uphill on C. Muntaner for 2 blocks and turn right on C. Plató. A blue-hued heaven for lesbians of all ages to chat it up by the female torso and orchids that decorate the bar or boogie on the dance floor to fun pop tunes. A touch of class, a dash of whimsy, and a ton of fun. Cover €6 (includes 1 drink). Beer €3.50, mixed drinks €6. Open Th-Sa 11pm-3:30am.

☖ **Bar Fly,** C. Plató, 15 (☎93 414 00 32). FGC: Muntaner. Same directions as D_Mer (see above). More popular in the winter than in the summer, when the locals stream out of the city. Cream-colored, boxy chairs and glass tables are strategically placed to allow enough room to mingle amidst the candles. Grab a drink at one of the 2 bars, hit the red-tinted dance floor, or shoot some pool out back. DJs spin rap, hip-hop, and funk. Drinks around €6. No cover. Open Th-Sa midnight-3:30am.

Bar Marcel, C. Santaló, 42 (☎93 209 89 48), at C. de Marià Cubí. Before midnight, this enormously popular bar masquerades as a quiet, unassuming cafe. But when the clock strikes 12, locals *pack* (we're talking overflowing, shoulder-to-shoulder action here) the place in search of cheap drinks. Certainly not the fanciest bar in the neighborhood, but quite possibly the most loved. Coffee €1.20. Tapas €1.10-3. Beer €1.80, mixed drinks €2.40-3. Open Su-W 8am-2am, Th-Sa 8am-3am.

Bubblic Bar, C. Marià Cubí, 183. (☎93 414 54 01; www.bubblicbar.com). With 2 dance floors downstairs, 1 upstairs, and outdoor drinking amidst the yellow glow of tiki torches, this bar/club manages to cater to almost every taste, chill and wild alike, miraculously leaving enough room for bargoers to breathe. DJs spin English and Spanish pop and house. Beer €3, mixed drinks €5. No cover. Open Th-Sa 11pm-3am.

Mas i Mas, C. Marià Cubí, 199 (☎93 209 45 02), at C. Sagues. The friendly bartenders seem to enjoy working almost as much as the patrons love hanging out. This small, simply decorated bar gets cramped, but that just adds to the fun. DJ/bartender spins hip-hop and pop when not serving up beer (€3) and mixed drinks (€5). Open Su-Th 7pm-2:30am, F-Sa 7pm-3am.

Entertainment

Barcelona offers a wide range of entertainment, from outdoor activities, sports, and bullfights to shopping, cinema, festivals, and performances of all sorts. Consult the invaluable
Guía del Ocio, €0.90 at newsstands, for info on movies (*Cine*), live concerts (*Música*),
nightlife (*Tarde/Noche*), and cultural events. While Barcelona proper has almost everything you could desire, those truly interested in outdoor activities should be sure to
peruse the **Daytrips** chapter (see p. 211) for information on nearby beaches, mountain
hikes, ski resorts, and other outdoor sports.

BEACHES

POBLE NOU

🏋 *Beach info ☎ 93 481 00 53. Dogs, camping tents, motorcycles, soap, music, and restaurant food are
not allowed on the beaches. Police, the Red Cross, and information are available on the promenade
between Nova Icària and Bogatell, and at Nova Mar Bella, June 18-Sept.15, 10am-7pm. Only Mar Bella
and Nova Mar Bella are fully wheelchair accessible.*

The beaches to the north of Port Olímpic (left, facing the water) include Platja Nova
Icària, Platja del Bogatell, Platja Mar Bella, and Platja Nova Mar Bella (from the port to
Nova Mar Bella is about a 20min. walk). Each of them has a lifeguard, shower stations, a
restaurant on the walkway above the sand, and a refreshment stand on the beach. There

from the
road

Topless Trauma

In many ways Western Europeans have a very accepting view of the body, especially when it comes to tanning and nudity. Topless and all-nude beaches dot the Mediterranean and Barcelona is no exception. Even the most public of its beaches, Platja de la Barceloneta, boasts its fair share of R-rated beauties. On my first visit to the beach, I listened to the old adage, "When in Rome . . .," and untied my bikini top and let it slide off along with my inhibitions. So there I was, half-naked and surrounded by men, women, and children who didn't give a hoot about my daring exploits. The only difference between me and the rest of the beach was that while they had spent a lifetime basking their breasts under the sun, my bright white headlights had never seen the light of day. As I didn't realize the repercussions of this and neglected to slather on sunblock, the biggest souvenir I took home from my liberating beach outing wasn't a new appreciation for the female body, but rather a new appreciation for aloe vera.

—Colleen Gargan

is usually someone selling sunbathing chairs (€3 per day) on Nova Icària, and people often bring volleyball nets and balls to the shore. Tops are very optional for female sunbathers, particularly at Mar Bella. The beaches are clean and safe for public use.

BARCELONETA

🚇 M: Barceloneta or any "Pg. Marítim" bus route. For daily information on the city's beaches, call 93 48 100 53. Police, Red Cross, and information services are all available in a booth behind the outdoor showers, open 10am-7pm.

Barceloneta's two main beaches, Platja San Sebastià and Platja Barceloneta (adjacent to one another), are the neighborhood's biggest draw, having been cleaned up and readied for public use during the Olympics. The beaches remain fairly clean, but you will still find plenty of cigarette butts and beer cans lying around. In the summer, natives and tourists alike flock to the area for a daily dose of sun and swim. One of the city's longest stretches of sand, San Sebastià is the beach at the end of Pg. Joan de Borbo, farthest from the Port Vell area. On weekends in particular, the center area near the entrance is the most crowded of all. Venture farther afield for a less congested area. Open space does have its price—be prepared for some hardcore nudity. Toplessness is common on all the city beaches, but people begin to lose their bottoms as well toward the nether regions of San Sebastià. The exposed beach bums of San Sebastià prefer sunbathing over leisure sports, so bring your volleyball elsewhere.

The central beach on the Barceloneta peninsula is Platja Barceloneta, which leads up to Port Olímpic and Frank Gehry's famous copper **Peix** (Fish) sculpture. Another public sculpture is **Homage to Barceloneta** by Rebecca Horn, which resembles a teetering stack of children's blocks. The proximity to the park and a pedestrian walkway along Pg. Marítim make the beach popular with tourists.

WATERFRONT ACTIVITIES

For those who would rather be active than lie in the sun, there are several options in the Vila Olímpica area, both on water and land. Boating and beach sports abound, and the coastal bike path runs about 4km in total length. Below is a list of beach clubs with different waterfront options, including plenty of nighttime beachfront fun.

BOAT TOURS

Las Golondrinas (☎93 442 31 06), on Portal de la Pau. M: Drassanes. At the foot of the Monument a Colom, in **Port Vell**. 2-decker ferries chug around the entire Port Vell, as far as Montjuïc and back. (35min.; July-Aug. daily every 35min. 11:35am-8pm, Sept.-June every hr. M-F noon-6pm, Sa-Su noon-7:30pm; €3.30, children €1.70.) A longer excursion includes a **tour of Port Olímpic**. (1½hr.; July-Aug. daily every hr. 11:30am-7:30pm; Sept.-June 3 per day 11am-5:30pm; round-trip €8.10, seniors and students €5.90, ages 4-10 €3.60.)

WATERSPORT RENTALS

Base Náutica de Mar Bella, Av. Littoral (☎93 221 04 32; www.basenautica.org), on Platja de la Mar Bella. The Mar Bella nautical base offers classes in windsurfing (€120.20 for 10hrs.), catamaran sailing (€150.25 for 16hr.), sailboat sailing (€186.37 for 16hr.), kayaking (€78.13 for 10 hr.), and diving and navigation (different prices for different categories). Membership (€141.25 per year) brings a 10-30% discount off all courses. The base also rents kayaks (€10.82), windsurfing boards (€15.03), catamarans (€21.04), and sailboats by the hour and leads group trips. Open daily May-Sept. 10am-8pm; Oct.-Apr. 10am-4:30pm.

Centre Municipal de Vela (☎93 225 79 40; fax 93 224 39 06; www.vela-barcelona.com; cmv@fcv.es), Moll de Gregal Port Olímpic. In the left corner of the port as you walk toward the water, lower level. Like the nautical base, the municipal sailing center offers lessons in windsurfing, sailing, and navigation for children and adults, as well as member services including saunas and massages. A more expensive, elite option than the nautical base, with a plethora of offerings; check the website or pick up an informational newsletter at the front desk. Open M-Th 9am-8pm, F-Su 10am-8pm.

OLYMPIC FACILITIES
MONTJUÏC

SOCCER

The **Estadi Olímpic de Montjuïc,** Pg. Olìmpic, 17-19, hosts soccer games for Barcelona's second beloved team, *R.C. Deportivo Espanyol,* a.k.a. los periquitos (parakeets), for **free.** (☎93 426 20 89, 24hr. ☎90 210 12 12. Stadium is open daily 10am-8pm. Obtain R.C. Deportivo Espanyol tickets from Banco Catalana or by phoning Tel- Entrada.)

Beach Near Olympic Port

Barceloneta Beach from Above

IMAX Port Vell

The Not-So-Great Outdoors

Though it may have held the Olympics, Barcelona is not a city bent on sports. While gyms abound and leftover Olympic arenas have been converted into state-of-the-art fitness facilities, for those who are more inclined toward the great (and free!) outdoors, Barcelona can prove frustrating. My first day in the city, I yanked on my Nikes and bopped out the door, ready for a fantastic and scenic run, only to discover a significant lack of trees (or parks that have actual grass) and that a rather high density of pollution from cars pervaded nearly every street. After multiple failures, where I returned home over-heated, coughing, and generally dissatisfied with the scenery (doesn't this city appreciate something green here and there?), I have discovered that indeed, Barcelona does have places to catch some free fresh-air fitness:

Montjuic: Probably the most accessible, prettiest place to run, filled with lush trees and flowering bushes that shade the pathways. For beginners, take the escalators all the way to the top and turn right for a downhill jog back to Pl. Espanya.

Park Güell: Fabulous for uphill running, with lots of ground, enough trees for shade, earthen pathways (softer on the knees), and a ton of ups and downs past Gaudí's whimsical designs.

Parc de Collserola: *The* place for trailrunning. Paths of varying intensity criss-cross the hills cradling Barcelona.

SWIMMING

Piscines Bernat Picornell, Av. Estadi, 30-40 (☎93 423 40 41; fax 93 426 78 18; www.picornell.com), to the right when facing the stadium. Test your swimming mettle in the Olympic pools—two gorgeous facilities nestled in stadium seating. A favorite for families and sunbathers. There is also a small cafe inside the complex. €4.40 for outdoor pool, €8 for pool and workout facilities including sauna, massage parlor, and gym. Outdoor pool open M-Sa 9am-9pm, Su 9am-8pm. Workout facilities open M-F 7am-midnight, Sa 7am-9pm, Su 7:30am-8pm.

THE GREAT OUTDOORS

The Collserola mountains at Barcelona's back door definitely compensate for the metropolitan area's lack of greenery. Hiking, biking, picnicking, and horseback riding abound in their moderate peaks. For other outdoor activities, such as skiing in the Pyrenees or hiking holy Montserrat, see **Daytrips**, p. 248.

PARC DE COLLSEROLA

The **Centro d'Informació,** Carretera de l'Església, 92, has all the information you'll need on activities in the park (see p. 100; FGC: Baixador de Vallvidrera, then follow signs to center. ☎93 280 35 52. Open daily 9:30am-3pm except Dec. 25-26 and Jan. 1 and 6.) The main **map** (€6; available in English) plots major roads and services in the park; the staff can advise you on various facilities and options in and around the park.

HIKING

The information center provides numerous useful guides to hiking paths in the park. For those who want to stay close to home, there are six hikes, marked with red, yellow, orange, blue, green, and purple, which start and end near the center itself. The red path to the **Font de la Budellera** (Budellera Spring), is an easy hike to the Torre de Collserola, Tibidabo, or the town of Vallvidrera. (At the top of the hill after passing the spring, once the tower is in sight, stay to the right of the house and continue straight along the road; at the intersection with C. Alberes, turn right and head downhill to get to Vallvidrera or up the dirt hill to the left for the tower and Tibidabo.) The full walk from the information center to Vallvidrera or the tower takes a little over an hour. To continue from the tower to Tibidabo will take another five to ten minutes; just walk uphill along the aptly named C. de Vallvidrera al Tibidabo. For more in-depth hiking, the *Parc de Collserola Guide Book* (€18.03) lists five hikes which traverse large portions of the park and begin and end at public transportation. Separate guided tours for children, teens, and adults are also available for €81 per person, or you can arrange a unique itinerary with a guide and negotiate the price (some guides do speak English). The park has few extremely challenging hikes and can be as rewarding for a beginner as for someone a bit more experienced.

BIKING

Biking in the park is limited to the wider paths, but there are plenty of them. The problem is locating them; the info office stopped publishing its bike guide. However, the main map (€6) notes road conditions and most roads are marked with signs as to whether they are bicycle-friendly. In another twist of bad luck for bikers, there is no bike rental shop near the park; you will have to rent one downtown and bring it up on an FGC train (see **Bike Rentals,** p. 313). Most FGC stations are equipped with escalators and ramps along the stairwells. One of the most popular paths for biking and jogging in the area, though not very far into the park, is the **Carretera de Aiges** (about 4km long). To get there, take the FGC from Pl. de Catalunya to the Peu del Funicular stop, catch the funicular, and press the request button to get out halfway up at C. de Aigües.

HORSEBACK RIDING

There are eight stables in the park, but most of them are far from public transportation. One exception is the **Hípica Severino,** Pg. Calado, 12, near the town of Sant Cugat. Guides here lead one-hour trips every hour on the hour. Call ahead to reserve a space. (From M: Lesseps catch the A6 bus to Sant Cugat; get off at the Vasconcell stop, before reaching the Sant Cugat monastery. ☎93 674 11 40. Open daily 10am-1pm and 4-7pm. €11.)

SPECTATOR SPORTS

EL BARÇA

◪ *The team plays at Camp Nou, on C. Aristides Maillol. M: Collblanc. Head down C. Francese Layret and take the 2nd right onto Trav. de les Corts. A block later, turn left onto C. Aristides Maillol, which leads to the ticket*

WE'RE IN THE CHAMPIONS, MY FRIENDS

Well, every great team needs an occasional dry spell to make the successes seem all the more sweet. And at the moment, Barça is in the midst of a dry spell which has many of its fans choking on their *chorizo*. The team has struggled, winning no major cups in the past 3 seasons (2000-2002), and has had several coaching changes since the late 1990s. Barça barely even qualified (for the second year in a row!) for the Champions' League, the league of top clubs that vie for the highly coveted European Cup the following season. For *barcelonistas*, devotees of the burgundy and blue, failure to qualify would have been the ultimate embarrassment, signaling the disappearance of the team from the elite company of Europe's clubs. With World Cup fever gone and with their inclusion into the 2003 Champion's League, this football-mad city is once again hoping that Barça will weather the long, arduous campaign for a major cup that has not been successful for a long, long time—as in 1992.

NO BULL

The average tourist leaves his first bullfight after only 2 of 6 bulls have been killed, but as fewer and fewer Spaniards attend *corridas* (bullfights), these inquisitive travelers are playing an increasingly important role in the economic survival of the sport. Anti-bullfighting sentiments among the native Spanish population are surprisingly strong. According to a 1992 survey by InterGallup S.A., 87% of Spaniards believe that it is wrong to make animals suffer for public entertainment or celebration, and 60% think that Spain has a bad reputation for its treatment of animals. Of those interviewed, 60% had not been to a single bullfight in the past decade, and more than 80% had not been even once in the past year. These numbers may be even higher in Catalunya, where there is no tradition of bullfighting and where the sport exists primarily to pacify tourists.

Formal anti-bullfighting groups could not form until Franco's anti-organization laws were lifted at his death, but the movement has since grown rapidly and is strongest in Barcelona. The international Anti-Bullfighting Campaign (ABC; www.adda-ong.org) organizes ringside protests at the first and last fight of the season in various cities, in addition to conducting ongoing political lobbies against the sport. It also circulates the *Bull Tribune* three times a year, in both English and Spanish.

office and museum entrance (see **Museums**, p. 122). ☎ 93 496 36 00; www.fcbarcelona.com. Tickets available for all club sport events. Ticket office open Sept.-June M-F (and the day before matches) 9:30am-1:30pm and 3:30-6pm; July-Aug. 8am-2:30pm.

FÚTBOL CLUB BARCELONA

The term *Fútbol Club Barcelona*, FCB for short, refers to Barcelona's soccer team and their fervently devoted fan club (see **Life and Times**, p. 55). A visit to Camp Nou, home of FCB, can be compared to a religious experience for many fans. The team, commonly referred to as el Barça, has a motto of *"més que un club"* (more than a club), and it's easy to see why. El Barça is a symbol of Catalunya and its proud people, and the team carries the political agendas of the entire region (see **More than a Rivalry**, p. 54). The club has a devoted worldwide following, and boasts more than 100,000 members. Even the Pope, when visiting in 1982, signed the membership book and became an honorary member.

The FCB also has teams in several other sports, including basketball, rugby, and roller hockey, who play in other buildings in the Camp Nou complex, which includes a ministadium and the Palau Blaugrana (Blue-Burgundy Palace).

GETTING TICKETS

Inaugurated in 1957, Camp Nou stadium was expanded in 1982 to hold 120,000 for the World Cup, and is today Europe's largest football ground. However, getting tickets to a Barça match is not always easy; hardcore FCB fans already have tickets, leaving slim pickings for visitors. Matches usually take place on Sunday evenings at 9pm, and the bigger the match, the harder it is to get in. Tickets *(entradas)* are available at the ticket office and usually go on sale to the public the Thursday before the match. A number of scalpers also try to unload tickets in the days before the match for copious amounts of cash. At the ticket office, expect to pay €30-60, and bring your binoculars, as most available seats are on the third level. The seats may be in the nosebleed section, but even at that height, any Barça match is an incredible sports-spectating experience. The cheap seats offer a bird's eye view of the action and gorgeous views of the mountains of Tibidabo and Montjuïc. Even if you can't tell which player scored the goal, you'll have just as much fun celebrating it with 70,000 newfound friends. For more on FCB, see **We're In the Champions, My Friends** (p. 175).

BULLFIGHTING

Catalunya is not the stronghold of bullfighting in Spain; bullfights will typically not sell out and will be dominated by tourists.

Plaza de Toros Monumental, Gran Via de les Corts Catalans, 743 (☎93 245 58 02; fax 93 232 71 58). M: Monumental. Built in 1915 by Ignasi i Morell, the bullring is one of the few prominent buildings in the city that draws overtly from Arabic architectural influences; it is a rare touch of Andalucia in Catalunya. The *corrida* (bullfighting) season runs Apr.-Sept., with fights every Su at 7pm. Tickets (€18-48 in the sun, €21-95 in the shade) may be purchased at the bullring; ticket window open daily 11am-2pm and 4-8pm. Tourist visits to the bull ring are also permitted during those hours; adults €4, children €3. Tickets may also be purchased at C. Muntanter, 24 (☎93 453 38 21; fax 93 451 69 98). Cash only. For more on the sport, see **Museu Taurí** (p. 115) and **No Bull!** (p. 176).

Balancing an Egg on the Fountain

THEATER, MUSIC, & DANCE

VENUES

Barcelona offers many options for theater aficionados, although most performances are in Catalan (*Guía del Ocio* lists the language of the performance). Reserve tickets through **Tel Entrada** (24hr. ☎902 10 12 12; www. telentrada.com) or any branch of **Caixa Catalunya** bank (open M-F 8am-2:30pm).

The **Grec** summer festival turns Barcelona into an international theater, music, and dance extravaganza from late June to the end of July (www.grec.bcn.com). For information about the festival, which takes place in venues across the city, ask at the tourist office, stop by the booth set at the bottom of Pl. de Catalunya for the duration of the festival, or swing by the **Institut de Cultura de Barcelona (ICUB),** Palau de la Virreina, Ramblas, 99. (☎93 301 77 75. Open for info year-round M-F 10am-2pm and 4-8pm. Grec ticket sales M-Sa 10am-9pm. Prices vary, but most performances €24.10.)

Dancing in the Dark

Another resource for tickets is the Internet: www.travelhaven.com/activities/barcelona/barcelona.html provides 10% discounts for performances at Palau de la Música Catalana, Gran Teatre del Liceu, and L'Auditori.

⚐ Palau de la Música Catalana, C. Sant Francesc de Paula, 2 (☎93 295 72 00; www.palaumusica.org). M: Jaume I. Off Via Laietana near Pl. Urquin-

Picornell Olympic Pool

kids
IN THE CITY

Family Fun

Here are some more suggestions for activities that can entertain families traveling with children:

Biking: see **p. 175**.

Bowling: see **p. 182**.

Horseback riding: see p. 175.

Movies: see p. 180.

Soccer Games: see p. 175 for FCB or p. 173 for a cheaper option.

Swimming: see p. 174 for pools and beaches.

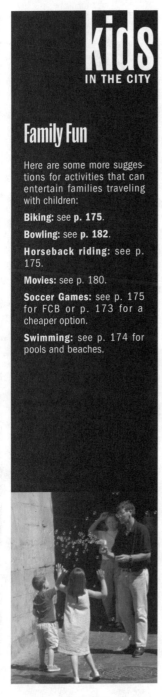

aona. Head up Via Laietana to the intersection of C. Ionqueres. Box office open M-Sa 9:45am-3pm, Su from 1hr. prior to the concert. No concerts in Aug.; check the Guía del Ocio for listings. Concert tickets €9-125. MC/V.

Centre Artesá Tradicionàrius, C. Trav. de Sant Antoni, 6-8 (☎93 218 44 85; www.personal4. iddeo.es/tramcat), in **Gràcia.** M: Fontana. Catalan folk music concerts Sept.-June F, 10pm. Building has a small cafe/bar and informational display on Catalan music. Tickets €10. Classes in traditional Catalan music (€84) and dance (€60) offered each trimester; call for information. Open M-F 11am-2pm and 5-9pm. Closed Aug. Wheelchair accessible.

Gran Teatre del Liceu, Las Ramblas, 51-59 (☎93 485 99 13; www.liceubarcelona.com. 24hr. ticket sales ☎902 332 211), on **Las Ramblas.** M: Liceu. Founded in 1847, the Liceu was one of the world's leading opera stages until its interior was destroyed by a fire in 1994. It recently reopened after extensive repairs and has regained its status as the city's finest concert hall (see **Smooth-Opera-ater,** p. 61). Tickets begin at €7and rise fast; be sure to reserve tickets well in advance.

Teatre Lliure, C. Montseny, 47 (☎93 218 92 51; www.teatrelliure.com), in **Gràcia.** M: Fontana. Showcases contemporary theater productions from summer festivals to Shakespeare. Call or check website for information. Tickets may be purchased at the theater or by calling Tel Entrada. Shows May-Oct. Tu-Sa 9pm, Su 7pm; Nov.-Apr. Tu-Sa 9pm, Su 6pm. Closed in Aug. Tickets M-W balcony €11.70, orchestra €15.60; Th-Su balcony €14.10, orchestra €18.80. 20% discount for students. Wheelchair accessible.

Teatre Grec, Pg. Santa Madron, 36 (Tel-Entrada ☎902 10 12 12; www.grec.bcn.es), across from the Museu d'Arqueològia. From M: Espanya, take bus #55 to **Montjuïc.** Located in the picturesque Jardins Amargós, the Teatre Grec was carved out of an old stone quarry in 1929 under the direction of Ramon Reventós. These days the open-air Grecian-style amphitheater is the namesake and occasional host of the Grec Barcelona Summer Theater Festival, which takes over Barcelona's major theaters from early June through July. Theater performances tend to be in Spanish or Catalan, but there are also plenty of music and dance shows to choose from. For information and tickets call Tel-Entrada or visit the Palau de la Virreina on Las Ramblas, 99. Outdoor cafe open July 8pm-3am.

Mercat de Les Flors, C. Lleida, 59 (☎93 426 18 75; www.bcn.es/icub/mflorsteatre). From M: Espanya, take bus #55 to **Montjuïc.** A converted flower market, now one of the city's major theater venues and a stage for the Grec festival. The Mercat de Les Flors and Teatre Grec will soon be incorporated into the

Ciutat del Teatre (City of Theater)—a home for theater performance and training in Barcelona. For tickets, call Tel Entrada or stop by the Palau de la Virreina at Las Ramblas, 99.

Teatre Nacional de Catalunya, Pl. de les Arts, 1 (☎93 306 57 00; info@tnc.es; www.tnc.es), near the intersection of Av. Diagonal and Av. Meridiana. M: Glòries, in **l'Eixample.** This national theater hosts classical theater and ballet in its main room (usually 1-2 months per show) and varied contemporary music, dance, circus, and textual performances in accompanying spaces. Tickets €16-20, 20% student discount, Th 25% discount. Available over the phone, through ServiCaixa, or at ticket windows (open M-Sa noon-8pm; Su noon-5pm; shorter hours in winter).

L'Auditori, C. Lepanto, 150 (☎93 247 93 00; www.auditori.com), between M: Marina and Glòries, next to the Teatre Nacional, in **l'Eixample.** Soon to be the new home of the city's Museu de la Música (currently closed to move), the Auditori is the dedicated performance space of the city orchestra (www.obc.es), although it occasionally hosts other concerts as well. Symphony season goes from the end of Sept. to mid-July, with performances F at 7pm, Sa at 9pm, and Su at 11am. Tickets €9.80-44.80, depending on the day and seating zone (Su is cheapest). Available by phone, through ServiCaixa, or at ticket windows (open M-Sa noon-9pm, Su 1 hour before show starts and 1 hour after it has begun).

Football Stadium Camp Nou

L'Espai de Dansa i Música de la Generalitat de Catalunya, Trav. de Gràcia, 65 (☎93 414 31 33; espai@qrz.net; cultura.gencat.es/espai), just above the intersection of Av. Diagonal and C. Aribau. M: Diagonal or FCG: Gràcia. Contemporary dance and musical performances, many from Catalunya but drawing from other regions as well. Tickets usually €10-14. Available at the ticket window or through ServiCaixa. Performances M-Sa 10pm, Su 7pm. Ticket window open M-Sa 7-9:30pm, Su 5-7pm.

Barça Fans

Palau d'Esports Sant Jordi (☎93 426 20 89) on **Montjuïc.** For concert information, check www.agendabcn.com or the *Guía del Ocio,* available at any newsstand.

Palau de la Generalitat (☎93 402 46 16), at Pl. Sant Jaume. M: Jaume I. The first Su of every month the Palau hosts a free bell concert at noon.

FLAMENCO

Although Catalunya does not have a tradition of flamenco, a dance which originated with the gypsies in southern Spain's Andalucia, the tourist industry has fed the demand for flamenco venues. Just because these venues may be geared to tourists should in no way reflect

Plaza del Toros Monumental

SONIC BOOM

Those who prefer something a little more avant-garde to sugary pop and cookie-cutter rock should consider hitting Barcelona's summer mainstay, the International Festival of Advanced Music and Multimedia Arts—more commonly known as **Sónar.** Considered by many to be the best electronic music festival on the planet, Sónar brings hundreds of the world's most cutting-edge DJs and audiovisual artists to Barcelona for a 3-day, 3-night, multiple-venue, non-stop party.

Aiming to provide a forum for musical experimentation and innovation, the festival includes far more than just the hottest turntable techno. A technology showcase, conferences and debates, interactive exhibits, and film screenings all add to the continuous stream of performances. Sónar 2002 (featuring, among many others, Pet Shop Boys, Yo La Tengo, and techno giant Jeff Mills) attracted tens of thousands of fans over three days and nights. By the time the dancing ends, at 10am on the festival's final night (morning?), exhausted fans were already eagerly anticipating Sónar 2003. Information and dates for Sónar 2003 were not available at the time of publication; for more information on Sónar, visit www.sonar.es.

poorly on their quality; some of the best flamenco musicians and dancers in Spain pass through these establishments.

El Patio Andaluz, C. Aribau, 242 (☎93 209 33 78), in **Gràcia.** M: Diagonal. From the Metro, take a left on Diagonal and turn right on C. Aribau. Lively Andalucian-themed restaurant showcases traditional Spanish flamenco dancing. Show and 1 drink €29.96; show and menú del día from €53.50. Daily shows at 9:30pm and midnight. Call 9am-7pm for reservations. El Patio's red-paneled bar, Las Sevillanas del Patio, stays open until 3am for drinks and dancing.

El Tablao de Carmen (☎93 325 68 95; www.tablaodecarmen.com), on Av. Marqués de Comillas, inside Poble Espanyol. From M: Espanya, go up the outdoor escalators, and to the right when facing the Palau Nacional, in **Montjuïc.** Spacious, Andalucian-style restaurant and flamenco performance space with paper lanterns and Picasso-esque paintings was built on the site where the great Carmen Amaya danced for King Alfonso XIII at the opening of Poble Espanyol in 1929. Families and couples enjoy the sexy, energetic flamenco dancing and lyrical guitar rhythms. A tourist spot that will not disappoint. Dinner and show €51; drink and show €27. Open Tu-Su from 8pm; shows Tu-Th and Su 9:30pm and 11:30pm, F-Sa 9:30pm and midnight. Call ahead for reservations, which include entrance into Poble Espanyol (see **Sights,** p. 90). MC/V.

Guasch Teatre, C. Aragó, 140 (☎93 323 39 50 or 93 451 34 62). M: Urgell, in **l'Eixample.** Often showcases flamenco; call for schedules.

CINEMA

MOVIE THEATERS

Movies in Spain come in two varieties and are marked accordingly in listings. The first is **vose** or **V.O. subtítulo** (versión original with subtitles); this indicates that the film will show in the original language with Catalan or Spanish subtitles. The second variety is **doblado** (dubbed), with the original language lines dubbed over into Spanish or Catalan; most major movies and theaters show movies this way and only indicate if they are shown otherwise. Movies in Spain are generally not shown until 4 or 5pm and continue showing well after midnight (listed as madrugada showings) on weekends. To find movie times and listings either check the Guía del Ocio (see p. 36; available at newsstands) or pass by the theater in question.

Icària-Yelmo Cineplex, C. Salvador Espriu, 61 (☎93 221 75 85; tickets ☎90 212 41 34; www.yelmocine-

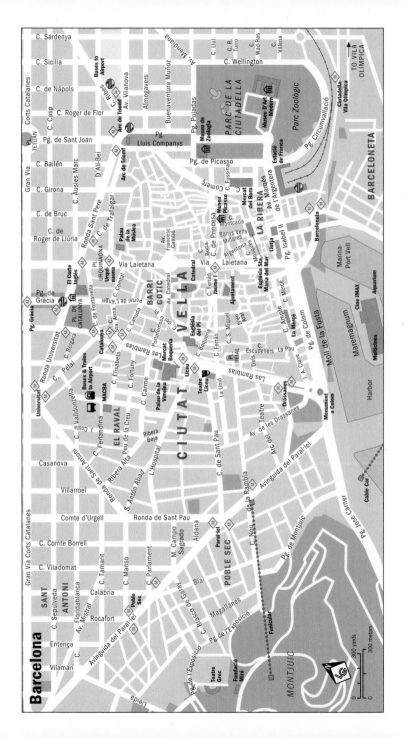

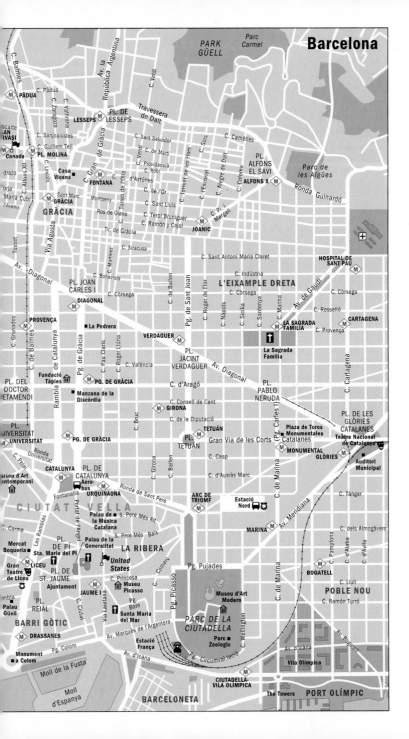

Barcelona Metro

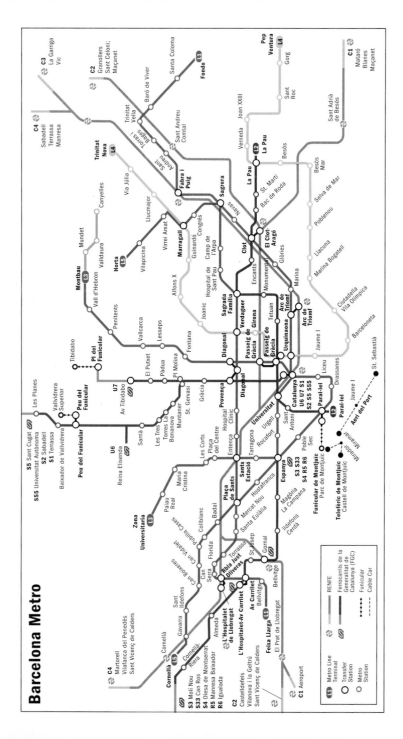

plex.es), in the **Vila Olímpica** mall. M: Ciutat-Villa Olímpica. Boasts 15 screens and a wide range of Spanish and international films, both in the subtitled original version and the ever-entertaining dubbed version. Weekend late-night showings usually feature American films in *V.O. subtítulo*. Tu-Su €5.50, M matinees €4. Open 11am-11pm.

Verdi, C. Verdi, 32 (☎93 238 79 90; www.cinemesverdi.com). M: Fontana, in **Gràcia.** Follow C. Astúries for several blocks and turn right on C. Verdi. Movie theater with plenty of subtitled films. International selection leans toward recent artsy releases. Tickets Tu-Su €5.50, M €4. Matinees M-Sa 4-7:30pm €4. Generally screens post-midnight shows F-Sa. Wheelchair accessible.

Cinesa Maremàgnum (☎902 33 32 31), Moll d'Espanya. M: Drassanes or Barceloneta. In the **Port Vell,** between the mall and the aquarium. 8 screens of dubbed Hollywood hits and a few Spanish-language originals. No English subtitles. M-Tu and Th-Su €5.25, W €4.05, F night €5.40.

Grec Festival

IMAX Port Vell (☎93 225 11 11), Moll d'Espanya, in the **Port Vell,** next to the aquarium and Maremàgnum. M: Drassanes or Barceloneta. One IMAX screen, an Omnimax 30m in diameter, and 3-D projection. Unfortunately for some, all features are in either Spanish or Catalan. Get tickets at the door, through ServiCaixa automatic machines, or by phone through Tel Entrada. Tickets €9.60, matinee €6.60. Showtimes 10:30am-12:30am.

Filmoteca: Cine Aquitania, Av. Sarrià, 33 (☎93 410 75 90). M: Hospital Clinic, in **l'Eixample.** Screens classic, cult, and otherwise exceptional films. Program changes daily. €2.70.

Méliès Cinemas, Villarroel, 102 (☎93 451 00 51). M: Urgell, in **l'Eixample.** 2 screens show classic films, generally spotlighting a particular director or actor. Tu-Su €4, M €2.70.

Live Band at London Bar

Casablanca, Pg. de Gràcia, 115 (☎93 218 43 45). M: Diagonal, in **l'Eixample.** Features recently released indie films in 2 theaters. Tu-F €5.25, Sa-Su €5.40, M €3.91.

Cine Malda, C. del Pi, 5 (☎93 317 85 29), just inside the Malda Galería. M: Liceu, in the **Barri Gòtic.** This is the only theatre in the city which lets you see two movies with one ticket. Two V.O. movies are screened in back-to-back pairs each week, including American and other international films; see the schedule flyers outside the ticket window. Tickets M €4, Tu-F €5, Sa-Su €5.25. Cash only.

Renoir-Les Corts, Eugeni d'Ors, 12 (☎93 490 55 10). M: Les Corts, in **Les Corts** in the **Zona Alta.** From Trav. de Les Corts, take C. Les Corts, then the first left. Independent international films in V.O. €5.25, M €3.90.

Devil at the Pride Parade

MOVIE RENTALS

Void, C. Santa Creu, 1 (☎93 218 56 60; www.void-bcn.com). M: Fontana. Above Pl. Virreina. If you're lucky enough to have access to a VCR in Barcelona, Void is the place to go for off-beat, interesting video rentals. If not, call ahead to reserve Void's big hot pink room and screen your favorite film on site (€2 per person). Pick up a video catalogue or check the web site for Void's cinematic offerings from Scorsese to Rossellini. Open W-Sa 5-11pm, Su noon-3pm and 5-9pm. Wheelchair accessible.

Blockbuster, Balmes, 129 (☎93 454 44 90), at C. Rossello. FGC: Provenca. Even Barcelona has been invaded by the global master of the video rental. Lots of DVDs in multiple languages. Overseas cardholders need to register in Barcelona with proof of address, passport, and phone number. Open Su-Th 11am-11pm, F-Sa 11pm-midnight.

Spanish Guitar

Liceu Opera House

OTHER DIVERSIONS

Not only are these establishments great for families, but they also draw decent crowds looking for an alternative to clubby nightlife.

BOWLING

Bowling Pedralbes, Av. Dr. Mariñón, 11 (☎93 333 03 52). M: Collblanc. 14 lanes and a bar just a block from the Camp Nou stadium make for a welcome late-night change of pace. Shoe rental €0.80. Call for prices. Open daily 10am-2am.

ICE SKATING

Skating Pista de Gel, C. Roger de Flor, 168 (☎93 245 28 00; www.skatingbcn.com), between C. Aragó and C. Consell de Cent, in **l'Eixample.** M: Pg. de Gràcia. One of only 2 ice-skating rinks in the city, and the only one open year-round and at night. €9.50 for entrance and skates; if you rent skates, you can bring 1 non-skate renter guest to the upstairs bar for free (€1.50). Day sessions Tu-F 10:30am-1:30pm, Sa-Su 10:30am-2pm. Night sessions with colored lights and music Su-Th 5-10pm, F-Sa 5pm-midnight. Cash only.

GYMS

Club Natació Atlètic-Barceloneta (☎93 221 00 10), on Plaça del Mar, Pg. Joan de Borbo, across the street from the Torre San Sebastià cable car tower. This athletic club, on Platje San Sebastià, offers outdoor and indoor pools in addition to beach access, a sauna, a jacuzzi, and a full weight room. Member-

Giant Figures at a Procession

ships start at €25.35 a month. Joining fee €53.35. Non-members €6.75 per day.

Nova-Icària Sports Club, Av. Icària, 167 (☎93 221 25 80), on the corner of C. Arquitecte Sert. A full-service sports club, with weight-lifting, aerobics, a pool, tennis courts, basketball courts, and more. Membership €32.10 per month. Non-members €6.50 per visit. Open M-F 7am-11pm, Sa 8am-11pm, Su 8am-4pm. Closed holidays.

Club Sant Jordi, C. París, 114 (☎93 410 92 61). M: Sants. Passes available for facilities, including a sauna, weights, and a stairmaster. Bring your passport. Pool €3.50 per hr. Open M-F 7am-9:45pm, Sa 8am-6pm, Su and holidays 9am-2pm. Closed first week in Aug.

Piscines Bernat Picornell, Av. Estadi, 30-40 (☎93 423 40 41; fax 93 426 78 18; www.picornell.com), to the right when facing the stadium. Test your swimming mettle in the Olympic pools—2 gorgeous facilities nestled in stadium seating. A favorite for families and sunbathers. There is a small cafe inside the complex. €4.40 for outdoor pool, €7.96 for pool and workout facilities including sauna, massage parlor, and gym. Outdoor pool open M-Sa 9am-9pm, Su 9am-8pm. Workout facilities open M-F 7am-midnight, Sa 7am-9pm, Su 7:30am-8pm.

Velodróm, Pg. Vall d'Hebron, 185-201 (☎93 427 91 42). M: Mundet. Take the right exit out of the Metro and turn left at the top of the stairs onto Pg. Vall d'Hebron. Turn left up the concrete steps toward the giant "A" sculpture; the Velodróm will be ahead on your right. Originally the Olympic cycling center, the Velodróm has since been converted into a community sports center. Annual membership is the only way to gain access; if you are interested, visit the offices at entrance 16 (up and around to the right of the building). Yearly dues €40. Facilities include a space for parties on the roof, soccer fields, basketball courts, a cycling track, a snack bar, and organized tournaments. Open M 4-11pm, Tu-F 4-6pm and 8:30-11pm.

Centre Muncipal de Tennis, Pg. Vall d'Hebron, 178. (☎93 427 55 00) and **Centre Muncipal d'Esports,** Pg. Vall d'Hebron, 166 (☎93 428 39 52). M: Montbau. Exit Metro opposite Jardins de Pedro Munoz Seca. Turn right down Pg. de Vall D'Hebron; the tennis center will be directly in front of you. The **tennis center** offers playing courts and a pool to members; non-members pay per visit to use the pool. Monthly membership €25-45 plus €35 joining fee. Pool €6.50 per day; under 12 €3.50. Wheelchair accessible. The **Municipal sports center** has a variety of facilities, including a gym, a pool, racquetball, yoga, and more. Monthly dues €20-25. Single use €6, children and over 65 €3.50. Open M-F 7am-11:30pm, Sa 9am-8pm, Su 9am-3pm. Wheelchair accessible.

Shopping

Barcelona is cosmopolitan, trendy, and trashy: shopping options reflect all these personalities. L'Eixample is full of designer stores, while other areas, like La Ribera and El Raval, have more unique, out-of-the-way shops. Below is an alphabetized list of categories of stores with listings beneath each category. If you're in the city during the first weeks of January and July, take advantage of the government-regulated sales. If you're wondering what European clothing or shoe size your American size corresponds to, check the **sizing chart** (see p. 320).

ARTS AND CRAFTS

Arlequí Máscares, C. Princesa, 7 (☎93 268 27 52). M: Jaume I, in **La Ribera.** Masks, marionettes, and puppets playfully greet customer from the crammed walls and shelves of this 19th-century Modernist building. Most goods on the premises, such as the *papier mâché* finger puppet, start at €3.40. Open M-Sa 10:30am-8:30pm and Su 10am-4pm.

Art Escudellers, C. Escudellers, 23-25 (☎93 412 68 01; export@escudellers-art.com; www.escudellers-art.com). M: Drassanes or Liceu, in the **Barri Gòtic.** C. Escudellers is a left off Las Ramblas between M: Liceu and Drassanes. Popular among the cruise-ship crowd, this warehouse-like tourist store sells local craftsmanship from every part of Spain, from pottery and glassware to tea sets and handmade jewelry. The goods are sorted by region and labeled clearly with highlighted maps, and the basement level holds an art gallery/wine cellar. Open daily 11am-11pm. AmEx/MC/V.

SHOPPING BY NEIGHBORHOOD

BARRI GOTIC AND LAS RAMBLAS

2Bis (186)	ART
Antique Market (192)	Market
Art Escudellers (185)	ART
Cap Problema Bicicletes (193)	SPORT
Casa Beethoven (192)	Music
Casa Ciutad (188)	C&A
Decathalon (193)	SPORT
H&M (189)	DC
L'Embruix (193)	Tattoos
Pl. del Pi (192)	Market
Pl. Reial (192)	Market
Santa Llúcia Market (192)	Market
Tattoo Dolar (193)	Tattoos

EL RAVAL

Discos Edison's (190)	Market
G.I. Joe Surplus (190)	DC
Llibreria del Raval (187)	BK
Mercat de Sant Antoni (192)	Market
Mies & Feji (190)	DC
Overstocks (192)	Music
Revolver (192)	Music
Zeus (190)	Market

GRÀCIA

Bell Books (187)	BK
Contribuciones (189)	DC
do.bella (186)	ART
Locura Cotidiana (186)	ART
QKbcn (188)	C&A

L'EIXAMPLE

Blanco (188)	C&A
Come In (187)	BK

L'EIXAMPLE CONTINUED

Crisol Libros y Más (187)	BK
don bolso (189)	DC
El Corte Inglés (190)	DPT
Factory Store (189)	DC
FNAC (192)	Music
Les Encants (192)	Market
LSD (192)	HW
Mango (188)	C&A
Mango Outlet (190)	DC
Next (191)	HW
Planet Music (192)	Music
Schindia (188)	C&A
Taxi Moda (189)	DC
Toy Market (192)	Market
Triangle (190)	DPT
Vinçon (191)	HW
WAE (191)	HW
Zara (188)	C&A

LA RIBERA

0,925 Argenters (188)	C&A
Arlequí Máscaras (185)	ART
Farcells (192)	Market
La Tienda de los Milagros (189)	DC
LAIE (187)	BK
Pl. St. Josep Oriol (192)	Market

PORT VELL

Maremàgnum (191)	DPT

ART = Arts and Crafts
BK = Bookstores
C&A = Clothing and Accessories
DC = Discount Clothing
DPT = Department Stores
HW = Housewares
SPORT = Sports Equipment

2Bis, C. Bisbe, 2 bis (☎93 315 09 54). M: Jaume I. Just off Pl. St. Jaume, in the **Barri Gòtic.** This bright, colorful store is filled to the brim with arts and crafts from Catalan artists, including varied figurines, ceramics, jewelry, painted masks, and a wide selection of glass creations. Open M-Sa 10am-8:30pm. AmEx/MC/V.

GRÀCIA

Gràcia has escaped conquest by chain stores and small, mom-and-pop establishments thrive among the crevices they call streets. **Trav. de Gràcia** hosts specialty shops carrying everything from traditional Catalan pottery and lamps to kitchen wares and used books.

■ **Locura Cotidiana,** Pl. Rius i Taulet, 12 (☎93 415 97 54). M: Fontana or Diagonal, FGC: Gràcia. Reasonably priced, unusual jewelry and crafts (many items €10-20). Most are made in the rear of the store in the workshop. Open M-Sa 10am-2pm and 4:30-8:30pm. D/MC/V.

do.bella, C. Astúries, 43 (☎93 237 33 88). M: Fontana. Stylish handmade beaded jewelry, bags, and silk scarves at affordable prices. All work done on the premises. Open M 5-8:30pm, Tu-Sa 11am–2pm and 5-8:30pm. AmEx/MC/V.

BOOKSTORES

Llibreria del Raval, C. Elisabets, 6 (☎93 317 02 93), off Las Ramblas. M: Catalunya, in **El Raval.** Literature and nonfiction in 4 languages (Catalan, Spanish, English, and French) fill the shelves of this spacious bookstore, born in 1693 as the Gothic-style Church of la Misericòrdia. Pocket Catalan/Spanish and Catalan/English dictionaries (€6.60) prove useful for travelers. Open M-F 10am-8:30pm, Sa 10am-2:30pm and 5-8pm.

LAIE, Av. Pau Claris, 85 (☎93 318 17 39; www.laie.es). M: Urquinaona, in **La Ribera.** Small but adequate English book section with a selection of travel guides and a cafe upstairs. Bookstore open M-F 10am-9pm, Sa 10:30am-9pm. Cafe open M-F 9am-1am, Sa 10am-1am.

Shopping on Pg. de Gràcia

Bell Books, C. Sant Salvador, 41 (☎67 889 15 81). M: Lesseps, in **Gràcia.** Follow Trav. del Dalt and make a right on C. Verdi and a left on Sant Salvador. Best used bookstore around, run by an eccentric British expat and her cat, Arnold Schwarzenegger. Trade-ins accepted. Video club including English films. Open M-F 1-8pm, Sa 10am-8pm.

Come In, C. Provença, 203 (☎93 453 12 04; casaidiomas@redestb.es). M: Diagonal or FGC: Provença, in **l'Eixample.** Primarily designed for people learning English, Barcelona's biggest English bookstore boasts an adequate, if slightly random, collection of literature, travel guides, board games, and language books. Peruse the message boards outside for apartment listings and postings for English-Spanish classes and conversation partners. Open M-Sa 10am-2pm and 4:30-8pm.

Twins Shopping

Crisol Libros y Más, La Rambla de Catalunya, 81 (☎93 215 27 20; www.crisol.es). M: Pg. de Gràcia, in **l'Eixample.** This Madrid transplant stocks a wide range of music (lots of international titles), books (fiction, self-help, cooking, travel guides, road maps), magazines, videos, DVDs, small gifts, and stationery. Also has a large children's section and some English novels and original English-version videos. Open M-Sa 8am-10pm. AmEx/MC/V.

CLOTHING & ACCESSORIES

In the **Barri Gòtic,** C. Portaferrissa and Av. Portal de l'Angel have lots of cheap, typical Spanish women's clothing stores. C. Avinyó also has a lot of trendy stores to buy gifts and accessories. C. Boqueria is chock full of jewelry, accessories, and beads. C. Call has jewelry, jewelry, and more jewelry.

Trying on Shoes

Talking Shop(ping)

Competition is usually the first word that comes to mind when one starts to think capitalism. That isn't necessarily the case when it comes to Barcelona shopping. While there are already laws in place preventing the proliferation of huge chains that would put smaller, private businesses out of business, the government has also chosen to regulate sales. By law, stores in Barcelona may only have sales (in Catalan *rebaixes* and in Spanish *rebajas*) twice a year, in January and July, where they may only discount their current merchandise (up to 30%). Not only can they not bring in special goods for the sales, but neither can they restock or change the type of merchandise on sale. As the sales progress, they may raise the discount. However, if the store jumps the gun and puts its stuff on sale before the officially designated start day, the fashion police crack down on them with hefty fines. What does this mean for the die-hard shopper visiting Barcelona? Hit the sales early even though the discounts will be greater in the end, as they are likely to have more and better merchandise. And if you happen to miss the fashion feeding frenzies, don't worry; there are still plenty of cheap and discount boutiques and chains waiting to be picked and pawed through (see **Discount Clothing**, p. 189).

Blanco, Diagonal, 572 (☎93 200 15 29; www.blancoint), at corner of C. d'Aribau. M: Diagonal, in **l'Eixample.** Of-the-minute styles at wallet-happy prices, with lots of mix and match options for big nights out. Cheap leather goods to be found for those who look carefully.

QKbcn, Trav. de Gràcia, 176-78 (☎93 210 40 00), near C. Torrent de l'Olla. M: Joanic or FGC: Gràcia, in **Gràcia.** Women's clothing boutique carries innovative and colorful designs by Basque and Catalan designers. Open M-Sa 10am-2pm and 5-9pm.

Zara, Pg. de Gràcia, 16 (☎93 318 76 75). M: Pg de Gràcia, in **l'Eixample.** With twelve locations in Barcelona alone (grab a directory brochure at the counter), more than 200 stores in Spain, and almost that many abroad, Zara has hit paydirt: snazzy, very Spanish of-the-moment designer styles, but in much cheaper materials than you will find on runways. The clothes you buy here may not last through next year, but you won't have spent too much, and by that time you'll want to come back for the newest look anyway. Expect to wait in line. Most skirts, pants, and shirts €12-30. Open M-Sa 10am-9pm. Wheelchair accessible.

Mango, Pg. de Gràcia, 8-10 (☎ 93 412 15 99). M: Pg. de Gràcia, in **l'Eixample.** Also boasts twelve other locations in the city; ask for a directory. The same idea as Zara, but done with a lot more flare: you'll find fewer staples and basic colors here and more funky dresses, sleek nighttime wear, and shiny accessories. Funky, nightwear shirts €15. Open M-Sa 10:15am-9pm. Wheelchair accessible.

Casa Ciutad, Av. Portal de l'Angel, 14 (☎93 317 04 33). M: Catalunya, in the **Barri Gòtic.** Founded in 1892, this elegant, old-fashioned accessories store sells quality hair clips and barrettes, brushes, nylons, men's and women's underwear, toiletry kits, and nail care sets at reasonable prices. Open M-F 10am-8:30pm, Sa 10:30am-9pm. AmEx/MC/V.

0,925 Argenters, C. Montcada, 25 (☎93 319 43 18). M: Jaume I, in **La Ribera.** Fashionable jewelry boutique nestled in one of C. Montcada's Gothic residences. Mainly silver designs, all by Spanish artists, start at €12. Friendly staff welcomes window shoppers. Open M-F 10:30am-8:30pm, Sa 11am-8pm, Su 11:30am-3:30pm.

Schindia, C. València, 167 (☎93 451 28 16). M: Hospital Clinic, in **l'Eixample.** Hippie-chic clothing and accessories imported from both India and China, low-priced silver jewelry, and funky yet comfy skirts with wild patterns. Open M-F 10:30am-9pm, Sa 11am-2pm and 5-8:30pm. Closed Sa in Aug. AmEx/MC/V.

DISCOUNT CLOTHING

There is not much concentrated discount shopping to be found inside the city proper; most is in the suburbs, accessible by car only. However these city stores will satisfy your need for high-powered labels.

Factory Store, Pg. de Gràcia, 81 (☎ 93 215 03 80). M: Diagonal, in **l'Eixample.** A fabulous find for budget-traveling label whores: high-class Italian and American brands from last year at 20-50% discounts. Men's and women's suits, pants, skirts, dresses, and shirts from Versace, Polo Ralph Lauren, Dolce & Gabanna, Hugo Boss, Alberta Ferreti, Guess?, and more. Don't worry, in Spain everything from last year is still in style. Be prepared to pick around for the best bargains. Open M-Sa 10:30am-8:30pm. MC/V. Wheelchair accessible.

El Corte Inglés

Taxi Moda, Pg. de Gràcia, 26 (☎93 318 20 70). M: Pg. de Gràcia, in **l'Eixample,** down a small passageway off the main street. The same business model as **Factory Store,** but a smaller selection, more conservative styles, and a few different brands. Open M-Sa 10:30am-8:30pm. MC/V. Not wheelchair accessible.

Contribuciones, C. Riera San Miquel, 30 (☎93 218 74 36). M: Diagonal, in **Gràcia.** High-end Spanish and Italian labels are half-off at this designer discount store, though prices are still quite steep. Check out the top floor for better bargains. Open M-Sa 11am-2pm and 5-9pm. AmEx/D/MC/V.

Fancy Mannequins

H&M, C. Portaferrissa, 16 (☎ 93 343 50 60). M: Catalunya, in the **Barri Gòtic.** A left off Las Ramblas. With its worldwide slogan of "fashion and quality at the best price," H&M is not unique to Barcelona and probably doesn't need an introduction; cheap and stylish, it is wildly popular in most of the 14 countries it has opened in. Shirts €5-15. Skirts and pants €15-40. Open M-Sa 10am-9pm. AmEx/MC/V.

La Tienda de los Milagros, C. Rera Palau, 7 (☎93 319 67 30). Off Pl. de les Olles, in **La Ribera.** M: Jaume I. Praise the clothing gods for these funky, retro finds at decent prices. The "shop of miracles" stocks accessories and outfits from casual to club wear. Open M-F 10am-3pm and 4-9pm, Sa 10:30am-3pm and 4-9pm.

don bolso, C. València, 247 (☎93 488 33 63), just to the right of Pg. de Gràcia when facing the Pl. de Catalunya. M: Pg. de Gràcia, in **l'Eixample.** If you must have lots of bags and purses, but don't want to waste money Kate Spade-style, come here; most handbags are under €20. No promise they'll last long, but they've got a colorful variety. Open M-Sa 10am-8:30pm. MC/V.

Revolver Records

CALLE GIRONA

One place to try for bargains is **Calle Girona,** between C. Casp and Gran Via, in **l'Eixample,** where you'll find a small line-up of discount shops offering girl's clothing, men's dress clothes, shoes, bags, and accessories. (M: Tetuán. Walk two blocks down Gran Via and take a left on C. Girona.) **Calle Bruc,** one street over, offers more retail delights for bargain hunters. Be aware of stores marked "Venta al Mejor;" these wholesale sellers aren't happy with windowshoppers.

Mango Outlet, C. Girona, 37 (☎93 412 29 35), between C. Casp and Gran Via. M: Girona or Tetuán, in **l'Eixample.** Last season's Mango clothes and accessories at 20-40% discounts, during clearance sales up to 50%. A great place to buy random shirts and throw-away night-club tanks, sometimes for as little as €3. Tax-free shopping. Open M-Sa 10:15am-9pm. MC/V. Wheelchair accessible.

MERCAT ALTERNATIU

Another area to try for discounts is the **Mercat Alternatiu (Alternative Market)** on C. Riera Baixa in **El Raval.** (M: Liceu. Take C. de l'Hospital—a right off Las Ramblas if you're facing the ocean—and follow it to C. Riera Baixa, the 7th right, shortly after the stone hospital building.) This street is crammed with second-hand and thrift stores covering everything from music to clothes.

▨ Mies & Felj, C. Riera Baixa, 5 (☎93 442 07 55). M: Liceu, in **El Raval.** This small store has a great selection of second-hand clothes, in good shape and at reasonable prices. The Adidas shirt and leather jacket collections are both worth a close look. Open M-Sa 11am-2pm and 5-9pm.

G.I. Joe Surplus, C. Hospital, 82 (☎93 329 96 52). M: Liceu. Off Las Ramblas, at the corner of Riera Baixa's Mercat Alternatiu, in **El Raval.** Offers a variety of army/navy-type alternative clothing, at low prices. Now you know. And knowing is half the battle. Open M-Sa 10:30am-2pm and 4:30-8pm.

Discos Edison's, C. Riera Baja, 9-10 (☎93 441 96 74). M: Liceu, in **El Raval.** All used, all the time. Buy or sell used CDs, records, or cassettes, most in the €3-€6 range. This is the place to unload regrettable past purchases and pick up that Paula Abdul tape you've been wanting all these years. Open M-Sa 10:30am-2pm and 4:30-8:30pm.

Zeus, Riera Alta, 20 (☎93 442 97 95). M: Sant Antoni, in **El Raval.** Specializes in gay videos (no lesbian action here), with an extensive collection in the front room. Venture into the back room for toys. Ask for the *plano gay,* a map of Barcelona and Sitges's main gay attractions. Open M-Sa 10am-9pm.

DEPARTMENT STORES & MALLS

Spain has a series of laws against franchises to protect the economic prosperity of small businesses. The theory is that if franchises are allowed to be open all the time, small business, whose limited staff must take off Sundays and *siesta,* will have no way to compete. Americans will be shocked to see that these monstrous department stores are only open six days a week; commercial law prevents them from being open on Sundays, except for the first Sunday of each month.

El Corte Inglés, Pl. de Catalunya, 14 (☎93 306 38 00). M: Catalunya, in **Pl. de Catalunya.** Behemoth department store has practically everything you could ever need or want. **Free map** of Barcelona available from the information desk. Also has English books, hair salon, rooftop cafeteria, supermarket, the *oportunidades* discount department, currency exchange, and telephones. Open M-Sa and first Su of every month 10am-10pm. M: Catalunya. Other branches: across the street from the tourist office, Portal de L'Angel, 19-2 (M: Catalunya); Av. Diagonal, 471-473 (M: Hospital Clinic); Av. Diagonal, 617 (M: Maria Cristina).

Triangle, Pl. de Catalunya, 4 (☎93 318 01 08; www.triangle.es). M: Catalunya, in **Pl. de Catalunya.** Since its opening in 1999, architecture buffs have bemoaned this shopping center's utter lack of imagination and style. Shopaholics, however, are more enthusiastic. The upper floor **FNAC** electronics store/bookstore and the first floor of clothing and sunglass shops are favorites. **Sephora**, the world's biggest cosmetics chain, is a warehouse-size beauty paradise. Open M-Sa 10am-10pm. On the corner near Las Ramblas sits the always-crowded **Café Zurich**, a recreation of the classic cafe that once occupied this site, torn down to accommodate the new mall.

Maremàgnum (93 225 81 00; www.maremagnum.es), Moll d'Espanya. M: Drassanes, in the **Port Vell.** Small stores fill the first 2 floors of Maremàgnum, the mall and all-around leisure superstop which dominates the skyline of the new waterfront. A must-see for *fútbol* (soccer) fans is the **Botiga del Barça**, a smaller version of the official F.C. Barcelona souvenir shop at the Camp Nou stadium (see p. 176), featuring posters, jerseys, and all varieties of memorabilia pertaining to the beloved Catalan team. Buddhism and the Buddha himself appear in posters, T-shirts, footwear, and any other possible commercialized form at trippy **Wae.** Stores open daily, most 11am-11pm (at night, the bars and clubs open as Maremàgnum transforms itself into a nightlife playground).

Zara

HOUSEWARES

The area around C. Banys Nou (M: Jaume I), in **La Ribera**, is a great place to look for antiques and cheap homegoods.

Vinçon, Pg. de Gràcia, 96 (☎93 215 60 50; fax 93 215 50 37; www.vincon.com). M: Diagonal, in **l'Eixample.** More of an experience than a mere store, Vinçon has been setting the house decor standard in Barcelona since 1941. Cutting-edge bedroom sets decorate 100-year-old rooms, and rows of funky lamps and knick-knacks entertain wandering shoppers. Modernisme fans will want to see the original interior of the **Casa Casas** (see **Sights**, p. 85) on display here. Open M-Sa 10am-2pm and 4:30-8:30pm. AmEx/MC/V. Partially wheelchair accessible.

Antique Store

WAE, La Rambla de Catalunya, 89 (☎93 487 14 13), on the corner of C. Mallorca. M: Diagonal or Pg. de Gràcia, in **l'Eixample.** Shop nearly bursts with brightly colored pillows, Eastern-influenced jewelry and housewares, and kitsch Mexican knick-knacks. Fun accessories and funny gifts. Open M-Sa 10am-8:30pm. AmEx/MC/V.

Next, C. Consell de Cent, 248 (☎93 451 40 32). M: Pg. de Gràcia, in **l'Eixample.** Funky home and bath accessories and gifts with colorful, sleek designs. *The* place for ladybug toilet seat covers, toilet paper with euros on it, and enough inflatable furniture to furnish your entire apartment with your own hot air. Open M 4:30-8:30pm, Tu-Th 10:30am-1:30pm and 4:30-8:30pm, F-Sa 10:30am-2pm and 4:30-8:30pm. MC/V.

Souvenir Shop

LSD, Gran de Gràcia, 56. M: Diagonal or Fontana, in **l'Eixample.** Though you won't find any drugs (as far as we know), the plastic grass-covered walls psychedelically illuminated by black and colored lights will have you thinking you are definitely on something. Take a trip here to pick up countless varieties of incense, candles, and wild home decor accents, along with kitschy trinkets that make perfect gifts. Open M-Sa 10am-9pm.

MARKETS, FAIRS, & FLEA MARKETS

Barcelona has a number of good weekly outdoor markets, as well as some more seasonal fairs and sales. Local **painters** display their work in the **Plaça St. Josep Oriol** (M: Jaume I, in La Ribera) every Sa 11am-7pm and Su 11am-2pm, while the **Plaça del Pi** (M: Liceu in Barri Gòtic) hosts a small **food market** on the first and third weekend of each month (F-Su 11am-2pm and 5-9pm). **Plaça Reial** (M: Liceu, in Barri Gòtic) is famous for its huge Sunday morning stamp and coin flea market (9am-2pm); its only real rival in size, perhaps, is the **Les Encants secondhand market** next to **Pl. Glòries** (M: Glòries, in L'Eixample; M, W, F, Sa 9am-7pm). **Antiques** are on sale every Thursday in front of the cathedral (9am-7pm). Christmastime brings a number of specialized fairs like the **Santa Llúcia market** in Plaça Nova (M: Liceu, in Barri Gòtic) and the **toy market** which takes place on the Gran Via. As always, particularly with the secondhand flea markets, watch your personal belongings in the shopping crowds.

Mercat de Sant Antoni. M: Sant Antoni, in **El Raval.** Barcelona's biggest flea market, with everything from antiques to anchovies. Visit M, W, F, or Sa for the best stuff. Book market Su mornings.

Farcells, C. Banys Vells, 9 (☎93 310 56 35). M: Jaume I, in **La Ribera.** Secondhand bazaar has low prices for everything from dishes to furniture to record albums to clothing. Sift through the mountainous junk to find some real treasures. Open M-F 10am-8pm and Sa 10am.

MUSIC

For music shopping in **El Raval,** the area around **C. Tallers** offers a good selection of new and used CDs and records.

Casa Beethoven, Las Ramblas, 97 (☎93 301 48 26; www.casabeethoven.com; ludwigvb@casabeethoven.com). M: Catalunya, on **Las Ramblas.** At last, the secrets to performing Ricky Martin's greatest hits revealed! This unique music shop specializes not in recorded music, but in written. Books of sheet music fill the shelves, featuring greats such as Mozart, Clapton, Hendrix, and Martin. The impressive collection of scores to more traditional music ranges from tangos to string quartets, spanning centuries. Open in summer daily 9:30am-5pm; winter 9am-1pm and 4-7:30pm.

FNAC, Pl. de Catalunya, 4 (☎93 344 18 00). M: Catalunya, in **Pl. de Catalunya.** Multi-level one-stop book, electronics, and music shop. Well-stocked English books, CD and video section. Has listening stations and a cafe. Credit card users beware: your transaction requires a passport as ID. Open M-Sa 10am-10pm. Branch at Av. Diagonal, 549 (M: Maria Cristina).

Planet Music, C. Mallorca, 214 (☎93 451 42 88; www.planetmusic.es). M: Diagonal, in **l'Eixample.** A huge selection of new music, including electronic, alternative, jazz, rock, pop, folk, and classical. A bright, easy-shopping store with several locations in the city. Open M-Th 10:30am-8:30pm, F 10:30am-9pm, Sa 10:30am-3pm and 4:30pm-9pm. AmEx/MC/V.

Overstocks, C. Tallers, 9 (☎93 412 72 85) in **El Raval.** Has the area's widest and most eclectic collection of CDs, from Spanish, English, and Catalan pop to trip-hop to jazz-funk. T-shirts, records, books, and music videos make this a one-stop music-lover's dream. Ticket office for BBVA tickets to most major club shows. Open M-Sa 10am-8:30pm.

Revolver, C. Tallers, 11 (☎93 412 73 58), in **El Raval.** Specializes in used CDs and vinyl. There is some pop, but the emphasis here is on punk and metal, with a nod to 60s psychedelica. Ticket office for BBVA tickets to most major club shows. Open M-Sa 10am-9pm.

SPORTS EQUIPMENT

Cap Problema Bicicletes, Pl. Traginers, 3 (☎93 310 00 82; tiend
www.capproblema.com). M: Jaume I, in the **Barri Gòtic.** Follow Via La
a right onto C. d'Angel Baixeras, and then a right on C. Sots to get to
shop offers a great deal for long-term visitors to Barcelona. You can bu
ance and a padlock starting at €200; after 1 month they'll buy it bac
after 2 months for 35%, and after 3 months for 30%. They also offer th
ton folding bicycles. Best of all, if you bring a cut padlock to prove t
they'll replace it for free. They charge €22 per hour for repair work. Ope
10am-9:30pm. MC/V.

Decathlon, Pl. Villa de Madrid, 1-3 (☎ 93 342 61 61). M: Catalunya, in **Barri Gòtic.** A le
off Las Ramblas onto C. Canuda. This sports megastore takes "one-stop shopping" to a whole
new level. Whatever you might need, from a tennis racket, basketball, or windbreaker to just
a new pair of running socks, they have it. Bicycle rental €5 per hour, €12.02 per day, €18.03
per weekend, €55 per week. Open M-F 10am-9pm, Sa 10am-9:30pm. AmEx/MC/V.

TATTOOS, ETC.

Tattoo Dolar, C. Boquería, 11 (☎93 268 08 29). M: Liceu, in the **Barri Gòtic.** A left off Las
Ramblas. An extremely hygienic, sleek tattoo and piercing parlor. Tattoos €48-240, depending on design. Piercing €42-120, depending on location. Open in winter M-Sa 10:30am-2pm
and 4:30pm-9pm, in summer 10:30am-9pm. AmEx/MC/V.

L'Embruix, C. Boquería, 18 (☎93 301 11 63; fax 93 412 58 74; www.lembruix.com; lem-
bruix@yahoo.es). M: Liceu, in the **Barri Gòtic.** A left off Las Ramblas coming from the metro.
Extremely popular among rebellious kids trying to sneak in a tongue ring while away from
home; the waiting area is almost a self-contained social scene. Minimum for tattoos €36;
some designs go up to €240. Minimum for henna tattoos €12. Normal piercing flat-rate €36
plus pendant; genitalia €60 plus pendant. Walk-in piercing; reservations required for tattoos.
They also offer specialized piercing courses. Open M-Sa 9:30am-9:30pm. MC/V.

Accommodations

While accommodations in Barcelona are easy to spot, finding a room in one can be more difficult. If it is one of the busier travel months (June-September or December), just wandering up and down Las Ramblas looking for a place to stay can quickly turn into a frustrating experience. If you want to stay in the touristy areas—Barri Gòtic or Las Ramblas—you should make reservations weeks in advance. Consider staying outside the tourist hub of the Ciutat Vella; there are plenty of great hostels in the Zona Alta, like Gràcia (see p. 206), that will have more vacancies.

Hostels in Spain are generally not of the dorm variety, but rather a private, basic room, with or without a private bathroom. Because heat and electricity are expensive in Spain, travelers should not assume that rooms have A/C, TV, or phone in the rooms unless specified; also be aware that some places do not have heat in the winter. Many establishments demand credit cards over the phone, while others accept only cash; be sure you know the policy where you are staying so you can cover your bill. The IVA tax is not necessarily included in these quotes. The following accommodations are listed by neighborhood and ranked within neighborhood by decreasing value; for a list of accommodations by price, see p. 197.

BARRI GÒTIC & LAS RAMBLAS

see map p. 338-339

The Barri Gòtic and Las Ramblas are the most sought-after destination for tourists; consequently, reservations are always recommended and usually necessary, weeks in advance. The neighborhood also has more dorm-style hostels than other areas.

the BIG $plurge

Ciutat Vella

If you're willing to spend a bit more for a central location, breakfast, and A/C, try one of the following:

Hostal Plaza, C. Fontanella, 18 (☎/fax 93 301 01 39; www.plazahostal.com). Savvy, super-friendly Texan owners, fun, brightly painted rooms with wicker furniture, and a great location make this place unbeatable. The common room boasts black leather couches, a drink/coffee/breakfast bar, a kitchen and tables, TV, phone, and Internet access with video-telephone. Laundry €9. 24hr. reception, but they prefer to do business 10am-10pm. Singles €52, with bath €65; doubles €58\€67; triples €68\€86. 12% discount Nov. and Feb. AmEx/MC/V. ❺

Hotel Principal, Junta de Comerç, 8 (☎93 318 89 70; fax 93 412 08 19; www.hotelprincipal.es). M: Liceu, in **El Raval.** From the Metro, head down C. Hospital and take a left onto Junta de Comerç. For a few extra euros, Hotel Principal offers far more comfort and amenities than most. 120 big rooms complete with A/C, telephone, satellite TV, and safes (€1.50 per day); ask for a balcony. Breakfast included. Singles €60, new singles €85; doubles €76, new doubles €95; €24 per extra person. MC/V. ❺

LAS RAMBLAS

Hostal Benidorm, Las Ramblas, 37 (☎93 302 20 54; www.barcelona-on-line.es/benidorm). M: Drassanes. With phones and complete baths in each of the very clean rooms, balconies overlooking Las Ramblas, and excellent prices, this is probably the best value on Las Ramblas. Singles €25-29; doubles €33-45; triples €50-60; quads €65-70; quints €75. ❷

Mare Nostrum, Las Ramblas, 67 (☎93 318 53 40; fax 93 412 30 69). M: Liceu, on Las Ramblas. Visible from Las Ramblas, Mare Nostrum lives somewhere between the realm of hostel and hotel. Its 30 rooms are about the same size as ordinary hostel rooms (some with shared bath), but all of them feature A/C, a view of Las Ramblas (with double-crystal windows to keep out the noise), and satellite TV with CNN and BBC. This is definitely the swankiest hostel on the strip. High-season prices include breakfast in the very pretty dining room overlooking the Miró Mosaic on Las Ramblas. Prices vary by season, but in the high season (summer and holidays) doubles €57, with bath €67; triples €77/€87; quads €93/€107. ❹

Hotel Toledano/Hostal Residencia Capitol, Las Ramblas, 138 (☎93 301 08 72; fax 93 412 31 42; reservas@hoteltoledano.com; www.hoteltoledano.com). M: Catalunya, just off Pl. de Catalunya. This family-owned, split-level hotel/hostel has been making tourists happy for almost 80 years. Rooms are quite nice, with cable TV, phones, and some balconies. Hotel rooms include full bath, hostel rooms do not. English-speaking owner. Reservations can be made over the website; book early. 4th-floor Hotel Toledano: singles €26, €29 with bath; doubles with bath €50; triples with bath €63; quads with bath €71; small room for a couple with bath €40. 5th-floor Hostel Residencia Capitol: singles €22; doubles €34, with shower €39; triples €44/€49; quads €51/€56. Add 7% for tax. AmEx/MC/V. Wheelchair accessible. ❸

Hostal Parisien, Las Ramblas, 114 (☎93 301 62 83). M: Liceu. Smack in the middle of the excitement (and noise) of Las Ramblas, 13 well-kept rooms with heat keep young guests happy. Balconies provide front-row seats to the street's daily pedestrian spectacle. Friendly owner speaks a bit of English, German, Dutch, and Italian. TV lounge; quiet hours after midnight. Prices vary, but generally singles €30, doubles with bath €38, triples with bath €48. ❸

Hotel Internacional, Las Ramblas, 78-80 (☎93 302 25 66; hinternacional@husa.es). M: Liceu, across from the Teatre Liceu. 60 standard rooms, all with private bath, safe, and telephone. Not quite as nice as they should be for these prices, but you can't beat the location. Full breakfast included. High season singles €56; doubles €97; triples €127; quads €154; quints €184. ❺

ACCOMMODATIONS BY PRICE

UNDER €15 PER PERSON ❶

Albergue Juvenil Palau (198)	BG
Albergue Mare de Déu (207)	GR
Casa de Huéspedes Mari-Luz (198)	BG
Hostal Avinyó (199)	BG
▨ Hostal Fernando (198)	BG
Ideal Youth Hostel (203)	ER
Pensión Bienestar (199)	BG
▨ Pensión Fani (202)	EIX

UNDER €25 PER PERSON ❷

Albergue de Juventud Kabul (198)	BG
Barcelona Mar Youth Hostel (203)	ER
Gothic Point Youth Hostel (202)	LR
Hostal Australia (205)	EIX
Hostal Béjar (207)	SA
Hostal Benidorm (196)	Rmbl
Hostal Bonavista (206)	GR
▨ Hostal de Ribagorza (201)	LR
Hostal Felipe II (205)	EIX
Hostal Hill (204)	EIX
Hostal La Terrassa (203)	ER
Hostal Layetana (200)	BG
▨ Hostal Levante (198)	BG
Hostal Malda (200)	BG
Hostal Marítima (198)	Rmbl
Hostal Marmo (199)	BG
Hostal Paris (200)	BG
Hostal-Residencia Europa (200)	BG
Hostal Residencia Neutral (204)	EIX
▨ Hostal Residencia Oliva (203)	EIX
Hostal-Residencia Rembrandt (199)	BG
Hostal-Residencia Sants (207)	SA
Pensión 45 (203)	ER
Pensión Aris (200)	BG
Pensión Arosa (200)	BG
Pensión Canadiense (199)	BG
Pensión Cliper (205)	EIX
▨ Pensión l'Isard (202)	ER
Pensión Iniesta (206)	MJ
Pensión Lourdes (202)	LR
Pensión Noya (198)	Rmbl
Pensión Puebla de Arenoso (205)	EIX
Pensión Rondas (202)	LR
Pensión Santa Anna (200)	BG

UNDER €35 PER PERSON ❸

▨ Hostal Eden (205)	EIX
Hostal Fontanella (200)	BG
Hostal Girona (204)	EIX

Hostal La Palmera (203)	ER
▨ Hostal Lesseps (206)	GR
Hostal Nuevo Colón (201)	LR
Hostal Opera (202)	ER
Hostal Orleans (201)	LR
Hostal Parisien (196)	Rmbl
Hostal Qué Tal (204)	EIX
▨ Hostal-Residencia Barcelona (206)	MJ
▨ Hostal-Residencia Capitol (196)	Rmbl
Hostal-Residencia Windsor (204)	EIX
Hostal San Remo (205)	EIX
▨ Hostal Sofia (207)	SA
Hostal Valls (207)	GR
Hotel Call (201)	BG
Hotel Peninsular (203)	ER
Hotel Toledano (196)	Rmbl
Pensión Aribau (205)	EIX
Pensión Ciutadella (201)	LR
Pensión Francia (205)	BAR
Pensión Port-bou (202)	LR
Pensión San Medín (206)	GR
Residencia Victoria (200)	BG

UNDER €45 PER PERSON ❹

Hostal Campi (199)	BG
Hostal Cisneros (205)	EIX
Hostal Palermo (200)	BG
Hostal-Residensia Lausanne (200)	BG
Hostal Rio de Castro (206)	MJ
Hotel Transit (208)	SA
Hotel Triunfo (202)	LR
Hotel Universal (204)	EIX
Mare Nostrum (196)	Rmbl
Pensión Dalí (200)	BG

OVER €45 PER PERSON ❺

Aparthol Silver (207)	GR
California Hotel (199)	BG
Hostal del Mar (206)	BAR
▨ Hostal Ciudad Condal (203)	EIX
▨ Hostal Plaza (196)	BG
Hotel Everest (205)	EIX
Hotel Internacional (196)	Rmbl
Hotel Lloret (197)	Rmbl
Hotel Paseo de Gràcia (204)	EIX
Hotel Principal (196)	ER
Hotel Roma (207)	SA

NEIGHBORHOOD LEGEND

BG = Barri Gòtic	LR = La Ribera
BAR = Barceloneta	MJ = Montjuïc
EIX = l'Eixample	Rmbl = Las Ramblas
ER = El Raval	SA = Sants
GR = Gràcia	

Hotel Lloret, Las Ramblas, 125 (☎ 93 317 33 66). M: Catalunya, at the head of La Rambla. Standard one-star hotel with 52 clean and decent rooms with private bath, A/C, heat, and TV. Slightly nicer than most of the hostels in the area, Hotel Lloret also puts you right next to Plaça Catalunya and near some of Barcelona's more upscale shopping and nightlife. Singles €46; doubles €69; triples €83; quads €97 (includes tax). ❺

the hidden deal

Youth Hostels in the Barri Gòtic

Albergue Juvenil Palau (HI), C. Palau, 6 (☎93 412 50 80). M: Liceu. A tranquil refuge in the heart of the Barri Gòtic for the budget set. Kitchen (open 7-10pm), dining room, and 45 clean dorm rooms with lockers (3-8 people each). Breakfast included. Showers available 8am-noon and 4-10pm. Linen €1.50. Reception 7am-3am. Curfew 3am. No reservations. Dorms €13. Cash only. The nearby **Alberg J. New York**, C. Gignàs, 6 (☎93 315 03 04) has similar accommodations and prices. ❶

Albergue de Juventud Kabul, Pl. Reial, 17 (☎93 318 51 90; fax 93 301 40 34; www.kabul-hostel.com). M: Liceu. Head to the port on Las Ramblas, pass C. Ferrán, and turn left onto C. Colon Pl. Reial; Kabul is on the near right corner of the *plaça*. This place is legendary among European backpackers; the cramped co-ed dormitory rooms can pack in up to 200 frat boys at a time. The tavern-like common area includes a satellite TV, a small restaurant/snack bar, free email for residents, a pool table, blaring pop music, and even beer and french-fry vending machines. Key deposit €10. Be sure to lock up your valuables in the free in-room lockers. Laundry €2.50. No reservations. Dorms €20. Cash only. ❷

Hostal Marítima, Las Ramblas, 4 (☎93 302 31 52). M: Drassanes, down a tiny alley off the port end of Las Ramblas. Follow the signs to Museu de Cera (See p. 104), which is next door. Nothing to write home about, but the location is convenient, the rooms are comfortable, and the prices are dirt cheap for Las Ramblas. No reservations. Singles €16, doubles €28. ❷

Pensión Noya, Las Ramblas, 133 (☎93 301 48 31). M: Catalunya, above the noisy Núria restaurant. If you don't have a lot of money to spend but still want to be in the center of all the action, this is the place for you. This 10-room hostel has time-warped back to the colors and styles of the 1950s. Bathrooms and hallways are cramped. No heat in winter. Singles €18; doubles €28; extra person €15. ❷

LOWER BARRI GÒTIC

The following hostels are located in the lower part of the Barri Gòtic, between C. Ferran and the waterfront. Backpackers flock here to be close to the port and hip Las Ramblas; it is an ideal place to experience the Old City's heady, fast-paced atmosphere. You'll find a lot of the best deals around C. Avinyó. Be careful with your wallet at night, especially in the Pl. Reial and below C. Escudellers.

🛏 **Hostal Levante**, Baixada de San Miguel, 2 (☎93 317 95 65; fax 93 317 05 26; www.hostalle-vante.com). M: Liceu. Walk down C. Ferran, turn right onto C. Avinyó, and take the 1st left onto Baixada de San Miguel (you'll see the sign from C. Avinyó). Probably the best deal in lower Barri Gòtic: 50 large, tastefully decorated rooms with light wood interiors and balconies or fans, and a relaxing TV lounge. Ask for one of the newly renovated rooms. Singles €27; doubles €46, with bath €52. Six apartments also available for 4 to 8 people each (kitchen, living room, laundry machines), €25 per person per night. MC/V. ❷

🛏 **Hostal Fernando**, C. Ferran, 31 (☎/fax 93 301 79 93; www.barcelona-on-line.es/fernando). M: Liceu. On the left on C. Ferran coming from Las Ramblas. This clean hostel is so well located it fills almost entirely from walk-in requests. Dorm beds come with free lockers in the room; otherwise storage lockers near the front desk are €1.50 per 24hr. Guests get keys. TV/dining room. High season, dorms €17, with bath €18; doubles €40, with bath €54; triples with bath €60. MC/V. ❶

Casa de Huéspedes Mari-Luz, C. Palau, 4 (☎/fax 93 317 34 63). M: Liceu. From Las Ramblas, follow C. Ferran, go right on C. Avinyó, left on C. Cervantes, and then right on tiny C. Palau. With over 25 years under their belt, Mari-Luz and husband Fernando know how to run a clean and efficient hostel. Narrow hallways flanked by tidy dorm rooms for 4-6 people and a few comfortable doubles. Kitchen available June-Aug. (open only 8-10:30am). Guests get keys, and each dorm bed comes with a locker. Laundry €5.50. Reservations require a credit card number. In summer dorms €16, doubles €37. MC/V. ❶

Hostal Avinyó, C. Avinyó, 42 (☎93 318 79 45; fax 93 318 68 93; reservas@hostala-vinyo.com; www.hostalavinyo.com). M: Drassanes. Just a stone's throw from Plaça "Trippy," this hostal puts you near the center of the action (which may also mean some noise at night). 28 bedrooms with couches, high ceilings, fans, in-room safes, and stained-glass windows. Singles €16; doubles €28, with bath €40; triples €42, with bath €60. Cash only. ❶

California Hotel, C. Rauric, 14 (☎93 317 77 66). M: Liceu. Enjoy the 31 clean, sparkling rooms, all with TV, phone, full bath, and A/C. Take the price plunge, and you'll add comfort to the convenience of the Barri Gòtic. Breakfast included. Singles €47, doubles €76, triples €95. ❺

Pensión Bienestar, C. Quintana, 3 (☎93 318 72 83). M: Liceu. A left off C. Ferrán, coming from Las Ramblas. Located on a less-traveled sidestreet, the building looks uninviting and brown is the dominant color inside. However, the friendly owners, decent rooms, and good location make this a solid choice (plus it probably won't fill up as fast as the others). Prices vary by season, but generally singles €16-18, doubles €28, triples €39-42. Cash only. ❶

Hostal Marmo, C. Gignàs, 25 (☎93 310 59 70). M: Jaume I. A right off Via Laietana from the Metro. 17 rooms in an old house still bedecked with plenty of plants, lacy curtains, and tiled floors. All rooms have balconies. Reservations only accepted 2 days in advance. Singles €18, doubles €32. Cash only. ❷

Pensión Canadiense, Bajada de San Miguel, 1 (☎93 901 74 61). M: Liceu. Across the street from Hostal Levante. This small hostel has dark hallways but a friendly owner and clean, quiet rooms with showers and balconies located in the heart of Barri Gòtic. Prices vary by season, but generally singles €22-24, doubles with shower €44-48. Cash only. ❷

UPPER BARRI GÒTIC

This section of the Barri Gòtic encompasses the area south of Pl. de Catalunya, bounded by C. Fontanella to the north and C. Ferrán to the south. **Portal de l'Angel,** the better-behaved little brother of Las Ramblas, is a broad pedestrian thoroughfare avenue running through the middle, southward from Pl. de Catalunya. Accommodations here are a bit pricier than those in the lower Barri Gòtic, but tend to have a more serene ambiance and are much quieter at night. As with the lower Barri Gòtic, early reservations are essentially obligatory in June, July, and August. The nearest Metro stop is Catalunya, unless otherwise specified.

Hostal Campi, C. Canuda, 4 (☎/fax 93 301 35 45, hcampi@terra.es). The first left off Las Ramblas (bearing right at the fork) coming from M: Catalunya. A great bargain for the quality and location. The rooms are spacious, with light, comfortable furniture and lacy curtains. Reservations accepted 9am-8pm. Prices tend to vary by season and availability, but generally doubles €40, with bath €48; triples €60. ❹

Pensión Dalí, C. Boquería, 12 (☎93 318 55 90; fax 93 318 55 80; pensiondali@wana-doo.es). M: Liceu. C. Boquería intersects with Las Ramblas right at the Metro. Designed as a religious house by Domènech i Montaner, the architect of the Palau de la Música Catalana, and originally run by a friend of Dalí's, Pensión Dalí still retains the stained glass and gaudy iron doors of its early years. A crowned Dalí stares down at you from above the reception desk. The 57 gold-and-brown hued rooms are a bit past their prime, but all have TVs and windows onto the street. Huge, couch-filled common room and great location, in the center of all the action in Barri Gòtic. In the high season, doubles €44.80, with bath €50.80; triples with bath €68.40; quads with bath €82.40. AmEx/MC/V. ❹

Hostal-Residencia Rembrandt, C. Portaferrissa, 23 (☎/fax 93 318 10 11). M: Liceu. Make the 2nd left off of Las Ramblas coming from Pl. Catalunya; the hostel is on the left. New owner is currently undertaking renovations to spruce the place up, although the hostel is already nice. Ask for a room with a balcony. Fans €2 per night. Singles €25; doubles €42, with bath €50; triples €52, with bath €60. One suite with 2 balconies, a marble tub, and a sitting area €78. Cash only. ❷

Hostal Fontanella, Via Laietana, 71 (☎/fax 93 317 59 43). M: Urquinaona. Tastefully decorated and clean, with a floral waiting room, wood furniture, fans in the 11 rooms, and a big fluffy dog named Benji waiting for you to rub his belly. Safe for valuables available, as well as information on planning excursions. Singles €26, with bath €31; doubles €41, with shower €47, with bath €55; triples €57.40, with shower €65.80, with bath €65.80; quads €71.75, with shower €82.25. AmEx/MC/V. ❸

Hostal-Residencia Lausanne, Av. Portal de l'Angel, 24 (☎93 302 11 39 or 93 302 16 30). M: Catalunya. Main entrance framed by 2 Zara display windows; walk left past the grand staircase in front to the smaller stairs in back by the elevator. A single-hallway hostel with basic rooms and a posh living room overlooking one of Barcelona's most popular shopping streets. Doubles €45, with bath €55. Cash only. ❹

Hostal Malda, C. Pi, 5 (☎93 317 30 02). M: Liceu. Go down C. Casañas from Las Ramblas, walk through Pl. del Pi, and make a left on C. Pi; the stairwell up to the hostal is inside a shopping center. With a dark green, antique motif, Hostal Malda offers 15 rooms of the same quality as elsewhere in the Barri Gòtic, but at about half the price. Reservations recommended. Doubles with shower €24-26, triples with shower €36. Cash only. ❷

Hostal Layetana, Pl. Ramón Berenguer el Gran, 2 (☎/fax 93 319 20 12; hostallayetana@hotmail.com). M: Jaume I. A short walk from the Metro going up Via Laietana toward the mountains. Look for the multinational flags on the third-floor balcony in the plaça. A sophisticated, peaceful hostel with extremely clean bathrooms and very spacious rooms. Rooms with bath have fans; for others they cost €1.20. In the high season (summer and holidays) singles €22.60; doubles €37.80, with bath €48.70. MC/V. ❷

Pensión Aris, C. Fontanella, 14 (☎93 318 10 17). About 100m from Pl. de Catalunya. 13 huge, clean, sparse rooms with fans and white washed walls. Basic hostel but with prices that are unbeatable for this location. Laundry €9. Singles €18; doubles €36, with bath €45. Cash only. ❷

Hostal Paris, Cardenal Casañas, 4 (☎93 301 37 85; fax 93 412 70 96). M: Liceu. The bright yellow sign is visible from Las Ramblas, right across from the Metro. 42 decent rooms and a common area overlooking the street. All rooms facing the inside patio have A/C, all exterior ones have fans, and all with bath have TVs. No reservations. Singles €22, with shower €24, with bath €44; doubles €39, with shower €43, with bath €55. MC/V. ❷

Residencia Victoria, C. Comtal, 9 (☎93 317 45 97 or 93 318 07 60). From Pl. de Catalunya, walk down Av. Portal de l'Angel and take a left on C. Comtal. Cafeteria-style lounge/dining room with outdoor terrace, large and fully equipped kitchen, TV, and small library. Rooms are basic but more spacious than usual for this part of town. Laundry €2.50 (no dryer). Singles €26-29, doubles €39-42, triples €52, quads €63, quints €69. Cash only. ❸

Pensión Santa Anna, C. Santa Anna, 23 (☎/fax 93 301 22 46). Tight quarters, but the floors and bathrooms are clean and the rooms are cheap. All rooms have fans. Guests get keys. Singles €20; doubles €40, with bath €50; triples €55. Cash only. ❷

Hostal Palermo, C. Boquería, 21 (☎/fax 93 302 40 02). M: Liceu. Watch your head on the way up the stairs. Large, party-conducive rooms with green plaid bedspreads. Small, plastic-chaired turquoise TV room and white washed walls. Laundry €2.50, safe €1.50 per day. Reservations require a credit card number. Singles €39, with bath €47; triples with bath €93; quads with bath €120. MC/V. ❹

Pensión Arosa, Av. Portal de l'Angel, 14 (☎93 317 36 87; fax 93 301 30 38), through a shared entrance with Andrew's Tie Shop. 7 bright and airy rooms in a homey private flat, some of them overlooking Av. Portal de l'Angel. Guests get keys. Singles €20; doubles €35, with shower €40; triples with shower €50. AmEx/MC/V. ❷

Hostal-Residencia Europa, C. Boquería, 18 (☎/fax 93 318 76 20). M: Liceu. Walk up the stairs past the headless nude statue. The hallways and TV lounge here are cramped and gloomy, but the 44 rooms inside have just enough light and air, and the location's unbeatable. Try to get a room overlooking C. Boquería. Prices vary by season, but in summer, singles €22; doubles €38, with bath €44; triples €54; quads with bath €80. Cash only. ❷

Hotel Call, Arco San Ramón del Call, 4 (☎93 302 11 23; fax 93 301 34 86). M: Liceu. From Las Ramblas, take C. Boquería to its end, then veer left onto C. Call; the hotel sign will be on your left. Nice lobby area and quiet, pleasant rooms, all with firm beds, phones, safes, A/C, and bath, although only some have windows (and those which do have small windows with no view). Singles €35, doubles €47, triples €60; add 7% for IVA. MC/V. ❸

LA RIBERA

see map p. 341

Pension Dalí

🏠 **Hostal de Ribagorza,** C. Trafalgar, 39 (☎93 319 19 68; fax 93 319 19 68). M: Urquinaona. With your back to Pl. Urquinaona, walk down Ronda Sant Pere and turn right on C. Méndez Núñez. Hostal is 1 block down on the corner. 12 rooms in an ornate Modernist building complete with marble staircase and tile floors. Rooms have TVs, fans, and homey decorations. Doubles only. Oct.-Feb. €26.50, with bath €38.50; Mar.-Sept. €35.50/€47.50. ❷

Hostal Orleans, Av. Marqués de l'Argentera, 13 (☎93 319 73 82). From M: Barceloneta, follow Pg. Joan de Borbó and turn right on Av. Marqués de l'Argentera. Spotless, newly renovated hostel with comfortable common area. Singles with TV €31, with bath €39.50; doubles €53, with A/C €54; triples €60-67; quads €80. ❸

Inside a Hotel Room

Pensión Ciutadella, C. Comerç, 33 (☎93 319 62 03). M: Barceloneta, follow Pg. Joan de Borbó, turn right on Av. Marqués de l'Argentera, and make the 6th left onto C. Comerç. Small hostel with 6 spacious rooms, each with fan, TV, and balcony. Family feel. Doubles only. Oct.-May €37, with bath €42; June-Sept. €39/€48. Each additional person (up to 4) €9. ❸

Hostal Nuevo Colón, Av. Marqués de l'Argentera, 19 (☎93 319 50 77). M: Barceloneta. Follow Pg. Joan de Borbó and turn right on Av. Marqués de l'Argentera. Newly renovated hostel with very clean, modern rooms and a large common area with TV and balcony. Singles €27; doubles €36, with bath €48. 6-person apartments with kitchens €110. ❸

Pensión Lourdes, C. Princesa, 14 (☎93 319 33 72). M: Jaume I. Cross Via Laietana and follow C. Princesa. Popular backpacker destination in the heart of La Ribera. 32 adequate, no-frills rooms with telephones. Common area with TV. Singles €23; doubles €33, with bath €42. Cash only. ❷

Balcony

the hidden deal

🔖 Pensión Fani

C. València, 278 (☎93 215 36 45). M: Catalunya. Just off Pg. de Gràcia on the left (facing Pl. de Catalunya). This long-term pension is dirt cheap and oozing with character and quirky charm, from colorful floor tiles and rows of hanging plants to a huge cage of birds in the sunroom. Rooms are generally rented by the month but can be used for a single night as well, if available. Three shared bathrooms, full kitchen with refrigerator, pots, pans, and utensils, dining room/TV room, laundry room (handwash and air-dry) with ironing board and iron, and pay phone. Bring your own towel. Not wheelchair accessible. Singles €276 per month; doubles €490 per month; triples €760 per month. One-night stay €20 per person. Payments due the 1st of each month. Cash only. ❶

Pensión Rondas, C. Girona, 4 (☎93 232 51 02; fax 93 232 12 25). M: Urquinaona. With your back to Pl. Urquinaona, walk down Ronda Sant Pere and turn left on C. Girona, hostel is on the right. Clean, basic rooms, some with balconies. English-speaking owner. Singles €22; doubles €31, with shower €42. Cash only. ❷

Pensión Port-bou, C. Comerç, 29 (☎93 319 23 67). From M: Barceloneta, follow Pg. Joan de Borbó, turn right on Av. Marqués de l'Argentera, and make the 6th left onto C. Comerç. Small hostel in 150-year-old building with high ceilings and balconies. Simple rooms with eclectic, mismatched furniture. Sept.-June Singles €26-29; doubles €33-35, with bath €44-46. July-Aug. singles €33; doubles €38, with bath €52. Extra person in double room €10. Reservations suggested. Cash only. ❸

Gothic Point Youth Hostel, C. Vigatans, 5 (☎93 268 78 08; badia@intercom.es). M: Jaume I. Walk down C. de l'Argentera; C. Vigatans is the 1st street on your left. Large Modernist building with orange and black lobby area boasting picnic tables, free Internet access, art posters, and large TV. A/C dorm-style rooms have individual curtained-off bed compartments, each with its own table and light. Rooftop terrace. Breakfast included. Sheet rental €1.80. Lockers €3. Beds €23. MC/V. ❷

Hotel Triunfo, Pg. Picasso, 22 (☎93 315 08 60). M: Barceloneta. Walk up Pg. Joan de Borbó, turn right on Av. Marqués de l'Argentera, and left on Pg. Picasso. Hotel is across from the Parc de la Ciutadella. Budget hotel with whitewashed walls and heavy floral curtains. All rooms have full bath, TV, and A/C. Singles €41; doubles €65. MC/V. ❹

EL RAVAL

see map p. 340

Hostels in El Raval, the area west of Las Ramblas, are harder to come by and less-touristed; staying here will give you a better feel for the Catalan lifestyle. Be careful in the area at night, particularly near the port and farther from Las Ramblas.

🔖 **Pensión L'Isard,** C. Tallers, 82 (☎93 302 51 83; fax 93 302 01 17). M: Universitat. Take the C. Pelai Metro exit, turn left at the end of the block, and then left again at the pharmacy. A simple, elegant, and unbelievably clean find. Bright rooms have enough closet space for even the worst over-packer. Ask for a room with a balcony. Singles €19; doubles €33, with bath €42; triples €48. ❷

Hostal Opera, C. Sant Pau, 20 (☎93 318 82 01). M: Liceu. Off Las Ramblas. Like the Liceu opera house next door, Hostal Opera has been renovated, making its sunny rooms feel like new. All rooms come with bath, telephone, and A/C. Handicapped accessible. Singles €31; doubles €50. MC/V. ❸

Pensión 45, C. Tallers, 45 (☎93 302 70 61). M: Catalunya. From Pl. de Catalunya, take the first right off Las Ramblas onto Tallers. What "45" lacks in name-choice originality, it makes up for in simple charm. Old paintings and photographs decorate the walls of its 25 small rooms. Singles €20; doubles €33, with bath €40. Cash only. ❷

Hotel Peninsular, C. Sant Pau, 34 (☎93 302 31 38). M: Liceu. Off Las Ramblas. This venerable building, now one of the 50 sights on the Ruta del Modernisme (see **Sights,** p. 60), served as the monastery for the Augustine order of priests in the mid-1800's. The rooms still have a certain austerity about them, although they are located off a fabulous inner patio with a bright skylight and numerous hanging plants. The 80 rooms all come with telephones and A/C, and most have baths. Breakfast included. Singles €25, with bath €45; doubles €45, with bath €65; triples with bath €80. MC/V. ❸

Hostal La Terrassa, Junta de Comerç, 11 (☎93 302 51 74; fax 93 301 21 88). M: Liceu. From the Metro, take C. Hospital and turn left after Teatre Romea. A hostel experience for the minimalist, with 50 small, aging, but clean rooms. The social courtyard is rare for a non-youth hostel. Singles €18; doubles €28, with bath €34; triples €36, with bath €45. MC/V. ❷

Ideal Youth Hostel, C. Unió, 12 (☎93 342 61 77; fax 93 412 38 48; ideal@idealhostel.com; www.idealhostel.com). M: Liceu. Off Las Ramblas, on the street next to the Gran Teatre Liceu. Somewhat dim dorm rooms and shared baths would make ideal air-raid shelters. Lobby with cafeteria (breakfast €1.50) and two computers with free Internet access. Laundry service €6. Co-ed and single-sex rooms available. €16.05 per person. ❶

Barcelona Mar Youth Hostel, C. Sant Pau, 80 (☎93 324 85 30; fax 93 324 85 31; info@youthostel.com; www.youthostel.com). M: Parallel. Situated in a peaceful area far from the late-night noise, this brand new hostel crams 120 dorm-style beds into air-conditioned rooms. Laundry service. Internet €1 per 45min. Breakfast included. €21 per person. ❷

Hostal La Palmera, C. Jerusalén, 30 (☎93 317 09 97; fax 93 342 41 36). M: Liceu. From Las Ramblas, just behind and to the right of the Boquería market (see **Sights,** p. 60). Somewhat spartan rooms feature new wood paneling, decent beds, and clean bathrooms. Breakfast included (9-11am). Singles €27; doubles €42, with bath €48; triples €60. ❸

L'EIXAMPLE

see map p. 344-345

Barcelona's most beautiful accommodations lie along l'Eixample's wide, safe avenues—style is of the essence in this famously bourgeois neighborhood. Many hostels have colorfully tiled, carpeted interiors and Modernist elevators styled with wood and steel; most rooms have high ceilings and lots of light. L'Eixample is one of the more expensive places to stay in the city; as a newer neighborhood full of Modernist sights, classy restaurants, and fancy shops, it's a popular destination for tourists with a comfortable budget. L'Eixample is divided by Passeig de Gràcia into left and right sections: *l'Eixample Esquerra* and *l'Eixample Dreta.*

AROUND PASSEIG DE GRÀCIA

⧆ **Hostal Ciudad Condal,** C. Mallorca, 255 (☎93 215 10 40). M: Diagonal. Just off Pg. de Gràcia, 2 blocks from La Pedrera. Prices reflect the generous amenities and prime location. All 11 rooms have full bath, heat, TVs, and phones; A/C soon to come. 24hr. reception with beer and soda (€1.25). Must reserve with a credit card for late arrivals. Wheelchair accessible. Singles €65; doubles €90. Prices often drop in winter. MC/V. ❺

⧆ **Hostal Residencia Oliva,** Pg. de Gràcia, 32 (☎93 488 01 62 or 93 488 17 89; fax 93 487 04 97). M: Pg. de Gràcia. At the intersection with C. Diputació. Elegant wood-worked bureaus, mirrors, and a light marble floor give this hostel a classy ambiance. All sixteen rooms have color TVs, and some of them overlook the Manzana de la Discòrdia. Reservations a must. Laundry €12. Singles €24; doubles €45, with bath €52; triple with bath €72. Cash only. ❷

LGB ▼
BARCELONA

How *You* Doin'?

Hostal Qué Tal, C. Mallorca, 290 (☎/fax 93 459 23 66; www.hotelsinbarcelona.net/hostalquetal), near C. Bruc in **l'Eixample Dreta.** M: Pg. de Gràcia or Verdaguer. This extremely high-quality gay and lesbian hostel has one of the best interiors of all the hostels in the city, with landscape painted walls in the coffee room, a chill, plant-filled inner patio for coffee or reading, and 14 carefully decorated rooms with their own distinctive colors and personality. Guests get keys. Morning tea and coffee included. Singles €35; doubles €55, with bath €66. Cash only. ❸

Hostal Residencia Windsor, Rambla de Catalunya, 84 (☎93 215 11 98). M: Pg. de Gràcia. On the corner with C. Mallorca. With carpeted hallways, gilded mirrors, and a plush TV room, this hostel lives up to its royal name. Rooms come equipped with comfy sleep sofas and heat in winter (no A/C). Singles €31, with bath €37; doubles €47, with sink and shower €51, with bath €55; extra beds €10 each. Cash only. ❸

Hostal Girona, C. Girona, 24 (☎93 265 02 59; fax 93 265 85 32). M: Urquinaona. Between C. Casp and C. d'Ausiàs Marc. A medieval twist on royal decor, with a cavernous stone entry foyer and dark carpeted and tiled hallways. Most of the 16 rooms have TVs, some have bath. Singles €25, doubles €50. MC/V. ❸

Hotel Paseo de Gràcia, Pg. de Gràcia, 102 (☎93 215 58 24; fax 93 215 37 24). M: Diagonal. On the corner with C. Rosselló. Double rooms here are a good deal for a 3-star hotel on the same block as La Pedrera. The decor is definitely a step up from any hostel, especially the plush, old-fashioned waiting area, leaving guests feeling closer to the lap of luxury so representative of L'Eixample. Try to get a room with a balcony on Pg. de Gràcia. Breakfast €3.25. Wheelchair accessible. Singles €55, doubles €68. AmEx/MC/V. ❺

Hotel Universal, C. Aragó, 281 (☎93 487 97 62). M: Pg. de Gràcia. 1 block to the left of Pg. de Gràcia when facing Pl. de Catalunya. This relaxing, tiny, one-star hotel offers better bang for your buck than many hostels. All 18 rooms have bath, heat, fans, TVs, phones, and free safes; most have windows overlooking the street. Reservations are highly recommended. Wheelchair accessible. Singles €47, doubles €55, triples €65 (IVA included). MC/V. ❹

Hostal Residencia Neutral, Rambla de Catalunya, 42 (☎93 487 63 90; fax 93 487 68 48). M: Pg. de Gràcia. On the corner of C. Consell de Cent. With Modernist mosaic floor tiles, a TV room just like home, and a classy breakfast dining area, this feels more like an old l'Eixample house than a hostel. All 28 rooms have fans, heating, and TVs. Laundry €12. Continental breakfast €3.60. Snacks and drinks available 24hr. (€1.20). Reserve with a credit card. Singles €23; doubles €33, with bath €39; triples €41, with bath €47. Cash preferred. ❷

L'EIXAMPLE DRETA

Hostal Hill, C. Provença, 323 (☎93 457 88 14; hostalhill@apdo.com), between C. Girona and C. Bailen. M: Verdaguer. A great deal for the location, with funky, modern furniture and fans in the rooms. Guests get keys. Reservations with a credit card number. Singles €25, with bath €32.50; doubles €41, with bath €49. V. ❷

Hostal San Remo, C. Bruc, 20 (☎93 302 19 89; fax 93 301 07 74), on the corner with C. Ausiàs Marc. M: Urquinaona. This tiny hostel fills up quickly, with 7 rooms decked out with TVs, A/C, light blue curtains and bedspreads, spotless new furniture, and soundproof windows in the street-side rooms. Reserve at least a month ahead of time. Singles €30; doubles €48, with bath €57. Nov. and Jan.-Feb.€6 less. MC/V. ❸

Hostal Felipe II, C. Mallorca, 329 (☎93 458 77 58), between C. Girona and C. Bailèn. M: Verdaguer. 11 well-kept rooms with lace curtains, new furniture, fans, TVs, and extremely clean bathrooms. Singles €23, with bath €30; doubles (shower and sink only) €45, with bath €51. Cash only. ❷

Hotel Everest, Trav. de Gràcia, 441 (☎93 436 98 00), to the left of the main entrance to the Hospital de St. Pau. M: Hospital de St. Pau (see p. 83). This simple, recently redecorated hotel feels slightly more clinical than Domènech's lush Modernist creation next door, but the price isn't bad for the hotel amenities: TV, A/C, phones, heat, huge bathrooms, and even some balconies. Singles €48, doubles €72, triples €90. Cash only. ❺

Hostal Australia, Ronda Universitat 11 (☎93 317 41 77; thomaslorenzo@thomaslorenzo.com). M: Universitat. Guests are family at this 5-room hostel, and the rooms make you feel that way; all rooms have embroidered sheets, curtains, balconies, artwork, and fans. Be prepared for the equally family-style quiet time, starting at 10pm. Reservations recommended. Singles €23; doubles €39, with bath €48. MC/V. ❷

L'EIXAMPLE ESQUERRA

🔲 **Hostal Eden,** C. Balmes, 55 (☎93 452 66 20; fax 93 452 66 21; hostaleden@hotmail.com; www.eden.iberica.com). M: Pg. de Gràcia. From the Metro, walk down C. Aragó past Rambla de Catalunya to C. Balmes and turn left. Modern, well-kept rooms are equipped with TVs, lockboxes, and fans; most have big, brand-new bathrooms. Free internet available in 2nd floor lounge. May-Oct. singles €29, with bath €39; doubles €39, with bath €55. Nov.-Apr. singles €23, with bath €32; doubles €29, with bath €45. AmEx/MC/V. ❸

Hostal Cisneros, C. Aribau, 54 (☎93 454 18 00). M: Pg. de Gràcia. From the Metro, walk down C. Aragó past La Rambla de Catalunya to C. Aribau. Large, bustling hostel with standardized hotel-like furniture and decorations. Aging rooms are kept clean; all have telephones and a few have balconies. Peaceful lounging and dining area. Breakfast included. Singles €38, with bath €45; doubles €53, with bath €59; triples with bath €80. MC/V. ❹

Pensión Aribau, C. Aribau, 37 (☎/fax 93 453 11 06). M: Pg. de Gràcia. From the Metro, walk down C. Aragó past La Rambla de Catalunya to C. Aribau, and turn left. Basic rooms have all the necessities plus TVs and fans. A few doubles even have A/C. Friendly owner speaks English. Singles €30; doubles €40-48, with bath €52; triples with bath €65. AmEx/V. ❸

Pensión Puebla de Arenoso, C. Aribau, 29 (☎93 453 31 38). M: Pg. de Gràcia. Walk down C. Aragó past La Rambla de Catalunya to C. Aribau and turn left. Small family-run *pensión* offers adequate rooms and clean, tiled bathrooms. Singles €18; doubles €30. Cash only. ❷

Pensión Cliper, C. Rosselló, 195 (☎93 218 21 88). M: Diagonal. Follow C. Rosselló for 3½ blocks. *Pensión* in Modernist building offers large, aging rooms with high ceilings that have seen better days. €20 per person, €40 with bath. ❷

BARCELONETA

see map p. 350

Lodging is not Barceloneta's forte, and places to stay here are few and far between. A couple places can be found in the area around M: Barceloneta, but not in the neighborhood itself, which is purely residential.

Pensión Francia, C. Rera Palau, 4 (☎93 319 03 76). M: Barceloneta. From Estació de França, turn left onto the main avenue (Av. Marqués de l'Argentera); C. Rera Palau is the 5th right. From the Metro, head right toward Pl. Palau, cross Pl. Palau, and turn right onto Av. Marqués de l'Argentera; C. Rera Palau is the 2nd left. A young crowd fills the 14 rooms of this out-of-the-way gem, which features balconies and satellite TV in every room, gleaming furniture, and a friendly owner. Its location allows easy access to both the Barceloneta and La Ribera neighborhoods, as well as the train station. Doubles €37, with shower €38.50, with complete bath €48; triples with shower €48.50. ❸

Hostal del Mar, Plaza Palacio, 19 (☎93 319 33 02; www.gargallo-hotels.com; reserve@gargallo-hotels.com). M: Barceloneta. Make a right as you exit the metro station, walk up the street into the Pl. de Palau, turn left and cross the plaza in front of the palace; it will be on the other side of the plaza (look for a sign). Private bathrooms in every room distinguish this busy hostel, which will cost you a little bit extra. Comfortable but not luxurious. Singles €45; doubles €55; three people 35% extra. ❺

MONTJUÏC

see map p. 348

The neighborhood of **Poble Sec,** at the foot of Montjuïc, is a diverse, working class community crammed with theaters and other nightlife options. Although Poble Sec does not have a particularly bad reputation, it is less touristed and may therefore require a little more confidence and awareness in terms of safety. The hostels listed here are close to the attractions on Las Ramblas and Montjuïc, but far enough away from the tourist hot spots to still be good deals.

🔲 **Hostal-Residencia Barcelona,** C. Roser, 40 (☎93 443 27 06; fax 93 442 50 75; hostal-barcelona@terra.es). M: Parallel. C. Roser is one block up Parallel in the direction of Pl. Espanya. The hostal is one block ahead on the right. Verging on hotel-like in quality and size, the Hostal Residencia has 63 rooms—all with TV and bath, most with A/C. Large, comfortable breakfast area with extensive buffet (€4). Friendly, English-speaking staff. Reservations suggested.Singles €30, doubles €50, triples €68, quads €78. AmEx/MC/V. ❸

Pensión Iniesta, C. d'En Fontrodona, 1 (☎93 329 10 15). M: Parallel. Look for hostel sign across from the Metro on the corner of Fontrodona and Parallel; enter on Fontrodona. Slightly cramped hallways give way to spacious rooms with TV and fans. Singles €18; doubles €30, with bath €40. ❷

Hostal Rio de Castro, Av. Parallel, 119 (☎93 441 30 46; hrcastro@teleline.es). Across from M: Poble Sec. Quiet, 15-room hostel offers doubles only. All rooms have TVs and sinks, and are nicely furnished. Owner speaks English. Doubles €44, with bath €53. MC/V. ❹

ZONA ALTA

see map p. 346

GRÀCIA

Locals outnumber travelers in Gràcia, a 5-10min. walk from M: Diagonal. Gràcia is Barcelona's deceptively quiet "undiscovered" quarter, but native 20-somethings have definitely discovered, and subsequently taken over, Gràcia's lively weekend nightlife. The accommodations listed here are small and well kept. Last-minute arrivals might have better luck finding vacancies here during high season.

🔲 **Hostal Lesseps,** C. Gran de Gràcia, 239 (☎93 218 44 34). M: Lesseps. Spacious, classy rooms sport red velvet wallpaper. All 16 rooms have a TV and bath, 4 have A/C (€5.60 extra per day). Singles €34, doubles €52, triples €70, quads €90. MC/V. ❸

Pensión San Medín, C. Gran de Gràcia, 125 (☎93 217 30 68; fax 93 415 44 10; www.sanmedin.com; info@sanmedin.com). M: Fontana. Embroidered curtains and ornate tiling adorn this family-run pension; 12 newly renovated rooms have nice furniture, sinks, and phones. Common room with TV. Owner speaks English. Singles €30, with bath €39; doubles €48, with bath €60. MC/V. ❸

Hostal Bonavista, C. Bonavista, 21 (☎93 237 37 57). M: Diagonal. Head toward the fountain at the end of Pg. de Gràcia and take the 1st right; the hostel is just off the traffic circle. Nine well-kept rooms with sinks, decorated with grandmotherly knick-knacks. TV lounge. Showers €1.50. No reservations. Singles €18; doubles €25, with bath €34. Cash only. ❷

Albergue Mare de Déu de Montserrat (HI), Pg. Mare de Déu del Coll, 41-51 (☎93 210 51 51; fax 93 210 07 98; www.tujuca.com), beyond Parc Güell (way out there). Bus #28 from Pl. de Catalunya and Nitbus N4 stop across the street from the hostel. Otherwise, from M: Vallcarca, walk up Av. República d'Argentina and cross the bridge at C. Viaducte de Vallcarca; signs point the way up the hill. This 180-bed government-sponsored hostel is absolutely gorgeous, complete with exquisite stained-glass windows and intricate tile work. Its fatal flaw is its location but the silver lining of being in the boonies is private woods and a hilltop view of Barcelona. Restaurant, Internet access, vending machines, and multiple common spaces. **HI members only.** Breakfast included. Sheets €2.10. Flexible 3-day max. stay. Reception 8am-3pm and 4:30pm-11:30pm. Lockout 10am-1:30pm. Midnight curfew, but doors open every 30min. Reservations suggested. Dorms €15, over 25 €19.23; prices drop approx. €5 in the winter. Full and half board available. AmEx/MC/V. ❶

Hostal Valls, C. Laforja, 82 (☎93 209 69 97). FGC: Muntaner. Walk downhill on C. Muntaner for 4 blocks and turn left on C. Laforja. Remote location is a drawback, but the building is beautiful. Has several large common spaces with marble floors and Modernista details. TV lounge. Singles €30; doubles €50, with bath €54-56. Cash only. ❸

Aparthotel Silver, C. Bretón de los Herreros, 26 (☎93 218 91 00; www.hotelsilver.com; silver@comfortable.com). From M: Fontana, walk downhill on C. Gran de Gràcia for 1 block, and turn right on C. Bretón de los Herreros; Aparthotel is on your right at the end of the block. Catering to short-term tourists and longer-term residents, Aparthotel Silver boasts 49 rooms, each with A/C, bath, TV, phone, and cleverly concealed mini-kitchens. Breakfast €5.50. Price range includes "inside" rooms (singles €59, doubles €62); standard rooms (singles €62, doubles €68.50), with terrace (singles €65, doubles €71.50); and large rooms with terrace (singles €78.50, doubles €84.50). A third person can be added to the large rooms with terrace and the standard rooms for €16.50 per day. AmEx/MC/V. Wheelchair accessible. ❺

SANTS

The neighborhood around Sants-Estació is not Barcelona's most exciting, but there is plenty of safe lodging for late-night arrivals, and it is well connected by Metro to Pl. de Catalunya and Las Ramblas.

🏠 **Hostal Sofia**, Av. Roma, 1-3 (☎93 419 50 40; fax 93 430 69 43). Directly across from the front of the station; cross C. Numància on the left and look up for the blue sign. A sun-lit, breezy hostel with 18 rooms heated in winter. TVs and safes available. Prices vary by season. In summer, singles €30-35, with bath €42; doubles €48, with bath €60; triples €60, with bath €72. MC/V. Wheelchair accessible. ❸

Hostal Residencia Sants, C. Antoni de Campany, 82 (☎93 331 37 00; fax 93 421 68 64). Leave the station from the back and follow C. Antoni through Pl. Sants, across C. Sants; look for the large vertical yellow sign on the left as you cross the *plaça*. A huge, clean, and inexpensive hostel with serviceable rooms and a convenient location. The cheapest and largest hostel this close to the station. All 75 rooms have heat but no A/C. Singles €18, with bath €22; doubles €28, with bath €34; double room for one person €21, with bath €27; triple €35, with bath €43. MC/V. Wheelchair accessible. ❷

Hostal Béjar, C. Béjar, 36-38 (☎93 325 59 53). Exit the front of the station to the right, onto C. Rector Triado, go immediately left onto C. Mallorca, and then right on C. Béjar. In an out-of-the-way and rather unassuming brick building with a cool, plant-lined interior stairwell. Clean, cheap rooms relatively close to the train station. All 21 rooms have desks and heaters, most have fans, and some have balconies. Singles €24; doubles with bath €48. MC/V. Wheelchair accessible. ❷

Hotel Roma, Av. de Roma, 31 (☎93 410 66 33; fax 93 410 13 52; www.hoteles-catalonia.es; cataloni@hoteles-catalonia.es). Same directions as Hostal Sofia (see above), but farther down Av. de Roma (on the same side). If you have the money to spend and feel like staying somewhere a bit more luxurious but near the train station, this is the place to go. A 3-star hotel with bright, clean rooms and a good location with easy access to Sants and L'Eixample. Singles with bath €82-114, doubles with bath €100-132. AmEx/MC/V. ❺

Hotel Transit, C. Rector Triado, 82 (☎93 424 60 13), the street immediately to the right out of the front of the station. 33 rooms with heat, bath, phones, and TVs. Doubles and triples have A/C. Cheapest hotel in the area, and close to the train station, but hostels offer better value. Singles €45, doubles €64.30, triples €77.60. AmEx/MC/V. Wheelchair accessible. ❹

CAMPING

Although there are no campsites within the city, intercity buses (€1.50) run to all the following locations in 20-45min. For more info, contact the **Associació de Càmpings de Barcelona,** Gran Vía de les Corts Catalanes, 608 (☎93 412 59 55; www.campings-bcn.com).

El Toro Bravo, Autovía de Castelldefells, km 11 (☎93 637 34 62; fax 93 637 21 15; info@eltorobravo.com; www.eltorobravo.com). Take bus L95 (€1.50) from Pl. de Catalunya to the campsite, 11km south. Offers beach access, laundry facilities, currency exchange, 3 pools, 2 bars, a restaurant, and a supermarket. Possibility for long-term stays. Reception 8am-7pm. Sept.-June 14 €4.55 per person, €4.85 per site, €4.55 per car, €3.65 electricity charge. June 15-Aug. €4.80 per person, €5.10 per site, €4.80 per car, €3.65 electricity charge. IVA tax not included. AmEx/MC/V.

Filipinas, Autovía de Castelldefells, km 12 (☎93 65 828 95; fax 93 658 17 91), 1km down the road from El Toro Bravo (see above), accessible by bus L95. Same prices and services as El Toro Bravo. AmEx/MC/V.

LONG-TERM ACCOMMODATIONS

Care to stay a while? With a little research, footwork, and phone-calling, a person can find a place to live in Barcelona without too much trouble. Securing a *habitación* (room) or *piso* (apartment) from outside the city can be difficult, however, so it's best to book a hostel for the first week of hunting. The easiest route is to check the many **bulletin boards** to look for possible sublets, often with English-speaking expats. Many rooms are available to sublet year-round. Those seeking a private apartment for only a few months will have a more arduous time. In general, the shorter the stay, the harder it is to rent, with the summer months being particularly difficult. The city's **accommodation agencies** are a big help, and can refer you to other sources of information. The city **newspapers** are another option; *La Vanguardia* has a large classified section. Depending on the location and the apartment, good prices range from €200 to €350 per person per month. There are plenty of short-term establishments that also cater to long-term guests, such as Aparthotel Silver (p. 207), El Toro Bravo (p. 208), and Pensión Fani (p. 202).

In addition to rent, expect to pay an agency or contract fee (where applicable), which can increase actual prices substantially, as well as monthly utilities. For convenience to public transportation and services, reasonable rents, and neighborhood safety, ⓔl'Eixample is a good all-around choice.

BULLETIN BOARDS

International House, C. Trafalgar, 14 (☎93 268 45 11, 93 268 02 39). M: Urquinaona. Open daily 8am-9:30pm.

Centre d'Informació Assesorament per a Joves (CIAJ), C. Ferrán, 32 (☎93 402 78 00; www.bcn.es/ciaj), off Las Ramblas. M: Liceu. Open M-F 10am-2pm and 4-8pm.

RENTAL AGENCIES

🗹 **Habit Servei,** C. Muntaner, 206 (☎93 209 50 45; habitservei@habitservei.com), between Londres and París. M: Hospital Clínic. From the Metro, walk north on Villarroel for 2 blocks, take a right on París, and take a left on Muntaner after 2 blocks. The helpful, patient staff speaks English, and understands if you know nothing about renting an apartment in Spain. Wide range of prices and lengths of stay (including homestays and shared apartments), according to the client's needs. Open M-F 10am-2pm and 4-7:30pm.

Barcelona Allotjament, C. Pelai, 12 (☎93 268 43 57; www.barcelona-allotjament.com), off Pl. de Catalunya. M: Catalunya. Reasonably priced apartments throughout the city. Open M-F 10am-2pm.

Habitatge Jove, C. Calàbria, 147 (☎93 483 83 92; www.habitatgejove.com). M: Rocafort. The multilingual web site can locate an apartment, room, or host family before you even visit the office, often at an excellent price. However, the minimum length of rental for an apartment is one year. Open M-F 9am-2pm and 3-5:30pm.

HOME EXCHANGES & HOME RENTALS

Home exchange offers the traveler various types of homes (houses, apartments, condominiums, villas, even castles in some cases), plus the opportunity to live like a native and to cut down on accommodation fees. For more information, contact **HomeExchange.com** (US ☎800-877-8723; www.homeexchange.com), **Intervac International Home Exchange** (93 453 31 71; www.intervac.com), or **The Invented City: International Home Exchange** (US ☎800-788-CITY, elsewhere US ☎+1 415-252-1141; www.invented-city.com). **Home rentals** are more expensive than exchanges, but they can be cheaper than comparably serviced hotels. Both home exchanges and rentals are ideal for families with children or travelers with special dietary needs; you often get your own kitchen, maid service, TV, and telephone.

Daytripping

COSTA BRAVA

Tracing the Mediterranean Sea from Barcelona to the French border, the Costa Brava's jagged cliffs and pristine beaches draw throngs of European visitors, especially in July and August. Early June and late September can be remarkably peaceful; the water is still warm but the beaches are much less crowded. In the winter Costa Brava lives up to its name, as fierce winds sweep the coast, leaving behind tranquil, boarded-up and almost empty beach towns. Unlike its counterparts, Costa Blanca and Costa del Sol, Costa Brava offers more than just high-rises and touristy beaches. The rocky shores have traditionally attracted romantics and artists, like Marc Chagall and Salvador Dalí, a Costa Brava native. Dalí's house in Cadaqués and his museum in Figueres display the largest collections of his work in Europe.

GETTING AROUND THE COSTA BRAVA

Transportation on the Costa Brava is seasonal, with frequent service during July and August, sporadic service May-June and Sept.-Oct., and little to no service from November to April. **RENFE trains** (☎902 24 02 02; www.renfe.es) stop at Blanes, Figueres, and then farther north at Llançà and Portbou (near the French border). **Buses** are the preferred mode of transportation, as they often run along beautiful winding roads and connect large and small towns with frequent and inexpensive service. **Sarfa** (☎97 230 02 62; www.sarfa.com), **Pujol i Pujol** (☎97 236 42 36), and **Teisa** (☎97 220 48 68) are Costa Brava's principal carriers.

FIGUERES (FIGUERAS)

In 1974, the mayor of Figueres (pop. 35,000) asked native Salvador Dalí to donate a painting to an art museum the town was planning. Dalí refused to donate a painting; he was so flattered by his hometown's recognition that he donated an entire museum. With the construction of the Teatre-Museu Dalí, Figueres was catapulted to international fame; ever since, a multilingual parade of Surrealism fans has been awed and entranced by Dalí's bizarre perspectives and erotic visions.

Though it is a beachless sprawl, Figueres hides other quality museums and some pleasant cafes. If you choose to extend your Figueres visit beyond Dalí's spectacle, the town's lovely Rambla is a good place to start for food, accommodations, and further sightseeing. It is also a convenient base for visiting the Costa Brava.

TRANSPORTATION

Trains: ☎90 224 02 02. To: **Barcelona** (2hr., 23 per day 6:11am-8:59pm, €8.05); **Girona** (30min., 23 per day 6:11am-8:59pm, €2.40); **Portbou** (30min., 11 per day 6:09am-9:24pm, €1.85).

Buses: All buses leave from the **Estació Autobuses** (☎97 267 33 54), in Pl. Estació. **Sarfa** (☎97 267 42 98; www.sarfa.com) runs to **Cadaqués** (1¼hr.; July-Aug. 5 per day, Sept.-June 2-3 per day; €3.45) and **Llançà** (25min.; July-Aug. 4 per day, Sept.-June 2 per day; €2). **Barcelona Bus** (☎97 250 50 29) drives to **Barcelona** (2¼hr., 2-6 per day, €12.90) and **Girona** (1hr., 2-6 per day, €3.40).

Taxis: (☎97 250 00 08 or ☎97 250 50 43). Taxis line the Rambla and the train station.

Car Rental: Hertz, Pl. Estació, 9 (☎90 240 24 05). All-inclusive rental from €44 per day. 24+. Open M-F 8am-1pm and 4-8pm, Sa 8am-1pm and 5-8pm. AmEx/D/MC/V.

ORIENTATION & PRACTICAL INFORMATION

Trains and buses arrive at **Plaça de Estació** on the edge of town. Cross the plaza and bear left on C. Sant Llàtzer, walk several blocks to Carrer Nou, and take a right to get to Figueres's tree-filled Rambla. To reach the **tourist office,** walk up the Rambla and continue on C. Lasauca straight out from the left corner. The blue, all-knowing **"i"** beckons across the rather treacherous intersection with Ronda Frial.

Tourist Office: Main office, Pl. Sol (☎97 250 31 55). Good map and free list of accommodations. Open Nov.-Mar. M-F 9am-3pm; Apr.-June and Oct. M-F 9am-3pm and 4:30-8pm, Sa 9:30am-1:30pm and 3:30-6:30pm; July-Aug. M-Sa 9am-8pm, Su 9am-3pm; Sept. M-Sa 9am-8pm. Two **branch offices** in summer, one at Pl. Estació (open July-Sept. 15 M-Sa 10am-2pm and 4-6pm), and the other in a yellow mobile home in front of the Dalí museum (open July-Sept. 15 M-Sa 9am-8pm, Su 9am-3pm).

Currency Exchange: Banco Santander Central Hispano, Rambla, 21. **ATM.** Open Apr.-Sept. M-F 8:30am-2pm; Oct.-Mar. M-F 8:30am-2pm, Sa 8:30am-1pm.

Luggage Storage: At the train station, large lockers €3.60. At the bus station €1.80. Bus station open daily 6am-10pm; train station open daily 6am-11pm.

Emergency: ☎112. **Police:** Ronda Final, 4 (☎97 251 01 11).

Internet Access: Tele Haddi, C. Joan Reglá, 1 (☎97 251 30 99). €1 per 15min., €1.80 per 30min., €3 per 1hr. Open daily 9am-1am.

Post Office: C. Santa Llogaia, 60-62 (☎97 250 54 31). Open M-F 8:30am-2:30pm, Sa 9:30am-1pm.

Postal Code: 17600.

ACCOMMODATIONS

Most visitors to Figueres make the journey a daytrip from Barcelona, but affordable accommodations in Figueres are easy to find. Most tend to be on the upper floors of small bars or restaurants. Some cluster on C. Jonquera, around the Dalí museum; others are located

Modernist Architecture in Figueres

Dalí Museum's Mae West Installation

Dalí Museum

PRAYING TO A PORCE-LAIN GOD

Visitors are often surprised by the infamous *caganer* (literally, "shitter"), a fixture of Catalan nativity scenes. The traditional nativity figures are all still there: the baby Jesus, Mary, Joseph, the kings, the shepherds...and hidden behind a bush or tree is the *caganer*, a little ceramic guy with his pants around his knees, squatting down to do his business—and yes, there is even a ceramic business beneath him.

While this character may seem shocking, even offensive, to outsiders, Catalans swear the little dude has nothing but the best intentions. Catalans value regularity and regard the well-formed stool as the ultimate good, a sign of fertility and fortune. The *caganer* is, after all, fertilizing the earth and ensuring the health of the land. Some people collect these figures, which come in a variety of forms: Santa Claus, bride and groom, political figures such as Bill Clinton or José Maria Aznar, and even a man using the Internet as he squats, to name a few. So instead of cursing the next time you step in a mess left behind by a Catalan dog, stop and think how fortunate you are.

closer to La Rambla and C. Pep Ventura. The tourist office has an annually updated list of all pensions and hostels.

Hostal La Barretina, C. Lasauca, 13 (☎97 267 64 12 or ☎97 267 34 25). From the train station, walk up the left side of La Rambla to its end and look for C. Lasauca directly ahead. A luxury experience—each room has TV, A/C, heat, and private bath. Reception is downstairs in the jointly owned restaurant. Reservations recommended. Singles €22.50, doubles €38.60. AmEx/MC/V. ❷

Hostal San Mar, C. Rec Arnau, 31 (☎97 250 98 13). Follow C. Girona off La Rambla and continue as it turns into C. Jonquera; take the 5th right onto C. Isabel II and then take the 2nd left; it's down the street on the right. Enter through the bar. If you make it all the way out here, you will be rewarded with a clean, modern room that has a bath and TV. Ask for a room with a view of the countryside. Singles €13, doubles €26. Cash only. ❶

Pensión Mallol, C. Pep Ventura, 9 (☎97 250 22 83). Follow the Rambla toward the tourist office, turn right on Castell at its end, and take the 2nd left. Look for the "Habitaciones-Chambres" sign. Spacious, clean, and simply decorated rooms with shared bathrooms and firm mattresses. A very good value. Singles €14.50, doubles €24.50. Cash only. ❶

FOOD & NIGHTLIFE

After the sun goes down, a youngish crowd fills up the string of bars and outdoor tables on the Pl. del Sol. Occasionally there is live music, but even without it, Pl. Sol is where it's at. Restaurants near the Dalí museum serve overcooked *paella* to the masses; better choices surround the Rambla on small side streets. The **market** is at Pl. Gra and near Pl. de Catalunya (open Tu, Th, and Sa 5am-2pm, with the widest selection on Th). Buy your own food at supermarket **Bonpreu,** Pl. Sol, 5. (☎97 251 00 19. Open M-Th 9am-2pm and 5-9:30pm, F-Sa 9am-9:30pm. MC/V.)

Hotel Duran Restaurant, C. Lasauca, 5 (☎97 250 12 50). From the train station, walk up the left side of La Rambla to its end and look for C. Lasauca directly ahead. Relax in the elegant and regally decorated dining room and enjoy carefully prepared traditional Catalan cuisine with a distinctive French influence. Lunch *menú* €10.25. Meat and seafood entrees €11.15-40.85. Open daily 1-3:30pm and 8:30-10:30pm. ❹

La Llesca, C. Mestre Falla, 15 (☎97 267 58 26), just beyond Pl. Sol. Family-run restaurant specializes in *llesques*, toasted sandwiches topped with just about anything (€3.35-10.25). *Menú* is a reasonable €7.20; salads €2.70-4.10. Open M-Sa 8am-midnight, Su 6pm-midnight. AmEx/MC/V. ❷

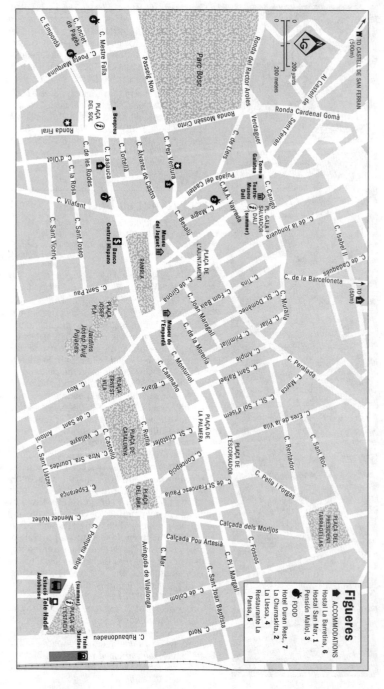

Figueres

ACCOMMODATIONS
Hostal La Barretina, **6**
Hostal San Mar, **1**
Pensión Mallol, **3**

FOOD
Hotel Duran Rest., **7**
La Churrasksita, **2**
La Llesca, **4**
Restaurante La Pansa, **5**

GET sm**art**

Decoding Dalí

Although Dalí's paintings can be confusing at first, aspects of their symbolism are consistent enough to be translated. Here a few examples:

Look carefully at Dalí's **women.** Those portrayed in a cubist style pose no threat to Dalí.

Most of Dalí's **landscapes** portray the rocky shores of Cadaqués.

A rotting **donkey** or **fish** is a symbol of the bourgeoisie.

The **crutches** propping up bits of soft flesh are symbols of masturbation.

The **grasshopper** is a symbol of terror, as Dalí had a great fear of the insect.

Staircases are a Freudian image, representing the fear of intercourse.

A **melting candle** is a symbol of impotence.

Lions represent animal aggression and **knives** are meant to be phallic symbols.

A **fish hook** (found in Dalí's head) is a symbol of his entrapment.

When asked about the famous **melting clocks,** Dalí replied, "the famous soft watches are nothing else than the tender, extravagant, solitary, paranoia-critical Camembert of time and space" (*Conquest of the Irrational,* 1969).

La Churraskita, C. Magre, 5 (☎97 234 11 71). Hammocks and handweavings adorn the colorful walls of this popular Argentinian restaurant. A romantic terrace hides out back. Offers a wide selection of grilled meats (€4.70-15) as well as plenty of vegetarian options like pizza and salads (€3.50-6.60). Open Tu-Su 1-4pm and 8pm-midnight. AmEx/MC/V. ❷

Restaurante La Pansa, C. l'Empordá, 8 (☎97 250 10 72). A comfortable, slightly more upscale restaurant serves meat and fish dishes and a popular 4-course *menú* (€7.50). Open Nov.-Apr. M-Sa 1-3:30pm; May-Oct. M-Sa 1-4pm and 8-10pm, Su 1-3:30pm. AmEx/MC/V. ❷

SIGHTS

▧ TEATRE-MUSEU DALÍ

🛈 ☎97 267 75 00; fax 97 250 16 66; www.salvadordali.org. From the Rambla, take C. Girona from the end farthest from the tourist office. C. Girona goes past Pl. Ajuntament and becomes C. Jonquera. Steps by a Dalí statue to your left lead to the pink and white, egg-covered museum. Open Oct.-June daily 10:30am-5:15pm; July-Sept. daily 9am-7:15pm. €9, students and seniors €6.50. Call ahead about night hours during the summer.

Welcome to the enchanting world of the Surrealist master. This building was the municipal theater for the town of Figueres before it burned down in 1939—hence the name Teatre-Museu ("theater-museum") Dalí. When Dalí decided to donate a museum to Figueres, he insisted on using the ruins of the old theater, which was where he showed his first exposition as a teenager. The resulting homage to his first gallery is the reconstructed theater, covered in sculptures of eggs and full of Dalí's paintings, sculptures, other creations, even his own tomb.

Dalí was infamous for being a fascist self-promoter and his personally designed mausoleum/museum/monument to himself dramatically lives up that reputation. It's all here: Dalí's naughty cartoons, his dramatically low-key tomb, and many paintings of Gala, his wife and muse, one of which, when viewed through a telescope (€0.20), transforms into a portrait of Abraham Lincoln. Be careful when you look up at this work; if you're on the ground level, you're actually standing on Dalí's grave. The treasure-trove of paintings includes, among others, the remarkable *Self Portrait with a Slice of Bacon, Poetry of America, Galarina,* and *Galatea of the Spheres.* Don't miss the spectacular *Sala de Mae West,* created by Dalí for the museum; when viewed from the lookout in the plastic camel, the furnished room resembles the face of actress Mae West. Other works include the surreal appearance of his own Cadillac in the middle of the museum. There is also a small offering of works by other artists selected by Dalí himself, including pieces by El Greco, Marcel Duchamp, and the architect Peres Piñero. While the museum is full of interesting art, not all the works are on the walls; be sure to look up as well.

MUSEU DEL JOGUET (TOY MUSEUM)

🚩 *Sant Pere, 1, off La Rambla.* ☎ *97 250 45 85; www.mjc-figueres.net. Open June-Sept. M-Sa 10am-1pm and 4-7pm, Su 11am-1:30pm and 5-7:30pm; Oct.-May Tu-Sa 10am-1pm and 4-7pm, Su 11am-1:30pm. €4.70, students and children under 12 €3.80.*

Castell de Sant Ferran

Delight in the wonders of your favorite childhood toys at this small toy museum, the winner of Spain's prestigious 1999 National Prize of Popular Culture. The collection includes antique dolls, blocks, board games, comics, rocking horses, toys for the blind, and more, as well as toys donated by famous Catalans such as Joan Miró and Salvador Dalí. Don't miss the impressive selection of Christmastime *caganers* (shitters), a Catalan favorite (see **Praying to a Porcelain God,** p. 214).

MUSEU EMPORDÁ

🚩 *Rambla, 2.* ☎ *97 250 23 05. Open Tu-Sa 11am-7pm, Su 11am-2pm. €2, students and seniors €1. Free entrance with presentation of Teatre-Museu Dalí ticket (see above).*

Though small, this museum's permanent exhibition manages to offer a satisfying taste of over 2000 years of the Alt Empordà region's art, from Neolithic to modern. On display are ancient Roman artifacts, 16th-century frescoes, Baroque paintings, and works by Casas, Tàpies, Dalí, and Miró, among others. Although most pieces have descriptions only in Catalan, the museum still merits at least a short visit by art-lovers.

Arches at Castell de Sant Ferran

CASTELL DE SANT FERRÁN

🚩 *Av. Castell de Sant Ferrán; follow Pujada del Castell from the Teatre-Museu Dalí.* ☎ *97 250 60 94. Open July-Sept. 15 daily 10:30am-8pm; Nov.-Feb. daily 10:30am-2pm; Mar.-July and Sept. 16-Oct. daily 10:30am-2pm and 4-6pm. €2.10.*

A 10min. walk from the Museu Dalí, this massive 18th-century castle/fortress commands a spectacular view of the surrounding countryside and, at 12,000 sq. m, is the largest stone fortress in Europe.

After the Festival

FESTIVALS

In September, classical and jazz music come to Figueres during the **Festival Interna-cional de Música de l'Empordà**. (Tickets available at Caixa de Catalunya. Call ☎97 210 12 12 or get a brochure at the tourist office.) From September 10th to 14th, the **Mos-tra del Vi de L'Alt Empordà**, a tribute to regional wines, brings a taste of the local vine-yards to Figueres. Around May 3, the **Fires i Festes de la Santa Creu** sponsors cultural events and art exhibitions. Parties and general merrymaking can be expected at the **Festa de Sant Pere**, held June 28-29, which honors the town's patron saint.

GIRONA (GERONA)

Girona (pop. 70,000) is a world-class city that the world has yet to notice. First a Roman settlement and then an important medieval cultural center, Girona was one of the few Spanish cities where Christians, Arabs, and Jews were able to peacefully coexist—for a time. Girona was the founding place of the renowned *cabalistas de Girona*, a group of 12th-century rabbis who created an oral tradition called the *Kabbala*, which was based on numerological readings of the Torah (see **The Jewish Sepharad**, p. 220). Visit Girona for a peerless glimpse into medieval Catalan culture.

TRANSPORTATION

Trains: RENFE (☎97 224 02 02; www.renfe.es), in Pl. de Espanya. Info open daily 6:30am-10pm. To: **Barcelona** (1½hr., 6:12am and 9:29pm, €4.90); **Figueres** (30-40min., 23 per day 6:15am-10:44pm, €2.05); **Madrid** (10½hr., 8:21pm, €31); **Portbou** (1hr., 10 per day 6:15am-10:44pm, €3.20); and **Paris** (11hr.; 10:17pm; €106, under 26 €85).

Buses: Next to the train station. Station police ☎97 221 23 19. **Sarfa** (☎97 220 17 96; open daily 8am-8:30pm; all prices are between €3 and €5; 10% discount for students; cash only) to: **Palafrugell** (1hr., 17 per day), for connections to Begur, Llafranc, Calella, and Tam-ariu and **Tossa de Mar** (40min.; July-Aug. 2 per day, Sept.-June 1 per day). **Teisa** (☎97 220 02 75; open M-F 9am-1pm and 3:30-7:15pm, Sa-Su 9am-1pm; cash only) drives to: **Lerida** (3½hr.; 2 per day; €14.30, students €12.90); **Olot** (1¼hr., 9 per day, €4.30); **Ripoll** (2hr., 3 per day, €7.50). **St. Feliu** (45min., 9-14 per day, €3). **Barcelona Bus** (☎97 220 24 32; open M-F 6:30-10am, 11am-2:25pm, and 4:30-7:10pm; MC/V) sends express buses to **Bar-celona** (1¼hr.; M-F 6 per day, €10; Sa-Su and holidays 3 per day; €11.45) and **Figueres** (50min.; M-F 6 per day, €3.95; Sa 2 per day, €4.55; Su and holidays 2 per day, €4.55).

Taxis: ☎97 222 23 23 or 97 222 10 20. Try Pl. Independència or Pont de Pedra.

Car Rental: Europcar is inside the train station. Other companies cluster around C. Barce-lona, right outside. Must be 21+ and have had a license for at least 1-2 years. **Avis** is also inside the train station. Must be 23+ and must have had a valid licence for at least one year. €16.63 per day. Extra charge of €6 per day for those under 25. Open M-Sa 8am-9pm. AmEx/MC/V; credit cards only.

ORIENTATION & PRACTICAL INFORMATION

The **Riu Onyar** separates the new city from the old. The **Pont de Pedra** (bridge) con-nects the two banks and leads into the old quarter by way of C. Ciutadans, C. Per-alta, and C. Força, which lead to the cathedral and **El Call,** the historic Jewish neighborhood. The **RENFE** and **bus terminals** are situated off C. de Barcelona, in the modern neighborhood. To get to the old city from the stations, head straight out through the parking lot, turn left on C. Barcelona and continue to follow C. Barce-lona for two blocks until it forks at the traffic island. Take the right fork via C. Santa Eugenia to Gran Via de Jaume I, across the Gran Via to C. Nou, which leads to the Pont de Pedra.

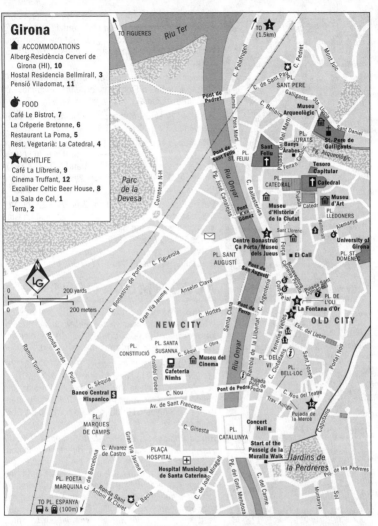

♠ ACCOMMODATIONS
Alberg-Residència Cerverí de
Girona (HI), **10**
Hostal Residencia Bellmirall, **3**
Pensió Viladomat, **11**

🍎 FOOD
Café Le Bistrot, **7**
La Crêperie Bretonne, **6**
Restaurant La Poma, **5**
Rest. Vegetarià: La Catedral, **4**

★ NIGHTLIFE
Café La Llíbreria, **9**
Cinema Truffant, **12**
Excaliber Celtic Beer House, **8**
La Sala de Cel, **1**
Terra, **2**

DAYTRIPPING ORIENTATION & PRACTICAL INFORMA-

Tourist Office: Rambla Llibertat, 1 (☎97 222 65 75; fax 97 222 66 12), in an American cheese-colored building directly on the left as you cross Pont de Pedra from the new town. Tons of free info on the city and region. English spoken. Pick up a free map and the free bi-weekly La Guía, in Catalan but with easy-to-follow listings of local events. Open M-F 8am-8pm, Sa 8am-2pm and 4-8pm, Su 9am-2pm. Another **branch** located nearby in Plaça del Vi. Open in winter M-F 9am-7pm, Sa 9am-2pm; in summer M-F 9am-3pm, Sa 9am-2pm.

Bank: Banco Central Hispano, At C. Nou and Gran Via, has an **ATM.** Open Oct.-Mar. M-F 8:30am-2:30pm, Sa 8:30am-1pm; Apr.-Sept. M-F 8:30am-2:30pm.

Luggage Storage: Lockers in train station €4.50 per 24hr. Open M-F 6:30am-10pm.

Travel Bookstore: Ulysses, C. Ballesteries, 29 (☎/fax 97 221 17 73), on the left as you walk up Ballesteries toward the Pl. Cathedral. Thorough offering of guides to Girona, Spain, and most of Europe; some in English (€18-27). Open M-Sa 10am-2pm and 4:30-8:30pm. MC/V. **219**

THE JEWISH SEPHARAD

Though Girona has a reputation for tolerance, the Jews of Girona were still victims of discrimination, ostracism, and eventual expulsion. Despite it all, they contributed ineradicably to the city's culture. The *aljama* (Jewish quarter) in Girona, once populated by 300 people, became a leading center for the study of the **Kabbala,** a mystical reading of the Torah in which number values are assigned to each Hebrew letter and numerical sums are interpreted to reveal spiritual meaning. Operating like a tiny, independent country within the city (inhabitants answered to their King, not the city government), El Call (see p. 221) was protected by the crown of Catalunya in exchange for financial tribute.

Until the 11th century, Christians and Jews coexisted peacefully, occasionally even intermarrying. Unfortunately, this did not last. Historical sources cite attacks and looting of the Jewish quarter in eight separate years, the first in 1276 and the last in 1418. Eventually, almost every entrance to El Call was blocked off. The reopening of the streets of El Call began only after Franco's death in 1975. In recent years, eight Spanish mayors have created a network called *Caminos de Sepharad,* an organization aimed at restoring Spain's Jewish quarters and fostering a broader understanding of the Sephardic legacy. for more on Jews in Catalunya, see **Catalan Jews,** p. 68.

Supermarket: Hipercor (☎97 218 84 00), on C. Barcelona; from the train station take a right and walk for 15 min. Groceries, clothing, telephones, currency exchange, English books, and cafeteria. Open M-Sa 10am-10pm.

Emergency: ☎112. **Police: Policía Municipal,** C. Bacià, 4 (☎092). From Banco Central Hispano, turn right on the Gran Via, then right on Bacià.

Hospital: Hospital Municipal de Santa Caterina, Pl. Hospital, 5 (☎97 218 26 00).

Internet Access: Corado Telephone, C. Barcelona, 31 (☎97 222 28 75), across from the train station. €2 per hr. Open M-Sa 9am-2pm and 5-9pm. **Café la Llibreria,** C. Ciutadans, 15 (see **Nightlife and Entertainment,** p. 224). €1 per 20 minutes, €3 per hr.

Post Office: Av. Ramón Folch, 2 (☎97 222 21 11), at the start of Gran Via de Jaume I. Turn right on Gran Via coming from the old city. **Second office,** Ronda Ferrán Puig, 17 (☎97 222 34 75). **Lista de Correos** only. Both open M-F 8:30am-8:30pm and Sa 9:30am-2pm. **Postal Code:** 17070.

ACCOMMODATIONS

Rooms are only hard to find in July and August, when reservations are a good idea on weekends. Budget accommodations in the old quarter are very well located and reasonably priced.

Pensió Viladomat, C. Ciutadans, 5 (☎97 220 31 76; fax 97 220 31 76), next to the youth hostel. Light, open, sparking clean and well-furnished rooms and dining/reading area with balcony. Rooms with bath have TVs. Singles €16; doubles €31, with bath €50. Cash only. ❷

Hostal Residencia Bellmirall, C. Bellmirall, 3 (☎97 220 40 09). With the cathedral directly behind you, C. Bellmirall is straight ahead to the left; look for the blue hostel sign. Expensive but absolutely worth the splurge. Features delightful rooms in a 14th-century stone house. Breakfast included and served in the cozy dining area or plant-filled garden patio. The perfect, romantic environment from which to enjoy Girona. Reservations recommended. Closed Jan. 6-Feb. 28. Singles €32; doubles €49, with bath €56; triples €75; family room (for 4) €96 (IVA included). Cash only. ❸

Albergue-Residència Cerverí de Girona (HI), C. Ciutadans, 9 (☎97 221 80 03; fax 97 221 20 23; www.tujuca.com). From the new city, cross Pont de Pedra, take a left on Ciutadans; it's about a block up on your left. The sterile, whitewashed walls and blue metal bunks in this college dorm building may cause flashbacks to sleep-away camp, but the price and location make it worthwhile. A good choice if you want to meet other travelers. 8 beds available Oct.-

June; 82 beds July-Sept. Sleek sitting rooms with TV/VCR; rooms of 3 and 8 beds with lockers. Breakfast €2.70; other meals €4.81. Sheets €2.10; towel rental €2.10; combined sheets and towel rental €3.01. Laundry €3. Internet €1.20 per hr. **Members only,** but HI cards for sale. Make reservations at the Barcelona office (☎93 483 83 63). Dorms for under 25 or groups €11.57; for over 25 €15.63. MC/V. ❶

FOOD

Considered home to some of the best cuisine in Catalunya, Girona's specialties are *botifarra dolça* (sweet sausage with pork, lemon, cinnamon, and sugar) and *xuixo* (sugar-sprinkled pastries filled with cream). Popular throughout Spain, *xuixo* originated in C. Argenteria, the continuation of La Rambla. By far the best place to find good, cheap food is on C. Cort Reial, at the top of C. Argenteria; La Rambla is home to rows of tourist cafes with ubiquitous terrace seating. Health food and vegetarian options also abound on both sides of the river. In summer, an open **market** can be found near the Polideportivo in Parc de la Deversa (open Tu and Sa 8am-3pm). Get your **groceries** at **Caprabo,** C. Sequia 10, a block from C. Nou off the Gran Via. (☎97 221 45 16. Open M-Sa 9am-9pm.)

🔳 **La Crêperie Bretonne,** C. Cort Reial, 14 (☎97 221 81 20). Potent proof of Girona's proximity to France, this popular crêpe joint combines a funky atmosphere with great food and cheap prices. Old French posters decorate the stone walls, and your food is cooked inside a small bus bound for "Cerbère." *Menú* €8.71. Crêpes €2.25-5.65. Unusual salads €5.56-6.31. Open Su 8pm-midnight, Tu-Sa 1-4pm and 8pm-midnight. ❶

Restaurante La Poma, C. Cort Reial, 16 (☎ 97 221 29 09). Internationally-influenced sandwiches, crêpes, pasta, pizza, and salads at unbelievable prices, in a cozy restaurant decked out in primary colors. Salads and pasta €3.90-4.50. Pizza €4. Crêpes €3-3.40. Open W-M 7:30pm-midnight. Cash only. ❶

Café Le Bistrot, Pujada Sant Domènech, 4 (☎97 221 88 03), a right off C. Ciutadans. An elegant, turn-of-the-century atmosphere, with a great view overlooking one of the old city's slanting streets. Excellent food. Fresh specialty pizzas €3.60-4.20. Crêpes €3-4.20. Lunch *menú* €12. Terrace costs 10% extra. Open M-Th 1-4pm and 8pm-1am, F-Sa 1-4pm and 7pm-2am, Su 1-4pm and 8pm-midnight. ❶

Restaurant Vegetarianà La Catedral, Lluis Batlle i Prats, 4 (☎97 221 83 38). Walk straight out the side exit to the Cathedral (Plaça des Apóstols), down Lluis Batlle i Prats; the restaurant is on the left. If you're looking to escape the more touristy area of the city, check out this out-of-the-way vegetarian restaurant serving creative vegetable, rice, and tofu dishes. The terrace offers a view of the cathedral. Lunch *menú* €9, €1 extra for terrace. Open M-W 1-3pm, Th-Sa 1-3pm and 8:30-11pm. ❷

SIGHTS

🔝 *At any one of the following museums, you can buy a combined ticket which gets you access to all 6 city museums for only €4.80 (good for 1 month).*

The narrow, winding streets of the medieval city, interspersed with steep stairways and low arches, are ideal for wanderers, but a bit much for those not used to climbing stairs. Start your self-guided historical tour at the **Pont de Pedra** and turn left at the tourist office down tree-lined **Rambla de la Llibertat.** Continue on C. Argenteria, bearing right across C. Cort Reial. Up the flight of stairs, C. Força begins on the left.

🔳 EL CALL

🔝 *The entrance to the center is off C. Força, about halfway up the hill. ☎97 221 67 61. Center and museum open May-Oct. M-Sa 10am-8pm, Su 10am-3pm; Nov.-April M-Sa 10am-6pm, Su 10am-3pm. Museum €2, students and over 65 €1, under 16 free. The tourist office offers guided tours of El Call in July and Aug. (€6 during the day, €12 at night).*

The part of the old town around C. Força and C. Sant Llorenç was once the center of Girona's medieval Jewish community ("call" comes from *kahal*, "community" in Hebrew), a city within a city where Jews led a segregated existence. The site of the last synagogue in Girona now serves as the **Centre Bonastruc Ca Porta**, named for Rabbi Moshe Ben-Nahman (Nahmanides), a scholar of Jewish mysticism and the oral tradition known as the *Kabbala* (see **The Jewish Sepharad**, p. 220). The center includes the **Museu d'Història dels Jueus Girona**, notable for its detailed wooden model of the original Call and its collection of inscribed Hebrew tombstones.

CATHEDRAL COMPLEX

🛈 *Tesoro* ☎ *97 221 44 26. Cathedral and Tesoro open Mar.-Sept. Tu-Sa 10am-2pm and 4-7pm, Oct.-Mar. Tu-Sa 10am-2pm and 4-6pm; open year-round Su-M and holidays 10am-2pm. Tesoro and cloister €3.*

Farther uphill on C. Força and around the corner to the right, Girona's imposing Gothic **cathedral** rises a record-breaking 90 steps (its Baroque stairway is the largest in Europe) from the *plaça*. The **Torre de Charlemany** (bell tower) and **cloister** are the only structures left from the 11th and 12th centuries; the rest of the building dates from the 14th-17th centuries. The most unique feature of the cathedral is its interior, where the three customary naves have been compressed into one, creating a single, large, hauntingly dark space that would make an ideal theater for a Catalan screening of the Rocky Horror Picture Show. The Cathedral contains the world's widest Gothic **nave** (22m) and is surpassed in sheer size only by St. Peter's in Rome. A door on the left leads to the trapezoidal cloister and the **Tesoro Capitular (treasury)**, home to some of Girona's most precious possessions. The *Tesoro's* (and possibly Girona's) most famous piece (judging by the thick glass protecting it) is the **Tapis de la Creació**, an 11th-century tapestry depicting the creation story, the only one of its kind in the world. For €1, the voice of a British woman with a mesmerizing accent will tell you everything you want to know about the tapestry.

MUSEUMS

MUSEU DEL CINEMA

🛈 *C. Sèquia, 1, one block north of C. Nou off C. Santa Clara. ☎ 97 241 2 777. Open Oct.-Apr. M-F 10am-6pm, Sa 10am-8pm, Su 11am-3pm; May-Sept. daily 10am-8pm. Museum entrance €3, students and over 65 €1.50, under 16 free. AmEx/MC/V.*

This unusual collection, the best of its kind in Europe, documents the rise of cinema from the mid-17th to the 20th century, with a few pieces from as early as the 11th century (Chinese shadow theater). It walks you through the chronological development of the *camera obscura* (9th-12th century), magic lantern (1659), panorama (1788), diorama (1822), Thomas Edison's kinetoscope (1891), and more. The hands-on visual displays will get you in touch with your early modern childhood, as you play with trick-of-the-eye technologies from yesteryear and watch early cartoons.

CITY MUSEUMS

In addition to the Jewish Museum, the Cathedral *Tesoro*, and the cinema museum, Girona boasts four small city-related treasures: the Museu d'Història de la Ciutat, Banys Arabs, Museu Arqueològic, and the Museu d'Art, worth visiting in that order.

The remarkably well-done **Museu d'Història de la Ciutat**, C. Força 27, showcases 2000 years of Girona's history, from the first settlers in Catalunya to the present day; check out the festival giants and the room dedicated to Napoleonic War. (☎ 97 222 22 29. Open Tu-Sa 10am-2pm and 5-7pm, Su and holidays 10am-2pm. Some descriptions in English. €2, under 16 free.) To get to the **Banys Arabs** from the cathedral, with your back to the stairs, take a right on C. Ferrán Catòlic. Inspired by Muslim bath houses, the graceful 12th-century structure once contained saunas and baths of varying temperatures; now they occasionally host art outdoor art exhibits. (☎ 97 221 32 62.

Open Apr.-Sept. M-Sa 10am-7pm, Su 10am-2pm; Oct.-Mar. daily 10am-2pm. €1.50, students €0.75.) The **Museu Arqueològic** complements its archeological displays with detailed booklets on the history of the area (available in English). The **Museu d'Art** holds medieval and modern art, including themed rooms on glass, ceramics, and liturgical art. Both offer some unique glimpses into Catalonian culture in Girona and are worthwhile stops for history and art history fans. The **Museu Arqueològic** is past the Banys Arabs through Pl. Jurants, on the right. (☎97 220 26 32. Open Tu-Sa 10:30am-1:30pm and 4-7pm, Su 10am-2pm. €1.80, students €1.40, under 16 free.) The Museu d'Art is next to the cathedral. (☎97 220 38 34. Open Mar.-Sept. Tu-Sa 10am-7pm, Oct.-Feb. Tu-Sa 10am-6pm; Su and holidays 10am-2pm. €1.80, students or over 65 €1.40.)

Catalan Flag

WALKS & TOURS

Girona's renowned **⛫Passeig de la Muralla,** not for the faint of heart, begins at the bottom of La Rambla in Pl. de la Marvà. The walk features some breathtaking views of Girona, but involves a lot of stair climbing and can be exhausting (there are places to climb down along the way if you get too tired). Take the steps up to the guard's rampart atop the old Roman defense walls and follow them around the entire eastern side of the old town. (Passeig de la Muralla open daily 8am-10pm.) The walk ends behind the Cathedral, where the equally beautiful **Passeig Arqueològic** begins, featuring well-preserved medieval gardens and buildings. Partly lined with cypresses and flower beds, this path skirts the northeastern medieval wall and also overlooks the city. For the less athletically inclined, a small trolley gives a 30min. guided tour of the main sights of the old town, including the town hall, the Cathedral, St. Feliu church, El Call, and the walls. (In summer, it leaves daily every 20-25min. from the Pont de Pedra, 10am-8pm or so. In winter, it runs less frequently, sometimes only weekends; check in the tourist office. Available in English. €3.)

Matador

NIGHTLIFE

The concentrated nightlife locales in Girona are the **Pl. de l'Oli** (and nearby streets), the old quarter, and in summer, the expansive, impeccably designed **Parc de la Devesa**, which explodes with *carpas*, temporary outdoor bars. (Across the river from the old town, several blocks to the left. Open June-Sept. 15 Su-Th 10pm-3am and F-Sa 10pm-4:30am. Drinks €4.20-5.40. Cash only.)

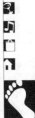

Seafood

Gala-vanting

Anyone even remotely interested in Salvador Dalí inevitably wonders what is up with the artist's strange obsession with his wife, Gala. Originally born Helena Deluvina Diankoff in Kazan where she frequented sanatoriums, Gala possessed a voracious sex drive, jumping from lover to lover her entire life. Dalí first met Gala in 1929 in Cadaqués, where she was vacationing with her then-husband, surrealist poet Paul Éluard. Gala had already peppered that relationship with boy toys, even convincing Éluard to participate in a threesome with German Dadaist Max Ernst. Although Gala's relationship with the impotent Dalí seems perplexing, the Russian nymphomaniac was lucky because Dalí, a voyeur, got off on her sexual infidelities (Dalí himself is known to have had homosexual tendencies). Some argue that as her material greed grew, Gala destroyed her husband's integrity just to make a buck. In 1970, Dalí left Gala to her sexual whims at Púbol, where she remained taking lovers well into her 80s. After a 4 year affair with actor William Rothlein, she fell for singer Jeff Fenholt (Jesus in *Jesus Christ Superstar*), for whom she built a recording studio at Púbol and bought a house on Long Island despite his sexual distaste for her. Her obsession (including its monetary repercussions) infuriated Dalí enough to break 2 of her ribs with a beating (she was 87). When Gala died in Barcelona rather than at her castle, her corpse was propped up in the back seat of her grandiose Cadillac and and chauffeured back to Púbol.

The bars and cafes in the old quarter are particularly mellow and relaxing, a good way to start the evening. For a more relaxed evening out, visit the movie theater, **Cinema Truffaut,** C. Portal Nou, 7, to catch the weekly foreign movie. (☎97 222 50 44. From C. Nou, go right on C. Subida de la Merced, and then left right after the stairs. Open daily 6pm-12:30am. €4.50, under 23 €3.50, 65+ €1.80. Cash only.)

Café la Llibreria, C. Ciutadans, 15 (☎97 220 10 82). Behind the bookstore; enter on C. Ferreires Vellas, parallel to C. Ciutadans. Cocktails (€3.60), beer (€1.40), and tapas (€2.10-2,70) served to chic intellectual types, or those who think they are. Live music (usually guitar) W and F after 11pm. Internet €1 per 20min., €3 per hr. Open M-Sa 8:30am-1am, Su 8:30am-midnight. MC/V.

Excalibur Celtic Beer House, Pl. de l'Oli, 1 (☎97 220 82 53), at the top of C. Ciutadans. The only authentic place in Girona to go for a pint of Guiness (€4) and English-speaking expat company. Irish rock and American pop from the speakers, lots of European sports on the TV, and a chalkboard outside advertising what games will be showing. Drinks €4.20. Open M-Th 6pm-12:30pm, F-Su 4pm-3am. MC/V.

La Terra, C. Ballestries, 23 (☎97 221 57 64). Serious women dressed all in black serve fresh-squeezed juices at this understated hang-out decorated with mismatched ceramics. Try their fruit juices (€2.40) or a hamburger (€3). Free ticket to Cinema Truffaut with a purchase of €7 or more. Open M-Th 5pm-1am, F-Su 5pm-2am. Cash only.

La Sala del Cel, C. Pedret, 118 (☎97 221 46 64). A 15min. walk upriver from the Pont de St. Feliu, on the old town side. A complex more than a mere club, with 3 techno and house-blasting dance floors, a huge hangout area with black leather couches, a pool and slide, Play Station computers, and a free massage room. Cover €12 (includes 1 drink). Open F-Sa midnight-5:30am. MC/V.

FESTIVALS

During the second half of May, government-sponsored **flower exhibitions** spring up in the city; local monuments and pedestrian streets swim in blossoms, and the courtyards of Girona's fine old buildings open to the public. Summer evenings often inspire spontaneous *sardana* dancing in the city *plaças* (see **May I Have This Dance,** p. 51). Like the rest of Catalunya, Girona also lights up on June 24 for the **Focs de Sant Joan,** an outdoor party featuring fireworks and campfires.

NEAR GIRONA: PÚBOL

🚩 *From Girona, take the train or bus to Flaça and pick up a taxi to Púbol, 3km away (approx. €7); taxis will usually arrange to bring you back to the station at your designated time. **Sarfa** (☎ 97 220 17 96 or 97 264 09 64) runs **buses** from Girona to Flaça (30min.; every 30min. M-F 7:45am-8:30pm, every hr. Sa-Su 9am-8:30pm; €2). **RENFE** (☎ 902 24 02 02) trains go from Barcelona Estació-Sants to Flaça (1¾hr., every 30min.-1hr. 5:50am-9:20pm, €5.86); and from Girona to Flaça (15min, several per hour 6:15am-9:36pm, €1-1.40).*

In the late 1960s, the adoring Salvador Dalí bought a crumbling 14th-century castle in the tiny village of Púbol for his beloved wife and muse, Gala. The Surrealist master set about restoring the castle to its former glory, while insuring that it maintained a slightly time-worn appearance which he and his wife prized. When Gala moved into her Púbol mansion, Dalí declared he would never visit without her written request. Rumors suggest that in Dalí's absence, Gala entertained her fair share of male visitors (see **Gala-vanting,** p. 224). The **Casa-Museu Castell Gala Dalí,** Púbol's major—and only—attraction, has been open to visitors since 1996. Besides Gala's tomb, tastefully sandwiched between the garage and gardens, the castle contains several of Dalí's works, including a colorful ceiling painting, a chess set made to resemble thumbs, and an elaborate gold and blue throne. The artist lived in the castle after Gala's death in 1982 and was almost killed when he accidently set fire to his bedroom two years later. One of his last works, a refined painting with strong, contrasting colors, sits on an easel in the castle's dining room. (☎ 97 248 86 55. Open Mar. 15-June 14 and Sept. 16-Nov. 1 Tu-Su 10:30am-5:15pm; Jun. 15-Sept. 15 daily 10:30am-7:15pm. €5, students and seniors €4. Free guided tours at noon in Catalan and at 5pm in Spanish. Wheelchair accessible.) There is little else to see in tiny Púbol, but if you get hungry before or after visiting the castle, **Can Bosch ❷,** on C. Fera Muralia next to the castle, offers solid Catalan fare and is about the only option. (☎ 97 248 83 57. Daily *menú* €7.20. Open July 15-Aug. 31 daily 9am-11pm, kitchen open 1-4pm and 8-11pm. Sept.-June M-W 9:30am-6pm, kitchen open 1-4pm; Th-Su 9:30am-8pm, kitchen open 1-4pm.)

CADAQUÉS & PORT LLIGAT

The whitewashed houses and small bay of Cadaqués (pop. 2000) have attracted artists, writers, and musicians ever since **Dalí** built his summer home in neighboring Port Lligat in the 1930s. Cadaqués is the bigger of the two towns (Port Lligat is basically just Dalí's house), which are so close to each other that they are virtually superimposed. To preserve the towns' authentic Mediterranean flavor, an affluent crowd of property owners and renters have kept at bay the commercial influx of sprawling condos, big hotels, and trains. Cadaqués has not been immune, however, to the trendy influence of the hordes of French tourists and Barcelona daytrippers who flock there in the summer to see Dalí's house; chic galleries and shops have cropped up to suit the cosmopolitan crowd. The rocky beaches and dreamy landscape attract their share of tourists, but Cadaqués preserves a pleasantly laid-back atmosphere. Be forewarned: if you're traveling to Cadaqués between September and May, most food and entertainment options will be shut down. It is best to make it a daytrip only, though the bus schedule may make it difficult to do so (see below).

TRANSPORTATION

Buses: Cadaqués has no train station. Sarfa buses (☎ 97 225 87 13) run to: **Barcelona** (2½hr., 11:15am and 4:15pm, €15.20); **Figueres** (1hr., 5-7 per day, €4.30); **Girona** (2hr., 1-2 per day, €7).

Bike and Boat Rental: Escola de Vela Ones (☎ 93 753 25 12 or 93 232 18 90), on the beach directly in front of the tourist office, rents kayaks, sailboats, and windsurfing gear. Choose from 3, 4, or 6hr. guided kayak excursions (€27-60), or head out on your own in a

GET smart

Dalí or not Dalí?

When Spanish police busted into the Centre d'Art Perrot-Moore in Cadaqués in April 1999, they arrested Captain Peter Moore and his wife Catherine Perrot on charges of art forgery. Moore, a British Army captain, was a friend and assistant to Salvador Dalí for 20 years until the artist passed away in 1989. The private collection of Captain Moore was on display at the Centre d'Art Perrot-Moore, which was quietly shut down following the couple's arrest and subsequent release on bail. Police, aided by a team of art historians, are collaborating in their efforts to discover whether over 10,000 prints ready for sale at the Centre d'Art Perrot-Moore are fakes. Authorities believe that Moore pressured an ailing Dalí into signing thousands of blank pieces of paper which were then printed with "limited edition" lithographs and sold as Dalí originals. Dalí thus continues to be the scandal-monger of the art world, even in death.

single kayak (€9 per hr., €24 half-day, €42 full day) or a double kayak (€12 per hr., €36 half-day, €60 full day). Windsurfing gear (€9 per hr.) and sailboats (€18-30) also available. Open July-Sept. 15 daily 10am-8pm. Bike rental also available at **Rent@bit** (see below).

ORIENTATION & PRACTICAL INFORMATION

The bus to Cadaqués halts to the right of the Sarfa office. With your back to the Sarfa office, walk right and downhill on Av. Caritat Serinyana to the waterfront square, **Plaça Frederic Rahola,** where a signboard map with indexed services and accommodations will orient you.

Tourist Office, C. Cotxe, 2 (☎97 225 83 15; fax 97 215 94 42), off Pl. Frederic Rahola, has a helpful map of Cadaqués and the surrounding beaches. Open July-Aug. M-Sa 9:30am- 1:30pm and 4-8pm, Su 10:30am-1:30pm; Sept.-June M-Sa 9am-2pm and 4-7pm.

Currency Exchange: Banco Central Hispano, C. Caritat Serinyana, 4 (☎97 225 83 62). Open Oct.-Mar. M-F 8:30am-2:30pm, Sa 8:30am-1pm; Apr.-Sept. M-F 8:30am-2:30pm. There are many **ATMs** along the waterfront promenade.

Police: (☎97 215 93 43), on Pl. Frederic Rahola.

Medical Assistance: ☎97 225 88 07.

Internet Access: on@, C. Miquel Rosset, 3 (☎97 225 10 42), just off Av. Caritat Serinyana. €0.75 per 10min., €2.50 per 30min., €4.75 per hr. Open Su-Th 11am-2pm and 4-7pm, F-Sa 11am-2pm and 5pm-midnight or 1am. **Rent@bit,** Av. Caritat Serinyana, 9 (☎97 225 10 23; www.rentabit.net). €2.75 per 30min., €4 per hr. Also rents bikes (€3 per hr., €12 per day) and scooters (€15 per 2hr., €35.50 per day). Open daily 10am-1pm and 3-10pm.

Post Office, Av. Rierassa (☎97 225 87 98), off Av. Caritat Serinyana. Open M-F 9:15am-2pm, Sa 9:30am-1pm.

Postal code: 17488.

ACCOMMODATIONS & CAMPING

As Cadaqués is a beach town, many accommodations are open only during the summer. The irony is that most places close in August; plan accordingly. Though room prices soar in these summer months, accommodations in Cadaqués can still be found for relatively reasonable prices.

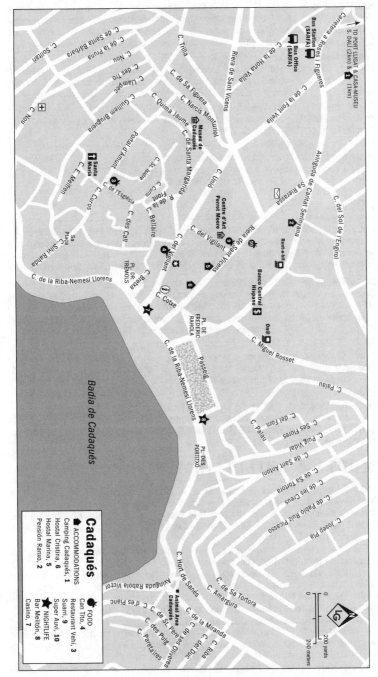

Badia de Cadaqués

Cadaqués

ACCOMMODATIONS
Camping Cadaqués, **1**
Hostal Cristina, **6**
Hostal Marina, **5**
Pensión Ranxo, **2**

FOOD
Can Tito, **4**
Restaurant Vehi, **3**
Super Auvi, **9**
Bar Meliton, **8**

NIGHTLIFE
Casino, **7**

0   200 yards
0   200 meters

Hostal Cristina (☎97 225 81 38), on C. Riera. Right on the water, to the right of Av. Caritat Serinyana. Bright, newly renovated rooms; rooftop terrace overlooks the water. Summer prices include breakfast. May-Sept. singles €26; doubles €40, with bath €52, with TV €57. Oct.-Apr. singles €20; doubles €27, with bath or terrace €38, with TV €50. MC/V. ❸

Pensión Ranxo, Av. Caritat Serinyana, 13 (☎97 225 80 05), on the right as you walk down from the bus stop. Potted plants and whitewashed hallways lead to clean and comfortable rooms. All rooms come with bath. Breakfast included. July-Sept. 15 singles €26, doubles €49.50; Sept. 15-June singles €20, doubles €43. Traveler's checks accepted. MC/V. ❸

Hostal Marina, C. Riera, 3 (☎97 225 81 99 or 97 215 90 91), boasts clean rooms with modern furniture. Some rooms have balconies. Open Apr.-Dec. Singles €19, with bath €25; doubles €35, with bath €45. MC/V. ❷

Camping Cadaqués, Ctra. Portlligat, 17 (☎97 225 81 26), 100m from the beach on the left on the way to Dalí's house; follow the signs for Hotel Port Lligat. Popular and crowded camp-site. Amenities include pool, supermarket, and bungalows (€24-33). Open Apr.-Sept. €4 per person, €5 per tent, €4 per car; IVA not included. ❶

FOOD

Cadaqués harbors the usual slew of overpriced, unexciting tourist restaurants on the waterfront; wander into the back streets for more interesting options. **Groceries** can be purchased at **Super Auvi,** C. Riera. (☎97 225 86 33. Open July 15-Aug. M-Sa 8am-2pm and 4:30-9pm, Su 8am-2pm; Sept.-July 14 M-Sa 8:30am-1:30pm and 4:30-9pm.)

▓ **Can Tito,** C. Vigilant, 8 (☎97 225 90 70). An exceptional historic and culinary experience. The stone archway at the entrance to this elegant restaurant is 1 of 5 portals dating back to AD 1100 when Cadaqués was still a fortified village at the mercy of roving pirates. Try the house specialty, *pastel de escalivada,* a *soufflé* of onions, peppers, eggplant, and pepperoni (€6.60). Lunch *menú* €12. Fish and meat entrees €4.80-14. Open Mar.-Jan. daily 1:30-3pm and 8-10:30pm. MC/V. ❷

Suarri, C. Vigilant, 3. An elegant, spacious place to escape from the heat of the sun for a wide range of Catalan and Italian dishes. Spinach and cheese ravioli with nut sauce (€11) can sooth tummies tired of Spanish cuisine. Entrees €8.50-24. Open daily 11am-1pm and 7-11pm. ❹

Restaurant Vehí, C. de l'Església, 6 (☎97 225 84 70). 2nd-floor restaurant with panoramic windows offering lovely views. Serves up traditional Catalan fare with an emphasis on sea-food. Split a 2-person dish (€18.50-21) with that special someone. *Menú* (€10.50-12) includes wine. Entrees €6-20. Open Mar.-Oct. ❸

SIGHTS & ENTERTAINMENT

The local church, **Església de Santa Maria,** is a 16th-century gothic building with a Baroque altarpiece. Unfortunately, the church is only open for services. Nearby, the **Museu de Cadaqués,** C. Narcis Monturiol, 15, has changing exhibits, often with a Dalí theme. (☎97 225 88 77. Open late-June to Sept. daily 10:30am-1:30pm and 3-8pm. €4.50; students €3.)

From the museum, take a pleasant walk (30min.) to ▓**Casa-Museu Salvador Dalí,** in Port Lligat, the home where Dalí and his wife Gala lived until her death in 1982. With your back to the Sarfa station looking uphill, take the right fork and follow the signs to Port Lligat; eventually Casa de Dalí signs appear. At C. President Lluís Companys, where signs point to the house in two different directions, follow the one to the right—the other road is the auto route. Originally a modest fisherman's abode, the house was transformed to meet the aesthetic and eccentric lifestyle led by Dalí and his treasured wife. The egg-covered building flaunts Dalí's favorite lip-shaped sofa and more stuffed snakes and swans than you bargained for. Though only two (unfin-ished) Dalí originals remain in the house, the decorating style is a work in itself. (☎97 225 10 15. Open June 15-Sept. 15 daily 10:30am-9pm; Sept. 16-Nov. and Mar. 15-

June 14 Tu-Su 10:30am-6pm. Tours are the only way to see the house; make reservations 1-2 days in advance. Ticket office closes 45min. before closing. €7.80; students, seniors, and children €4.80.)

Lucky for you, the **Centre d'Art Perrot-Moore,** C. Vigilante, 1, once closed because of a huge artistic fraud scandal (see **Dalí or not Dalí?,** p. 226), is reopening to the public, replacing exhibits of Dalí with other artists who can be contrasted with Picasso. If you can't get enough Dalí, **boat rides** in Dalí's boat *Gala* leave in front of the house on the hour for a 55min. trip to Cap de Creus. (☎617 46 57 57. Open daily 10am-7pm. €9.) Outdoor activities in Cadaqués are popular, and in addition to **water sports** and **biking,** a map of various 2-8km **hikes** is available at the tourist office.

NIGHTLIFE

When the sun sets, head to one of Cadaqués's beachfront bars for drinks and music. **Bar Melitón** (☎97 225 82 01) on the *passeig* has a popular terrace with plenty of tables. The oldest bar in town, **Casino** (☎97 225 81 37), on Pl. Doctor Tremols, has high ceilings, big windows, and a stream of drink-sippers all day and into the night (pool table and coin-op Internet also available).

PALAFRUGELL

In the year AD 988, inhabitants of the beach town of Llafranc founded inland Palafrugell, seeking refuge from the constant plundering of Mediterranean pirates. Today, budget travelers come here to flee the wallet-plundering of seaside hotels and restaurants. Forty kilometers east of Girona, Palafrugell serves as a base for trips to the picturesque nearby beach towns of **Calella, Llafranc,** and **Tamariu,** which cater to wealthy Europeans whose idea of a budget accommodation is any hotel that doesn't leave mints on the pillow. To save some euros, stay in admittedly bland (and beachless) Palafrugell and daytrip to the beaches. The small beaches are connected by the **Camino de Ronda,** a series of stone footpaths allowing exploration of the rocky, wooded coast.

TRANSPORTATION

Buses: Sarfa, C. Torres Jonama, 67-79 (☎97 230 06 23). Prices rise on weekends. To: **Barcelona** (2hr.; 17 per day, last bus 8:30pm; €11.40); **Calella** and **Llafranc** (15min.-20min.; 12-24 per day, in winter months 4-5 per day; €1); **Figueres** (1½hr., 3-4 per day, €5.65); **Girona** (1hr., 18 per day, €3.75).

Taxis: Radio Taxi (☎97 261 00 00). 24hr. service throughout the area.

ORIENTATION & PRACTICAL INFORMATION

To get from the bus station to the center of town, turn right and walk down C. Torres Jonama to C. de Pi i Maragall. Then turn right and walk past the Guardia Civil and the market until you hit **Pl. Nova,** the main square of the town, off of which are C. San Sebastià and C. Cavallers. On your way you'll pass the **Pl. l'Església** on the right. To get to the nearby beach towns of Calella, Llafranc, and Tamariu, take a bus (see **Transportation,** above), spin away on a moped or mountain bike, or take a pleasant, if lengthy, walk through the countryside (about 1hr. to each town).

Tourist Office: (☎97 261 18 20; fax 97 261 17 56) Can Rosés, Pl. l'Església. First right off C. Cavallers walking away from Pl. Nova. Ask for the indispensable *Guía Municipal.* A **larger branch** is at C. Carrilet, 2 (☎97 230 02 28; fax 97 261 12 61). From the bus station, go left on C. Torres Jonama, left again at the traffic circle, and walk about 200m. An inconvenient location, but loaded with info. Both open May-Sept. M-Sa 10am-1pm and 5-8pm, Su 10am-1pm; Oct.-Apr. M-Sa 10am-1pm and 4-7pm, Su 10am-1pm; Carrilet branch also open July-Aug. M-Sa 9am-9pm, Su 10am-1pm.

Currency Exchange: Banesto, C. Torres Jonama, 43 (☎97 230 18 22), at the corner of C. l'Estrella. **ATM.** Open M-F 8:30am-2pm.

Roadside Emergency: ☎112. **Police:** ☎092. **Municipal police:** ☎97 261 31 01, at Av. Josep Pla and C. Cervantes. Call them for **24hr. pharmacy** info.

Medical Services: Centro de Atención Primaria, C. d'Angel Guimerà, 6 (☎97 261 06 07; emergencies/ambulance 97 230 00 23). Open 24hr.

Internet Access: Internet Papereria Palé, C. Cavallers, 16 (☎97 230 12 48). €1 per 15min. Open July-Sept. Su 10am-1pm, M-Sa 9am-1pm and 5-9pm.

Post Office: C. Barris i Buixó, 23 (☎97 230 06 07). **Lista de Correos.** Open M-F 8:30am-2:30pm, Sa 9:30am-1pm.

Postal Code: 17200.

ACCOMMODATIONS & CAMPING

Though options are few, accommodation prices are reasonable and room quality high in Palafrugell. Be sure to call ahead on summer weekends.

▨ **Fonda l'Estrella,** C. Quatre Cases, 13-17 (☎97 230 00 05), at the corner of C. La Caritat, a right off C. Torres Jonama. High-ceilinged, well-lit rooms with sinks off a Moorish courtyard bursting with plant life. Common baths, but even the bathrooms of this carefully preserved 1605 historic building are gorgeous. Breakfast €4. Singles €24 (available only Apr.-May and Sept.), doubles €37, triples €54. Open Apr.-Sept.

Hostal Plaja, C. Sant Sebastià, 34 (☎97 230 05 26), off Pl. Nova. Grand, frescoed foyer gives way to a broad courtyard surrounded by spotless rooms, all with balconies, bathrooms, TVs, bottled water, clotheslines, and new beds. Singles €24, doubles €44. ❷

Residencia Familiar, C. Sant Sebastià, 29 (☎63 626 36 03), off Pl. Nova. Clean and colorful rooms have sinks and some have high ceilings. No private baths. Singles €18.50, doubles €37; less for longer stays and for families. ❷

Camping: Moby Dick, C. Costa Verda, 16-28 (☎97 261 43 07). Take the Sarfa bus to Calella and ask the driver to let you off. No white whale in sight, but it is close to the water. €4.20 per adult, €3.30 per child, €4.20 per tent, €4.20 per car. Open May-Sept. ❶

FOOD

Restaurants near the beach are predictably expensive, making meals in Palafrugell proper a wiser option. For some reason, the town has a disproportionately high number of pizzerias and Italian restaurants. Shrugs one local, "We just really like pizza." **L'Arcobaleno** ❷, C. Mayor, 3, brings a touch of Tuscany to Catalan classics. The delicious all-inclusive lunchtime *menú* (€8.10) has everything from lasagna to roast chicken. (☎97 261 06 95. Open Apr.-Sept. 14 daily 11am-4pm and 6:30pm-12:30am; Sept. 15-Mar. closed M. AmEx/MC/V.) **Pizzeria Vapor** ❷, C. de les Botines, 21, is a popular restaurant with, in addition to the requisite pizza (€4.50-5.50), a fresh *menú* for €7. (☎97 230 57 03. Entrees €4.50-10. Open June-Aug. daily noon-4pm and 8pm-midnight; Sept.-May Tu-Su noon-4pm and 8pm-midnight.) Ice-cream shops and restaurants with terraces dominate the **Pl. Nova.**

SIGHTS & ENTERTAINMENT

In addition to nearby beaches, Palafrugell boasts one of the world's few cork museums. The **Museu del Suro,** C. Tarongeta, 31, has everything you ever (never?) wanted to know about cork. (☎97 230 78 25. Open June 15-Sept. 15 daily 10am-2pm and 4-9pm; Sept.16-June 14 Tu-Sa 10am-1pm and 5-8pm, Su 10:30am-1:30pm. €1.20, students and seniors €0.60. English explanations available.)

A Palafrugell Friday evening stroll ends up at the *plaça*, where young and old often dance the traditional Catalan *sardana* (see **May I Have This Dance**, p. 51)

Palafrugell

ACCOMMODATIONS
Fonda l'Estrella, 1
Hostal Plaja, 5
Residencia Familiar, 4
Camping Moby Dick, 6

FOOD
L'Arcobaleno, 2
Pizzeria Vapor, 3

around 10:30pm in July and August. The tourist office prints a monthly bulletin of upcoming events; also check the *Guía Municipal.* The town's biggest party takes place July 19-21, when the dance-intensive **Festa Major** bursts into the streets. Calella honors **Sant Pere** on June 29 with lots of *sardana* dancing, and Tamariu celebrates on August 15, coinciding with the Assumption of the Blessed Mother. The **Festivals of the Hanaveres** (Spanish-Cuban sea songs) come to town the first Saturday of every July.

BEACH TOWNS

🚩 *Take a Sarfa bus from Palafrugell to* **Calella** *(15min., 12-24 per day, €1). From Calella, follow the Camino de Ronda (see below) and walk 20min. to* **Llafranc***. From Llafranc,* **Tamariu** *is a 2hr. walk farther along the path.*

CALELLA

Calella is the largest and liveliest of the three beach towns near Palafrugell, with lots of small restaurants and shops in the streets around the beach. The town is also a great starting point for a trip to Llafranc. The bus stops in town, and the small beach at **Port Bo** is only a short walk downhill. From there, take a left to get to the bigger **Canadell** beach, at the far end of which begins the Camino de Ronda path to Llafranc. Calella's **tourist office,** C. Voltes, 6, provides maps of paths that criss-cross the area, including the **Camino de Ronda,** which climbs the coast from Calella to Llafranc. (☎97 261 44 75. Open daily July-Aug. 10am-1pm and 5-9pm; Apr.-June and Sept.-Oct. 12 M-Sa 10am-1pm and 5-8pm, Su 10am-1pm.)

The **Jardí Botànic de Cap Roig,** the botanical garden in front of Hotel Garbí, has an excellent view of the coast. (☎97 261 45 82. Open daily June-Aug. 9am-8pm; Sept.-May 9am-6pm. €1.80.) To get to the garden, take a right at Port Bo and follow the road as far as Hotel St. Roc. There the Camino de Ronda starts up again—look for signs, and when in doubt, look for the small red and white parallel stripes painted along the path as markers. The hike ends in a steep climb up a set of steps (45min. in all). The castle also hosts regular concerts and the **Festival de Jazz de la Costa Brava** in July and August. For tickets and info, contact the tourist office or call ☎902 44 77 55.

LLAFRANC

The most popular of the beaches, Llafranc and its coarse sand are usually covered with French and German tourists. To get there from Calella, take a pleasant 15-20min. hike from Calella along the Camino de Ronda. There is a tourist office branch in Llafranc, C. Roger de Llúria. (☎97 230 50 08. Open July-Aug. daily 10am-1pm and 5-9pm; Apr.-June and Sept.-Oct. 12 M-Sa 10am-1pm and 5-8pm, Su 10am-1pm.) Although prices for rooms in resorty Llafranc tend to reach for the sky, ◾**Hostal Celi-mar ❸,** C. Carudo, 12-14, is the lone exception, offering clean, florally decorated rooms with balconies and bathrooms only two blocks from the beach. To get there from the tourist office, go down Passeig de Cípsela along the beach. Take the first left at Plaça del Promontori, and continue down for two blocks; it will be on your right. (☎/fax 97 230 13 74. Singles €27.05, doubles €45.08.) On the port side of the beach, **Barracuda Diving Center** (☎97 261 15 48) offers scuba diving courses (5 days, €330) and rents equipment. Every two hours from 11am onward, they also have two-hour boat excursions to caves and inlets along the coast, with snorkeling and swimming (€13, children €10). For an outdoor adventure, take a 30min. walk from Llafranc to the ◾**Ermita de San Sebastià.** Crowning the mountain of the same name (50m from the lighthouse), the hermitage offers views of the entire Palafrugell valley, beaches, and sea. From the far end of the Llafranc beach, hop onto the good old Camino and head up. At the paved road, wind up and up (and up) 30 minutes to the lighthouse (unfortunately not open to visitors) and to lookout points. After the climb up and a nice rest at the peak, the remaining hour and fifteen minute hike to Tamariu will be a relative cinch.

TAMARIU

The beaches get quieter the farther you walk from Calella; Tamariu is the most peaceful, a reward for anyone who makes the challenging two-hour hike. From the far end of the Llafranc beach, take the Camino de Ronda and then the paved road up the mountain to the Ermita de San Sebastià. From there, the remaining 1 hour 15 minutes, along the wooded Camino de Ronda to Tamariu, are easier. Be sure to follow the red and white parallel stripes along the way, especially when in doubt. For all the tranquility but none of the blisters, take the **bus,** which loops to Tamariu and back four times a day from Palafrugell (15min.; 8:20am, 10am, 5:20pm, 7:45pm; last bus leaves Tamariu at 8pm) from the town bus stop. Tamariu's **tourist office** is on C. Riera (☎97 262 01 93. Open June-Sept. M-Sa 10am-1pm and 5-8pm, Su 10am-1pm.)

Beachbums

TOSSA DE MAR

Falling in love in (or in love with) Tossa de Mar is easy. In 1934, French artist Marc Chagall commenced a 40-year love affair with this seaside village, deeming it "Blue Paradise." When *The Flying Dutchman* was filmed here in 1951, Ava Gardner fell hard for Spanish bullfighter-turned-actor Mario Cabrera, much to the chagrin of Frank Sinatra, her husband at the time. (A statue of the actress in Tossa's old city commemorates her visit.) Like many coastal cities, Tossa (pop. 4000) suffers from the usual tourist industry blemishes: souvenir shops, inflated prices, and crowded beaches. That said, it resists a generic beach town ambiance, drawing from its historical legacy and cliff-studded landscape to preserve a unique small-town feel. Built in the 12th century as a fortified medieval village, the sun-baked walls of Vila Vella continue to overlook Tossa's blue Mediterranean water.

Summertime Frolicking

TRANSPORTATION

Buses: (☎97 234 09 03) on Av. Pelegrí at Pl. de les Nacions Sense Estat. Ticket booth open 7am-12:40pm and 2:20-8:10pm. **Pujol i Pujol** (☎61 050 58 84) goes to **Lloret del Mar** (20min.; June-Aug. every 30min., Sept.-May every hr. 8am-9:10pm; €1.05). **Sarfa** (☎97 234 09 03) goes to **Barcelona** (1½hr., 18 per day 7:25am-8:10pm, €7.55) and **Girona** (1hr.; 2 per day, offseason 1 per day; €4).

Car Rental: Viajes Tramontana, Av. Costa Brava, 23 (☎97 234 28 29; fax 97 234 13 20). **Avis** (☎90 213 55 31), their affiliates **Olimpia** (☎97 236 47 10) and **SACAR** (☎97 236 60 16) operate from the same

Bikini-Watcher

Rolled Hay in the Countryside

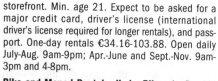

Fountain

Country Scene

storefront. Min. age 21. Expect to be asked for a major credit card, driver's license (international driver's license required for longer rentals), and passport. One-day rentals €34.16-103.88. Open daily July-Aug. 9am-9pm; Apr.-June and Sept.-Nov. 9am-3pm and 4-8pm.

Bike and Moped Rentals: Jimbo Bikes, La Rambla Pau Casals, 12 (☎97 234 30 44). Staff gives bike route information. Bring license for moped rental. Mountain bikes €3.50-4.50 per hr., €17-22 per day. Open M-Sa 9am-9pm, Su 9:30am-2pm and 4-8pm. AmEx/MC/V.

Boat rentals: Kayaks Nicolau (☎97 234 26 46), on the beach at Mar Menuda, offers 1½hr. kayak excursions to Cala Bona (10am, noon, and 4pm; €10.30). Kayak rental €5 per hr., paddle boats €7. Open Apr.15-Oct.15 daily 9am-6pm.

Taxis: ☎97 234 05 49. Wait outside the bus station.

ORIENTATION & PRACTICAL INFORMATION

Buses arrive at **Pl. de les Nacions Sense Estat** where **Av. del Pelegrí** and **Av. Ferrán Agulló** meet at a giant Modernist sculpture that looks like a big ball of thick noodles; the town slopes gently down from there to the waterfront. Walk away from the station down Av. Ferrán Agulló and turn right on Av. Costa Brava; as Av. Costa Brava turns into Pou de la Vila, take a right on any of the side streets and continue until your feet get wet (10min. total). **Pg. del Mar,** to the right at the end of Av. Costa Brava, curves along the **Platja Gran** (Tossa's main beach) to the old quarter, **Vila Vella.**

Tourist Office: Av. Pelegrí, 25 (☎97 234 01 08; fax 97 234 07 12; www.infotossa.com), in the bus terminal at Av. Ferrán Agulló and Av. Pelegrí. Grab a handy, thoroughly indexed (and free!) map. English spoken. Offers advice on hiking trails and tourist sights, and a posted schedule of upcoming events. They also lead guided hikes and walks on weekends (€6-9). Open June 15-Sept. 15 M-Sa 9am-9pm, Su 10am-2pm and 5-8pm; Apr.-May and Oct. M-Sa 10am-2pm and 5-8pm, Su 10:30am-1:30pm; Mar. and Nov. M-Sa 10am-1pm and 5-7pm; Dec.-Feb. M-F 10am-1pm and 5-7pm, Sa 10am-1pm.

Currency Exchange: Santander Central Hispano, Av. Ferrán Agulló, 2 (☎97 234 10 65). Open Apr.-Sept. M-F 8:30am-2pm; Oct.-Mar. M-F 8:30am-2:30pm, Sa 8:30am-1pm.

Police: Municipal Police, Av. Pelegrí, 14 (☎97 234 01 35), down the street from the tourist office. English spoken. They'll escort you to a **24hr. pharmacy.** For non-emergency pharmacy needs, **Farmàcia Castelló,** Av. Ferrán Agulló, 12, is open 9:30am-1:30pm and 4:30pm-9pm.

Medical Services: Casa del Mar (☎97 234 18 28 or 97 234 01 54), Av. de Catalunya. Primary health care and immediate attention. The nearest hospital is in Blanes, 30min. south.

Internet Access: Tossa Bar Playa, C. Socors, 6 (☎97 234 09 22), off the main beach. €1 per 14min., €2 per 28min. Open May-Oct. 15 daily 9:30am-midnight. **Scuba Libre,** Av. Sant Raimón de Penyafort, 11 (☎97 234 20 26). Cafe has several Internet terminals. €3.60 per hr. Open daily May-Oct. 8am-2am; Nov.-Apr. Sa-Su 10am-6pm.

Post Office: C. Maria Auxiliadora, 4 (☎97 234 04 57), down Av. Pelegrí from tourist office. Open M-F 8:30am-2:30pm, Sa 9:30am-1pm.

Postal Code: 17320.

ACCOMMODATIONS & CAMPING

Tossa is a seasonal town, and therefore many hostels, restaurants, and bars are open only from May to October. During July, August, and festivals, Tossa fills quickly; make reservations in advance. The **old quarter** hotels are the only ones really worth considering. The tourist office website (www.infotossa.com) also offers rooms.

Fonda/Can Lluna, C. Roqueta, 20 (☎97 234 03 65; fax 97 234 07 57). From Pg. del Mar, turn right onto C. Peixeteras, veer left onto C. Estalt, walk up the hill until the dead-end, go left, and then head straight. Delightful family offers immaculate single, double, and triple rooms, all with private baths. Breakfast included—eat on the rooftop terrace and enjoy a breathtaking view of the water. Washing machine €6. A popular choice with Spanish tourists; rooms are booked months in advance in summer. Oct.-Mar. and July-Aug. €16 per person. Mar.-June and Sept. €12. Cash only. ❶

Pensión Carmen Pepi, C. Sant Miguel, 10 (☎97 234 05 26). Turn left off Av. de Pelegrí onto Maria Auxiliadora and veer to your immediate right through the Pl. de l'Antic Hospital and onto C. Sant Miguel. This old, traditional house with its small, greenery-covered courtyard has an authentic feel and good location. The high-ceilinged rooms, each with private bath, are somewhat beyond their prime, but are spacious and comfy. Breakfast €1.50. July-Aug. singles €19.50, doubles €39; May-June singles €17, doubles €34; Sept.-Apr. singles €14.50, doubles €29. Cash only. ❷

L'Hostalet de Tossa, Pl. de l'Església, 3 (☎97 234 18 53; fax 97 234 29 69; www.tossa.com/hostalettossa), in front of the Sant Vicenç church. Clean and annually renovated with hotel-quality rooms. Many of L'Hostalet's 32 double rooms overlook its orange tree terrace and face the church. Rooms have baths and include breakfast. 2 common areas boast foosball, pool table, and TV. In-room TV €4 per day. Doubles Apr.-May and Oct. €15, with balcony €18.50; June and Sept. €19.50, with balcony €21.50; *Setmana Santa* (Holy Week) and July-Aug. €25.50, with balcony €27. MC/V. ❷

Pensión Moré, C. Sant Telmo, 9 (☎97 234 03 39). Downstairs sits a dim, cozy sitting room with TV. Upstairs, large doubles and triples with views of the old quarter. July-Aug. €12 per person; Sept.-June €10 per person. Cash only. ❶

Can Tort, C. Pescadors, 1 (☎97 234 11 85 or 97 234 22 40). Friendly owner maintains 14 very clean double rooms in her pottery-filled restaurant-hostel. All rooms have bathrooms, homey furnishings, and views of Tossa's old quarter. Breakfast included. Doubles Apr.-May €30; June €32; July €37; Aug. €46; Oct.-Sept. €33. Cash only. ❸

Camping: Can Martí (☎97 234 08 51; fax 97 234 24 61), at the end of La Rambla Pau Casals, off Av. Ferrán Agulló, 15min. from the bus station, is the closest site. Popular, tree-lined campsite on fringes of a wildlife reserve. Hot-water showers, telephones, swimming pool, and restaurant. Minutes from the municipal sports area. June 20–Aug. €5.50 per person, €6 per tent, €3.50 per car; May 12-June 19 and Sept. 1-16 €4.50 per person, €5 per tent, €2.70 per car. Traveler's checks or cash only. ❶

FOOD

Restaurants catering to tourists serve up *menús* at reasonable prices in the old quarter. Dining on **Pg. del Mar** offers the best people watching; **Mar Menuda** has the same ocean views with a quieter, less touristy feel. If it's food quality and diversity you're after, you'll have to sojourn into town. If you need groceries, head to **Magatzems Palou,** C. Enric Granados, 4. (☎97 234 08 58. Open daily June-Sept. 8am-9pm.)

Restaurant Santa Marta, C. Francesc Aromi, 2 (☎97 234 04 72), just inside entrance to old fortress off C. Portal. Housed in one of the medieval dwellings long ago inhabited by the city's elite, log-cut tables and chairs spill out of the stone-walled, romantically dimmed interior and onto an elegant patio covered by soft, shady leaves. The contemporary cuisine proves a delectable contrast to the historic building, with such winners as salmon with raspberry and kiwi sauce (€12.46). Entrees €9.92-26.90. Open daily 12:30pm-4pm and 7:30pm-11:30pm. AmEx/MC/V. ❸

La Taberna de Tossa, C. Sant Telm, 26 (☎97 234 14 47). In the heart of the old quarter, right off La Guardia. Serves up inexpensive house wine (€3.61 per 1L), traditional tapas (€1.65-3.16), and provincial meat and fish specialities (sandwiches €2.61-3.46) in a large old world style-dining room. Popular among Spanish tourists. *Menús* €7.18-8.38. Open Apr.-Sept. daily 1-4pm and 7pm-1am; Oct.-Mar. F-Su 1-4pm and 7pm-1am. V. ❷

Restaurant Marina, C. Tarull, 6 (☎97 234 07 57). Faces the Església de Sant Vincenç and has outdoor seating for prime people-watching. A nice family restaurant with benches bedecked with green checkered tablecloths. Multilingual menu features pizza, meat, fish dishes, and lots of *paella*. Entrees €3.75-12.30. *Menús* €8.50 and €10.50. Open *Setmana Santa* (Holy Week) to Oct. daily 11:30am-11:30pm. MC/V. ❷

Pizzeria Anna, Pont Vell, 19 (☎97 234 28 51). Turn right on Pont Vell from Pg. Mar; it's the small restaurant on the left-hand corner. Though homesick Italians might be a bit disappointed, the seafood-sick traveler will be in heaven. Pasta €4.25-5.50; pizza €5.25-6.70. Open Apr.-Sept. daily noon-4pm and 7:30-11:30pm. AmEx/MC/V. ❶

Restaurant Baserri, C. Codolar, 18 (☎97 234 30 81). Near the Museu Municipal (see below). A romantic dark wood and warm peach interior compliments the gourmet food. Vegetarian-friendly, creative food with a Mediterranean flavor. Appetizers €10-15. Entrees €15-18. Open July-Aug. daily 1-4pm and 8-11pm; Sept.-June W-M 1-4pm and 8-11pm. MC/V. ❸

Dino's, Sant Telm, 28 (☎972 34 07 02). Italian fare with German flare. Open for late-afternoon dining when everything else is closed. Pizzas €5-6.60. Open daily 1pm-midnight. ❷

SIGHTS

The prime destination in Tossa (besides the beach) is the **Vila Vella,** a medieval fortress that wraps around the base of the town. Built in the 12th century, then restored in 1387, the fortress defended the Spanish elite from Moorish attack in the 16th century. Inside, a spiral of medieval alleys leads to tiny Pl. Pintor J. Roig y Soler, where the first contemporary art museum in Spain, the ▓ **Museu Municipal,** Pl. Pintor Roig i Soler, 1, has a breezy, rather large collection of 1920s and 1930s art, including—because the artist had a house here—one of the few Chagall paintings still in Spain. In addition, Tossa's Roman mosaics (dating from the 4th to the first century BC), and other artifacts from the nearby Vila Romana are displayed in the museum, originally a 12th-century palace. (☎97 234 07 09. Open June 1-15 and Sept. 16-30 M-F 11am-1pm and 3-5pm, Sa-Su 11am-6pm; June 16-Sept. 15 daily 10am-8pm; Oct. M-F 11am-1pm and 3-5pm, Sa-Su 11am-5pm. €3, students and seniors €1.80.)

BEACHES

Tossa's main beach, **La Platja Gran,** is surrounded by cliffs and the dreamy Vila Vella, and draws the majority of beach-goers. To escape the crowds, visit some of the neighboring *calas* (small coves), accessible by foot. The tiny ▓**Es Codolar** sits just under the tower of the Vila Vella palace, hugged by precipices cloaked in foliage, and lacks the throngs of swimmers and sunbathers on the main beach. To get there, follow C. Portal to end. Snorkeling and diving are popular sports; pick up gear at **Andrea's Diving Center,** C. San Raimon de Penyafort, 11 (☎97 234 20 26). Well-marked hiking and mountain-biking paths also criss-cross the **Massif of Cadiretes** wildlife reserve and offer impressive views of the coastline. For less strenuous activity, several companies, like **Fonda Cristal,** send glass-bottomed boats to nearby beaches and caves, where you can sometimes jump in for a swim. Tickets are available at booths on the Platja Gran. (☎97 234 22 29. 1hr., 17 per day, €7.50 per person, children €5.) **Club Aire Libre,** on the highway to Lloret, organizes various excursions and rents equipment for water sports. (☎97 234 12 77. Canoeing and kayaking €13, water skiing €26 for 2 lessons, scuba diving €264 for 5-day certification course, sailing €11 per hr., windsurfing €10.30 per hr.)

NIGHTLIFE

Bars line the streets of the old quarter and offer live music from time to time. At 🏠**Bar Trinquet,** C. Sant Josep, 9, flirt over drippy candles and under romantic chandeliers or enjoy the stars in the flower- and ivy-drenched interior courtyard. **Bar El Pirata,** C. Portal, 32, and its companion bar **Piratín,** C. Portal, 30, have outdoor tables overlooking the sea at Es Codolar. (☎97 234 14 43. Open Apr.-Oct. daily 11pm-3am.) DJs spin acid jazz and house on weekend nights. (☎61 638 55 87. Open Apr.-Oct. daily 9pm-3am.) For live music try **Don Pepe,** C. Estolt, 6, a small bar which hosts a flamenco guitarist every night. (☎97 234 22 66. Open Apr.-Oct. daily 9:45pm-4:30am.)

MATARÓ

As far north of Barcelona as Sitges is south of Barcelona, the city of Mataró (pop. 100,000) has nearly comparable beaches to Sitges in a far more low-key, family-friendly setting. This wonderfully easy daytrip from Barcelona will have you out of the train station and onto the beach minutes after arrival.

TRANSPORTATION

Cercanías Trains (☎93 490 02 02) **Line #3** runs to Mataró frequently from Barcelona-Sants and Pl. de Catalunya (40min., every 10-20min. 5:54am-11:29pm, €2.15). The last train from Mataró back to Barcelona leaves at 10:40pm. **Mataró Bus,** C. Francesc Layret, 72 (☎93 757 53 94), has an extensive network of buses that hits almost all points of the town. Lines #1-5 all originate at the train station, with Line #0 running across town. €0.85 per ride. For a **taxi,** call ☎93 798 60 60 or 93 799 14 14.

ORIENTATION & PRACTICAL INFORMATION

The RENFE train station is considerably located right on the coast, just a few meters from the town beaches. Upon exiting the station, turn right, descend the ramp at the end of the block, and cross under the train tracks to get to the beach. To get to the town center, cross Av. Maresme, the street in front of the train station, head right, and take the second left onto C. Lepanto. This street leads to La Rambla (5min.), the main street that circles around the commercial district. A right onto La Rambla cuts through Pl. Santa Anna to C. La Riera, the home of the **Ajuntament,** La Riera, 48, the town hall of Mataró. Come here for basic **tourist information.** They are not well-stocked with printed info, but there is a huge map posted at the back of the foyer (www.infomataro.net; open M-F 9am-7pm). The nearby cultural center, **Patronat Municipal de Cultura de Mataró,** C. Sant Josep, 9, also has information on upcoming events and festivals, usually in Catalan. (Take a left off C. La Riera in front of the Ajuntament. ☎93 758 23 61. Open M-F 9am-2pm and 6-8pm.) Services include **Police:**

A NIGHT OUT

Sitges's gay nightlife scene is considered one of the best in Europe. Any evening should begin at **Parrot's Pub** on C. Primer de Maig, a place to relax with a drink outside before hitting the clubs (☎93 894 78 81. Opens at 5pm). Ask here for a copy of the *plano gay*, a free map of gay establishments in Sitges and Barcelona. **Mediterráneo,** C. Sant Bonaventura, 6, off C. Sant Francesc, shakes every summer night with one jam-packed floor of drinking and dancing and another of pool and cavorting. (Open 10pm-3:30am.) After hours, the crowds move to **Trailer,** C. Angel Vida, 36, the hottest disco party in town, with DJs nightly and foam parties W and Su. (☎61 055 94 40. Cover with drink €12. Opens at 1am, but the crowds don't arrive until 3:30am on weekends.)

☎092 and **Emergencies:** ☎112. **Internet access** is available on two coin-fed machines at **Flin's Burger Restaurant,** La Rambla, 22, in Pl. Santa Anna. (☎93 790 49 84. €0.70 per 10min. Open daily noon-midnight). Farther from the beach, **Cyber@Mataro,** C. Miquel Biada, 50, is less crowded. (☎93 757 88 05. €1.20 per 30min. Open daily 9am-11pm.) The **post office** is at C. Lepanto, 31. (☎90 219 71 97. Open M-F 8:30am-8:30pm, Sa 9:30am-2pm.) **Postal code** is 08302.

ACCOMMODATIONS

Most people travelling to Mataró make it a day-trip because of its proximity to the big city. There are a few options, though few are close to the sandy shores or cheap. **Hostal Cerdanyola ❸,** Pl. Isla Cristina, 1, is relatively inexpensive and tidy, but a 30min. walk from the beach. To get there, walk down St. Josep, turn right onto C. Ronda Prim, then left on Puid i Cadafalch until Pl. Isla Cristina; or take bus #1 or 2 from the train station. (☎93 798 20 45. Doubles €34.) **Castell de Mata ❺,** Ctra. N-II, Km. 649, lies on a highway that leads away from town, and it is only reachable by taxi, but is the only hotel right on the water. The hotel has a pool, a terrace, and a restaurant; 52 rooms with A/C, satellite TV, and phones. (☎93 790 10 44. Singles €74, doubles €95.)

FOOD

Both on the beach and in town, quick-service cafes and tapas restaurants thrive by getting the beach crowd fed and back on the sand where they belong. **Racó d'en Margarit ❷,** Pg. Callao, 15, on the beach at the beginning of Platja del Callao, has a standard tapas selection (€2.50-5.70) as well as a variety of *paellas* (€6.60-7.50), with fast-food service and beachside seating. (☎93 790 66 78. Open daily noon-midnight.) **Restaurant Bar Iluro ❸,** La Rambla, 14, on Pl. Santa Anna, is a shady break from the sun near the center of town. (☎93 790 32 08. Coffee or beer €1.50-3. Seafood entrees €8.90-14.70, meats €5.40-15.90. Open daily 9am-2pm and 5-9pm.)

BEACHES

Mataró's beaches are the town's biggest draw, with soft sand, refreshing waves, and plenty of room to spread out, but they do tend to fill up on weekends and steamy afternoons. The first, **Platja del Varador,** is the widest, with enough room for three full beach-soccer fields behind its sunbathers. Though it is speckled with people, that means there are many more amenities, like food and water, available within reach. An outcropping of rocks, easily circumvented, separates it from the town's remaining two beaches, **Platja del Callao** and **Platja de St. Simó.** This long stretch extends more than a kilometer down the coast. Outdoor showers are everywhere, and Red Cross stations (open 9am-6pm) are found on Varador and Callao beaches.

FESTIVALS

On the last weekend in July (25-28) Mataró pulls out all the stops in celebrating **Les Santes** (The Saints), its Festa Major in honor of patroness saints Juliana and Semproniana. Nearly a week of activities includes parades, concerts, fireworks, and all-night beach dance parties. The Saturday afternoon parade is worth catching, with regal giants, spinning bulls with fireworks for horns, and the 400-year-old tradition of the Mataró eagle performing a jig in front of the Ajuntament.

COSTA DORADA

SITGES

Forty kilometers south of Barcelona, the beach town of Sitges merits its self-ordained title, "jewel of the Mediterranean," with its prime tanning grounds baked by 300 sunny days a year, lively cultural festivals, and an electric atmosphere of sexual liberty. First prominent in the late 19th century as one of the principal centers of the *Modernisme* art movement, Sitges today is swarmed by tourists from around the world who have heard the tales of its thriving gay community and vibrant nightlife. However, whereas this flood of daytripping Spaniards, tourist families, and twenty-something partiers tends to drown many towns in the banalities of commercial tourism, in Sitges it only seems to add to its exhilarating flavors. So close it's in the same area code as Barcelona, Sitges is the ideal daytrip for when the big city's crowded beaches just aren't cutting it, and is well worth a couple of days' stay.

TRANSPORTATION

Cercanías Trains (RENFE; ☎93 490 02 02) run from Estació Barcelona-Sants to Sitges (40min., every 15-30min. 5:27am-11:52pm, €2.15) and continue on to **Vilanova** (7min.; every 15-30min.,

Fish

Hiking in the Country

Strolling in the Park

...in from Sitges at 12:44am; €1). The last train from Sitges returns to Barce-
...a at 10:26pm. To get to the beaches in between the two cities, rent a car in Barcelona (see **Service Directory**, p. 314) or in Sitges at **Europcar** (☎93 811 19 96), on the 1st
fl. of the Mercat next to the train station. For a **taxi,** call ☎93 894 13 29. A taxi
between Barcelona and Sitges costs €40-45.

ORIENTATION & PRACTICAL INFORMATION

Most everyone coming into Sitges starts out at the RENFE train station, on **C. Carbonell,** in the north of town. From here, the town center is a five-minute walk, the beach
about ten minutes. To get to both, take a right as you leave the station, and then your
third left onto **C. Sant Francesc.** This will lead straight to the old town, and **C. Parellades,** the main path of stores and restaurants, which runs parallel to the ocean. Any
street off of Parellades will lead you to the waterfront. **Pg. Ribera** runs along the central and most crowded beaches.

For a good free map and info on accommodations, stop by the **tourist office,** Sínia
Morera 1. From the station, turn right onto C. Carbonell and take the first big right a
block later. The office is across the street, a block to the left—look for the sign with
the big "i". (☎93 894 50 04. Open July-Aug. daily 9am-9pm; Sept.-June W-M 9am-2pm,
and 4-6:30pm.) In summer, a smaller branch opens by the museums on C. Fonollar.
(☎93 894 42 51. Open W-F 10:30am-1:45pm, Sa 11am-2pm and 4-7pm, Su 11am-2pm.)
Super Avui, C. Carbonell, 24, is a supermarket across from the train station. (Open
M-Sa 9am-2pm and 5-8pm.) Services include: **medical assistance** (☎93 894 64 26) and
emergency assistance (☎93 894 39 49). **Internet access** and **fax** service are available at
Sitges Internet Access, C. Espanya, 7. (☎93 811 40 03. €4.50 per hr., €1.20 per 15min.
Open daily 11am-1am.) The **post office** is in Pl. Espanya. (☎93 894 12 47. Open M-F
8:30am-2:30pm, Sa 9:30am-1pm. No packages Sa.) The **postal code** is 08870.

ACCOMMODATIONS

Accommodations are expensive and difficult to find on summer weekends, so consider daytripping to Sitges from Barcelona and reserve early if you plan to stay.
Prices listed are for the high season, unless otherwise indicated.

Hostal Parellades, C. Parellades, 11 (☎93 894 08 01), one block from the beach. Offers
clean rooms and an airy terrace that are dirt cheap for Sitges. Singles €20; doubles €32,
with bath €38; triples with bath €45. ❷

Hotel El Cid, C. Sant Josep, 39 (☎93 894 18 42). From the train station, take the 4th left off
C. Carbonell. One of the best deals in town. All the colorful and comfortable rooms come with
bathrooms and A/C. Small pool. Breakfast included. Su-Th singles €29; doubles €37.30. F-
Sa singles €34; doubles €48. ❸

Hostal Internacional, C. Sant Francesc, 52 (☎93 894 26 90), off C. Carbonell. Bright rooms
not far from the train station. Doubles €36, with bath €42. ❸

Hostal Bonaire, C. Bonaire, 31 (☎93 894 53 26), off Parellades, toward the beach. Though
the 9 rooms are somewhat cramped, ceiling fans and TVs in every room make amends. Singles €30, with bath €37; doubles with bath €45. ❸

Pensión Maricel, C. Tacó, 13 (☎93 894 36 27), 1min. from the beach, close to the museums. Big double rooms all come with phones and fans, much needed on the occasional
sticky summer night. Breakfast included. Doubles with bath €55. ❺

FOOD

Izarra, C. Mayor, 24 (☎93 894 73 70), behind the museum area. This Basque tapas bar provides a quick food fix before a long night of club-hopping. Ask for a *plato* and grab whatever
tapas look tastiest, from Basque fish tapas to more traditional Spanish *croquetas* to chicken
wings (€0.75 each). Big entrees (€4.20 and up) and Basque *sidra* (cider, €1.80) also available. Open daily 1:30-4pm and 8:30-11pm. ❶

Sites

ACCOMMODATIONS
Hostal Bonaire, 6
Hostal Internacional, 5
Hostal Parellades, 7
Hotel El Cid, 12
Pensión Maricel, 9

FOOD
Izarra, 10
Restaurante El Pozo, 8
Restaurante La Oca, 3
La Santa Maria, 1

NIGHTLIFE
Mediterraneo, 4
Parrot's Pub, 2
Trailer, 11

SECTOR VINYET

LA GRANJA

SANT CRISPI

SINIA MORERA

"OASIS"

C. Josep Roig i Reventos

Av. Mare de Deu de Montserrat

C. Prat de la Riba

C. Soler Carbó

C. Mare de Deu del Vinyet

C. Antoni Castro

C. M. Joan Llopis

C. Maria Rafols

Avinguda de Sofia

Passeig Marítim

C. St. Antoni

C. Sant Mus.

C. Sta. Barbara

Passeig de Vilanova

C. de Sinia Morera

C. Salvador Olivella

C. Espanya

PLAÇA ESPANYA

C. Espalter

C. 1er. de Maig

C. M. Montroig

C. J. Tarrida

C. Parellades

Museu Romàntic

C. St. Bonaventura

C. St. Josep

C. Pau Benazet

Passeig de Villafranca

TO PACHÁ

C. de Bonaire

Passeig de la Ribera

C. Sant Pere

C. Sant Pau

C. Sant Francesc

C. St. Gaudenci

Av. Carbonell

RENFE
PLAÇA E. MARISTANY

PLAÇA DEL HOSPITAL

C. del Hospital

Av. Cami dels Capellans

Av. de les Flors

C. F. Guma

C. Jesús

C. Illa de Cuba

C. St. Bartomeu

Modernist Clock Tower
PL. CAP. DE LA VILA

C. Carreta

C. Tacó

C. Nou

C. Major

C. d'Angel Vidal

C. Santiago Rusiñol

C. Rafael Llopart

C. St. Sebastià

C. St. Isidre

PLAÇA DEL BALUARD

St. Bartolomeu i Sta. Tecla

PL. AJUNTAMENT
C. Devallada

Palau Maricel (summer)

C. Fonollar

Museu Cau Ferrat

Museu Maricel del Mar

C. Joan Maragall

C. Isabel Julia

C. Port Alegre

Platja de St. Sebastià

Platja de la Fragata

Platja de la Ribera

Platja de la Bassa Rodona

Platja de l'Estanyol

TO PLATJA DE LA BARRA & PLATJA DE TERRAMAR (500m)

0   200 yards
0   200 meters

241

Restaurante La Oca, C. Parellades, 41 (☎93 894 79 36). Chickens roasting on an open fire attract long lines of hungry tourists. Try the succulent *half-pollo al ast* (roasted chicken) for €4.95 or cover one with sauce for €5.60. The chicken *croquetas* (€2.45) are outstanding. Open Su-F 1pm-midnight, Sa 1pm-1am. ❷

Restaurante El Pozo, C. Sant Pau, 3 (☎93 894 11 04), off C. Parellades, is a throwback to the town's days as a quiet fishing village. Art on the walls of this tiny tavern depicts rustic scenes, and the food tastes as if it's fresh out of the water. Seafood-heavy menu, with wine or beer. Entrees (€6.50-12) include lobster soup, sole, shrimp, and squid. Open F-W 1:30-4pm and 7-11pm. ❷

La Santa Maria, Pg. Ribera, 52 (☎93 894 09 99), near the waterfront, at the corner of C. Espanya. A leisurely lunch on the shaded terrace is worth the lost hour of tanning time. Enjoy the casually elegant atmosphere, carefully prepared dishes, and views of the crowded beach. *Menú* €9.10. Seafood dishes €6-20, meats €7-14. Open daily 1-4pm and 7-11:30pm. ❸

SIGHTS

The pedestrian walkway **C. Parellades,** which features shopping, eating, and drinking galore, is the central attraction. Cultural activities may seem as undesirable as rain to some beachgoers, but Sitges has some can't-miss attractions, including Morell's whimsical **Modernist clock tower,** Pl. Cap de la Vila, 2, above Optica at the intersection of Parellades and Sant Francesc. Behind it, on C. Fonollar, the **Museu Cau Ferrat** (☎93 894 03 64) hangs over the water's edge. Once home to Catalan modernist Santiago Rusinyol and a meeting point for young Catalan artists Pablo Picasso and Ramon Casas, the building is a shrine to Modernist iron work, glass work, and painting. Next door, the **Museu Maricel del Mar** (☎93 894 03 64) has a selective collection of Romanesque and Gothic painting and sculptures. Farther into town, the **Museu Romàntic,** C. Sant Gaudenci, 1, off C. Parellades, is a 19th-century bourgeois house filled with period pieces like music boxes and 17th- to 19th-century dolls. (☎93 894 29 69.) All 3 museums open in summer Tu-Su 10am-2pm and 5-9pm; rest of the year Tu-F 10am-1:30pm and 3-6:30pm, Sa 10am-7pm, Su 10am-3pm. Combo entrance good for 30 days €5.40, students €3; otherwise €3 per museum, students and seniors €1.50.) Across the street from the museums, the stately **Palau Maricel,** on C. Fonollar, built in 1910 for American millionaire Charles Deering, wows visitors with its sumptuous halls and rich gardens. Guided tours are available on summer nights and include a glass of *cava* (champagne); on Friday, Saturday, and Sunday nights, a piano and soprano concert complete the evening. Call ahead for reservations. (☎93 811 33 11. Tours and glass of *cava* €5.40; F-Su concert, tour and *cava* €7.20.)

BEACHES

Plenty of soothing sand accommodates hordes of sun worshippers on hot summer days. At **Platja de la Fragata,** the beach farthest to the left as you face the sea, sand sculptors create new masterpieces every summer day. By midday, the beaches closest to downtown can become almost unbearably crowded. The best beaches, with calmer water and more open space, are a kilometer or two walk further down, at **Platja de la Barra** and **Platja de Terramar.** Rocks shield the beach here from waves, creating a shallow ocean swimming pool ideal for children. Showers and Red Cross stations abound. In case of **emergency,** call ☎93 811 76 25.

NIGHTLIFE

The place to be at sundown is **Carrer Primer de Maig** (which runs directly from the beach and Pg. Ribera) and its continuation, **Carrer Marquès Montroig,** off C. Parellades. Bars and clubs line both sides of the small street, blasting pop and house from

10pm until 3am. The clubs here are wide-open and accepting, with a mixed crowd of gay people, straight people, the occasional drag queen, and families. There's no cover anywhere, making for great bar- and club-hopping. Beers at most places go for about €3, mixed drinks €6.

Even crazier is the "disco-beach" **Atlàntida**, in Sector Terramar (☎93 894 26 77; foam parties on Th and Su nights), and the legendary **Pachá**, on Pg. Sant Didac in nearby Vallpineda (☎93 894 22 98). Buses run all night on weekends to the two discos from C. Primer de Maig. Other popular nightspots can be found on C. Bonaire and C. Sant Pau, but most open only on weekends.

FESTIVALS

Sitges celebrates holidays with all-out style. During the **Festa de Corpus Christi** in June, townspeople collaborate to create intricate fresh-flower carpets. For *papier-mâché* dragons, devils, and giants dancing in the streets, visit during the **Festa Major,** held August 22-27 in honor of the town's patron saint Bartolomé. Nothing compares to the **Carnaval,** a preparation for Catholic fasting during the first week of Lent (Feb. 27-Mar. 5). Spaniards crash the town for a frenzy of dancing, outrageous costumes, and vats of alcohol. The last night is the wildest, as hundreds parade through the streets dressed in drag. On the first Sunday in March, a pistol shot starts the **Rally de Coches de Epoca,** an antique car race from Barcelona to Sitges. June brings the **International Theater Festival** (€9-21 per show), and July and August the **International Jazz Festival** (€10.20 per concert). From September 12 to 14, competitors trod on fresh grapes on the beach for the annual **Grape Harvest.** October 1-12 brings the world-famous **Festival Internacional de Cinema de Catalunya.**

DAYTRIP FROM SITGES: VILANOVA I LA GELTRÙ

↗ *Cercanías trains (RENFE) run from Vilanova to Sitges (7min., every 15-30min., €1), and continue to Barcelona (50min., €2.15). Mon Bus (☎93 893 70 60) connects Vilanova to Sitges (€1.20), Vilafranca (€1.60), and Barcelona (€2.90). The bus station is in the plaza in front of the train station. A taxi (☎93 893 32 41) from Vilanova to Sitges costs about €9-12.*

One of Catalunya's most important ports, **Vilanova i la Geltrù,** actually turns out to be two cities in one: an industrial center and a well-groomed beach town. There is little in the dusty uptown area except for old churches and stone facades; most visitors spend the day on the beach (10min. from the train station). In the evening, Vilanovans generally forgo late-night madness for beach volleyball or soccer at Parc de Ribes.

To get to the **beaches,** exit the station, turn left on C. Forn de Vidre, take the third left onto the thoroughfare Rambla de la Pau, head under the overpass, and follow the *rambla* all the way to the port and onto **Passeig del Carme.** The **tourist office,** about 100m to the right, off Passeig del Carme in a small park called **Parc de Ribes Roges,** offers excellent **maps.** (☎93 815 45 17. Open July-Aug. M-Sa 10am-8pm, Su 10am-2pm; Sept.-June 10am-2pm and sometimes 4-7pm.) The wide **Platja de Ribes Roges** is past the tourist office; to the left is the smaller **Platja del Far.** Expect fine sand, sun, and company.

If you decide to stay in town, the popular **Can Gatell,** C. Puigcerdà 6-16, has clean rooms and full baths. With your back to the station, head down C. Victor Balaguer, the leftward of the two parallel streets; at the end, turn right onto La Rambla and then take the first left. (☎93 893 01 17. Singles €28; doubles €45, with A/C €51. Extra bed €10.) The hostel's *menú* (€8, served M-F, includes wine) is popular with locals. (Open daily 7-10:30am, 1-5pm, and 8:30-10pm.) Numerous restaurants serving fresh seafood line Passeig del Carme, but they can be quite pricey. A less-expensive alternative is **Supermarket Orangutan,** Rambla de la Pau 36, on the way to the beach. (Open M-Sa 9:30am-2pm and 5:30-9pm.)

I'VE GOT THE TOWER

Imagine the difficulty you had the time you tried to lift a heavy-set friend on your shoulders. Now, imagine that person standing on your shoulders rather than sitting. And now just picture another guy on his shoulders...and another one on top of that. Shoulders hurt yet? With this in mind, consider in wonder Catalunya's *castellers*—the castle makers. The sport of creating *castells*—human towers (literally, "castles") is a popular competition in the province of Tarragona, usually performed at the most important town festivals in the main *plaça*.

Castell-making teams, called *colles*, wear a traditional costume called the *xiquet*, consisting of white pants, a shirt of the team color, and a cloth belt, which serves as a foothold for teammates. Hundreds of people crowd together to form the bottom layer, and the *colle* begins its grueling work. *Castells* vary in height, width, and degree of difficulty; the best teams can create up to nine stories of three to four people each, clinging tightly to each other's arms. The tower is topped off by a small girl or boy, called the *anxaneta* (weather vane), who fearlessly scrambles to the top and waves upon completion. Even trickier, the *castell* must then disassemble without collapsing into a jumble of tangled limbs. The *colles* are a source of great town pride.

TARRAGONA

Before Barcelona was even a twinkle in anyone's eye, Tarragona was an emerging city, key to Rome's colonization of Iberia (see **Life & Times,** p. 40). In 218 BC, the Carthaginian general **Hannibal** and his troops were tearing through Spain in a march toward Rome. The Romans, led by the **Scipio brothers** Gnaeus and Publius, set out (successfully) to cut them off and turn them back to North Africa. They set up headquarters and began building giant, impenetrable stone walls in a small coastal port, then called Tarraco, and a provincial capital was born. Tarragona's strategic position made the city a thriving provincial power in ancient times; today, an amphitheater and other ruins pay homage to the city's imperial glory days. These vestiges of Tarragona's Roman past are the city's most compelling attractions, but plenty of visitors are satisfied with lolling on the beaches in one of Catalunya's most important port cities.

TRANSPORTATION

Trains: ☎902 24 02 02. On Pl. Pedrera by the water. Info open daily 6am-9pm. The best transportation option. To: **Alicante** (4hr., 10 per day, €27); **Barcelona** (1¼hr., 30 per day, €4.15); **Madrid** (6½-8hr., 4 per day, €37); **Sitges** (45min., 20 per day, €2.60); **Valencia** (2-3hr., 15 per day, €11.40); **Zaragoza** (4hr., 10 per day, €12.30).

Buses: ☎97 722 91 26. Pl. Imperial Tarraco. **Alsa Enatcar** (☎902 42 22 42) serves most destinations. To: **Barcelona** (1½hr., 8 per day, €7.50) and **Valencia** (4hr., 6 per day, €15.20).

Public Transportation: EMT Buses (☎97 754 94 80) run daily 6am-11pm. €1, 10-ride *abono* ticket €4.70.

Taxi: Radio Taxi (☎97 722 14 14).

ORIENTATION & PRACTICAL INFORMATION

Most sights are clustered on a hill, surrounded by remnants of Roman walls. At the foot of the hill, **La Rambla Vella** and **La Rambla Nova** (parallel to one another and perpendicular to the sea) are the main thoroughfares of the new city. La Rambla Nova runs from **Passeig de les Palmeres** (which overlooks the sea) to **Plaça Imperial Tarraco,** the monstrous rotunda and home of the bus station. To reach the old quarter from the train station, turn right and walk 150m to the killer stairs parallel to the shore.

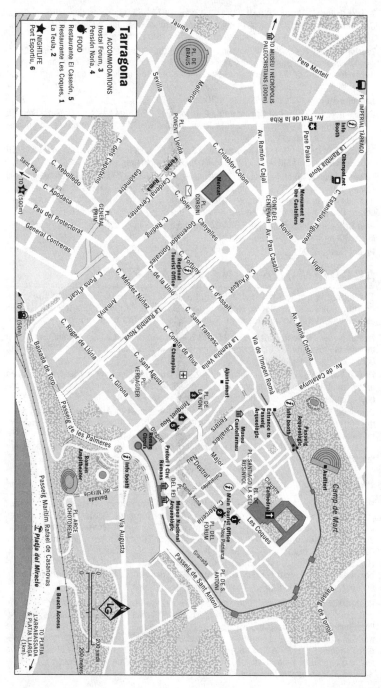

Tarragona

ACCOMMODATIONS
- ▶ Hostal Fòrum, 3
- ▶ Pensión Noria, 4

FOOD
- ✦ Restaurante El Caserón, 5
- La Teula, 2
- Restaurante Les Coques, 1

NIGHTLIFE
- ★ Port Esportiu, 6

Tourist Office: C. Major, 39 (☎97 724 52 03; fax 97 724 55 07), below the cathedral steps. Crucial **free map** and a guide to Tarragona's Roman ruins. Open July-Aug. M-Sa 9am-9pm, Su 10am-2pm; Sept.-June M-Sa 10am-2pm and 4-7pm, Su 10am-2pm.

Tourist Information booths: Pl. Imperial Tarraco, at the bottom of La Rambla Vella, just outside the bus station; another at the intersection of Av. Catalunya and Via de l'Impera Romi; a 3rd at the corner of Via Augusta and Pg. Sant Antoni. Open July-Sept. daily 10am-1:30pm and 4:30-8pm; Nov.-June Sa-Su 10am-2pm.

Luggage Storage: At the train station 4:30am-midnight; €3.

Emergency: ☎091 **Police: Comisaria de Policía** (☎97 724 98 44), on Pl. Orleans. From Pl. Imperial Tarraco on the inland end of La Rambla Nova, walk down Av. Pres. Lluís Companys, and take the 3rd left to the station.

Medical Assistance: Hospital de Sant Pau i Santa Tecla, La Rambla Vella, 14 (☎97 725 15 70). **Hospital Joan XXIII** (☎97 729 58 00), on C. Dr. Mallafré Guasch.

Internet Access: Ciberspai.net, C. Estanislao Figueras, 58 (☎97 724 57 64), off the Imperial Tarraco rotunda. €0.75 per 15min., €1.50 per 30min., €1.80-2.40 per 1hr. Open M-F 9am-midnight, Sa-Su 10am-midnight. **Biblioteca Pública,** C. Fortuny, 30 (☎97 724 05 44). Public library; free use of the computers with passport.

Post Office: Pl. Corsini, 12 (☎97 724 01 49), below La Rambla Nova off C. Canyelles. Open M-F 8:30am-8:30pm, Sa 9:30am-1pm.

Postal Code: 43001.

ACCOMMODATIONS & CAMPING

Tarragona is not known for its abundance of cheap beds, as most of the city's accommodations are two- to four-star hotels near the center. Still, a few good deals can be had in the old quarter in Pl. Font (parallel to La Rambla Vella).

Hostal Noria, Pl. de la Font, 53 (☎97 723 87 17), in the heart of the historic town. Enter through the restaurant. 24 clean and bright rooms with pretty-in-pink bathrooms. Singles with bath €22, doubles with bath €39. ❷

Hostal Forum, Pl. de la Font, 37 (☎97 723 17 18), upstairs from the restaurant. Clean rooms and bathrooms don't leave space for spreading out, but a decent place to sleep for the night. Singles with bath €19; doubles with bath €37. ❷

Camping: Several campsites line the road toward Barcelona (Via Augusta or CN-340) along the northern beaches, especially around km 1.17. Take bus #9 (every 20min., €1) from Pl. Imperial Tarraco. **Tarraco** (☎97 729 02 89) is the closest campsite, at Platja de l'Arrabassada. Well-kept facilities near the beach. 24hr. reception. €3.50 per person, per car, and per tent. Open Apr.-Sept. ❶

FOOD

Pl. Font and Las Ramblas Nova and Vella are full of cheap *menús* (€5-7.50) and greasy *platos combinados*. Tarragona's indoor **Mercado Central** (market) takes place in Pl. Corsini next to the post office. (☎97 723 15 51. Open M-W and Sa 8am-2pm, Th-F 7am-2pm and 5:30-8:30pm. Flea market Tu and Th.) For **groceries,** head to **Champion,** C. Augusta at Comte de Rius, between Las Ramblas Nova and Vella. (Open M-Sa 9am-9:15pm.) **El Serrallo,** the fisherman's quarter right next to the harbor, has the best seafood. Try your food with Tarragona's typical *romesco* sauce, simmered from red peppers, toasted almonds, and hazelnuts.

Restaurant Les Coques, Nou Patriarca, 2 (☎97 722 83 00), off Pl. La Seu near the cathedral. Enveloping you in its eclectic interior of ancient Roman wall, wooden beams, chandeliers, paintings, antiques, and wine bottles, Les Coques offers a peaceful refuge from the world in which to enjoy some of the best food and wine in Tarragona. Try the cod filet with garlic sauce (€17.13), grilled baby goat (€11.62), or fresh Tarragonan *cigalitas* (a native shellfish related to shrimp) sauteed in a garlic sauce (€16). Entrees €9.62-31.65. Open M-Sa 1:15-3:45pm and 9-10:45pm. ❹

La Teula, C. Mercería, 16 (☎ 97 723 99 89), in the old city near Pl. del Fórum. Great for salads (€3-€4.50) and toasted sandwiches with interesting Catalan veggie/meat combos (€5.86-9.01). Lunch *menú* €6.60. Open daily noon-4pm and 8pm-midnight. MC/V. ❷

Restaurant El Caserón, C. Ces Del Bou, 9 or Trinquet Nou, 4 (☎ 97 723 93 28), parallel to La Rambla Vella (off Pl. Font). This popular local diner serves home-style food. Entrees €4.25-12.10. *Menú* €7.50. Open Tu-F 1-4pm and 8:30-10:30pm, Sa-M 8:30-11pm. ❷

SIGHTS

Tarragona's status as provincial capital transformed the small military enclosure into a glorious imperial port. Countless Roman ruins stand silently amid 20th-century hustle and bustle, all just minutes from the beach.

■ ROMAN RUINS

⑦ *All ruins open May-Sept. Su 9am-3pm, Tu-Sa 9am-9pm; Oct.-Apr. Tu-Su 9am-7pm. Admission to each €1.87, students €0.62.*

Below Pg. Palmeres and set amid gardens above Platja del Miracle beach is the **Roman Amphitheater** (☎ 97 744 25 79), where gladiators once killed wild animals and each other; this barbaric but popular activity dates back to the founding of the city. In AD 259, the Christian bishop Fructuosus and his two deacons were burned alive here; in the sixth century, these martyrs were honored with a basilica built in the arena.

Next to the Museu Nacional Arqueològic in Pl. Rei is the entrance to the **Pretori I Circ Romans** (☎ 97 724 19 52), which houses the **Praetorium Tower,** the former administrative center of the region, and the **Roman Circus,** the site of chariot races and other spectacles. Visitors descend into the long, dark tunnels that led fans to their seats, and see a model reconstruction of what the complex looked like. The Praetorium was the governor's palace in the first century BC. Rumor has it that the infamous hand-washer Pontius Pilate was born here. Ascend to the top of the tower for a view of the entire city.

The scattered **Fòrum Romà,** with reconstructed Corinthian columns, lies near the post office on C. Lleida. Once the center of the town, its distance clearly demonstrates how far the walls of the ancient city extended. To see what remains of the 2nd-century BC walls, stroll through the **Passeig Arqueològic.** The walls originally stretched to the sea and fortified the entire city.

OTHER SIGHTS

The **Pont del Diable (Devil's Bridge),** a Roman aqueduct 10min. outside of the city, is visible on the way in and out of town by bus. Take municipal bus #5 (every 20min., €1) from the corner of C. Christòfer Colom and Av. Prat de la Riba or from Pl. Imperial Tarraco. Lit by octagonal rose windows flanking both arms of the cross is the gigantic Romanesque-Gothic ■**cathedral,** which dates from 1331 and is one of the most magnificent cathedrals in Catalunya. The stunning interior, which was fully restored only in 1999, is filled with lavishly decorated altars, paintings, sculptures, and 16th-century tapestries, as well as the tomb of Joan d'Aragó. The adjoining **Diocesian Museum** showcases religious relics from the last 700 years. (Entrance to both on C. Claustre, near Pl. La Seu. Open mid-Mar. to May M-Sa 10am-1pm and 4-7pm; mid-June to Oct. M-Sa 10am-7pm; mid-Oct. to mid-Nov. M-Sa 10am-5pm; mid-Nov. to mid-Mar. M-Sa 10am-2pm. €2.40, students €1.50.)

MUSEUMS

The worthwhile **Museu Nacional Arqueològic,** across Pl. Rei from the Praetorium, displays ancient architecture, utensils, statues, and mosaics, and offers interesting descriptions of daily life in the Roman Empire. (☎ 97 723 62 09. €2.40, students €1.20; includes admission to the Necropolis. Open June-Sept. Tu-Su 10am-8pm;

Oct.-May Tu-Su 10am-1:30pm and 4-7pm.) The huge early Christian burial site at the **Museu i Necròpolis Paleocristians,** Av. Ramón y Cajal, 78, has yielded a rich variety of urns, tombs, and sarcophagi, the best of which are in the small museum. (☎97 721 11 75. €2.40, students €1.20; Tu free; includes admission to Museu Arqueològic. Open June-Sept. Tu-Sa 10am-8pm, Su 10am-2pm; Oct.-May Su 10am-2pm, Tu-Sa 10am-1:30pm and 4-7pm.) If you've had too much Roman roamin', descend the steps in front of the cathedral and take the third right onto C. Cavellares to visit the **Casa-Museu Castellarnau.** It housed the Viscounts of Castellarnau in the 18th century, and features a breathtaking ceiling painting in the main room. (☎97 724 22 20. €1.87, students €0.62. Open May-Sept. Tu-Sa 9am-9pm, Su 9am-3pm; Oct.-Apr. Tu-Su 9am-7pm.)

BEACHES

The hidden access to **Platja del Miracle,** the town's main beach, is along Baixada del Miracle, starting off Pl. Arce Ochotorena, beyond the Roman theater. Walk away from the theater until you reach the underpass, under the train tracks, to the beach. The beach is not on par with other Costa Dorada stops, nor even with the beaches of Barcelona—but it's not bad for a few hours of relaxation. A bit farther away are the larger beaches, **Platja l'Arrabassada,** with dirt-like sand, and the windy **Platja Llarga** (take bus #1 or 9 from Pl. Imperial Tarraco or any of the other stops).

NIGHTLIFE & ENTERTAINMENT

Weekend nightlife in Tarragona is on a much smaller scale than that of its northern neighbors, Sitges and Barcelona. Between 5 and 9pm, Las Ramblas Nova and Vella (and the area in between) are packed with strolling families. After 9pm, the bars start to liven up; around 10pm on Saturdays in summer, fireworks brighten the skies. The most popular place to be is **Port Esportiu,** a portside plaza full of restaurant-bars and mini-discos. Heading up La Rambla Nova away from the beach, take a left onto C. Unió; bear left at Pl. General Prim and follow C. Apodaca to its end. Cross the tracks; the fun will be to the left.

The end of July ushers in the **Fiesta de Tarragona,** which goes through the first week of August (☎97 724 47 95; 24hr. tickets ☎902 33 22 11). Pyromaniacs shouldn't miss the first week of July when the beach is lit up with fireworks in **El Concurso Internacional de Fuegos Artificiales.** On even-numbered years, the first Sunday in October brings the **Concurs de Castells,** an important regional competition featuring tall human towers, as high as seven to nine "stories," called *castells* (see **I've got the Tower,** p. 244). *Castells* also appear amid beasts and fireworks during the annual **Fiesta de Santa Tecla** (Sept. 23). If you're unable to catch the *castellers* in person, don't miss the monument to the *castellers* on La Rambla Nova, an impressive life-size *castell* of bronze Tarragonans.

INLAND

MONTSERRAT

With a saw of gold, the angels hewed twisting hills to make a palace for you.
　　—Jacint Verdaguer, *Virolai*

With its 1236m peak protruding from the flat Río Llobregat Valley and its colorful interplay of limestone, quartz, and slate stone, Montserrat (Sawed Mountain) has long inspired poets, artists, and travelers. As the story goes, in AD 888, a shepherd wandering the crags of Montserrat had a blinding vision of the Virgin Mary. His story spread, attracting pilgrims to the mountain in droves. In 1025 an opportunistic bishop-abbot named Oliba founded a monastery to worship the Virgin, who had become the spiritual patroness of Catalunya. Today, 80 Benedictine monks tend the building, most of which dates from the 19th century (although two wings of the old Gothic cloister survive). During the Catalan *Renaixença* of the early 20th century (see p. 44), politicians and artists like poets Joan Maragall and Jacint Verdaguer turned to Montserrat as a source of Catalan legend and tradition. In the Franco era the monastery became a center for Catalan resistance—Bibles were printed here in Catalan, and nationalist demonstrations were held on the mountain. Today, the site attracts devout worshipers and tourists who come to see the Virgin of Montserrat, her ornate basilica, the accompanying art museum, and perhaps most of all, the panoramic views of the mountain's awesome rock formations.

TRANSPORTATION

The R5 (Manesa-bound) line of the **FGC trains** (☎93 205 15 15) connects to Montserrat from M: Espanya in Barcelona (1hr., 1 per hr. 8:36am-5:36pm, round-trip including cable car €11.30); be sure to get off at Aeri de Montserrat, not Olesa de Montserrat. From there, catch the heart-stopping **Aeri cable car** to get up to the monastery. (July-Aug. every 15min. daily 9:35am-6:35pm, Mar. and Oct. 9:25am-1:45pm and 2:20-6:45pm; price included in train fares or €6 round-trip by itself. Cable car schedules change frequently; call ☎93 877 77 01 for current times.) **Autocars Julià** runs a daily bus to the monastery, from right near the Estació Sants train station in Barcelona. (Leaves daily at 9am and returns at 5pm. Call ☎93 317 64 54 for reservations. €10. MC/V.) If you plan to use the funiculars at Montserrat to reach hiking paths, the **Tot Montserrat** is a good investment: available at tourist offices or in M: Espanya, it gets you round-trip tickets for the FGC train, the Aeri cable car, both mountaintop funiculars, entrance to the Museu de Montserrat and audiovisual display (see below), and a meal at the *cafetería*, all for €34 (€20 if you buy it at Montserrat without the train fare included, or €19.50 without audiovisual and museum entrance and lunch). If you miss the last cable car or bus down the mountain, call ☎93 835 03 84 or 93 828 43 43 for a **taxi.**

PRACTICAL INFORMATION

Montserrat is not a town; it is a monastery with adjacent housing and food for pilgrims, both religious and of the camera-toting variety. Most visitor services are in **Pl. Creu**, the area straight ahead from the top of the steps at the Aeri cable car. The **info booth** in Pl. Creu provides free maps, schedules of daily religious services, and advice on mountain navigation. (☎93 877 77 77. Open July-Sept. daily 9am-7pm; Oct.-June M-F 9am-5pm, Sa-Su 9am-7pm.) For more detailed information, buy the *Official Guide to Montserrat* (€6.40) or the official guide to the museum (€6.30). Other services in Pl. Creu include **currency exchange** with poor rates (open M-F 9:15am-2pm, Oct.-May Sa 9:15am-1:30pm), **ATMs**, and a **post office** (open daily 10am-1pm). For an **ambulance** or the **mountain rescue team**, call ☎904 105 555.

ACCOMMODATIONS

For those who choose to spend the night at Montserrat, there aren't many options: choose from camping, an apartment in one of two different buildings, or a room in the three-star hotel. All but the campsite are wheelchair accessible, and all prices listed include the IVA. For reservations (a must) for the apartments or hotel, contact the **Central de Reserves i Informació** (☎93 877 77 01; fax 93 877 77 24; www.abadiamontserrat.net). The apartment administration office, **Administració de les Celles**, is located in the corner of the *plaça*. (Open daily 9am-1pm and 2-6pm; after 6pm they're at the Hotel Abat Cisneros reception. 2-day minimum stay, 7-day in July and August.)

Abat Marcet ❷, the newer, nicer building, has rooms for one to five people, all with full bath, phone, TV, heat, a dining room, and a kitchen with microwave. (Singles €11.50-30.10; doubles €23.60-38.60, students €19.20-32.) **Abat Oliva ❷**, which is much older than Marcet, has rooms for two to seven people, but the kitchens have only hotplates for cooking, and there is no heat, so it closes in winter. (Doubles €23.36-25.40; quads €36.80-40.) The **Hostal Abat Cisneros ❸**, next to the basilica, has a restaurant and more comfortable bedrooms than the apartments. (Singles €24.15-43.75; doubles €40.70-76.30. Breakfast included.) The **campsite ❶** is a 5min. walk up the hill from the monastery level of the Sta. Cova funicular station. (☎93 835 02 51. Open Apr.-Oct. Office open daily 8am-9pm. €2.50 per person, under 12 €2; €2.25 per tent. No fires allowed.)

FOOD

Food options on Montserrat remain limited and are all marked clearly on the free map available from the info counters. If you want to take food hiking with you, the 2-aisle **Queviures supermarket** in Pl. Creu (open daily 9am-7:45pm) offers a pretty good selection of grocery goods, including fruit, utensils, yogurt, and cookies. Meat and cheese is available at the **Pastisseria** (open daily 9am-7:45pm). For quick, informal food, try the **Bar de la Plaça ❶**, next to the supermarket (*bocadillos* and hamburgers €2.60-3.60; open M-F 9:30am-5pm, Sa 9:30am-4:40pm), or the main **cafeteria ❶** at the top of the steps from the cable car, with ample seating and a large selection of sandwiches and hot foods (most under €3; open Apr.-Nov. daily 9am-8pm; Dec.-Mar. daily 9am-5pm; MC/V). For a larger lunch with a gorgeous panoramic view of the valley, the **self-service cafeteria ❷** (the included meal for *Tot Montserrat* card-holders but open to anyone for €9) is up the hill to the right from the cable car steps (open Feb.-Dec. daily noon-4pm), as is the scenic **Restaurant de Montserrat ❷**. (*Menú* €12, kids €5.40; IVA included. Open Mar. 15-Nov. 15 daily noon-4:30pm. MC/V. Wheelchair accessible.) Despite the price difference you'll get the same view from both. The **Restaurant Hotel Abat Cisneros ❺** offers the most expensive *menú* (€23.30) in the nicest setting; a stone-walled, brightly lit dining room. (Entrees €11.89-15.70. Wheelchair accessible. Open daily 1-4pm and 8-10pm. AmEx/MC/V.)

SIGHTS

The **monastery** is the biggest sight in Montserrat. Above Pl. Creu, the entrance to the **basilica** looks out onto Pl. Santa Noría. Austere and somber in its dark, ornate glory, the basilica was consecrated in 1592. To the right of the main chapel, a route through the side chapels leads to the Romanesque **La Moreneta** (the black Virgin Mary), Montserrat's venerated icon of Mary, the mother of Jesus. (Walkway open Nov.-June M-F 8-10:30am and noon-6:30pm, Sa-Su 8-10:30am and noon-6:30pm; July-Sept. daily 8-10:30am and noon-6:30pm.) Legend has it that St. Peter hid the figure, carved by St. Luke, in Montserrat's caves. When in AD 888 the shepherd boy had his blinding vision in a cave, upon seeking out its source, all he found was this statue. Though they tried, the icon could not be removed, and therefore the monastery at Montserrat was built in order to give this miracle its proper home. However, Mary's story seems as "hole-y" as Spanish lace, as it was indeed removed from Montserrat, twice, once after the Napoleonic Wars and again during the Spanish Civil War (see p. 46), and, as carbon dating has revealed, was sculpted in the 12th century, not the 7th. But faith defies reason and the little mother is now showcased in an elaborate silver case. For good luck, rub the orb in Mary's outstretched hand, and if you can, schedule your visit so that you can hear the renowned **Escalonia boys' choir** sing *Salve Regina* in the basilica. (Daily at 1pm and 7:30pm, except late June and July.)

Also in Pl. Santa María, the **Museo de Montserrat** exhibits a wide enough variety of art, ranging from a mummified Egyptian woman to works by Picasso, including *Sardana of Peace*, painted just for Montserrat, and *Old Fisherman*. The museum's Impressionist paintings deservedly steal the spotlight; Ramon Casas's famous

Madeline Absinthe is one of many evocative portraits, and may make you think twice about indulging in the little green fiend. (Open Nov.-June M-F 10am-6pm, Sa-Su 9:30am-6:30pm; July-Sept. M-F 10am-7pm, Sa-Su 9:30am-7pm. €4.50, students and over 65 €3.50, children 10-14 yr. €3, under 10 free; combo ticket with Espai Audiovisual €5.50, students and over 65 €4.40, children 10-14 yr. €3.30.) The **Espai Audiovisual,** at the top of the steps by the cable car, offers a brief view, through CD-ROMs and video, of the life of a monk on Montserrat, but is poorly organized and is available free at the gift shop. (€2. Open daily 9am-6pm.)

WALKS

A visit to Montserrat is not complete without a walk along the "mountain of a hundred peaks." Some of the most beautiful areas of the mountain are accessible only on foot. The **Santa Cova funicular** descends from Pl. Creu to paths that wind along the sides of the mountain to ancient hermitages. (Apr.-Oct. daily every 20min. 10am-6pm; Nov.-Mar. Sa-Su only, 10am-5pm. Round-trip €2.50.) Take the **St. Joan funicular** up for more inspirational views of Montserrat. (Apr.-Oct. daily every 20min. 10am-6pm; Nov.-Mar. M-F 11am-5pm, Sa-Su 10am-5pm. Round-trip €6.10; joint round-trip ticket with the Sta. Cova funicular €6.90, over 65 €6.20, children 10-14 €3.50.) The dilapidated **St. Joan monastery** and **shrine** are only a 20min. tromp from the highest station. But be forewarned; the "monastery" appears to have become the stomping grounds for late-night boozing and garbage dumping. The real prize is **Sant Jeróni** (the area's highest peak at 1236m), with its mystical views of Montserrat's rock formations. The enormous domes and serrated outcroppings resemble a variety of human forms, including "The Bewitched Friars" and "The Mummy." The hike is about 2½ hours from Pl. Creu or a one-hour trek from the terminus of the St. Joan funicular. The paths are long and winding but not all that difficult—after all, they were made for guys wearing long robes. En route, make sure you take a sharp left when, after about 45min., you come to the little old chapel—otherwise, you're headed straight for a helicopter pad. On a clear day the hike offers spectacular views of Barcelona and surrounding areas.

For **guided visits** and hikes, call ☎93 877 77 01 at least two weeks in advance. (Hiking tour in English €6.50, museum tour €5, joint tour €14. In Spanish, hiking and museum tour €4 each, joint tour €7.) For rock climbing and more athletic hiking in the area, call Marcel Millet at ☎93 835 02 51 or stop by his hiking/climbing office next to the Montserrat campsite.

CATALAN PYRENEES

RIPOLL

In the heart of Catalunya sits sleepy Ripoll (pop. 11,000), the region's strongest link to its proud early history. Ripoll houses the ninth-century monastery founded by Guifré el Pilós (Wilfred the Hairy; see p. 40), the founding father of Catalunya, as well as the tomb of the legend himself. The Monasterio de Santa Maria, built in the 9th century, attracts visitors in search of Spain's Romanesque architectural legacy; its elaborately carved portal is one of the most famous in all of Spain. Ripoll also serves as a convenient base for excursions to the nearby town of Sant Joan de las Abadesses; the convent at Sant Joan and Ripoll's monastery are the two great architectural relics of the age of Guifré.

TRANSPORTATION AND PRACTICAL INFO

RENFE, Pl. Mova, 1 (☎97 270 06 44), runs **trains** to Barcelona (1¾hr., 9-12 per day 6:32am-8:04pm, €4.90) and Puigcerdà (1hr., 6 per day 8:56am-8:54pm, €2.51). The bus station (separated from the train station by a small park) sends **Teisa buses** (☎97

220 48 68) to: Barcelona (4hr., 1 per day, €10.80); Girona (2hr., 1 per day, €6.60), via Olot; Sant Joan de las Abadesses (15min., 8-10 per day, €1.10). The **tourist office,** next to the monastery on Pl. Abat Oliba, gives out free maps. (☎97 270 23 51. Open M-Sa 9:30am-1:30pm and 4-7pm, Su 10am-2pm and 4-7pm.) Connect to the **Internet** at **Xarxtel,** Pl. d'Espanya, 10, a computer-electronics store that charges customers for use of their network connection. The **public library,** C. de les Vinyes, 6, offers free use of their computers. (Open M-Tu and Th-F 4-8:30pm, W 9am-1:30pm, Sa 10am-1:30pm.) Other services include: **emergency** (☎112); **police,** Pl. Ajuntament, 3 (☎97 271 44 14); and the **post office,** C. d'Estació, facing the tree-lined park. (☎97 270 07 60. Open M-F 8:30am-2:30pm, Sa 9:30am-1pm.) The **postal code** is 17500.

ACCOMMODATIONS AND FOOD

Ripoll is an ambitious daytrip; you can sleep at the luxurious and friendly ◙**Fonda La Paula** ❷, C. Berenguer, 4, on Pl. Abat Oliba alongside the tourist office, which has cream-colored rooms with comfortable beds, TVs, and spacious, tiled bathrooms. (☎97 270 00 11. Singles €21.40, doubles €36.38, triples €50.29, quads €64.20. V.) The few other accommodations in town are pricey. From the monastery's plaza, follow C. Sant Pere for two blocks to **Hostal del Ripollès** ❺, Pl. Nova, 11, which provides small but well-furnished rooms with TV, phone, and full bath. (☎97 270 02 15. Breakfast included. Doubles €48.) **La Trobada Hotel** ❸, Pg. de Honorat, 4, offers similar rooms at slightly higher prices, in a convenient location, on the right as your approach the Pont d'Olot, the bridge between the train/bus stations and the center of town. (☎97 270 23 53. Singles €28.36, doubles €50.49, triples €58.)

Restaurants surround Pl. Gran. Follow C. Bisbe Morgades and take a right before the river on C. Mossen; the *plaça* is to the left. If you are looking for fancy Catalan fare, try ◙**Reccapolis** ❸, Ctra. Sant Joan, 68 (about a 10-15 minutes walk down Ctra. Sant Joan from Pl. Ajuntament. Entrees €10.82-16.83. ☎97 270 21 06. Open Th-Tu 1-4pm and 8:30-10:30pm, W 1-4pm.) At **La Piazzetta** ❷, Pl. Nova, 11, the ambience and menu may Catalan, but the food is Italian; same owners and location as the Hostal del Ripollès. (Pizzas €5.10-8.75, pasta €5.35-7.25. ☎97 270 02 15. Open M-Sa 1-3:15pm and 8:15-11:30pm, Su 8:15-11:30pm.) Stock up on **groceries** at the supermarket across from the bus station, **Champion,** C. Progress, 33-37. (☎97 270 26 32. Open M-Th 9am-9pm, F-Sa 9am-9:30pm, Su 10am-2pm. AmEx/MC/V.)

SIGHTS

Almost everyone who visits Ripoll comes to see the incredibly intricate 11th-century portal of the ◙**Monasterio de Santa María.** To reach the monastery, take a left on C. Progrés from the train and bus stations, then follow it until it merges with C. Estació. Take the first left after the "metal dancers" (the colorful modern statues) onto Pont d'Olot, cross the river, and continue straight on C. Bisbe Morgades to the Pl. Ajuntament and Pl. Abat Oliba. (Church open daily 10am-1pm and 3-7pm. €2, with student card €1; includes entrances to the cloister.)

Founded in AD 879 by Count Guifré el Pilós (Wilfred the Hairy), the Santa María monastery was once the most powerful in all of Catalunya. The arched doorway, nicknamed the "Stone Bible," is considered perhaps the finest piece of Romanesque architecture in all of Spain, and is definitely worth a look (English brochure available €1 at the entrance which tells you what everything means; there is also a verbal explanation available for €1). It depicts scenes from the Old and New Testaments, as well as a hierarchy of the cosmos and a 12-month calendar. The panels directly around the door are representations of the 12 months, and the panels next to the arch depict the Exodus. After centuries of battering from the elements, the worn portal is now sheltered in a climate-controlled glass enclosure.

Inside you'll find the Romanesque basilica, very different from its original form due to extensive renovations. A number of tombs line the interior, the most famous (and most modern looking) of which lies to the left of the altar: that of Guifré el

Pilós, Catalonia's beloved first count Wilfred the Hairy (see p. 40). Killed in battle in AD 897, his bones were regathered and honored here in the early 1980s. The Catalan inscription reads "Here lies Wilfred the Hairy, Count of Barcelona...[and seven other regions], Founder of the National Catalan dynasty, and Rebuilder of Our Land."

Adjoining the church is a beautiful two-story Romanesque and Gothic **cloister,** with artifacts from the monastery dating back hundreds of years, surrounding a quiet courtyard. The cloister also sometimes hosts temporary exhibits. Next door to Santa Maria is the **Museu Etnogràfic de Ripoll,** which houses a hodgepodge collection of artifacts from Ripoll's history, focusing on the industries of the town and its surrounding areas. (Open Tu-Sa 9:30am-1:30pm and 3:30pm-7pm.)

DAYTRIP FROM RIPOLL: ST. JOAN DE LAS ABADESSES

🚌 *TEISA buses in Ripoll or Sant Joan (☎ 97 274 02 95) connect Sant Joan to Ripoll (15min., 8-10 per day, €1.10), stopping next to the church. The helpful **tourist office,** Pl. l'Abadia, 9 (☎ 97 272 05 99) is next door to the monastery alongside a 15th-century cloister. Office open M-F 10am-2pm and 4-7pm. The convenient bus schedule from Ripoll allows for a visit the complex in one or two hours.*

Wilfred the Hairy was nothing if not an equal-opportunity employer. After founding Ripoll's first monastery, he went on to endow a convent 10km away, to which he appointed his daughter Emma as the first abbess in 887. Sant Joan de las Abadesses (pop. 3700) developed around the nuns, but unfortunately some of The Hairy's successors were not so keen on female independence; their community was ousted in the 11th century and it took 100 years before anyone was allowed to move back. The Augustines who eventually took over turned the convent into a monastery. Today it contains a Romanesque **church** and adjoining **museum,** which proudly display religious art and artifacts from throughout Catalunya. (☎ 97 272 23 53. Open daily July-Aug. 10am-7pm; Nov.-Feb. M-F 10am-2pm, Sa 10am-2pm and 4-6pm; Mar.-Apr. and Oct. M-Sa 10am-2pm and 4-6pm; May-June and Sept. M-Sa 10am-2pm and 4-7pm. Museum and church €2.) The highlight of the candlelit church may be the haunting **Santíssim Misteri,** a 13th-century wooden sculpture depicting Christ's removal from the cross. On Christ's forehead is a piece of the Host that has been preserved for over 700 years. In addition to the 12th-century Romanesque church and the 15th-century Gothic cloister, the small complex also includes an 18th-century Baroque **Chapel of the Virgin of Sorrow.** The museum contains an eleventh-century prayer book as well as a particularly evocative 16th-century portrait of Christ by Joan Gascó.

PUIGCERDÀ

A challenging name for foreigners, Puigcerdà (pop.7000; Pwee-chair-DAH) has become a popular town by virtue of its stunning location in the mountainous Cerdanya region. Puigcerdà's view of the valley is beautiful, and the town serves as a cheap base for hiking, biking, or skiing the surrounding hillsides. Puigcerdà is perhaps best known for appearing in the 1993 *Guinness Book of World Records* for the world's longest *butifarra* (sausage), a Freudian nightmare measuring 5200m.

TRANSPORTATION

RENFE trains (☎ 97 288 01 65) run to: Barcelona (3hr., 6 per day, €6.90) and Ripoll (1¼hr., 6 per day, €2.60). **Alsina Graells buses** (☎ 97 335 00 20) run to Barcelona (3¼hr., 2-4 per day, €12) and La Seu d'Urgell (1hr., 7 per day, €4). Buses depart in front of the train station and from Pl. Barcelona; purchase tickets on board. See the schedule in Bar Estació, to the right as soon as you walk into the train station. Taxis (☎ 97 288 00 11) wait on Pl. Cabrinetty. For **bike rental,** try **Sports Iris,** Av. de França, 16. (☎ 97 288 23 98. Bikes €9 per half day, €15 per day. MC/V.)

ORIENTATION & PRACTICAL INFORMATION

Puigcerdà's center is at the top of a hill. **Plaça Ajuntament,** located off the main *plaça*, is nicknamed *el balcón de Cerdanya* for its view of the valley and the less picturesque **train station** at the foot of the slope. It's best to get off buses at Pl. Barcelona, not at the train station. To reach Pl. Ajuntament from the inconvenient train station, walk past the stairs in the station's *plaça* until you reach the first real flight of stairs (between two buildings). Walk up and turn right at the top; then look for the next set of stairs on your left, just before a sign for C. Hostal del Sol. Climb these to the top and turn left on C. Raval de les Monges, where the final set of stairs winds up to the right. From the *plaça*, walk one block on C. Alfons I to **C. Major,** the principal commercial street. Turn left on C. Major to Pl. Santa Maria. From Pl. Santa Maria, with your back to the bell tower, walk diagonally to the left to Pl. Barcelona.

The **tourist office,** C. Querol, 1, a right off Pl. Ajuntament with your back to the view, has an English-speaking staff that gives out maps and lodging listings. (☎97 288 05 42; info@puigcerda.com. Open M-Tu and F-Sa 9am-2pm and 3-8pm, W-Th 10am-1:30pm and 4:30-7:30pm, Su 10am-2pm.) **Banco Central Hispano** is on Pl. Cabrinetty. (Oct.-Mar. M-F 8:30am-2pm, Sa 8:30am-1pm; closed Sa Apr.-Sept.) Other services include: **emergency** (☎091 or 092); **municipal police,** Pl. Ajuntament, 1 (☎97 288 19 72); and the **Centre Hospitalari** (☎97 288 01 50 or 97 288 01 54), in Pl. Santa Maria. Log on at **Punt com,** C. Espanya, 10. (☎97 288 31 55. €1.20 per 30min. Open daily 10am-1pm and 4-8pm.) The **post office,** Av. Coronel Molera, 11, is off Pl. Barcelona on the left after a block and a half. (☎97 288 08 14. Open M-F 8:30am-2:30pm, Sa 9:30am-1pm.) The **postal code** is 17520.

ACCOMMODATIONS AND FOOD

Rooms in Puigcerdà come easily, if not cheaply. Most less-expensive *pensiones* hole up off Pl. Santa Maria, in the old town. **Alfonso Habitaciones ❷,** C. Espanya, 5, offers decent, dimly lit rooms with TVs, bathrooms, and colorful bedspreads. Take a left off C. Alfons I when heading away from the church. (☎97 288 02 46. Singles €21; doubles €42. Cash only.) If you're looking for something a bit nicer, try the **Hotel Avet Blau ❺,** Pl. Santa Maria, 14, right next to the bell tower, which has six spacious and comfortable doubles. (☎97 288 25 52. Rates vary by season from €70.74 to €96.46.) **Camping Stel ❷,** 1km from Puigcerdà on the road to Llivia, offers full-service camping with the benefits of a chalet-style restaurant-bar and lounge. (☎97 288 23 61. Site with tent and car €15, €4.45 per person. 220V electricity for €3. Open Sa-Su only June 1-Sept. 30 and Oct. 27-May 1.) If you're planning to ski in La Molina, try **Mare de Déu de les Neus (HI) ❷,** on Ctra. Font Canaleta, which has modern facilities and a beautiful location just 500m from the La Molina RENFE station and 4km from the slopes. In winter a bus goes up to the slopes every 30 minutes. (☎97 289 20 12, reservations 93 483 83 63. Breakfast included. Sheets €2. Reserve in high season. Jan.-Nov. dorms €12, over 25 €16; Dec. dorms €14, over 25 €18. Doubles and triples available, same price per person. MC/V.)

The neighborhood off C. Alfons I is filled with markets and restaurants. For fresh produce, try the weekly **market,** at Pl. 10 d'Abril (Su 6am-2pm). Get **groceries** at **Bonpreu,** C. Colonel Molera, 12, the small supermarket diagonally across from the post office. (Open M-Th 9am-1:30pm and 5-9pm, F-Sa 9am-9pm, Su 10am-2pm. MC/V.) **◼El Pati de la Tieta ❷,** C. dels Ferrers, 20, serves large portions of pasta and pizzas (€6-9.60) and heavenly desserts in an ivy-covered outdoor patio. (☎97 288 01 56. Fish and meat entrees €11.50-17. Open daily 1-3:30pm and 8-11:30pm. MC/V.) At **Cantina Restaurant Mexicà ❷,** Pl. Cabrinetty, 9, you can kick back with a margarita and take in some excellent tacos, fajitas, and quesadillas. (☎97 288 16 58. Entrees €4-15. Open M 9-11:30pm, Tu-W and F-Su 2-4pm and 9-11:30pm. MC/V.)

SIGHTS AND OUTDOOR ACTIVITIES

Between ski runs and cycling, dash over to the **campanario,** the octagonal bell tower in Pl. Santa Maria. This 42m high 12th-century tower is all that remains of the **Església de Santa Maria,** an eerie reminder of the destruction wreaked by the Civil War. Climb to the top for 360° views of Puigcerdà and the Pyrenees. (Open July-Aug. M-F noon-2pm and 5-8pm; Sa-Su 11am-noon and 5-8pm. Free.) The 13th-century **Església de Sant Domènec,** on Pg. 10 d'Abril, contains several Gothic paintings considered to be among the best of their genre. (Open 9:30am-8pm. Free.) Puigcerdà's picturesque **Lake Estany,** a 2min. walk up C. Pons i Gasch from Pl. Barcelona, was created in 1380 for irrigation purposes. It now serves the town well as a lovely place to rent a boat (€2 per person per 30min.; inquire at the cafe).

Puigcerdà calls itself the "capital of snow." **Ski** in your country of choice (Spain, France, or Andorra) at one of 19 ski areas within a 50km radius. The closest and cheapest one on the Spanish side is **La Molina** (☎97 289 20 31; www.lamolina.com). Nearby **Masella** (☎97 214 40 00; www.masella.com) offers the longest run in the Pyrenees at 7km. For cross-country skiing, the closest site is **Guils** (☎97 219 70 47). A little farther out, try **Lles** (☎97 329 30 49) or **Aransa** (☎97 329 30 51). The Puigcerdà area is also popular for **biking;** the tourist office has a brochure with 17 potential routes mapped out. La Molina opens trails up for biking in the summer months, and provides rentals for €12.62 per day. You can also navigate the trails on horseback for €12 for an hour-long excursion. For indoor sports, the **Club Poliesportiu Puigcerdà,** on Av. del Poliesportiu, has a pool, tennis courts, basketball courts, and a skating rink. (☎97 288 02 43. Open M-F 11am-10pm, Sa 11am-9:30pm, Su 11am-8pm. €3.80 per sports facility or €6 per day.)

NIGHTLIFE & FESTIVALS

Cafes and bars crowd the *plaças*, particularly the adjacent Pl. Santa Maria and Pl. Herois. **Bar Miami** (☎97 288 00 13) and **Kennedy** (☎97 288 11 91) sit next to each other on Pl. Herois and have popular outdoor patios with good people-watching both day and night. **Central,** Pl. Santa Maria, 6, is a hip bar with eclectic and cozy furniture.

Puigcerdà hosts several festivals throughout the year, including the popular **Festival de Música Clásica** during the last two weeks of July, the **Festa de L'Estany (Festival of the Lake),** with grand fireworks displays at the end of August, and at Easter, the **Antic Puigcerdà,** the town's biggest market and fair.

THE BALEARIC ISLANDS

Every year discos, ancient history, and beaches—especially beaches—draw nearly two million of the hippest Europeans to the *Islas Baleares*, 100km off the east coast of Spain. Culture-philiacs and shopaholics will fall for the high-class act and stunning natural beauty of **Mallorca.** A counterculture haven since the 1960s, **Ibiza** offers some of the best nightlife in all of Europe. The smaller islands of **Formentera** and **Menorca** hold unspoiled sands, hidden coves, and mysterious Bronze Age megaliths.

GETTING TO THE ISLANDS

Flights to the islands prove the easiest way to get there. Those under 26 often get discounts from **Iberia** (☎902 40 05 00; www.iberia.com), which flies to Palma de Mallorca and Ibiza from Barcelona (40min., €60-120). **Air Europa** (☎902 24 00 42) and **SpanAir** (☎902 13 14 15; www.spanair.com) offer budget flights to and between the islands. **SOM** (Servicios de Ocio Marítimo; ☎97 131 03 99) lines up bus companies, ferry lines, and *discotecas* for packages to Ibiza designed for disco fiends who seek transportation and an all-night party but have no use for lodging. Book tickets through a Barcelona travel agency. Another option is **charter flights,** which can be the

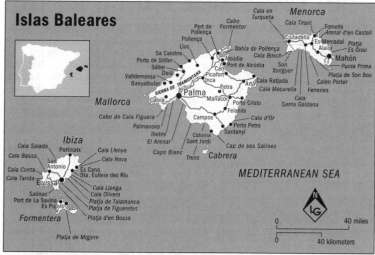

Islas Baleares

cheapest and quickest means of travel. Most deals include a stay in a hotel, but some companies (called *mayoristas*) sell unoccupied seats on package-tour flights. The leftover spots ("seat only" deals) can be found in newspaper ads or through travel agencies (check TIVE and other budget travel havens in Barcelona). Prices are much higher during summer and *Semana Santa* than in the off-season (Oct.-May). Off-season, tickets are not hard to get a week before departure. Those traveling in July or August should reserve several weeks in advance.

Ferries to the islands are less expensive but slower and less popular. **Trasmediter-ránea** (☎902 45 46 45; www.trasmediterranea.com) departs from Barcelona's Estació Marítima Moll for Mallorca, Menorca, and Ibiza (€43-58). **Buquebus** (☎902 41 42 42) goes from Barcelona to Palma (4hr., 2 per day, €49). Book tickets through a travel agency.

The same companies which fly to the islands fly between them. **Ferries** are the most cost-efficient way to travel between islands. **Trasmediterránea** (see above) sails between Palma and Mahón (6½hr., Su only, €23) and between Palma and Ibiza (2½hr., 7am, €37). There is no direct Mahón-Ibiza connection. **Trasmapi** (☎97 131 20 71) links Ibiza and Formentera (fast ferry 25min., 12 per day). **Umafisa Lines** (☎97 131 45 13) runs car ferries on the same route. **Car rental** costs around €36 per day, **mopeds** €18, and **bikes** €6-10.

MALLORCA

A favorite with Spain's royal family, Mallorca has been a popular member of the in-crowd since Roman times. Today, European package tourists have converged on the island, in some areas virtually suffocating the coastline. Nevertheless, there are legitimate reasons for such Mallorca lust. Lemon groves and olive trees adorn the jagged cliffs of the northern coast, and lazy beaches sink into calm bays to the east. The capital and undisputed cultural center of the Balearics, **Palma** (pop. 323,000), embraces conspicuous consumption and pleases with its well-preserved old quarter, colonial architecture, and local flavor.

TRANSPORTATION

Flights: Aeroport Son San Juan (☎97 178 90 00), 8km from downtown Palma. Buses #17 and 25 go to and from Pl. Espanya (€1.80). A taxi to the center costs about €5.

Ferries: Trasmediterránea, Estació Marítim, 2 (☎902 45 46 45). Daily ferries to Barcelona. Ferries dock at Moll Pelaires (south of the city). Bus #1 goes through Pg. Marítim. Tickets sold M-F 9am-1pm and 5-7pm, Sa 9am-noon.

Trains: Ferrocarril de Sóller (☎97 175 20 51), Pl. Espanya. Runs to **Sóller** (1hr., 5 per day 8am-8:05pm, €2.40). Avoid the 10:40am "tourist train" when prices inflate to €4.80 for a 10min. stop in Mirador del Pujol d'en Banya. **Servicios Ferroviarios de Mallorca (SFM),** Pl. Espanya, 6 (☎97 175 22 45), departs to **Inca** (35min., 22 per day 5:45am-10pm, €1.80).

Buses: Bus travel to and from Palma is not too difficult, but travel between most other areas is inefficient and restrictive. Nearly all buses stop at the main stop on C. Eusebi Estada, several blocks down from Pl. Espanya; buy tickets on the bus. The tourist office has a detailed schedule of all buses. Some of the more popular destinations include: **Alcúdia** and **Port d'Alcúdia** (1hr.; M-F 16 per day 8am-9pm, Sa-Su 5 per day 9:30am-9pm; €3.70); **Covetes/ Es Trenc** (M-F 3 per day 10am-5pm, Sa-Su 10:30am; €3.84); **Cuevas Drac** (M-F 4 per day 10am-1:30pm, Sa-Su 10am; €5.40); **Port Pollenca** (1hr.; M-F 5 per day 9am-7:15pm, Sa-Su 3 per day 10am-8:30pm; €4.30); **Sóller** and **Port de Sóller** (45min.; M-F every hr. 7am-7pm, Sa-Su 1 and 4:30pm; €2.10); **Valldemossa** (30min.; M-F every 2 hr. 7:30am-7:30pm, Sa-Su 4 per day 8:30am-7:30pm; €1.20).

Public Transportation: Empresa Municipal de Transportes (EMT; ☎97 175 22 45). Pl. Espanya is the hub. Stops around town and as far as Palma Nova and Arenal. €1; 10 tickets €9. Buy tickets onboard. Buses run approx. 6am-10pm. Bus #17 runs until 1am (€1.80). Bus #25 also goes to the airport but stops running at 10pm.

Taxis: ☎97 175 54 40.

Car Rental: Mascaro Crespi, Av. Joan Miró, 9 (☎97 173 61 03). €30 per day with insurance. Open M-Sa 8am-1pm and 3-8pm, Su 9am-1pm and 5-8pm.

ORIENTATION AND PRACTICAL INFO

To get to town from the airport, take bus #17 or 25 to **Pl. Espanya** (15min., every 20min., €1.80). From the dock, take Pg. Marítim (a.k.a. Av. Gabriel Roca), or bus #1 to Av. D'Antoni Maura, which leads to **Pl. Reina** and **Pg. Born.** From the sea, Pg. Born leads to **Pl. Rei Joan Carles I,** the center of the old town, and **Av. Rei Jaume III,** the business artery. To the right, C. de la Unió leads (after some stairs) to **Pl. Major,** the center of Palma's pedestrian shopping district.

Tourist Offices: Palma branch, C. Sant Dominic, 11 (☎97 172 40 90). From Pl. Reina, take C. Conquistador until C. Sant Dominic; office is at bottom of stairway, below street level. Open M-F 9am-8pm, Sa 9am-1:30pm. **Info booth** in Pl. Espanya. **Island tourist office,** Pl. Reina, 2 (☎97 171 22 16). Open M-F 9am-8pm, Sa 10am-2pm.

El Corte Inglés: Av. Rei Jaume III, 15 (☎97 177 01 77). Open M-Sa 10am-10pm.

Emergency: ☎112. **Police:** (☎091 or 092) Av. Sant Ferrá.

Internet Access: La Red, C. Concepció, 5 (☎97 171 35 74), 2 blocks off of Av. Jaume III near the intersection of Pg. Born. €2.40 for 30min. Open daily 10am-midnight. **Cyber Central,** C. Soletat, 4 (☎97 171 29 27), in Pl. Reina. €4.80 per hr., students €3.60 per hr. Open M-Sa 9am-10pm, Su noon-8pm.

Post Office: C. Constitució, 5 (☎902 19 71 97), 1 block off Pl. Reina. Parcels upstairs. **Fax** service. Open M-F 8:30am-8:30pm, Sa 9:30am-2pm.

Postal Code: 07080.

ACCOMMODATIONS

This resort town has few *hostals* or bargains. Call in advance for summer stays.

Hostal Ritzi, C. Apuntadores, 6 (☎97 171 46 10), next door to Hostal Apuntadores, conveniently situated above "Big Byte" cybercafe. Centrally located *hostal* with cheerfully-decorated rooms overlooking an interior patio that can get noisy at night. Laundry service €7 per load. Singles €23; doubles €34, with bath €49. ❷

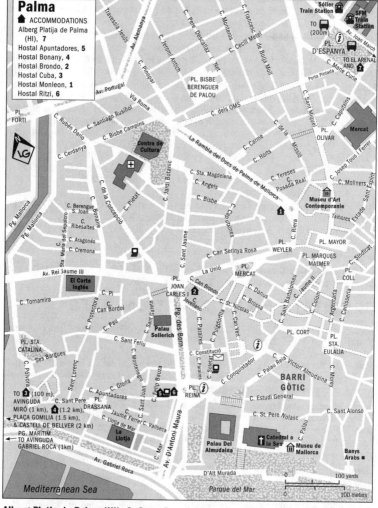

Palma

🏠 ACCOMMODATIONS
Alberg Platija de Palma (HI), **7**
Hostal Apuntadores, **5**
Hostal Bonany, **4**
Hostal Brondo, **2**
Hostal Cuba, **3**
Hostal Monleon, **1**
Hostal Ritzi, **6**

Alberg Platja de Palma (HI), C. Costa Brava, 13 (☎97 126 08 92), in the beach town El Arenal. Take bus #15 from Pl. Espanya (every 8min., €1), and get off at the corner of C. Costa Brava. Lively crowd. 4-person dorms with shower. **HI card required.** Breakfast included. Sheets €2.40. Laundry service €6. Reception 8am-3am. Curfew midnight. Dorms €9-12, over 26 €10.20-14. ❶

Hostal Apuntadores, C. Apuntadores, 8 (☎97 171 34 91), less than a block from Pl. Reinain in a great location. Rooms are airy and bright. Dorms €12; singles €18; doubles €30, with shower €33. ❷

Hostal Cuba, C. San Magí, 1 (☎97 173 81 59), at C. Argentina, on the edge of town center. From Pl. Joan Carles I, turn left and walk down Av. Jaume III, cross the river, and turn left on C. Argentina. Look for the "Restaurant Cuba" sign several blocks down. First floor rooms are more basic than 2nd floor. Prices may change as renovations are completed. Singles €15-18; doubles €30-33. ❷

Hostal Monleon, La Rambla, 3 (☎971 71 53 17). Dimly lit, noisy rooms, but cheap for the area. Singles €15, with shower €16, with bath €20; doubles €27, with bath €31, with shower €34. ❷

Hostal Bonany, C. Almirante Cervera, 5 (☎971 73 79 24), in a wealthy residential area 3km from the town center. Take bus #3, 20, 21, or 22 from Pl. Espanya to Av. Joan Miró and walk up C. Camilio José Cela. Take the 1st right, then the 1st left. Spacious rooms with bath and balcony. Singles €26, doubles €40. ❸

Hostal Brondo, C. Can Brondo, 1 (☎97 171 90 43), off Pl. Rei Joan Carles I. Each room has character; all have beautiful wooden furniture, tasteful artwork, and clean bathrooms. Common lounge. 2 wheelchair accessible rooms. Reception M-Sa 9am-2pm and 6-8pm, Su 10am-1:30pm. Singles €21, doubles €33. ❷

FOOD

Palma's multi-ethnic restaurants are paradise for those sick of tapas. Pricey but popular outdoor restaurants fill **Pl. Mayor** and **Pl. Llotja,** but budget eaters head to the side streets off **Pg. Born,** to the cheap digs along **Av. Joan Miró,** or to the pizzerias along **Po. Marítimo.** Make sure to try the *ensaimadas* (pastries smothered in powdered sugar) and the *sopas mallorquinas* (a pizza-like snack of stewed vegetables over brown bread). Two **markets** vie for customers: one is in Pl. Olivar off C. Padre Atanasio, the other is across town at the corner of C. Pou and C. Dameto. For **groceries,** try **Servicio y Precios** on C. Felip Bauzá, near C. Apuntadores and Pl. Reina (open M-F 8:30am-8:30pm, Sa 9am-2pm), or the supermarket in **El Corte Inglés,** Av. Rei Jaume III, 15. (☎97 177 01 77. Open M-Sa 10am-10pm.)

Bon Lloc, C. San Feliu, 7 (☎97 171 86 17), a left off C. Born, heading away from water. Ultra-hip vegetarian restaurant. Menu features salads (€5.70), falafel (€7.20), and dishes like basmati rice with chinese-style sauteéd vegetables (€9.60). Midday *menú* €9.60. Open M-Tu 1-4pm, W-Sa 1-4pm and 9-11:30pm. MC/V. ❷

Pizzeria Restaurante Vecchio Giovanni, C. San Juan, 3 (☎97 172 28 79), right off C. Apuntadores. Lively family restaurant with excellent pizzas (€5-8) and pastas (€7-10). Gets crowded for dinner, especially on weekends. Open daily 5pm-midnight. ❷

Cellar Montenegro, C. Montenegro, 10, off of C. Apuntadores. Heaping portions of great *comida típica* in a family setting. *Menú* €9. Entrees €6-9. Open M-F 1-4pm and 8:30pm-midnight. AmEx/MC/V. ❷

Cantina Mariachi, C. Ramon y Cajal, 2 (☎97 173 30 33), across the river (and Pg. Mallorca) from the old quarter, off Av. de l'Argentina. Decent, inexpensive Mexican food served in a lively, cheerfully-decorated locale. Tacos €7.50, fajitas (chicken or lamb) €10. Open daily 8pm-midnight. ❷

SIGHTS

Palma's architecture is a medley of Arabic, Christian, and Modernist styles: a reflection of the island's multicultural past and present. Many of the landmarks are nestled amidst the narrow streets of the Barri Gòtic (Gothic Quarter).

◾ CATEDRAL O LA SEA

◪ *C. Palau Reial, 29, off Pl. Reina. ☎97 172 31 30. Cathedral and museum open Apr.-Oct. M-F 10am-6pm, Sa 10am-2pm; Nov.-Mar. M-F 10am-3pm. €3.*

This Gothic giant towers over Palma and its bay. The cathedral, dedicated to Palma's patron saint San Sebastián, was begun in the 1300s, finished in 1601, and then modified by Gaudí in Modernist fashion in 1909. Now the interior and the ceiling ornamentation blend smoothly with the stately exterior. The southern facade, perhaps the most impressive, overlooks a reflective pool and the ocean.

■ PALAU DEL'ALMUDAINA

🔲 *On C. Palau Reial, just off Pl. Reina. ☎ 97 172 71 45. Open M-F 10am-6:30pm, Sa 10am-2pm. Guided visits €3.91, unguided €3.16. Students and children €2.25. EU citizens free on W.*

Built by the Moors, this imposing, austere palace was a stronghold of *los Reyes Católicos*, Fernando and Isabel. Guided tours, which pass through the museum, are given in numerous languages. The pleasant garden off Pl. Reina directly in front of the palace also merits a visit.

CASTELL DEL BELLVER

🔲 *Bus #3, 21, or 22 from Pl. Espanya. ☎ 97 173 06 57. Castle and museum open Apr.-Sept. M-Sa 8am-8:30pm, Su 10am-5pm; Oct.-Mar. M-Sa 8am-7:15pm, Su 10am-5pm. €1.68.*

Overlooking the city and bay, Castell de Bellver was a summer residence for 14th-century royalty; it also housed Mallorca's most distinguished prisoners. The castle contains a municipal museum with paintings and archaeological displays, as well as models of archaeological digs.

MUSEU D'ART ESPANYOL CONTEMPORANI

🔲 *C. Sant Miquel, 11. ☎ 97 171 35 15. Open M-F 10am-6:30pm, Sa 10am-1:30pm. €3.*

Now part of the March Foundation, this mansion-turned-museum displays modern art from some of the twentieth century's most iconic Spanish artists, including Picasso, Dalí, Miró, Juan Gris, and Antoni Tápies. Also houses temporary exhibits as well.

OTHER MUSEUMS

Palma is filled with museums. Inaugurated in December 1992, **Fundació Pilar i Joan Miró** displays the works from Miró's Palma studio at the time of his death. (C. Saridakis, 29. From Pl. Espanya, take buses #3, 21, or 22 to C. Joan Miró. ☎ 97 170 14 20. Open May 16-Sept. 14 Tu-Sa 10am-7pm, Su 10am-3pm; Sept. 15-May 15 Tu-Sa 10am-6pm, Su 10am-3pm. €4.20.) **Fundació "la Caixa"** hosts a collection of Modernist paintings as well as other exhibits in Doménech's Modernist Gran Hotel. (Pl. Weyler, 3. ☎ 97 117 85 00. Open Tu-Sa 10am-9pm, Su 10am-2pm. Free.) The **Casal Solleric** houses modern art. (Pg. Born, 27. ☎ 97 172 20 92. Open Tu-Sa 10:30am-1:45pm, Su 10am-1:45pm. Free.) **Centre de Cultura "Sa Nostra"** features rotating exhibits and cultural events such as lectures, concerts, and movies. (C. Concepción, 12. ☎ 97 172 52 10. Open M-F 10:30am-9pm, Sa 10am-1:30pm.) **Museu de Mallorca** is ideal for travelers interested in archaeology or medieval painting. (C. Portella, 5. ☎ 97 171 75 40. Open Apr.-Sept. Tu-Sa 10am-2pm and 5-8pm; Oct.-Mar. Tu-Sa 10am-1pm and 4-8pm, Su 10am-2pm. €1.80.) For those fed up with being inside, there's always **Poble Espanyol,** a small village with replicas of famous Spanish architecture, which is identical to its namesake in Barcelona. (C. Poble Espanyol, 39. Buses #4 and 5 pass on C. Andrea Doria. ☎ 97 173 70 75. Open daily 9am-8pm; Dec.-Mar. 9am-6pm. €4.80.)

BEACHES

Mallorca is a huge island, and many of the best beaches are a haul from Palma. Still, several picturesque (albeit touristy) stretches of sand are accessible by city bus. The beach at **El Arenal** (Platja de Palma, bus #15), 11km to the southeast (toward the airport), is the prime stomping grounds of Mallorca's most sunburnt German tourists. The waterfront area is full of German signs for restaurants, bars, and hotels—think Frankfurt am Mediterranean. The beach is one of the longest and most crowded in the area, with white sands and intensely turquoise water. Other beaches close to Palma include **Palma Nova** (bus #21), 15km southwest, and **Illetes** (bus #3), 9km southwest, which are smaller than El Arenal, but equally popular. The tourist office distributes a list of over 40 nearby beaches.

NIGHTLIFE AND ENTERTAINMENT

Nightlife and entertainment *à la Mallorca* have a Spanish flavor often missing in the other isles, but they are still well-documented for visitors. The tourist office keeps a comprehensive list of sporting activities, concerts, and exhibits. Every Friday, *El Día del Mundo* (€0.75) publishes an entertainment supplement with listings of bars and discos, and *La Calle* offers a monthly review of hotspots.

In the past, Pl. Reina and La Llotja were the place for bar-hoppers, but a recent law requiring bars to close by 3am has shifted the action to the waterfront. Nevertheless, many partiers still start their night in the *casco viejo*. **La Bodeguita del Medio,** C. Vallseca, 18, plays Cuban rhythms. (Open Th-Sa 8pm-3am, Su-W 8pm-1am.) Follow the Aussies to **Bar Latitude 39,** C. Felip Bauza, 8, a "yachtie" bar. (Beer €1.50. "Twofer nights"—two for the price of one—Tu, Th, and Sa 9-10pm. Open M-Sa 7pm-3am.) **Barcelona,** C. Apuntadores, 5, jams with live music from midnight to 3am. (Cover €1.80 for live concerts. Open daily 11pm-3am).

Palma's clubbers start the night in the *bares-musicales* on the **Po. Marítimo** strip. Each mini-disco boasts different tunes, but Spanish pop dominates. Come 2am, two of the best places by the water include the salsa-happy **Made in Brasil,** Po. Marítimo, 27 (mixed drinks €3.60-4.80; open daily 8pm-4am), and dance-crazy **Salero,** Po. Marítimo, 31 (open daily 8pm-6am). Several clubs and bars are also centered on Pl. Gomilia and along C. Joan Miró—but take caution here at night, as there have been a number of reported instances of petty crime occurring here in recent years. The bars and clubs around **El Arenal** are German-owned, German-filled, and German-directed. But if you don't mind partying with Deutschland, possibly the best deal for entertainment in Palma is here at ◼**Riu Palace,** one block in from the beach. Two huge rooms, one playing techno and the other spinning hip-hop, fill nightly with hip, young, fashion-conscious German disco-fiends. All guests receive free t-shirts, "Rapper caps," necklaces, and coupons for free food at a nearby beer garden. (Cover €15; open bar, all you can drink. Themed parties every weekend. Open daily 10pm-6:30am.)

When the bar scene fades at 3am, partiers migrate to Palma's *discotecas*, which attract more locals than tourists. **Tito's Palace,** Po. Marítimo, is Palma's hippest disco, with two floors of house in an indoor colosseum of mirrors and lights overlooking the water. (Cover €15-18. Open daily 11pm-6am). **Pachá,** Av. Gabriel Roca, is a toned-down version of the Ibiza landmark, but even this little sibling has a massive dance floor, tropical terrace, and enthusiastic patrons. (Cover €12-18. Open daily 11pm-6:30am.)

Mallorcans use any and every occasion as an excuse to party. One of the more colorful bashes, **Día de Sant Joan** (June 24), brings singing, dancing, and drinking to Parc del Mar. The celebration begins with a fireworks display the night before.

DAYTRIPS ON MALLORCA

The west coast of Mallorca is one of the most beautiful landscapes in the Mediterranean. The small town of **Sóller** basks in a fertile valley lined with orange groves. The town, with a backdrop of spectacular mountains, is a pleasant change from Las Palmas's more touristed beaches. From Sóller, a 30min. walk down the valley will bring you to **Puerto de Sóller,** a pebble and sand beach where windsurfers zip back and forth. Old-fashioned trolleys also connect the two (every 30min. 7am-9pm, €0.75). On the southeast coast, scalloped fringes of bays and caves are investors' most recent discovery. The ◼**Cuevas Drach,** near Porto Cristo in the southeast, are among the most dramatic natural wonders in Mallorca. The caves amaze with their droopy, finger-like rock formations, illuminating the cave in a spectrum of red and pink color. A 30min. walk into the depths of the cave leads to one of the largest **underground lakes** in the world. The performances given by classical musicians boating across the lake can be classified somewhere between absurd and bizarre; audience members can take free boat rides at the concert's end. A bus runs from Palma to the caves, leaving from the main station by Pl. Espanya (M-Sa 4 per day 10am-1:30pm, Su 10am; €5.40). **261**

MENORCA

Menorca's 200km coastline of raw beaches, rustic landscapes, and well-preserved ancient monuments draws ecologists, photographers, and wealthy young families. Unfortunately, the island's unique qualities and ritzy patrons have resulted in elevated prices. The nightlife here is quieter than in its more rambunctious neighbors. Perched atop a steep bluff, **Mahón** (pop. 25,000) is the main gateway to the island.

TRANSPORTATION

Flights: Airport (☎97 115 70 00), 7km out of town. **Iberia/Aviaco** (☎97 136 90 15); **Air Europa** (☎97 124 00 42 or 97 115 70 31); **SpanAir** (☎97 115 70 98). In summer advance booking is essential.

Ferries: Estació Marítima (☎97 136 60 50), on Moll Andén de Ponent. Open M-F 8am-1pm and 5-7pm, Sa 8am-noon, Su 8-10:30am and 3:30-5:15pm. **Trasmediterránea** (☎97 136 29 50) sends ferries daily to Barcelona.

Buses: Check the tourist office or the newspapers *Menorca Diario Insular* and *Menorca* for schedules. There is no central bus station; buses stop around Pl. s'Esplanada. **Transportes Menorca (TMSA),** C. José M. Quadrado, 7 (☎97 136 03 61), off Pl. s'Esplanada. Check schedules for Sunday service. To: **Ciutadella** via **Ferreries** and **Es Mercadal** (1hr., 6 per day 8am-7pm, €3.51); **Es Castell** (every 30min. 7:45am-8:45pm, €0.87); **Platja Punta Prima** (9 per day 8:30am-7:30pm, €1.02); **Son Bou** (7 per day 8:45am-7pm, €1.65). Some depart from Pl. s'Esplanada, some from nearby C. Quadrado; check signs at the bus stop. Tickets available when boarding the bus or at office on C. Quadrado. **Autobuses Fornells Roca Triay** (☎97 137 66 21) buses depart from C. Vassallo, off Pl. s'Esplanada, to: **Arenal d'en Castell** (7 per day 9:30am-7pm); **Es Grau** (4 per day 10am-6:15pm); **Fornells** (4 per day 11am-7pm); **Son Parc** (3 per day 1-7pm). Buy tickets on board.

Taxis: Main stop at Pl. s'Esplanada (☎97 136 12 83), or call **Radio Taxi** from anywhere on the island (☎97 136 71 11).

Car Rental: Autos Menorsur, C. Luna, 23 (☎97 136 56 66), off C. Hannóver. July-Aug. €36 per day, €180 per week; substantial discounts in low season. English spoken. Open M-F 9am-2pm and 5-9pm, Sa-Su 9am-2pm.

Bike and Scooter Rental: Motos Menorca, Moll de Levante, 35-36 (☎97 135 47 86), in Puerto de Mahón. Summer prices are higher than spring. Bicycles €9 per day, €37-42 per week. Scooters €21-27 per day, €93-150 per week. Open Apr.-Sept. daily 9:30am-1:30pm and 5-7:30pm.

ORIENTATION AND PRACTICAL INFO

Take a taxi (€7.80) between the **airport** and Mahón. To get to the heart of the city from the **ferry station**, go left (with your back to the water) about 150m, then turn right at the steps that cut through the serpentine **Costa de ses Voltes.** The steps end between Pl. Conquesta and Pl. Espanya. To reach **Pl. de s'Esplanada,** take Portal de Mar to Costa de Sa, which becomes C. Hanóver and C. Ses Moreres, and continue to the *plaça.* To reach **Pl. de la Miranda,** walk through Pl. Espanya and Pl. Carme; when you reach Pl. Princep, turn left, and Pl. Miranda is 100m ahead.

Tourist Office: Sa Rovellada de Dalt, 24 (☎97 136 37 90; fax 97 136 74 15). From Pl. s'Esplanada, head down C. Ses Moreres one block, and take the first left. English spoken. Open M-F 9am-1:30pm and 5-7pm, Sa 9am-1pm. Summer office at the airport (☎97 115 71 15) provides similar materials. Open Mar.-Oct. daily 8:30am-10:30pm.

Internet Access: Menorca Compunet, C. Vasallo, 48, four blocks from Pl. s'Esplanada. €3 per hr. Open M-F 10:30am-2pm and 4:30-7:30pm, Sa 10:30am-1pm.

Post Office: C. Bon Aire, 11-13 (☎97 135 66 34), at C. Esglésias. From Pl. s'Esplanada, take C. Moreres until it turns into C. Hanover, then take the first left. Open M-F 8:30am-8:30pm, Sa 9:30am-2pm.

Postal Code: 07703.

Port Mahón

TO FORNELLS (15km)

TO CIUTADELLA (40km), ALAIOR (20km)

TO CIUTADELLA (40km), Sta.

TO (11km)

0   200 yards
0   200 meters

PL. EIVISSA

Es Mercadal

Costa de Ponent

Fornells

Dr. Guàrdia

Ciutadella, Sta.

Escolàstica

Sta. Victòria

Sol — la Clota

Museu de Menorca (St. Francesc)

Xoriguer Gin Distillery

Aquarium

PL. D'ES MONESTIR

Moll de Ponent

Costa d'es General

Vassallo

S'Arraval

Frares

S'Arraval

Negres

Sa Rovellada de Dalt

Cardona i Orfila

PL. DE S'ESPLANADA

de ses Moreres

St. Antoni

D'es Rector Mort

St. Roc

PL. de l'Esglèsia

Isabel II

Bon Aire

Militar CONSTITUCIÓ

Gobierno

PL. CONSTITUCIÓ

Ferry Terminal

Costa d'es General

C. Sant Jordi

Hannover

Cos de sa plaça

del Rosari

BASTIÓ de San Roc

COLOM

Nou

Teatre Principal

Es Freginal

Santiago Ramón y Cajal

Verge de Gràcia

Cos de Gràcia

REAL

Portal de Mar

Santa Maria

PL. ESPANYA

PL. s'Arravaleta

Costa de Deià

PL. CONQUESTA

Voltes

Claustre del Carme

Fish Market

PL. DEL CARME

PL. DE LA MIRANDA

PL. DEL PRÍNCEP

D'Anunnzivoy

de la Infanta

d'es Comerç

de la Reina

St. Josep

Av. de Menorca

Av. Josep M. Quadrado

Vives

Lluíl

Av.

Sta. Anna

PL. ST. ROC

PL. Sta. Catalina

de la Concepció

del Carme

Costa de ses Voltes

Costa de Llevant

Sta. Cecília

St. Nicolau

PL. J. CLARET

Barcelona

Madrid

St. Sebastià

Passeig Marítim

Moll de Llevant

Av. Fort de l'Eau

Passeig Marítim

Moll de Llevant

Sailing Club

Mahón

ACCOMMODATIONS
Hostal la Isla, **3**
Hostal Orsi, **1**
Hostal-Residencia Jume, **2**

263

ACCOMMODATIONS

It's easier to find a room in Menorca than on the other islands, but it's still a good idea to call ahead, especially in July and August.

Hostal-Residencia Jume, C. Concepció, 6 (☎97 136 32 66; fax 97 136 48 78), off Pl. Miranda. Bright hallways lead to rather boring rooms in tip-top shape, all with full baths. Breakfast included. June-Aug. singles €18; doubles €35. Sept.-May €17.20/€32. Closed Dec. 15-Jan. 5. ❷

Hostal La Isla, C. Santa Catalina, 4 (☎/fax 97 136 64 92). Take C. Concepció from Pl. Miranda. Immaculate rooms; all with private bath. Restaurant downstairs (see **Food,** below) has a cheap, typical *menú*. Singles €15, with breakfast €18; doubles €30, with breakfast €34. MC/V. ❷

Hostal Orsi, C. Infanta, 19 (☎97 136 47 51). From Pl. s'Esplanada, take C. Moreres as it becomes C. Hanover. Turn right at Pl. Constitució and follow C. Nou through Pl. Reial; Orsi is on the left. Friendly American expats keep clean rooms. Owners aren't always in, so call before arriving. Breakfast included. Laundry €6. Singles €15-21; doubles €26-35, with shower €30-42. MC/V. ❸

FOOD

Cafe-bars around Pl. Constitució, Reial, and s'Esplanada serve *platos combinados* (€2.70-5.10) to sidewalks of hungry customers, though the majority of tourists head to the scenic restaurants on the port, where prices match the atmosphere. Seafood is a big hit among chefs here, but restaurants serve myriad other favorites. Regional specialties include *sobrassada* (soft sausage spread), *crespells* (biscuits), and *rubiols* (turnovers filled with fish or vegetables). *Mahónesa* (mayonnaise), which was invented on the island, is popular in many of the more exotic dishes. There is a produce **market** in the cloister of the church in Pl. Espanya (open M-Sa 9am-2pm). **Groceries** are sold below the produce market at **Eurospar** (open M-Sa 8am-8pm) and at **Miny Prix,** C. J.A. Clavé and Av. Menorca (open M-Sa 8am-2pm and 5-8:30pm). **Grand General Delicatessen ❶,** Moll de Llevant, 319, has fresh, cheap vegetarian dishes, fish and meat entrees, and Italian sandwiches. The 20min. walk from the port is well worth it. (Sandwiches €1.50-2.10, entrees €3.90-6. Open daily noon-midnight.) In town, **La Oca ❷,** C. Sa'Ravaleta, 27, off Pl. del Carme, serves reasonably priced pizzas (€5.65-7.50) and pastas (€7-10) in a pleasant atmosphere. (☎97 135 37 45. Open daily 1-4pm and 6-11pm.)

SIGHTS

The most awe-inspiring sights in Menorca lie outside of its cities, although Mahón does have a few attractions. The **Museo de Menorca,** Av. Dr. Guàrdia, an old Franciscan monastery closed in 1835, displays excavated items and exhibits on Menorcan history dating back to Talayotic times. (☎97 135 09 55. Open Tu-Su 10am-2pm and 5-8pm. €1.80.) Founded in 1287 and rebuilt in 1772, the **Església de Santa María La Major** trembles from the 51 stops, four keyboards, and 3210 pipes of its über-organ, built by the Swiss Juan Kilburz in 1810. Mahón's **Festival de Música de Maó** in July and August showcases the immense instrument. (Pl. Constitució. Festival concerts start at 9:30pm; see tourist office for upcoming events. Seat "donation" €3.) The **Arc de Sant Roc,** up C. Sant Roc from Pl. Constitució, the last fragment of the medieval wall built to defend the city from marauding Catalan pirates, straddles the streets of Mahón. You can get sauced off free liquor samples at the **Xoriguer Gin Distillery** on the port. Through glass windows at the back of the store, visitors watch their drinks bubble and froth in large copper vats. (☎97 136 21 97. Open M-F 8am-7pm, Sa 9am-1pm.) Mahón is close to numerous **archeological sites,** including prehistoric caves, settlements, and monuments, but they are only accessible by car; see the tourist office for information on a self-guided driving tour. Perhaps the most famous of these monuments is **Torre d'en Galmes**, off the road to Platges de Son Bou from Alaior. Perched atop a hill overlooking the island's interior, this Talayotic city from 1400 BC served as a religious and commercial center for Menorca's original inhabitants. Many of the monuments have yet to be fully excavated and seem to be nothing more than piles of disorganized rubble. One exception of special interest is the eerie **Sala Hipostila**, a prehistoric house whose roof is suspended by columns which are narrower at their bases than at their crowns. (Open daily 10am-8pm. €1.80.)

NIGHTLIFE AND ENTERTAINMENT

Mahón is not known for its nightlife. Weekdays are quiet except in August. A string of *bares-musicales* line the **Costa d'els Generals** near the water. The colorful, lively **Tse Tse Bar,** Moll de Ponent, 14, fills nightly with a young, energetic 18-20 year-olds eager to take advantage of the ample dance floor. An upstairs terrace with a bar has an unbeatable view of the harbor. (Beer €2.40, mixed drinks €4.80. Open daily 10pm-4am; in winter Th-Sa 10pm-4am.) One of the more fashionable places on the strip is **Akelarre**, a spacious, trendy bar and jazz and dance club. Dancing begins at midnight, while occasional free jazz concerts start earlier. A mixed straight and gay crowd fills the dance floors upstairs. (Open daily June-Oct. 8am-5am; Nov.-May 7:30pm-4am. Live music W-Th 11pm-2am. No cover.) Away from the port, **Discoteca Sí,** C. Virgen de Grácia, 16, turns on the strobelight only after midnight, while **Nou Bar,** C. Nou, 1, 2nd fl., serves drinks to a calm, older crowd. (Open daily noon-3pm and 7:30pm-3am.)

From May to September, merchants sell shoes, clothes, and souvenirs in **mercadillos** held daily in various town squares (Tu and Sa Mahón; F and Sa Ciutadella; Th Alaior; Su Mercadal; Tu and F Ferrerias; M and W Es Castell). On July 16, Mahón's **Verge del Carme** celebration brings a colorfully trimmed armada into the harbor.

DAYTRIPS FROM MAHÓN

The coves and beaches near Mahón are best explored with a rental car and the *Let's Go to the Beach* brochure and map available at the tourist office. Though the highway from Mahón to Ciutadella is straight and well-maintained, the local roads are curvy, pot-holed, and oftentimes unpaved. Take caution if driving here at night.

THE NORTH SHORE

ARENAL D'EN CASTELL. Breathtaking views, calm water, and packed sands make this tiny cove a popular destination for daytrippers from Mahón and the vacationing families who populate the upscale resorts and condos above the beach. From the bus stop in Arenal, the "Arenal Na Macaret Express" tourist train makes the short trip across a narrow strip of land to **Macaret,** a tiny fishing village with an even tinier beach. (Autocares Fornells buses leave from C. Vasallo in Mahón. 30min.; M-Sa 7 per day 9:30am-7pm, Su 11am and 7pm; €1.59.)

ES GRAU. A large natural reserve, Albufera Es Grau entices visitors with lagoons, pine woods, and farmland, as well as diverse flora and fauna. Recreational activities include hiking to the coves across the bay. The best swimming areas are across from the main lagoon and uphill from the town, along a series of bluffs that form secluded coves where only the sound of the clear water lapping at the rocks can be heard. **Illa d'en Colom,** a tiny island with more beaches, is a boat ride away. **Viajes Isla Colom** sends four boats per day (☎971 35 98 67; 10:30am-5pm, last boat returns at 7pm) from the marina on the lagoon in Es Grau to the island. (Autocares Fornells buses leave from C. Vasallo in Mahón. 20min., 4 per day 10am-6:15pm, €1.02.)

CAP DE CAVALLERIA. Off the main road to Fornells, along a lonely, windswept highway that is more frequently used by goats than tourists, is the breathtaking landscape of Cap de Cavalleria. With a striking resemblance to parts of the British Isles, the green hills dotted with medieval ruins lead to a series of white limestone cliffs crowned by a beautiful lighthouse overlooking the deep blue water below. Though there are several beaches along the cape, it is best to come here for a relaxing picnic on the seaside bluffs or to watch the sun dip down into the sea from the lighthouse. To get to the lighthouse of Cap de Cavalleria, you must pass a gate which warns against trespassing. Disregard this sign (it is merely to deter the tourist hordes from ruining the pristine, rugged beauty of the place), and remember to close the gate behind you as you enter or exit.

THE SOUTH SHORE

■ PLATGES DE SON BOU. The longest beach on the island, Son Bou offers 4km of sand on the southern shore, covered with throngs of sunburned tourists. The most popular of Menorca's beaches, it is also the most visitor-friendly, with frequent bus service to and from Mahón and Ciutadella, beach chairs and umbrellas for rent, cafes, and even *discotecas* two blocks from the sand. Be aware, though, that part of the beach is for nudists, and the farther you walk away from the commercial center, the more naked it gets. **Disco/Bar Copacabana,** in the Nuevo Centro Comercial, on the left when heading away from the water, is the best place to rock your evening while enjoying a great view of the water. (No cover. Open May-Oct. daily 11pm-3:30am.) If you're just in the mood for a relaxing frozen drink, head across the street to the big rattan chairs and couches of **Bou Hai Hawaiian Bar,** which serves margaritas and daiquiris for €5.50. (Open daily 4pm-3am.) Make sure you have a rental car or a place to stay—there is no public transportation back to Mahón until the morning. (Transportes Menorca buses leave from C. Josep Quadrado, on the corner of Pl. s'Esplanada in Mahón to the beaches. 30min., 7 per day 8:45am-7pm, €1.65.)

CALEN PORTER. Expansive and extremely touristy, Calen Porter greets thousands of visitors each summer with its gleaming whitewashed houses, orange stucco roofs, and red sidewalks. Its small but well-used beach lies at the bottom of a steep, bouldered hillside, but pedestrian access is easy via the main road and a marked staircase. A 10min. walk away, the ■ **Covas d'en Xoroi** caves dominate cliffs high above the sea. A popular disco (which attracts a largely young British crowd) rules the night. (☎971 37 72 36. Foam parties every Th. Cover for bars €3.50, includes one drink. Cover for disco €15. Bars open Apr.-Oct. daily 10:30am-9pm, disco opens at 11pm.) The cove is inhabited by a network of bars by day. (TMSA buses run to and from C. Josep Quadrado, on the corner of Pl. s'Esplanada in Mahón. 7 per day 9:30am-7:30pm, €1.02.)

PUNTA PRIMA. While this popular beach may not be as secluded or expansive as some of the island's others, it draws a crowd with its proximity to Mahón, shallow waters, and local atmosphere. A lighthouse on a narrow strip of land across from the beach overlooks the coastline. (TMSA buses run to and from Pl. s'Esplanada in Mahón. 8 per day 9:30am-7:30pm, €1.02.)

ES CANUTELLS. Situated right off the road from Mahón to Cala en Porter (a 15min. drive from Mahón), Es Canutells is a pleasant and relatively secluded cove with calm, turquoise waters that make for good swimming and snorkeling. A couple of bars and restaurants lie on the road above the cove. (Es Canutells cannot be reached by public transportation.)

CALASCOVES. Past Es Canutells and off the road from Mahón to Cala en Porter (a 20min. drive from Mahón), this pristine serpentine cove has rocky cliffs and a small beach whose turquoise waters create a most refreshing swim. Equally refreshing is this area's lack of tourist inundation. (Calascoves cannot be reached by public transportation. Leave your car at the top of the hill, and continue down the dirt path for about 20min. until you reach the rocky part of the cove. The beach is over the cliffs to your right.)

CALA MITJANA AND CALA MITJANETA. This beach overlooks a dramatic cove bordered by white limestone cliffs that plunge into the turquoise sea. Though it's not totally secluded, if you climb the staircase on your right upon entering the cove and head down the dirt path for about 5min., you get to **Cala Mitjaneta**, a smaller cove that affords even more dramatic views of the limestone cliffs and the wide expanse of the Mediterranean beyond the inlet. While some wade into the water here, others prove their bravery (or recklessness) by diving from the rocks. (On the main highway from Mahón to Ciutadella, head toward Ferreries, and then take the road to Santa Galdana. Directly on your left before reaching the roundabout above the town is the dirt road that leads to **Cala Mitjana**, a 30min. drive from Mahón. Park your car in the small dirt lot and continue on foot to the small beach.)

IBIZA

EIVISSA (IBIZA CITY)

Perhaps nowhere on Earth does style rule over substance more than on the island of Ibiza (pop. 84,000). **Eivissa** (Ibiza City; pop. 35,000) is the world's biggest 24-hour party. The town itself is like Dr. Jekyll and Mr. Hyde. During the day, families meander and sightsee through the walled Dalt Vila, and it could easily be mistaken for any other seaside village in Spain. At night, however, there's no mistaking this town for any other. Disco fiends, high-fashion gurus, movie stars, and party-hungry backpackers arrive in droves to debauch in the island's outrageous, sex- and substance-driven summer culture. Flashy bars appear seemingly out of nowhere, filling street after street with neon lights, blasting music, and fast-talking club promoters. Come 3am, the scene migrates to the clubs, where parties last until dawn—and often well into the next day...then it all begins again. Although a thriving gay community still lends credence to its image as a center of "tolerance," the island's high price tags preclude economic diversity. As shocking as it may sound, there is more to Ibiza than just nightlife—its beaches and mountains are some of the most spectacular in the Balearics.

TRANSPORTATION

Flights: Airport (☎97 180 90 00), 7km south of the city. Bus #10 runs between the airport and Av. Isidor Macabich, 20, in town (30min., every hr. 7:30am-10:30pm, €0.75). Information booth open 24hr. for tickets and reservations. **Iberia,** Pg. Vara de Rey, 15 (☎902 40 05 00 or 97 130 03 00), has flights to Barcelona. Both **Air Europa** and **Spanair** offer similar options.

Ferries: Estació Marítima, at the end of Av. Bartolomé Rosselló. Across from the tourist office. To get to the city center and bus stop from the waterfront, take Av. Bartolomé Rosselló, which becomes Av. Isidor Macabich. **Trasmediterránea** (☎97 131 51 00) sells tickets at Estació Marítima. **Umafisa Lines** (☎97 121 02 01) sends ferries to and from Barcelona 3-4 times per week. **Trasmapi-Balearia** (☎97 131 40 05) runs between Eivissa and Palma.

Buses: The bus system in Ibiza is much more organized than those of her Balearic sisters. The 3 main stops in Eivissa are Av. Isidor Macabich, 42; Av. Isidor Macabich, 20; and Av. Espanya (Voramar buses). For an exact schedule, check the tourist office or *El Diario de Ibiza*. Buses to the beaches cost €0.75 and leave from Av. Isidor Macabich, 20.

Taxis: ☎97 130 70 00 or 97 130 66 02.

Car and Motorbike Rental: Casa Valentín, Av. B.V. Ramón, 19 (☎97 131 08 22), the street parallel to Pg. Vara de Rey. Mopeds €18-30 per day. Cars from €39. Open daily 9am-1pm and 3:30-8:30pm.

PRACTICAL INFORMATION

Three distinct sections make up Eivissa. **Sa Penya,** in front of Estació Marítima, is mobbed with bars and boutiques. Atop the hill behind Sa Penya, high walls circle **Dalt Vila,** the old city. **Sa Marina** and the commercial district occupy the gridded streets to the far right (with your back to the water) of the Estació. **Av. Espanya,** continuing from Po. Vara de Rey, heads toward the airport and local beaches. The local paper *Diario de Ibiza* (www.diariodeibiza.es; €0.75) features an *Agenda* page with everything you need to know about the island.

Tourist Office: C. Antoni Riquer, 2 (☎97 130 19 00; www.ibizaonline.com), across from where the ferries come in. Open M-F 9:30am-1:30pm and 5-8pm, Sa 10:30am-1pm. Also a **booth** at the airport arrival terminal (☎97 180 91 18; fax 97 180 91 32). Open May-Oct. M-Sa 9am-2pm and 3-8pm, Su 9am-2pm.

Laundromat: Wash and Dry, Av. España, 53 (☎97 139 48 22). Wash and dry €4.20 each. Internet access €5.40 per hr. Open M-F 10am-3pm and 5-10pm, Sa 10am-5pm.

Emergency: ☎112. **Police:** (☎97 131 58 61) C. Vicent Serra.

Internet Access: Centro Internet Eivissa, Av. Ignacio Wallis, 39 (☎97 131 81 61). €3 per hr. Open M-Sa 10am-midnight, Su 5pm-midnight. **Ciber Matic,** C. Cayetano Soler, 3 (☎97 130 33 82), off Pl. Parc. €1.80 per 30min., €3 per hr. Open M-Sa 10am-11pm. Also at **Wash and Dry** (see above).

Post Office: (☎97 131 43 23) Av. Isidor Macabich. With your back to the port, follow Av. Isidor Macabich to its end. **Lista de Correos.** Open M-F 8:30am-8:30pm, Sa 9:30am-2pm.

Postal Code: 07800.

ACCOMMODATIONS

Decent, cheap hostels in town are rare, especially in the summer. Call several weeks in advance for summer stays, when prices climb and hostels fill fast. Eivissa has a relatively safe and up-all-night lifestyle, and owners offer keys for 24hr. entry. All prices listed below are for high-season and can drop by as much as €12 in the off-season. The tourist office offers an extensive list of all the lodging options available in the city. If all else fails, nearby San Antonio offers cheap accommodations and is well-connected to Eivissa through public transportation (see p. 272).

Hostal Residencia Sol y Brisa, Av. B. V. Ramón, 15 (☎97 131 08 18; fax 97 130 30 32), parallel to Pg. Vara de Rey. Upstairs from Pizzeria da Franco (signs point the way to the pizzeria). Clean and in a central location, but rooms are sweltering hot in summer. Very social atmosphere. Singles €21, doubles €36. ❷

Hostal La Marina, C. Barcelona, 7, Puerto de Ibiza (☎97 131 01 72; fax 97 131 48 94), across from Estació Marítima and right in the middle of the raucous bar scene. Don't stay here if you plan on going to bed before the wee hours of the morning. 4 buildings offer different levels of lodging, ranging from stark to plush. The best (and most expensive) have TV, A/C, private bath, carpeting, and balcony. Singles €27-48, doubles €42-96. ❸

Hostal Residencia Ripoll, C. Vicente Cuervo, 14 (☎97 131 42 75). Fastidiously clean hallways and bathrooms and unusually large, fan-cooled rooms are among the best in town. The singles are a bit pricey though. July-Sept. singles €27; doubles €39; 3-person apartments with TV, patio, and kitchen €72. ❸

Hostal Parque, Pl. del Parque, 4 (☎97 130 13 58). Located in a pleasant square close to the Dalt Vila, Hostal Parque offers expensive but spotless rooms and an attentive staff. July-Sept. singles €48; doubles with bath €100; triples with bath €135. Prices drop Oct.-July. ❹

Hostal Juanito and Hostal Las Nieves, C. Juan de Austria, 17-18 (☎97 119 03 19). Run by the same owner, both hostels offer cheap housing in a central area. Rooms are basic and bare-walled, but more than adequate for sleeping off a hangover. Singles €21; doubles €42, with bath €45. ❷

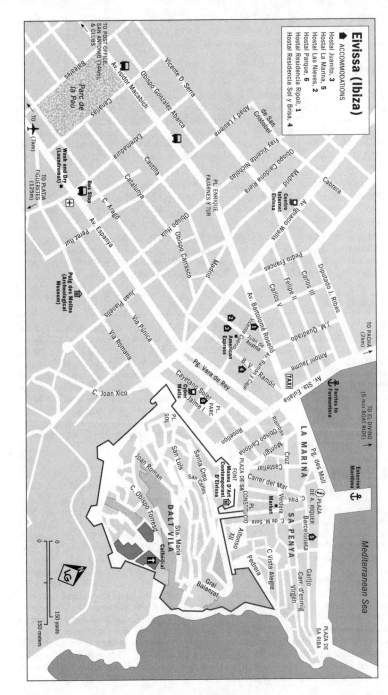

Eivissa (Ibiza)

ACCOMMODATIONS

Hostal Juanito, **3**
Hostal La Marina, **5**
Hostal Las Nieves, **2**
Hostal Parque, **6**
Hostal Residencia Ripoll, **1**
Hostal Residencia Sol y Brisa, **4**

Camping: **Es Cana** (☎97 133 21 17; fax 97 133 99 71). Reserve via fax. €3 per person, €1.80 per site, €2.70 to rent a tent. Bungalow €14. **Cala Nova** (☎97 133 17 74). €3 per person, €2.85 per tent. Both sites close to Sta. Eulária del Río. ❶

FOOD

Inexpensive cuisine is hard to find. Ibizan dishes worth hunting down are *sofrit pagès*, a deep-fried lamb and chicken dish; *flao*, a lush lemon- and mint-tinged cheesecake; and *graxonera*, cinnamon-dusted pudding made from eggs and bits of *ensaimada* (candied bread). The **market** at C. Extremadura and C. Canarias sells meat, fruits, and vegetables (open M-Sa 7am-1pm). For **groceries,** try **Hiper Centro,** C. Ignacio Wallis, near C. Juan de Austria. (☎97 119 20 41. Open M-Sa 9am-2pm and 5-9pm.)

🦑 **Mama Pat's Curry y Más,** C. Espanya, 43. Not only does Mama Pat's have some of the cheapest food around, it also has some of the most creative. Authentic Caribbean cuisine or awesome chicken, veggie, and lamb curry entrees (€6-9). Vegetarian options. *Menú* €6. Open M-Sa 8am-3am. ❷

Restaurante La Oliva, C. Santa Cruz, 2 (☎97 130 57 52). Situated on a crowded street in the lower part of the Dalt Vila. Serves pricey but delicious Italian fare to the island's jet-set. Grab a candle-lit outdoor table and enjoy some people-watching as you wait for your meal. Pasta €5-7, meat and fish entrees €9-18. Open daily 8pm-1am. ❸

SIGHTS

Wrapped in 16th-century walls, the **Dalt Vila** (High Town) rises gracefully above the town. Its twisting streets lead to the 14th-century **Cathedral,** built in several phases and styles. (Open daily 10:30am-1pm.) Next to the Cathedral stands the **Museu Arqueològic D'Eivissa,** home to a variety of regional artifacts. (Open Tu-Sa 10am-1pm and 5-10pm, Su 10am-2pm. €1.80, students €0.90.) Amid stone walls, the small **Museu D'Art Contemporani D'Eivissa** displays a wide range of art exhibitions. (C. Sa Carrosa, on the left when entering through Dalt Vila's main entrance. ☎97 130 27 23. Open M-F 10am-1:30pm and 5-8pm, Sa 10am-1:30pm. €1.20, students free.) The archaeological museum, **Puig des Molins,** Vía Romana, displays Punic, Roman, and Iberian artifacts. Adjoining the Puig is the Punic-Roman **necropolis.** (Both open M-Sa 10am-2pm and 5-8pm, Su 10am-2pm. €1.20.)

BEACHES

The power of the rising sun draws thousands of topless solar zombies to nearby tanning grounds. **Platja Figueretes,** a thin stretch of sand in the shadow of large hotels, is the best foot-accessible beach from Eivissa. To get there, walk down Av. Espanya for about 10min., and take a left on C. Juan Ramón Jiménez. Farther down, **Platja d'en Bossa** is the liveliest of Ibiza's beaches, home to numerous beach bars, as well as throngs of sun-seeking tourists. **Platja des Duros** is tucked across the bay from Sa Penya and Sa Marina, just before the lighthouse. At **Platja de Talamanca,** the water—more an enclosed bay than open sea—is accessible on foot by following the road to the new port and continuing to the beach (20min.). **Platja de ses Salinas** is one of Ibiza's most popular and famous beaches, although others are actually more scenic. Bask among the beautiful people, and groove to the house music pulsating from **Sa Trincha** bar at the end of the beach. Neighboring **Platja des Cavallet** is clothing-optional and attracts a beautiful and largely gay crowd. To get to both, take the bus from Eivissa to Salinas; for Es Cavallet, get off at the stop before Salinas (look for the T-intersection to the left or just ask the bus driver) and walk to the beach (10min.) or just walk from Salinas (20min.).

More private coastal stretches lie in the northern part of the island and are accessible by car or scooter. Among these, the German enclave at **Cala de Sant Vicent** (past Santa Eularia on the road to St. Carles de Peralta) offers white sands and breathtaking views that are far from secluded, but peaceful nonetheless. The small coves in the rocky northernmost point of the island (between Portinatx and St. Agnes de Corona) are worth visiting if you seek serenity or the company of modern-day flower children. **Cala Xarraca** is a beautiful EU *bandera azul* cove, popular with families who fight for spots on its small beach. Quite possibly the most dramatic views on the island are those from **Cap Rubio**. On the road from Sant Miquel to Sant Mateu, take the left fork up a semi-paved road; the road rises and then drops suddenly to a rocky path, which leads to impressive limestone cliffs. Hike down to any of the coves at the bottom of the paths next to the abandoned mine shafts, and you'll be rewarded with your own private swimming hole.

NIGHTLIFE

The crowds return from the beaches by nightfall, an hour when even the stores dazzle with throbbing techno and flashing lights. Herds of men and women representing each club parade through the streets, advertising their disco and trying to outdo others. **Bars** in Eivissa are crowded between midnight and 3am and are everyone's first stop before hitting the discos. The scene centers around **C. Barcelona** and spins outward from there into the sidestreets. **C. Virgen** is the center of gay nightlife and utterly outrageous fashion.

The island's ⊠**discos** (virtually all have a mixed gay/straight crowd) are world-famous—veterans claim that you will never experience anything half as wild or fun. The best sources of information are disco-goers and the zillions of posters that plaster the stores and restaurants of Sa Marina and Sa Penya. There is something different each day of the week, and each club is known for a particular theme party—be sure to hit up a club on a popular night, or you'll end up shelling out a lot of money for a not-so-happening party. For listings, check out *Ministry in Ibiza* or *DJ*, free at many hostels, bars, and restaurants. Drinks at Ibiza's clubs cost about €10 and covers start at €30. If you know where you're going ahead of time, buy your disco tickets from a promoter at or in front of the bars in town; you'll save anywhere from €6-18 off what you would pay at the door, and it's legit. Generally, disco-goers bar-hop in Eivissa and jet off to clubs via bus or taxi around 3am. The **Discobus** runs to all the major hotspots (leaves Eivissa from Av. Isidoro Macabich every hr. 12:30am-6:30am, schedule for other stops available at tourist office and hotels; €1.50).

⊠ **Privilege,** on the Discobus to San Antonio or a €9 taxi from Eivissa. The world's largest club, according to the Guinness Book of World Records. This enormous complex packs in up to 30,000 partiers and has everything from double-digit bars to a stage set in a pool for bizarre acrobatics. *The* place to be on M for its world-infamous "Manumission" parties. Though the live sex shows of years past have stopped, "Manumission" is still the hottest night in Ibiza. Cover €30-48, includes 1 drink. Open June-Sept. daily midnight-7am. V.

Pachá, a 5min. walk from the port, 2min. in a cab. The most famous club chain in Spain, and the most elegant of Ibiza's discos. F night's "Ministry of Sound" party brings the biggest crowd. The "Made in Italy" night on Th is, not surprisingly, very popular with Italian tourists. The only club in Ibiza open year-round. Cover €30-42. Open daily midnight-7:30am.

Amnesia, take the Discobus to San Antonio. Converted warehouse with psychedelic lights and movie screens has two gigantic rooms; a largely gay crowd tends to congregate in the one to the left of the entrance. Legendary foam parties Su and W. Best known for its Cream and MTV Dance Presents parties on Th, when London DJs play hard house or trance. Cover €30-42. Open daily midnight-7am.

Space, Platja d'en Bossa. Starts hopping around 8am, peaks mid-afternoon, and doesn't wind down until past 5pm. The metallic get-up and techno music is almost as hardcore as the dancers. An outdoor dance terrace has a more low-key atmosphere. Known for its Su morning show, Sa-Tu mornings are all popular too. Hosts the official after-parties for "Ministry of Sound" at Pachá, "Manumission" at Privilege, and "La Troya Asesina" (the infamous drag-queen party) at Amnesia. Cover €30 and up.

Eden, C. Salvador Espíritu, across from the beach in San Antonio. Gaining in popularity, Eden pulls out all the stops for "Judgement Sunday," when DJ Judge Jules attracts huge crowds. Popular among British visitors. Retro nights on Tu feature house from the past decade. Cover €30-42. Open daily midnight-7am.

El Divino, Puerto Ibiza Nueva. Small but energetic, this terraced club right on the water over-looking Eivissa is worth coming to just for the view, although the exotic dancers, thumping house, and lively crowd aren't too shabby either. Spanish crowd. El Divino fliers serve as free passes for the disco shuttle boat—otherwise, it costs €0.90 one-way. Cover €30. Open mid-June to mid-Sept. daily midnight-6am.

SAN ANTONIO

Every summer, masses of young Brits migrate to San Antonio. The rowdy nightlife and down-to-earth atmosphere combined with its proximity to some of the island's best beaches have turned the town into a twenty-something enclave. With two clubs, plenty of bars, and cheaper food and accommodations than in Eivissa, San Antonio provides the perfect budget alternatives to its sister city's high prices and lifestyle.

TRANSPORTATION AND PRACTICAL INFO

San Antonio is connected to the rest of the island by the **buses** from Pg. Mar. Buses go to: **Cala Bassa** (10min., 8 per day 9:30am-6:30pm, €1); **Cala Conta** (15min., 7 per day 9:10am-6pm, €1); **Cala Tarida** (10min., 8 per day 9:30am-6:30pm, €1); **Eivissa** (25min.; every 30min. M-Sa 7-9:30am and 10-11:30pm, every 15min. 9:45am-9:30pm, Su every 30min. 7:30am-10:30pm; €1.35); and **Santa Eulária** (35min., M-Sa 4 per day 10:15am-6:45pm; €1). Smaller companies run daily **boats** to nearby beaches. Signs posted daily along the port have schedules. For a **taxi,** call ☎97 134 07 79. San Antonio is very easy to get around, as major streets lie on something of a grid. For **car** and **moped rental,** try **Motos Luis,** Av. Portmany, 5. (☎97 134 05 21. Mopeds €20 and up. Cars €38 and up. Open M-Sa 9am-2pm and 4-8pm, Su 9am-2pm.) The **tourist office** is a stone building in the middle of the pedestrian thoroughfare by Pg. Fonts. (☎97 134 33 63. Open M-F 9:30am-2:30pm and 3-8:30pm, Sa 9am-1pm, Su 9:30am-1:30pm.) In an **emergency,** call ☎112 or the **police,** Av. Portmany, km 14 (☎97 134 08 30). There is a **Centro de Salud** on C. Alicant (☎ 97 134 51 21).

ACCOMMODATIONS AND FOOD

Hostels in San Antonio, full of Brits, are numerous and cheap. In the height of summer, call well in advance for any summer stay; in the low season prices drop. **Hostal Residencia Roig ❷,** C. Progreso, 44, has gorgeous, clean rooms all with private bath. (☎97 134 04 83. Singles €21; doubles €42.) The large bedrooms, huge TV lounge, and great location make **Hostal Salada ❷,** C. Soletat, 34, one of the best bargains in town. Walk up C. Bartolomé Vicente Ramon from the port and turn left on to C. Soletat. (☎97 134 11 30. Singles €15; doubles €24; triples €30.) Another option is the more basic **Hostal Rita ❷,** C. Bartolomé Vicente Ramon, 17B. Doubles and triples have private baths; singles share common bathrooms. (☎97 134 63 32. Singles €20; doubles €39; triples €53.) **Restaurants** are everywhere in San Antonio. A variety of choices are available at the outdoor cafes along Pg. Mar or on its sidestreets leading uphill. Of the more trendy beachfront establishments, ◪**Terraza Kiwi Beach ❶,** Av. Doctor Fleming, 2-4, stands out. The orange building right on the water serves a combination of cheap sandwiches, salads, blended fruit drinks and milkshakes, as well as wide range of alcoholic favorites. (Entrees €2.40-4. Alcoholic milkshakes €5.40, non-alcoholic shakes and smoothies €2.70-4. Open daily 10am-4am.)

BEACHES AND NIGHTLIFE

The **beaches** near San Antonio are some of Ibiza's best and are fairly accessible. The town itself is situated on a long, narrow strip of sand, but better beaches are only a stone's throw away. Check out **Cala Bassa,** one of the more popular tanning spots, for a gorgeous (and sometimes nude) beach accessible by bus. **Cala Gració,** 1½km from San Antonio, is easily reached by foot. **Santa Eulária** is more built up, but it's substantially larger than some of the other beaches nearby. Hoof it or bike to the small coves of **Es Pouet** and **Caló des Moro.** If you have a car or moped, head to **Cala Salada,** just a few km north of town, for calm, beautiful waters and a picturesque hippie community. San Antonio's **nightlife** revolves largely around three main areas. The area on the far end of town, near the littered beach of Es Ganguil, has several waterfront bars. Crowds gather on the small beach to watch the **sunset** and chill to mellow house music. **Café del Mar,** "the original sunset bar," serves overpriced drinks. The chic **Cafe Mambo** is a popular pre-party bar, and, much farther down toward Calo des Moro, **Kanya** offers a lively scene. The crowded streets of town are packed with low-key watering holes and drunk pre-partiers. The clubs **Eden** and **Es Paradis Terrenal,** beach bars including the popular and upscale **M Bar,** and mini-discos facing the main beach round out the nightlife scene. Compared to the competitive club scene of Eivissa, the nightlife options in San Antonio can be much more casual and relaxed.

FORMENTERA

The tiny island of Formentera is Spain's version of island paradise. Despite the recent invasions by bourgeois, beach-hungry Germans and Italians, the island's stunning beaches maintain a sense of hypnotic calm. Join Formentera's "save our island" spirit by hiking or renting a bike—the tourist office offers a comprehensive list of "Green Tours" for hikers and cyclists, and bike paths are plentiful. The island itself is pricey, and is often visited simply as a daytrip from Ibiza.

TRANSPORTATION

Ferries at Estació Marítima, near the Burger King in Eivissa, offer transportation. **Pitra** car ferries (☎97 119 10 88), **Trasmapi-Balearia** (☎97 131 20 70), and **Umafisa** car ferries (☎97 131 45 13) all run to and from Formentera. If you're in a hurry, choose **Línea Jet's** speedy ride (25min., 16 per day 7:45am-8:30pm, €13) or ride with the trucks on the cheaper, slower mother ship (1hr.; M-Sa 9 per day 6:45am-8pm, Su 5 per day 9am-8pm; €7.95). **Buses** run from La Savina to **Es Pujols** (9 per day 8:30am-7:15pm, €1.05); **Platja de ses Illetes** (10:30am and 5pm, €0.85); **Platja Migjorn** (7 per day 9:45am-7:15pm, €1.05); **San Francisco** (12 per day 8:30am-7:15pm, €0.85). For a **taxi,** call ☎97 132 80 16. Car, scooter, and bike **rental booths** line the dock in La Savina. (Cars €30-36 per day. Scooters €18-21. Bikes €3-6.) Although all rental agencies are more or less the same, **Autos Ca María** offers friendly service and advice on routes. (☎97 132 29 21. Cars €33. Scooters €18. Bicycles €3-6. Open daily 9am-9pm. MC/V.)

ORIENTATION AND PRACTICAL INFORMATION

On the northern side of the island is the main port, **La Savina.** The main artery runs from the port (km 0) to the eastern tip, **Punta D'Esfar** (km 20). The island's "capital," **San Francisco,** off the main artery at km 3.1, has the basics but little else. **Es Pujols,** km 4, is the liveliest town on the island. All the main roads have lanes for scooters to putter along freely with bicycles. The **tourist office,** Edificio Servicios La Savina, is at the port. (☎97 132 20 57. Open M-F 10am-2pm and 5-7pm, Sa 10am-2pm.) For **police** call ☎97 132 20 22; for the **medical center** call ☎97 132 23 69. The **Postal code** is 07870.

ACCOMMODATIONS AND FOOD

Formentera offers the top shelf of hostel-living—and prices certainly reflect it. Almost all of the island's hostels are hotel-quality with attentive staff; the best of them are tucked away on their own stunning, deserted beaches. At **Hostal Costa Azul ❸**, Platja de Migjorn, km 7, serene rooms are complemented by a quiet beach. (☎97 132 80 24. Doubles before July 15 €41, after July 15 €58.) **Hostal Mayans ❺**, in Es Pujols, has spacious doubles with fridges, balconies, and large bathrooms. (☎97 132 87 24. Breakfast included. Doubles €73.) Gobble down *paella* (€7.80) at **El Mirador ❷**, km 14.3, overlooking both the island and the water. (☎97 132 70 37. Open daily 12:30-4pm and 7-11pm.) Check out the varied restaurants in Es Pujols for both *comida típica* and more international cuisine. **Supermarkets** line all the major roads.

BEACHES

To bask on Formentera's best beaches, take Av. Mediterránea from the port, turn left at the sign pointing toward Es Pujols, and take another left onto the dirt road at the sign marking Verede de Ses Salines. Paths to the right lead to **Platja de Llevant,** a long strip of fine sand. Farther up the peninsula, roads to the left lead to **Platja de Ses Illetes,** with its more popular, but rocky, swimming holes. **Platja de Migjorn,** the longest beach on the island, is slightly rocky but less crowded than others. A tourist boat also runs to Ses Illetes and Espalmador from La Savina (leaves La Savina 10:15, 11:45am, 1:15pm; returns 4:15, 5:30, 6:45pm; round-trip €9). For sailing, windsurfing, or canoeing rental try **Wet 4 Fun** on Es Pujols beach. (☎97 132 18 09. Sailboats €35.60 per hr.; windsurfing €13 per hr.; canoes €5.40 per hr., €12 per half-day.) For stunning dry-land sightseeing, those with mopeds should drive through the mountainous regions of **La Mola** to the **lighthouse** at **Far de la Mola** and **Punta de Sa Ruda** on the easternmost extreme of the island or cruise by the groves of olive trees to Cap de Barbaria just south of La Savina. Those seeking a less-touristed beach should head to **Cala Saona,** a pleasant cove on the western part of the island.

Planning Your Trip

DOCUMENTS & FORMALITIES

EMBASSIES & CONSULATES

For foreign embassies and consulates in Barcelona, check the **Service Directory** (p. 314).

SPANISH EMBASSIES & CONSULATES ABROAD

Questions concerning visas and passports go to consulates. Embassies handle weightier matters.

Australia: Embassy: 15 Arkana St., Yarralumla, ACT 2600; P.O. Box 9076, Deakin, ACT 2600 (☎02 62 73 35 55; fax 62 73 39 18). **Consulates:** Level 24, St. Martin's Tower, 31 Market St., Sydney, NSW 2000 (☎02 92 61 24 33 or 92 61 24 43; fax 92 83 16 95); 540 Elizabeth St., 4th fl., Melbourne, VIC 3000 (☎02 93 47 19 66; fax 93 47 73 30).

Canada: Embassy: 74 Stanley Ave., Ottawa, ON K1M 1P4 (☎613-747-2252; fax 744-1224). **Consulates:** 1 Westmount Sq., Suite 1456, Montreal, PQ H3Z 2P9 (☎514-935-5235; fax 935-4655); Simcoe Place, 200 Front St., Suite 2401, P.O. Box 15, Toronto, ON M5V 3K2 (☎416-977-1661; fax 593-4949).

Ireland: Embassy: 17A Merlyn Park, Ballsbridge, Dublin 4 (☎01 269 1640; fax 269 1854).

New Zealand: See **Australin Embassy,** p. 277.

South Africa: Embassy: 169 Pine St., Arcadia, P.O. Box 1633, Pretoria 0083 (☎012 344 3875; fax 343 4891). **Consulate:** 37 Shortmarket St., Cape Town 8001 (☎021 222 415; fax 222 328).

ONE EUROPE

The idea of European unity has come a long way since 1958, when the European Economic Community (EEC) was created to promote solidarity and cooperation between its six founding states. Since then, the EEC has become the European Union (EU), with political, legal, and economic institutions spanning 15 member states: Austria, Belgium, Denmark, Finland, France, Germany, Greece, Ireland, Italy, Luxembourg, The Netherlands, Portugal, Spain, Sweden, and the UK.

So what does this mean for the average non-EU tourist? In 1999 the EU established **freedom of movement** across 15 European countries—the entire EU minus Ireland and the UK, but plus Iceland and Norway. This means that border controls between participating countries have been abolished, and visa policies harmonized. While you're still required to carry a passport (or government-issued ID card for EU citizens) when crossing an internal border, once you've been admitted into one country, you're free to travel to all participating states. Britain and Ireland have also formed a common travel area, abolishing passport controls between the UK and the Republic of Ireland. This means that the only place you'll see a border guard within the EU is traveling between the British Isles and the Continent.

For more consequences of the EU for travelers, see **The Euro** (p. 282) and **EU customs regulations** (p. 280).

UK: Embassy: 39 Chesham Pl., London SW1X 8SB (☎020 7235 5555; fax 7235 9905). **Consulates:** 20 Draycott Pl., London SW3 2RZ (☎020 7589 8989; fax 7581 7888); Suite 1A, Brook House 70, Spring Gardens, Manchester M2 2BQ (☎016 1236 1262; fax 1228 7467); 63 N. Castle St., Edinburgh EH2 3LJ (☎013 1220 1843; fax 1226 4568).

US: Embassy: 2375 Pennsylvania Ave. NW, Washington, D.C. 20037 (☎202-738-2330; fax 738-2302; www.spainemb.org). **Consulates:** 150 E. 58th St., 30th fl., New York, NY 10155 (☎212 355-4080; fax 644-3751); others in Boston, Chicago, Houston, Los Angeles, Miami, New Orleans, Puerto Rico, and San Francisco.

TOURIST OFFICES

Spain's official tourist board operates an extensive website at www.tourspain.es. It also has offices in Canada, the US, and the UK.

Canada: Tourist Office of Spain, 2 Bloor St. W., Suite 3402, Toronto, ON M4W 3E2 (☎416-961-3131; fax 961-1992).

UK: Spanish Tourist Office, 22-23 Manchester Sq., London W1U 3PX (☎207 486 8077; fax 486 8034; londres@tourspain.es).

US: Tourist Office of Spain, 666 Fifth Ave., 35th fl., New York, NY 10103 (☎212-265-8822; fax 265-8864). Additional offices in Chicago, IL (☎312-642-1992), Beverly Hills, CA (☎323-658-7188), and Miami, FL (☎305-358-1992).

PASSPORTS

REQUIREMENTS

Citizens of Australia, Canada, New Zealand, South Africa, and the US need valid passports to enter Spain. For citizens of some countries, Spain does not allow entrance if the holder's passport expires in under six months; check with the appropriate consulate to see if this applies to you. Returning home with an expired passport is illegal. European Union citizens need a National Identification Card.

NEW PASSPORTS

Citizens of Australia, Canada, Ireland, New Zealand, the United Kingdom, and the United States can apply for a passport at any post office, passport office, or court of law. Citizens of South Africa can apply for a passport at any office of Foreign Affairs. Any new passport or renewal applications must be filed well in advance of the departure date, although most passport offices offer rush services for a very steep fee. Note that as of April 2002, new security measures require all US passports to be printed domestically rather than at foreign embassies and consulates, significantly extending the processing time. Temporary passports issued in cases of emergency are now limited in validity and can no longer be extended.

PASSPORT MAINTENANCE

Be sure to photocopy the page of your passport with your photo, as well as your visas, traveler's check serial numbers and any other important documents. Carry one set of copies in a safe place, apart from the originals, and leave another set at home. Consulates recommend carrying an expired passport or an official copy of your birth certificate in a part of your baggage separate from other documents.

If you lose your passport, immediately notify the local police and the nearest embassy or consulate of your home government. To expedite its replacement, you will need to know all information previously recorded and show ID and proof of citizenship. In some cases, a replacement may take weeks to process, and it may be valid only for a limited time. Any visas stamped in your old passport will be irretrievably lost. In an emergency, ask for immediate temporary traveling papers that will permit you to re-enter your home country. Lost passports may be replaced in a matter of days, quicker with a copy of the passport. Your passport is a public document belonging to your nation's government. You may have to surrender it to a foreign government official, but if you don't get it back in a reasonable amount of time, inform the nearest mission of your home country.

VISAS & WORK PERMITS

VISAS

As of August 2000, citizens of South Africa need a visa—a stamp, sticker, or insert in your passport specifying the purpose of your travel and the permitted duration of your stay—in addition to a valid passport for entrance to Spain; citizens of the Australia, Canada, the Republic of Ireland, the UK, and the US do not need visas for brief stays. All tourists need a visa for any stay of 90 days or longer in Spain.

Double-check on entrance requirements at the nearest embassy or consulate of Spain (see **Embassies & Consulates,** p. 277) for up-to-date info before departure.

WORK PERMITS

Admission as a visitor does not include the right to work, which is authorized only by a work permit. For more information, see **Working,** p. 307.

IDENTIFICATION

When you travel, always carry two or more forms of identification on your person, including at least one photo ID; a passport combined with a driver's license or birth certificate is usually adequate. Many establishments, especially banks, may require several IDs in order to cash traveler's checks; some stores in Spain require a passport if you want to use a credit card. Never carry all your forms of ID together, and keep photocopies of them in your luggage and at home.

TEACHER & STUDENT IDENTIFICATION

The **International Student Identity Card (ISIC),** the most widely accepted form of student ID, provides discounts on sights, accommodations, food, and transport; an ISIC card in Barcelona will cut admission to many museums and sights in half. All cardholders have access to a 24hr. emergency helpline (in North America call ☎877-370-ISIC (4742); elsewhere call US collect ☎1-715-345-0505) and have insurance benefits (see **Insurance,** p. 287). The ISIC is preferable to an institution-spe-

CUSTOMS IN THE EU

As well as freedom of movement of people within the EU (see p. 278), travelers in the countries that are members of the EU (Austria, Belgium, Denmark, Finland, France, Germany, Greece, Ireland, Italy, Luxembourg, The Netherlands, Portugal, Spain, Sweden, and the UK) can also take advantage of the freedom of movement of goods. This means that there are no customs controls at internal EU borders (i.e., you can take the blue customs channel at the airport), and travelers are free to transport whatever legal substances they like as long as it is for their own personal (non-commercial) use—up to 800 cigarettes, 10L of spirits, 90L of wine (60L of sparkling wine), and 110L of beer. You should also be aware that duty-free was abolished on June 30, 1999 for travel between EU member states; however, travelers between the EU and the rest of the world still get a duty-free allowance when passing through customs.

cific card (such as a university ID) because it is more likely to be recognized and honored abroad. Applicants must be degree-seeking students of a secondary or post-secondary school and must be of at least 12 years of age. Because of the proliferation of fake ISICs, some services (particularly airlines) require additional proof of student identity, such as a school ID or a letter attesting to your student status, signed by the registrar and stamped with the school seal.

The **International Teacher Identity Card (ITIC)** offers teachers the same insurance coverage as well as similar but limited discounts. For travelers who are 25 years old or under but are not students, the **International Youth Travel Card (IYTC;** formerly the **GO 25** Card) also offers many of the same benefits as the ISIC.

Each of these identity cards costs US$22 or the equivalent. ISIC and ITIC cards are valid for roughly one and a half academic years; IYTC cards are valid for one year from the date of issue. Many student travel agencies (see p. 289) issue the cards, including STA Travel in Australia and New Zealand, Travel CUTS in Canada, usit in the Republic of Ireland and Northern Ireland, SASTS in South Africa, Campus Travel and STA Travel in the UK, and Council Travel and STA Travel in the US. For a listing of issuing agencies, or for more information, contact the **International Student Travel Confederation (ISTC)**, Herengracht 479, 1017 BS Amsterdam, Netherlands (☎31 20 421 28 00; fax 421 28 10; istcinfo@istc.org; www.istc.org).

CUSTOMS

Upon entering Spain, you must declare certain items from abroad and pay a duty on the value of those articles that exceeds the allowance established by Spain's customs service. Goods and gifts purchased at duty-free shops abroad are not exempt from duty or sales tax at your point of return and thus must be declared as well; "duty-free" merely means that you need not pay a tax in the country of purchase. Duty-free allowances were abolished for travel between EU member states on July 1, 1999 (see **Customs in the EU,** p. 280), but still exist for those arriving from outside the EU. Upon returning home, you must similarly declare all articles acquired abroad and pay a duty on the value of articles in excess of your home country's allowance. In order to expedite your return, make a list of any valuables brought from home and register them with customs before traveling abroad. Also be sure to keep receipts for all major purchases abroad.

MONEY

CURRENCY & EXCHANGE

The currency chart below is based on August 2002 exchange rates between local currency and Australian dollars (AUS$), Canadian dollars (CDN$), Irish pounds (IR£), New Zealand dollars (NZ$), South African rand (ZAR), British pounds (UK£), and US dollars (US$). Check the currency converter on financial websites such as www.bloomburg.com and www.xe.com, or a large newspaper for the latest exchange rates.

EUROS (EUR€)		
AUS$1 = EUR€0.61		EUR€1 = AUS$1.65
CDN$1 = EUR€0.69		EUR€1 = CDN$1.45
IR£1 = EUR€1.27		EUR€1 = IR£0.79
NZ$1 = EUR€0.52		EUR€1 = NZ$1.93
ZAR1 = EUR€0.11		EUR€1 = ZAR9.25
US$1 = EUR€1.06		EUR€1 = US$0.94
UK£1 = EUR€1.54		EUR€1 = UK£0.65

As a general rule, it's cheaper to convert money in Spain than at home. However, you should bring enough foreign currency to last for the first 24 to 72 hours of a trip to avoid being penniless should you arrive after bank hours or on a holiday. Travelers from the US can get foreign currency from the comfort of home: **International Currency Express** (☎ 888-278-6628) delivers foreign currency or traveler's checks second-day (US$12) at competitive exchange rates.

When changing money, go to banks or *casas de cambio* that have at most a 5% margin between their buy and sell prices. Since you lose money with every transaction, **convert large sums, but no more than you'll need.**

If you use traveler's checks or cash, carry some in small denominations (the equivalent of US$50 or less) for times when you are forced to exchange money at disadvantageous rates, but bring a range of denominations since charges may be levied per check cashed. Store your money in a variety of forms; ideally, at any given time you will be carrying some cash, some traveler's checks, and an ATM and/or credit card. All travelers should also consider carrying some US dollars (about US$50 worth), which are often preferred by local tellers.

TRAVELER'S CHECKS

Traveler's checks, one of the safest and least troublesome means of carrying funds, are readily accepted in Barcelona. American Express and Visa are the most widely recognized brands. Many banks and agencies sell them for a small commission. Check issuers provide refunds if the checks are lost or stolen, and many provide additional services, such as toll-free refund hotlines abroad, emergency message services, and stolen credit card assistance. Ask about toll-free refund hotlines and the location of refund centers when purchasing checks, and always carry emergency cash.

American Express: Checks available with commission at select banks and all AmEx offices. US residents can also purchase checks by phone (☎ 888-887-8986) or online (www.aexp.com). Checks available in American, Australian, British, Canadian, Euro, and Japanese currencies. *Cheques for Two* can be signed by either of 2 people traveling together. For purchase locations or more information contact AmEx's service centers: in Barcelona ☎ 93 301 1166; in Australia ☎ 800 25 19 02; in New Zealand 0800 441 068; in the UK ☎ 0800 521 313; in the US and Canada ☎ 800-221-7282; elsewhere US collect ☎ 801-964-6665.

THE EURO

The official currency of 12 members of the European Union—Austria, Belgium, Finland, France, Germany, Greece, Ireland, Italy, Luxembourg, The Netherlands, Portugal, and Spain—is now the euro.

The currency has some important—and positive—consequences for travelers hitting more than one euro-zone country. For one thing, money-changers across the euro-zone are obliged to exchange money at the official, fixed rate (see the **Currency Chart,** p. 281), and at no commission (though they may still charge a small service fee). Second, euro-denominated traveler's checks allow you to pay for goods and services across the euro-zone, again at the official rate and commission-free.

Visa: Checks available (generally with commission) at banks worldwide. For the location of the nearest office, call Visa's service centers: in the US ☎800-227-6811; in the UK ☎0800 89 50 78; elsewhere UK collect ☎020 7937 8091. Checks available in American, British, Canadian, Japanese, and Euro currencies. To report lost or stolen checks in Spain, or to find the location of their nearest office, call ☎900 974 414.

Travelex/Thomas Cook: In the US and Canada call ☎800-287-7362; in the UK call ☎0800 62 21 01; elsewhere call UK collect ☎1733 31 89 50.

CREDIT, DEBIT, AND ATM CARDS

Credit cards are widely accepted in Barcelona, and often offer superior exchange rates—up to 5% better than the retail rate used by banks and other currency exchange establishments. Credit cards may also offer services such as insurance or emergency help. While credit cards are sometimes necessary to reserve hotel rooms or rental cars, cash is often required at budget establishments. **MasterCard** (a.k.a. EuroCard or Access in Europe) and **Visa** (a.k.a. Carte Bleue or Barclaycard) are the most welcomed; **American Express** cards work at some ATMs, AmEx offices and at major airports. The AmEx national number in Spain is ☎900 994 426.

ATM cards are widespread in Spain and everywhere in Barcelona. Depending on the system that your home bank uses, you can most likely access your personal bank account from abroad. ATMs get the same wholesale exchange rate as credit cards, but there is often a limit on the amount of money you can withdraw per day (around US$500), and unfortunately computer networks sometimes fail. There is typically also a surcharge of US$1-5 per withdrawal.

Debit cards are a relatively new form of purchasing power and are as convenient as credit cards but have a more immediate impact on your funds. A debit card can be used wherever its associated credit card company (usually Mastercard or Visa) is accepted, yet the money is withdrawn directly from the holder's checking account. Debit cards often also function as ATM cards and can be used to withdraw cash from associated banks and ATMs throughout Spain. Ask your local bank about obtaining one.

The two major international money networks are **Cirrus** (to locate ATMs contact US ☎800-424-7787 or www.mastercard.com) and **Visa/PLUS** (to locate ATMs US call ☎800-843-7587 or www.visa.com).

GETTING MONEY FROM HOME

If you run out of money while traveling, the easiest and cheapest solution is to have someone back home make a deposit to your credit card or cash (ATM) card. Failing that, consider one of the following options.

WIRING MONEY

It is possible to arrange a **bank money transfer,** which means asking a bank back home to wire money to a bank in Spain. This is the cheapest way to transfer cash, but it's also the slowest, usually taking several days or more. Note that some banks may only release your funds in local currency, potentially sticking you with a poor exchange rate; inquire about this in advance. The rates for sending cash are generally US$10-11 cheaper than with a credit card, and the money is usually available at the place you're sending it to within an hour. Money transfer services like **Western Union** are faster and more convenient than bank transfers—but also much pricier. Western Union has many locations worldwide. To find one, visit www.westernunion.com, or call in Australia ☎800 501 500, in Canada ☎800-235-0000, in New Zealand ☎800 27 0000, in South Africa ☎0860 100031, in Spain ☎900 633 633, in the UK ☎0800 83 38 33, or in the US ☎800-325-6000. There are Western Union representatives all over Barcelona, including one at **Admon Manuel Martín,** Las Ramblas, 41 (open daily 9:30am-midnight). Money transfer services are also available at **American Express** and **Thomas Cook** offices.

US STATE DEPARTMENT (US CITIZENS ONLY)

In dire emergencies only, the US State Department will forward money within hours to the nearest consular office, which will then disburse it according to instructions for a US$15 fee. If you wish to use this service, you must contact the Overseas Citizens Service division of the US State Department (☎202-647-5225; nights, Sundays, and holidays ☎202-647-4000).

COSTS

The cost of your trip will vary considerably depending on where you go, how you travel, and where you stay. The single biggest cost of your trip will probably be your round-trip (return) **airfare** to Spain (see **Getting to Barcelona: By Plane,** p. 289). A **rail pass** (or **bus pass**) will be another potential expense (see **Getting to Barcelona: By Train,** p. 294). Before you go, calculate a reasonable per-day **budget** that will meet your needs.

STAYING ON A BUDGET

To give you a general idea, a bare-bones day in Barcelona (camping or sleeping in hostels/guesthouses, buying food at supermarkets) would cost about US$35/€37; a

TRAVEL ADVISORIES

The following government offices provide travel information and advisories by telephone, by fax, or via the web:

Australian Department of Foreign Affairs and Trade: ☎1300 555135; faxback service 02 6261 1299; www.dfat.gov.au.

Canadian Department of Foreign Affairs and International Trade (DFAIT): In Canada and the US ☎800-267-6788, elsewhere ☎+1 613-944-6788; www.dfaitmaeci.gc.ca. Call for their free booklet, *Bon Voyage...But.*

New Zealand Ministry of Foreign Affairs: ☎04 494 8500; fax 494 8506; www.mft.govt.nz/trav.html.

United Kingdom Foreign and Commonwealth Office: ☎020 7008 0232; fax 7008 0155; www.fco.gov.uk.

US Department of State: ☎202-647-5225; faxback service 202-647-3000; http://travel.state.gov. For *A Safe Trip Abroad*, call ☎202-512-1800.

slightly more comfortable day (sleeping in hostels/guesthouses and the occasional budget hotel, eating one meal a day at a restaurant, going out at night) would run US$50/€53; and for a luxurious day, the sky's the limit. Don't underestimate the cost of partying in Barcelona; while some clubs may charge no cover, drink prices can get out of hand. Also, don't forget to factor in emergency reserve funds (at least US$200) when planning how much money you'll need.

TIPS FOR SAVING MONEY

Saving just a few dollars a day over the course of your trip might pay for days or weeks of additional travel. Take advantage of freebies: **museums** will typically be free once a week or once a month, and Barcelona often hosts free open-air **concerts** and **cultural events.** If possible, do your **laundry** in the sink; buy food in **supermarkets** instead of restaurants; split **accommodations** costs with trustworthy fellow travelers. With that said, don't go overboard with your budget obsession. Staying within your budget is important, but not at the expense of your sanity or health. For more tips on staying on a budget, check the **On the Cheap** sidebars scattered throughout this book.

TAXES

Spain has a 7% **Value Added Tax,** known as IVA, on all restaurants and accommodations. The prices listed in *Let's Go* (and on price tags) include IVA unless otherwise mentioned. Retail goods bear a much higher 16% IVA, although again, listed prices are usually inclusive. Non-EU citizens who have stayed in the EU fewer than 180 days can claim back the tax paid on purchases at the airport. Ask the shop where you have made the purchase to supply you with a tax return form.

SAFETY AND SECURITY

PERSONAL SAFETY

To avoid unwanted attention, try to blend in as much as possible. Respecting local customs (in many cases, dressing more conservatively) may placate would-be hecklers. Familiarize yourself with your surroundings before setting out, and carry yourself with confidence. If you are traveling alone, be sure someone at home knows your itinerary, and never admit that you're traveling alone. When walking at night, stick to busy, well-lit streets and avoid dark alleyways. If you feel uncomfortable, leave as quickly and directly as you can.

If you are using a **car**, learn local driving signals and wear a seatbelt. Children under 18kg/40lbs. should ride in a specially-designed carseat, available for a small fee from most car rental agencies.

The main terrorist group in Spain is the ETA, a Basque Separatist group. Their violent protests are usually aimed against Madrid or high-profile political events, however, there have been several bombings in Catalunya in the past. For more information about their history and cause, see **Current Events**, p. 48. Catalunya has its own separatist group; however, they generally work through peaceful political action and are relatively happy with the internal autonomy that the Generalitat of Catalunya enjoys. There is a small contingent of hard-core separatists, but the group's last known violent act occurred more than 15 years ago.

FINANCIAL SECURITY

To minimize the financial risk associated with traveling, **bring as little with you as possible,** buy a few combination **padlocks** to secure your belongings, **carry as little cash as possible,** and keep all valuables on your person in a **money belt.** For back-up, **keep a small cash reserve separate from your primary stash.** This should be about US$50 sewn or stored in the depths of your pack, along with your traveler's check numbers and important photocopies.

In large cities **con artists** often work in groups, and children are among the most effective. Beware of certain classics: sob stories that require money, rolls of bills "found" on the street, mustard spilled (or saliva spit) onto your shoulder to distract you while they snatch your bag. **Don't ever let your passport or your bags out of your sight.** Beware of **pickpockets** in city crowds, especially on public transportation.

Never leave your belongings unattended; crime occurs in even the most demure-looking hostel or hotel. Bring your own **padlock** for hostel lockers, and don't ever store valuables in any locker. Be particularly careful on **buses** and **trains;** horror stories abound about determined thieves who wait for travelers to fall asleep. Carry your backpack in front of you where you can see it.

HEALTH

Common sense is the simplest prescription for good health while you travel. Drink lots of fluids to prevent dehydration and constipation, wear sturdy, broken-in shoes and clean socks, and use talcum powder to keep your feet dry. For a basic **first-aid kit,** pack: bandages, pain reliever, antibiotic cream, a thermometer, a Swiss Army knife, tweezers, moleskin, decongestant, motion-sickness remedy, diarrhea or upset-stomach medication (Pepto Bismol or Imodium), an antihistamine, and sunscreen.

In your **passport,** write the names of any people you wish to be contacted in case of a medical emergency, and also list any allergies or medical conditions a doctor would need to know about. Matching a prescription to a foreign equivalent is not always easy, safe, or possible. Carry up-to-date, legible prescriptions or a statement from your doctor stating the medication's trade name, manufacturer, chemical name, and dosage. While traveling, be sure to keep all medication with you in your carry-on luggage.

ESSENTIAL INFORMATION

CURRENT & ADAPTERS

In Barcelona, electric current is 220 volts AC, enough to fry any 110V North American appliance. Americans and Canadians should buy an adapter (which changes the shape of the plug) and a converter (which changes the voltage; US$20). Don't make the mistake of using only an adapter (unless appliance instructions explicitly state otherwise). New Zealanders and South Africans (who both use 220V at home) as well as Australians (who use 240/250V) won't need a converter, but will need a set of adapters to use anything electrical.

IMMUNIZATIONS

Travelers over two years old should be sure that the following vaccines are up to date: MMR (for measles, mumps, and rubella); DTaP or Td (for diptheria, tetanus, and pertussis), OPV (for polio), HbCV (for haemophilus influenza B), and HBV (for hepatitis B). For recommendations on immunizations and prophylaxis, consult the CDC (see below) in the US or the equivalent in your home country, and check with a doctor for guidance.

USEFUL ORGANIZATIONS & PUBLICATIONS

The US **Center for Disease Control and Prevention** (**CDC**; ☎877-394-8747; tollfree fax 888-232-3299; www.cdc.gov/travel) maintains an international travelers' hotline and an informative website. The CDC's comprehensive booklet *Health Information for International Travel*, an annual rundown of disease, immunization, and general health advice, is free online or US$25 via the Public Health Foundation (☎877-252-1200). Consult the appropriate government agency of your home country for consular information sheets on health, entry requirements, and other issues (see the box on **Travel Advisories,** p. 284). For quick information on health and other travel warnings, call the **Overseas Citizens Services** (☎202-647-5225, after-hours 202-647-4000), or contact a passport agency, embassy, or consulate abroad. US citizens can send a self-addressed, stamped envelope to the Overseas Citizens Services, Bureau of Consular Affairs, #4811, US Department of State, Washington, D.C. 20520. For information on medical evacuation services and travel insurance firms, see the US government's website at http://travel.state.gov/medical.html or the **British Foreign and Commonwealth Office's** website at www.fco.gov.uk.

For detailed information on travel health, including a country-by-country overview of diseases, try the **International Travel Health Guide,** by Stuart Rose, MD (US$19.95; www.travmed.com). For general health info, contact the **American Red Cross** (☎800-564-1234; www.redcross.org).

MEDICAL ASSISTANCE ON THE ROAD

There are no particular health risks associated with traveling in Spain. The public health care system in Spain is very reliable; in an emergency, seek out the *urgencia* (emergency) section of the nearest hospital. For smaller concerns, it is probably best to go to a private clinic to avoid the frustration of long lines. Expect to pay cash up front (though most travel insurance will pick up the tab later) and bring your passport and other forms of identification. A single visit to a clinic in Spain can cost anywhere from US$40 to US$100, depending on the service. Ask the tourist office or your consulate for help finding a doctor or clinic.

Farmacias (pharmacies) in Spain are also very helpful. A system has been set up so that at least one *farmacia* is open at all times in each town; look for a lit green cross. Spanish pharmacies are not the place to find your cheap summer flip-flops or greeting cards: they sell contraceptives, common medications, and many prescription drugs. They can also answer simple medical questions and help find a doctor.

If you are concerned about obtaining medical assistance while traveling, you may wish to employ special support services. The *MedPass* from **GlobalCare, Inc.,** 2001 Westside Pkwy. #120, Alpharetta, GA 30004, USA (☎800-860-1111; fax 770-677-0455; www.globalems.com), provides 24hr. international medical assistance, support, and medical evacuation resources. The **International Association for Medical Assistance to Travelers** (**IAMAT;** US ☎716-754-4883, Canada ☎416-652-0137, New Zealand ☎03 352 20 53; www.sentex.net/~iamat) has free membership, lists English-speaking doctors worldwide, and offers detailed info on immunization requirements and sanitation. If your regular **insurance** policy does not cover travel abroad, you may wish to purchase additional coverage (see p. 287).

Those with medical conditions (such as diabetes, allergies to antibiotics, epilepsy, heart conditions) may want to obtain a **Medic Alert** membership (first year US$35, annually thereafter US$20), which includes a stainless steel ID tag, a 24hr. collect-call number, and other benefits. Contact the Medic Alert Foundation, 2323 Colorado Ave., Turlock, CA 95382, USA (US ☎ 888-633-4298; elsewhere ☎ 209-668-3333; www.medicalert.org).

INSURANCE

Travel insurance generally covers four basic areas: medical/health problems, property loss, trip cancellation/interruption, and emergency evacuation. Although your regular insurance policies may extend to travel-related accidents, you may consider purchasing travel insurance if the cost of potential trip cancellation/interruption is greater than you can absorb. Travel insurance generally runs about US$50 per week for full coverage, while trip cancellation/interruption may be purchased separately at a rate of about US$5.50 per US$100 of coverage.

Medical insurance often covers costs incurred abroad; check with your provider. **US Medicare** does not cover foreign travel. **Canadians** are protected by their home province's health insurance plan for 90 days abroad; check with the provincial Ministry of Health or Health Plan Headquarters for details. **Homeowner's insurance** often covers theft during travel and loss of travel documents (passport, plane ticket, rail pass, etc.) up to US$500.

ISIC and **ITIC** (see p. 279) provide basic insurance benefits, including US$100 per day of in-hospital sickness for up to 60 days, US$3000 for accident-related medical reimbursement, and US$25,000 for emergency medical transport. Cardholders have access to a toll-free 24hr. helpline (run by the insurance provider **TravelGuard**) for medical, legal, and financial emergencies overseas (US and Canada ☎ 877-370-4742, elsewhere US collect ☎ 715-345-0505). **American Express** (US ☎ 800-528-4800) grants most cardholders automatic car rental insurance (collision and theft, but not liability) and ground travel accident coverage of US$100,000 on flight purchases made with the card.

INSURANCE PROVIDERS

Council and **STA** (see p. 289) offer a range of plans that can supplement your basic coverage. Other private insurance providers in the US and Canada include: **Access America** (☎ 800-284-8300), **Berkely Group/Carefree Travel Insurance** (☎ 800-323-3149; www.berkely.com), **Globalcare Travel Insurance** (☎ 800-821-2488; www.globalcare-cocco.com), and **Travel Assistance International** (☎ 800-821-2828; www.europ-assistance.com). For a provider in the **UK** contact **Columbus Direct** (☎ 020 7375 0011). In **Australia**, try **AFTA** (☎ 02 9375 4955).

CONTACTING SPAIN

BY MAIL

Spain's postal service is good, although it may not be quite as fast as other countries. A letter should take about 7-8 working days to reach Spain from North America, 3-4 days from Europe, or 9 days from anywhere else with a decent postal system. Packages should hypothetically take the same amount of time, but are much more susceptible to enigmatic delays, and may take up to three weeks to get anywhere.

BY PHONE

Remember before you call that Barcelona is one hour ahead of Greenwich Mean Time, two hours ahead during Daylight Savings Time. To place an international call:

20,160 minutes floating (in the sun).
5 minutes to book online (Boston to Fiji).

Save money & time on student and faculty
travel at StudentUniverse.com

 StudentUniverse.com   Real Travel Deals

first, dial the international dialing prefix of the country you are calling from (from Australia, dial 0011; Canada or the US, 011; the Republic of Ireland, New Zealand, or the UK, 00; South Africa, 09); second, dial the country code of the country you are calling to (to Spain, 34); third, dial the city code (for Barcelona, 93) and the local number. For more info on phones in Barcelona, see **Once In Barcelona**, p. 31.

GETTING TO BARCELONA

BY PLANE

When it comes to airfare, a little effort can save you a bundle. If your plans are flexible enough to deal with the restrictions, courier fares are the cheapest. Tickets bought from consolidators and standby seating are also good deals, but last-minute specials, airfare wars, and charter flights often beat these fares. The key is to hunt around, to be flexible, and to ask persistently about discounts. Students, seniors, and those under 26 should never pay full price for a ticket.

AIRFARES

Airfares to Barcelona peak between June and August; major Catholic holidays are also expensive. The cheapest times to travel is during the winter, November to February. Midweek (M-Th morning) round-trip flights run US$40-50 cheaper than weekend flights, but they are generally more crowded and less likely to permit frequent-flier upgrades. Not fixing a return date ("open return") or arriving in and departing from different cities ("open-jaw") can be pricier than round-trip flights. Patching one-way flights together is the most expensive way to travel.

Fares for round-trip flights to Barcelona from the US or Canadian east coast may cost US$700 or more in peak months or US$350-500 in winter months; from the US or Canadian west coast US$800 to well over US$1000; from the UK, UK£100 to UK£450; from Australia AUS$1800 to AUS$2500.

BUDGET & STUDENT TRAVEL AGENCIES

While knowledgeable agents specializing in flights to Spain can make your life easier and help you save money, they may not spend the time to find the lowest possible fare—they get paid on commission. Travelers holding **ISIC and IYTC cards** (see p. 279) qualify for big discounts from student travel agencies. Most flights from budget agencies are on major airlines, but in peak season some may sell seats on less-reliable chartered aircraft.

CTS Travel, 44 Goodge St., **London** W1T 2AD, UK (☎0207 636 0031; fax 0207 637 5328; ctsinfo@ctstravel.co.uk).

Council Travel (www.counciltravel.com). Countless US offices, including branches in Atlanta, Boston, Chicago, L.A., New York, San Francisco, Seattle, and Washington, D.C. Check the website or call 800-2-COUNCIL (226-8624) for the office nearest you. As of May 2002, Council had declared bankruptcy and was subsumed under STA. However, their offices are still in existence and transacting business.

STA Travel, 7890 S. Hardy Dr., Suite. 110, Tempe AZ 85284, USA (☎800-781-4040; www.sta-travel.com). A student and youth travel organization with over 150 offices worldwide (check the website for a listing of all their offices), including US offices in Boston, Chicago, L.A., New York, San Francisco, Seattle, and Washington, D.C. Ticket booking, travel insurance, railpasses, and more. In the UK, walk-in office, 11 Goodge St., **London** W1T 2PF or call ☎0207 436 7779. In New Zealand, Shop 2B, 182 Queen St., **Auckland** (☎09 309 0458). In Australia, 366 Lygon St., **Carlton** Vic 3053 (☎03 9349 4344).

Travel CUTS (Canadian Universities Travel Services Limited), 187 College St., **Toronto,** ON M5T 1P7 (☎416-979-2406; fax 979-8167; www.travelcuts.com). 60 offices across Canada.

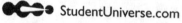

Also in the UK, 295-A Regent St., **London** W1R 7YA (☎0207 255 1944).

usit world (www.usitworld.com). Over 50 **usit campus** branches in the UK, including 52 Grosvenor Gardens, **London** SW1W 0AG (☎0870 240 10 10); **Manchester** (☎0161 273 1880); and **Edinburgh** (☎0131 668 3303). Nearly 20 usit NOW offices in Ireland, including 19-21 Aston Quay, O'Connell Bridge, **Dublin** (☎01 602 1600; www.usitnow.ie); and **Belfast** (☎02 890 327 111; www.usitnow.com). Offices all over the world, including a gateway office (offering full travel service) in Barcelona; see **Service Directory**, p. 317.

Wasteels, Skoubogade 6, 1158 **Copenhagen** K. (☎3314 4633; fax 7630 0865; www.wasteels.dk/uk). A huge chain with 165 locations across Europe. Sells Wasteels BIJ tickets discounted 30-45% off regular fare, 2nd-class international point-to-point train tickets with unlimited stopovers for those under 26 (sold only in Europe).

COMMERCIAL AIRLINES

The commercial airlines' lowest regular offer is the **APEX** (Advance Purchase Excursion) fare, which provides confirmed reservations and allows "open-jaw" tickets. Generally, reservations must be made seven to 21 days ahead of departure, with a seven- to 14-day minimum-stay and up to 90-day maximum-stay restrictions. These fares carry hefty cancellation and change penalties (fees rise in summer). Book peak-season APEX fares early; by May you will have a hard time getting your desired departure date. Use the Internet (see **Internet Flight Planning**, p. 291) to get an idea of the lowest published fares, then use the resources outlined here to try and beat those fares. The Air Travel Advisory Bureau in London (☎020 7636 5000; www.atab.co.uk) provides referrals to travel agencies and consolidators that offer discounted airfares out of the UK. All major international airlines offer service to Barcelona, but the most popular carriers are listed here.

DISCOUNT AIRLINES

Air France: US ☎800-237-2747; www.airfrance.com. Connections to Barcelona from Paris.

British Airways: US ☎800-247-9297, UK ☎0845 77 999 77; www.british-airways.com. Flights through the UK from Europe and the east coast of North America.

British Midland Airways: UK ☎0870 607 05 55; www.flybmi.com. Departures from throughout the UK.

easyJet: UK ☎0870 600 00 00; www.easyjet.com. London to Barcelona UK£47-136.

Iberia: US and Canada ☎800-772-4642, UK ☎020 7830 0011, Spain ☎902 400 500, South Africa

INTERNET FLIGHT PLANNING

The Internet is one of the best places to look for travel bargains—it's fast and convenient, and you can spend hours exploring options without driving your travel agent insane.

Many airline sites offer special last-minute deals on the Web:

www.travelpage.com

www.lastminute.com

Other sites do the legwork and compile deals for you:

www.bestfares.com

www.onetravel.com

www.lowestfare.com

www.travelzoo.com

For **student quotes,** try:

www.studentuniverse.com

www.sta-travel.com

www.counciltravel.com

Full travel services:

Expedia (msn.expedia.com)
Travelocity (www.travelocity.com)

Priceline (www.priceline.com) allows you to specify a price, and obligates you to buy any ticket that meets or beats it; be prepared for antisocial hours and odd routes.

Skyauction (www.skyauction.com) allows you to bid on both last-minute and advance-purchase tickets.

Cambios

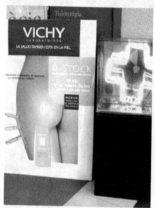

Farmacy

Information at Casa Robert

☎11 884 92 55, Ireland ☎1 407 30 17; www.iberia.com. Serves all domestic locations and major international cities. **Aviaco,** a subsidiary of Iberia, covers only domestic routes. Ask about youth and other discounts—youth under 12 often get a 25% discount, and Iberia usually offers a range of ticket types with different restrictions and prices. Some fares purchased in the US require a 21-day minimum advance purchase.

SpanAir: US ☎888-545-5757, Spain ☎971 745 020; fax 971 492 553; www.spanair.com Offers international and domestic flights.

AIR COURIER FLIGHTS

Those who travel light should consider courier flights. Couriers help transport cargo on international flights by using their checked luggage space for freight. Generally, couriers must travel with carry-ons only and must deal with complex flight restrictions. Most flights are round-trip only, with short fixed-length stays (usually one week) and a limit of one ticket per issue. Generally, you must be over 21 (in some cases 18). In summer, the most popular destinations usually require an advance reservation of about two weeks (you can usually book up to two months ahead). Super-discounted fares are common for "last-minute" flights (three to 14 days ahead). Not all courier services fly to Barcelona; flying into Madrid and taking a train to Barcelona is still an economical option (US$30 and up).

FROM NORTH AMERICA

Round-trip courier fares from the US to Barcelona run about US$200-500. Most flights leave from New York, Los Angeles, San Francisco, or Miami in the US; and from Montreal, Toronto, or Vancouver in Canada. The organizations below provide members with lists of opportunities and courier brokers for an annual fee. Prices quoted below are round-trip.

Air Courier Association, 350 Indiana St. #300, Golden, CO 80401, USA (US☎800-282-1202; www.aircourier.org). Ten departure cities throughout the US and Canada (high-season US$150-360). One-year membership US$49.

International Association of Air Travel Couriers (IAATC), P.O. Box 980, Keystone Heights, FL 32656, USA (US☎352-475-1584; fax 475-5326; www.courier.org). From 9 North American cities. One-year membership US$45.

Global Courier Travel, P.O. Box 3051, Nederland, CO 80466, USA (www.globalcouriertravel.com). Searchable online database. Six departure points in the US and Canada to Madrid. Lifetime membership US$40, 2 people US$55.

NOW Voyager, 315 W. 49th St., New York, NY 10019, USA (☎212-459-1616; fax 262-7407). Flights to Madrid US$499-699. Usually one-week max. stay. One-year membership US$50. Non-courier discount fares also available.

FROM THE UK AND IRELAND

The minimum age for couriers from the **UK** is usually 18. **Brave New World Enterprises,** P.O. Box 22212, London SE5 8WB (info@courierflights.com; www.courierflights.com) publishes a directory of all the companies offering courier flights in the UK (UK£10, in electronic form UK£8). **Global Courier Travel** (see above) also offers flights from London and Dublin to Madrid. **British Airways Travel Shop** (☎0870 240 0747; info@batravelshops.com; www.batravelshops.com) arranges some flights from London to destinations in continental Europe (specials may be as low as UK£60; no registration fee).

TICKET CONSOLIDATORS

Ticket consolidators, or **"bucket shops,"** buy unsold tickets in bulk from commercial airlines and sell them at discounted rates. The best place to look is in the Sunday travel section of any major newspaper (such as the *New York Times*), where many bucket shops place tiny ads. Call quickly, as availability is typically extremely limited. Not all bucket shops are reliable, so insist on a receipt that gives full details of restrictions, refunds, and tickets, and pay by credit card (2-5% fee) so you can stop payment if you never receive tickets. For more information, see www.travel-library.com/air-travel/consolidators.html.

FROM THE US & CANADA

Travel Avenue (☎800-333-3335; www.travelavenue.com) searches for best available published fares and then uses several consolidators to attempt to beat that fare. **NOW Voyager,** 74 Varick St., Suite 307, New York, NY 10013 (☎212-431-1616; fax 219-1793; www.nowvoyagertravel.com) arranges discounted flights from New York to Barcelona. Other consolidators worth trying are **Interworld** (☎305-443-4929; fax 443-0351); **Pennsylvania Travel** (☎800-331-0947); **Rebel** (☎800-227-3235; travel@rebeltours.com; www.rebeltours.com); **Cheap Tickets** (☎800-377-1000; www.cheaptickets.com); and **Travac** (☎800-872-8800; fax 212-714-9063; www.travac.com). Yet more consolidators on the web include the **Internet Travel Network** (www.itn.com); **Travel Information Services** (www.tiss.com); **TravelHUB** (www.travelhub.com); and **The Travel Site** (www.thetravelsite.com). Keep in mind these are just suggestions to get you started in your research; *Let's Go* does not endorse any of these agencies. As always, be cautious, and research companies before you hand over your credit card number.

FROM THE UK, AUSTRALIA, & NEW ZEALAND

In London, the **Air Travel Advisory Bureau** (☎0207-636-5000; www.atab.co.uk) can provide names of reliable consolidators and discount flight specialists. From Australia and New Zealand, look for consolidator ads in the travel section of the *Sydney Morning Herald* and other papers.

STANDBY FLIGHTS

Traveling standby requires considerable flexibility in arrival and departure dates and cities. Companies dealing in standby flights sell vouchers rather than tickets, along with the promise to get you to your destination (or near your destination) within a certain window of time (typically 1-5 days). You call in before your specific window of time to hear flight options and the probability that you will be able to board each flight. You can then decide which flights you want to try to make, show up at the appropriate airport at the appropriate time, present your voucher, and board if space is available. Vouchers can usually be purchased for both one-way and round-trip travel. You may receive a monetary refund only if every available flight within your date range is full; if you opt not to take an available (but perhaps less convenient) flight, you can only get credit toward future travel. Carefully read agreements with any company offering standby flights as tricky fine print can leave you in a lurch. To check on a company's service record in the US, call the Better Business Bureau (☎212-533-6200). It is difficult to receive refunds, and clients' vouchers will not be honored when an airline fails to receive payment in time. One established standby company in the US is Whole Earth Travel, 325 W. 38th St., New York, NY 10018, USA (☎800-326-2009 or 888-247-4482; fax 212-864-5489; www.4standby.com). Offers one-way flights to Europe from the Northeast (US$169), West Coast (US$249), Midwest (US$219), and Southeast (US$199). Intracontinental connecting flights within the US or Europe cost US$79-139.

CHARTER FLIGHTS

Charters are flights a tour operator contracts with an airline to fly extra loads of passengers during peak season. Charter flights fly less frequently than major airlines, making refunds particularly difficult, and are almost always fully booked. Schedules and itineraries may also change or be canceled at the last moment (as late as 48 hours before the trip, and without a full refund), and check-in, boarding, and baggage claim are often much slower. However, they can also be cheaper.

Discount clubs and **fare brokers** offer members savings on last-minute charter and tour deals. Study contracts closely; you don't want to end up with an unwanted overnight layover. **Travelers Advantage** specializes in European travel and tour packages. (☎203-365-2000; www.travelersadvantage.com. A US$60 annual fee includes discounts and cheap flight directories).

BY TRAIN

Spanish trains are clean, relatively punctual, and reasonably priced. Spain's national railway is **RENFE** (☎902 24 02 02, international ☎93 490 11 22; www.renfe.es). RENFE offers extensive service in Spain and all of Europe, with a variety of trains. (Open daily 7am-10pm.) *Tranvía*, *semidirecto*, and *correo* trains are very slow. The Euromed has the fewest stops, while the Estrella, Talgo, Arco, Diurno and the Regional usually take much longer. The prices listed below are for the sitting *turista* class only (*preferente* and beds cost more.) Non-smokers (and non-chain-smokers) should consider buying a *no-fumador* (non-smoking) seat a few days in advance, as they are apt to sell out. For more details on prices and routes, ask at an information window for an *horario*—schedule. Some of the most popular connections to and from Barcelona include: **Alicante** (4-5hr., 8 per day, €30-41); **Bilbao** (8-9hr., 5 per day, €30-32); **Granada** (11-12hr., 4 per day, €46-47); **Madrid** (7-8hr., 7 per day, €31-42); **Pamplona** (6-7hr., 2 per day, €27.50); **Salamanca** (10-12hr., 5 per day, €37.50); **San Sebastian** (8-9hr., 5 per day, €29.50-31); **Sevilla** (11-12hr., 6 per day, €47-51); **Valencia** (3-5hr., 15 per day 7am-9pm, €27.50-32). International destination include **Milan** (through **Figueres** and **Nice**) and **Montpellier** with connections to **Geneva, Paris**, and various stops along the French Riviera. There is a 20% discount on round-trip tickets.

There is absolutely no reason to buy a Eurail pass if you are planning on traveling just within Spain. Trains are cheap, so a pass saves little money, and may actually be more expensive than buying individual tickets. Ages 4-11 are half-price; children under four are free. There are several passes that cover travel within Spain. You must purchase rail passes at least 15 days before departure. Call ☎1-800-4-Eurail (38-7245) in the US or go to www.raileurope.com.

Spain Flexipass offers 3 days of unlimited travel in a 2-month period. 1st-class US$200; 2nd-class US$155. Each additional rail-day (up to 7) US$35 1st-class, US$30 2nd-class.

Iberic Railpass is good for 3 days of unlimited 1st-class travel in Spain and Portugal for US$205. Each additional rail-day (up to 7) US$45.

Spain Rail n' Drive Pass is good for 3 days of unlimited 1st-class train travel and 2 days of unlimited mileage in a rental car within a 2-month period. US$255-365, depending on how many people are traveling and the type of car. Up to 2 additional rail-days and extra car days are also available, and a 3rd and 4th person can join in the car using only a Flexipass.

BY CAR

For more information on traveling by car once you get to Spain, check out **Once in Barcelona,** p. 28.

INTERNATIONAL DRIVING PERMIT (IDP). If you plan to drive a car in Barcelona, you must be over 18. An International Driving Permit (IDP) is recommended, though Spain allows travelers to drive with a valid American or Canadian license for a limited number of months. It is a good idea to get one, in case you're in a situation (e.g. an accident or stranded in a small town) where the police do not know English; information on the IDP is printed in ten languages, including Spanish. AAA members and non-members alike can call US ☎800-AAA-HELP (800-222-4357) or visit www.aaa.com for info.

Your IDP, valid for one year, must be issued in your own country before you depart. An application usually needs to include one or two photos, a current local license, an additional form of identification, and a fee.

CAR INSURANCE. Most credit cards cover standard insurance, though you should always ask before when renting. If you rent, lease, or borrow a car, you will need a **green card,** or **International Insurance Certificate,** to certify that you have liability insurance and that it applies abroad. Green cards can be obtained at car rental agencies, car dealers (for those leasing cars), some travel agents, and some border crossings. Rental agencies may require you to purchase theft insurance in countries that they consider to have a high risk of auto theft.

RENTING. You can rent a car from a US-based firm with European offices, from a European-based company with local representatives, or from a tour operator which will arrange a rental for you from a European company at its own rates. Multinationals offer greater flexibility, but tour operators often strike better deals. Most available cars will have standard transmission—cars with automatic transmission are difficult to find and much more expensive. Reserve well before leaving for the region and pay in advance if at all possible. It is always significantly less expensive to reserve a car from the US than from Barcelona. Ask your airline about special fly-and-drive packages; you may get up to a week of free or discounted rental. The minimum age in Spain is usually 25 with the larger agencies (Hertz, Avis) and 21 at smalle, local businesses. At most agencies, all that's needed to rent a car is a US license and possibly an international driver's license (see above).

RENTAL AGENCIES. You can generally make reservations before you leave by calling major international offices in your home country. However, occasionally the price and availability information they give doesn't agree with what the local offices in your country will tell you. Try checking with both numbers to make sure you get the best price and accurate information. Local desk numbers are included in town listings; for home-country numbers, call your toll-free directory. Rental agencies in Barcelona include:

Avis/Auto Europe, Casanova, 209 (☎93 209 95 33). Will rent to ages 21-25 for an additional fee of about US$5 a day.

Budget, Av. Josep Tarradellas, 35 (☎93 410 25 08). Must be 25. **Branch** in El Prat de Llobregat airport (see p. 35).

Docar, C. Montnegre, 18 (24hr. ☎93 439 81 19). M: Les Corts. Free delivery and pickup. From €13.80 per day plus €9 insurance and €0.15 per km. Open M-F 8:30am-2pm and 3:30-8pm, Sa 9am-2pm.

Hertz, C. Tuset, 10 (☎93 217 80 76; www.hertz.es). M: Diagonal or FCG: Gràcia. Open M-F 9am-2pm and 4pm-7pm, Sa 9am-2pm. **Branch** in El Prat de Llobregat airport (☎93 298 36 37; see p. 35).

Tot Car, C. Berlín, 97 (☎93 430 01 98). Free delivery and pickup. From €27 per day, plus €0.13 per km. Insurance included. Open M-F 8am-2pm and 3-8pm, Sa 9am-1pm.

SPECIFIC CONCERNS

FEMALE TRAVELERS

Women exploring on their own inevitably face some additional safety concerns, but it's easy to be adventurous without taking undue risks. If you are concerned, consider staying in hostels which offer single rooms that lock from the inside or in religious organizations with rooms for women only. Communal showers in some hostels are safer than others; check them before settling in. Stick to centrally-located accommodations in well-lit areas. Avoid solitary late-night treks or Metro rides, and if carrying a purse, make sure it has a zipper or other secure closure and wear it across your body, as purse snatchings are not a rarity.

Always carry extra money for a phone call, bus, or taxi. **Hitchhiking** is never safe for a lone woman, or even for two women traveling together. Choose train compartments occupied by women or couples. Look as if you know where you're going and approach older women or couples for directions if you're lost or uncomfortable.

Generally, the less you look like a tourist, the better off you'll be. Trying to fit in can be effective, but dressing to the style of an obviously different culture may cause you to be ill at ease and a conspicuous target. Wearing a conspicuous **wedding band** may prevent unwanted overtures.

Your best answer to verbal harassment is no answer; the perpetrators generally lose interest quickly if you do not respond at all. The extremely persistent can sometimes be dissuaded by a firm, loud, and very public *"Vete"*—"Go away" in Spanish. However, don't hesitate to seek out a police officer or a passerby if you feel uncomfortable. Memorize the relevant emergency numbers, and consider carrying a whistle on your keychain. A self-defense course will not only prepare you for a potential attack, but will also raise your level of awareness of your surroundings as well as your confidence.

TRAVELING ALONE

There are many benefits to traveling alone, including independence and greater interaction with locals. On the other hand, any solo traveler is a more vulnerable target of harassment and street theft. Lone travelers need to be well-organized and look confident at all times. Try not to stand out as a tourist, and be especially careful in deserted or very crowded areas. If questioned, never admit that you are traveling alone. Maintain regular contact with someone at home who knows the number of your hostel and what you'll be doing from day to day. For more tips, pick up *Traveling Solo* by Eleanor Berman (Globe Pequot Press, US$17) or subscribe to **Connecting: Solo Travel Network,** 689 Park Road, Unit 6, Gibsons, BC, V0N 1V7 Canada (☎604-886-9099; www.cstn.org; membership US$35). **Travel Companion Exchange,** P.O. Box 833, Amityville, NY 11701, USA (☎631-454-0880, in the US ☎800-392-1256; www.whytravelalone.com; US$48), links solo travelers with companions with similar travel habits and interests.

OLDER TRAVELERS

Senior citizens are eligible for a wide range of discounts. If you don't see a senior citizen price listed, ask, and you may be delightfully surprised. The books *No Problem!*

Worldwise Tips for Mature Adventurers, by Janice Kenyon (Orca Book Publishers; US$16) and *Unbelievably Good Deals and Great Adventures That You Absolutely Can't Get Unless You're Over 50*, by Joan Rattner Heilman (NTC/Contemporary Publishing; US$13) are both excellent resources. For more information, contact one of the following organizations:

Elderhostel, 11 Ave. de Lafayette, Boston, MA 02111 USA (☎877-426-8056; www.elderhostel.org). Organizes 1- to 4-week "educational adventures" in Barcelona for those 55+.

The Mature Traveler, P.O. Box 15791, Sacramento, CA 95852 USA (☎800-460-6676). Deals, discounts, and travel packages for the 50+ traveler. Subscription $30.

BISEXUAL, GAY, & LESBIAN TRAVELERS

As a predominantly Catholic country with a recent history of fascism, Spain leans toward the conservative side when it comes to recognizing the variety of the sexuality spectrum. However, Barcelona is perhaps the most accepting, most comfortable, and most exciting city in Spain for BGL travelers; it's proximity to gay-friendly **Sitges** is another plus (see **Daytripping,** p. 239). No special precautions should be necessary for gay travel in Barcelona.

For the inside scoop on all things gay and lesbian in Barcelona—from gay-friendly hostels to the best gay nightlife—check out the BGL Barcelona sidebars scattered throughout this guide. Listed below are contact organizations, mail-order bookstores, and publishers that offer materials addressing some specific concerns. **Out and About** (www.planetout.com) offers a bi-weekly newsletter and a comprehensive site addressing gay travel concerns.

Gay in Spain: www.gayinspain.com. A webpage that offers comprehensive coverage of LGB resources and establishments in Spanish and English in Barcelona, Sitges, and Girona.

Gay's the Word, 66 Marchmont St., London WC1N 1AB (☎20 7278 7654; www.gaystheword.co.uk). The largest gay and lesbian bookshop in the UK, with both fiction and nonfiction titles. Mail-order service available.

Giovanni's Room, 1145 Pine St., Philadelphia, PA 19107, USA (☎215-923-2960; www.queerbooks.com). An international lesbian/feminist and gay bookstore with mail-order service (carries many of the publications listed below).

International Lesbian and Gay Association (ILGA), 81 rue Marché-au-Charbon, B-1000 Brussels, Belgium (☎2 502 2471; www.ilga.org). Provides political information, such as homosexuality laws of individual countries.

FURTHER READING

Spartacus International Gay Guide 2001-2002. Bruno Gmunder Verlag (US$33).

Damron Men's Guide and *The Women's Traveller.* Damron Travel Guides (US$14-19). For more info, call ☎800-462-6654 or visit www.damron.com.

Ferrari Guides' Gay Travel A to Z, Ferrari Guides' Men's Travel in Your Pocket, and *Ferrari Guides' Inn Places.* Ferrari Publications (US$16-20). Purchase online at www.ferrariguides.com.

The Gay Vacation Guide: The Best Trips and How to Plan Them, Mark Chesnut. (US$15).

TRAVELERS WITH DISABILITIES

Because sections of Barcelona are so old, it can be difficult to get around in certain neighborhoods, specifically the Ciutat Vella, which includes the Barri Gòtic, La Ribera, and El Raval. Hostels, mostly in aging buildings, tend to have narrow doorways and only a few boast elevators. Restaurants and shops, particularly in the Ciutat Vella, also tend to have unmanageable entrances. In this medieval area, the sidewalks are narrow and the streets marred with cobblestones. Spain has made huge improvements over the last ten years, but wheelchair accessibility does not mean the same thing in Spain as in the US. Those with disabilities should inform airlines, hotels, and hostels of their disabilities when making reservations; some time may be needed to prepare the necessary arrangements. Call ahead to restaurants, museums, and other facilities to find out about the existence of ramps, the widths of doors, the dimensions of elevators, etc. *Let's Go* has investigated the accessibility of the sights and establishments we review; be advised, however, that when something is labeled "wheelchair accessible," that term may only denote an adequate width of doors and absence of steps, and not necessarily an accessible bathroom.

The **train** is probably the most convenient form of travel for disabled travelers in Europe; many (but not all) stations have ramps, and some trains have wheelchair lifts, special seating areas, and specially equipped toilets. For those who wish to rent cars, some major **car rental** agencies (Hertz, Avis, and National) offer hand-controlled vehicles. Most buses and trains are accessible, but may not function easily or properly. For wheelchair accessibility, major museums and sites tend to be the most reliable. The **Institut Municipal de Disminuits**, C. Llacuna, 171, provides specific information on accessibility (☎93 291 84 00). The Ajuntament information office has a map of wheelchair accessible routes, available at Pl. Sant Miquel or the TMB office in the Universitat Metro stop. For information about wheelchair access points and adapted bus routes, call the **transport information phoneline** (☎93 486 07 52.)

Guide dog owners will not need to quarantine their dogs, but they will need to provide certificates of immunization, and those coming from the US must have their health certificates stamped by the USDA.

USEFUL ORGANIZATIONS

Directions Unlimited, 123 Green Ln., Bedford Hills, NY 10507, USA (☎800-533-5343). Books individual and group vacations for the physically disabled; not an info service.

Mobility International USA (MIUSA), P.O. Box 10767, Eugene, OR 97440 USA (☎541-343-1284, voice and TTD; www.miusa.org). Sells *A World of Options: A Guide to International Educational Exchange, Community Service, and Travel for Persons with Disabilities* (US$35).

Society for the Advancement of Travel for the Handicapped (SATH), 347 Fifth Ave., #610, New York, NY 10016, USA (☎212-447-7284; www.sath.org). An advocacy group that publishes free online travel information and the travel magazine *OPEN WORLD* (US$18, free for members). Annual membership US$45, students and seniors US$30.

MINORITY TRAVELERS

The Spanish suffer from little interaction with different ethnicities. Barcelona is perhaps the most international city in Spain, with a growing immigrant community and increasing diversity; however, minority travelers may encounter a certain degree of curiosity with respect to their skin color, even in the city. In general, comments or reactions that minority travelers perceive as offensive are not meant to be hostile on the part of the offending party. This factor of intention does not excuse ignorance, which a minority traveler must unfortunately be prepared to encounter.

TRAVELERS WITH CHILDREN

Family vacations often require that you slow your pace, and always require that you plan ahead. When deciding where to stay, remember the special needs of young children; if you pick a hostel a small hotel, call ahead and make sure it's child-friendly. **Be sure that your children carries some sort of ID** in case of an emergency or in case they get lost.

Museums and tourist attractions in Barcelona frequently offer discounts for children. Children under two generally fly for 10% of the adult airfare on international flights (this does not necessarily include a seat). International fares are usually discounted 25% for children from two to 11. Finding a private place for **breast feeding** is often a problem while traveling, so plan accordingly.

Barcelona is full of children and full of activities for families to do together; *Let's Go: Barcelona* features a special **Kids in the City** sidebar with suggestions for family- and kid-oriented activities. For more information, consult one of the following books or check with a local library:

Backpacking with Babies and Small Children, Goldie Silverman. Wilderness Press (US$10).

Take Your Kids to Europe, Cynthia W. Harriman. Cardogan Books (US$18).

How to Take Great Trips with Your Kids, Sanford and Jane Portnoy. Harvard Common Press (US$10).

Have Kid, Will Travel: 101 Survival Strategies for Vacationing With Babies and Young Children, Claire and Lucille Tristram. Andrews McMeel Publishing (US$9).

Trouble Free Travel with Children, Vicki Lansky. Book Peddlers (US$9).

DIETARY CONCERNS

Spain can be a difficult place to visit as a strict vegetarian; meat or fish is featured in the vast majority of popular dishes. Most restaurants serve salads, and there are also many egg, rice, and bean based dishes that can be requested without meat. Be careful, though, as some servers may interpret a "vegetarian" order to mean "with tuna instead of ham." While you have to be careful to avoid miscommunications in non-vegetarian restaurants, Barcelona has a respectable number of vegetarian and vegan establishments to choose from, especially in Gràcia. Check the table of **Restaurants by Type**, p. 127, for more info.

The **North American Vegetarian Society**, P.O. Box 72, Dolgeville, NY 13329, USA (☎518-568-7970; www.navs-online.org), publishes information about vegetarian travel, including *Transformative Adventures, a Guide to Vacations and*

Retreats (US$15), and the *Vegetarian Journal's Guide to Natural Food Restaurants in the US and Canada* (US$12). For more resources, visit your local bookstore, health food store, or library, and consult *The Vegetarian Traveler: Where to Stay if You're Vegetarian*, by Jed and Susan Civic (Larson Publications; US$16) or *Europe on 10 Salads a Day*, by Greg and Mary Jane Edwards (Mustang Publishing; US$10).

Travelers who keep kosher should contact synagogues in larger cities for information on kosher restaurants. Your own synagogue or college Hillel should have access to lists of Jewish institutions across the world. If you are strict in your observance, you may have to prepare your own food on the road. A good resource is the *Jewish Travel Guide*, by Michael Zaidner (Vallentine Mitchell; US$17). For information on Jewish life in Barcelona, contact the *Communidad Israelita de Barcelona* at ☎93 200 85 13. This synagogue is located at C. Porvenir, 24, and also houses a community center.

OTHER RESOURCES

Let's Go tries to cover all aspects of budget travel, but we can't put *everything* in our guides. Listed below are books and websites that can serve as jumping off points for your own research.

TRAVEL PUBLISHERS & BOOKSTORES

Hippocrene Books, Inc., 171 Madison Ave., New York, NY 10016, USA (☎718-454-2366; www.hippocrenebooks.com). Publishes language dictionaries and language learning guides.

Hunter Publishing, 470 W. Broadway, Fl. 2, South Boston, MA 02127, USA (☎617-269-0700; www.hunterpublishing.com). Has an extensive catalog of travel guides and diving and adventure travel books.

Rand McNally, P.O. Box 7600, Chicago, IL 60680, USA (☎847-329-8100; www.randmcnally.com), publishes road atlases.

Adventurous Traveler Bookstore, P.O. Box 2221, Williston, VT 05495, USA (☎800-282-3963; www.adventuroustraveler.com).

Bon Voyage!, 2069 W. Bullard Ave., Fresno, CA 93711, USA (☎800-995-9716, from abroad 559-447-8441; www.bon-voyage-travel.com). Specializes in European travel. Free newsletter.

Travel Books & Language Center, Inc., 4437 Wisconsin Ave. NW, Washington, D.C. 20016, USA (☎800-220-2665; www.bookweb.org/bookstore/travelbks). Over 60,000 titles from around the world.

WORLD WIDE WEB

Almost every aspect of budget travel is accessible via the web. With 10min. at the keyboard, you can make a reservation at a hostel, get advice on must-see Modernist sights, and get the latest soccer scores from the FCB website.

Listed here are some sites to start off your surfing; other relevant web sites are listed throughout the book. Because website turnover is high, use search engines (such as www.google.com or www.yahoo.com) to strike out on your own.

THE ART OF BUDGET TRAVEL

How to See the World: www.artoftravel.com. A compendium of great travel tips, from cheap flights to self defense to interacting with local culture.

Recreational Travel Library: www.travel-library.com. A fantastic set of links for general information and personal travelogues.

Backpacker's Ultimate Guide: www.bugeurope.com. Tips on packing, transportation, and where to go. Also tons of country-specific travel information.

Backpack Europe: www.backpackeurope.com. Helpful tips, a bulletin board, and links.

INFORMATION ON BARCELONA

The City of Barcelona Online: www.bcn.es/english/ihome.htm. The city's official webpage, covering everything from shopping and beaches to current events.

Tourist Office of Spain: www.okspain.org. The tourist office's official American webpage, full of links for everything from media to gastronomy.

Tourist Office of Barcelona: www.barcelonaturisme.com. Barcelona's own tourist office webpage offers basic information about the city and its culture, as well as a hotel booking service and virtual tours of the city's main sights.

Barcelona On Line: www.barcelona-on-line.es. This new travel agency provides a useful online guide about Barcelona.

Fútbol Club Barcelona: www.fcbarcelona.com. For those soccer enthusiasts among us, El Barça's official webpage is your guide to Catalunya's favorite team.

Spanish Cheese: www.cheesefromspain.com. Complete with photos of some of Spain's most succulent dairy products. Lactose-intolerants beware.

Foreign Language for Travelers: www.travlang.com. Provides free online translating dictionaries and lists of phrases in both Spanish and Catalan.

PlanetRider: www.planetrider.com. A subjective list of links to the "best" websites covering the culture and tourist attractions of Spain.

The Crapper: www.caganer.com. Get in touch with the Catalan celebration of regularity.

Floquet de Neu: www.zoobarcelona.com. The Barcelona Zoo's website, featuring a live feed of the world's only albino gorilla.

& OUR PERSONAL FAVORITE...

Let's Go: www.letsgo.com. Our constantly expanding website features photos and streaming video, online ordering of all our titles, info about our books, a travel forum buzzing with stories and tips, and links that will help you find everything you ever wanted to know about Barcelona.

Alternatives to Tourism

Working, volunteering, or studying for an extended period of time can be a better way to understand life in Barcelona. Most people pass through the city on vacation, but there are plenty of options for those who want to stretch their stay out to a few months or more. Unfortunately, some concerns, like finding a job and an apartment, are easier taken care of in Barcelona than from home.

LONG-TERM VISAS

Any stay over 90 days in Spain requires a visa; what you are doing with your time in Spain will dictate what sort of a visa you will get. It is always better to get these papers in advance; making arrangements for a longer stay while you are already in Spain will involve a lot of long lines and angry, intimidating visa personnel. Spain has good border control and travelers crossing back and forth from Spain in a period of over 90 days will not be permitted to re-enter without the appropriate visas. Getting a visa is straight-forward, but also a hassle. Call to inquire about the necessary documents before going to the consulate to avoid having to make multiple trips. It is difficult to get an appointment during the study abroad crunch months of September and January; if you'll need a visa then, call at least one month in advance.

Upon arrival in Spain, all long-term visitors must register at the *comisaria* (police station) immigration authority for an alien residency identification card. All persons staying in Spain more than 90 days must complete this process **in addition to** having a visa. Your

303

job/program/school will have to file papers with the *comisaria*, and will be able to direct you to the *comisaria* in question. At the station you will provide fingerprints, a photo, and a signature; in return you will get an ID. Be prepared to wait in line.

STUDY VISAS

To obtain a study visa for Spain, you must be enrolled in a program. Most study abroad programs are accustomed to dealing with foreign students, and will send everything needed for your visa automatically; if you are enrolling directly in a Spanish university, getting a visa may require a little more initiative. At the very least, be prepared to present a visa application form (best filled out in advance), your passport, passport photos, a medical letter, two letters from an institution verifying your full-time enrollment, and copious amounts of copies of these documents. In the interest of saving time, it is imperative to discuss visa requirements with both your program and your resident Spanish consulate. Be forewarned that most consulates are only open in the morning and some may require you to file for a visa in person.

STUDYING ABROAD

Many options are available for study abroad in Barcelona. For students with strong Spanish or Catalan skills, enrolling directly in a Spanish University in Barcelona may be the cheapest and best option. The instructional language is a controversial point at public universities in regions like Catalunya and País Vasco, which have their own languages. Despite what they might prefer, professors at public universities in Catalunya are required to offer classes in Spanish—not Catalan—if even one student is uncomfortable with Catalan. Consequently, the choice between enrolling in a public or a private university may depend on whether a student wants to study Spanish or Catalan.

Study abroad programs designed for foreign students are particularly popular for summer study. Some study abroad programs are affiliated with universities in Barce-

lona and allow students to take classes directly through the university; other programs for foreigners are more self-contained, with instruction in various combinations of English and Spanish. These programs may be affiliated with an American university, but are open to other students as well. While they have a reputation for creating self-contained social circles void of Spanish nationals, they often offer great benefits. Most arrange housing, with a family or in a dorm, and excursions, both within the city and throughout Spain. Some also offer an internship placement program for part-time work to compliment class work. Barcelona is also a fantastic place to study art; most study abroad programs offer an art component, and students with a stronger interest can enroll directly in an art school.

Art School, Pl. Veronica

Study abroad students should contact individual programs and universities to find out the requirements for their stay. Websites such as www.studyabroad.com are excellent resources, as are the following books, available at most libraries and many university career/study abroad offices: *Academic Year Abroad* (Institute of International Education Books; US$47); *Vacation Study Abroad* (Institute of International Education Books; US$43); and the encyclopedic *Peterson's Study Abroad* and *Summer Study Abroad* (Peterson's; US$30 each).

AMERICAN PROGRAMS

Central College Abroad, Office of International Education, 812 University, Pella, IA 50219, USA (☎800-831-3629 or 641-628-5284; studyabroad.com/central). Offers semester- and year-long programs in Barcelona. Application fee US$25.

A Bite to Eat in the Sun

School for International Training, College Semester Abroad, Admissions, Kipling Rd., P.O. Box 676, Brattleboro, VT 05302, USA (☎800-336-1616 or 802-257-7751; www.sit.edu). Semester- and year-long programs in Barcelona run US$10,600-13,700. Also runs the **Experiment in International Living** (☎800-345-2929; fax 802-258-3428; eil@worldlearning.org), 3- to 5-week summer programs that offer high school students homestays, community service, ecological adventure, and language training. Program fee US$1900-5000.

International Association for the Exchange of Students for Technical Experience (IAESTE), 10400 Little Patuxent Pkwy, Suite 250 L, Columbia, MD 21044-3510, USA (☎410-997-2200; www.aipt.org). 8- to 12-week programs in Spain for college students who have completed 2 years of technical study. Application fee US$25.

Hanging Out on C. Portaferrisa

Shopper with Cell Phone

Little Girl at Poble Espanyol

Birdcage in Window

International Studies Abroad, 901 W. 24th, Austin, TX 78705, USA (☎800-580-8826; www.studiesabroad.com). Programs at the University of Barcelona in Hispanic Studies or Spanish Language and Culture. Costs range from $3,300 (summer) to $13,750 (full-year).

PROGRAMS IN BARCELONA

University of Barcelona (☎93 403 53 79; fax 93 403 53 87; www.ub.es; ori-dir@pu.ges.ub.es). For academic exchange programs within the EU, contact ☎93 403 53 86; fax 93 403 53 87; bec-soc@pu.ges.ub.es. For academic exchange programs outside of the EU, ☎93 403 55 81; fax 93 403 53 87; elo@pu.ges.ub.es. Foreign students looking for information about enrolling in the University of Barcelona and the procedure for obtaining a student visa, ☎93 403 55 62; fax 93 403 53 87; gema@pu.ges.ub.es.

LANGUAGE SCHOOLS

Unlike American universities, language schools are frequently independently-run international or local organizations or divisions of foreign universities that rarely offer college credit. Language schools are a good alternative to university study if you desire a deeper focus on the language or a slightly less-rigorous courseload. They generally cost anywhere from US$500 to US$15,000, depending on the length of the program and whether they include lodging, food, and side trips. These programs are also good for younger high school students that might not feel comfortable with older students in a university program. Some good programs include:

Eurocentres, 101 N. Union St. #300, Alexandria, VA 22314, USA (☎703-684-1494; fax 684-1495; www.eurocentres.com). In Europe, Head Office, Seestr. 247, CH-8038 Zurich, Switzerland (☎41 1 485 50 40; fax 481 61 24; info@eurocentres.com). Language programs for beginning to advanced students with homestays in Barcelona. 2-week class $302, with homestay $616.

Language Immersion Institute, 75 South Manheim Blvd., SUNY-New Paltz, New Paltz, NY 12561, USA (☎845-257-3500; www.newpaltz.edu/lii). 2-week summer language courses and other programs for college credit in Spanish. Program fee US$750 per 2 weeks, including homestay and full board.

S.O.L. Barcelona, Entenza, 320, ent. 1a, 08029 Barcelona, Spain (☎93 405 12 00; www.solbarcelona.com). Classes in business Spanish and preparation for the D.E.L.E. exam for Spanish proficiency. Program fee US$500.

Consorci per a la Normalització Lingüística, C. Mallorca 272, 8a planta, 08037 Barcelona, Spain (☎93 272 31 00; www.cpnl.org/presentacio/welcome.htm). Organizes programs for adults learning Catalan.

BCN Languages, Av. Diagonal, 407 ent. 2a, 08008 Barcelona, Spain (☎93 218 21 77; www.bcnlanguages.com). Organizes a variety of courses, from standard to super intensive. Choose between host family accommodations or student residence.

WORKING ABROAD

WORK PERMITS

American, Canadian, South African, and Australian citizens need a work visa to work in Spain. Those desiring such a visa should contact the Spanish consulate in their country for the exact requirements, which include: a passport valid for at least six months, a job offer in Spain filed at the Ministry of Labor in Spain, a letter of good conduct from the police department in the city of original residence, a letter from a physician affirming good health and freedom from addiction, four passport photos, and approximately US$45. These visas may take four months or more to process, although certain cases may be rushed; if necessary, call the consulate multiple times to make sure you have the necessary paperwork or you will have to wait and wait and wait. European Union citizens can work in Spain, and if your parents were born in an EU country, you may be able to claim the right to a work permit.

WORK OPTIONS

There are two main schools of thought. Some travelers want long-term jobs that allow them to get to know another part of the world in depth (e.g. teaching English, working in the tourist industry). Other travelers seek out short-term jobs, usually in the service sector, working for a few weeks at a time to finance the next

Back Doors

Feeding Pigeons in Pl. Catalunya

View of the Street

leg of their journey. This section discusses both short-term and long-term opportunities for working in Barcelona.

Popular temporary jobs for foreigners include being an au pair, teaching English, or waiting tables. Irish pubs are almost always staffed with English-speaking expats, and the demands for English tutors is high. A good way to line up a more permanent job from home is to get a job with an international corporation with offices in Barcelona; large consulting and investment banking firms generally have offices abroad.

It is much easier to line up a job in Spain when you are already there; invaluable resources like "help wanted" signs just aren't visible from other countries, and the Internet can only get you so far. Get your hands on a copy of Catalunya's leading newspaper, *La Vanguardia*, to look at job ads; other publications are *El Periódico* and the English-language *Barcelona Metropolitan*.

For US college students, recent graduates, and young adults, the simplest way to get legal permission to work abroad is through **Council Exchanges Work Abroad Programs.** For a US$300-425 fee Council Exchanges can help you obtain a three- to six-month work permit/visa and provide assistance finding jobs and housing.

LONG-TERM WORK

If you're planning on spending a substantial amount of time (more than three months) working in Barcelona, search for a job well in advance. International placement agencies are often the easiest way to find employment abroad, especially for teaching English. **Internships,** usually for college students, are a good way to segue into working abroad. They are often unpaid, but many say the experience is well worth it. Search for internship options at www.internabroad.com.

AU PAIR

Au-pairs are typically women, aged 18-27, who work as live-in nannies, caring for children and doing light housework in foreign countries in exchange for room, board, and a small spending allowance or stipend. Most former au-pairs speak favorably of their experience, and of how it allowed them to really get to know the country without the high expenses of traveling. Drawbacks, however, often include long hours of constantly being on-duty, and mediocre pay. Much of the au pair experience depends on the family you're placed with. The agencies below specialize in looking for employment as an au pair.

Au Pair Homestay, World Learning, Inc., 1015 15th St. NW, Suite 750, Washington, D.C. 20005, USA (☎ 800-287-2477; fax 202-408-5397).

Au Pair in Europe, P.O. Box 68056, Blakely Postal Outlet, Hamilton, Ontario, L8M 3M7 Canada (☎ 905-545-6305; fax 905-544-4121; www.princeent.com).

Childcare International, Ltd., Trafalgar House, Grenville Pl., London NW7 3SA, UK (☎ 44 020 8906 3116; fax 8906-3461; www.childint.co.uk). UK£100 application fee.

interExchange, 161 Sixth Ave., New York, NY 10013, USA (☎ 212-924-0446; fax 924-0575; info@interexchange.org; www.interexchange.org).

TEACHING ENGLISH

Teaching jobs abroad are rarely well-paid, although some elite private American schools can pay somewhat competitive salaries. Volunteering as a teacher in lieu of getting paid is also a popular option, and even in those cases, teachers often get some sort of a daily stipend to help with living expenses. In almost all cases, you must have at least a bachelor's degree to be a full-fledged teacher, although often times college undergraduates can get summer positions teaching or tutoring.

Many schools require teachers to have a **Teaching English as a Foreign Language (TEFL)** certificate. This does not necessarily exclude you from finding a teaching job, but certified teachers often find higher paying jobs. Native English speakers working in private schools are most often hired for English-immersion classrooms where no Catalan or Spanish is spoken. Those volunteering or teaching in public schools, are more likely to be working in both English and Catalan. Placement agencies or university fellowship programs are the best resources for finding teaching jobs in Barcelona. The alternative is to make contacts directly with schools or to try your luck once you get there. If you are going to try the latter, the best time of the year is several weeks before the start of the school year. The following organizations help place teachers in Barcelona.

International Schools Services, Educational Staffing Program, P.O. Box 5910, Princeton, NJ 08543, USA (☎ 609-452-0990; www.iss.edu). Recruits teachers and administrators for American and English schools in Barcelona. US$150 program fee.

Office of Overseas Schools, US Department of State, Room H328, SA-1, Washington, D.C. 20522, USA (☎ 202-261-8200; fax 261-8224; www.state.gov/m/a/os/). Keeps a comprehensive list of schools abroad and agencies that arrange placement for Americans to teach abroad.

Teach Abroad (www.teachabroad.com). Posts listings of positions for English-speaking instructors and offers courses to prepare participants to be English language teachers.

SHORT-TERM WORK

Traveling for long periods of time can get expensive; therefore, many travelers try their hand at odd jobs for a few weeks at a time to make some extra cash to carry them through another month or two of touring around. Unemployment is high in Spain, so it may be difficult for someone just passing through to get a job in any Spanish city. An added impediment in Barcelona is that many employers require that their workers speak Catalan as well as Spanish and English. A better bet would be to travel to the beach towns which cater specifically to sun-loving tourists but whose employees take their month off in August. Most often, these short-term jobs are found by word of mouth, or simply by talking to the owner of a hostel or restaurant.

VOLUNTEERING

Volunteering can be one of the most fulfilling experiences in life, especially when combined with foreign travel. Many volunteer services charge a fee to participate in the program. These fees can be surprisingly hefty (although they frequently cover airfare and most, if not all, living expenses). Try to research a program before committing—talk to people who have previously participated and find out exactly what you're getting into, as living and working conditions vary greatly. The more informed you are and the more realistic your expectations, the more enjoyable the program will be.

Most people choose to go through a parent organization that takes care of logistical details and frequently provides a group environment and support system. Volunteer jobs are readily available in Barcelona, and many provide room and board in exchange for labor. You can sometimes avoid high application fees by contacting the individual work camps directly. The ⬛**Centre d'Informació i Assessorament per a Joves (CIAJ)**, Via Laietana, 39, 6e (☎93 319 23 00; www.bcn.es/ciaj) is the best place to look for volunteering opportunities once in Barcelona.

Earthwatch, 3 Clocktower Pl. Suite 100, Box 75, Maynard, MA 01754, USA (☎800-776-0188 or 978-461-0081; www.earthwatch.org). Arranges 1-3 week programs in Mallorca to promote conservation of natural resources. Fees vary based on location and duration. Costs average $1900 plus airfare.

Elderhostel, Inc., 11 Avenue de Lafayette, Boston, MA 92111-1746, USA (☎877-426-8056; fax 877-426-2166; www.elderhostel.org). Sends volunteers age 55 and over around the world to work in construction, research, teaching, and many other projects. Costs average $100 per day plus airfare.

Service Civil International Voluntary Service (SCI-IVS), SCI USA, 3213 W. Wheeler St., Seattle, WA 98199, USA (☎/fax 206-350-6585; www.sci-ivs.org). Arranges placement in work camps in Barcelona for those 18+. Registration fee US$65-125.

Volunteers for Peace, 1034 Tiffany Rd., Belmont, VT 05730, USA (☎802-259-2759; www.vfp.org). Arranges placement in work camps in Barcelona. Membership required for registration. Annual *International Workcamp Directory* US$20. Programs average US$200-500 for 2-3 weeks.

Volunteer Abroad (www.volunteerabroad.com). Posts and searches listings of volunteer opportunities worldwide. In Barcelona these opportunities usually involve teaching English.

Service Directory

ACCOMMODATIONS

For information on **rental agencies, home exchanges,** and how to acquire **long-term accommodations** in Barcelona, see p. 208.

AIRLINES

See also **Transportation Services,** p. 317.

Air Europa (24hr. reservation and info ☎902 40 15 01; www.air-europa.com).

British Airways, El Prat de Llobregat Airport (☎93 298 34 55, 24hr. reservation and info ☎902 11 13 33; open 6am-7pm). **Branch** at Pg. de Gràcia, 16.

Delta (24hr. reservation and info ☎901 11 69 46; www.delta-air.com).

Easy Jet (24hr. reservation and info ☎902 29 99 92; www.easyjet.com)

Iberia/Aviaco, Diputació, 258. (24hr. reservation and info ☎902 40 05 00). Student discounts.

Spanair, Pg. de Gràcia, 57 (24hr. reservation and info ☎902 13 14 15) offers fares that are often cheaper than Iberia.

BANKS

Banco de Espanya, Pl. de Catalunya 17 (☎93 482 47 00). Charges no commission on traveler's checks.

Caixa de Catalunya, Pl. Espanya, 6-8 (☎93 426 08 73). The most helpful with cash advances from credit cards without PINs.

La Caixa (☎902 223 040). Practically an office on every corner. Phone lines open M-F 10am-8pm; call for hours of specific branches.

BICYCLE AND MOPED RENTAL

Vanguard Rent a Car, C. Viladomat, 297, between Londres and París (☎93 439 38 80). Mopeds start at €36.95 per day, if renting for 3 days or less, €34.56 per day for more than 3 days, and €32.80 per day for more than 7 days. More expensive 2-person motos also available. Insurance, helmet, and IVA included. Must be 19, with identification, to rent. Open M-F 8am-1:30pm and 4-7:30pm, Sa-Su 9am-1pm.

BUSES

See also **Transportation Services**, p. 317.

Alsa Enatcar (☎902 42 22 42; www.alsa.es), Estació Nord.

Eurolines (☎902 40 50 40; www.eurolines.es), Estació Nord.

Linebús (☎93 265 07 00), Estació Nord. Discounts for travelers under 26 and over 60. Open daily 8am-8pm, Sa 8:30am-1pm and 5-8pm.

Sarfa (☎902 30 20 25; www.sarfa.com), Estació Nord. Open daily 8am-9pm.

CAR RENTAL

See **Planning Your Trip**, p. 295.

CLINICS

see also **Hospitals**, p. 315.

Barcelona Centro Médico (BCM), Av. Diagonal, 437, #14 (☎93 414 06 43), M: Maria Cristina. Coordinates referrals, for Spaniards and foreigners.

CRISIS AND HELP LINES

Crisis Lines: Oficina Permanente de Atención Social (24hr. toll-free ☎900 70 30 30).

DISABILITY RESOURCES

Ajuntament, Pl. Sant Miquel. Information office has a map of wheelchair accessible routes and establishments. (Also available at TMB office in the Universitat Metro.)

Centre d'Aternció a Disminuits, Badal, 102 (☎93 331 21 62). General information on help for disabilities.

Institut Municipal de Disminuits, C. Llacuna, 171 (☎ 93 291 84 00). Provides specific information on accessibility of sites, restaurants, etc.

Taxi: ☎93 420 80 88.

EMBASSIES AND CONSULATES

American Consulate, Pg. Reina Elisenda de Montcada, 23 (☎93 280 22 27; fax 93 280 61 75; www.embusa.es). FCG: Reina Elisenda.

Australian Consulate, Gran Via Carlos III, 98, 9th fl. (☎93 490 90 13; fax 93 411 0494; www.embaustralia.es/hours.htm). M: Maria Cristina.

British Consulate, Edificio Torre de Barcelona, Av. Diagonal, 477 (☎93 366 62 00; fax 93 366 62 21; www.fco.gov.uk/directory/posts). M: Hospital Clinic.

Canadian Consulate, Elisenda de Pinós, 10 (☎93 204 27 00; fax 93 204 27 01; www.canada-es.org). FCG: Reina Elisenda.

Irish Consulate, Gran Via Carlos III, 94 (☎93 451 90 21; fax 93 411 29 21; www.goireland.com/low/visitorsguide/irembassies.html). M: Maria Cristina.

New Zealand Consulate, Trav. de Gràcia, 64 (☎93 209 03 99; fax 93 201 08 90).

South African Consulate, C. Teodora Lamadrid, 7 (☎93 418 64 45 ; fax 93 418 05 38; www.sudafrica.com).

EMERGENCY SERVICES

see also **Clinics** (p. 314), **Crisis Lines** (p. 314), and **Hospitals** (p. 315).

Emergency: ☎112

Local Police: ☎092

National police: ☎091

Medical: ☎061

Police: Las Ramblas, 43 (☎93 344 13 00), across from Pl. Reial and next to C. Nou de La Rambla. M: Liceu. Tourists in need of assistance should visit the department labeled "Tourist attention," where they will find helpful multilingual officers. Open 24hr., tourist assistance open 8am-2am. Branches beneath the Pl. de Catalunya on the side facing the Banco Nacional, and at the Barcelona-Nord bus station.

GAY AND LESBIAN SERVICES

Antinous, C. J. Anselm Clavé, 6 (☎93 301 90 70; www.antinouslibros.com). M: Drassanes. On the right as you walk down C. Clavé from Las Ramblas. A large bookstore and cafe specializing in gay and lesbian books, including several guide books. Decent selection of books in English. Open M-F 11am-2pm and 5-9pm, Sa noon-2pm and 5-9pm.

Cómplices, C. Cervantes, 2 (☎93 412 72 83). M: Liceu. From C. Ferrán, take a left onto C. Avinyó and then the 2nd left. A small gay and lesbian bookstore with publications in English and Spanish as well as a decent selection of gay and lesbian films. Also provides an informative **map** of Barcelona's gay and lesbian bars and discos. Open M-F 10:30am-8:30pm, Sa noon-8:30pm.

HOSPITALS

Hospital Clinic, Villarroel, 170 (☎93 227 54 00). M: Hospital Clinic. Main entrance at the intersection of C. Roselló and C. Casanova.

Hospital de la Santa Creu i Sant Pau (☎93 291 90 00; emergency ☎93 291 91 91), at the intersection of C. Cartagena and C. Sant Antoni Maria Claret. M: Hospital de Sant Pau.

Hospital Vall d'Hebron (☎93 274 61 00) M: Vall d'Hebron.

INTERNET ACCESS

bcnet (Internet Gallery Café), Barra de Ferro, 3 (☎93 268 15 07), right down the street from the Picasso museum. M: Jaume I. €1.50 per 15min., €3.61 per hr.; 10hr. ticket available for €18. Open daily 10am-1am.

Café Interlight, Av. Pau Claris, 106 (☎93 301 11 80; interlight@bcn.servicom.es). M: Urquinaona. €0.60 per 15min., €1.50 per hr. Open 9am-3pm.

CiberOpción, Gran Via, 602 (☎93 412 73 08), across from the Universitat building. M: Universitat. €0.60 per 30min. Open M-Sa 9am-1am, Su 11am-1am.

Conèctate, C. Aragó, 283 (☎93 467 04 43). M: Pg. de Gràcia. One block to the right of the Metro, facing away from Pl. de Catalunya. Internet midnight-9am €1.20 for 2hr., 6pm-9pm €1.20 for 45min., and the rest of the time €1.20 per hr. Most other services an additional €0.60. Open 24hr. Wheelchair accessible.

Cybermundo Internet Centre, Bergara, 3 and Balmes, 8 (☎93 317 71 42). M: Catalunya. Just off of the Pl. de Catalunya, behind the Triangle shopping mall. Allows uploading of disks. €1 per hr. Open M-F 9am-1am, Sa 10am-1am.

▓ Easy Everything, Las Ramblas, 31 (www.easyeverything.com). M: Liceu. €1.20 for about 40min.—price fluctuates according to the number of computers in use. Open 24hr. Also on Ronda Universitat, 35, right next to Pl. de Catalunya, at the same prices.

El Pati d'Internet, C. Astúries, 78 (☎93 292 02 45). M: Fontana. €0.90 per 15min.,

€1.35 per 30min., €2.40 per hr., €0.60 per 15min. after 1 hr.; 5hr. tickets cost €8, 10hr. goes for €15. M-F 11am-2pm and 4-10pm, Su 4-10pm.

h@ppy world, C. Muntaner, 122 (☎93 454 91 69). M: Hospital Clinic. €1.20 for 30min., €2.40 per hr.,€9 for 5 hr., €17.45 for 10 hr., €39.10 for 25 hr. Open M-Sa 10am-10pm, Su 5-10pm. Closed Su in Aug.

Idea, Pl. Comercial, 2 (☎93 268 87 87; www.ideaborn.com). From M: Jaume I, follow C. Princesa almost to its end and turn right on C. Comerç; the *plaça* is ahead on the right. €1.50 per 30min., €2.50 per hr. Open M-Th 10am-11pm, F-Sa 10am-3am, Su 10am-10pm. Internet access until 10:30pm daily.

Intergame, Pl. Rius i Taulet, 8 (☎93 416 01 71). M: Fontana. €1.20 per hr. Open daily 10am-midnight.

Internet Exchange, Las Ramblas, 130 (☎93 317 73 27). M: Catalunya. €0.06 per minute; €12 for 5hr., €27 for 20 hr.; students €15 for 10hr., €30 for 30hr.

Locutorio, Gran Via, 820 (☎93 246 36 07), right near the Monumental bullring, en route to Pl. Glòries, in **l'Eixample.** M: Monumental. Internet 3pm-11pm €2 per hr.; noon-3pm €1 per hr. Black-and-white printing €0.60 per page. Color printing €1 per page. Open daily noon-11pm. Cash only.

Music Center-Internet, C. Córsega, 171. M: Hospital Clinic. €1.20 per 30min. Open M-Th 8am-10pm, F-Sa 8am-3am.

Travel Bar, C. Boqueria, 27 (☎93 342 52 52; www.barcelonatravelbar.com). M: Liceu. Just off Las Ramblas. €1 per 15 min. Open daily 9am-2am.

Workcenter, Av. Diagonal, 441 (☎902 11 50 11; www.workcenter.net). M: Hospital Clinic or Diagonal. Another **branch** is at C. Roger de Lluria, 2. M: Urquinaona. €0.52 per 10min. Large range of printing and computer services. Open 24hr.

LAUNDROMATS

Lavandería Roca, Joaquín Costa, 14 (☎93 442 59 82). Full service €8.42, available in 2-4hr. Open M-F 8:30am-7:30pm, Sa 8:30am-2pm.

Tintorería Ferran, C. Ferran, 11. M: Liceu. Ferran runs off Las Ramblas, just below Liceu. Open M-F 9am-8pm.

Tintorería San Pablo, C. San Pau, 105 (☎93 329 42 49). M: Parallel. Wash, dry, and fold €10; do-it-yourself €7.25. Open July-Sept. M-F 9am-2pm; Oct.-June M-F 9am-2pm and 4-8pm.

LIBRARIES

Biblioteca Sant Pau, Carrer de l'Hospital, 56 (☎93 302 07 97). M: Liceu. Take C. Hospital off Las Ramblas and walk a few blocks to a castle on your right; enter the courtyard and walk to its far end; the library is on the left. Open M, W, F 3:30-8:30pm; Tu, Th, Sa 10am-2pm and 3:30-8:30pm.

Institut Nord-americà, Via Augusta, 123 (☎93 240 51 10). Open Sept.-July M-F 9am-2pm and 4-7pm.

MEDICAL SERVICES

See also **Clinics** (p. 314), **Hospitals** (p. 315), and **Emergency Services** (p. 314).

Association Ciutadana Anti-SIDA de Catalunya, C. Junta de Comerç, 23 (☎93 317 05 05). AIDS information. Open M-F 10am-2pm and 4-7pm.

MOTO RENTAL

See **Bike and Moped Rental**, p. 313.

PHARMACIES

Pharmacies open 24hr. on a rotating basis; look for the green and red neon crosses to find one. Check pharmacy windows for current listings.

POST OFFICES

Lista de Correos (general info on Barcelona post offices ☎902 19 71 97, for this specific office ☎93 486 80 50; www.correos.es), Pl. de Antoni López, at the corner of Pg. Colom (the street that runs along the port from the Columbus Monument), and Via Laietana. Across the street from the port. M: Jaume I or Barceloneta. Fax and *lista de correos*. Open M-F 8:30am-9:30pm. A little shop in the back of the post office building, across the street, wraps packages for mailing (about €1.80). Shop open M-Sa 9am-2pm and 5-8pm. **Postal Code:** 08003.

Lista de Correos, C. Aragó, 282, across from the Amena cell phone store, near Gaudí's Casa Batlló. M: Pg. de Gràcia. Fax and *lista de correos* services. Open M-F 8:30am-8:30pm, Sa 8:30am-1pm. **Postal Code:** 08007.

Lista de Correos, Ronda Universitat, 23, off Pl. de Catalunya. M: Catalunya. Open M-F 8:30am-8:30pm. Sa 9:30am-1pm.

RELIGIOUS RESOURCES

Comunidad Israelita de Barcelona (Jewish services), C. Avenir, 29 (☎93 200 61 48).

Comunidad Musulmana (Muslim services), Mosque Toarek Ben Ziad, C. Hospital, 91 (☎93 441 91 49). Services daily at prayer times.

Església Catedral de la Santa Creu, in Pl. Seu, up C. Bisbe from Pl. St. Jaume. M: Jaume I. Cathedral open daily 8am-1:30pm and 4-7:30pm. Cloister open 9am-1:15pm and 4-7pm.

Església Santa Maria del Mar (☎93 310 23 90), on Pl. Santa Maria del Mar. M: Jaume I. Services in Spanish Su and Holy days noon and 7:30pm. Open M-Sa 9am-1:30pm and 4:30-8pm, Su 9am-2pm and 5-8:30pm.

Església Sant Pau de Camp, at the intersection of C. Sant Pau and C. Carretes, 2 blocks off Av. Parallel. M: Parallel. Open W-M 5-8pm.

SUPERMARKETS

Champion Supermarket, Las Ramblas, 113 (☎93 302 48 24). M: Liceu. From Liceu, walk up Las Ramblas and look to the left. All the essentials, as well as an inexpensive menu of ready-to-eat foods (meats €6 per kg and up) and a salad bar. Open M-Sa 9:15am-10pm.

Condis, Junta de Comerç, 19, in **El Raval**, off of C. Hospital. Open M-Th 9am-2pm and 5pm-9pm, F-Sa 9am-9pm.

El Corte Inglés, Pl. de Catalunya, 14 (☎93 306 38 00). M: Catalunya. The Spanish superstore has in its basement level a sizable supermarket, with a more exotic variety of items than most local places.

TAXIS

RadioTaxi (☎93 225 00 00).

Servi Taxi (☎93 330 03 00; www.servi-taxi.com).

Taxi Barcelona (☎93 090 09 08; www.taxi-barcelona.com).

Taxigroc (☎93 490 22 22; www.taxigroc.com).

Taxi 033 (☎93 303 30 33; www.taxi033.com).

Disabled travelers should call ☎93 420 80 88.

TELEPHONE INTERNATIONAL ACCESS NUMBERS

See **Once In**, p. 32

TICKETS

See also theater venues in **Entertainment**, p. 177.

Tel Entrada (☎902 10 12 12). Call for information, listings, and reservations to theatrical and musical performances.

TOURS

Bus Turístic: The easiest place to hop on the Bus Turístic is Pl. de Catalunya, in front of El Corte Inglés. Buses run daily (except Dec. 25 and Jan. 1) every 10-30min., 9am-9:30pm. Purchase tickets on the bus, the Pl. de Catalunya tourist office, or at Estació Barcelona-Sants. 1-day pass €14, ages 4-12 €8; 2-day pass €18.

Ruta del Modernisme: Passes (€3; students, over 65, and groups over 10 people €2 per person) are good for a month and give holders a 25-30% discount on entrance to major Modernist attractions. Purchase passes at Casa Amatller, Pg. de Gràcia, 41 (see p. 57), near the intersection with C. Consell de Cent (☎93 488 01 39). For information on which sights the pass offers discounts to, see p. 57.

Walking Tours of the Barri Gòtic (☎906 301 282). Sa-Su at 10am in English and noon in Catalan and Spanish. Group size is limited; buy tickets in advance. €6.60, ages 4-12 €3.

TOURIST OFFICES

Tourist Info Line: ☎90 730 12 82, from abroad ☎93 368 97 31 30.

Aeroport El Prat de Llobregat (☎93 478 05 65), in the international terminal. English-speaking agents offer information on Catalunya and Barcelona, maps, and hotel reservations. Open daily 9am-9pm.

Informació Turística Plaça Catalunya, Pl. Catalunya, 17S, below Pl. de Catalunya. M: Catalunya. Open daily 9am-9pm.

Informació Turística Plaça Sant Jaume, Pl. Sant Jaume, 1, off C. Ciutat. M: Jaume I. Open M-Sa 10am-8pm, Su 10am-2pm.

Oficina de Turisme de Catalunya, Palau Robert, Pg. de Gràcia, 107 (☎93 238 40

00; fax 93 292 12 70; www.gencat.es/probert). M: Diagonal. Open M-Sa 10am-7pm, Su 10am-2pm.

TRANSPORTATION SERVICES

See also **Airlines** (p. 313), **Bike and Moped Rental** (p. 313), **Buses** (p. 314), **Car Rental** (p. 314), and **Taxis** (p. 316).

Airport: El Prat de Llobregat airport (☎93 298 38 38; www.aena.es/ae/bcn/homepage), 12km (8 mi.) southwest of Barcelona; see **Once in Barcelona**, p. 24.

Buses: Barcelona Nord Estació d'Autobuses, C. Ali-bei, 80 (☎90 230 32 22). M: Arc de Triomf, exit to Nàpols. Info office open daily 7am-9pm.

Trains: Estació Barcelona-Sants, in Pl. Països Catalans. M: Sants-Estació. Buses to the station include #30 from Pl. de Espanya 44 through l'Eixample (stops at La Sagrada Família), and N2. Station open M-F 4:30am-midnight, Sa-Su 5am-midnight. See p. 25.

Estació França (☎902 24 02 02), Av. Marqués de l'Argentera. M: Barceloneta. Buses include #17 from Pl. de Catalunya and N6. Open daily 7am-10pm.

RENFE. (24hr. info ☎902 24 02 02; www.renfe.es.)

TRAVEL AGENTS

See Budget and Student Travel Agencies, p. 289.

WESTERN UNION

Most *Correos y telégrafos* (post offices) offer Western Union services. Check www.westernunion.com for exact locations.

Admon Manuel Martín, Las Ramblas, 41. Open daily 9am-midnight.

YOUTH SERVICES

Centre d'Informació Assessorament per a Joves, C. Ferrán, 32 (☎93 402 78 00; www.bcn.es/ciaj). M: Liceu. 1 block off Las Ramblas. More of a student assistance office than a travel agency. No tickets for sale, but plenty of free advice and a bulletin board with youth events and opportunities. Excellent library of travel guides for browsing. Open M-F 10am-2pm and 4-8pm.

Appendix

SPANISH & CATALAN PHRASEBOOK

THE BASICS

ENGLISH	CATALAN	SPANISH
Hello	Hola	Hola
Good morning	Bon dia	Buenos días
Good afternoon	Bona tarde	Buenas tardes
Good night	Bona nit	Buenas noches
Goodbye	Adéu	Adiós
Please	Si us plau	Por favor
Thank you	Gràcies	Gracias
You're welcome	De res	De nada
Excuse me	Perdoni	Perdón
I don't understand Catalan/Spanish	No entenc català/castellà	No entiendo catalán/castellaño
Do you speak English?	Parleu anglès?	¿Hablaís inglés?

DIRECTIONS

ENGLISH	CATALAN	SPANISH
Where is/are...?	On és/estan...?	¿Dónde está/estan...?
...the bathroom	...els lavabos	... los aseos/servicios
...the train station	...estació de trenes	...la estación de trenes
...the church	...l'església	...la iglesia
...the hostel	...l'hostal	... el hostal
...the store	...magatzem	...la tienda
...the museum	...el museu	...el museo
...the market	...el mercat	...el mercado
...the pharmacy	...la farmàcia	...la farmacia
...the hospital	...l'hospital	...el hospital

ACCOMMODATIONS & TRANSPORTATION

ENGLISH	CATALAN	SPANISH
Do you have...?	Té...?	Teneís...?
...a room	...una habitació	...una habitación
...for one person	...per una persona	...para una persona
...for two people	...per dues persones	...para dos personas
...with a double bed	...amb un llit per dues persones	...con una cama matrimonial
...with two beds	...amb dos llits	...con dos camas
...with a bath	...amb bany	...con baño
How much does it cost?	Quan és?	¿Cúanto cuesta?
I would like a train ticket.	Voldria un bitlet	Quisiera un billete
a round-trip ticket	un bitlet d'anar i tornar	un billete de ida i vuelta

DAYS & MONTHS

ENGLISH	CATALAN	SPANISH
Monday	dilluns	lunes
Tuesday	dimarts	martes
Wednesday	dimecres	miercoles
Thursday	dijous	jueves
Friday	divendres	viernes
Saturday	dissabte	sábado
Sunday	diumenge	domingo
January	gener	enero
February	febrer	febrero
March	març	marzo
April	abril	abril
May	maig	mayo
June	juny	junio
July	juliol	julio
August	agost	agosto
September	septembre	septiembre
October	octobre	octubre
November	novembre	noviembre
December	desembre	diciembre

NUMBERS

ENGLISH	CATALAN	SPANISH
1	un/una	uno
2	dos/dues	dos
3	tres	tres
4	quatre	quatro
5	cinc	cinco
6	sis	seis
7	set	siete
8	vuit	ocho
9	nou	nueve
10	deu	diez
11	onze	once
12	dotze	doce
13	tretze	trece
14	catorze	quatorce
15	quinze	quince
16	setze	dieciseis
17	disset	diecisiete
18	divuit	dieciocho
19	dinou	diecinueve
20	vint	veinte
30	trenta	treinta
40	quaranta	quarenta
50	cinquanta	cincuenta
60	siexanta	sesenta
70	setanta	setenta

80	vuitanta	ochenta
90	novanta	noventa
100	cent	cien

AVERAGE TEMPERATURES

AVG TEMP	JANUARY	APRIL	JULY	OCTOBER
F°	40-55	50-64	69-79	54-70
C°	4-13	10-18	22-26	12-21

SIZE CONVERSIONS

WOMEN'S CLOTHING

US SIZE	4	6	8	10	12	14	16
UK SIZE	6	8	10	12	14	16	18
EUROPE SIZE	36	38	40	42	44	46	48

WOMEN'S SHOES

US SIZE	5	6	7	8	9	10	11
UK SIZE	3	4	5	6	7	8	10
EUROPE SIZE	36	37	38	39	40	41	42

MEN'S SUITS/JACKETS

US/UK SIZE	32	34	36	38	40	42	44
EUROPE SIZE	42	44	46	48	50	52	54

MEN'S SHIRTS

US/UK SIZE	14	14.5	15	15.5	16	16.5	17
EUROPE SIZE	36	37	38	39	40	41	42

MEN'S SHOES

US SIZE	6	7	8	9	10	11	12
UK SIZE	5.5	6.5	7.5	8.5	9.5	10.5	11.5
EUROPE SIZE	38.5	39.5	40.5	41.5	42.5	43.5	44

METRIC CONVERSIONS

1 foot (ft.) = 0.30 meter (m)	1m = 3.28 ft.
1 mile (mi.) = 1.61 kilometers (km)	1km = 0.62 mi.
1 pound (lb.) = 0.45 kilogram (kg)	1kg = 2.2 lb.
1 gallon (gal.) = 4 quarts (qt.) = 3.78 liters (L)	1 L = 1.06 qt.= 0.264 gal.

Index

R

S

T

Maps

MAP LEGEND

✚ Hospital	✈ Airport	🏛 Museum	▲ Mountain
✪ Police	🚌 Bus Station	🏨 Hotel/Hostel	Park
✉ Post Office	🚂 Train Station	⛺ Camping	
ⓘ Tourist Office	M METRO STATION	🍴 Food & Drink	Beach
🛈 Bank	⚓ Ferry Landing	🛍 Shopping	
⚑ Embassy/Consulate	✝ Church	★ Nightlife	Water
▪ Site or Point of Interest	✡ Synagogue	🍺 Pub	
☎ Telephone Office	☪ Mosque	💻 Internet Café	
♜ Theater	⛱ Beach	••••••• Pedestrian Zone	The Let's Go compass always points NORTH.

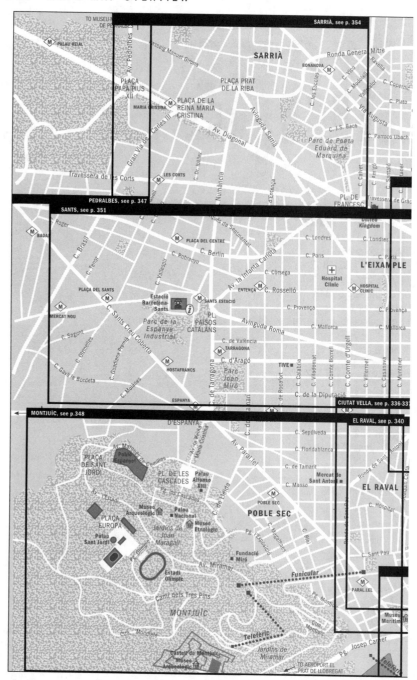

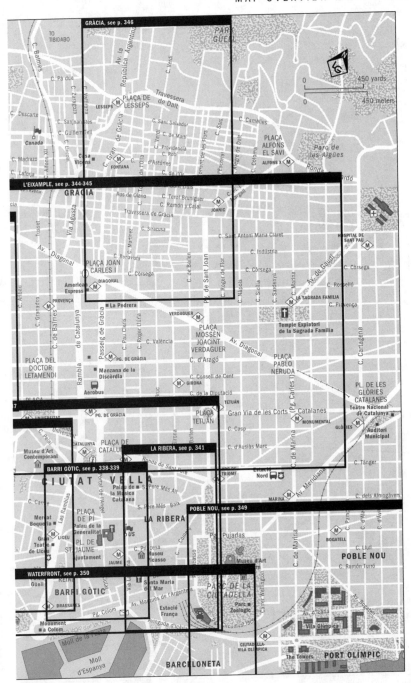

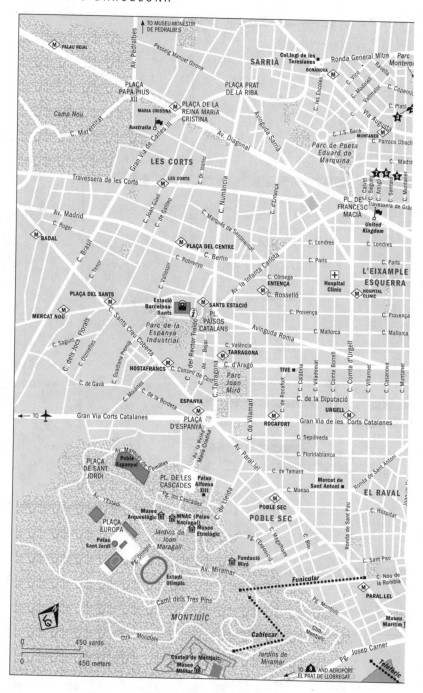

TO MUSEU-MONESTIR
DE PEDRALBES

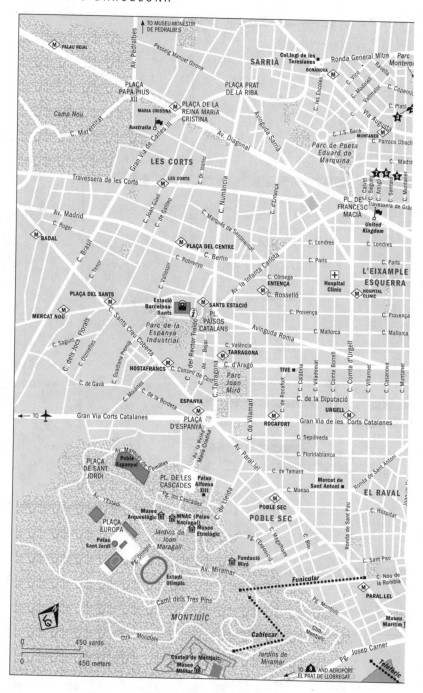 PALAU REIAL

Av. Pedralbes

Passeig Manuel Girona

SARRIÀ

Col.legi de les
Teresianes

Ronda General Mitre

Parc
Montero

BONANOVA

Ravella

C. Vico

C. les Escoles

C. Modolell

C. Vallmador

C. Copernic

PLAÇA
PAPA PIUS
XII

PLAÇA PRAT
DE LA RIBA

C. Plató

MARIA CRISTINA

PLAÇA DE LA
REINA MARIA
CRISTINA

Via Augusta

Camp Nou

Australia

Avinguda Sarrià

C. J.S. Bach

MUNTANER

C. Parroco Ubach

Gran Via de Carles III

Av. Diagonal

Parc de Poeta
Eduard de
Marquina

C. Madra

LES CORTS

Travessera de les Corts

LES CORTS

C. Dr. Ibáñez

C. Numància

Av. Diagonal

Calvet

C. Sague

C. Amigo

C. Santa

C. Muntaner

Av. Madrid

C. Roger

C. Joan Güell

C. de Galileo

C. d'Entença

PL. DE
FRANCESC
MACIÀ

Travessera de Grà

BADAL

C. Brasil

C. Tenor

C. Vallespir

PLAÇA DEL CENTRE

C. Robrenyo

C. Berlin

Av. la Infanta Carlota

United
Kingdom

C. Londres

C. Londres

C. Paris

C. Paris

C. Còrsega

L'EIXAMPLE
ESQUERRA

PLAÇA DEL SANTS

C. dels Jocs Florals

C. Sants Creu Coberta

Estació
Barcelona-
Sants

SANTS ESTACIÓ

ENTENÇA

C. Rosselló

Hospital
Clinic

HOSPITAL
CLINIC

MERCAT NOU

C. Sagunt

C. Olzinelles

Parc de la
Espanya
Industrial

PL.
PAÏSOS
CATALANS

C. Provença

C. Provença

C. del Rector Triadó

C. Guadiana Premia

HOSTAFRANCS

C. de Gavà

C. Molàns

C. de Centença

C. Bejar

C. de la Bordeta

C. Tarragona

C. València

C. d'Aragó

TARRAGONA

Parc
Joan
Miró

C. Mallorca

C. Mallorca

Avinguda Roma

TIVE

C. de Rocafort

C. Calabria

C. Viladomat

C. Comte Borrell

C. Comte d'Urgell

C. Villarroel

C. Casanova

C. Muntaner

ESPANYA

C. de Vilamarí

C. de la Diputació

URGELL

TO ✈

Gran Via Corts Catalanes

PLAÇA
D'ESPANYA

Av. Paral·lel

ROCAFORT

Gran Via de les Corts Catalanes

C. Sepúlveda

Av. la Reina Maria Cristina

C. Floridablanca

PLAÇA
DE SANT
JORDI

Av. Marques de Comillas

Poble
Espanyol

PL. DE LES
CASCADES

Palau
Alfonso
XIII

C. de Lleida

C. de Tamarit

C. de Manso

Mercat de
Sant Antoni

Ronda de Sant Antoni

EL RAVAL

Av. l'Estadi

Museo
Arqueològic

MNAC (Palau
Nacional)

POBLE
SEC

POBLE SEC

C. Hospital

PLAÇA
EUROPA

Palau
Sant Jordi

Museo
Etnològic

Jardins de
Joan
Maragall

Pg. de Mont

Pg. l'Exposició

C. Magallanes

C. Blai

Ronda de Sant Pau

C. Sant Pau

Estadi
Olímpic

Fundació
Miró

Av. Miramar

Funicular

C. Nou de
la Rambla

PARAL.LEL

Camí dels Tres Pins

Ctra. Mondials

MONTJUÏC

Cablecar

Cta.
Montjuic

Pg. Montjuic

Museu
Marítim

0 ___ 450 yards
0 ___ 450 meters

Castell de Montjuic

Museo
Militar

Jardins de
Miramar

TO 🔲8 AND AEROPORT
EL PRAT DE LLOBREGAT

Pg. Josep Carner

Telefèric

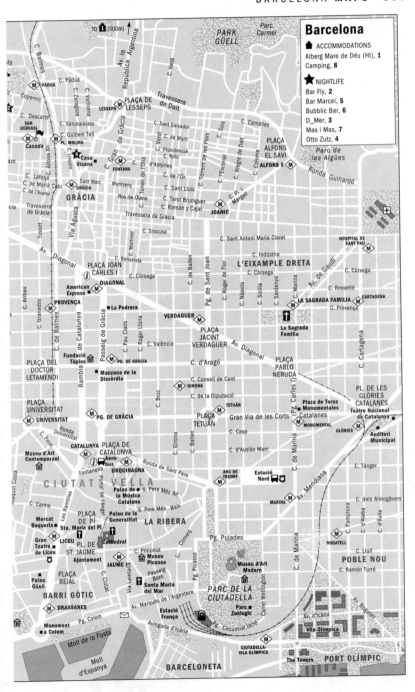

TO ⌂ (500m)

PARK GÜELL

Parc Carmel

Barcelona

⌂ ACCOMMODATIONS
Alberg Mare de Déu (HI), 1
Camping, 8

★ NIGHTLIFE
Bar Fly, 2
Bar Marcel, 5
Bubblic Bar, 6
D_Mer, 3
Mas i Mas, 7
Otto Zutz, 4

Av. la República Argentina

C. Balmes

C. Pàdua

M PÀDUA

Copernic

C. Verdi

Travessera de Dalt

PLAÇA DE LESSEPS

LESSEPS

SAN GERVASI

C. Descartes

C. Sanjoanistes

C. Guillem Tell

Canada

PL. MOLINA

C. Alfons XII

C. Lincoln

Casa Vicens

FONTANA

C. Sant Salvador

C. Verdi

C. de Martí

C. Providència

C. Robí

d'Astúries

C. de l'Or

C. Sant Lluís

C. Sant Salvador

C. Camèlies

C. Sos

PLAÇA ALFONS EL SAVI

ALFONS X M

Parc de les Aigües

Ronda Guinardó

C. Gran de Gràcia

C. Zaragoza

C. Valltranca

C. Laforja

C. de Maria Cubí

C. de l'Avenir

GRÀCIA

Sant Marc

GRÀCIA

Montseny

Ros de Olano

C. Terol Bruniguer

C. Ramón y Cajal

Travessera de Gràcia

Travessera de Gràcia

C. Torrent de l'Olla

C. Torrent de les Flors

C. l'Escorial

C. Alegre de Dalt

C. Coloma

C. Pi i Margall

JOANIC M

C. Martínez

C. Siracusa

C. Sant Antoni Maria Claret

HOSPITAL DE SANT PAU M

Via Augusta

Tusset

Av. Diagonal

C. Bonavista

PLAÇA JOAN CARLES I

C. Còrsega

C. de Ballén

C. Indústria

L'EIXAMPLE DRETA

C. Còrsega

Av. de Gaudí

C. Còrsega

C. Rosselló

C. Anbau

i DIAGONAL

American Express

PROVENÇA

C. Granados

C. de Balmes

Rambla de Catalunya

Passeig de Gràcia

C. Pau Claris

C. Roger Lúria

■ La Pedrera

C. València

VERDAGUER

PLAÇA JACINT VERDAGUER

Av. Diagonal

Pg. de Sant Joan

C. Roger de Flor

C. Nàpols

C. Sicília

C. Sardenya

C. Marina

M SAGRADA FAMILIA

C. Cartagena

C. Provença

La Sagrada Família

PLAÇA DEL DOCTOR LETAMENDI

Fundació Tàpies

M PG. DE GRÀCIA

■ Manzana de la Discòrdia

C. d'Aragó

PLAÇA PABLO NERUDA

C. Cartagena

PLAÇA UNIVERSITAT

M UNIVERSITAT

C. Pelai

Ronda Universitari

M PG. DE GRÀCIA

C. Bruc

M GIRONA

C. de la Diputació

C. Consell de Cent

M TETUÁN

PLAÇA TETUÁN

Gran Via de les Corts Catalanes

Plaza de Toros Monumentales

MONUMENTAL

PL. DE LES GLÒRIES CATALANES

Teatre Nacional de Catalunya

GLÒRIES M

Auditori Municipal

Pg. Carles I

C. de Marina

Museu d'Art Contemporani

CATALUNYA PLAÇA DE CATALUNYA

i Aero-bus

Fontanella

URQUINAONA

CIUTAT VELLA

C. Casp

C. d'Ausiàs Marc

C. Tànger

C. dels Almogàvers

Ronda de Sant Pere

M MARINA

Av. Meridiana

C. Pamplona

C. d'Àlaba

C. d'Àvila

Palau de la Música Catalana

S. Pere Més Alt

S. Pere Més Baix

ARC DE TRIOMF

Estació Nord

C. Carme

C. Girona

C. Ballén

Portal de l'Àngel

Las Ramblas

Mercat Boqueria

PLAÇA DE PÍ

Sta. Maria del Pí

Palau de la Generalitat

LA RIBERA

Pg. Pujades

Museu d'Art Modern

M ROGATELL

C. Llull

POBLE NOU

C. Ramón Turró

Gran Teatre de Liceu

LICEU

PL. DE ST. JAUME

Cathedral

C. Princesa

M JAUME

Ajuntament

Museu Picasso

Passeig Born

Santa Maria del Mar

C. Comerç

Pg. Picasso

C. de Marina

Carrer Wellington

PARC DE LA CIUTADELLA

PLAÇA REIAL

Palau Güell

BARRI GÒTIC

M DRASSANES

Via Laietana

C. Ciutat

PARC DE LA CIUTADELLA

Parc Zoològic

Monument a Colom

Pg. Colom

Moll de la Fusta

Estació França

Av. Marquès de l'Argentera

Avinguda d'Icària

Pg. Circumval·lació

Av. d'Icària

Av. Bogatell

Vila Olímpica

Moll d'Espanya

BARCELONETA

CIUTADELLA-VILA OLÍMPICA

M

The Towers

PORT OLÍMPIC

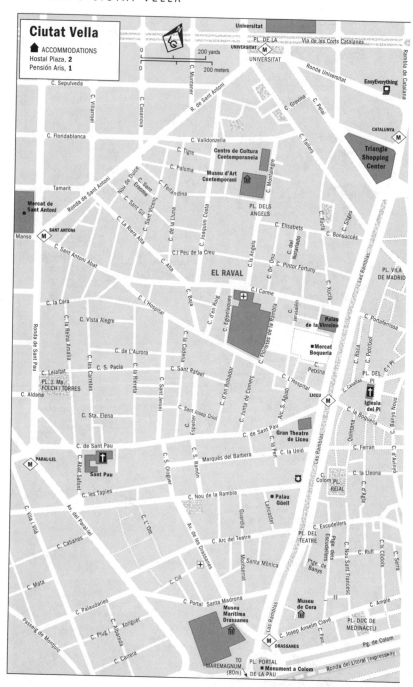

Ciutat Vella

ACCOMMODATIONS
Hostal Plaza, **2**
Pensión Aris, **1**

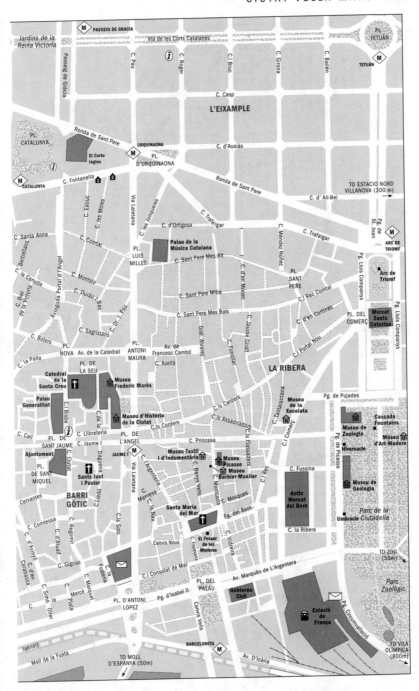

Barri Gòtic

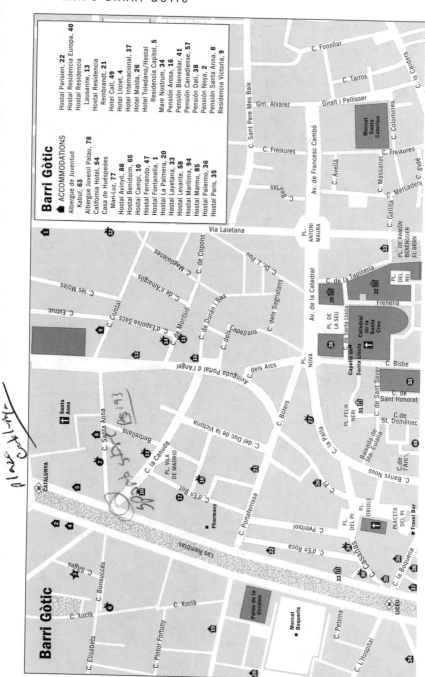

Barri Gòtic

♦ ACCOMMODATIONS
Albergue de Juventud
Kabul, 63
Albergue Juvenil Palau, 78
California Hotel, 54
Casa de Huéspedes
Mari-Luz, 77
Hostal Avinyó, 88
Hostal Benidorm, 65
Hostal Campi, 10
Hostal Fernando, 47
Hostal Fontanella, 1
Hostal La Palmera, 20
Hostal Layetana, 33
Hostal Levante, 58
Hostal Marítima, 94
Hostal Marmo, 85
Hostal Palermo, 36
Hostal Paris, 35

Hostal Parisien, 22
Hostal Residencia Europa, 40
Hostal Residencia
Lausanne, 13
Hostal Residencia
Rembrandt, 21
Hotel Call, 49
Hotel Lloret, 4
Hotel Internacional, 37
Hotel Malda, 26
Hotel Toledano/Hostal
Residencia Capitol, 5
Mare Nostrum, 34
Pensión Arosa, 16
Pensión Bienestar, 41
Pensión Canadiense, 57
Pensión Dalí, 38
Pensión Noya, 2
Pensión Santa Anna, 8
Residencia Victoria, 9

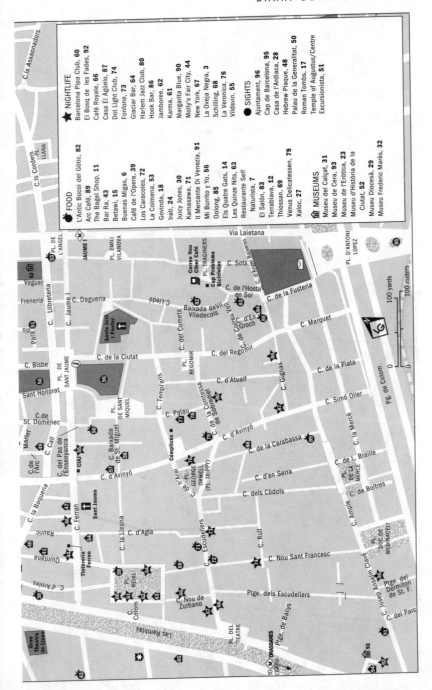

★ **NIGHTLIFE**
Barcelona Pipa Club, **60**
El Bosq de les Fades, **92**
Café Royale, **66**
Casa El Agüelo, **87**
Dot Light Club, **74**
Fontone, **73**
Glaciar Bar, **64**
Harlem Jazz Club, **80**
Hook Bar, **86**
Jamboree, **62**
Karma, **61**
Margarita Blue, **90**
Molly's Fair City, **44**
New York, **67**
La Oveja Negra, **3**
Schilling, **68**
La Veronica, **76**
Vildsvin, **55**

● **SIGHTS**
Ajuntament, **96**
Cap de Barcelona, **95**
Casa de l'Ardiaca, **28**
Hebrew Plaque, **48**
Palau de la Generalitat, **50**
Roman Tombs, **17**
Temple of Augustus/Centre
Excursionista, **51**

★ **FOOD**
L'Antic Bocoi del Gòtic, **82**
Arc Café, **89**
The Bagel Shop, **11**
Bar Ra, **43**
Betawi, **15**
Buenas Migas, **6**
Café de l'Opera, **39**
Los Caracoles, **72**
La Colmena, **53**
Govinda, **18**
Irati, **24**
Juicy Jones, **30**
Kamasawa, **71**
Il Mercante Di Venezia, **91**
Mi Burrito y Yo, **56**
Oolong, **85**
Els Quatre Gats, **14**
Les Quinze Nits, **63**
Restaurante Self
Naturista, **7**
El Salón, **83**
Terrablava, **12**
Thiossan, **69**
Venus Delicatessen, **79**
Xaloc, **27**

🏛 **MUSEUMS**
Museu del Calçat, **31**
Museu de Cera, **93**
Museu de l'Eròtica, **23**
Museu d'Història de la
Ciutat, **52**
Museu Diocesà, **29**
Museu Frederic Marès, **32**

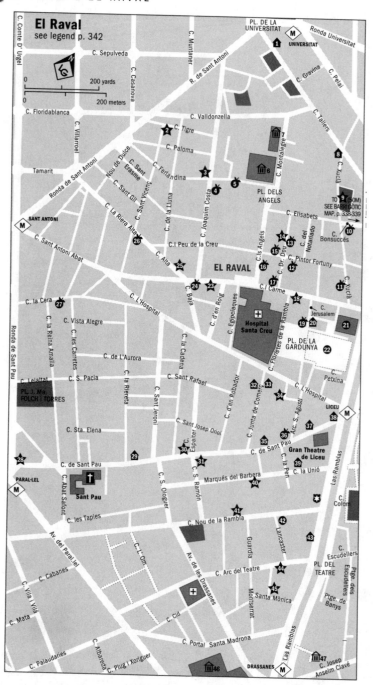

El Raval
see legend p. 342

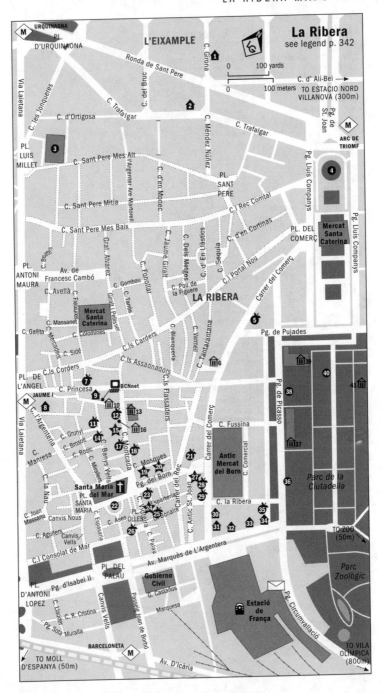

La Ribera
see legend p. 342

El Raval
see map p. 340

🏠 ACCOMMODATIONS

Barcelona Mar
  Youth Hostel, 29
Hostal Benidorm, 43
Hostal Opera, 37
Hostal La Palmera, 20
Hostal La Terrassa, 33
Hotel Principal, 32
Hotel Peninsular, 35
Ideal Youth Hostel, 39
Mare Nostrum, 38
Pensión 45, 8
Pensión L'Isard, 1

🍴 FOOD

Bar Ra, 19
Bar Restaurante
  Los Toreros, 11
Bar Restaurante Romesco, 36
Buenas Migas, 10
Carmelitas, 17
Colibri, 26
L'Hortet, 15
mamacafé, 13
Pla dels Angels, 5
Restaurante Biocenter, 12
Restaurante Can Lluís, 27
Restaurante Riera, 4
Shalimar, 24
Silenus, 16

⭐ NIGHTLIFE

El Cafe que pone Muebles
  Navarro, 25
Casa Almirall, 3
La Confiteria, 28
London Bar, 41
Lupino, 18
Marsella Bar, 31
Moog, 44
Muy Buenas, 23
La Paloma, 2
Pastis, 45
La Oveja Negra, 9
The Quiet Man, 40
Raval-Bar, 14
Rita Blue, 34
Sant Pau 68, 30

⬤ SIGHTS

Mercat Boqueria, 22
Palau Güell, 42
Palau de la Virreina, 21

🏛 MUSEUMS

Centre de Cultura
  Contemporània, 7
Museu d'Art Contemporani, 6
Museu de Cera, 47
Museu Marítima Drassanes, 46

La Ribera
see map p. 341

🏠 ACCOMMODATIONS

Gothic Point Youth Hostal, 8
Hostal de Ribagorza, 2
Hostal Nuevo Colón, 33
Hostal Orleans, 32
Hotel Triunfo, 34
Pensión Ciutadella, 31
Pensión Lourdes, 9
Pensión Port-bou, 30
Pensión Rondas, 1

🍴 FOOD

Barcelónia, 29
Café del Born, 28
Cal Pep, 26
Euskal Etxea, 18
Gades, 25
La Cocette, 23
La Habana Vieja, 11
Sandwich and Friends, 21
Suborn, 35
Taira, 5
Tèxtil Café, 12
Txirimiri, 7
Va de Vi, 14
Xampanyet, 17

⭐ NIGHTLIFE

El Copetin, 19
Mudanzas, 24
Palau Dalmase, 15
Pitin Bar, 27
Plàstic Café, 20

⬤ SIGHTS

Arc de Triomf, 4
Cascada Fountains, 40
El Fossar de les Moreres, 22
Hivernacle, 38
Palau de la Música Catalana, 3
Umbracle, 36

🏛 MUSEUMS

Museu Barbier-Mueller, 16
Museu d'Art Modern, 41
Museu de Geologia, 37
Museu de la Xocolata, 6
Museu de Zoologia, 39
Museu Picasso, 13
Museu Textil i d'Indumentària, 10

L'Eixample

see map pp. 344-345

♠ ACCOMMODATIONS

Hostal Australia, **87**
Hostal Bonavista, **10**
Hostal Cisneros, **42**
Hostal Ciudad Condal, **35**
Hostal Eden, **63**
Hostal Felipe II, **38**
Hostal Girona, **98**
Hostal Hill, **26**
Hostal Qué Tal, **36**
Hostal Residencia Neutral, **68**
Hostal Residencia Oliva, **76**
Hostal Residencia Windsor, **34**
Hostal San Remo, **97**
Hotel Everest, **3**
Hotel Paseo de Gràcia, **18**
Hotel Universal, **55**
Pensión Aribau, **59**
Pensión Clíper, **14**
Pensión Fani, **46**
Pensión Puebla de Arenoso, **60**
Pensión Rondas, **99**

♦ FOOD & DRINK

A-Tipic, **70**
ba-ba-reeba, **83**
La Bodegueta, **28**
Café Miranda, **85**
Café Torino, **45**
Campechano, **49**
Can Cargol, **56**
Casa Dario, **106**
Chicago Pizza Pie Factory, **29**
Comme-Bio, **82**
El Criollo, **32**
Cullera de Boix, **96**
dahabi, **78**
La Flauta, **62**
Ginza, **24**
Giorgio, **53**
Hard Rock Café, **92**
Harmony, **93**
Hostal de Rita, **54**
Laie Llibreria Café, **90**
Madrid-Barcleona, **69**
Mandalay Café, **30**
Mauri, **21**
La Muscleria, **37**
La Provença, **27**
El Racó d'en Baltá, **17**
El Raconet, **13**
Restaurante Terrani, **8**
El Rodizio Grill, **72**
Thai Gardens, **75**
Txapela, **89**
Wok & Bol, **86**
Vips, **88**

★ NIGHTLIFE

Aire (Sala Diana), **43**
La Boîte, **7**
Buenavista Salsoteca, **15**
Illusion, **2**
Luz de Gas, **4**
Salvation, **95**
Sol, **6**
Topxi, **57**

◗ PUBS

Aloha, **22**
berlin, **5**
Caligula, **61**
Dietrich, **105**
domèstic, **77**
Fuse, **85**
La Filharmónica, **33**
La Fira, **23**
Les Gens que J'Aime, **50**
Let's Go, **39**
The Michael Collins Irish Pub, **40**
The Pop Bar, **31**

● SIGHTS

L'Auditori, **102**
Can Serra, **11**
Casa Amatller, **65**
Casa Batlló, **64**
Casa Calvet, **94**
Casa Comalat, **12**
Casa de las Punxes, **19**
Casa Golferichs, **79**
Casa Lactància, **80**
Casa Lleó Morera, **67**
Casa Milà (la Pedrera), **25**
Casa Olano, **52**
Casa Vidua Marfà, **51**
El Corte Inglés, **91**
Joieria Roca, **84**
Let's Go Bull (Meditation), **81**
The oldest house in L'Eixample, **71**
Palau del Baló de Quadras, **16**
Plaza de Toros Monumental, **101**
La Sagrada Família, **41**
Skating Pista de Gel, **73**
Teatre Nacional de Catalunya, **103**
Torre de les Aigües, **74**
Vinçon/Casa Casas, **20**

🏛 MUSEUMS & GALLERIES

Fundació Godia, **48**
Fundació Tàpies, **44**
Museu de Clavegueram, **58**
Museu de l'Esport, **104**
Museu del Perfum, **66**
Museu del Còmic i de la Il.lustració, **1**
Museu Egipci, **47**
Museu Taurí, **100**

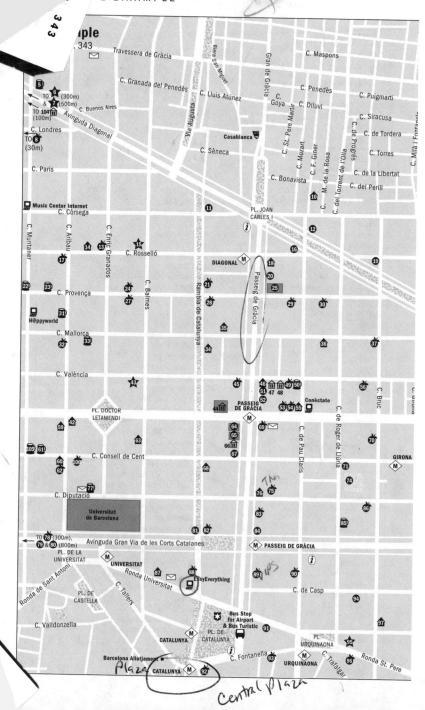

L'Eixample p. 343

Travessera de Gràcia

C. Granada del Penedès

C. Lluis Atúnez

C. Maspons

C. Penedès

C. Puigmarti

C. Goya

C. Diluvi

C. Siracusa

C. Buenos Aires

C. de Tordera

Avinguda Diagonal

Casablanca

C. de Progrés

C. Torres

C. Londres

C. Sèneca

C. de la Libertat

C. Paris

C. Bonavista

C. del Perill

Music Center Internet

C. Còrsega

PL. JOAN CARLES I

C. Rosselló

DIAGONAL

Passeig de Gràcia

C. Provença

Rambla de Catalunya

C. Balmes

H@ppyworld

C. Mallorca

C. València

PL. DOCTOR LETAMENDI

PASSEIG DE GRÀCIA

Conèctate

C. de Roger de Llúria

C. Bruc

C. Consell de Cent

C. de Pau Claris

GIRONA

C. Diputació

Universitat de Barcelona

Thai

TO 78 (300m), 79 & 80 (800m)

Avinguda Gran Via de les Corts Catalanes

PASSEIG DE GRÀCIA

PL. DE LA UNIVERSITAT

UNIVERSITAT

Ronda Universitat

EasyEverything

C. de Casp

Ronda de Sant Antoni

PL. DE CASTELLA

C. Tallers

C. Valldonzella

Bus Stop for Airport & Bus Turistic

PL. DE CATALUNYA

PL. URQUINAONA

URQUINAONA

CATALUNYA

Barcelona Allotjament

Plaza

CATALUNYA

C. Fontanella

C. Trafalgar

Ronda St. Pere

Central Plaza

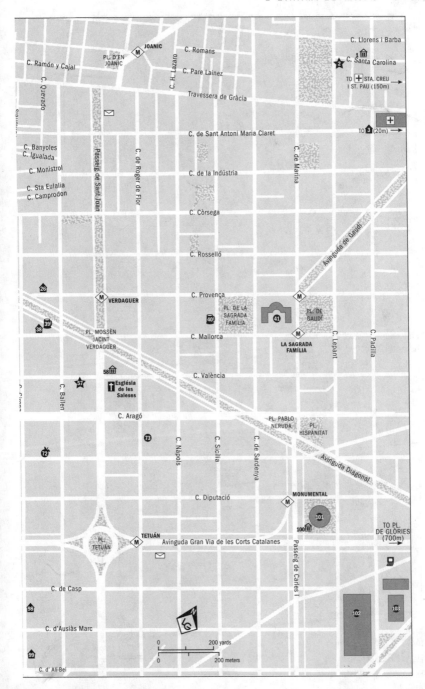

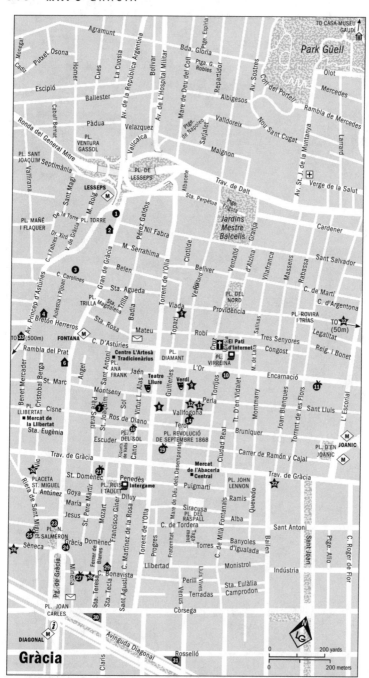

Gràcia

Gràcia

ACCOMMODATIONS
Aparthotel Silver, **4**
Hostal Bonavista, **29**
Hostal Lesseps, **2**
Hostal Valls, **33**
Pensión San Medín, **6**

FOOD
El 19 de la Riera, **25**
La Buena Tierra, **11**
Equinox Sol, **16**
La Gavina, **7**
Nut, **14**
Restaurant Illa de Gràcia, **21**
El Tastavins, **19**
Xavi Petit, **27**

NIGHTLIFE
Bahía, **26**
Bamboleo, **5**
Blues Café, **12**
Buda, **8**
Café de la Calle, **20**
Casablanca, **28**
Gasterea, **9**
Ikastola, **13**
KGB, **32**
Pirineus Bar, **22**

SIGHTS
Casa Cama, **23**
Casa Comalat, **30**
Casa de les Punxes, **31**
Casa Fuster, **24**
Casa Ramos, **1**
Casa Rubina, **10**
Casa Vicens, **3**

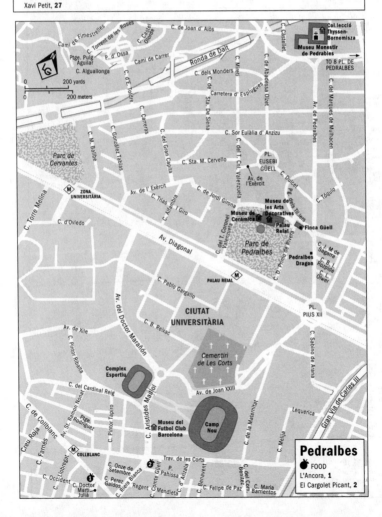

Pedralbes

FOOD
L'Ancora, **1**
El Cargolet Picant, **2**

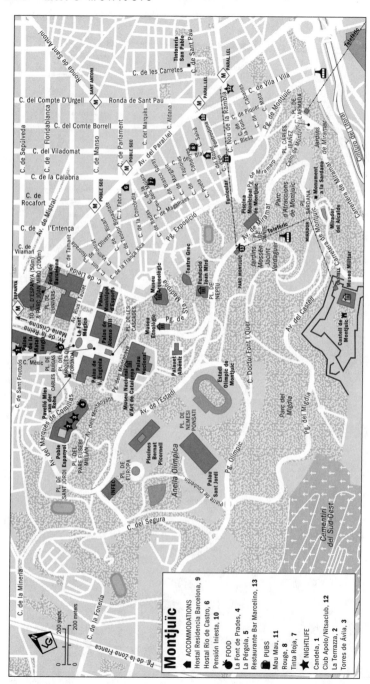

Montjuïc

ACCOMMODATIONS
Hostal Residencia Barcelona, **9**
Hostal Río de Castro, **6**
Pensión Iniesta, **10**

FOOD
La Font de Prades, **4**
La Pérgola, **5**
Restaurante Bar Marcelino, **13**

PUBS
Mau Mau, **11**
Rouge, **8**
Tinta Roja, **7**

NIGHTLIFE
Candela, **1**
Club Apolo/Nitsaclub, **12**
La Terrrazza, **2**
Torres de Ávila, **3**

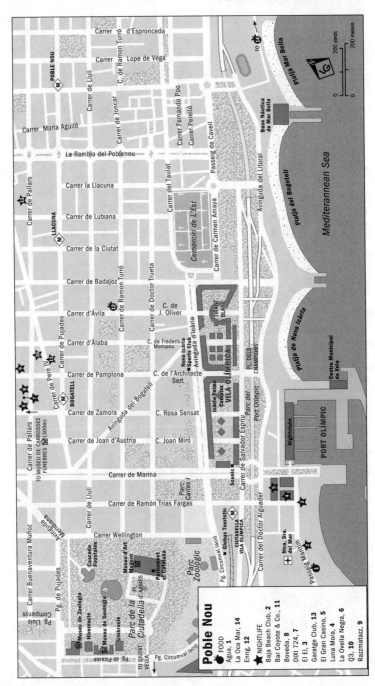

Carrer Turró d'Espronceda
Carrer Lope de Vega
C. de Ramon Turró
POBLE NOU M
Carrer de Llull
Carrer de Joncar
Carrer Maria Aguiló
Carrer de Joncar
Carrer Fernando Poo
Carrer Perelló
La Rambla del Pobllenou
Passeig de Cavell
Carrer del Taulat
Base Nàutica
de Mar Bella
platja Mar Bella
200 yards
200 meters
200 meters

Carrer la Llacuna
Carrer de Pallars
LLACUNA M
Carrer de Lutxana
Avinguda del Litoral
platja del Bogatell
Mediterannean Sea
Carrer de la Ciutat
Cementiri de l'Est
Carrer de Carmen Amaya
Carrer de Badajoz
Carrer de Ramon Turró
Carrer de Doctor Trueta
C. de
J. Oliver
TIRANT
LO BLANC
Carrer d'Àvila
platja de Nova Icària
Carrer de Pujades
C. de Frederic
Mompou
Carrer d'Àlaba
Nova Icària
Sports Club
Avinguda d'Icària
Carrer de Pamplona
C. de l'Architecte
Sert
Icària-Yelmo
Complex
VILA OLÍMPICA
Parc del
PL. DELS
CHAMPIONS
Port Olímpic
Centre Municipal
de Vela
Carrer de Pere IV
BOGATELL M
Carrer de Zamora
C. Rosa Sensat
Avinguda del Bogatell
Carrer de Joan d'Austria
C. Joan Miró
Carrer de Salvador Espriu
Carrer de Marina
Parc del
Nightclubs
PORT OLÍMPIC
Carrer de Pallars
TO MUSEU DE CARROSSES
FÚNEBRES (300m)
Carrer de Llull
Carrer de Ramón Trias Fargas
Parc
Carles I
Scenic
5
Carrer Wellington
Carrer del Doctor Aiguader
Ntra. Sra.
del Mar
3
Carrer Buenaventura Muñoz
Avinguda
Meridiana
Cascada
Fountains
Museu d'Art
Modern
Parlament
of Catalunya
Parc
Zoològic
Globus Touristic
CIUTADELLA M
VILA OLÍMPICA
Pg. Circumval·lació
Passeig Marítim
Pg. de Pujades
Museu de Zoologia
Hivernacle
Museu de Geologia
Umbracle
PL.
D'ARMES
Parc de la
Ciutadella
Pg. Lluís
Companys
TO CIUTAT
VELLA
Pg. Circumval·lació
Pg. de Picasso

Poble Nou

🍴 FOOD
Agua, **1**
La Oca Mar, **14**
Enng, **12**

⭐ NIGHTLIFE
Baja Beach Club, **2**
Bar Coyote & Co., **11**
Boveda, **8**
DIXI 724, **7**
El El, **3**
Garatge Club, **13**
El Gran Casino, **5**
Luna Mora, **4**
La Ovella Negra, **6**
Q3, **10**
Razzmatazz, **9**

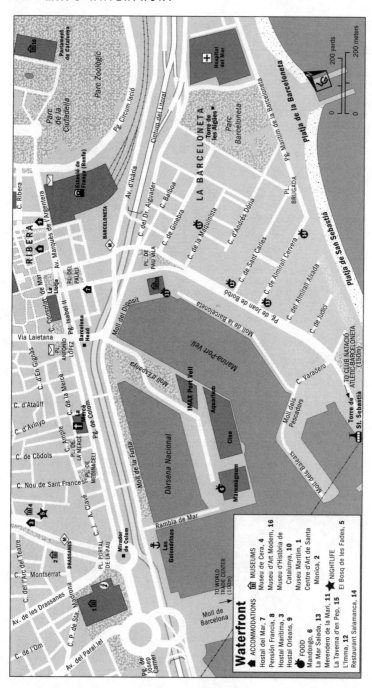

Waterfront

ACCOMMODATIONS
Hostal del Mar, **7**
Pensión Francia, **8**
Hostal Marítima, **3**
Hostal Orleans, **9**

FOOD
Mandongo, **6**
La Mar Salada, **13**
Merendero de la Marí, **11**
La Taverna d'en Pep, **15**
L'Imma, **12**
Restaurant Salamanca, **14**

MUSEUMS
Museu de Cera, **4**
Museu d'Art Modern, **16**
Museu d'Història de
    Catalunya, **10**
Museu Marítim, **1**
Centre d'Art de Santa
    Monica, **2**

NIGHTLIFE
El Bosq de les Fades, **5**